CW01465975

ESTONIA

Baltic Sea

LATVIA

Riga

Dünaberg

Krottingen

LITHUANIA

Kowno

Wilna

EAST
PRUSSIA
Danzig (GER.)

Hochwald

Augustow

Grodno

Minsk

Moscow

U S S R

Kursk

Graudenz

Wolfsschanze

romberg

Soldau

Bialystok

Prokhorovka

taren

Plock

Warsaw

POLAND

Pripyat

Teterewino

Belgorod

Kutno

Tomassow

Krasnoborki

Sabolot

Radomyshi

Alexandrowka

Ljubotin

Kharkov

Lodz

Kielce

Lublin

Bug R.

Pekartschina

Kiev

Federowka

Smijew

Donetsi R.

Oppeln

Zhitomir

Tortschin

Stanitschnoje

Jefremowka

hwitz

Vistula R.

Krakau

Przemysl

Jaroslaw

Pivd. Buh R.

Staroverowka

Dnieper R.

Taganrog

Rostov

VAKIA

Dniester R.

Mariupol

Greigova

Budapest

HUNGARY

ya

Cherson

ROMANIA

Black   Sea

Danube R.

OSLAVIA

BULG.

ALBANIA

GREECE

Larissa

onian
Sea

Athens

NETH.

Antwerp

Venlo

Düsseldorf

Rhine R.

GERMANY

Hasselt

Cologne

Brussels

Maastricht

Düren

Weilwerwist

Bonn

Altenkirchen

BELGIUM

Huy

Meuse R.

Aachen

Rheinbach

Charleroi

Liege

La Gleize

Malmedy

Bad Münstereifel

Blankenheim

Koblenz

Ligneuville

Thirimont

Petit Thier

Losheim

Marienfels

St. Vith

Prüm

Mosel R.

Rhine R.

Bastogne

Lutrebois

LUX.

Osweiler

FRANCE

Colmar-Berg

Trier

0   40 miles

Luxembourg City

0   40 kilometers

PEIPER'S WAR

For Ann Hamilton Shields

PEIPER'S WAR

THE WARTIME YEARS OF SS LEADER
JOCHEN PEIPER: 1941–1944

Danny S. Parker

FRONTLINE
BOOKS

ff

PEIPER'S WAR
The Wartime Years of SS Leader Jochen Peiper: 1941–1944

First published in Great Britain in 2019 and reprinted in 2021
by Frontline Books,
an imprint of Pen & Sword Books Ltd, Yorkshire - Philadelphia

Copyright © Danny S Parker
ISBN: 978-1-52674-342-8

Typeset in India by Vman Infotech Private Limited
Printed and bound by CPI Group (UK) Ltd, Croydon, CR0 4YY

Pen & Sword Books Ltd incorporates the imprints of Pen & Sword Archaeology,
Air World Books, Atlas, Aviation, Battleground, Discovery, Family History, History,
Maritime, Military, Naval, Politics, Social History, Transport, True Crime, Claymore
Press, Frontline Books, Praetorian Press, Seaforth Publishing and White Owl

For a complete list of Pen & Sword titles please contact:

PEN & SWORD BOOKS LTD
47 Church Street, Barnsley, South Yorkshire, S70 2AS, UK.
E-mail: enquiries@pen-and-sword.co.uk
Website: www.pen-and-sword.co.uk

Or

PEN AND SWORD BOOKS,
1950 Lawrence Road, Havertown, PA 19083, USA
E-mail: Uspen-and-sword@casematepublishers.com
Website: www.penandswordbooks.com

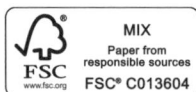

MIX
Paper from
responsible sources
FSC
www.fsc.org FSC® C013604

Contents

Preface

*P*eiper's War is the third in my quadrilogy of books on the infamous SS colonel Jochen Peiper. In Germany in the Second World War, Peiper was known as a handsome Aryan prodigy, a witness to the inner working of the Nazi elite, Waffen SS warrior and favourite to Hitler. He had been Heinrich Himmler's personal adjutant in the early years of the war, and once procuring a field command, Peiper had become well known for his flamboyant and brutal style of warfare on the Eastern Front. I have already written two books dealing with Peiper. *Fatal Crossroads* (DaCapo, 2011) covered the infamous Malmédy massacre perpetrated by Peiper's troops. That volume attempted to reconstruct the event in detail, from varied perspectives, rendered as a meticulous warcrime investigation. The Malmédy incident would define Peiper; indeed, it would beleaguer him for the rest of his days.

In contrast, *Hitler's Warrior* (DaCapo, 2014) dealt with Peiper's life before and after the war but not primarily with the conflict itself. As Peiper fought on all war fronts, many readers have requested an accounting of these years. This third volume fills that void, covering the period from 1941 through the summer of 1944. The final volume will cover the Ardennes fighting in detail.

Peiper's War looks to provide a unique view of the span of the European conflict through the eyes of the controversial SS colonel—ostensibly a view from the wrong side of history. Invariably, readers will see some duplication within *Peiper's War* from *Hitler's Warrior*—a necessary expedient for a full accounting of the war years. Yet, different from fringe books on German military personalities and similar subjects, *Peiper's War* provides a substantial and nuanced military history of the Second World War from the netherworld of Hitler's Germany.

How did Peiper view the war in the East? This is from the perspective of a well-connected SS officer—a favourite of Hitler. What went wrong within Peiper's command in Northern Italy in autumn 1943 when his command burned down a small village, with many put to death? How did the experience in the East contrast with the Normandy battlefields in France against the Americans and British in 1944? In what context did Peiper and his comrades candidly see the crushing defeat of D-Day and the German expulsion from France?

My aim is that *Peiper's War* will serve as a serious historical work on the Second World War as told from a central participant in Hitler's legions. Peiper has long served as a powerful icon, glorifying German participation within 'the myth of the Eastern Front'[1] At the same time, as befitting my controversial subject, I have approached the story in a purposefully unbiased fashion, thoroughly documenting evidence to encourage confidence. Our view of the war is from top to the bottom-from Hitler and Himmler themselves all the way down to SS officer comrades like Kurt Meyer to panzer men like Fritz Kosmehl who rode in the command tank with Peiper.

Now, I welcome the reader to another world, and one with frightful parallels to our world today. Motivated by radical racial ideologies, Adolf Hitler in 1941–44 attempted the ruthless total conquest of Europe during the Second World War. Our view of that tumultuous past is through the eyes of an infamous Waffen SS warrior who endeavoured to help translate Hitler's terrifying vision into reality: Jochen Peiper.

—Danny S. Parker
Cocoa Beach, August 2019

---

1 Ronald Smelser and Edward L. Davies: *The Myth of the Eastern Front: The Nazi-Soviet War in American Popular Culture,* (Cambridge University Press, Cambridge, 2007.)

Chapter 1

The Goths are Riding Again

'What the Goths, the tribes and all single marchers of Germanic blood were not able to accomplish, will now be done. This is a new German crusade that will be realized by our leader—the leader of all Germanics. Now, the assault of the [Russian] plain will be beaten back. Now, it will be fulfilled, what Germanic fighters in the forests and the greater regions of the East previously dreamed. A 3,000-year-old chapter of history now comes to a glorious end. The Goths are riding again—since the 22nd of June 1941—every one of us a Germanic warrior!'
—Heinrich Himmler, summer 1941[1]

On 1 March 1941, Jochen Peiper did not realize he was personally witnessing a pivotal event in what would become known as the beginning of one of the most horrific and infamous episodes of the Second World War.

That cold Saturday morning a dark-green Junkers Ju 52 aircraft flying from Berlin touched down at the hard-frozen airfield in the industrial town of Gleiwitz in Upper Silesia, Germany. Inside the aircraft was Heinrich Himmler, the head of the Schutzstaffel, or SS; SS Gruppenführer Karl Wolff, his chief of staff; and 26-year-old Jochen Peiper, Himmler's devoted personal adjutant. On that date Adolf Hitler's Second World War in Europe was a year and a half old. Ironically, Gleiwitz was the location of an undercover operation staged by National Socialist SS agents posing as Poles against the German radio station there on the last day of August 1939. The subversive operation enacted there became a pretext for invading Poland and ostensibly the start of the Second World War.

Hitler, the authoritarian leader of Germany, was involved in a titanic war of conquest in Europe. Himmler, the SS Reichsführer, was key to the German dictator's ideological aims of racial transformation because the SS was tasked with bringing about his plans to establish

Germanic racial superiority from England all the way to Russia, and for that assignment Himmler intended to remove vast segments of society he deemed unworthy. At first those imprisoned consisted of political prisoners, but soon they included Himmler's designated 'racially undesirable elements': Jews, Poles and homosexuals were being moved to his expanding system of concentration camps.[2] Accordingly, the assignment for Himmler's retinue on 1 March was to visit the new *Konzentrationslager*—the KZ—in Upper Silesia.

Peiper, as a young SS officer, was Himmler's adjutant—his *Edelknappe*— his devoted noble servant and single-minded assistant. In December 1940 Himmler had shared with Peiper that plans were under way for the invasion of the Soviet Union—a colossal struggle that Himmler suggested would decide the entire war and even the fate of Germany.

Once the aircraft had noisily taxied about and the tri-motor Junkers' propellers fluttered to a stop, out stepped Himmler, followed by Wolff and Jochen Peiper. It was bitterly cold outside.[3] Since the deep freeze in February the German battleship *Bismarck*, with Peiper's brother-in-law, Dr Rolf Hinrichsen, on board, had been frozen in the harbour near Hamburg. Adolf Hitler, who was secretly planning a rapid war against the USSR, convened a climate workshop in Berlin with meteorologists expected to provide statistical assurances that the following winter, 1941– 1942, would be milder.[4] After a brief combat assignment in France the previous June, Jochen Peiper, a Waffen SS officer of Hitler's Praetorian Guard, the Leibstandarte Adolf Hitler, was now back on seemingly endless tours with the Reichsführer SS. Although the assignment as an SS adjutant to the second-most powerful man in Hitler's Reich might have been considered a plum assignment, it was hardly soldierly. Still, as always, Peiper followed obediently along; indeed, as his comrade recognized, he was one of the few officers in the Waffen SS 'who appreciated Himmler as a person'.[5]

Leaving the airstrip, Himmler, Wolff and Peiper were met by the local National Socialist political official, or Gauleiter, of Upper Silesia, Fritz Bracht. With him was High SS and Police Leader (HSSPF) Erich von dem Bach-Zelewski, a bespectacled Prussian SS leader under Himmler known for embracing unsavoury assignments, as well as the inspector of the expanding Concentration Camp System, Richard Glücks. After eating a prepared lunch, the uniformed SS officers drove 65km across the border with Poland to the town of Auschwitz in Upper Silesia. There, a new concentration camp had been established at the site of an old artillery barracks, established by Bach-Zelewski 1940. The location was now just inside the expansion of Hitler's Reich since the conquest of Poland in 1939.

Over the previous two years Peiper had been with the Reichsführer SS to one concentration camp after another—Dachau, Oranienburg, Mauthausen, Neuengamme, Ravensbrück. Although it was Himmler's first visit to this new site, Peiper's boss seemed to take unusual interest in Auschwitz.

Himmler enthusiastically told the Concentration Camp Commandant, Rudolf Höss, that the concentration camp would be dramatically expanded. Currently, the major activity at the concentration camp was agriculture, but Himmler seemed to have other ideas. Höss was previously from Sachsenhausen concentration camp and seemed slightly surprised. Himmler explained that place must be built out to hold at least thirty thousand prisoners and the surrounding swamps be drained. Moreover, a second section of the facility would be expanded to nearby Brzezinka, where Auschwitz II would incarcerate 'dangerous criminals'. He decreed that workshops be expanded, venturing that a new ammunition plant there would be helpful so that the SS would be central to a strong German arms industry. Yet, beyond just being another concentration camp, Himmler was thinking about opportunities through German chemical industries.

Since the beginning of the year one of Himmler's old schoolmates, Otto Ambros, a ranking chemist at the industrial chemical giant I.G. Farben, had petitioned the Reichsführer for a massive new industrial park. Ambros wanted to locate a chemical factory near Auschwitz to produce synthetic rubber (Buna) out of reach of Allied bombers. Farben was enthused about the prospects for cheap labour, and Himmler directed Höss to immediately send ten thousand prisoners to the adjoining village of Dwory by Oświęcim, where the new Buna factory would be built. Did Himmler already have inklings about the potential use of Auschwitz for killing? Ambros was not only a high-ranking official in I.G. Farben, but also an authority on the nerve gas sarin and other toxic compounds.

Indeed, a year before, Peiper had accompanied Himmler to Posen, Poland, to witness a new 'humane' method by which to rid the Reich of *lebensunwerten Lebens*—lives not worth living. The victims of the carbon monoxide gassing were twenty insane Jewish inmates from Tiegenhof Asylum—an event that Peiper would discuss later in life, where a circle of guests was invited to watch the 'mercy killing' through a plexiglass window.[6]

Peiper later described himself as victim 'I cannot deny that, as an escort of the Reichsführer that I was not ever everywhere present,' he would later admit, 'but often I had no knowledge ... As a solider I was, so to say, forced into it.'[7]

In the meantime, the head of the German air force, the Luftwaffe, Hermann Göring, had ordered the Germanization of the locale: that meant the removal of all Jews and Poles. Himmler intended Auschwitz to be a German model town for the settlement of the East. Indeed, on 20 March Peiper would be photographed as Himmler lectured high-ranking Nazi officials Rudolf Hess, Gottlob Berger and Martin Bormann on his plans for *Lebensraum* (living space) for the Reich. The group huddled over detailed models of buildings, farms, barns and outlying buildings at an SS exhibition in Berlin.[8] As Himmler envisioned it, after deporting or eliminating Poles from the conquered lands in the East, German *Wehrbauer*, or SS soldier peasants, would be settled on the model farms along a fortified line in Poland. If silent, Peiper may have been dubious.[9]

For now Himmler, Bracht, Glücks and Bach-Zelewski were pleased enough to provide housing for the construction workers for the I.G. Farben factory. There was no immediate indication that Auschwitz was being prepared as an elimination camp where over a million human beings would be murdered, but Himmler clearly had plans in mind. Himmler ordered Höss to establish a gigantic new KZ in nearby Birkenau with a capacity of one hundred thousand prisoners.[10] He was thinking ahead to Hitler's plan to invade Soviet Russia.

Later that Saturday afternoon Himmler, Wolff, Bracht and Peiper examined the concentration camp itself. Conducting a walking inspection tour, they passed the long line of barracks, kitchen and carpentry shop. It must have made a depressing sight: prisoners wearing coloured triangular badges used in Himmler's concentration camp system moving about inside the electrified barbed-wire fences that made up the perimeter. Still, it seems Peiper hardly disapproved of the KZ system itself, as he would clearly state after the war.[11]

The group later drove on to the nearby Kattowitz with the Gauleiter of Upper Silesia to dine at the renowned Café Central and stay over at the luxurious Hotel Monopol, where they would celebrate the forty-second birthday of Bach-Zelewski. Since November 1939, the SS chief had served Himmler the 'Commissioner for the Strengthening of Germandom in Silesia', where he was charged with the mass resettlement and the confiscation of Polish private property. Known for his lack of scruples, by August 1940 at least eighteen thousand Poles had been cast out of their homes. Himmler was delighted with Bach-Zelewski, who continued to be pliant to his wishes, if mentally unstable. Although Bach-Zelewski remained embarrassed that each of his sisters had married Jewish men, all that was forgotten for his birthday.[12] The Monopol was one of the finest hotels in Poland, and sought out by artists and the upper-crust aristocracy.

4

After an easy-going evening celebration, the group retired to a sitting room to puff on cigars.

Strangely, it was only a few months later, from 13–15 July, just after the war with Russia had begun, that Höss recalled that Jochen Peiper called him back to Berlin to meet with Himmler. 'The Führer has ordered that the Jewish question be solved once and for all,' Höss said, 'and that we, the SS, are to implement that order. The existing extermination centres in the East are not in a position to carry out the large actions anticipated. I have therefore earmarked Auschwitz for this purpose.'[13] Peiper, who liked to fancy himself a 'pure soldier', had briefly fought against the French in June 1940, but was now firmly back in Himmler's orbit.[14] Even if familiar with Himmler's direction to pursue a 'war of annihilation' against the Jews and other races, such an assignment may have been unwelcome. Chances to get back into the shooting war seemed to dim with each concentration camp tour.

How had he gotten to this point? Named Joachim—but preferring the more common nickname Jochen—Peiper had been born in 1915 in the Berlin suburb of Wilmersdorf into a middle-class family with two brothers. His father, Woldemar, was a gruff veteran of the First World War. The older Hans-Hasso, an aesthete and likely a homosexual, had violent arguments with his father. In 1931 he unsuccessfully attempted suicide and was left in a vegetative state. Meanwhile, at school Jochen had not completed the *Abitur* that would have allowed admission to a university and instead followed his older brother Horst (born in 1912) into the German Scouting movement, both developing an interest in the outdoors and a military career. Peiper turned 18 years old on 30 January 1933, when Adolf Hitler was appointed as chancellor of Germany, and he immediately volunteered for the Hitler Youth, known as the Hitler Jugend.[15]

Interested in horses and speed, Peiper longed to join the cavalry units of the German Reichswehr. Encouraged by a family friend, General Walther von Reichenau, Peiper joined the 7th SS Reiterstandarte in October 1933, quickly developing proficiency. In January 1934, he became an SS Mann and later that same year, at the Nuremberg Party Rally, attracted the attention of Heinrich Himmler, who encouraged him to become an SS officer.

In 1935, Peiper went to a camp for prospective SS officers near Jüterborg and then attended the SS *Junkerschule* (officer's training school) at Braunschweig from 24 April until 30 March 1936, including training stints at Dachau Concentration Camp during the last two months before his graduation. On 20 April 1936 Peiper was promoted to SS Untersturmführer and posted to the Leibstandarte Adolf Hitler under Sepp Dietrich.

He would remain with the Leibstandarte for two years, after which he would join Heinrich Himmler as his adjutant in the summer of 1938, nominally working out of the Berlin offices of the Reichsführer SS on Prinz-Albrecht-Straβ.

Peiper was a favourite of Himmler and, in the next three years, became familiar with many of the high-ranking SS officers and personalities in Hitler's Third Reich. In 1938 he met his future wife, Sigurd Hinrichsen, who was a secretary for Himmler along with her friend Hedwig Potthast, who would become not only very close to Peiper but also the future mistress to Heinrich Himmler.

In 1939, at the outbreak of the war, Peiper accompanied Himmler in his train that moved through Poland. Given SS loyalty and proficiency with weapons, Peiper drew an assignment to provide personal protection to Hitler's command car as it moved through the Polish countryside in the wake of the invasion. However, as the campaign wound down, he also became intimate with Himmler's plans for eliminating Jewish Polish intellectuals and what Himmler termed 'racial undesirables'. Peiper was also with Himmler near Blomberg on 20 September, when they witnessed the shooting of twelve to fifteen Poles. Of the condemned, Peiper professed himself 'astonished by their composure as they died', relating that Himmler was so shocked that afterwards he was unable to speak for days.[16]

Spring 1940 found Peiper touring the Buchenwald and Flossenburg concentration camps and later the brutal Mauthausen concentration camp near Linz, Austria, but without overt post-war criticism for the hardships witnessed, merely saying that: 'I did not see cruelties there, but the work at Mauthausen seemed excessively strenuous.'

In the war in France in 1940 Peiper received leave from Himmler to join the fighting with the Leibstandarte, which was already in combat, and received the Iron Cross for seizing a French artillery battery on the heights of Wattenberg in France. Promoted to SS Hauptsturmführer, in June 1940 Peiper returned back to Himmler as adjutant, with triumphant tours to the Berhof to see Hitler as well as again continuing the tours of the concentration camps (Dachau and Ravensbrück) and even the ghettos in Lublin and Łódź.[17] The tours and communications developing for the racial cleansing of Poland hardly seemed soldier-like, and Peiper seems to have pursued a potential return to a military command. The death of his brother, Horst, in June 1941 under murky circumstances seems to have cemented the deal.

Before the war Horst Peiper decided that the Luftwaffe was not devoted enough to National Socialism. Like Jochen, Horst joined Himmler's SS to later serve as a leader in the SS Totenkopf (Death's Head) division and fought in France in 1940. However, he seems to have been accused of being a homosexual and likely committed suicide on 11 June 1941, just before the invasion of the Soviet Union.[18]

Meanwhile, the specific SS military establishment to which Peiper returned, the Leibstandarte SS Adolf Hitler, was groomed for the largest military operation in history: the invasion of Russia. The Leibstandarte was the only military formation carrying Hitler's name, and the assignment was considered the height of prestige in the armed or Waffen SS. Peiper, like Hitler, saw the clash as inevitable. 'Germany declared war on Russia in 1941', the young SS officer would later write, 'as a last attempt to eliminate the increasing political threat from the East.'[19] Peiper looked to be released from assisting Himmler so he could fight his way to victory and glory in Hitler's war.

Hitler's armies had invaded Poland in 1939 and then swept across France and then Norway, Holland and Denmark in the fast-paced Blitzkrieg campaign of 1940. It was in France that Peiper had displayed his mettle as a successful fighting adjutant for Himmler. But while Germany rolled over Greece and the Balkans, Peiper remained with Himmler and away from the fighting, even as he was very aware that Operation Barbarossa, the invasion of the Soviet Union, was near.

In the meantime, in the early summer of 1941 the SS troopers of the Leibstandarte rushed from engagements in Greece and Yugoslavia to an assembly area near what is now Brno, Czechoslovakia, to be hurriedly reorganized on the Führer's orders.[20] According to plans, Hitler's personal command swelled to a full motorized division: ten thousand fanatically dedicated political soldiers. Even in the third year of the war the Leibstandarte maintained an all-volunteer composition, with rigidly enforced entrance standards based on fabled National Socialist notions of a rarefied racial purity. According to Hitler, the recruits must possess exceptional physical strength and mental toughness. The Leibstandarte sought to meet that challenge. Within its ranks devotion soared to their namesake leader and to his aim of European domination. More than that, the Leibstandarte felt totally superior to all other combat forces: they could translate Hitler's will into reality. 'The units of the Waffen SS were small in number and not yet watered down,' Peiper himself would later claim. 'They were, in every respect, an elite.'[21]

Even with Hitler's blessing, the reorganization was rushed. By the time Operation Barbarossa began on 21 June, the tables of organization for weapons and equipment remained a paper plan of guns and promised vehicles.[22] Regardless, the command was to join Field Marshal Gerd von

Rundstedt's Army Group South and Panzer Group I in its advance on Kiev. Yet, when the legions moved off for the initial attack, the Leibstandarte was left behind. Hadn't Hitler promised them they would be at the forefront of every great offensive?

Grumbles within the self-proclaimed elite Leibstandarte ended when orders arrived to move east. As the division crossed Silesia, enthusiastic crowds showered the SS men with flowers, while old German comrades from the Russian campaign in the First World War provided wisdom on how to defeat the Cossacks. Spirits ran high as they crossed the border. If anyone worried, it was those confused readers of *Mein Kampf*. The author–turned German chancellor had decried a two-front war. Of course, the overwhelming expectation for the summer of 1941 was that there would be a swift victory. 'We'll be in Moscow in six weeks if Ivan moves fast enough!' gushed one SS trooper.[23]

Peiper was still stuck with Himmler. At mid-summer 1941 he remained with the SS Reichsführer at his East Prussian headquarters he called Hochwald.[24] There, in the small forest directly north of Grosgarten and not far from Hitler's nearby headquarters, he and Werner Grothmann, the second assistant, operated in Himmler's command train. Himmler kept Peiper and Grothmann on as adjutants, along with a secretary and a very small office staff, but no chief of operations, as he was obsessed with control. As part of the inner circle, Peiper's relationship with Himmler remained close; indeed, as personal adjutant, little was hidden from the youthful SS Hauptsturmführer. Each morning on Himmler's special train, the *Sonderzug Heinrich*, began with the morning briefing. It was Peiper's job to describe the operations over the past twenty-four hours that made up Himmler's personal war. Marked maps at the headquarters neatly showed the positions of the various SS cavalry regiments and the police battalions, all with intricate lines depicting radio communication.[25]

On the surface it looked military.[26] Although the Reichsführer SS was obsessed with his Waffen-SS, his Weltanschauungskrieg in the East was not a soldierly operation but rather a far-reaching operation of racial genocide—a grand play for the complete ethnic cleansing of the conquered regions. As Himmler saw it, when his killing teams—police squads and security service, *Sicherheistdienst* (SD security service), or *Einsatzgruppen*—were done, the Russian racial slate would be clean. Adolf Hitler agreed: 'The war with Russia will be such that it cannot be conducted in a chivalrous fashion. This struggle is one of ideologies and racial differences and will have to be conducted with unprecedented merciless and unrelenting harshness.'[27]

The *Einsatzgruppen* and 1st and 2nd SS Infantry Brigades 1 and the SS Cavalry Regiments would translate 'unrelenting harshness' into reality. These units, though part of the Waffen SS, did not belong to any regular unit but were instead at Himmler's personal disposal for his nihilistic campaign.

Peiper knew well the cast of characters doing Himmler's dirty work. SS officer Hermann Fegelein was in charge of the SS Cavalry Brigade, and Sturmbannführer Gustav Lombard was in command of its Riding Regiment and was Peiper's former riding instructor from his early SS days in Berlin. On 27 July 1941 Lombard and his staff sent back a fantastic complaint by radio to *Sonderzug Heinrich*: 'The order to drive women and children into swamps was without success because the swamps were not deep enough. The total number of plunderers shot by the Riding Battalion was 6,526.'[28] Ever the meticulous technocrat, Himmler wanted to be confident with the numbers. In the end, the SD groups killed over six hundred thousand people.

What of claims that Hitler did not know of these goings-on? One key fragment of information seems telling. In a radio telegram to Himmler's *Einsatzgruppen* on 1 August, Gestapo Chief Heinrich Müller ordered that 'illustrative material—photos' should be sent to Hitler in Berlin because 'the Führer should be presented with continuous reports on the work of the *Einsatzgruppen*.'[29] At the same time, however, Himmler looked to shield Hitler from direct connection. Although he had told a collection of generals in Koblenz that, 'I do nothing of which the Führer is not aware', on another occasion he stated, 'The person of the Führer must not be mentioned in this context under any circumstances. I will assume all responsibility.'[30] Himmler would be the bad guy; Peiper was his aide-de-camp. And then there was the real war.

When the great torrent of the German Wehrmacht was unleashed on the Russians on 21 June, the initial blast collapsed the Russian border forces. Generalfeldmarschal Ewald von Kleist's tanks of the Panzer Group I surged forward, as if expanding in a limitless vacuum. Within two days, however, Soviet resistance stiffened, and when the Leibstandarte was committed on 1 July, the army group was tangled in heavy fighting as the Soviets threw one mechanized corps after another into the German path. There was heavy fighting to repulse almost continuous enemy counterattacks; in three weeks the unit suffered some 683 casualties. 'They are', one SS veteran dourly noted, 'the best fighters we have ever met ... They fought to the last drop of blood!'[31]

In August Hitler had made the fateful decision to give additional weight to quicken the progress of von Rundstedt's Army Group South in the Ukraine. Strongly contested by the German general staff, the change would come at the expense of the Army Group Centre's advance on Moscow. Yet for the German leader, the Ukraine, with its rich grain fields, metals and the all-important oil in the Caucasus beyond, was the distant key to Barbarossa's success. Why else would the Russians there be fighting so stubbornly?[32]

At the end of July 1941, Peiper had an argument of an unknown nature with Himmler and then resigned his position as adjutant. Unofficially, by the end of the first week of August Peiper was back with the Leibstandarte Adolf Hitler as an observer for Himmler. The SS Reichsführer said farewell to Peiper at a Berlin airport in early August, and Himmler flew back to Angerburg, East Prussia, on 5 August.[33] As Himmler's eyes were on the ground, Peiper seems to have acted as an operations officer with the divisional staff—albeit one free to come and go at will. At Dietrich's office, Peiper encountered SS Hauptsturmführer Max Wünsche, another hyper-arrogant SS officer in the inner circle of National Socialism. While Peiper was Himmler's adjutant, Wünsche seemed even more favoured, as he was an SS Ordonnanz officer reporting directly to Hitler himself. Indeed, his birthday was on the same day as Hitler's, he had served on the Führer Escort Battalion in Poland, and he was now adjutant to Sepp Dietrich in Russia.[34] The two SS men seemed to be in an unspoken competition for who would be the most celebrated SS officer warrior. Wünsche had the deep penetrating stare, while Peiper had perfected the arrogant frown, and both men were glory hounds.

Yet far apart from rivalries, Peiper's aim was to get back to the fighting. On 19 August he was photographed with SS Sturmbannführer Wilhelm Weidenhaupt, Max Hansen and Albert Frey as they observed the shelling of an 88mm gun against the Russians clinging to the banks of the Dnieper River, part of the wider effort to capture the Black Sea port of Cherson.[35]

Later that day Peiper seems to have taken at least temporary command of the 11th Company to reinforce the isolated reconnaissance battalion. Kurt Meyer had flung his armoured cars against strong resistance at a fruit jam factory on Cherson's eastern edge and, after breaking through, boldly fought his way to the centre of town, but with nobody behind him. The infantry advance towards Cherson was done in rushes across the open ground—completely exposed and devoid of cover, save the occasional stands of sunflowers. The roar of artillery fire boomed, periodically punctuated by louder explosions as the Russians, pulling back, detonated ammunition dumps. In the late afternoon Peiper's men managed to reach the railway line to the north-west of the port city, supported by 21cm artillery fire. The big guns fired as they moved forward, and 'shorts' wounded several in his company.[36] By 1800 hours Peiper and the rest of III Battalion reported linking up with 'Schneller' Meyer.[37] They were pitted against Russian sailors impressed as infantry, fighting them from one house to the next and across gardens and public squares. By nightfall it was over—the darkness illuminated by burning streets.

In the Russian war everything always seemed to be burning. The air was filled with the odour of burning houses and the acrid stink of gunpowder. Where the stubbly plains met the late summer horizon, there was an ever-present pall of flame and smoke. Russian homes' thatched roofs blazed and crackled to the rumble of guns and exploding shells. In Cherson big, black, ugly clouds of smoke rose overhead. Russians were leaving, having put the torch to two fuel depots. To Peiper it was likely the oily smell of conquest.

The war seemed to be closing fast on a German victory. When Cherson fell into SS hands later that day, the captured scuttled several Russian ships to the bottom of the Black Sea, while Soviet hopes similarly sunk—so much so that on 21 August the Leibstandarte was even temporarily pulled out of combat for rest and refitting.

At first Peiper's time away from the front line appeared temporary. With the fighting over for at least the moment—perhaps soon for good—Peiper took his leave to report on the war in the East to his former boss; Himmler always valued a colourful first-hand account. While Peiper regaled Himmler with tales from the front of a war seemingly on the verge of ending, the SS men of the Leibstandarte motored by the sand dunes of Chulakovka along the Black Sea coast. Civilians lined the roads, showering the SS men with autumn flowers and enthusiastic calls. A festive air prevailed. The natives were decked out in colourful traditional Ukrainian costumes; some brought food—melons, eggs and grapes—while others danced to balalaika music. They greeted the German invaders as liberators. This war looked just like France the summer before.

Peiper was thinking longingly of his time with Himmler when he wrote in saccharine tones to Hedwig 'Häschen' Potthast on 23 September 1941. Potthast, one of Himmler's secretaries, had been Peiper's very close friend before the war and during its opening phases, and by 1940 she became Himmler's mistress. Yet Hedwig's relationship with Peiper remained exceedingly close—perhaps even intimate: 'I always hoped you would send sometime short greetings into our desolate Steppe,' he jotted. 'Unfortunately, you seem to have forgotten me totally. But, here, for me, it feels very different. Desire and the feeling of loyalty are growing in relation to the distance.' But then Peiper became more serious in his note to Himmler's mistress, almost as if he had to provide a reason for his departure: 'I am happy to be permitted participation in this war that is so necessary for our people and for you to be taken care of at home. I am glad to have come out again to the fighting in the field which promises to be the last great campaign of our generation.' But then he wrote almost with a note of caution: 'I am not a "war junky" looking for and desiring war.' If this is the case, why did he leave Himmler's services? Would he come back again?[38]

> The long activity under the conditions well known to you has built up an immense pressure, which now demands a valve and some distance in time. But already today, I notice that one cannot get away from the stable in which one snorted through one's nostrils and pointed one's ears for three years—Should I bring my *skin* home undamaged—this, by the way, is not that simple—I shall be available again unconditionally.
>
> For today and as always, I wish you the best; please greet the *Somebody* heartily from me and I am
>
> Your faithful little brother[39]

Peiper did perhaps return—at least for a short visit. On 17 September 1941, at Hochwald, Peiper again took over his adjutant responsibilities with the SS Reichsführer long enough to jot down the daily entry in the office calendar.[40] Two days before, Himmler had been in Minsk to receive a demonstration of what 'liquidation of undesirables' really meant. However, Peiper had not been along for that infamous episode, as Werner Grothmann had taken his place. In any case, soon after Peiper reappeared at the Angerburg headquarters for the Reichsführer SS, Himmler set off in a fleet of cars, replete with military escort and a wireless car, on a multi-day tour of the South Russian Front: Uman, Krivoi-Rog, Nikolaijew and Cherson. Himmler's tour included a visit to the region conquered by Leibstandarte just weeks before where Peiper had personally followed the division. From Cherson Peiper likely set off from Himmler's cortège from one of the field airports, to arrive at the division positions some 350km to the east near Berdjansk on 1 October, as shown in his service record.

For Himmler a high point was to be the tour of Berditschew (Berdichev) in the Zhitomir district, where he waxed effusive about the German Volhynian settlements to be seen there. Officially there were more pressing concerns relative to his private war, so from the field he sensibly warned his leaders on 13 September that 'the danger of their messages being decoded is great ... sensitive matters that should not be sent by wireless include the number of executions carried out'.[41]

Himmler's war continued relentlessly. By the end of 1941 the death toll among the non-combatants in the Soviet Union reached a zenith that strained credulity. Upwards of eight hundred thousand Jewish civilians had been killed, and entire regions were declared *judenfrei*—free of Jews.[42] Many of those remaining were confined to ghettos, where they would eventually perish. All the while the killing frenzy in the 'first sweep' in the East grew in intensity and violence, moving from men of military age to eventually encompass Jews or 'racial undesirables' of any age or sex.

One of those participating in the expanding series of pogroms in the East was SS-Sturmbannführer Emil Sator, one of Peiper's first tactical instructors at Jüterbog. Sator had spent time with the Totenkopfstandarte 'Thüringen' at Buchenwald in 1937 and later became a tactical teacher at Braunschweig. In the summer of 1941 he moved to Totenkopfstandarte 10 for the invasion of Russia. The man who had pronounced Peiper to be 'definitely suitable to be an officer' in 1935 was such a fanatical Nazi that the hard-driven men under his thumb nicknamed him 'Satan'. As if to prove it, on 4 August Sator orchestrated a mass shooting of over two thousand Jews just outside Ostrog some 35km south-east of Rowno in the Ukraine, telling his men that it was 'a good preparation to see such blood; that would get them ready for the front'.[43] Elsewhere, Peiper's first cavalry instructor, Gustav Lombard, was engaged in a far-reaching campaign of annihilating 'enemies of the Reich'.

The situation in the Ukraine that was a focus for the Nazi pogroms differed fundamentally from that in the Great Byelorussian areas in the north-eastern regions. Intensely nationalist, the Ukrainians had been a thorn in the side of the Moscow government for decades, although Western Ukraine had only been part of the Soviet Union since 1939, having been snatched from Poland. Before the Bolshevik Revolution, Cossack leaders such as Simon Petlyura had established independent regimes in Kiev and Kharkov, and fought the Communist regime during the bloody civil war. In particular, the populace detested Nikita Khrushchev, Stalin's first secretary of the Ukrainian Communist Party. Under his iron hand the Soviets closed their churches and persecuted local intellectuals and the upper class. Further, between 1932 and 1939 Stalin had engineered a diabolical famine in the Ukraine by seizing and collectivizing so many farms that famine swept the area, costing at least five million lives.[44] Thus, many of the Ukrainians welcoming the Germans were tired of the excesses of Stalinism and its cruel commissars. What's more, the Ukrainians had something else in common with the Nazis: a long-standing hatred of the Jews: Petlyura's Cossack bands had also slaughtered tens of thousands in the Civil War.

Yet, more than anything else, it was the Red commissars who turned the Ukrainian populace against Stalin.[45] On 20 July Stalin had authorized the Russian secret police, the NKVD, to purge 'unreliable' elements from the army. This they had done with reckless abandon, murdering hundreds of political prisoners when forced to yield territory to the Germans.[46] Almost every family had lost someone. Whole villages had been stripped of men when they were shot or impressed into the Soviet Army. Even local priests were executed. As the commissars pulled out, they also took the cattle which were herded alongside a pitiful line of political prisoners. Few returned.

Could the Germans be any worse? The Ukrainians invited the soldiers of conquest into their whitewashed peasant homes. Many spoke the German tongue and shared the Nazi commonality of hating the Communists. Some became fast friends. At the same time, many dejected Russian soldiers were inclined to desert. In July, after the devastating encirclement at Smolensk, no fewer than one hundred thousand Russians marched into captivity. At first the invading soldiers treated the local populace well, and the Ukrainians uneasily accepted their fate as part of the new Reich—or at least many German soldiers believed that. Perhaps, the Ukrainians reasoned, the Germans would re-establish civilization, the Orthodox church and an independent government.

Hitler's minister in the East, Alfred Rosenberg, was convinced that Ukraine was the key to the war: keep the Ukrainians happy, peacefully administer its rich grain land and productive industrial region, and Germany's advantage over the Soviets would be insurmountable.[47] At stake was the viability of the German army in the East: Would they have forty million friends or foes at their back?

Hitler and Himmler, however, did not share Rosenberg's view of the Ukrainians as allies in the war on Russia. Even while Peiper was away fighting the French campaign in May 1940, Himmler drafted a memo to Hitler that would provide guidelines on how to carve up territories in the East:[48] 'Like the skimmed fat at the top of a pot of bouillon, there is a thin intellectual layer on the surface of the Ukrainian people; do away with it and the leaderless mass will become an obedient and helpless herd.'[49]

Five days after the Ukrainians formed a separatist government, the National Socialists dissolved it and appointed party autocrat Erich

14

Koch to take charge as Reichskommissar of the region. Called a 'golden pheasant' for his signature brown shirts with golden braids, Koch, an ex-railway official from the Rhineland, set about to eliminate the Jews from the region as well as anyone else of the slightest suspicion. He was not only arrogant and stubborn but also a rabid extremist, totally fixated on the Aryans as the 'master race'. His was a policy of wanton killing so extreme that even the SS complained of its darkness. 'I am known as a brutal dog,' he boasted that summer. 'Our job is to suck from the Ukraine all the goods we can get a hold of. I am expecting from you the utmost severity towards the native population,' said Koch.[50]

With the unleashing of new savage policies, however, the smiling, handkerchief-waving Ukrainians quickly transformed into bitter enemies.[51] In short months a wave of partisans materialized in the German rear, bent on vengeance at any cost. It was a total reversal. At its root stood a wider ideological gulf between the two cultures. To Hitler and Himmler the Ukrainians were *Untermenschen*, just like the Russians. Hermann Göring cut to the chase. 'The best thing,' he said, 'would be to kill all men in the Ukraine over 15 years of age, and then to send in the SS stallions.'[52]

What's more, promises were broken. The collectivized farms were not turned over to the people as soldiers had said they would be. And those disillusioned Southern Ukrainians who wanted to volunteer to join the German side were not accepted. Worse yet, Koch considered the locals—even those who spoke German—to be Neanderthal-like and ripe for elimination. That Hitler approved is clear: he originated the so-called Commissar Order in June 1941, which called for the elimination of Russian commissars, Jews and intellectuals. The mission was left to Himmler's *Einsatzgruppen* and police killing detachments. These excesses in turn delivered Stalin a 'patriotic war' that unified the nation in a Napoleonic fervour. No matter that the Ukrainians hated NKVD and the commissars; the conflict now became one for 'Mother Russia'. 'The first Germans were liberators,' ventured one Ukrainian. 'The second group were enslavers and the third were hangmen.' Peiper saw it much same way:

> The Ukraine received us as liberators and waited to inherit their independence. The short-sighted set-up of our civil administration created an enemy in our rear and also partisan fighting and in my opinion was a decisive error. It is my conception [*sic*: view] that the backbone of the Soviet Army was broken in the autumn of 1941 … Good treatment of the subjugated enemy would have started the mass

desertion of the enemy. Instead the contrary was done ... and handed Stalin the slogan for a unifying national goal.[53]

Fire met fire. If the Germans started the war, the Russians helped to bring the conflict to a more barbaric level. On 3 July, while pushing their motorcycles through the thatched-roof villages of Olyka and Broniki, the Leibstandarte reconnaissance battalion came upon 153 members of a German bicycle company of the 25th Motorized Division who had been captured, stripped naked and 'slaughtered like beasts' in a clover field by the road.[54] Kurt Meyer described the disturbing scene:

> We passed through the woods along the road leading to Klewan. The village was taken and we proceeded towards Rowno. The road there ran straight like as a string heading south-east. From Klewan the road went down gently and after a few kilometres it went up again towards Broniki. Over the horizon some clouds of smoke were rising straight to the sky. I was with the leading platoon and was looking at the field around me through my binoculars. I could see a truck over there on the slope and some light shadows close to it.
>
> Now we could see a light gun ready to fire. For the first time we could see an abandoned German weapon on the battlefield, it was very depressing. After passing by the gun we could see a field ambulance, it had its doors wide open with blood's trace on it. We saw all this in silence. We could not see any German soldier, neither dead nor alive. We went along the slope and the light shadows could be seen clearly now. I put my binoculars down, I scrubbed my eyes and rising the binoculars I looked again.
>
> My God, it could not be possible. The head platoon detrucked and went to those light spots without words. Before us were lying the naked corpses of at least one German company. We took off our helmets holding them in ours hands as we would be praying. The corpses had the hands tied on his backs with wire strings. Their eyes wide open as if they were looking steady to us. Surely the company's officers have got a horrible end, they lain some metres away from their comrades. We marched past in silence in front of our dead comrades.[55]

This already brutal war blossomed into a conflict of full barbarity, with the Leibstandarte serving as flammable tender. The official account claimed that Sepp Dietrich forbade retribution, but the battlefield reality was very different. The Russians had not signed the Hague Convention on the Rules of War, and the intensity of the conflict slowly eroded whatever battlefield ethos had existed before then.[56] For instance, in the late summer fighting in the Uman pocket, two companies of a neighbouring division could not be located during the advance on Cherson. Erich Kernmayer, a Viennese SS war reporter, travelled with the IV Battalion of the Leibstandarte. According to his account, on the morning of 15 August they found the missing ninety-eight German soldiers killed in a cherry orchard in the village of Grejgova near Nowo Danzig. They had been ghoulishly executed: strung up in trees and their stockinged feet doused with gasoline and set afire—'Stalin-socks'. Retribution came swiftly:

> At noon the next day, an order was received by division to the effect that all prisoners captured during the next three days would be shot as a reprisal for the inhumane atrocities which the Red Army had committed in our sector. It so happened that we had taken very many prisoners during those fatal days and so the lives of four thousand men fell forfeit. They scarcely looked up when our interpreter told them of their fate.[57]

According to Kernmayer, grim firing squads carried out the executions, felling one line of eight after another into anti-tank ditches. While documentation of the Russian atrocity is complete, no direct evidence of reprisals can be found in German archival material—which is hardly surprising.[58] 'The other side carries it out with the meanest means,' wrote home one contemporary of Peiper's in the Leibstandarte. 'One gets very angry seeing again and again beastly massacred soldiers, who somewhere got lost or were taken prisoner.'[59] Himmler had more to say:

> Soldiers of the Army and the Waffen SS! On 1 September, six SS officers were found in the Weniza forest in the following condition: They had been stripped of their clothing and hanged with their legs up. Their entrails had been taken out. Such an act demands revenge, and since it was Jews who did it, we will utterly extirpate them. Even the brood in the cradle must be crushed like a swollen toad. We are living in an iron time and have to sweep with iron brooms. Everybody has therefore to do his duty without first asking his conscience.[60]

Jochen Peiper himself admitted that there was some truth to the episode, although he attributed no specific guilt to the Leibstandarte. After the war Peiper prepared a rebuttal on many war crimes issues levelled at his division:

> At that time, a bicycle company of the Kleist armoured spearhead was murdered and mutilated. As a reprisal, the army ordered that

for the next three consecutive days 'no prisoners would be taken'. Although the Leibstandarte was assigned to Group Kleist, the order did not apply to it, because during that time it was not in action, but in transit towards the south.[61]

Sturmbannführer Theodor Wisch made a personal report to his commander on the bestial murders. Dietrich was emphatic: 'We don't have a right, and can't afford to let the enemy take advantage of these murders by repaying these hideous deeds with similar actions.'[62]

Nevertheless, the rough-hewn Dietrich likely knew that such pronouncements would make little impact in tempering the cycle of killings accelerating in Russia. For instance, there were many incidents involving executing villagers for 'partisan sympathies'—a terrible recurring theme. Hitler himself had enjoined such reprisals in an order dated 16 December 1942:

> If the repression of the bandits in the East, as well as in the Balkans, is not pursued by the most brutal means, the forces at our disposal will, before long, be insufficient to exterminate this plague. The troops, therefore, have the right and the duty to use any means, even against women and children, provided they are conducive to success. Scruples of any sort are a crime against the German people and against the German soldiers … No German participating in action against the bandits and their associates is to be held responsible for acts of violence.[63]

After the war Leibstandarte veterans steadfastly insisted this order had been ignored, however to believe that Hitler's most dedicated command would ignore his bidding seems naive. The implications were clear: the war in the East was a barbaric conflict in which both sides learned to give little mercy to the other. As SS officer Max Wünsche would later pronounce: 'Someone who did not participate in the Russian Campaign cannot know or have any concept of what it meant.'[64]

What Wünsche meant was that the war in the East had become a racial conflict—a nihilistic clash of ideologies: *Weltanschauungskrieg*. The partisan war in Russia was really the first large-scale guerrilla conflict. It was a frustrating and unconventional armed battle for control of supposedly conquered territory that had to be fought continuously from the local villages and forests against an enemy that repeatedly struck like an apparition, only to evaporate when challenged. The problems this created, both for the Russian populace and for the German foe, is alarmingly familiar to the queasy indistinct gulf between civilians and guerrillas that U.S. armed forces in Vietnam found themselves entangled with some thirty years later.

Beyond that, partisan warfare had a time-honoured history in Russia. Peasant bands constantly harassed Napoleon's failed legions during his expulsion from that frigid land in 1812, and guerrilla operations had been a part of the civil war that had won the Revolution. At first Stalin saw the partisans as a threat to his power, yet in July of 1941, in desperation he embraced them, appealing for a patriotic fight by an irregular civilian army fighting for Mother Russia. His appeal to basic patriotism worked. With each passing month the partisans in the East became bolder in draining the German war effort. By the end of 1943 there were some 220,000 armed partisans operating in the Ukraine, wrecking rail lines, ambushing motor columns, interrupting supply and killing the unwary.[65] Some of this was spontaneous, but much was furtively coordinated by Stalin's Machiavellian state. The German forces, aware that the partisans wreaking havoc behind their lines, could not function without either support or safe haven, descended upon the local populace with brutal retribution.

On 16 September 1941, Hitler's chief of staff, Wilhelm Keitel, announced the notorious hostage order: fifty Russians would be executed for every German death at the hand of partisans. Hitler dismissed the severity of his decree, contending instead that human life counted for little in the Soviet Union. Although arguably a truism under Stalin's callous regime, the whole moral conflict was now caught in a quickening death spiral. Neither side could expect any leniency from the other. Terrible inhumanity would be met by greater barbarism, and that with unspeakable terror. Peiper saw it that way as well:

> Being asked about any shootings, I would like to emphasize that I saw these things then within the framework of legality. If, e.g. partisans were shot, then I had no doubt that such shootings were justified as one could read in the daily press that acts of sabotage were committed against Germans. Later on, in the environment of total war, these things spiralled up, so that later on it was very difficult to see the proper limit.[66]

This 'proper limit' denied any reason or morality. Russian soldiers had been told to expect no quarter from the invader, and captured SS soldiers could hardly expect humane treatment. In one example, a Leibstandarte patrol of six men had been captured on 13 October 1941. In March 1942, when the Germans again moved into Taganrog, they found that the six missing SS men had been thrown down a well near the local commissar's headquarters. Surviving civilian witnesses described how the Soviet secret police led the men to a courtyard and then beat and hacked them to death with rifle butts, bayonets and axes before casting their bodies down the well.[67]

Knowing the price of capture, during the hasty retreats of December 1941 many German soldiers shot themselves rather than be taken captive. Even generals felt this way: General Erich von Manstein confessed to preferring to take his own life in Russia rather than being made prisoner: 'On the very first day of the war ... our German troops came across a German patrol which had been cut off by the enemy ... All of its members were dead and gruesomely mutilated.'

Von Rundstedt's Army Group South reported similar savagery. 'Prisoners of Infantry Regiment 35 mishandled by the Russians', went the evening report of 1 July, 'other prisoners bestially murdered.'[68] Although the German reportage of the brutalities was obviously biased, the killings that took place were gruesomely summarized in photographic evidence compiled by the Oberkommando der Wehrmacht. In particular, many of the compiled offences came from the Nikolayjew area—a convenient cover to the much greater excesses soon perpetrated by Himmler's *Einsatzgruppen.*[69]

Clearly the Germans won the contest to see who could kill more. In addition to the savage battle against the partisans was Himmler's vast campaign to eliminate the Jews, which went further than anything the Russians could do. Murder was institutionalized. In one example similar to many, a 50-year-old professional soldier from Göttingen, General Walter Brüns, was shocked to witness the mass murder of ten thousand women and children at Skirotawa near Riga in December 1941: 'The victims were stripped of all their belongings and of their clothes, down to a shirt, and were herded into ditches in the woods where they were shot by SS personnel. After one group of victims had been finished off, Brüns saw a drunken SS man still shooting wildly at the corpses in the ditch.'[70]

Uncontrolled barbarism prevailed on both sides—atrocities on the German side that extended beyond the SS and beyond ready comprehension.[71] Following behind the conquering armies, the *Einsatzgruppen* totalled only three thousand men, yet they managed to kill over half a million people in six months. On this subject SS apologists have remained discreetly silent other than to claim that the *Einsatzgruppen* were distinctly separate from the Waffen SS. However, up to a third of the participants in the *Einsatzgruppen* came from the Waffen SS—usually for disciplinary indiscretions.[72]

Following in the wake of Army Group South was Einsatzgruppe D, under the command of Dr Otto Ohlendorf. 'At present, the Jewish problem is being solved in Nikolayev and Cherson', he dutifully reported to Himmler and Heydrich in October. 'About 5,000 Jews were processed at either place.' Here 'processed' was synonymous with murder, which became clear in his report the following January, when Ohlendorf tersely announced that '3,176 Jews, 85 partisans, 12 looters and 122 Communist officials were shot.' Significantly, just a few weeks earlier the Leibstandarte had pulled back from Nikolayev and Cherson.[73] Himmler toured the latter town just after the actions were complete, on 4 and 5 October, profusely complimenting those in command and promoting Ohlendorf to SS Oberführer on the spot.[74]

Some may wonder: by way of his front-line duty, was Jochen Peiper now conveniently insulated from intimate knowledge of the genocide in progress? It appears not. For on Himmler's birthday, on 7 October 1941, Peiper was photographed standing behind the SS Reichsführer and Karl Wolff as they walked along an unpaved road.[75] Although Peiper had earlier been with the Leibstandarte, he would not take over official command of the 11th Company until mid-October. That Peiper, an intimate of Himmler, would have been at his superior's forty-first birthday party should come as no surprise. He had been with Himmler again filing reports only two weeks prior. That his adjutant was photographed with Himmler immediately after his tour of the Police Battalion 311 killing zones in Nikolayev and Cherson must be seen as strong circumstantial evidence that Peiper had either been along for the previous trip or certainly would have learned about it in detail.

To the extent feasible, Himmler and Heydrich endeavoured to keep the killings secret. Indeed, as the war continued, Himmler made an effort to move the war against the partisans from his immediate control and, eventually, to that of SS officer Erich von dem Bach-Zelewski, who would be put in charge of such *Bandenbekämpfung* (bandit fighting) operations. Yet, Himmler's desires were schizophrenic. 'He always wanted to do everything himself and keep everything under his control,' one of his staff remembered. 'This wasted his time to such a degree that he could not take care of the uniformed regular police, for which he did not have a high regard anyway. The combating of partisan activity seemed to him … as a harmless game of 'cops and robbers', the control of which he felt was utterly below his dignity.'[76]

Realistically, Himmler could not bring himself to give up micro-management of the SS genocidal operations, the magnitude of which made such butchery impossible to conceal. At Kiev, at the end of

September, some 33,800 Jews were shot in a ravine called Babi Yar. In the autumn of 1941 one *Einsatzkommando* reported, 'rumours regarding the shootings have made actions considerably more difficult. Information regarding our action against the Jews is gradually filtering through via fugitive Jews, Russians and talkative German soldiers.'[77] Even Himmler's conscience seemed disturbed by the magnitude of the developing pogrom. On 11 November 1941 his masseuse Felix Kersten, wrote in his diary of a near confession: 'Today Himmler is very depressed. He has just come from the Führer Reich Chancellery. I gave him treatment ... He told me the destruction of the Jews is being planned.'[78]

Indeed, on the last day of November 1941 Himmler was phoning SD Leader, Reinhard Heydrich in Prague to warn him that a special trainload of Jews from Berlin to Riga contained the supposed son of Russian foreign minister Molotov. 'No liquidation,' he implored to the train's keepers. That was a telling fact, for without Himmler's *'keine liquidierung'* proviso, they were executing them all.[79] After all, on that same day fifteen thousand Jews were shot into mass graves in the woods outside Riga.

After 17 October Jochen Peiper may not have observed what was happening to the rear, but that he was aware of the shootings is beyond doubt. Concrete evidence of intimate knowledge of the ongoing pogrom comes from one of Peiper's tough contemporaries, Sturmbannführer Jakob Hanreich, who fell into Allied hands in August 1944. This strapping Austrian had been with the Leibstandarte since 1933 and fought with Dietrich's command from Poland through France and Greece with the 14th Company. In the autumn of 1941 he joined the Leibstandarte in Russia, where he learned of the shocking dimensions of the warfare there:

> During the time Hanreich had first seen action in Russia in November of 1941, he was told by the commander of III Battalion, Hauptsturmführer Albert Frey, that thousands of Jews had been murdered south of Mariupol and in Taganrog by the SD Einsatzkommandos. They were brought out of towns by being told that they were to be transferred, but were brought in front of some anti-tank ditches. There they had to undress, descend into the ditch and were shot. The anti-tank ditches were afterwards covered with earth. Hanreich stated that, as far as he knew, members of the LSSAH were not concerned [i.e., involved] in this crime.[80]

Even so, the officers of the Leibstandarte certainly knew about what was happening. In fact, in recent years new evidence has come out showing that Sepp Dietrich and the Leibstandarte *assisted* Einsatzkommando

10a in the killings. Indeed, on 18 October 1941, just after Peiper arrived with Himmler, both the Leibstandarte and Einsatzkommando 10a made their headquarters in Taganrog. And one of the Leibstandarte intelligence interpreters, SS Unterscharführer Georg Blunder, when taken captive would report that Einsatzgruppen 10a coordinated closely with the division, which 'carried out the death sentences imposed on civilians ... rounding them up, undressing them, shooting them and burying them in mass graves'.[81]

On 25 and 26 October 1941 Dietrich supported these actions by helping to seal off the town of Taganrog and deliver Jews to the terrain feature called the Petrushina Balka while the killing teams of Obersturmführer Heinz Otto Seetzen did their dirty work.[82] What did Seetzen report of that operation? '1,800 Jews were shot.'[83] Meanwhile, Dietrich had personally requested his own SD team from Himmler in their meeting earlier that month and readily accepted when Seetzen, a close friend of Heydrich, agreed to follow his division towards Mariupol. Thus, similar killings began in the village of Mariupol, with over eight thousand killed over the following days—a pogrom in which some members of the Leibstandarte purportedly took part and Albert Frey was witness.[84] Associated operations took place on 21 November 1941, when Einsatzgruppe D reported that the 'commandos are proceeding via Taganrog, and Rostov ... The cities of Mariupol and Taganrog are free of Jews'.[85]

The abuses were not solely an SS problem. That German army generals enjoined the genocide—even by starvation—was clearly in evidence from none other than Generalfeldmarschal Erich von Manstein in an order he issued to the German Eleventh Army on 20 November 1941:

> The Jewish Bolshevist system must be exterminated ... The German soldier comes as the bearer of a racial concept. [He] must appreciate the necessity for harsh punishment of Jewry ... In enemy cities, a large part of the population will have to go hungry. Nothing, out of a misguided sense of humanity, may be given to prisoners of war or to the population unless they are in service of the Wehrmacht.[86]

Over two million Russian prisoners starved.

Chapter 2

On the Savage Plain

'You will be home before the leaves fall from the trees.'
—Kaiser Wilhelm II, August 1914

Could the war in the East be won before winter? Just as with the last war, Hitler's field marshals knew of the danger but still recommended Operation Barbarossa.[1] With winter's cold and snow, wouldn't the wheels of the offensive advance slowly? Hitler had advocated a short, sharp summer campaign in Russia that would slay Stalin's Soviet Union by autumn, even as the head of the Luftwaffe, Herman Goering, had reminded the German leader of Napoleon's disastrous Russian campaign. 'But Napoleon did not have Stukas and tanks,' Hitler protested.

Still, unlike Poland and France before it, the war in the East seemed to lurch and sputter.

In early autumn, on 4 October 1941, the Leibstandarte Adolf Hitler, to which Peiper had moved, conducted a motorized south-east pursuit across the vast Ukrainian plains towards Berdjansk—land as flat as a table. That day the commander of III Battalion, Wilhelm Weidenhaupt, was wounded after driving over a mine and was replaced by Albert Frey from the 11th Company, with leadership of that formation passing to the soon-to-be assigned Jochen Peiper.[2] Yet, for the moment Peiper was again off to see Himmler at his headquarters, as he had been requested to attend the birthday celebration of the Reichsführer SS. When Peiper officially assumed command of 11th Company on 17 October 1941, the Leibstandarte had just wrested the Ukrainian industrial port city of Mariupol from the Russians and were pushing east along the Azov coast.[3] They plodded through a vast sea of sunflowers and grasslands.

Again on the military front, Peiper knew perhaps better than any other soldier in the Leibstandarte that the conflict in the East was an

Advance on Taganrog

17 October 1941

ideological war. His rowdy contemporaries in Russia knew the same. One of them, Kurt 'Panzer' Meyer, continued to enhance his dashing reputation in combat. Boasting he had once broken twenty-five bones in his body, this short, slim SS officer was known for his bold and courageous approach to fighting on the battlefield. Tough and totally without fear, Meyer was immensely popular with his men and widely admired as a keen commander, although some claimed he was also a Schnapps-loving womanizer.[4] He had been accused of having ordered the shooting of fifty Poles in Modlin in October 1939, but this accusation was later discredited.[5] In any case, Meyer, for his part, saw himself as a dedicated enforcer of the ethos of the Waffen SS, of which he immodestly saw Hitler's Own as a peerless elite.

The Leibstandarte was now assigned to Eberhard von Mackensen's III Panzer Corps. Mackensen's immediate objective was Rostov. During the first week of October the Leibstandarte, along with the 3rd Romanian Army and the XXX Army Corps, pounded at the southern front along the Sea of Azov. Then, on 4 October, Dietrich, without armour himself, came upon prepared Soviet anti-tank positions. So rapid had been the Leibstandarte advance, outpacing the 8th Romanian Mountain Division to the north and the 72nd Infantry Division to the south, that the 13th Panzer Division took some time to catch up to Dietrich's faster SS grenadiers.[6] Sepp Dietrich ordered defences to be set up; meanwhile a hundred kilometres to the north Army Group Centre was bearing down on Moscow. The Russians retreated as in a rout, and soldiers in the streets of the spired city seemed seized with panic.

As Jochen Peiper and his men motored east, a steady stream of prisoners choked the dusty roads as they headed for assembly areas to the rear. Even hardened Soviet soldiers looked beaten. Captured Ukrainians appeared docile and resigned to defeat. Some of the SS troopers bought vodka, sugar and beer from the populace. Could the end of this war be far away?

As usual, Hitler kept a close watch on his namesake formation, but he was clearly ahead of himself on 11 October, when he envisioned Dietrich's SS task force crossing the Don River and into the Caucasus— they had not even crossed the Mius River. While the Führer warned about Russian gunboats firing on the bridge south of Rostov, the Leibstandarte's commanders, including Jochen Peiper, were more concerned with the immediate objectives in their binoculars: Mariupol and Taganrog.[7]

Most famous as the birthplace of the great Russian playwright Anton Chekhov, few of the Germans thought of Taganrog as a rallying point for the enemy. Did they know that Tsar Peter the Great established the first Russian navy in the cold-water port in 1698? And near Rostov the Russian military tribesmen—the dreaded Don Cossacks—fought a series of bloody wars with the Turks to lay claim to the plains along the Azov coast. That the Cossacks had vehemently fought the Bolsheviks in the civil war and hated them even now was one good sign for the Germans. Moreover, the region took on a sacred significance to the southern peoples of Russia, who were known for their ferocity and stubborn defiance—a lost historical lesson for the Germanic warriors of 1941.[8] Instead, Sepp Dietrich, who some derided as a Bavarian country yokel, found he had developed a taste for Russian ballet. He reorganized the theatre in Taganrog—a little culture and civilization amid the war.[9]

In October Soviet resistance stiffened as a series of bitter battles were fought amid the endless stands of dying unharvested corn that became a killing ground for both sides. Recognition emerged that the ethos of the fight was reaching a terrible extreme not yet seen in the conflict. Wilhelm Canaris, the chief of German intelligence—the *Abwehr*—would darkly warn Hitler of the increasing cycle of killing–retribution–more killings:

> Our own treatment of Russian prisoners is having awful consequences. In the retreat from Moscow we had to abandon German field hospitals as well. The Russians dragged out the sick and injured, hanged them upside down, poured gasoline over them and lit them on fire. Some uninjured German soldiers had to watch this torture; they were then kicked in the groin and sent back to German lines with instructions to describe how the Bolsheviks were reacting to news of mass executions and barbaric treatment to their comrades in German captivity.[10]

Ominous signs came as summer faded. Cold winds blew in from the Sea of Azov. Finding billets for the German troops became a problem. And now, along the banks of the Mius River, the Soviets began to counterattack with elements of the 31st Rifle Division. As the first thrusts were crude and lacking tactical finesse, they were repelled. Yet the courage of the Russian enemy and their toughness—particularly the Siberians—made a firm impression on the Germans. Artillery fire grew in intensity, as did the menacing blasts from armoured trains that sallied forth from Taganrog and the adjacent hamlet of Nikolajewka. Even Russian fighter aircraft—supposedly vanquished from the Eastern skies by Göring's Luftwaffe—pestered from the air. Were these not the 'beaten enemy'?

At times, even with its limitations, the steel of the German advance seemed too much for Stalin. Even amid a defiant defence, the Germans managed to seize Nikolajewka. The southward pursuit towards Taganrog on 17 October was another matter, however. As Peiper and his company rushed that morning towards the railway line between that town and Rostov, huge Russian armoured trains hove into view and began bombarding his infantry with gunfire. Caught on the open embankment with no cover, the German ranks were shredded. The juggernauts defied even the heaviest calibre guns immediately available. Eventually Peiper's superiors were able to bring some powerful 88mm flak guns up to silence the trains, and by evening the port town was in German hands.[11] Still, losses were high.

Dark mushroom-like clouds of smoke from burning gasoline and exploding ammunition darkened the azure sky as the Russians hastened to evacuate the combine factories, heavy industry and metal works. As they arrived in Taganrog, the Germans opened fire on the gunboat *Krenkel*, which sank in the seaport. In the meantime the Russians blew up everything otherwise left behind—a sure sign of retreat. Even the remainders of the 44th Home Guards Detachment fought nihilistically against the Germans who would vanquish them. Casualties in the 11th Company were great.[12] The losses were not solely confined to Peiper's command: the 3rd Company under Heinrich 'Hein' Springer came out of the fighting for Taganrog with only seven unwounded men.[13]

Beyond that, the changing weather dashed German plans. On 20 October heavy rains turned the Russian roads to quagmire. Worn-out German transport vehicles sank up to their hubs in mire.[14] 'The mud season, in the whole of Russia, made an advance nearly impossible,' the division commander surmised. Within a week disease cost the Leibstandarte more dead than wounded. Most of Dietrich's vehicles as well as those of the neighbouring 13th Panzer Division now stood stuck for want of fuel and worn out from weeks of uninterrupted advance.[15] So perilous was the transport shortage that Dietrich personally signalled his adversary, Himmler, for help.[16]

The Leibstandarte stood on the Tusloff River only 25km north of Rostov when they received urgent orders to advance. But on 13 November the thermometer plummeted, revealing a summer-clothed German army ill prepared for the monstrous Russian winter. No one had sufficient warm clothing; the men had neither greatcoats nor proper footwear; indeed, Peiper's men wore Russian peasant clothing to keep from freezing. There wasn't enough antifreeze to restart their frozen engines. SS troopers huddled under icy tarpaulins as the winds blew waves of powdered snow.[17] On 27 November Dietrich reported thirty-one cases of frostbite, and he himself nearly lost the toes of his right foot.[18] Many, like experienced SS machine gunner Hans Siptrott, were weakened and made ill by the cold Russian winter and then sent home to recuperate.[19]

While the wheels of the Blitzkrieg froze in place, orders came for Dietrich to swoop down on Rostov in a lightning stroke. For the task, assistance came from a tank group in the adjacent 13th Panzer Division. Even under the atrocious conditions, the attack roared off in a snow storm on the morning of 17 November, even as the corps commander darkly reminded his superior, Ewald von Kleist, that his formations were too spent to hold off any large-scale enemy counterattack. Peiper's company was at point, with the fortified village of Sultan Saly as the immediate objective. Daybreak saw a total white-out from an ice fog; visibility was near zero. That delayed the advance until afternoon, when they could make out what lay before them. Although they promptly seized the town, a savage Russian counterattack in the late afternoon nearly overpowered elements of the IV Battalion just outside it. The Germans were caught out in the open fields. Soon the white-clothed Soviet forces surged around the Nazi defences and began to methodically shoot down the encircled prey. Winter war, Russian style.

With every gunner wounded and all nearly out of ammunition, Peiper suddenly arrived with the infantry of his company and three self-propelled assault guns. His counterattack knifed into the surprised enemy. Peiper called for more tanks from the neighbouring Panzer Regiment 4. Abruptly the enemy gave up, and Peiper himself brought in eleven hundred prisoners.[20]

> We lay there with our bayonets fixed, waiting for the enemy. Then suddenly they appeared, but were holding their hands up high, sur- rendering and not attacking, and shouting at us not to shoot. They had had enough. We could see their political commissars behind them, running away. We fired at them, but they were too quick. I think on that day that both sides were happy to just have survived.[21]

The fighting grew increasingly desperate. The Russians threw in batta- lions of women soldiers, whose ferocity and bravery shocked Peiper.[22] The retreating Russians left behind little of value. Factories were evacuated to Siberia, and those that were left behind, such as the tractor works in Kharkov, were so immense that 'it made those at Krupp look like a tiny blacksmith's shop'.[23] Crops, parts, or munitions were burned or destroyed:

> The same tactics that were so successfully used against Napoleon were also used against the invading German armies. All villages,

artificial installations and crops were burned down in the path of the approaching enemy. This left the German forces with few villages and buildings that could be used for warmth and survival from the severe Russian winter.[24]

On 20 November the SS division flung itself towards Rostov using every trick its troopers had up their sleeves. The remarkably tall commander of 3rd Company, SS Hauptsturmführer Heinrich Springer, planned a surprise attack on a railway bridge with his men arrayed in captured Russian clothing and Russian rifles. Peiper knew 'Hein' Springer well. Both audacious and impulsive, they were cut from the same cloth. By noon the SS men had captured the airfield, running hot on the heels of the retreating Russians. Clad in Russian uniforms, Springer and his improvised commandos suddenly found themselves charging into the heart of Rostov:

> The city was in a complete uproar, with streams of retreating Russians, vehicles, horses and civilians all mixed together. Everything was streaming towards the bridge over the River Don. Still in front of the public buildings were Russian guards with guns at their feet. The enemy did not suspect how close we were to the bridge.[25]

It was growing dark as Springer and his disguised combat team approached the double-arch steel-rail bridge. They could make out Soviet engineers preparing it for demolition. At that moment a large locomotive packed with Russian soldiers and a full head of steam roared out of the city. Springer immediately ordered his men to open fire on the engine with everything they had. There was an unworldly racket of bullets slamming into steel—like hail on a metal roof. The crippled iron beast staggered to a halt just before the bridge, clouds of hot steam spouting from the holes cut in its boilers. On the Russian side was total bedlam. Springer dashed across the steel girders and ripped away primer cords from the barrels of dynamite along the bridge pilings. His grenadiers swept to the south bank so quickly that they disarmed the bridge guard unit as they also ate their dinner.[26]

Meanwhile, amid the swirling maelstrom, savage street fighting erupted in the heart of Rostov with Peiper and his men. Fire poured out of building windows, the air choked with smoke and the streets were alive with the crackle of gunfire. Many were wounded in the bitter fighting. Eventually Peiper and what was left of his 11th Company—just thirty men—managed to reinforce Springer's position. They stayed in place through the night, taking refuge in basements as the Russians pounded their positions with gusts of artillery fire.[27]

Wild fighting still raged in Rostov—'solid chaos', judged one platoon leader. So fierce were the Russian counterattacks against the bridgehead on 21 November that Dietrich ordered it relinquished to the enemy. So Peiper and the 11th Company pulled back to the west bank to watch bitterly as the enemy blasted the hotly contested span. It was so cold that the waters of the Don froze solid, and what had been a natural military obstacle was now pervious to assault by infantry or raiders on horseback. During that day the final resistance in the center of Rostov was mopped up, with the Russians later claiming that the German invaders treated its citizens abominably.[28] 'The Battle of Rostov has been won,' crowed von Mackensen, the old cavalry general.[29] One SS man with Peiper even waxed poetic: 'Rostov is ours—roaring rolls of our gunfire and grenades fly though the air like organ music through the night!'[30]

At Hitler's East Prussian headquarters, the *Wolfsschanze* near Rastenburg, his adjutants watched as their chief's enthusiasm ebbed and flowed with the battle. On 5 October Heinrich Himmler stopped by to proffer insights from his recent tour to Kiev, Nikolayev and Cherson.[31] He called on the Leibstandarte as well as 'business' sojourns to his grim-tasked *Einsatzgruppen*. Werner Koeppen, a liaison officer, was present at Hitler's lunch to listen in the Führer extolled the beauty of his multi-coloured vegetarian table compared with one covered by butchered carcasses, while Himmler pronounced the Ukrainians expendable: 'In Kiev ... the number of inhabitants is still very large,' Himmler began. 'These people overall made a very poor proletarian impression, so that a good 80 to 90 per cent of them could be dispensed with!'[32] Himmler was thinking of Ohlendorf and his execution squads.

Two days later Himmler was again with Hitler to celebrate his forty-first birthday, with both of them astonished to witness a massive military encirclement of a full Russian army just completed near Vyazma only 240km west of Moscow. Heinz Guderian's revolutionary tactics, with their penetrating Panzer thrusts without regard for flanks, was again paying dividends. Jodl announced that some seventy-two enemy divisions were trapped. All caught in the net would later surrender—a staggering blow for the Russians. 'The military victory in the East has been won', Hitler blustered, 'and Russia is finished!'[33]

Six weeks later, however, in late November, all was changed. General Gerhard Engel, the army adjutant in Hitler's headquarters, noted his leader's increasing anxiety regarding future military prospects in the East:

'The Führer explains his great concern about the Russian winter and its weather, saying we started one month too late ... time is his greatest nightmare now.'[34]

Rostov infused Hitler's bad dream. As long as the Germans controlled the city, the Russians were intent on making the occupation costly: the garrison came under continuous artillery fire, punctuated by strong Russian armoured counterattacks from the north. Both the Leibstandarte and III Panzer Corps were weak, holding the won city against growing enemy forces. The usually irrepressible Kurt Meyer was down with dysentery, and his replacement, Hugo Kraas, found the Leibstandarte reconnaissance battalion repelling one reckless Russian divisional tank assault after another. Although the SS men stood their ground, von Kleist, in charge of the army group, saw that the Rostov bridgehead was dangerously overextended. On 22 November he ordered preparations to pull back to the Mius River.[35] On 1 December, General Field Marshal Gerd von Rundstedt, in charge of Army Group South, gave the orders to pull back from Rostov. Pull back? A pullback was ... a German retreat. Rostov was the first major reverse in Hitler's war.

The German leader bristled upon learning of von Rundstedt's order. He immediately telegraphed Heeregruppe South, which was already pulling out its forces: 'Remain at the front, retreat no further.'

'It is madness to attempt to hold,' von Rundstedt responded. 'I request this order be rescinded or you will find someone else.'[36] Someone else was Generalfeldmarschal Walther von Reichenau. Although a venerated icon in German military tradition, von Rundstedt, the wrinkled old field marshal, tendered his resignation. Hitler saw von Reichenau as a fearless and 'politically reliable' replacement for von Rundstedt.[37] Although unquestioning his own abilities, Hitler correctly sensed that leadership was not the only problem—he needed to further affix blame for Rostov.

How had his namesake division let him down? Perpetually focused on the fortunes of the Leibstandarte, Hitler immediately ordered a complete accounting of the strength of the division. On the last day of November, Dietrich reported 157 German officers and 4,556 men against an established strength of 290 Russian officers and 9,704 men.[38] He also estimated that only fifteen per cent of the two thousand assigned motorized vehicles were operational—now some 1,200km deep inside enemy territory. But most important, Dietrich told von Reichenau that the Rostov salient could not be held. He insisted that his personal assessment be transmitted directly to Hitler.[39]

For Hitler, Sepp Dietrich was difficult to ignore. 'He is one of my oldest companions in the struggle,' Hitler said, harkening back to the 1923 Munich putsch. Upon receiving Sepp's report, Hitler promptly boarded a plane and set off to Mariupol to get the word personally from his old comrade. Hitler met Dietrich at the airport on 2 December 1941, and the two rode together to Mackensen's field headquarters. Outside was the cold Russian winter. When they reached warmth and privacy, Dietrich, the old fighter, was candid. Even if distasteful, the retreat to the Mius had been necessary. Von Kleist was not a defeatist, Dietrich insisted. What Hitler told him is not recorded, yet on the last day of 1941 Hitler ordered Dietrich to his quarters, where he stayed for three days as Hitler's personal guest and received the Oak Leaves to the Knight's Cross.[40] Soon he would be off to Berlin to marry his second wife, Ursula Brenner. Said Hitler,

> Sepp Dietrich is unique ... A man who is simultaneously cunning, energetic and brutal ... And what care he takes with his troops! He's a phenomenon in the class of people like von Frundsberg, von Zeihten and von Seydlitz ... He is a Bavarian von Wrangle, someone who is irreplaceable.[41]

Amid the insufficiency of von Rundstedt in the south and Guderian before Moscow, Hitler had begun to turn increasingly to the likes of men such as von Reichenau and Dietrich, in whom the Prussian calculation and planning of the officer caste—which had failed—were substituted with loyalty and fanaticism. Charisma and determination, Hitler increasingly believed, could overmatch numerical superiority. The haughty von Rundstedt would later call Dietrich 'a cigarette roller' and 'decent, but stupid'.[42] It was the best an old deposed Prussian junker could say.

For the National Socialist social clutch in Berlin, Sepp was a celebrity. Before assembled guests at Hermann Göring's birthday party on 12 January 1942, the Reichsmarschall pronounced Dietrich 'the pillar of the Eastern front!'[43] 'Sepp Dietrich is a real trooper and makes one think of a Napoleonic general,' lauded propaganda minister Joseph Goebbels. 'If we had twenty men like that as divisional commanders, we wouldn't have to worry about the Eastern Front.' Even if old Sepp, the 'national institution', defended von Rundstedt and von Kleist publicly, his candid private opinion was less friendly. On 27 January Dietrich confided in Goebbels that 'the bourgeois generals on the southern front had lost their nerve and ... this weakness naturally communicated itself to the troops'.[44] Kurt Meyer evidenced even greater Waffen SS contempt for the army's general staff, stating, 'Mistrust of our generals … is by no means groundless, because they have not accepted National Socialism as a *religion*, as we have.'[45] Politically lukewarm to the cause and without *loyalty*, the regular army generals had *lost their nerve*. Said Peiper,

> The first voices of discontent were raised and the seed of disintegration fell on fertile ground. It is my conviction that the Chief of the General Staff [General Franz Halder] was the driving motive in this case. Held together by a strong caste spirit, he often stood indifferently above the factions and regarded the developments more from a scientific rather than a national viewpoint. As they further regarded the Führer from the beginning as a political adventurer, many of them now felt a certain vindication without considering that they were sawing off the branch on which they themselves were sitting … Hitler once christened the Chief of Staff, 'an order of Jesuits in red pants' and thought it to be the only lodge of Freemasons not yet dissolved![46]

But there was plenty of time for recrimination during the long months that the Leibstandarte sat in the winter wasteland along the icy Black Sea. The Blitzkrieg was over.

Jochen Peiper and the men of his 11th Company spent a frigid winter holiday on the banks of the icy Sambek River. For Peiper and the others, it was a winter of frozen foxholes, starkly similar to trench warfare of the previous war—only colder. There was no covering terrain, and Russian lines were clearly visible to anyone who could look. For this a portable periscope was recommended, as Russian sharpshooters were ever on the watch for an opportunity. 'There is nothing more miserable than the area where we now have been stuck for weeks,' wrote home another member of the division. 'And the "Red Insanity" still fights with total doggedness and lets itself be killed in its foxhole. What good fortune that we anticipated the Russian intentions—poor Germany, what would have become of us, if this multitude had rolled on first … We are going to spend our "holidays" in this wasteland in the East correspondingly and the band of godless will prepare for us a celebration.'[47]

Word that Hitler had declared war on the United States on 11 December 1941 seemed remarkably inauspicious as Peiper's company dug deeper into the frozen river banks. After all, the war had gone wrong that Christmas. The mood in Hitler's headquarters was as gloomy as it was in the icy foxholes around Taganrog. 'A dejected Christmas,' diplomatic liaison Walther Hewel recorded in his diary. '[T]he Führer's thoughts are elsewhere. No candles are lit.'[48] Peiper was now writing to Himmler's mistress again, this time having finally been let in on the secret of her pregnancy:

10 December 1941
Dear Little Sister:
Your dear letter arrived while we were still sitting on our proud steeds in Rostov—the first sign of life from you in almost four months. After the hasty steps of our advance have been checked, the opportunity arises while sitting in a comfortable hole in the ground to thank you. I want to do even more, now that peaceful festival of Christmas stands before the door and I can thank you as a part of my close family. The knowledge of not being forgotten, and being let in on a tender secret, has made me happy. You have no idea how sincerely happy I am for you all—Happiness, blessings, and health for the future are my honestly meant wishes, especially for you. I hope you can enjoy Christmas with soulful happiness ... I myself am doing well under the circumstances. We all have much to do together!

We all have survived everything so far, what has become daily custom during the recent months, just a cake walk!—Despite all dangers and privations, it is a great fortune for a young person to be given the opportunity to pass through this great smelting process, which frequently *forges* the spirit. I believe this experience enriches our inner self very much. I would not want to miss it for my later development! Without exception, my boys are heroes! Their quiet readiness for sacrifice always is worthy of admiration! Now, dear Hasenkind, enough about the cruel war. Do not forget me, remain healthy and cheerful and—be happy!—All this is to wish for you in old heartfelt warmth.

Your Jochen[49]

Meanwhile, back at Himmler's headquarters at Hochwald, the racial war was never far from the top of the Reichsführer's agenda.[50] On the first day of the month Himmler was on the phone with Heydrich discussing the massive 'executions in Riga'.[51] It was on 18 December, at *Wolfsschanze* that Himmler jotted down a terse and revealing note of his conversation with Hitler:

Führerhauptquartieier
Wolfsschanze 18.XII. 41. 16:00 hrs
Führer

Judenfrage | als Partisanen auszurotten
[Jewish question | exterminate as partisans][52]

36

Soon thereafter Himmler flew on to Taganrog and the Leibstandarte on 24 December 1941.[53] What did Peiper and the others of the division know of the recent killings of Jews nearby? Likely, quite a lot.

Around the same time Peiper attempted to provide a little levity for his men over the holidays, playing the role of *Weihnachtsmann*—Santa Claus—for his soldiers in the snowy trenches.[54] That Christmas Eve was a dreary mixture of cold rain, frost, snow and fog. When the snow paused, the Russian guns took over. Radio operator Sturmmann Hermann Riegamer recounted,

> Tomorrow is Christmas, the Holy Eve! In years past, one was full of expectation on this day. Would I ever have thought a year ago that I would be with my many comrades in another great family of comradeship in Russia on this most German of German holidays? … German Christmas deep in Russia, 200 metres from the Soviet's front posts! Father Christmas came to us at the last minute. Today one comrade from the unit went to the division to be decorated with his Iron Cross Second Class by Sepp … Our comrade came back from the Division Headquarters with his EK. He looked just like Father Christmas to us, for he had a huge postal sack on his back. In an instant it became Christmas. Candles burned and threw ghostly flickers on the white walls, which were hastily painted with hand-drawn fir branches … At 9:00 hours the Russian blessing set in like never before … Hit after hit, the damned artillery … At 10:00 hours the neighbouring house collapses under a direct hit … Blindly we clambered out of the rubble of our clay house which must have been hit. We lurched into the dark cellar, half stupefied. I took an unharmed bottle of schnapps along so we could toast each other.[55]

Awkwardly Himmler also did his part to cheer the flagship command of the Waffen SS. On 24 December 1941 he flew with his inner circle to Mariupol, where he spoke briefly with the ostracized leader of Panzer Group I, Generaloberst von Kleist. From there he flew to Taganrog, where he met Dietrich at the airport.[56] He spent the next day at the division headquarters at Nikolajewka and, with Dietrich, toured the front lines to convey greetings. The severe winter dismayed Dietrich: 'The ground, frozen down to 1.1 metres and the cold to minus 45 degrees very much deteriorated the health of the troops who were without winter equipment.'[57]

Later Himmler visited forty wounded soldiers of the Leibstandarte in a large hall in Taganrog that was being used as a hospital. On 26 December a somewhat ironic complimentary greeting arrived from the III Panzer Corps commander, von Mackensen:

I realized the demands on your time and the glorious roads of this Soviet paradise will not allow a visit ... Herr Reichsführer, I can assure you that the Leibstandarte is held in high regard ... This truly is an elite unit which I am proud and happy to have under me ... Whether you convey this message to the Führer, I leave to you.[58]

On Christmas Day Himmler was at the divisional post at Nikolajewka and speaking with Dietrich. (According to Himmler, Christmas was not a holiday for SS men—that was reserved for the *Julfest*, the festival of the winter solstice.) But Dietrich's tolerance of Himmler's quasi-military airs was strained. 'You have never been a soldier,' Dietrich told Himmler with growing impatience. 'You are no soldier and you will never be a soldier.'[59]

But some, like Kurt Meyer, overlooked Himmler's martial short-comings and remained enamoured with his steady demeanour. 'He is an extremely objective,' Meyer said, and a 'cool, calculating man'.[60] The Reichsführer then visited with his former adjutant to provide requisite Julfest greetings.[61] What Peiper told him is not recorded, but some inkling can be gleaned from Peiper's sarcastic assessment. 'The incredibly severe winter of 1941–1942 forced the German army to halt the offensive and was the beginning of the end,' Peiper began. 'At an average [below] freezing temperature of -30°Celsius, I remained with my company in the foremost ditches without a day of relief. Our winter clothing was almost entirely of Russian origin and the food consisted only of millet.'[62]

When Himmler prepared to fly back from Taganrog to Lódz on 28 December, the field airport gave him a taste of the Russian cold. He arrived at the frozen field to find big, ducted heaters in use to keep the engines of the Junkers warm enough to start. From Lódz Himmler and his escort drove on to see Hitler at the *Wolfsschanze* at eight o'clock that evening. There he grimly informed the German leader of the conditions he had seen the Leibstandarte enduring. With supply columns frozen, Dietrich had instituted strict rationing for meat and bread.[63] This must have done little to cheer Hitler's mood, who was now grappling with the prospect of the entire Eastern front disintegrating. He was now so convinced that his generals lacked the nerve to win the war, he announced that he was taking over leadership of the army himself.

* * *

Peiper, now sporting a moustache, was elated from Himmler's holiday visit, so much so that he took the opportunity to pen another letter to

Hedwig Potthast. In the letter he would covertly refer to Himmler in confidence as K.H.—König Heinrich, as the SS Reichsführer preferred from his inner staff. Himmler saw himself as the reincarnation of King Heinrich the 1st:

30 December 1941

My Dear Little Sister:

Your Christmas package, above all your nice writing was a great pleasure for me. Many people thought of me in a touching manner and in such an overflowing quantity, that the overtaxed Saint Nicholas had to take a break on his way and arrived one day late to me. One should recognize them by their gifts! This time, too. As usual, you bestowed upon me an especially thoughtful present (100 years old!). Presents of that kind always are reminders, which revive memories and from time to time encourage writing. If in the morning I shake the straw out of my head, I reach [into] the pocket and take out my comb with silver border. Do you still remember? It also will go this way in [the] future, when I shall reach into my breast pocket to feel the cognac still gurgling.

While I am writing these lines—lying on my back—outside a mighty snowstorm has been raging all night. This morning, everything was snowed under. Only with great effort did we fight our way out to daylight! Today a snowstorm—tomorrow streaming rain and the day after tomorrow crackling frost—these are the weather characteristics of our neighbourhood here. Otherwise, nothing new from the trench war. As before, the Russian is after our lives and we are thinking hard about how to make his existence difficult for him and spoil their efforts.

All of us, were naturally surprised on 24 December by the visit of the SS Reichsführer to the division. You can imagine my surprise, when I, unsuspecting, was called to the telephone and suddenly heard the familiar voice of K.H. [Himmler]. Being together the next day not only was a change from my life in a hole but beyond that a present that made me happy! (Please do not tell that to anybody!! [anybody is a euphemism for Himmler himself]) As you will have told to other ones everything, I would like to ask you how things went for you and what you are doing, reading, etc. In this frozen land here, one is glad about every word from at home!—Especially from you! I have a great yearning and am immensely anxious for Elke [Peiper's daughter]! Sigurd writes that people see in the very playful Elke, her mother, and in the serious Elke her Pappi. Is that correct? Nobody gives me an objective report and I am always depending on my miserable fantasy!

In other respects, time flies. The days are so short, that we spent most of our time in darkness. Things around me are full of activity: two men are sitting at the writing table, four are catching lice, and one is grinding coffee. The latter I must explain better. The preparation of this invigorating elixir is done in an old welding urn. Naturally, we do not have a coffee mill. So, the beans are wrapped into a relatively clean foot-wrapping rag, rolled and crushed with a hand grenade with a wooden handle. After that, we serve it with a *Stollen* sent by the Führer.

We have become wild mercenaries. We celebrate festivities as they occur, are rough and soft—Callous and sometimes a little sentimental. For you, my dear distant little sister, are all my heartfelt thoughts! Strength and health for the coming, fortune and fulfilment for the year 1942; those are my wishes! Don't forget me and write soon.

Always, your Jochen[64]

Nor did the Reichsführer SS forget his meeting with his former squire. Mindful of his extended SS family, the following morning Himmler personally phoned Sigurd Peiper in Berlin to extend wishes from her husband—likely leaving out the inglorious details of her man's holidays in a frozen Russian trench. 'Greetings from Jochen,' the telephone register recorded. On Friday, 2 January 1942 Himmler thoughtfully had his personal secretary, Erika Lorenz, pay a special visit to 'Mother Peiper'.[65] Sigurd Peiper was pregnant again and due in the spring. All the while, during those dark days at the end of 1941, Sigurd burned a bright yellow flame in the earthenware *Julleuchter* candle holder that had been a gift from the Reichsführer SS on the occasion of the solstice.[66] In spite of hearts and Hagall runes under the candle, her husband was not home, and she was raising her daughter alone. She did keep in close contact with Hedwig Potthast, who had some surprising news.

Jochen now heard again from 'Bunny' that she too was expecting a baby—a baby from her extramarital affair with Heinrich Himmler.[67] As Himmler's former secretaries, she and Sigurd remained close. Now both were due to have children within weeks of each other while he crouched in an icy Russian foxhole:

10 February 1942
Dear Häschen:
These days your detailed letter of 20 January arrived, with which you caused me a lot of pleasure! While we here stumble around in miserable stupidity, I often think about home and you too! All the things you all are doing! When you and Sigurd are together, there will be 300 pounds swaying along. And the Elke baby is growing from a baby into a small human child. And great events are about to happen and I cannot be there even once to make sure everything goes right. But knowing you and your vanity, I think you are quite pleased with that!

40

Sigurd thinks that I shall receive leave at the earliest in fall. Should this happen, you will again have gone back to being 'girdle slim'. Then we shall push through the streets with our Kinderwagen caravan and let our three kids be admired!

But until then, a lot of water is going to flow under the bridge. During the last weeks we had a snow storm of until now unknown force! Now, it is raining since yesterday! On both sides of our ditches, snow is piled up 3 metres high! Now, all this will turn to water! I trudge through the mud worrying and prepare my men for action as 'Technical Emergency Support'. We all have a little bit of 'bunker tantrums'. We have been lying around here for already 2½ months! Now, three months of rain and mud weather are coming! But there is an end to everything! As long as you at home think of us so faithfully, nothing can happen to us! While I am thanking you again heartily for your loving lines and especially for the small, nice little book, I am with many heartfelt greetings.

Always Your
Jochen[68]

Peiper's twenty-seventh birthday on 30 January 1942 was celebrated in a cold trench on the Sambek. SS Haupsturmführer Hugo Kraas shared the small celebration with Jochen, his own birthday having been only five days before. The thin-faced Kraas was quickly making more of a name for himself, having been the first Leibstandarte officer to win the Iron Cross first class in 1940 in France. More recently he had stood in for the ill Kurt Meyer and had performed dashingly well—earning himself the German Cross in Gold.[69] But on Peiper's birthday both men were likely thinking more about warmth than medals. On the Sambek there was a fierce wind blowing in a snowstorm from the East. The thermometer sunk to -30 degrees Celcius.[70]

Peiper's birthday on 30 January came on the *Machtergreifung*, the annual birth celebration of National Socialism. Far away from Berlin, Hitler spoke words to inspire his nation—words to which Peiper felt some fateful annual link. Far off in Russia Peiper may have not heard the broadcast, but he most certainly was able to read of Hitler's words in the *Völkischer Beobachter*, as a copy always made the rounds. But the focus of Hitler's speech was not Russia—it was the racial war:

I do not even want to speak of the Jews. They are simply our old enemies, their plans have suffered a shipwreck through us and they rightly hate us, just as we hate them. We realize that this war can only end either in the wiping out of the Germanic nations, or by the disappearance of all Jews from Europe![71]

As Hitler made the clarion call for expanding the racial clash, others found themselves trying to get the military back on track. That same day Sepp Dietrich and Albert Speer flew one of Hitler's personal Heinkel 111s from Berlin to the industrial city of Dnepropetrovsk. Speer was Hitler's architect and soon-to-be armaments minister who had been charged with supervising railway repair in Ukraine. Russian partisans had ripped up the rails, and consequently much of Army Group South was nearly without food, fuel or ammunition. Dietrich, returning to the Leibstandarte after a month of awards, a honeymoon and a glitzy slate of partying and social fanfare, watched Russia pass by with Speer as their plane droned along:

> To keep our direction, we flew along the railway line. Scarcely a train could be seen; the stations were all burned out and the roundhouses were destroyed. Beneath us the dreary, snow-covered plains flowed by … The great stretches of land we passed over were frightening in their deathly silence, which could be felt even inside our plane … The trip brought home to me the danger to the armies almost cut off from supplies.

After the Heinkel transport crunched onto the whitened airstrip, the passengers stepped out to find that snow was coming down like a river of white. Speer and Dietrich found themselves snowed in by a Siberian blizzard, making it impossible for either to escape the airfield. Speer, the intellectual, marvelled at Dietrich's rapport with the men on the rail construction crew. All gathered around, sang songs and tried to keep warm. A momentary scare came when word arrived that Russian tanks were approaching. The enemy apparition disappeared, with the Soviet armour itself lost in the blinding snow.[72] The chunky Bavarian general made a simple speech. Even amid near-comic disarray, all the workers cheered. Here was the Russian winter.

Meanwhile, Peiper and his men were equally marooned. The elite, cocky Leibstandarte officers, so daring and fixed on the glory of attack, sat for four long months in static trench warfare on the Donets River. Peiper and the rest of the Leibstandarte huddled in their frozen holes, pummelled sporadically by Russian artillery, with its characteristic sound—a thunder like a gigantic door being slammed in the sky. 'Unfortunately, the quality of the Russian war materiel quite often is good,' wrote Peiper's contemporary Heinz von Westernhagen:

> For instance, the Russians have plenty of artillery, of good quality and rather nimble. They caused us some damned problems … You are correctly asking where the Russian gets all his war materiel. We, too, again and again have been astonished and cursed … in spite of that, what is left to be done is no problem. I no longer consider the final destruction of the Red Army a problem after the return of normal weather, because the Russians lost too many men and materiel; one can notice their shortages.[73]

Regardless of their enemy's suffering, the Russians had by no means given up. Indeed, at night enemy patrols harassed Peiper's men while blaring Russian folk music over loudspeakers, which would pause only for unanswered calls for defection. Against that, there were lonely hours of sentry duty in sub-zero temperatures at gun positions clad in what SS men saw as unseemly Polish winter wear. Snowstorms, lice and hunger added even more misery. And Peiper himself would develop dysentery like most of the others.[74]

If the German situation seemed desperate, then the view from the Russian side was equally dismal. Stalin sent out peace feelers to Foreign Minister Rudolf von Ribbentrop, and Hitler reciprocated. Would the frigid stalemate end with a diplomatic stroke? Indeed, in February 1942 Peiper's old superior at Himmler's headquarters, Karl Wolff, was sent to Mtsensk in Belarus for a super-secret meeting with an NKVD (secret police) representative sent by Stalin himself. Wolff, the shrewd upper-class negotiator, heard Stalin's proposal: a ceasefire on the Eastern Front beginning May of 1942 with a German pull-back to the Russian border. In return the Soviet Union would become an ally of the German forces to begin military actions against England and the United States in 1943–44, 'with the goal of creating a new world order'. Stalin agreed that Germany and the USSR could collectively blame 'international Jewry' for the war, then carve up the entirety of the planet for ownership by the Germans, Russians and Japanese.

Nevertheless, in the eventual meeting Wolff counter-proposed. Although enthusiastically embracing Stalin's offer to 'put an end to Jewry,' the Germans would only pull back to the positions occupied at the end of 1941. This snag—specifically the clash over surrendering won territory—effectively put an end to the futile negotiations after one week, on 27 February 1942. Although Wolff agreed with Stalin that the war might stretch on for several more years, he was convinced it would be the Germans who would emerge victorious. The frozen crusade in the East would go on.[75]

Peiper likewise saw that a fleeting opportunity was passing in the East—a point he would reflect on in later years:

> The incredibly severe winter of the year 1941–1942 forced the German army over to the defensive and was the beginning of the end. As no one believed or contended that a continuous line of defence running from the Polar Sea to the Asonic Sea would become necessary, all of the preparations and especially the foundations for supply were non-existent … A peace at this time without a doubt could have been within reach and also would have provided a time gains of several years and given us protection in the rear for a one front war in the West.[76]

Amid the icy boredom of Russia, there was both good and bad news from Berlin. On 14 April 1942 Peiper learned that his second child, Hinrich, was born—a happy event. Yet, less than a month later officials informed Jochen that his eldest brother, Hans-Hasso, had died in Berlin on 11 May. Under treatment at a sanatorium, the official cause of death was tuberculosis. However, his father would later claim that Hans-Hasso had been 'a victim of war … sterilized by the Nazis according to a decision of the court and he died a short time later'. The 62-year-old father was relieved from his job at the tank repair facility in Poland and sent to a reserve hospital in Wilmersdorf. The reason given: heart strain. And Jochen Peiper was now the sole surviving son.[77]

From the winter cold, a long line of trains jangled to the West, with the SS legions aboard longing for revenge, but on their guard.

Chapter 3

France and Back

'We developed a firm, practical feeling of solidarity, which grew, on the battlefield, into the best thing that the war produced—comradeship in arms.'

—Erich Maria Remarque

By spring 1942 Peiper and his men had been so long in Russia that Heinrich Himmler began to fear that his racial warriors might start to lose a sense of what it meant to be German. Moreover, there was now the very real threat of an Allied invasion in France. Even with the conflict in the East demanding most of the military resources, Hitler decided that the most trustworthy formations needing refitting and should be moved to the West to rehabilitate. There they could reorganize unfettered while being ready as a reliable emergency force. Thus, Peiper and the Leibstandarte Adolf Hitler could be moved to the West to help take care of both needs.

At the end of May 1942 Peiper and the rest of the Leibstandarte were pulled from the front line to Mariupol on the shores of the Sea of Azov. There they were to rest, refit and serve as a mobile reserve. Food was short, but at last the men could relax. Dietrich received word that his tired command would be outfitted to a full division. A fifth battalion returned, which originally had been Hitler's guard battalion in Berlin and more recently had detached temporarily on the Leningrad front.[1] As Dietrich celebrated his fiftieth birthday on 28 May 1942, the entire newly expanded division received its own gift: moving to the rest area near Mariupol. Dietrich gushed: 'While our losses have not been exactly light, we have borne them proudly for our Führer and our homeland … Wherever we have fought, we have successfully passed the test of strength … And be assured we will continue to endure … You can depend on us.'[2]

Weary SS soldiers greeted the break with delight. Some had not been on leave in two years. There was a chance to bathe and relax. As most other units pulled out, on 29 May Kurt Meyer's reconnaissance battalion organized a 'sports festival'. Everyone stripped off their shirts in the warm spring sun and cackled with laughter as they watched Haupsturmführer Gustav Knittel and Gerhard Bremer's antics: 'motorized sausage catching'—literally trying to snatch a *wurst* dangling on a string in their mouths while driven around in a motorcycle sidecar. Other events included a blindfolded whipped cream eating contest and a colourful Roman-style chariot race.[3]

More than that, Hitler had personally decreed that the reorganized division would be outfitted with an Mk IV tank battalion and another of artillery, anti-tank and assault guns. There would be more hand-picked SS troopers allocated. The unit would be brought to 100 per cent effectiveness and would nearly double in size. As the new Panzer command would be organized in Wildflecken, the opportunity presented itself to have the entire command moved for a complete reorganization.[4]

SS machine gunner Hans Siptrott, temporarily back in Berlin as an honour guard in 1942 at the Reichs chancellery, saw the opportunity to go to the tanks. Originally SS officer Rudi Sandig requested he return to Russia to lead an infantry platoon at Leningrad, but Siptrott protested. 'I want to go to a unit that doesn't have to march,' he said, considering the invitation from Rudolf von Ribbentrop, the son of Hitler's foreign minister, and another well-known comrade, Ralf Tiemann. Changing to the tanks was easy, he remembered. There was no 30lb MG-34 with a tripod to carry, and approaching the enemy behind iron sides seemed better. After all, a machine gunner was highly vulnerable; Siptrott had lost an assistant gunner in Russia.

But going back home, Siptrott was agog at the contrast. The atmosphere at the Wildflecken training ground was totally unlike the Eastern Front. There were over a dozen canteens in the area with plentiful food and drink—and drink particularly. 'By the time you had made it through all 21 canteens,' Siptrott joked, 'you were burned out.'[5] Soon 'Old Spitz'— Siptrott's new nickname—was in Sennelager with the others to be trained by the army as a tanker on the 25-ton Panzer IV.

Hitler quickly decided where best to reorganize his personal elite. With the move of U.S. forces to Great Britain after Pearl Harbor, Hitler became worried that the Allies might attempt a surprise invasion of France. Deciding that his forces in the West must be strengthened, he decreed that France would be an excellent location to train his namesake division into a fanatical tank force.

Being the former adjutant of the Reichsführer SS had other privileges. Peiper came away frequently from the front—this time as soon as they pulled out of the line. On 1 June 1942 Peiper appeared at Himmler's field quarters at Hochwald at 1500 hours for an hour meeting to be followed later with a cosy dinner with Himmler, Rudolf Brandt and SS General Heinz Lammerding.[6] The scar-faced SS officer was on the staff of the heartless Theodor Eicke within the concentration camp system and was more recently the 1st staff officer with Eicke's Totenkopf Division, where he was organizing a tank battalion.

The conversation between the four almost certainly involved the medical condition of Reinhard Heydrich, who had been mortally wounded in an assassination attempt in Prague on 27 May. Peiper knew Heydrich from his days on Prinz Albrechtstrasse and, of course, because Sigurd and Lina Heydrich were old school chums with Heydrich from Kiel. Some said that in years past Heydrich had even courted Sigurd Hinrichsen. The dinner and conversation that night went on for three hours. The very next day Himmler and those with him flew to Prague to be at the side of the dying Heydrich.

On Sunday, 7 June 1942, as the flag-draped caisson bearing Heydrich's body passed through the streets of Prague, Himmler stood in the foreground with one of Heydrich's blond-haired sons on either arm. The music corps of the SS Leibstandarte provided the dirge as well as the honour guard.[7] 'Our friend Heydrich is now under the sod,' Himmler pronounced. 'Now the whole SS ... will march on with beating drums and helmets donned. So long as one man in any positions ... remains who can crook a finger around a trigger, all is not lost.'[8]

Still, the death of Heydrich weighed on Himmler. Heydrich had always carried out the very worst of Himmler's edicts. What Peiper learned from his former boss that summer can only be guessed; however, Peiper was with Himmler often in those months. Beyond his official presence on 1 June, Peiper's location at Himmler's field headquarters emerged a month later. This information comes from a discovered document in which a member of Himmler's office notes having received files from Peiper regarding the need for a rapid decision on whether or not to allow Vera Hinrichsen, the widow of Sigurd's brother Rolf, to remarry her other brother, SS Haupsturmführer Kurt Hans Hinrichsen. The letter, dated 11 July 1942, clearly indicates that Peiper was at Himmler's field headquarters the previous day.[9]

Later, on 22 June 1942, Peiper and the other high officers of the Leibstandarte Adolf Hitler came into close contact with those involved in the dirty work of killing Jews and what they derisively referred to as the *Untermenschen* just behind their front lines. The contact was a drinking party at the church-command post of Sepp Dietrich for Heinrich Seetzen on the occasion of the latter's birthday. Seetzen was the head of Sonderkommando 10a, which was involved in expansive killings that took place in the wake of Dietrich's men. Dietrich brought all his higher SS officers to the *Trinkgelage*: Fritz Witt, Theodor Wisch, Alfred Bludau and Jochen Peiper. SS Hauptsturmführer Hermann Müller-John, who was close to Seetzen's men, provided music for the festivities, where the Leibstandarte and the Sonderkommandos did a lot of socializing—drinking and blowing off steam.[10] In the drunken carousing, Peiper and the others heard more about what the Einsatzkommando had been up to for the last year—if one could even naively imagine they did not know before. Peiper's former boss was divulging much as well.

In the following weeks hesitant communication from SS Reichsführer Himmler to those around him revealed a secret too large to conceal: the mortally wounded Heydrich had spawned a terrible plan, and Himmler now inherited the responsibility of carrying it out. 'The occupied territories must be cleared of Jews,' he wrote to Gottlob Berger. 'The Führer has charged me with carrying out this very difficult task. No one can relieve me of the responsibility.'[11] Peiper's old superior in Himmler's office, Karl Wolff, was drawn into the quagmire, smugly thanking by letter a minister of transport for verifying that thousands of Jews were being transported from Warsaw to Treblinka and, ultimately, unspoken extermination: 'My warm thanks, also in the SS Reichsführer's name, for your letter of 28 July. I was especially delighted to hear from you that already for a fortnight there has been a daily train, taking 5,000 of the *Chosen People* to Treblinka, thus enabling us to carry out this movement of populations with increasing tempo.'[12]

Since March 1942 mass executions using carbon monoxide from diesel engines had been taking place at Belzec elimination camp near Lublin as well as near Mariupol in the south-eastern Ukraine. However, systematic murder using the pesticide Zyklon-B quickly became the preferred means of mass slaughter: by May 1942 Sobibor became operational, Treblinka in June, and Auschwitz by July. Each camp had the capability of killing thousands each day and cremating their remains—a process so diabolical that it defied belief.[13]

Indeed, Himmler and a fleet of others flew from the East Prussian headquarters to Kattowitz, Poland, on 17 July to see how the elimination camp at Auschwitz functioned. The commandant, Rudolf Höss, escorted the SS Reichsführer and an entourage around the death camp 'so he got a good look at everything'. Although Himmler had supposedly gone weak at the knees after witnessing the gassing operations using the Zyklon B insecticide, he later pronounced himself pleased with the operation, announcing to those around him that 'those were battles the coming generations wouldn't have to fight'.[14]

We know that Peiper had been with Himmler the week before. Had he accompanied his former boss on 17 July 1942? One photograph taken of Himmler's visit to Auschwitz shows Peiper's successor, Werner Grothmann, standing just behind Himmler in front of one of the ugly brick buildings of the elimination camp complex.[15] Some accounts have confused Peiper for Grothmann in these photos. Although this remains an academic question as to whether Peiper personally visited Auschwitz that summer, there is no question that Peiper learned what was going on there and at the other Polish extermination camps during those weeks. Peiper later made this clear by his own admission to his battalion adjutant, Otto Dinse.[16] There was no forgetting that dark secret.

Now, having learned about the *Endlösung* from Himmler, Peiper journeyed to France to meet his division at the end of the July. The Leibstandarte had been loaded into trains in mid-July near Mariupol. On 26 July 1942 they debouched to the sunny warm French countryside near Fontainebleau, east of Paris. Three days later, on 29 July, Dietrich's men put on a flamboyant parade through the streets of Paris. To impress Allied eyes, the procession featured all the new tanks, armoured cars, guns and motorcycles of Dietrich's revamped command. The impression—particularly of Schönberger's Panzer battalion—was formidable. Arrayed in neatly pressed uniforms and standing resolutely in each tank hatch, the Panzer men flowed down the Parisian streets, their arms raised in the Hitler salute as they passed. Message: the German army is strong in occupied France.

Presiding over the whole affair was the new commander of German forces in the West, none other than venerable old Generalfeldmarschal Gerd von Rundstedt. Looking the part of the Prussian field marshal, von Rundstedt stood ramrod straight; on his right side was Sepp Dietrich, and flanking the other was the father of the Waffen SS, Paul Hausser. As von Rundstedt held his baton for the stone-faced grenadiers passing by, Jochen Peiper had to be thinking of the irony: fresh from the Rostov debacle, the vanquished commander of Army Group South was now back in charge.[17]

For Peiper and the men of the Leibstandarte, gliding down the Champs Élysées, the troop may as well have been in another world—there was no snow, no lice, no enemy or primitive days wallowing in holes. The

French air was warm and clean, the green trees were lush, and attractive women—even with pensive smiles—beamed from under awnings lining the sidewalks. The Leibstandarte glided through the Arc de Triumph. The entire parade took nearly six hours, as witnessed by Guenther Borchers of Peiper's troop:

> The entire LSSAH Division rolled in an unbroken column through Paris. French people stood in thick crowds on the city sidewalks. Heavy antiaircraft weapons were positioned on the Concorde Place, to protect us from surprise attacks in the air. We rolled through the Arch of Triumph through Poissy, Nantes, Loynes, Ivery, St. Andre, Daimoille toward our present barracks in Creton. We ate melons and peaches, and bought chickens and fried them.[18]

The division then assembled for its work-over near Evreux. Peiper and his troops were billeted in and around Verneuil-sur-Avre. Rather than an icy trench, Peiper set up in a lovely chateau just behind the main square, surrounded by a bright green lawn and manicured park.[19] His wife even came to France to join him. His satisfaction that summer must have been palpable: a happy Sigurd bringing along their new son and daughter. Jochen, with his wife, greeted the men of his company with champagne and a chorus of cheers.[20] Regardless of the official toast, the unofficial one must have been: to the warmth of France. There were other cheers upon Peiper's arrival. On 10 August 1942, at Verneuil, Peiper took part in the ceremony celebrating the official assignment of the 1st SS Infantry Regiment to SS Standartenführer Fritz Witt.[21]

Verneuil was heaven—a charming French town with the beautiful old l'Eglise de la Madeleine from the twelfth century and the lattice of ancient moats separated by lime-green lawns. Even the houses were cute, with the criss-cross timbered architecture of the Maisons à colombages. There were also the trappings of culture. For a budding Francophile there was the old La Tour Grise castle from the thirteenth century, and for the deprived palate there were the patisseries and crusty French bread and sidewalk cafés along the flowered cobble-stoned streets of the big centre town market. For the ears there was the lovely sing-song of the church bell tower at seven o'clock every morning and evening. Flowers burst from every balcony. Verneuil was art for the senses.

The Germans lucky enough to be there occupied over a dozen houses in the village and took over the École des Roches outside of town. 'They were all over the place, but we got used to them,' said one young French boy, Jacques Derlon. The French didn't see the Germans as all that bad. 'We tolerated them,' Derlon, recalled. In 1942 the war didn't seem all that close in Verneuil. True, a stray bomb had levelled the train station in 1940 and created a lot of boyhood excitement, but mainly the French way of life—long hours for the older men every day at the same café—went on. For the locals it was easy to recognize the SS guys, as they had 'Adolf Hitler' written on their sleeves. 'They weren't nasty,' recalled one. 'The officer at the villa chateau gave me candy and cakes.' Jacques Bayet remembered that one kid had a bike stolen, and the Germans helped replace it. 'But we had to be careful as we were secretly listening to de Gaulle on Radio London.'

Beyond helping local kids and soaking up French culture, some of Peiper's men opted for more fecund diversions. They were men, after all. Recreation French-style: wine, beer and the opposite sex.

> Some French women clustered around the gate and invited us to chat for a while. But we had already heard great things about France. Some of us wanted to know for sure, though, and went off with them. After they came back we weren't laughing anymore. Just great! The French came with wine and champagne to sell, and made a lot of sales with us. We stayed the night in the city. Then one of the French women came back and wanted to speak with the 'Commander' because 'your friend didn't pay his bill.' 'The Commander isn't here,' was our answer. It was really funny to us, and that night passed very quickly. There was accordion music on the square.[22]

The Café de Europe was particularly essential in this role, with its plentiful weak beer and continuing popularity with the French locals—particularly the women.[23] Excessive drinking would not be tolerated, decreed Peiper, and at first he forbade close contact with French women. But the battalion doctor challenged the young SS officer. 'You can't do this,' he told him, 'because it would be too hard for the men. The married men are used to sex and it would be too much pressure for the others.'[24] Peiper let it go.

Himmler agreed with Peiper's priggish ways. On 5 January 1943, the Reichsführer SS wrote to Carl Oberg, the senior SS and police commander in France, complaining that Dietrich admitted that seven thousand members of the Leibstandarte had come down with venereal disease in France. It was common knowledge that many SS men in the East had kept a plump Ukrainian *devochka*—a friendly local mistress. Still, unlike Peiper, Himmler acknowledged the carnal needs of his high-strung SS thoroughbreds. Properly controlled military brothels, Himmler opined, were the solution to this mess.

Dietrich hastily revised the numbers, informing Himmler that the true number of cases was only 244—a fantastic reduction. But Himmler was not at all satisfied. For the real concern of the SS Reichsführer was not sex but that his pure stock of SS manhood was fooling around with untempered races. Himmler proposed that Waffen SS men be forbidden to have sex with non-Germanics. However, Dietrich, knowing that many of his officers kept a mistress, intended to ignore the edict, calling it an 'order issued by theoretical experts'.[25] In the meantime, Fritz Witt went to Paris to source select prostitutes for his men in order to put a stop to the sexually transmitted diseases from local 'ladies of the night'. He installed selected ladies in a brothel/hotel near his regimental headquarters. That move was more popular.[26]

Beyond the drinking and libidinous affairs that summer, the big excitement in August came when the Canadians landed on French beaches at Dieppe. For a time the division was put on full alert—with many training for the possibility of an Allied airborne assault. But German forces quickly smashed the actual small Allied landing team near the beachhead, and high command rescinded the alert.[27] 'No action was required on our part,' a Leibstandarte man jotted in his diary, 'which was a shame as we would have gladly "greeted" those gentlemen.' At least, he ventured, the assigned SS man in his company had shown up with the promised Schnapps delivery.[28]

Hitler dispatched Dietrich to inspect the scene of the Canadian disaster. Along with Albert Speer, Dietrich toured the failed beachhead on 19 August 1942. The weather was beastly hot as they poked about. The French sands were littered in a macabre display of broken Canadian tanks and equipment.[29] Was this the invasion that Hitler predicted? Command nerves were jittery.

That August Himmler himself, at his Hegewald Headquarters near Zhitomir, confessed his worries to Walter Schellenberg, his head of the *Sicherheitsdienst* Ausland (SD intelligence) and increasingly a confidant since the demise of Heydrich. 'How do you think this will end?' he posed ominously to his underling. Many things now seemed to go wrong on all fronts in the war for Germany. Schellenberg darkly suggested that Germany strive for an armistice with England—or else the war seemed lost now that America was coming in on the side of the British—just like with the previous war. What kind of deal would be acceptable to the British empire? The two men bent over maps and whispered about arrangements. What if they gave back France, except for Himmler's beloved Alsace Lorraine? Burgundy in France was another sore point. They would keep Austria and south-west Czechoslovakia and hold Poland as a bargaining chip. Could it work? Himmler lamely suggested Schellenberg quietly explore feelers via his spy network.[30] Even in October 1942, Hitler was convinced that the Allies were about to land in Normandy. That Canaris's *Abwehr* mistakenly predicted this event likely prevented the division from being shipped off to North Africa, where, at El Alamein, Field Marshal Erwin Rommel teetered on the edge of defeat.[31] So the Leibstandarte alerted and stood down, over and over. On 13 September von Rundstedt inspected their new tanks. An omen for North Africa?

No one knew, but on the next day, 14 September 1942, Peiper was promoted to leader of the III Battalion of SS Infantry Regiment 2. Many whispered that Peiper continued to receive help from his former boss. Earlier in the summer of 1942 the battalion—mostly composed of men from the SS Totenkopf Standarte 8 and 10—had been commanded by 36-year-old SS Sturmbannführer Günther Anhalt. But the old fighter's performance had been unsatisfactory. He was not popular with his men; one characterized him as 'famously insufferable'.[32] What's more, Anhalt had a *big* drinking problem—something that rubbed Himmler the wrong way. Drinking was already a concern in the Waffen SS—much less having leaders weaving in their cups. Even if Hitler said he cared much more how fast a soldier could march than how many litres of beer he could drink, the propensities of male German youth deemed otherwise. Thus, it seems hardly surprising that Anhalt was relieved of command in early September 1942 by order of Himmler himself.[33] Indeed, Anhalt did not even say farewell; he just disappeared.

The opening was now there for Peiper, but he was only an SS captain—an SS Hauptsturmführer—and he was young even for that post. In the meantime, his former commander, Fritz Witt, made an application for Peiper's promotion with the usual glowing endorsements. 'The character is clear and clean,' he stated with obvious contrast to Anhalt. 'He observes critically; hard and also cynical in his criticism … He leaves a company that in every respect is of high quality.'[34] Peiper counted on his connections.

This time it didn't work, however. Himmler denied the application in November, allegedly because of Peiper's youth. Possible consolation came on 1 September 1942, when Peiper received the *Winterschlacht im Osten* medal, disparagingly known as the *Gefrierfleischmedaille*—frozen flesh medal. Even without the promotion, Peiper took command of the battalion on 14 September. Rank or not, he now had a full battalion of supposedly elite troops.

Although his command featured relatively less experienced men (most of the IV Battalion, which had only been formed in June 1941), he knew they would ride into battle on armoured halftracks. As a dedicated horseman, Peiper saw these fast, all-terrain vehicles as a modern embodiment of the cavalry.[35] He would teach the men saddled on the *Schützenpanzerwagen*, or SPWs, to attack at his tempo—a three-beat gait of a war stallion. If a massed cavalry charge of SPWs was halted, he would soon have a proper battering ram nearby. In November at Evreux the Leibstandarte was allocated a company of the new super-heavy Tiger tanks—a telling indicator of the favour of Dietrich's command.[36] For Peiper, who knew he would fight alongside the tanks, there was only one touchy thing about the Panzer regiment: there, again, was Max Wünsche, an SS officer with an ego as big as Peiper's. The more medals the better.

Training soon became an obsession. On the day Peiper took over leadership the battalion formed up in a courtyard in Verneuil. As Peiper paced nervously, the short battalion adjutant, the blond-headed SS Obersturmführer Otto Dinse, made a short speech calling for a dedication similar to what the former commander enjoyed.

Peiper already knew Dinse. Like himself, Dinse had signed up early for the SS. Peiper had met Dinse with Himmler at the launching of the battleship *Bismarck* on 14 February 1939, when he was the adjutant of the police chief of Bremen. They met again in Lódz in Poland in October 1940 while Peiper was with Himmler and Karl Wolff. At that time SS Captain Dinse was busy helping to round up Jews—ostensibly to be resettled elsewhere. As a typical SS man, he did not speculate on their fate. Only after the war would he express any remorse.

When Peiper spoke, any hesitation from any under him visibly disappeared; he reminded each man of his allegiance. Look at your sleeve, he told them, you have a reputation to uphold as 'a unit that the Führer could always rely on'.[37] Each morning Peiper insisted on overseeing training exercises and conducting parade drills—even for veterans. 'We were not thrilled,' remembered one. However, Dinse, the old-timer, recognized Peiper as 'a true leader of troops'.[38] Everyone drilled the Leibstandarte way: accuracy with weapons, speed in firing and fast manoeuvre.

Peiper made his quarters in a small castle behind the town marketplace even more cosy. In September new BMW motorcycles were delivered for their new terrain reconnaissance platoon under SS Untersturmführer Georg Preuss, who enjoyed puttering around to the castles of France and engaging Frenchmen in conversation. Now with leisure time, Peiper also took in the French countryside on motorcycle or, upon returning home, struck up a quick game of table tennis. Even in the hectic training pace, the Waffen SS found time for their cherished athletic events. In November Peiper himself presided over the events at Verneuil, addressing participants in everything from marksmanship and a 15km forced march to a competition for the best singers in the battalion.

France was casual. That autumn there was time to get a dog, to see Sigurd and even to write to Hedwig Potthast—Himmler's mistress and close friend of Peiper's wife. Potthast was now with her new boy-child, Helge:

19 October 1942

Dear Häschen:

Heartfelt thanks for your letter of 15 September, which recently arrived here. I could not find an explanation for your silence and thought I had put my foot into my mouth somewhere. I have written to everyone (Erika [Lorenz], Kurt, Hermann Dörner, Grothmann, Sepp Kiermaier, Franz Lucas, Rudi Brandt) and none honoured me with an answer. It does show that one has been away for over a year! Time flies! Imagine, in eight weeks it will be Christmas again. As you are never writing a word about yourself and Helge, I must obtain information about you via Sigurd. Apparently, you did not do so well during the recent days. I know absolutely nothing about your crown prince. Does he already have teeth, hair; can he already walk; does he have a sharp tongue?

All these things interest me, inasmuch as in our rough surrounding one needs some balance. For this reason, I bought a puppy. He is precious, a droll little guy of two months (Cocker Spaniel), who has conquered here the hearts of the girls in no time at all. Say! How does one get such a brat housebroken? Every ten minutes, every bit of excitement causes him to sprinkle on the carpet! Sometimes, I am totally desperate and I get up three times during the night to take him upstairs. But the worries caused by my dog-boy are by far not the worst! The other 1,200, some of whom did not turn out so well, who had been given into my care, commit everyday things that suffice to wipe the last traces of youthful freshness from my face. Every evening, I pray for good weather and beg Providence to give us more of a long training period. Outside it looks very much like fall. Nevertheless, we are convinced that the Anglo-Americans still will do us the honour. Who knows where we are going to spend Christmas or the next spring, respectively? Somehow, one has become a restless mercenary!

Sometimes, I really cannot imagine that I am married and am supposed to have two children. Also, one cannot imagine that one day the war might be over! Fortunate are those who know their loved ones are cared for and under good protection in the homeland! Let us hope the Tommie will spare Berlin. As you finally have servant girls, now everything in winter will be easier for you. I am always pleased to hear from Sigurd that you two have undertaken something together. Don't you want to go to the theatre and to concerts together? It certainly should be possible to get the tickets! As there is no use thinking about leave, I shall continue to write diligently and in order to keep the connection from going to sleep—Don't forget me and you and your son are greeted heartily.

As always yours,
Jochen[39]

Peiper liked France. The entire restrained atmosphere, the cultural ambience and national egotism struck his Prussian upbringing just right. The French airs of pride and aloofness were a good fit to his temperament, too. When there was more free time Peiper made himself friendly to the townspeople of Verneuil, and one gesture he invited a parish priest to his battalion officers' mess to share a meal.[40] The French goodies: fragrant baguettes and patisseries ... well, they were wonderful, and there was Paris and its trappings. On 12 December, the Music Corps of the Leibstandarte put on a flamboyant musical event at the Trocadero in Paris—complete with a ninety-man chorus and orchestral music. Stodgy Germans? Sepp's Leibstandarte boys had added a saxophone section—big-band style. To the Germans the crowd seemed to love it—even Strauss' Festival March. In the rousing close to the William Tell Overture, every piece of the orchestra played as loudly and proudly as they could—*Kultur* to the Parisians.[41]

Yet, for the most part, the fun and games ended in November when the new armoured halftracks, or *Schützenpanzerwagen* (SPW), arrived. These SPWs were 9-ton machines with front tyres for turning and rear tracks for all-terrain manoeuvrability. The important thing for infantry-men was that they could now ride into battle in these protective steel boxes—no more marching towards the enemy through a rain of lead. For Peiper, who had experienced that terrible day exposed on the railway near Taganrog, any protection was good.

Sure, they weren't protected like a true Panzer, but they did make a formidable fighting machine all the same. Other than the driver and assistant driver, there was an open crew compartment to hold a heavily armed squad of Panzer grenadiers. The theory on that was better than reality: supposedly twelve would ride, but eight was about all that would go in without crowding—to be effective, the occupants had to be able to use their weapons. Looking like a lance, a deadly MG42 machine gun was usually mounted on the front on a swivel mount behind an armour-plated shield. The general idea was that after the tanks had broken through the front, these fast machines—they could reach up to 53km per hour—would race through the breach to consolidate the won territory and wreak havoc on the enemy rear. Certainly the enemy would be firing at the SPWs during all this, but the SPWs were designed to keep the dozen riding infantry safe—at least in theory.

The 12mm sloped armour plate on the SPWs was designed to repel enemy rifle fire, but veterans frowned. They turned their weapons on one of the steel-walled troop carriers to see if their small arms would penetrate the hull they would depend on for survival. Although conventional rounds were repelled, armour-piercing ammunition chopped right through the metal hull. So, during the quiet days in France, enterprising workmen modified some of the halftracks of the 11th Company with additional sections of armour plate.

The real frustration came from the shortage of fuel which prevented proper training—they always seemed to be in need of gasoline. There was not even enough to conduct a coordinated battalion-scale exercise. All this brought to mind, again, the situation in Russia: How were they coming along at conquering the Caucasus region with its promised oil? While Maikop had been captured that autumn, the Russians had sabotaged the oil fields, and it would take months to get them back into production. Still worse was the Pyrrhic victory there; against a massive Russian counterattack the German forces could barely hold on to the great prize.

When Peiper was promoted to battalion commander, SS Obersturmführer Paul Guhl took over his old charge, the 11th Company. The freckle-faced Guhl was one of the tough SS core types. When he took over that autumn, Guhl drove everyone relentlessly. In France his training was harsh and tough. Even the favoured veterans were not safe. Although Peiper had taken something of a shine to the boyish SS Untersturmführer Werner Wolff, Guhl called him a 'lout'. Having fought everywhere with the Leibstandarte, from Poland on, Guhl's experiences made an impression on the Stuttgart native. His motto was 'Sweat saves blood', and anyone who died in combat, he constantly reminded them, would not be pitied.[42] Instead, Guhl's hardened epitaph was 'There lies a poor soldier.'

Peiper's infantry would now be called *Panzer* grenadiers—from their steel mounts they would fight with the tanks. This would need coordination. Accordingly, in early December 1942, Peiper took in a two-day training at the tank battalion school in Putlos. While he was there word came that the division would soon ship out. But where to? In recent weeks everyone submitted to physical exams to determine fitness for tropical service. Most hoped for a stint with Genflm. Erwin Rommel in exotic Africa. But it was not to be. That November a great desert battle was fought in the sands of El Alamein, after which British general Bernard Montgomery blasted through the Afrika Korps. Scarcely a week later the

Americans began to land in North Africa to seal the fate of the Desert Fox. There would be little to salvage there.

Even more serious events soon transpired in Russia. Only weeks after the anniversary of the German invasion of Russia, Army Group South, without the Leibstandarte, had crossed once more into the vast Steppe land between the Donets and Volga Rivers in Ukraine. There had been high hopes at Hitler's headquarters that the victory that had eluded them in 1941 would at last be reached. At first the German assault repelled the Red Army from the Donets River line; Rostov was again recaptured, with Soviet Russia, again, seemingly on the verge of collapse. Yet, with coming autumn Stalin's armies somehow rallied along the Volga River. That was the turning point.

If the war in the East had taught anything so far, it was that the strength of the German war machine seemed to reach an apogee in summer while the Russian offensive opportunity seemed to grow as temperatures dropped. On 19 November 1942, in the midst of a raging snowstorm, the Soviets launched a furious counteroffensive with two army groups. Within a week over two hundred thousand German troops in twenty-two divisions were surrounded between the Volga and Donets Rivers. Even if aghast, Hitler forbade any retreat.

The Sixth Army was to make a defensive stand in the symbolic city of Stalingrad, 3,200km from the German border. Their only salvation would come from friendly forces capable of reaching the encirclement. There was little prospect for assistance from the neighbouring Army Group Center, staggering, as it was, from further Russian blows in front of Moscow. Although details were short, Peiper knew of the dire events for the Reich in both North Africa and Russia. Late in December railcars arrived, delivering winter clothing to those in France—that could only mean Russia.

At Christmas Peiper returned to Berlin for a final leave before redeployment.[43] There he found that war had come to the Peiper family doorstep. Even on holiday, everyone always kept an open ear for the air raid sirens. The Royal Air Force had begun a bombing campaign to hit Berlin; since May they boldly conducted frequent raids into German air space. Everyone strained to maintain seasonal appearances at 7 Rüdesheimerplatz. On 13 December, Himmler himself rang up the Peiper household to provide greetings and a personal invitation to join him for the *Julfest*. Like all SS families, Peiper had received his *Julleuchter*, the special rune-covered clay SS candle holders made by Allach and mailed out by Himmler each season; rather than the birth of Christ, the idea was to celebrate the child of the sun arising from the ashes of the winter solstice. But the new holiday borrowed heavily from Christmas. Even over *Julfest* there were the familiar victual accoutrements: goose, *Kartoffelklösse* and *Rotkohl*, and there were always the delicious sweets—*Stollen und Lebkuchen*—for the most hallowed of the German holidays.

Right after the winter festival Peiper headed back east, stopping for a couple of days to visit with Himmler at his East Prussia headquarters. He found his old boss distraught that Hitler had recently informed him that the war in Russia might not be over in a year or two; Himmler said it might last as long as thirty! Hardly festive news. On 27 December Peiper was a luncheon guest at Hochwald with Himmler and Andreas Schmidt, who was dedicated to helping the SS recruit members of the Romanian population. Himmler wanted to know what Peiper knew of the great battle in the East.[44] Later, Hermann Fegelein joined them, regaling all with stories from the cavalry front. Did he tell them of the partisan warfare, where the SS cavalry brigade had slaughtered thousands of Russian Jews?

Then there was the *Julfest* proper; twelve candles were lit, and everyone present recited verses: 'This candle is for all mothers … for all comrades in Europe and the world … and the German nation.' All SS men were expected to sing '*Hohe Nacht der klaren Sterne*' ('High Night of the Clear Stars'). Peiper stayed on to speak with Himmler until the early hours of the morning, retiring at 0200 hours. The next day he was back to spend time with Himmler, joining everyone for dinner at 1800 hours.[45]

Meanwhile, back with the Leibstandarte in France, the New Year was celebrated as rumours persisted that they might be sent to the Mediterranean. While the SS officers were away, the men took their fill of the season. SS man Günther Borchers celebrated:

> On New Year's Eve, we burned it up with the anti-tank platoon. The night turned into day as we whooped it up. By dawn all we could see were shadows. Since we could only celebrate one time, we celebrated New Year's Eve for the next year in advance. We knew that shortly we'd be back in action. We had tropical training and there was a rumour going around that we were going to Gibraltar.[46]

But just over a week later Borchers learned—on his birthday—that he and his men were receiving winter gear while still in France. Peiper then re-joined the Leibstandarte in France before they shipped out.[47] Last-minute training and equipment procurement was completed, and on 16 January 1943 Peiper informed his men of what they already suspected: prepare to move east. 'Today we loaded up in Verneuil,' Borchers wistfully jotted in his diary on 22 January 1943. 'Naturally, some of the men had to go see their "Janet". We would gladly come to France again.'

Still, for Peiper there was some reason to celebrate. On 30 January 1943, 28-year-old Jochen Peiper finally received his delayed promotion to SS major. On that day, with the assembled men, Sturmbannführer Peiper listened to speeches by Hermann Göring and Hitler about the *Machtergreifung*—the seizure of power. 'The address of the Führer moved us all,' platoon leader Erhard Gührs penned in his diary. 'The Führer is the Führer!'[48]

However, the sure knowledge of the closing fate of the German Sixth Army, now surrounded in a stranglehold deep in Russia, squelched any gaiety. The place of the fight had become tiresomely monotonous—a gruesome melodrama with an entire German army on the verge of collapse: Stalingrad. The bombastic message from Hermann Göring to mark the tenth anniversary of National Socialism could hardly have inspired optimism: 'Out of all this gigantic battle, now the fight for Stalingrad stands out like a monument. We know a great song of the heroes, it is the "fight of the Nibelungen". The law ordered them to die, that the race could go on and win.'[49]

The *Reichsmarschall* forlornly compared the disaster with the pyrrhic Persian victory over the Spartans at Thermopylae. Who was convinced? As if to underscore doubt, towards the end of the speech, British night bombers chased Göring himself into an air raid shelter.

At Hitler's headquarters the mood grew surreal. On 23 January, to the astonishment of those around him, the Führer proposed that a new battalion of heavy tanks, fresh off the assembly line, be used to cut through the Russian lines to the trapped German forces. Even so, it was a battalion of Panther tanks on a rescue mission where a Panzer army had failed. Meanwhile, messages from the embattled pocket described a hellish scene. On the evening of 29 January, Gen. Friedrich Paulus tensely radioed to Hitler: 'On the anniversary of your assumption of power, the Sixth Army sends greetings to the Führer. The swastika still flutters over Stalingrad.'

Not for long. Paulus's army was now cut in two pockets across the frozen streets, with the defenders in a ferocious, but pointless fight. There was almost no food for the Sixth Army, the air lift of the Luftwaffe having failed. The chief of staff at the Führer's headquarters instituted 'Stalingrad rations' for officers present, and Hitler ordered that a dirge of brooding Wagnerian music be played over the airwaves. It was as if the Siegfried Funeral March, or *Götterdämmerung*, would awaken Germans to the grave crisis.[50] Pointedly, Hitler replied to Paulus's anniversary gesture by promoting him to general field marshal. No field marshal,

Hitler ventured, had ever been taken prisoner—a perfect inducement for total sacrifice. It did not matter. Less than twenty-four hours later Paulus sent a final radio transmission: 'The Russians are at our bunker door.' The radio went dead; Paulus and the entire German Sixth Army marched into captivity.

On the day the Leibstandarte troopers heard of the great catastrophe, rain fell from a slate-grey French sky. With a soggy farewell, Peiper's battalion loaded onto the trains. They were wet and apprehensive. For any thinking person, to hear that an entire German army had been lost was terrible. Strangely, however, many of the SS men yearned all the more for the opportunity to throw back the Russians they now called *Untermenschen*.[51] Recalled a protégé to Peiper: 'It always seemed like coming home. The west was too civilized. Here you have to be a man again!'[52] As their trains pulled out of Verneuil, Erhard Gührs exuded enthusiasm: 'I believe we will swing things back our way again. We are all very confident.' They had their orders from their namesake leader and aimed to set things right. It was just like the SS marching song immortalized by SS-man Kurt Eggers:

> Comrade, when the Führer speaks,
> The SS is ready at the bell.
> The Führer's word is our duty;
> We're unafraid of death and hell![53]

In winter cold a long line of trains jangled to the East, with the SS legions aboard longing for revenge, but on their guard. For Jochen Peiper, Stalingrad—'moral turning point of the war'—eclipsed all before it.[54]

Chapter 4

Operation Peiper

'General Famine and General Winter, rather than Russian bullets, have conquered the Army.'

—Marshal Ney

Like many self-pronounced SS warriors, Jochen Peiper seemed to have found his new home in Russia.

It was there, in the land the Führer deigned most evil, that the ethos of the National Socialist fighter rose to centre stage. *Kampfkraft*—fighting strength, spirit, and audacity—were foremost. And so it was for those officers in the Waffen SS, whose vanity could only be assuaged by Iron Crosses and ever more prestigious military decorations. Seeing themselves as the blood heirs of Teutonic knights, they claimed to live for fighting—to exert their unshakable bravery in battle, their fierce demeanour to kill the enemy and to eagerly die in combat for Germany. For SS leaders such as Peiper, it was just as Seneca had pronounced: '*Vivire militare est!*'—To Live Is to Fight![1]

Yet the unsaid ethos for the SS man fighting for Hitler in the East was beyond military: a murderous one—a willingness to hunt down helpless Jews and civilians and murder them by the tens of thousands under the guise of 'anti-partisan campaigning'.

Hitler's response to the debacle at Stalingrad was to put someone he could trust in charge of larger SS forces to stabilize the deteriorating situation. That person was SS General Paul Hausser, who would have three SS divisions under his command. In the closing days of 1942 Hitler commanded the SS divisions to be speedily moved from France to attack the Russian forces ringing the beleaguered German Sixth Army. Hitler had personally called the surrounded commander, General Paulus, and enthusiastically described how the coming SS divisions would

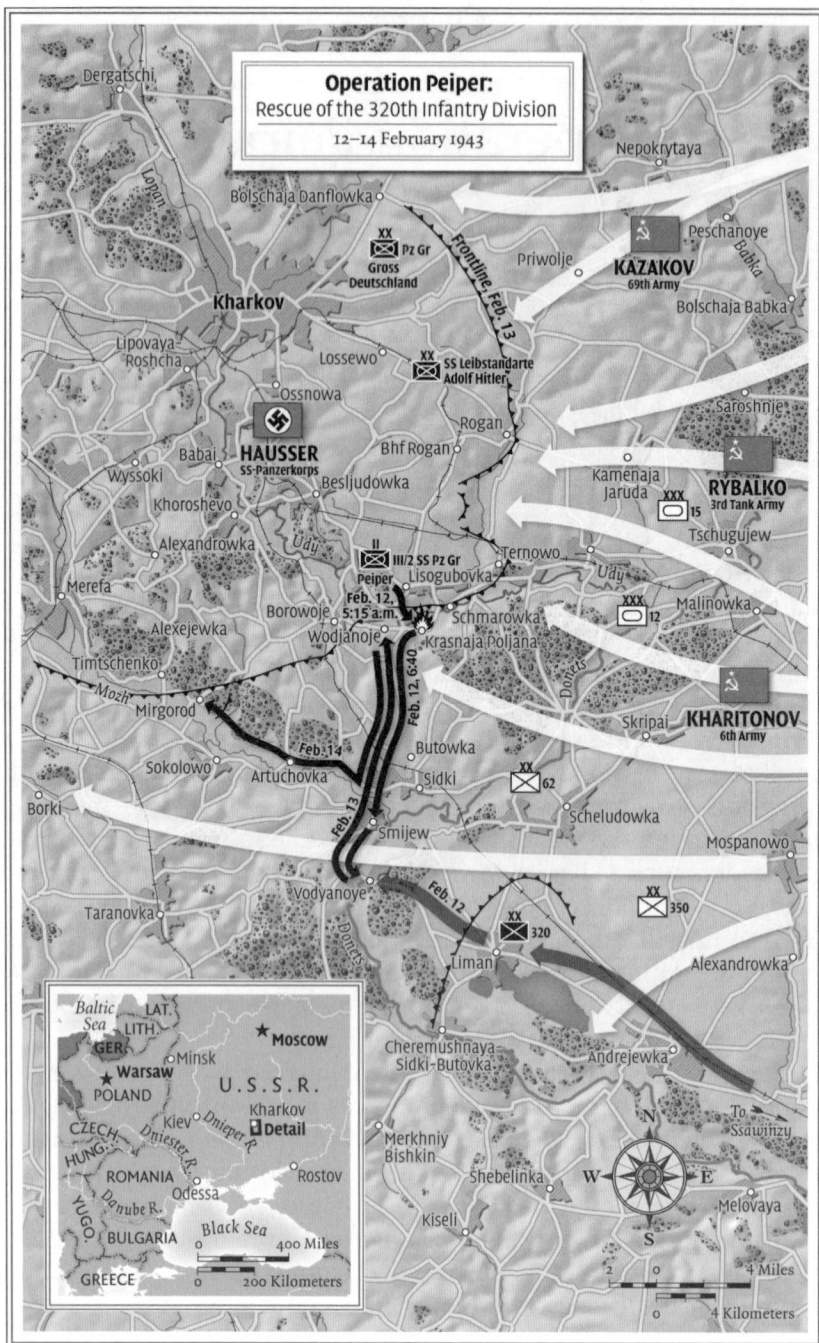

Operation Peiper:
Rescue of the 320th Infantry Division
12–14 February 1943

rout the Bolsheviks.[2] Hitler's phone call was hardly more than a bluster of encouragement.

In spite of great effort, Hausser, Dietrich and the Leibstandarte would arrive too late in the East to serve the intended role. By the time the division had arrived at the end of January 1943—on Peiper's birthday—the southern front in the East was in grave peril. Circumstances had moved from saving the Sixth Army to halting a colossal enemy stampede. Just 160km west of Stalingrad the Soviets had reached the River Donets line and prepared to launch another massive pincer to the west. Their aim was to gobble up von Manstein's army group that was attempting to come to Paulus's rescue. Even if von Manstein's forces should only be propelled backwards, the prospects for nearby Army Group A was more hazardous still. Yet, as always, Hitler appeared ready to hand the SS the impossible.

The Leibstandarte had the task within the newly formed SS tank corps to make a bold counteroffensive to halt the rot. In one sense the Soviets were ripe for riposte—the gigantic November–December northern offensive of Russian Field Marshal G.K. Zhukov, 'Operation Mars', having failed at a cost of nearly half a million casualties.[3]

The situation to the south remained critical. Paul Hausser and his SS troops were subordinated to a provisional two corps-sized formation called Army Abteilung Lanz under General Hubert Lanz. The plan of the army high command was soon forgotten by the fast-changing events. The SS divisions were forced onto the defensive 50km east of the city of Kharkov.

Meanwhile, the Leibstandarte train columns chugged through Russia, warily watching for partisans. Machine guns were mounted on the troop carriers, and the forward car, loaded with sand, had already found a mine days earlier. As Peiper and his men unloaded on 4 February at Smijew rail station, the thermometer stood at -31 degrees Celsius with blowing snow. There was no need for a briefing on the 'local conditions'—it was bitter cold, and everywhere the Russians were advancing, boldly striking for Kharkov.

When the reconnaissance battalion trundled off the rail cars, Peiper's comrade SS Haupsturmführer Gustav Knittel found his armoured vehicles ordered forward to cover the retreat of the 298th Infantry Division. Worse, a company of that division was trapped in the bitter cold behind the Russian lines. Moving forward on 4 February and attempting to reach the pocket near the village of Schewtschenkowo, Knittel was shocked to find his path blocked by retreating columns of their contemptible Italian *allies*. How demoralizing! They didn't have any winter clothing and dragged their belongings on sleds across the snow drifts.[4] The pathetic rabble was the otherwise-noble *Bersaglieri* marksmen of the Italian 8th Army.

Even circumventing the Italians, Knittel found his assigned road bristling with Russian infantry and cavalry. Running his armoured halftracks and armored cars at full speed like snow ploughs, he peeled the Russian infantry off the road and charged through surprised enemy road blocks and anti-tank gun positions. 'Speed! Speed!' the point leader shouted over the radio. Their tactics were primitive: charge ahead with every barrel blazing. It worked; they rescued the trapped men, but in so doing, they also lost a third of their number, including the SS leader who had spurred them on.[5]

That same evening, as it began to snow, Peiper and the arriving elements of his battalion quietly moved into the breach near the village of Skirpa some 30km south-east of Kharkov. As far as the eye could see, the landscape was covered with an icy white, only the stubble of the Steppe grasses and an occasional tree poking out of the brightness was visible. Everyone wore their new winter gear with white camouflage overcoats, but even the warmest apparel paled against the Russian cold. Leather jackboots invited frostbite unless stuffed with doubled heavy wool socks. Insulated gloves and winter anoraks were the preferred garb. With rifles and grenades at the ready, they huddled under blankets in icy foxholes carved out of snow. So frigid was the atmosphere that bread had to be thawed to make it edible. Small fires were built under the halftracks so the engines would turn over in the sub-zero dawn.

At the same time, Peiper's old 11th Company, with assigned assault guns under Obersturmführer Gühl, was ordered to clear the enemy in Andrejewka to the south and subdue the enemy headed for their positions. According to the historical record, Peiper went along. This was accomplished while also rescuing the bedraggled 298th Infantry Division—a frigid mission made difficult by blinding blizzards and deep snows. The rest of Peiper's battalion threw back a heavy Soviet night assault on their positions at Skirpa. The willingness of the Russians to sacrifice was shocking; hundreds of Russian dead were counted before the icy German positions at daybreak.

To the south of Peiper was nothing—a frozen Ukrainian plain and anything but friendly. The neighbouring SS division, Das Reich, warned that Soviets were concentrating there. The 320th and 298th Infantry Divisions had arrived in January, just in time for the winter onslaught. Now the mass of the Red Army offensive bypassed the 320th, leaving them many kilometres behind enemy lines. So bereft, they relied on an all-around 'hedgehog' defence as they attempted to sidestep back towards friendly lines, but they were limited by fuel shortages and enemy actions. On the end of 23 January the division reported that its 587th Regiment had been hit by a destructive raid of eight Soviet tanks supported by 'daredevil cavalry'. Included was a casualty report for the overall division, showing 969 wounded.[6] Like a circled Wild West wagon train, the most able-bodied men formed a tight defence perimeter; what little transport remained and the many wounded occupied the centre of the bastion. On 7 February, General Major Georg Postel, commander of the beleaguered division, landed in a spindly Fieseler Storch at Dietrich's frozen headquarters near Tschugujew. There he was given a bath, fresh clothes and a hot meal. So fortified, Postel told Dietrich he thought he could fight his way north to link up with the Leibstandarte. His wandering divisional pocket behind Russian lines had closed up to the area around Ssawinzy. Could Dietrich's SS men meet him halfway near Liman?[7]

That plan took little account of the rampaging enemy tank columns assailing German lines from the south and west. On the ground Peiper and those with him knew it. By 8 February the intrepid SS officer and Paul Guhl in Andrejewka were feeling quite alone. Profoundly overextended, Guhl's battle group appeared to be surrounded by their enemy. Time and time again his men in their halftracks fought off the waves of Russians. They seemed like men possessed, totally unafraid to die and bent on sacrifice. Guenther Borchers said,

> In Borowoje the Russians came at us like water out of a pipe, advancing toward us in a march column. Our Division was at full strength here. A Luftwaffe reconnaissance plane (HS 126), worked with us and gave us a report on the strength of the Russian's weapons, direction of march, and approximate time of arrival. He circled around the HQ for a long time and dropped a communication packet … He waved, we waved, and then he flew again toward the front. The whole operation with the Luftwaffe worked very well. We allowed the Russians to charge and bunch up, and then killed a lot of them like we did a few days ago. We had some enemy action but more injuries from the frostbite than combat.[8]

Near Peiper's positions, however, the Soviets brought up heavily armoured T-34 tanks. As the Soviet commander pushed their strength to the fore, the steel shot from the beasts pierced the thin-skinned *Schützenpanzer-wagen* like Swiss cheese. With Russian tanks blindly milling about within their positions, Peiper called for reinforcements, but none came. Guhl radioed back that supply columns should watch out: he could do nothing to stop the Russians he could see passing west on his right flank.[9]

Had he known, Peiper would have taken little comfort in the happenings beyond Andrejewka. The Russians were quickly surrounding Kharkov to the north and the south, just as they had encircled Stalingrad. Forget Andrejewka and the 320th—he was ordered to fight *his* way back to Liman and friendly lines. That was easier said than done: they were surrounded by two Soviet rifle regiments and a tank brigade. Recklessly throwing his halftracks forward, Peiper burst through the ring around his battalion and pulled back to the main battle line. He and his men shot down two enemy T-34s and 'caused the enemy heavy bloody losses'. Dietrich later wrote admiringly of Peiper's 'adroit leadership and singular personal courage'.[10]

The following day there were constant assaults all along the division line, with heavy artillery shelling. They threw back the Russian assaults near Lisogubovka, but it appeared the Leibstandarte was in danger of becoming surrounded themselves. On 10 February, the division was ordered to disengage and pull back to a position south-west of Kharkov—the city would be abandoned on 14 February on the orders of Hausser.

The Leibstandarte pulled back in the black cold of night—an operation so frigid that a third of the moved vehicles had to be towed due to frozen transmissions or dead batteries. Meagre rations of rye bread and butter were frozen solid like wood. In the meantime the retrograde movement was not unnoticed in Hitler's headquarters. The phone shrilled at Dietrich's headquarters—the Führer wanted to know what reserves the Leibstandarte had to stop the Russians. There were none, he was told. 'Behind me,' Dietrich flatly told Hitler, 'there are 400 kilometres of wind!'[11]

The 320th Berliner Herz—Heart of Berlin—Division appeared lost. A phalanx of Russian T-34 tanks cut right through the overextended right flank of the unit, leaving it cut off and many kilometres behind friendly lines. Meanwhile, Peiper and his III Battalion were still in reserve in a Ukrainian *kolkhoz*, or collective farm, near Alexandrowka. Dietrich came to give the orders to Peiper, entering the peasant hovel in which Peiper made his headquarters. Inside the men were shielded from the cold, the air filled with pungent smoke rings from Balkan cigars. With Dietrich was Rudolf Lehmann, Peiper's old friend from SS officer's training school.

Peiper greeted his superior formally. His battalion was honoured, he told Dietrich, to receive the mission and indicated his command's readiness. Could he get the 320th Division out of there? Yes, he told Dietrich. 'Operation Peiper' would proceed like cavalry to rescue the 320th Infantry Division. Dietrich turned approvingly to Theodor Wisch, Peiper's superior in charge of the SS Panzer Grenadier Regiment 2, and declared, 'With men such as this, we could carve our way to Vladivostok if not only for those stripe-trousered sods at OKW!'[12]

The next day, 11 February, Teddi Wisch met Peiper in the snow-packed street of Podolchow to give him some good news. Wisch wore a heavy overcoat, hat and gloves, but Peiper stood outside without a coat, bare-handed and with no head cover but hair perfectly in place. Wisch told Peiper that he would have help. The enemy, it seems were elements of the Soviet 12th Tank Corps that had swept south of Kharkov. For the operation, Jochen's halftracks would be reinforced by two platoons of assault guns, the divisional anti-tank platoon and a medical detachment to handle the expected casualties. Peiper's men hastily whitewashed the SPWs to camouflage their daytime moves. Air support would be available from the Luftwaffe to provide supply air drops or help with direct tactical air support through an assigned liaison. Afterwards Peiper had his adjutant line up his newly assigned units into a parade formation in the tiny village of Podolchow. He always met his newly assigned men before a mission, as it was important for them to know their commander's face. To Erhard Gührs, the plan of 'Operation Peiper' sounded 'crazy, but was one after our hearts'.[13] He considered whether to entrust his carefully composed diary to someone not participating in the operation. Would any of them return?

A radio message flashed from General Postel to the headquarters at *Armee Abteilung Lanz*, relaying the urgency: there were ten thousand, but that included fifteen hundred wounded and with little remaining transport, fuel and rations.[14] The beleaguered infantry division had none-theless reached Grigorijewka and were ordered to fight their way to the railway line near Sidki, where Kampfgruppe Peiper would meet them. Could they make it? At least there was air support, as General Postel watched German Stuka dive bombers pounding the Soviet-held village of Liman ahead of them, but his combat forces were exhausted.

Peiper's mission was to reach the trapped division by breaking through the Russian line near Smijew. According to the plan, the SS leader would escort sixty ambulances to evacuate the forlorn soldiers now encircled north-west of Liman. Every available surgeon and medic in the division would go with him. Radio reports indicated that hundreds were wounded. For surprise, Peiper would launch his halftracks out of the pre-dawn night of 12 February, but there was an obstacle on their route right at the start. The Udy River, a small tributary of the Donets, would need to be crossed right away—a sector thinly held by the I Battalion of the 2nd Panzer Grenadier Regiment. Even though the Udy was frozen under a packed field of white, there was only one bridge that would be needed for armoured vehicles. It was long, wooden, primitive and unsteady.

Searchlights provided illumination for assembling Peiper's troop, but these were cut off after everyone was loaded. In the darkness of the pre-dawn at 0430 hours, Peiper's halftracks lumbered ahead. Approaching the frozen river, the SPWs closed up, with Peiper directing them to hide behind the houses in the village until all were available for a rapid advance. At 0515 hours Peiper gave the order to go; the Maybach engines droned loudly as a fountain of fire spouted from every barrel. His column struck so quickly that they abruptly engulfed a small enemy force of the 111th Rifle Division holding a rickety wooden bridge and dashed into the riverside village of Krasnaja Poljana. In mere minutes they were through the enemy cordon and deep in unfriendly territory—the rolling snowy hills south-east of Kharkov. Peiper dropped off a medical detachment and a defence platoon to hold the bridge; they would need it for the passage back to safety and doctors to attend to the wounded. Yet some at the tail end of the truck column following in Peiper's wake arrived minutes after the SPWs had blown through Krasnaja Poljana. The Russians of the 399th Rifle Regiment in the snow-encrusted village recovered from their slumber and ambushed six trucks passing Peiper had left behind.

Peiper knew nothing of this reverse in fortune behind him. He was at the head of his steel cavalry, barrelling along. The way was clear for advance. The divisional staff officer, Rudolf Lehmann, had warned to avoid the roads—they were likely mined. However, sensing they had achieved surprise, Peiper ordered his halftracks to race down the snowy track as fast as they could drive. From the command vehicle Peiper's balled fist pumped in the air—forward. No halting for anything.

Peiper's iron-walled chariots barrelled down the road, firing wildly with bow-mounted machine guns, spitting flame and death. The surprised enemy fled from their path. By 0640 hours Peiper's rushing armour had captured Smijew without enemy resistance.

Where was Postel and the 320th?

Passing through the village, Peiper found that a contingent of the Leibstandarte, his old comrade Hans 'Hein' Hennecke, was already there, having been ordered to the village three days before. It was a strange war: neither knew of the other's mission, which was the same for both of them—save the 320th. The radio crackled: a pilot from the Luftwaffe had located the 320th not far from Liman.[15] His message: they hadn't moved![16]

By 0800 hours Peiper's radio rattled on again: orders were altered. Rather than wait on the west bank of the Donets River, he was to plunge on to Liman to link up with them. Worried the surprise would soon be lost, Peiper rushed ahead, while Hennecke and his crew would secure Smijew in their rear. The command: 'Bash on.'

> To liberate the comrades of the 'Ace of Hearts',
> We penetrated deeply behind the Russian lines.
> We sat on our tanks as fresh as in the old days.
> For us, that is just small potatoes.[17]

As Peiper's halftracks roared ahead through the blowing snow, there was no sign of the enemy. In Smijew the snow-covered thatch-roofed houses were eerily quiet as Peiper's column motored through. Soon Peiper reached the frozen shore of the Donets River near Vodyanoye, but there he stopped: there would be no complying with the divisional order. With their usual thoroughness, the Russians had torched the bridge; all that remained were ugly, charred stumps nearly covered by snow. Looking across the expanse of icy river, he knew there could be no advance to reach Liman. Yet, from the Luftwaffe report, he knew the 320th must be close by. Where were they? Just before 1400 hours a package floated down to General Postel by parachute: '*Spitze* of the SS Div. A.H. in contact with the western most elements of division at 13:50 ... Smijew, the next village east of you is free of the enemy!'

Peiper and his commanders stood pensively on the bank of the frozen river and waited for the leading group of the entrapped division to meet them. In the meantime he ordered their positions camouflaged—the Russians might appear at any moment. Presently a German Horch staff car approached. Out stepped a corpulent regular army general wrapped in a long fur coat and a white cape. It was General Postel.

'Why have you not crossed the river?' Postel demanded. Peiper explained that the ice did not seem sufficient to bear the weight of his vehicles. While the general was arguing the point, Postel's ordnance officer showed up to complain that one of their few remaining assault guns had just fallen through the ice. Peiper did not dare smile. A red-faced Postel declared that his division would set up a billet there for the night and ranted about their disastrous circumstances—marooned so far behind Russian lines. As they had run out of gasoline, all vehicles had been abandoned. Their improvised transport was now impressed Russian peasant horses drawing *panje* wagons. Food was nearly gone; his men were starving.

Did the SS officer realize the general had more than a thousand wounded, many nearly exhausted? Peiper listened silently; he had a capable medical staff with him and a whole column of ambulances as well as another medical detachment at Krasnaja Poljana. The afternoon in wintry Russia meant that the cold night was not far away. Under Postel's orders they would set up defences around the division's perimeter near Cheremushnaya–Sidki–Butovka as the wounded formation collected itself on the west bank of the Donets. Somehow they would also improvise ramps down to the frozen river so the wounded soldiers could make their way across. In the morning they would be prepared to escort the division back to friendly lines.

Postel lit a cigar, boarded his staff car and disappeared. Peiper and his officers waited uncomfortably in their halftracks. Peiper assigned Ehrhard Gührs as liaison to Postel, who was aghast at what he saw: 'The division was a wreck, it was hard to believe.' Nearly an hour had gone by. The success of Peiper's rescue raid was speed; staying here was a sure invitation for trouble. In the meantime Postel reappeared, escorting a gaggle of soldiers. To Peiper and others looking on the frozen scene, there was one thought: *Berezina*—Napoleon's retreat from Moscow translated to 1943.[18]

First in the line of march were those able to walk, then the wounded and lastly the seriously wounded to the rear. Many obviously had frostbitten feet and hobbled along on the icy roads, leaning on rifles, their uniforms now torn, bloody rags. It was a 'parade of misery on sleighs and sleds,' Peiper recalled. All the sleds and one-horse *panje* wagons were overloaded with wounded. Many looked like they were near death, and a fetid stench told of death and gangrene.

Before dark, Peiper's battalion surgeon, Dr Robert Brüstle, set up an emergency medical station. Operating under an ice-crusted tarpaulin illuminated by ambulance headlights, the doctor operated long into the night. Much of it was cutting away gangrenous frostbitten limbs—a horrible job. Peiper and the others kept watch, 'looking out with hollow cheeks into the ghostly night, convinced that it would not go well for long'.[19] 'Speed,' Peiper always lectured, 'is our safety!'

When would the Russians close in? It couldn't be long. Peiper toured the 320th's assembly perimeter and checked on Hans Hennecke in Smijew just to the west. All was still quiet, but Hennecke had bad news: reports came in that there had been fighting in Krasnaja Poljana since Peiper had passed through there, and the division indicated that the entire line of the Leibstandarte was under furious enemy assault. Theodor Wisch, fighting before Rogan, reported *waves* of Russians from the 15th Tank Corps attacking.

There was scarcely any tactics to the Russian assaults—simply whole battalions charging blindly for the German lines. They seemed to suddenly arise from trenches and foxholes shouting 'Hurrah!' in a startlingly defiant chorus. The result was hardly war—the Russians marched right into German killing zones, seemingly determined to exhaust German machine gun ammunition through maniacal sacrifice. Some fifteen hundred dead Russians were estimated to be piled before Gruppe Wisch at a single position—and still they came.[20] Such hordes were closing in on Kharkov. Peiper saw the battle as a clash of cultures—this was not any way to fight:

> 'Who is this monster? I do not comprehend him!' cried out soldiers and cold sweat broke out on their bodies. We started to retreat because the enemy had broken through at the right or the left, but not because the situation in front of our own sector had become untenable. 'The Russians are coming!' Like a rabbit in front of a snake, he sat with glazed eyes in his foxhole staring at the brown flood which rolled forward.[21]

Returning back to the north, Peiper hoped to find his medical detachment holding out. In the early morning hours on 13 February, Kampfgruppe Peiper, with sixty ambulances in tow and many vehicles of the 320th Division, set off to the west. Snow flurries and bitter cold obscured their way forward as they carried over a thousand wounded. The column bumped along cross-country—even the bold Peiper was not willing to test the old patrol wisdom: never return from a raid by the same route left. He reached Wodjanoje by noon, although he was increasingly slowed by the staggering pace of the exhausted and wounded soldiers of the 320th. And another disturbing development: all attempts to reach the medical detachment in Krasnaja Poljana by radio were met with silence. As Peiper's armour crunched towards the tiny Russian hovel, they momentarily expected contact with their rear-guard.

As they reached the first thatch-roofed buildings, Peiper's men pensively manned their weapons, fully expecting an enemy ambush. But there was nothing there. Peiper's halftracks rumbled into the dismal village. All was eerily quiet. No enemy, no medical detachment. A trap? Elements of the 320th were right behind his vanguard. Every vehicle manned its weapons as the men searched the village for the missing SS contingent. When they found them, it was a horrific discovery.

The enemy had brutally massacred and butchered the SS men and German medics. Some were hanging from trees; others were tied up and burned to death.[22] The defence platoon had obviously put up a fight; enemy dead scattered among the fallen SS were from the dreaded NKVD. Natural enemies, the SS could expect no mercy from their ideological opposites. One witness, an SS Rottenführer in Peiper's ration supply company, claimed that Peiper responded in kind: 'In the village the two petrol trucks were burnt and 25 Germans killed by partisans and Russian soldiers. As a revenge, Peiper ordered the burning down of the whole village and the shooting of its inhabitants.'[23]

Beyond Krasnaja Poljana, Peiper ordered his column forward to secure the bridge across the frozen Udy Creek. They needed it to pass the 320th to friendly lines. There, amid the snow-covered forests and hills by the crossing, they halted—the bridge was gone. The long wooden span Peiper and his men had so boldly captured two days before was now a line of smoking posts. As an improvised engineer platoon set about to undertake makeshift repairs, Peiper's attention to the burned-out bridge seemed to signal a Russian ski battalion to descend from the surrounding hills in an ambush. The enemy was firing at Peiper's column from all sides. There was little choice but to fight it out with the enemy in Krasnaja Poljana.

There was a wild melee, but with a flurry of 7.5cm rounds from their heavy SPWs, Peiper managed to hold the enemy away from the hastily repaired bridge. With that, the ambulances and bedraggled columns of infantry soldiers could begin to pass across the ice. The Germans maintained that the Russians were firing on the ambulances, even though they were clearly marked with red crosses.[24] Although fighting raged from house to house, Peiper eventually prevailed; the Russian ski battalion was listed as 'destroyed'. All through the night Waffen SS engineers struggled to install a somewhat stouter bridge across the frigid stretch of river.

That done, the following day the miserable collection of soldiery of the 320th Infantry Division passed across the frozen Udy Creek to friendly German lines. Meanwhile, the improvised bridge repair was able to support only one single truck with wounded at a time. Even so, by 1600 hours General Postel and his division were back to the friendly lines east of Kharkov. At 0825 hours on 14 February General Postel reported that the last of his rear-guard had reached friendly lines. Peiper would have dearly liked to follow Postel, but the improvised bridge was too flimsy for his steel halftracks.[25] After the last vehicle of the 320th had reached safety, Peiper's battle group detoured and roared back south. His battle group looped crazily behind Russia lines towards Butowka and nearly to Smijew before darting west to Mirgorod, moving parallel with the unsuspecting Russians.

In spite of heavy enemy counterattacks against Sidki, Peiper soon reached friendly lines, his halftracks suddenly appearing at the new division headquarters near Merefa.[26] Reporting to his superiors, Peiper described General Postel as reflecting the weakness of an army commander caught in a tough spot and 'experiencing a crisis in morale'. Even more infuriating was Postel's report on 14 February, stating that they had reached friendly lines relatively unmolested by the Russians.[27] There was no mention of Kampfgruppe Peiper, who had made his escape march possible.

One attribute not short in General Postel's demeanour was an arrogance to match Peiper's own. Both men would never have anything good to say about the other.

Chapter 5

The Sword of Damocles

'There is an East Wind coming ... and a good many of us may wither before its blast.'

—Sir Arthur Conan Doyle, 'His Last Bow'

There was little time to celebrate Peiper's feat of the winter rescue of the 320th Infantry Division with other comrades. Nor was there time to settle accounts between the 'Leibstandarte Adolf Hitler' with the equally arrogant General Postel.

After a single night of rest, Peiper was again ordered into action. By 15 February the Russian columns had reached Ossnowa, just south of Kharkov. Peiper's SPWs darted off that afternoon and, by 1800 hours, fought their way to the railway just west of Ossnowa. By then it was dark, and the Russians seemed to be everywhere. Peiper lost one halftrack to Russians boldly throwing a barrage of Molotov cocktails at suicide range. One of his best combat leaders had been badly burned, and others were killed. And there was worse. The elite army division Grossdeutschland reported that the Soviets were now in possession of the western part of the city. The SS Division Das Reich reported powerful enemy penetrations into the city from the east. Several of the assaults included heavy KV-1 tanks, and some reports claimed that the city's restless civilians had taken up weapons.

By 15 February the deepening thrust of the Soviet forces so endangered the SS Panzer Corps that orders took the Leibstandarte out of Kharkov, in spite of Hitler's orders and those of Lanz himself. 'Papa' Hausser called the shots—there was no sense losing good troops: 'A decision about pulling back must be made by 12:00 hours!' The chief of the army, General Schulz, agreed with Hausser: 'The danger of being surrounded is acute.'

SS Panzerkorps Counterattack
Below Kharkov
11–25 February 1943

Detail

Moscow

U.S.S.R.

Dnieper R.
Kiev
Kharkov
Rostov
Minsk
Black Sea
TURKEY
Odessa
Dniester R.
ROMANIA
Danube R.
BULGARIA
GREECE
YUGO.
HUNG.
CZECH.
POLAND
Warsaw
GER.
LAT.
LITH.
Baltic Sea

N E S W

4 Miles
4 Kilometers

Andrejewka
Shebelinka
Kiseli
Merkhniy Bishkin
Bereka
Oril'ka
Timtschenko
Alexejewka
298
15 Gd Cav
Oktjobrski
SS Rn
Meyer
KHARITONOV
6th Army
Dimirowka
Nichni Orel
Orel

Cheremushnaya
Sidki-Butovka
Bespalowka
Sokolowo
Taranowka
Ochochtale
Jefremowka
17 Feb. 1943
Front line, 19 Feb.
11-17 Feb
I/SS Pz Rn
Wuensche
Paraskoweja
Jeremejewka
Leninskij
Shliakhova
Wlassowka
Kardachewka
Vorochilova
Bahatia

11-17 Feb
KG Peiper
III/2 SS
Timtschenko
Mirgorod
Alexejewka
Mozh
Leibstandarte
Adolf Hitler
1 SS Pz Gr
Merefa
Borki
LAH
II/SS Pz LAH
Dzhhun
Riabuchtino
Bulachi
Karawanskoie
Vl'khuvatka
Peiper, 22 Feb.
Peiper, 20 Feb.
Medwedowka
Berestowaia
Berestowka
Kazatschij
Maidan
Feb. 19, night
Petrowka
23-25 Feb
Kegitchewka
Krutojarowka

Fedorowka
Nowo Wodolaga
Peressel
Mozh
Gawrilowka
Stanitschijo
Staroworowka
Jarotin
Berestowenka
Ziglerowka
Feb. 19pb.-predawn
Peiper, 18
Natalino
Krasnograd
3 SS Pz Gr
Totenkopf
HAUSSER
SS-Panzerkorps
2 SS Pz Gr
Das Reich
Bobrowka
Nikolskoie
Jelenowka

Hausser negotiated a tense conversation with Lanz. 'The enemy,' Hausser told him, 'had already seized the airstrip south of the city.' Peiper's group had been dispatched to retake the place but ran into a hornets' nest. At 1800 hours Hausser's phone jangled. It was General Lanz reminding him that, 'Kharkov is to be held, in accordance with the Führer's orders. Were positions held today?'

'At the moment, yes, but the order to retreat was given half an hour ago.'

'This contradicts the Führer's orders and must be rescinded!'[1] That couldn't be done, Hausser told him. Lanz countered that the 320th Division should be used to renew an assault against the enemy closing on Kharkov. That division was just north of Smijew, Hausser complained, and besides, its horses were too weak to march. No one made mention of its exhausted and frostbitten soldiers.

It wasn't long before word of Hausser's rebuff reached the *Wolfsschanze*. Hitler fumed. Here was an insubordinate Waffen SS general. So as the Reich propaganda minister Goebbels called for 'total war' back home, Hitler warned Army Group South to expect a house call. Hitler's staff advised Generalfeldmarschal Erich von Manstein that the visit would not be a pleasant one.

Meanwhile, Jochen Peiper was ordered to pull back to Merefa, making it one of the last battalions to leave Kharkov. He returned with his weary command in the early morning hours of 16 February. Other SS units were pulling back, too. In Peiper's opinion, paranoid German commanders were suffering from the 'getting-surrounded-complex': '[T]he Stalingrad sword of Damocles floated over his head. The fear of getting surrounded as well as a preoccupation with the flank and the rear became a mania … The retrograde movement itself became heroically tinted and legalized by false reports.'[2]

Kharkov could be just like Stalingrad. But Peiper was unaware of the controversy brewing for those above him. 'The Führer has ordered that all positions around Kharkov are to be held under all circumstances.'[3]

On 17 February Hitler flew from his *Wolfsschanze* headquarters to Zaporozhe to give von Manstein a piece of his mind. Von Manstein knew that Hitler seldom ventured to the front, so this appearance could not be a good sign. Sure enough, upon arrival Hitler declared that Kharkov must be recaptured, and at once. Von Manstein listened in patience, then told Hitler that the withdrawal would allow him a great victory by a counterstroke designed to slice off the Russian spearheads. Besides, the Totenkopf Division was stuck fast just beyond its unloading point. It seemed its pig-headed leader, Eicke, had ordered the entire armoured division off roads and out onto the Russian plains without realizing that the warm weather had turned the grassland into a sea of mud.

Hitler could hardly disagree. Von Manstein described an audacious plan in which pulling back to shorter lines allowed for the creation of a powerful operational reserve. With that he assured Hitler that Kharkov would 'fall like a ripe apple'.[4] As if to underscore the gravity, the Russian tank spearheads were pushing towards Zaporozhe—perilously nearby. As if to underscore the desperation, a group of marauding Russian T-34 tanks from the Soviet 25th Tank Corps came within gun range of the headquarters airfield before being dispatched by German flak guns. That was enough to send Hitler and his entourage to the nearby airfield. Without further prompting, the Führer's plane buzzed off, escorted by a pair of Messerschmitt 109 fighters. Von Manstein was glad when he left.

As Hitler confronted von Manstein, Peiper was hastily moving his battalion to Krasnograd, now ordered to strike the advancing enemy in the flank at Ziglerowka. To make ready for the attack, Peiper had to move his heavy battalion 60km in a single night. Von Manstein now collected his new reserve, strongly reinforced by the delayed arrival of the SS Totenkopf Division.

Attacking beneath the moonlight on 19 February, Peiper and the many others in the SS corps slammed into the advancing Russians and drove deep into their right flank. In spite of tough Russian resistance, Peiper's men managed to capture Ziglerowka in just under an hour. At 800m from the outermost house, the SPWs opened up with every gun they had. The surprised enemy responded with point-blank anti-tank fire. One SPW was lost to such suicidal gunnery, but Peiper's armour charged to the east: 'A wonderful picture, the moon is lighting the scenery. From 800 metres we open fire. There is only a weak defence by two Russian guns. One SPW after another, we quickly approach the village. In one hour we are through. It is half past midnight. Like a torch the village is burning behind us.'[5]

Peiper immediately thrust on to the village of Kasatschij Maidan, running headlong into an enemy battalion in a night march towards the front.

The enemy was surprised. Peiper took the frozen village and, before daybreak the following morning, launched an audacious attack on Jeremejewka—strongly garrisoned by a Russian cavalry force replete with tanks. Drifting snow provided protection to the enemy and slowed the speed of the assault. In wild fighting amid the naked frozen trees in the hamlet, Peiper and his grenadiers fought from atop their snow-encrusted

SPWs. Soon they had the upper hand, with the enemy fleeing from Jeremejewka in confusion:

> We are attacking at high speed. The enemy is fleeing. We try to reach them. Our SPW flies in the snow. We are successful and have already reached our target when suddenly an SPW is hit by an anti-tank gun at very close range. Uscha. Hesse is dead. Peiper gives the order to hold. We have taken two villages and annihilated a Russian regiment and have advanced 20 km. The main front line can be brought forwards ... This is a hard war. We want to sleep, but by 1800 I have to go to the command post.[6]

Leading from the front with headphones pressed over his ears, Peiper commanded from a 7.5cm cannon-bearing halftrack, pointing out targets to his gunners along the white horizon. After the rescue of the 320th Division, Peiper was now a minor SS celebrity. Accordingly, an SS *Kriegsberichter* followed along, snapping pictures of Peiper and his crew. Peiper peered through a scissors periscope. There he saw them. Scarcely pausing, Peiper chased the enemy streaming across the snowy plains towards Leninskij. Spinning tracks kicked up snow as Peiper's SPWs closed on the fleeing enemy, their guns at the ready. Caught in the open snowy fields, his machine guns mercilessly chopped down the Soviets— even those who attempted to surrender.[7] Later that day his guns felled three Russian tanks and six cannon. In a single night Peiper's troops had fought their way 20km behind enemy lines. His apothegmatic radio announcement: '0630 hours: Jeremejewka and the Leninskij Factory taken. Pushed another 5 km to the east. Enemy completely defeated and fleeing to the east-south-east.'[8]

Surveying the carnage, the III Battalion counted at least eight hundred enemy dead scattered about the frozen tundra. Even with three hundred hardy Russian horses captured, there was not a single Soviet prisoner. 'No quarter was given,' Gührs entered in his diary. 'A regiment of Waffen SS in the East in close combat felt no chance. We had to fight.'[9] There was another commendation for Peiper—and this one was big-time.[10] Accolades for a war without pity.

The arrival of part of the tank regiment and Meyer's reconnaissance battalion at Jeremejewka the next afternoon released Peiper for a new assignment. The village was to become a major divisional support point—albeit one that the stubborn enemy was intent on recapturing. The new mission for Peiper was to support SS Panzer Grenadier Regiment 1 to seize the bridge at Krasnograd. The Leibstandarte's defensive position by this city was to form the left hinge of the bold German counterstroke as the Das Reich and Totenkopf Divisions plunged deep into enemy territory south of Kharkov.

Peiper's whitewashed SPWs reached Borki in the late afternoon and paused for a break before the new assignment. By the night of 22 February his SPWs had moved another 70km south towards Krasnograd and set up defensive positions near Natalino by 24 February. The enemy was intent on breaking the developing noose of encirclement, and the commander of the 12th Company, Lukas 'Lex' Westrup, ran afoul of desperate Russians east of Krasnograd and was killed. Later Peiper himself presided over the burial of the popular commander when his swastika-draped body was lowered into the snowy ground at noon on 26 February. Peiper composed a short eulogy, read aloud in the cold noon air. The SS leader stiffly saluted over his grave. Another 'bright star', he said, was interred into the frozen Ukrainian earth.

At the same time that Peiper was putting another of his comrades into the ground, an infamous Waffen SS icon also met his end. This was SS-Obergruppenführer Theodor Eicke, who perished when enemy fire brought down his Fieseler Storch reconnaissance aircraft.[11] Everywhere in Peiper's sphere the news seemed bad. Heinz von Westernhagen with the Leibstandarte reacted bitterly to a letter from his mother:

> We all hope that all of the homeland understands what this is all about, and proves itself to be worthy! The man our here does not ask for his field kitchen portion, but for *ammunition*. Fourteen days and longer the infantry here had no warm meals, but the will to fight is unbroken. Our youngest soldier understands that this is about *everything* ... All everyday matters and all little things have fallen from us. Nothing anymore can frighten us—and you must change accordingly, so that we out here can calmly pursue our service ... I am sitting in a stinking mud hut, at least ten persons are crowded on the stove; below them pigs and a goat; chickens and pigeons perch on the wallboards. That is our war. I am not writing this to complain. We do not want to complain, but you at home should spread these words about what is being done here, so that the homeland gets to its senses. Nobody can take our humour away! If the homeland will be as strong as our young men, all of the world cannot overpower us.[12]

There was little time to mourn the dead or fix the home front. The Leibstandarte assumed positions in a wide arc before Krasnograd. Over the next three days Peiper's command threw back reckless Russian tank assaults against their positions near Kegitschewka. The Soviets were close to breaking through, but waves of Stuka dive bombers appeared out of the clouds to pummel the determined enemy, leaving three T-34s smoking in silence just in front of Peiper's positions. Even so, the pressure on Kegitschewka increased so dramatically that Peiper got on the phone to headquarters, recommending to Rudi Lehmann that his force pull back to the west bank of the Wshiwaja river—at least until dawn. Lehmann agreed, but there was even greater danger elsewhere.

On the other side of the defensive perimeter before Krasnograd, a pack of thickly armoured T-34s had surged through the lines of SS Panzer Grenadier Regiment 1 near Olchowatka and threatened the divisional supply road. Dietrich gave Ralf Tiemann an urgent assignment: gather up anything he could lay his hands on to stop the Soviet intrusion. The 24-year-old Panzer leader quickly improvised a Kampfgruppe formed around tanks under repair from the 7th Company and launched the armour into the side of the Russian flank. The Russians soon fell back after a sharp but costly tank battle. 'Eight days ago the company commander, my replacement, was killed,' he wrote in a letter home in March 1943. 'Many of my best previous enlisted men and NCOs are no longer alive.'[13] How long did any of them have? At night the evening sky was aflame with the eerie staccato flashes of far-off guns.

What Tiemann saw were the distant signs of battle as the other SS divisions cut scythe-like strokes through the steppes—parrying and destroying and splitting up the Russian army. While the Russians attempted to break the positions of the Leibstandarte, the 2nd SS division Das Reich plunged into their rear. In the meantime the 4th Panzer Army under General Hermann Hoth slammed into the overextended Soviet line from the South. Von Manstein's trap was sprung.

When the Russians attempted to force their way out to the east, they found the way barred. Peiper's doorstop held; for the trapped Russians, there was no escape. So while Sepp Dietrich was recommending Peiper and his marauders for the German Cross in Gold, the secretly assembled 7th and 11th Panzer Divisions crashed into the Russian left flank as the SS Wiking Division blunted the enemy thrust to the south-west.

Von Manstein's blow took the 1st Guards Tank Army, under Lieutenant General Markian Popov, completely by surprise. Between the SS and army divisions, Popov's great tank force was cut off from any supply and then sliced up and scattered. Massive Luftwaffe air support increased the slaughter of the trapped Russian pocket.

By the end of the month Popov's armour lay battered and abandoned across the snowy plains stretching from Krasnoarmeyskoye to Izyum: 615 wrecked tanks and 423 destroyed guns and anti-aircraft pieces. With over

80,000 casualties and over half or those killed or missing, 23,000 Russian corpses littered the battlefield.[14]

Each day that winter Peiper and his men assembled before dawn and prepared for another day's fighting on the savage plain. Typically it was below freezing, so they repurposed their blowtorches to heat the halftrack engines and transmissions so the oil and grease would become liquid enough to allow them to start. Faces were covered by mufflers or they froze; great clouds of steam rose from the men huddled together in fleece-lined parkas and crunching on frozen snow. By flashlight they reviewed plans for the day's attack with gloved hands across the spreading maps of the unending frozen tundra that was Russia. Breakfast was often a slice of black bread chased by a swig of Hennessy 'aggressive spirit' and a hastily smoked cigarette. Outnumbered and forced to give up ground for what he saw as an inferior enemy, Peiper was grimly burning villages to the ground:

> We pulled back again, as the pressure from the Russians got stronger day by day. Starowerovka went up in flames. As always, the Russians were dug-in at the Front—and their soldiers were not well supplied. There were 16- to 18-year-old youngsters, and 40- to 60-year-old civilians. They hardly had any uniforms, and their rifles had only a leather strap instead of the usual sling. In their rucksacks we found beef bones, sorghum, ammunition, and hand grenades.[15]

Peiper's perspective was less inspiring: 'The Germans and Russians launched desperate attacks completely lacking in sound military goals, for the sole purpose of securing warm buildings with a protecting roof … The village meant warmth, and warmth meant survival.'[16] The scale of the military operations on the *Ostfront* was vast and the distances enormous. Those who died in the winter fighting in Russia quickly disappeared from sight—covered by a blanket of white. Those not immediately buried were soon lost to winter. The blowing snow whipped up by the *buran*—the frozen east wind of the Russian steppes—covered all the dead—often within hours.

Only during the spring thaw did the blackened corpses from the terrible winter fighting grimly emerge from the melting snow.

Chapter 6

Kharkov

'Once more unto the breach dear friends, once more.'
—Shakespeare, *King Henry V*, Act III

At the end of February 1943 the Russian thermometer began to rise. Everywhere in the East the snow banks were dripping and the unpaved roads melted into a slurry of earthen slush. The greatest looming threat to German offensive plans was not the Russians but 'General Mud'.

Regardless of conditions, on 1 March 1943 Peiper, along with attached tanks, set off to wrest Jeremejewka once more from the enemy. The planned move to Wschiwaja was impossible—the approach roads there were nothing more than gooey tracks. Even a halftrack would mire down to its hubs. And the Russian weather had other surprises.

So thick was the fog that day that Peiper and his men could see no more than 100m ahead. At Kasatchij Maidan this worked to their favour; the blinded Russians were quickly overrun. Five km further, Peiper found his column under a blizzard of anti-tank shells coming out of the fog from every direction. The Russians had set up a line of anti-tank guns—a *Pakfront*, a formidable Russian innovation in which up to ten anti-tank guns were unified in fire control under a single commander that would have the guns fire simultaneously at a single target—and let loose at his bunched SPWs at a range impossible to miss. Two halftracks exploded instantly, with the crews bailing out to a deadly hail of gunfire. Peiper's group couldn't see a thing. They were left impotent before a nearby enemy who shot them to pieces. Peiper's troops licked their wounds and regrouped that night.

On 2 March Peiper attacked towards Loginwy. Again there was anti-tank fire, but the Germans flushed out the enemy gunners and then pursued them into the snowy fields. The SPWs advanced faster than

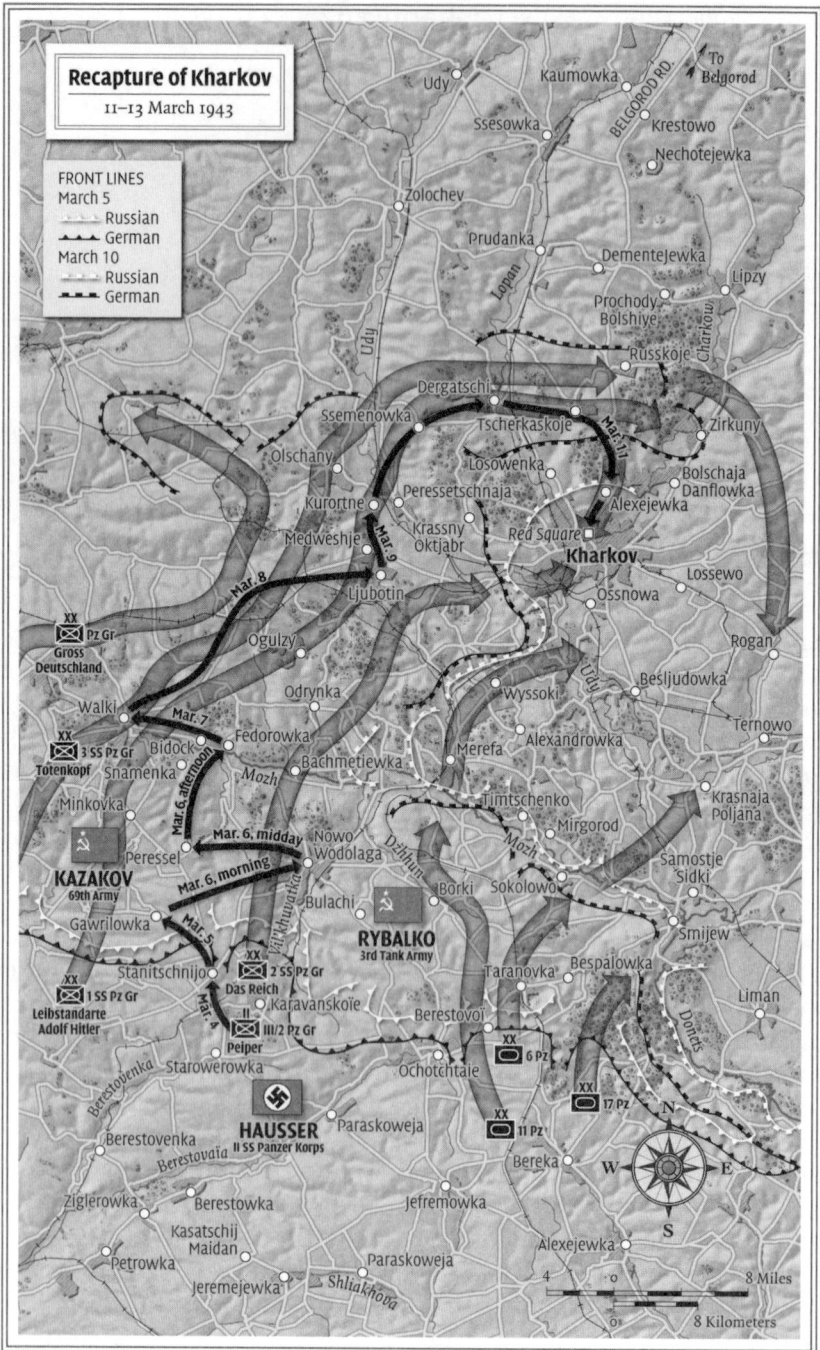

Recapture of Kharkov
11–13 March 1943

FRONT LINES
March 5
~~~~~ Russian
▲▲▲ German
March 10
━━━ Russian
━━━ German

Gross Deutschland
XX
Pz Gr

3 SS Pz Gr
XX
Totenkopf

1 SS Pz Gr
XX
Leibstandarte
Adolf Hitler

2 SS Pz Gr
XX
Das Reich

III/2 Pz Gr
II
Peiper

HAUSSER
II SS Panzer Korps

KAZAKOV
69th Army

RYBALKO
3rd Tank Army

6 Pz
XX

17 Pz
XX

11 Pz
XX

the Russians could disengage. Like feudal cavalry chasing down foot infantry, the men on the *Schützenpanzerwagen* slaughtered the fleeing Russian enemy. As they pressed on, they ran into Russian anti-tank guns again. One of the pierced SPWs shuddered to a stop, belching smoke. Almost simultaneously one of the attached self-propelled assault guns splintered and flew apart. Peiper laid down smoke in an attempt to blind the enemy gunners while he brought up his own. Squinting through the mist and smoke with binoculars, he saw them: two T-34s and three anti-tank guns. Mad minutes later, the enemy guns had been dispatched and the advance resumed. Now there was nothing left to stop Peiper. Against the frigid night they assaulted the village of Melechowka, seeking billets. Yet, the resourceful Russian enemy was not done. 'Ivan' boldly threw out *Holzkastenmine*—wooden box mines—in front of the lunging SPWs. Though rudimentary, metal mine detectors could not find them. Peiper, who found Soviet armoured tactics failing and crude, called the wooden mines 'the first effective defence measure' against the enemy.[1] More losses. On that day alone the 13th Company lost seven halftracks in fighting, making Peiper's brash, charging style of warfare too costly to sustain. 'It was a bloody day,' Erhard Gührs recorded wearily.[2] The result was a 40km advance, with many enemy, and others of their own, killed in battle. There had to be a way to keep the enemy infantry from daring too draw close to their war wagons. Could the enemy gunners be somehow shaken so their shooting accuracy suffered or they fled their guns?

After the losses on 2 March it was Peiper's enterprising 20-year-old mechanic, Unterscharführer Oswald Siegmund, who came up with an answer: mount the blowtorches (*Lötlampen*) on the front of the SPWs to create a new weapon. Although they were currently utilized to warm engines to start in the cold Russian winter, they could also be transformed into something of a flame-thrower. Siegmund and the maintenance staff altered the devices with pumps to give Peiper's SPWs improvised, short-range flame-throwers:

> Without orders, on the 3rd of March, the *Lötlampen* [blowtorches] were freed: out of every *Lötlampen* which each vehicle needed to warm up the engines, they became 'flame-throwers' which shot a stream of gasoline of 8–15 metres. The torches were used to light the streams and they could burst fire. Everyone had fear of this, especially the Russians.[3]

In fact, flame-throwers were the most dreaded weapon faced by fighting men everywhere. Death by gunshot, artillery blast or tank shells—for the lowly infantryman, those were appalling enough to contemplate. But a fiery death, burned alive in roiling gasoline—that horrifying prospect was enough to send sensible types running. This was what men of the 'Blowtorch' Battalion, as they came to be called, counted on: an enemy so terrified, so shaken by the fiery terror of Peiper's war that they would flee rather than fight.[4]

On Wednesday 3 March 1943, Peiper first used the new *Flammenwerfer* in the capture of Petscheiwka and Ster in a night assault. The following day the new weapon worked famously in the attack on Stanitschnoje. There Peiper's command ran again into a fearsome line of anti-tank guns—a *Pakfront*. Such fire was devastating, particularly when it caught German armour in the flank. This time Peiper's command rushed so quickly that the commander of the *Pakfront* couldn't even react. Several guns were crushed under their tracks. The largest losses came from charging across three minefields without reconnaissance. This impetuosity cost another three SPWs. Peiper and his command would later be accused of burning Stanitschnoje to the ground, with corroborating evidence coming from one of the engineers in his battalion who also proudly described how improvised flame-throwers were fashioned for the assault.[5]

That the fighting was savage is beyond doubt. The action report from 3 March showed that some four T-34 tanks and six hundred enemy dead had been counted, although only five prisoners were taken.[6]

Thus another terrifying new wrinkle was added to the combat technique of the III Battalion. When coming into an enemy-held village, shots from every barrel announced the SS arrival. Spurting jets of fire set buildings in their path aflame. Confronted by sheets of fire, the previously stalwart Russian infantry took to their heels. With the vanity of a *Herrenmensch*, Peiper had the profile of a blowtorch stencilled onto every halftrack. Far and wide in the Waffen SS, Peiper's command became known for the *Lötlampen*. Even those in the kitchen knew: 'Stubf. Peiper and his battalion distinguished themselves by using their blowtorches.'[7] They were the *Lötlampen Abteilung*—the Blowtorch Battalion.

While Peiper would later challenge the prevailing notion as to why his command was called the Blowtorch Battalion, those inside the organization knew the truth.[8] If one saw a smudge of smoke or blossom of flame on the snow-packed Russian horizon, there was but one conclusion: there is Peiper.[9] Although some SS veterans post-war denied that the blowtorch symbol had anything to do with Peiper's pyro-tactical style of warfare, those describing his command in 1946 said otherwise: 'Peiper, like Panzermeyer, was generally known for conducting a ruthless warfare. Wherever Panzermeyer or Peiper were, fire could be seen and flags of smoke would indicate their location. As a sign of this, his SPW (halftrack) battalion wore as its tactical sign the blowtorch.'[10]

There was more. When Sturmbannführer Jakob Hanreich was captured in France in August 1944, he told interrogators that, when he joined the Leibstandarte in Russia in February 1943,

> At the time, there existed an oral order that in case of retreat of the regiment, all villages were to be evacuated and burnt ... The III Battalion of the 2nd Regiment was particularly eager to execute the order to burn villages. The battalion burned down by means of blowtorches and called itself the 'blowtorch' battalion. It was led by Sturmbannführer Peiper, who was later promoted to commander of the Panzer Regiment.[11]

Peiper's later explanation stretched credulity: the reason they were famous for *Lötlampen* became: 'We will torch that thing, sure enough!'[12] Nonsense. Peiper's command was called the 'Blowtorch Battalion' because they were famous for fire. The real reason Peiper laid flaming waste to all in his path had an obvious explanation: it was 100 per cent effective. They entered each village shooting and burning. Jochen Peiper's flaming warfare was without mercy, but neither the commander nor anyone under him saw their actions as war crimes; instead, it was a ruthless and brutal style of combat—a modern embodiment of the terror of Genghis Khan. They were the embodiment of the Waffen SS song they had sung so gleefully in France: 'Where the Leibstandarte fights, everyone takes flight.'[13] Peiper himself had said it best: 'Our reputation precedes us as a wave of terror and is one of our best weapons,' he wrote in 1943. 'Even old Genghis Khan would gladly have hired us as assistants.'[14]

This mode of combat in Russia seems to have been the norm for Peiper. SS Rottenführer Paul Zwigart was an SPW driver in Peiper's battalion and later would tell his interrogators stories corroborated by those told by Jakob Hanreich. 'In Russia, generally we did not take any prisoners at all,' Zwigart began.

> When the fighting became heavier and the German advance slowed down, prisoners of war were only taken in special instances. On various occasions we burned down whole villages with our blowtorches. I remember two cases; one in the spring of 1943 when we expressly received the order near Kharkov to set a village afire and 'bump off' all inhabitants 'including women and children'. When I say we, I mean the third battalion, which at that time was led by Hauptsturmführer Peiper. As far as I know he originated the order personally. Our battalion was, at that time, cut off from the main unit, and operated on its

own ... I myself did not see Haupsturmführer Peiper, who was with us at the time, shooting at civilians. However, it was generally known that he actively participated in this action ... I saw in this village which was of medium size (approximately 500–600 inhabitants) how our battalion set the houses afire with the blowtorches. I was a tank [sic: SPW] driver and on that occasion I did not leave my tank. I stood with my SPW at the entrance of the village and watched the infantrymen of our battalion running around with blowtorches and saw at least one who set a house on fire ... [they] ran around between the burning houses with machine guns and rifles shooting into the houses.[15]

The justification for wiping out the village, Zwigart told his interrogators, was that an inhabitant in the gutted village had shot into a truck, causing several Germans to be wounded.

On 4 March, as Peiper burned his way into Stanitschnoje, the battle for the recapture of Kharkov began. 'The troop has tremendous trust in their commander's luck,' Erhard Gührs wrote in his diary that day. 'Jochen Peiper has become an idol!'[16] Peiper was one of the boys. Eschewing a rear headquarters, he fought right up front in a halftrack himself, exposed and in as much danger as anyone else. A day later Peiper's troops pushed into Garilowka. 'In 30 days the fortunes of war have changed,' Gührs wrote on 5 March. 'We cannot win this war!' he had written home a month before. Now, 'our panzer grenadier battalion has torn a bloody furrow in the Russian soil.'

We continued to attack, and for the most part the Russians pulled back. Once again our air support was right there. The Russians sighted their tanks behind walls of snow in their positions, but they could hardly shoot that way. Our artillery was always very quick to fire. We blew up the Russian tanks and cannons immediately. In the morning, the attack on Narva Wadalaga began.[17]

On 6 March Peiper reached Peressell by noon and, four hours later, wrested Federowka and an important bridgehead across the Msha River. Although he had only two SPWs left, Erhard Gührs boldly thrust across the bridge to wipe out two enemy guns, seven trucks and several mortars. When the enemy attempted to flee, Gührs gave chase, shooting down eighty in one place. No one gave a thought to the killing—neither side was taking many prisoners.[18] Indeed, privately most Germans fighting on the Russian Front, particularly SS men, confided that there was a very low likelihood of being able to surrender to the Soviets.[19]

In a frozen field outside the strategic prize, Peiper hopped off his halftrack to meet his superior Theodor Wisch, who was just driving up. With gloved hands Peiper pointed out to Wisch their progress on the horizon. His men had expanded the bridgehead as far as Bidock. That night Wisch and Peiper moved inside his snow-encrusted field headquarters to discuss the next move. At a bare wooden table they shared a simple meal in the warmth of a Russian home. Over cigarettes the two pored over maps and consulted front-line outposts over a field telephone. The thawing roads were a mess; they could count on little artillery help—perhaps a few salvos from the lighter Nebelwerfer rockets. Supply over the quagmire was also becoming a problem. All remained mindful, however, that the big prize of Kharkov was not far off. Wisch proposed to support Peiper's armoured battalion with his other Panzer grenadiers advancing on Minkowka. A jolt of Schnapps sealed the plan. The next objective would be Walki, a town was just east of Kharkov.[20]

In the morning a frozen ground fog turned the sun into an orange glowing ball that slowly rose over the frigid white hills. They chased a sizzling Schnitzel with hot ersatz coffee. Soon after that, Peiper and his command barrelled along as Wisch ordered. Near Walki they ran afoul of still another Russian *Pakfront*. But with help from concentrated rocket fire and a cannonade from tanks commanded by Max Wünsche, the enemy gunners soon fled their posts. The final assault into Walki took place in concert with the 1st Reconnaissance Battalion under Kurt Meyer, which had to cross the frozen river to reach the village. Frustrated at the lack of progress, Meyer himself rode up to the front line, jumped off an SPW, shouldered a rifle and began picking off enemy gunners on the other side of the river. That was the signal to go: 'Tanks provided the covering fire, and we went all at once across the ice and into the village. We were firing from every barrel we had and howling like maniacs. Ivan couldn't take it. He fled. But we were completely exhausted.'[21]

Soon the peasant huts blazed. Inside the hamlet fierce resistance continued near the collective farm headquarters, and several of the assisting assault guns became marooned in waist-deep snow. By the time the village was captured, the scene was macabre, with 'dead Russian soldiers lying everywhere'.[22]

On 8 March came another night assault to seize the enemy-held bridge at Ljubotin, west of Kharkov. 'Each day was another wild evening of fighting behind enemy lines,' remembered Peiper's adjutant, Otto Dinse. 'This became our normal way. Fighting at night with speed and surprise. We seemed to be out just about every night. The enemy never knew where we were.'[23]

The news spread quickly. On 9 March 1943 Jochen Peiper earned the Knight's Cross of the Iron Cross—in one month of fighting in Russia he had earned one of the highest military decorations of the German Wehrmacht. News of the award arrived by radio from the Reichsführer himself. And Unlike Himmler's typically emotionless homilies, this one gushed:

> Heartfelt congratulations for the Knight's Cross my dear Jochen!
> I am proud of you! May your soldier's luck continue.
> Sigurd is doing well. Heartfelt congratulations from everybody.
> Heil Hitler![24]

Jochen Peiper was the Reichsführer's 'poster boy' who had done well. Sigurd, Jochen's wife and his previous secretary, was thriving—still part of the inner family back in Berlin. The news thoughtfully closed with greetings to Peiper from the office *Zauberkreis*—Himmler's magic circle: 'everybody sends greetings'.[25]

Max Wünsche, too, was salting the medals away. He was styling in his own sort of East Front iconoclastic manner—outfitted in a Russian fur cap and looking the Waffen SS egotist. On the same day as Peiper was leading the 320th Division to safety over the Udy River, Wünsche was also tasked with a rescue mission 45km to the south.[26] This time, however, it was for one of their own. Obersturmbannführer Kurt Meyer, in command of the LAH's reinforced *Aufklarungsabteilung* (reconnaissance battalion),[27] was in desperate straits.

Surrounded by Russian forces in the village of Alexejewka, he had transmitted his final situation report, in which he outlined the impending demise of his encircled battle group. With fuel and ammunition running out, the Soviet forces were edging ever closer to their stricken quarry. Meyer then made the gut-wrenching decision to abandon his wounded and authorised that their precious stock of pistols be distributed amongst them. The implication was unspoken: better for an SS man to end one's own life than to fall into the hands of 'Ivan'.[28]

Meanwhile, Wunsche and his rescue party were ploughing ever closer through the deep snow, their armour laden with fuel drums and ammunition canisters. Four kilometres from Alexejewka they came under scattered mortar fire. Wünsche immediately forbade any engagement and ordered the men onwards, fearing that any distraction would mean arriving too late to save their beleaguered colleagues from annihilation.[29] Kurt Meyer recorded their fortuitous arrival:

> The sound of fighting to our rear, that is, to the west of Alexejewka, transformed our mood into one of happy excitement. The sound could

only mean Max Wünsche's advance had been successful. And so it was, the Panzer Abteilung had gnawed its way through heavy enemy forces … we were completely operational again.[30]

For this action and for those over the previous days' fighting in Merefa, Wünsche was awarded the German Cross in Gold on 25 February.[31] Coincidently, on that very same day, while Meyer was being bestowed his Oak Leaves by his grateful Führer at the 'Werewolf' headquarters near Vinnytsia, Wünsche led another charge against the Soviet lines near Jeremejewka while urging on his forces 'Forward! Forward, don't stop to fight their infantry! Their artillery is our goal.' The tanks punched ahead, spraying their path with machine gun bullets. The thrust destroyed fifty-four cannons and guns, leaving behind at least eight hundred Russian dead scattered among hundreds of horses and oxen still attached to sleighs. 'The Russian fled in droves,' remembered the adjutant of the Panzer battalion, 'easily visible in their brown uniforms as soon as they left their snow fortifications.'[32] This action earned Wünsche a further trinket for his growing haul, the coveted Knight's Cross of the Iron Cross.[33] Little wonder that during a post-war interrogation a Canadian intelligence officer sardonically declared him 'decorated like a Christmas tree'.[34]

There was little time for Peiper to savour his award or contemplate that received by his shadow, Wünsche. Even as some of his men decorated their SPWs with flowers as if to celebrate, on 9 March there was a new challenge—the recapture of Kharkov. Pushing beyond Ljubotin under a protective umbrella from a rocket barrage, Peiper linked up with the Totenkopf Division and destroyed another enemy battalion in close combat outside Komuna.

The taciturn Generaloberst Hermann Hoth, in charge of the 4th Panzer Army, wanted to encircle and starve out Kharkov—that was the prudent way. To go into Kharkov to fight in the city … well, that experiment had been run at Stalingrad. But, like it or not, Hausser saw himself in Hitler's dog house and thus desired rapid results—as did the Führer. On 10 March, Hitler called on Sepp Dietrich at his headquarters at Dergatschi, with Rudolf Lehmann, the divisional general staff officer, listening in on the conversation on the telephone. How was it going for 'his men?' Hitler asked of Dietrich. There was consternation over reported losses but then a challenge in Hitler's parting words: 'If my Leibstandarte attacks with its usual nerve, it cannot fail to tear Kharkov from the enemy's hands!'[35]

On his own initiative Paul Hausser would launch both the Leibstandarte and Das Reich into a direct battle to capture the city. Would the weather hold up for the attack? After all, mud from a thaw would stop everything. At 1900 hours Teddi Wisch met with Peiper and his other battalion commander. They would launch the attack in the dead of night—at 0330 hours Peiper's III Battalion was to punch into the north part of Kharkov as soon as the I Battalion secured the north edge of the city. According to the plan, the Totenkopf Division would attack from the north-west, Das Reich from the west, with the Leibstandarte essayed to collapse the enemy defences from the north.

Once the Totenkopf Division, Das Reich and Leibstandarte joined the battle on the main Belgorod road, SS Panzer Grenadier Regiment 1, under SS Standartenführer Fritz Witt, bludgeoned its way into Kharkov, while SS Standartenführer Wisch moved his regiment forward, with his left covered by Kurt Meyer and his reconnaissance battalion. The first battalion under Sturmbannführer Hugo Kraas seized the northern edge of the city, assisted by a wave of Stuka dive bombers that pounded the Soviet line amid the spindly trees. With the further support of tanks, Fritz Witt's SS Panzer Grenadier Regiment 1 reached the large buildings on the northern edge of the city after fighting through slushy fields and parks. Witt chomped on cigars, reviewing plans with Haupsturmführer Josef "Jupp" Diefenthal of the SS Panzer Grenadier Regiment 2 as engineers struggled to remove crude wrought-iron anti-tank obstacles. Once that was done, they could ram-rod the Panzers into the Ukrainian city. One member of the engineer company remembered,

Today we attacked into Kharkov, and now we had to take Alexejewka before the way into the city was clear. The village was taken quickly but then things really started to happen. The flat terrain dropped slowly toward Kharkov, but off to the right was a high area divided by a small stream. We received some heavy machine gun and mortar fire from well-defended Russian positions in that open area. We stayed where we were until the attack stopped. The Russians shot down on us, as we were clearly visible, like dark flecks in the white snow. When that happened, it was soon over for the whole Battalion. The Russians were positioned by a sawmill and we were able to shoot that up and set it on fire. One attack gun was blown up, the crew of a tank burned to death inside it, a Flak gun shot it out with a T-34, the flak flew through the air and a T-34 burned. We couldn't move forward. To the left of us was a sniper in a water tower, and we couldn't take him out. The road was mined but our Panzer had to go forward. A heavy gun was lost when it sagged though the ice crossing a stream while we moved cross-country. Four others made it across successfully, though. We broke out of there recklessly but didn't know whether we could make it—either way we would be fired on, walking or riding. Even when we walked we had to stay low. Metre by metre we crept forward. The Battalion Commander [Peiper] was in front of us—one by one we went forward with him.[36]

On the evening of 11 March, Peiper's SPWs pulled forward into the breach opened by Witt's assault and prepared to launch an attack the following morning. Supported by a pack of assault guns, their objective would be a propaganda coup: Red Square. Dietrich confidently radioed back: 'Enemy completely surprised by the rapid advance of the Leibstandarte and thrown back.'

Meanwhile, all was not well at headquarters. Hermann Hoth was furious with Paul Hausser, ordering that the Das Reich Division immediately come out of the assault on Kharkov from the west and swing around with Totenkopf to surround the city from the east. Although that order was followed, Hausser did not pull out the Leibstandarte, which was inextricably tangled in the Kharkov streets. It would be primarily Dietrich's responsibility to deliver the great prize.[37]

At 1000 hours on 12 March Peiper and the assault guns rolled headlong down the main thoroughfare leading into Kharkov. At one point they were faced with a menacing-looking road block—heaped with abandoned wagons and wood. Were they hiding anti-tank guns and mines? No matter. A platoon leader of the assault guns called to 'put it in high gear and don't stop'. Peiper's column crashed into the road block with all guns blazing, tearing away the wagons and surging on ahead. They suddenly debouched into a wide-open courtyard—Red Square.

Peiper then made contact with steely eyed SS Sturmbannführer Max Hansen already there. Binoculars dangling over a snow-camouflage poncho, Hansen assured Peiper that the work there was nearly done. This was in spite of the lively gunshots animating the background of their conversation. They puffed on cigars and briefly savoured the moment in the middle of Kharkov's wrecked and burning streets. And where was Kurt Meyer? He was usually in the middle of everything.

Sensing trouble, Peiper commanded three SPWs to link up with Meyer at a nearby key road intersection. Meyer would later credit Peiper with saving his surrounded battalion on 12 March:

Once again the entire Kampfgruppe had been surrounded and was struggling in desperate fighting. A circle of burning buildings pinpointed our position in that sector of the city. By the onset of night I no longer had much hope that we could hold out until the following morning. The enemy was within hand-grenade range … Jochen Peiper beat his way through to us with two SPW [*sic*], thus establishing contact with the remainder of the division. His escort SPW was knocked out by a T-34, but he succeeded in bringing the men out to safety.[38]

That done, Peiper ordered his assault guns and halftracks to resume smashing their way forward. Russian resistance was fierce; one SPW was destroyed as Peiper's men shot their way through the flames and debris from one house to the next. With escalating losses that afternoon, Peiper seized a small but strategic stone bridge across the Kharkov River, which flowed right through the northern section of the city.

Poking beyond the bridge, however—that was another matter. The windows of every house on the other side bristled with machine guns and sharpshooters ready to cut down anyone foolish enough to venture beyond. Snipers were everywhere. The dull rasping sound of the Russian machine guns chattered over the whipping, high-pitched stutter of the faster German MG 42s. Peiper's vehicles had just started to cross the span when the Russians blew it up. The fighting around the bridge swirled in a maelstrom of gunfire and explosions with choking smoke and dust which continued to rage into the night. The place was shortly immortalized in the nihilistic Waffen SS legend as 'Peiper Bridge'.[39]

German engineers toiled to repair Peiper's namesake bridge while under constant gunfire that night. Before dawn on Sunday, 13 March the fighting reached a tumult: an SPW crossed to the other side laden with Panzer grenadiers, who were then immediately met by a hail of bullets as they emerged. Meanwhile, Peiper himself dashed across the bridge and led a close-quarter infantry battle along Petinska Street; they cleared the brick buildings one by one. Rushing beyond the nearby tractor factory, each of the two squad leaders were wounded. SS Untersturmführer Heinz Tomhardt had his 13th Company temporarily surrounded by counterattacking Soviets and was himself wounded as well. And when an SPW mounting a 7.5cm cannon was driven across to subdue the enemy, it took a direct hit, instantly killing its commander, SS Unterscharführer Fritz Jobi. The 12th Company lost half its men in the street battle; the 7th Squad was killed to a man.

Something had to be done. Peiper's answer was to bring up big 88mm flak guns. Although arranging this took time, once they were in place the guns blasted apart the buildings from which the Russians defiantly fired. By the afternoon the following day Peiper had expanded his toehold on the opposite bank and cleared the road enough for the I Battalion under Hugo Kraas to get to the other side and clear the enemy from the buildings around the nearby church. The Luftwaffe even flew five hundred Stuka sorties to subdue the T-34s sallying out to Kharkov, while German tanks clattered down the streets, two abreast, blasting away at anything that challenged them. Machine gunners fired away from piles of rubble, and so it raged the next day: it was the evening on 14 March before the city was clear of the Russians. Peiper and his men ended the fight by overpowering the enemy at the local railway station.

> Early in the day we fought on. Our Company saw a lot of action, and some tough battles came our way. The Russians put up a stubborn defence but we attacked with dogged persistence. Over and over we had to fire in the streets, and the houses took some direct shots (at 100 metres and less). Nevertheless the Russians kept firing from the cellars of the destroyed houses. I took some more shots in my sidecar as we ricocheted through the streets. A grenade exploded in front of my moving motorcycle and I got a piece of shrapnel in my knee and more in the vehicle. It still ran nevertheless. Stubaf. Hansen in the 1st Regiment took the 'Red Square'. More and more T-34s kept coming into the fight from the side streets and gardens. Plaster busts of Stalin stood all over the place. We stuck like glue to the Russians and attacked them wherever they showed themselves. In this way we fought house by house, street by street through Kharkov! The 'Red Square' was renamed the 'Platz der Leibstandarte'.[40]

Kharkov, the fourth-largest city in Russia and the industrial centre of the Ukraine, was now again under German control. Clad in a thick, fur-lined coat, Dietrich showed up at the captured tractor works to congratulate everyone. Although it was a great victory, the cost was monumental; Hausser lamented that some twelve thousand Waffen SS soldiers were sacrificed in its conquest and the regiment to which Peiper belonged saw fourteen hundred officers and men become casualties.[41] Even so, there were plenty of accolades. After all, it was the kind of destructive clash that Hitler extolled. On the afternoon of 14 March a bulletin on *Sender Großdeutschland* (Greater German Radio) suddenly interrupted its classical playlist: 'The High Command of the Army announces that Army Group South … launched a campaign of encirclement and has succeeded in recapturing Kharkov after days of heavy fighting. The enemy's losses, in both men and material, is incalculable.'[42]

Von Manstein's counteroffensive at Kharkov with Hausser's SS corps ranks among the most strategically perfect military ripostes ever fought. After the humiliating defeat at Stalingrad and the near collapse of the front in February, the March counteroffensive once again seized the hallowed military initiative—the *Gesetz des Handelns*—and at least temporarily reversed the course of the war in the East. Hitler was exhilarated.

Dietrich got the big prize—'The Führer has recognized your service to the future of the German people ... the loyal companion of the Führer, the old SS leader and current general of the Waffen SS'—by awarding him the Oak Leaves with Swords to his Knight's Cross.[43] He was only the twenty-sixth soldier to be so decorated at that time.

Peiper was also among the anointed. The story of the 'Peiper Bridge' loomed large in Waffen SS lore, with the young SS commander already a favourite both to Himmler and Hitler.[44] Particularly to his own men, Peiper had become a hero to the Waffen SS. Peiper chafed to learn that the ungrateful General Postel of the 320th Infantry Division, whose ass he had bailed out without a nod of thanks, was now getting the Oak Leaves. SS General Hausser, who had delivered Kharkov—and where the army had been unwilling—got nothing. He was snubbed. Still in Hitler's dog house, Hausser would not be rewarded until months later, and then it would be the much-disparaged Gold Party Badge. The gratitude for a decisive victory—and certainly one of the most dramatic of the war—paled against Hausser's refusal to heed Hitler's order to hold Kharkov in the first place. Or at least that was the rumor.

Yet in capturing Kharkov, the enthusiasm of the Leibstandarte men for victory appeared to translate into horrific brutality.

An unidentified officer in the Leibstandarte ambulance detachment was accused of having set a Russian army hospital ablaze in Dzerzhinsky Square on Trinkler Street on 13 March 1943, with SS men then shooting any of the wounded who attempted to escape the flames. About thirty Red Army soldiers desperately jumping out windows were gunned down, and others attempting to escape were barricaded inside and the building set afire. Three hundred died.[45]

The next day nine SS men came into the remaining blocks of the hospital and, after driving all the medical personnel out, shot four hundred Soviet officers while they lay in their beds.[46]

Of course, after the war the Waffen SS flatly denied the horrific episode, and hundreds of the SS men later gave extensive depositions disputing the charges. The truth remained evasive, but the Frankfurt state attorney's inquiry concluded that 'it could well have been an act of retribution, since several witnesses reported that in the course of the Eastern campaign, including around Kharkov, captured members of the Leibstandarte were found dead with signs of horrible mistreatment having been inflicted on them before death'.[47] Even Peiper himself admitted that the Eastern Front had transformed the ethos of war.

While claiming 'old divisions of the Waffen SS performed amazing deeds,' there was a moral price: 'Severity against friend and foe became a necessity for survival and human life lost its value!'[48]

Nonetheless, beyond that brutality, even in retaking Kharkov, the German high command was painfully aware that the city was untenable if the Russians gathered forces for another counterattack. To offer any protection, the Germans needed to capture the bridgehead beyond the Donets River at Belgorod and restore their previous defensive line. With the weather so uncertain at that time of year, it would need to be done immediately. General Mud would stop everything. How to capture it quickly?

Three days after Kharkov was seized, the army announced that Belgorod would be snatched by its own army elite force, the Grossdeutschland Division, with the Leibstandarte SS Adolf Hitler and the Totenkopf Divisions assisting. However, upon receiving the mission of 'assisting', Peiper confided in staff officer Rudolf Lehmann that he intended to be first—they would win 'the race for Belgorod'.[49] It was another chance to rub the stodgy army noses in what Peiper saw as the natural SS superiority. 'We had a better spirit,' Peiper would later say of the SS versus the army. 'We weren't better, we were more desperate.'[50]

The key, they decided, was arranging good air support and extra firepower. Peiper and the SS Panzer Grenadier Regiment 2 slowly pushed north of Kharkov—the gelatinous roads were bad enough, but the thicket of Russian anti-tank guns dug into snow drifts south of Nechotejewka—that was something else. He needed some *Schlachtflieger* to blast the *Pakfront* from the air, and he needed some tanks—real tanks, not assault guns—to subdue the T-34s that must be lurking just beyond. That too was arranged. Peiper would have Rudolf von Ribbentrop's 7th Panzer Company along with a couple of the new super-heavy Tigers. Peiper knew von Ribbentrop well. This brave kid was the son of the German foreign minister. The new Tigers mounted the huge 88mm cannon and at last gave the Germans real tank superiority on the Eastern Front. With these arrangements, Peiper opined, he could take just about anything. The Tiger leaders were totally unafraid of the Soviet armoured concentrations. 'As a Panzer Man,' ventured Rolf Mobius, 'I cannot remember a Russian tank organization ever fighting a tank battle to a finish unless its numerical superiority was so unequivocal that the outcome could not be doubted.'[51] Mobius felt his Tiger I and those with him were superior to the Russian tanks in every way. They were never turned back, and the Russians always fled.

When 18 March dawned cold and bright, after a short radio call and punctually at 0700 hours, the Stukas zoomed out of the sky and furiously bombed the Russian line. Peering through binoculars, Peiper barely waited for the buzzard-like dive bombers to lift before ordering his tanks and SPWs forward across the snow pack. 'We floored it,' one tanker remembered.[52] SS Rottenführer Werner Wendt was with the new heavy Panzer company, featuring the confident behemoth Tiger tanks. He clanked right behind Peiper's lead Panzer IV. 'At 7 AM, we broke through the front Russian line,' he recalled. 'We turned on our engines and put ourselves in fast march. We caught the enemy by surprise.'[53] Battle group Peiper shot up half a dozen T-34s in as many minutes. At 0710 hours Peiper radioed that he was through the enemy line and rushing towards Otradnyj. 'Everyone', he radioed to those in his column, would need to 'keep it up at their fastest tempo'. That village, halfway between Kharkov and Belgorod, was soon in German hands.

Although the objective for the day had already been reached, Peiper saw no reason to pause. Soviet defences were completely confused. Peiper's team was advancing so quickly that several enemy T-34s were shot down in a Russian tank repair shop, the mechanics totally stunned during their breakfast. Peiper ordered his tank force to keep storming ahead—no stopping for anything. A small flock of Me 110 fighters roared over the snowy plain, providing cover.[54] By 1000 hours they were in Krassnoje—almost there. Peiper's voice crackled over the radio: 'Spearhead eight kilometres south-west of Belgorod on the march route. The Russians are retreating to the west. Two enemy tanks destroyed.' Said Guenther Borchers:

> We stormed forward again. On the square in Krassnoje we still saw some Ivans. Immediately we gave it the gas and drove right into a heavy mortar position. The surprised Russians threw up their hands, and we headed them back towards a collection point. We stayed there. Another battalion took over the point and on the same day took Belgorod. The Russians there were surprised, too. They weren't able to get their T-34s up and running fast enough, and over 20 anti-tank pieces fell into the hands of our Regiment—Peiper's unit. The Russian tank crews were still in the houses when Peiper's battalion came into the city. A few Russians were on the tanks but when they saw Peiper's men they took off into the field looking for cover.[55]

Peiper's armoured column zoomed forward so quickly that they surprised a Russian anti-tank crew and crushed the gun before the crew could do anything more than scatter. Looking out to their left, Peiper could see the endless slush-covered steppe, seemingly covered by Soviet soldiers running for the horizon, their great coats fluttering in the wind. On orders, Peiper's tanks and SPWs ignored them: Forward! Top speed! At 1135 hours his report electrified headquarters:

Belgorod taken in surprise attack. Eight enemy tanks destroyed.
—Commander of the III/2[56]

Peiper's column sped towards Belgorod with a Mk IV Panzer out in the lead, followed by a Tiger. The tanks saw signs in Russian Cyrillic letters. No one could read them, but there was no mistaking the size of the city nested between the bowl-like hills on the Donets plain—this had to be Belgorod. Approaching from the south-west, they gingerly drove across a wooden bridge; luckily it was able to support the hulking Tiger. Beyond that, however, Peiper encountered one Russian tank after another, each being shot down by the Tiger and Mk IV. By 1700 hours Peiper was able to radio that they had now destroyed fourteen enemy tanks and a bevy of anti-tank pieces. Friendly losses were light: one killed and six wounded. The Russians fled. The Germans had the town, but their advance had been so quick that headquarters had no idea that Belgorod was now in German hands. As a result, the Luftwaffe flew a 'beautiful bombing run' on their own positions.[57]

In any case, Peiper was at the top of his game. The army Grossdeutschland Division was still west of Belgorod, while Peiper spent the remaining daylight sealing his grip on the city and expanding a bridgehead across the Donets River. At night his men used their blowtorches to scramble eggs while others set up an all-around hedgehog defence, which was fortuitous, for the Russians counterattacked the next day in strength. By then, however, Peiper had brought up more flak guns. Seven Russian tanks smoked before Belgorod, although the T-34s blasted away at Peiper's SPWs.

In the battle on 19 March Peiper reinforced his bridgehead to the north, brushing aside resistance at Schopino. Soviet high command was now in something of a panic. If the enemy penetration continued north to Kursk, an entire Russian army might be trapped. Whatever could be spared—most of it artillery and tanks fresh from the factory—were hurried to the front before Belgorod. When Peiper set out the following day the roads were in a horrid condition, and his column slowly toiled forward. Near Gonki the Russians plastered Peiper's advance with artillery and tank fire—even Russian close support aircraft. One halftrack was hit and began to burn furiously. 'Withdraw!' Peiper called over

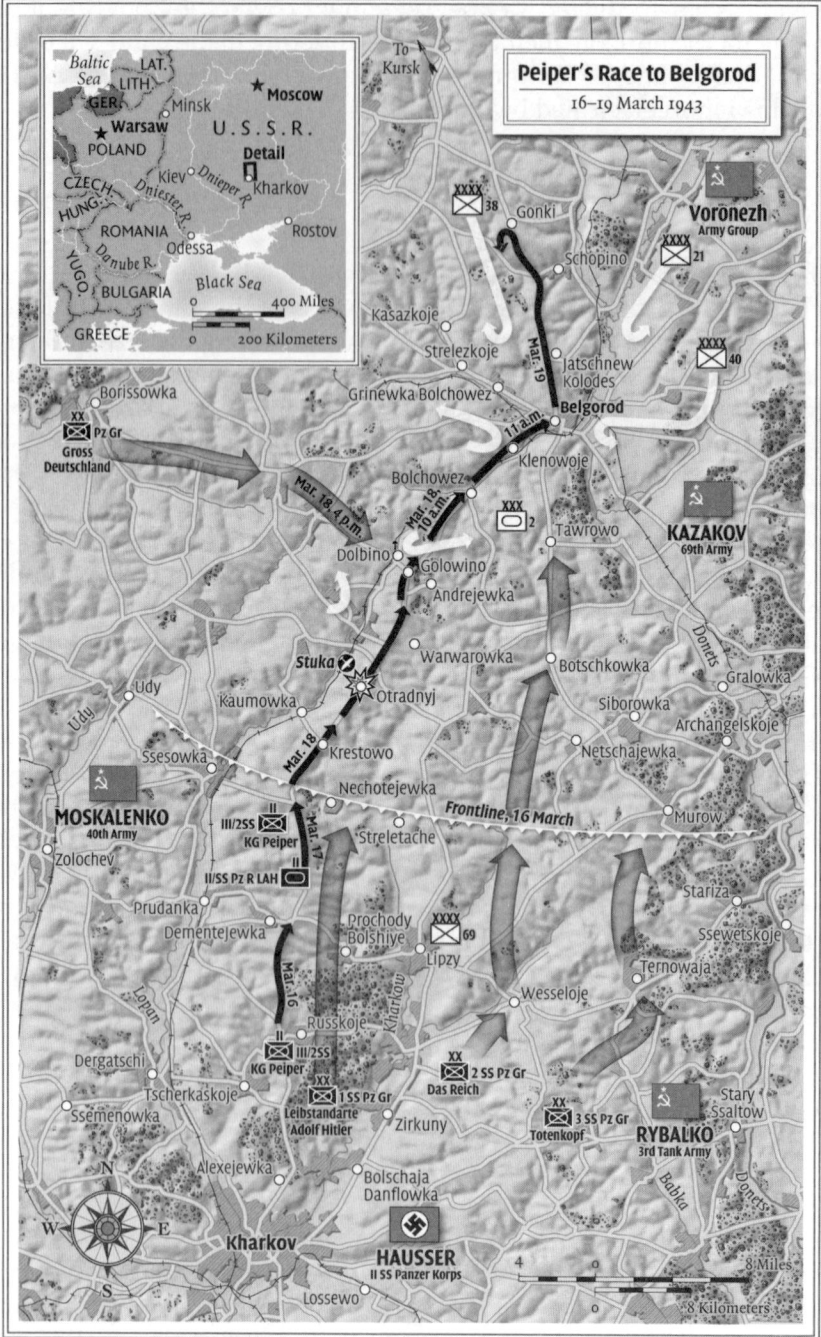

Peiper's Race to Belgorod
16–19 March 1943

the radio. 'Pull to the back side of the slope.' He told his battle group to set up a defence near Jatschnew-Kolodes north of Belgorod. 'There's nothing to be gained here!'[58]

The commander of the destroyed halftrack was a friend of Peiper's. Rudolf von Ribbentrop volunteered to take his Mk IV and go look for survivors. Peiper agreed reluctantly: 'Be careful, Ribbentrop.' Their Panzer zipped across the rise at high speed, catching the Russian artillery unware. But when von Ribbentrop reached the smouldering halftrack he found the wreckage true to its name—an 'iron coffin'. All were dead.[59]

He drove back to the others with only pay books and identity discs. Peiper thanked him; the big throw looked to be over.

The Ukrainian countryside warmed in the late winter sun. Peiper's battalion, like everyone else in the German army, was stuck fast. The reason was readily apparent to anyone familiar with the Ukrainian spring: the indigenous soil is a black podzolic mixture, which transforms into a liquid quagmire after the first real thaw. Every wheel, every track and every boot that set out from a road onto it marooned its owner in a gummy morass. Real movement was impossible. This was the seasonal circumstance that played out each spring during the war in Russia.

Peiper took the opportunity to write his 'little sister', Hedwig Potthast, who was now staying at the SS estate at Brückenthin, Pomerania, with Oswald Pohl and his family near the SS main hospital at Hohenlychen. The women's concentration camp at Ravensbrück was not far away— the kept mistress had been installed at the epicentre of Himmler's expansive world.[60] The father of her new son, the Reichsführer SS himself, came to visit on weekends when he was not in the East with Hitler. In March 1943 Hedwig had sent Jochen Peiper congratulations on his latest battlefield commendation along with a picture of her son, Helge, with herself and Himmler in the picture. Jochen Peiper was still on the inside track with the Reichsführer SS, and the former adjutant was feeling ebullient about his bold command:

Command Post
    24 March 1943
    Dear Little Sister:
    Thanks for the congratulation and above all for [the] charming little picture. Your demand to destroy it after having looked at it is an imposition I must reject with indignation. Should unauthorized eyes look on the picture, I shall brag of Helge and proudly present him as my son, who as an exception is permitted to sit on the arm of his godfather. You! The kid really is coming along well. I am a little envious

and regret again and again that we have not yet succeeded with a No. 3 child, inasmuch as out here in the combat environment one often pursues one's own thoughts.

Otherwise, everything is just fine. Seven weeks of very concentrated living are behind us. We are aware that things could not get any worse and calmly look into the uncertain future. I had many joyous events with my bunch. We have become known beyond the borders of our division because of our successes and because of our persistence and enduring matter-of-factness. But even a bad reputation has its obligations— (I freely quote Zarah Leander). Our reputation precedes us as a wave of terror and is one of our best weapons. Even old Genghis Khan would gladly have hired us as assistants.

For beautiful women and tender hearts of girls, however, watching and coming along on our daily work would not be appropriate. We rather would now spend our time relaxing with them on the reclining terraces of St. Anton [ski resort in the Austrian Alps]. Improbable and hardly imaginable—we all feel as we never had been away from Russia. The little intermezzo in France is already gone from our imaginations. Right now I am sitting in a Gypsy wagon, looking out the window, and dozing relaxed into the winter landscape. The rapid attacks with our weapons during the most recent days has led to some quiet time. There is even talk about us being taken out of here and exchanged. Sort of as a temporary conclusion, I took with my battle group the city of Belgorod in a bold stroke. It was a splendid success and Army, Corps, and division outdid themselves in honouring recognition. Otherwise my bunch and I are leading quite a robber's life. Because of my insubordination, quite well known to you, I was able to carry out my successful undertakings either with or without orders. Even though I had to look out every hour for ricochets from my extremely competent regimental commander.

We are worrying about air raids where you are! The Tommie rather should drop more bombs around here and spare you. Thank God, nothing has yet happened. Continue to remain healthy and well and be assured that my thoughts are often at home. Bunny child don't forget me totally and accept greetings for all your loved ones.

Always,
Your Jochen[61]

Heinz von Westernhagen, fighting with the assault gun beside Peiper, also wrote home of the cataclysmic fight but had a less sanguine view of the fighting:

What we left behind is appalling. A repetition of that is hardly possible. It could not get worse—you can't imagine .... If you were to come to Kharkov now, you would not recognize it. Hardly a house is left intact. Nobody is going to forget the street combat ... Nobody can describe what here happened during the winter fighting. Every single man deserves the Knights Cross. In Kharkov itself we drove to within 30 metres of fortified houses and fired directly into them with our panzer artillery. From above, the brothers bedevilled us with satchel charges on our heads. And after the dust from bricks and explosives had settled, these dogs continued to fire. From a distance of 100 metres we fired artillery into them and in places killed them with Cossack sabres.[62]

By the end of March 1943 the Eastern Front was again quiet—a lull between the two heavyweight champions, each looking to kill the other but exhausted by tremendous losses. The clash of titans would be stuck in limbo until the summer sun dried the fields and grasslands to free the antagonists from the muck. Until then, the German initiative was put on hold. Both sides could only prepare for the deadly summer season. And that was Hitler's quandary: What next?

At the end of the month Peiper and his III Battalion moved to Klenowoje to rest and refit. Far away from the fighting front they could relax, take a bath and even resume their cherished sporting events. Peiper's men organized a soccer tournament, but with a few wartime twists: penalty kicks were made more difficult by smoke grenades thrown into the goal area to complicate the kicker's shot. There was also an amphibious vehicle obstacle course. The whole thing was photographed by the SS cameramen and sent to the folks back home. One thing that did not receive press: some of the men developed May love affairs with the local Ukrainian girls in Klenowoje, many of whom were attractive and spoke fluent German—springtime in the East.

By any accounting, Kampfgruppe Peiper had succeeded brilliantly at Kharkov. Its commander earned the Knight's Cross for seizing Belgorod on his own initiative. The mineral-rich Donets Basin was again in German hands and the Eastern Front stabilized. Moreover, Hitler's appreciation of the Waffen SS reached new heights against falling expectations for his allies: 'The SS Panzer Corps,' he gushed to Generalfeldmarschal Hans von Kluge, 'is worth twenty Italian divisions.'[63] As Hitler planned future operations, he fussed that the Waffen SS must get the choice replacements, best equipment and the heaviest tanks.

Four more SS armoured divisions would be formed, many from East European volunteers. One, the 12th SS, or Hitlerjugend Panzer Division, would be composed of Hitler Youth with a more Germanic complexion and led by Fritz Witt from the Leibstandarte. Sepp Dietrich, whose reputation had reached a heady zenith, would command an entire SS Panzer Corps. Peiper's former commander, Theodor Wisch, would take charge of the Leibstandarte. All this annoyed the regular German army, but nothing could change the fact that Hitler's political soldiers—and Peiper among them—had delivered a very great victory in March 1943. But now, holding the baton of the initiative: How would Hitler capitalize?

To be sure, the Leibstandarte saw its supposedly elite composition weakened that spring. Not only did they lose 40 per cent of their strength—4,540 SS officers and men fallen in Kharkov's streets—but they now relinquished many of their senior officers and NCOs, who were to provide a veteran nucleus for the forming Hitlerjugend Division.[64] Not only would Sepp Dietrich be gone but also such motivating and fanatical personalities as Obersturmbannführer Kurt 'Panzer' Meyer and Max Wünsche. They all left for what old veterans cynically called the 'schoolboy' division.

The leadership drain promised to slip things a notch. Wünsche would take the entire I Battalion of the Panzer regiment as well as many experienced officers and NCOs. Perhaps worst, however, were the replacements delivered to the Leibstandarte. Many were transferred from the Luftwaffe and had only a modicum of infantry training. It was a sign of things to come. As the exigencies of a consuming war imperilled Hitler's Reich, the all-volunteer, super-elite status of the Leibstandarte seemed in danger. By 1942 individuals in Himmler's SS could reckon with suddenly being thrust into the Waffen SS. Ethnic Germans born outside the nominal borders of Germany were admitted into the organization. Gottlob Berger, in charge of recruitment, had obtained permission to accept 17-year-olds into the Waffen SS, even without their parents' permission. The Totenkopf units even had permission to take 16-year-olds. Kids, Luftwaffe clerks or ex-concentration camp guards were hardly the basic material of an elite. Some were even drafted. Regardless, Hausser encouraged the Leibstandarte combat leaders to indoctrinate the green replacements in the 'way of the SS'.[65]

The 'way of the SS' produced further tarnish that winter. Numerous charges arose of SS killings during the Kharkov campaign. Although most SS veterans insisted after the war that no atrocities transpired in Russia, a few slipped from the agreed-upon story. One of these was SS Hauptsturmführer Alfred Kilian, a member of the staff company of SS Panzer Grenadier Regiment 2. Wounded in action in the fighting with Peiper in February near Smijew, Kilian returned to Theodor Wisch's headquarters staff near the airfield south of Kharkov. There he observed many Russian prisoners being held nearby. About one week later Kilian returned and asked Untersturmführer Wilhelm Schermeng, the regimental signals officer, what had become of the prisoners who had been there before; also standing in the staff room was Teddi Wisch, Jupp Diefenthal and some dispatch riders. 'Schermeng answered that these prisoners had been shot.' To Kilian it seemed obvious that Wisch approved, as there was scarcely a reaction when Schermeng described the Russians' fate. Later a comrade told Kilian of having witnessed an interrogated Russian civilian shot down after he refused to give information near Lisabudowka.[66] Another grenadier with the Panzer grenadiers in the Leibstandarte named Röthling recalled his platoon leader bragged 'that in Russia they always assembled about a hundred Russian PW and then made them march ahead over the minefield. They made them blow up their own mines.'[67]

Peiper revealed in his letter to Hedwig Potthast how they looked at their fighting—a fighting that was so raw and savage that women and girls with tender hearts would best not witness it: 'Our reputation precedes us as a wave of terror and is one of our best weapons. Even old Genghis Khan would gladly have hired us as helpers.'[68]

What more could be said?

German Waffen SS veterans interviewed by the author in the 1990s agreed that there had been grim prospects for captives in the East. 'Yes, it is true that few prisoners were taken by either side in Russia towards the end of the war,' said one anonymous veteran, 'but that is what arises from a catastrophic situation!'[69] Even Peiper himself wrote, 'I concede, that in those days the ideological war and propaganda brain washing had progressed so far, that neither a commissar nor an SS man counted on being captured.'[70]

There is substantial evidence that the veteran officers of the Leib-standarte knew of the butchery going on behind the front lines.[71] Much of it had to do with anti-partisan activity—a fact of life in the intensely ideological war in the East. The increasingly destructive partisan activity, the SS maintained, justified the cruellest of responses.

One such 'Iron fist response' occurred in February 1943 in the Ukrainian villages of Jefremowka and Semenivka, an action so ruthless that it was later related in multiple German POWs' post-war testimonies.

After Kurt Meyer's *Aufklarungsabteilung* had been rescued from certain annihilation by Wünsche at Alexejewka, both forces united and jointly held off the Soviet onslaught for two more days. By the early hours of 16 February they were ordered to break out to the west and return to the village of Jefremowka from whence they had both come.[72]

Arriving back safely, complete with their dead and wounded, a quiet day followed, but this peace was not to last.[73] The first indication that something was amiss came the following morning on 17 February, when Erich Rumpf, a member of the Pioneer (Engineer) Battalion heard a pistol shot outside his billet on the outskirts of the village at 1030 hours. Running to the door, he saw a scar-faced Hauptsturmführer, approximately 30 years old, standing there in a snow camouflage outfit and fur cap.[74] The man seemed enraged, shouting that the company commander should be called there right away. Shortly, Hauptsturmführer Gerhard Nüeske arrived on the scene to have the SS captain dress him down: 'On the orders of Meyer this town is to be levelled to the ground, because this morning armed civilians attacked this locality. At this he shot a 25-year-old woman who was busy cooking our lunch.'

Later Rumpf heard other shots and learned that the same man had shot two other girls in the house nearby. Nüeske left, only to return thirty minutes later, confirming that Meyer had indeed made such orders. He was beside himself that the unnamed murderous Hauptsturmführer under Meyer 'behaved like a wild man'.[75]

What followed was a bloodletting so callous and horrific that not even the animals were spared. The women and children were summarily dispatched in an unimaginable orgy of violence and cruelty. Some were set alight while still alive; others thrown down wells or run over by the tracks of the heavy tanks. Children were beaten to death with iron bars, and old couples shot dead while entwined in their last desperate embrace.[76]

The males of the village had already been detailed to shovel snow on the approach roads. That afternoon they were brought to the church in Semenivka and ushered inside while snarling Alsatians dogs strained on their leashes. A machine gun had been set up on the straw-strewn floor. Once the last man was over the threshold, the shooting started. Those at the back threw themselves down, hoping to feign death. These were the unluckiest of all, for when the shooting was over, Meyer is purported to have called for gasoline to be poured over the bodies, and all victims, both dead and alive, were then set alight.[77]

It was a scene of unimaginable cruelty. Over eight hundred men, women and children were murdered that day, a larger number than at Oradour. An account of a survivor:

> The road to Semenovka was covered with snow ... the male population of the village was driven to clear the road. The people gathered up to two hundred people. In the church they kept horses, there was a lot of

straw, and after clearing the road already in the evening, all of us, like a herd, were driven into the church.

At the entrance two hand-held machine guns and a box with bottles were installed. Two soldiers lay at the machine gun, and an SS officer with a revolver in his hand. Two more soldiers took bottles from a box and threw at us. In the bottles was a self-igniting mixture, which was intended for the destruction of tanks. Everything around flared up. Several people rushed to the machine guns, but were immediately bevelled. Everywhere a fire raged, straw, walls, clothes and human bodies burned. There was a terrible, suffocating stench from burning human flesh. A horrible, heart-breaking death-cry was merged with the crackling and roaring of a raging flame. Even the executioners could not stand this sight, they left, closing the doors to the castle.

I was lucky. Of all those who were there, I was left alone. When ten men rushed to the exit, to the machine guns, I was somewhere between them in the middle. The bullet hit me in the leg, and I fell. Others fell on me and I was swamped with corpses. The bodies burned from above, I felt a burning pain on my head and cheek, but I was afraid to move. When the pain became unbearable, I sharply shook myself from the burning corpses, looked around, through a thick veil of smoke saw a closed door, crawled to it and immediately lost consciousness. I came to my senses already in our field hospital … At dawn our troops entered the village. In the hospital they told me, when they opened the church door, there was nothing to see from the smoke, and when the smoke cleared, they saw a terrible picture. Many veteran fighters could not hold back their tears.[78]

Elements of the story are further substantiated by a separate testimony from captured SS Sturmbannführer Jakob Hanreich:

The reconnaissance battalion of the LSSAH made an advance at the end of February [1943] towards the East and reached the village of Jefremovka. There they were surrounded by Russian forces. Fuel and ammo ran out and they were supplied by air until they were ordered to try to breakthrough towards the West. Before trying to do so, the entire civilian population was shot and the village burnt to the ground. The reconnaissance battalion was at that time lead by Obersturmbannführer Kurt Meyer.[79]

When the Germans eventually left, the few survivors crawled out of their homes over the mounds of dead. The moans of the dying competed with the bellowing of the mutilated cattle and the smell of burning, putrid flesh. All told, 865 died that day in the two villages, with 244 of these burnt in the church.[80]

In the aftermath the survivors tried to piece together what had prompted such brutality, but none could explain why such a calamity had been visited upon them. Years later one survivor searched in vain for the perpetrator. Helped by an Italian politician, he was eventually shown the evidence given against Peiper at his trial and thought he had found his culprit.[81] Peiper's name still appears in the local records as the man in command that day.[82] However, multiple testimonies and the LAH's own division records firmly establish that it was Kurt Meyer who had ordered Jefremowka's destruction. Meyer actually alluded to his motive in his own autobiography:

> During the fighting back to the west we got to know a new phase of this inhuman war. It was impossible to distinguish Soviet soldiers from harmless civilians. For the first time soldiers were ambushed in towns and in the countryside without being able to identify enemy units. We became nervous. The locals did not dare to betray the concealed Red Army soldiers ... My old comrade, Fritz Montag, who has been given command of the acting headquarters company, drove into a minefield and lost both legs above the knee. He was brought to me fully conscious in a motorcycle sidecar ... The fighting had taken on a treacherous character.[83]

Records show that Montag was fatally wounded on 17 February, the very day of the atrocity at Jefremowka.[84] Was this a coincidence or a a motive?

For many SS men fighting in Russia, pitiless killing became a way of life. An example comes from a letter home from the front by an SS Untersturmführer who died in Russia. The letter was published in the SS Leitheft by Himmler's office at the end of 1942 and was clearly meant to be inspirational for SS men:

> Dear Else:
> ... 24 hours later. It is night again, after an eventful day. I had to finish my day of work with an execution. I received the order to take three soldiers and execute two Red Army men, so that they can no longer be dangerous to us. Apathetic and tattered, like animals, they were handed to me. I hand each one a spade and they begin to dig their own graves. I quiet myself with a cigarette. Not a word is said. Russians are without a soul, they are animals. Better, they were made into that during the past years. They don't beg for their lives, they don't laugh and don't scream, they dig. Three rifle barrels are pointed at them; they are done; they are supposed to step into their grave. One turns around and flees. He got away as far as 20 metres, and he

drops ... The other stands motionless. Then he steps into the hole and also drops ... Two minutes later the good earth has covered everything. We light another cigarette ... We have learned to be terribly hard when it counts! Russia has taught us to extinguish a human life inexorably and ice cold.[85]

Was such brutal behaviour officially sanctioned by the leadership of the Waffen SS? In Berlin, in June of 1943, Albert Speer witnessed an indicator of Dietrich's reluctance for fighting in such a manner. While Hitler was soon launching a new offensive in the East, Speer was attending a dinner in the rear of the Chancellery. Dietrich quietly informed Speer that Hitler intended to issue an order that no prisoners would be taken in the great offensive. Speer was shocked. All this, Dietrich told him, was in response to units of the Waffen SS encountering repeated circumstances of the Russians butchering German prisoners. Hitler demanded revenge a 'thousand fold'. Speer had Hitler's ear, Dietrich suggested—perhaps he could change things. Speer confronted the German leader: these prisoners were needed as labour for his operations. Hitler seemed relieved to rescind the order just as the great offensive got under way.[86]

According to Dietrich, he did not officially sanction brutal reprisals against Soviet prisoners. However, the fact that he felt compelled to remind his senior SS commanders against such behaviour is a telling indicator of prevailing behaviour. 'We owe it to the title on our sleeve,' Dietrich reminded.[87] Not surprisingly, the exhortative did not filter down to all ranks of the men fighting the brutal war in the East.

There, no quarter was given or expected.

Chapter 7

'We Had Better Win this War'

'Our kingdoms lay in each man's mind, and as we wanted nothing material to live on, so perhaps we offered nothing material to the killing. It seemed a regular soldier might be helpless without a target.'
—T.E. Lawrence

In the Ukrainian spring of 1943 Jochen Peiper and his battalion rested. The mud and exhaustion demanded a halt. Kampfgruppe Peiper was billeted in the small villages and hovels in the rolling hills around Kharkov and the city itself. The relationship with the locals, if uneasy, was mostly cordial—even emotional: 'We lived in the old neighbourhoods where we had fought. The people were very friendly to us, and we gave them some tea from our rations which they quickly cooked for us in their Samovars. It was good enough ... When we left before Easter, they wept.'[1]

The boss himself made quarters in a thatched hut with a Ukrainian couple. Such were the oddities of the war. For in war's strange circumstance of extremes and desperation, now they were friends:

Naturally, the Russian knew how to capitalize on the advantages his own country offered. The civilian populations was right away forced to take part in the fighting and it did not matter that they were old men or women ... Talk about civilians! After the recapture of a city like Kharkov ... a full evacuation could not be put into practice. The German soldier sleeping in a house today, knew that tomorrow his host would pursue him on a T-34. The fighting became more ferocious all the time and the conception [idea] of a 'civilian' disappeared.[2]

On 24 April his old chief, Heinrich Himmler, came to visit Kharkov and addressed officers of the three victorious SS divisions. There was at least one personal meeting with Peiper to display the latter's signature cynicism. Losses in the Leibstandarte were extraordinarily heavy, Peiper explained to his former boss. The Russians were more numerous than ever. Himmler explained that many new recruits would be obtained to redress the balance. 'Reichsführer,' Peiper sarcastically suggested, 'if you want to win the war, you might consider creating battalions of women!'[3] If reflecting Peiper's cynical and macabre sense of humour, he spoke from experience:

> I remember two specific cases where we were attacked by tanks manned by women. One of the women introduced to me with the rank of 1st Lieutenant appeared with painted lips and fingernails. She explained to me that ... as punishment [for a small crime] she was ordered to take part in the front line fighting ... One merely has to hand out a weapon to any Russian citizen, whether a man or a woman and another soldier is ready![4]

The Reichsführer SS had more than gender on his mind. There, in the devastation of Kharkov, Himmler visited the university where the SS officers, including Jochen Peiper, were lectured on the usual themes. Uncharacteristically, his remarks this time revealed things he was usually careful not to speak about.

> We have only one task, to stand and pitilessly lead this race battle ... the reputation for horror and terror which preceded us in the battle for Kharkov, this outstanding weapon we want never to allow it to diminish, but only want to strengthen it. The world may call us what they will.[5]

'The reputation for horror and terror.' Himmler's choice of words reflected a heartfelt notion. To the devil with chivalry—he wanted the Waffen SS to be proud of its unmerciful reputation, one that struck terror into the hearts of their opponents, and a little later he spoke of a hygienic justification of the campaign for annihilation of the Jews: '[I]t is now a *Weltanschauung* question to rid oneself of lice.' How could anyone pretend not to know about the murderous goings-on?

A final indictment for the behaviour of the Waffen SS in and around Kharkov in the winter and spring of 1943 came from the Soviets after they recaptured the city later that August. Finding several mass graves, they accused the SS of having slaughtered twenty thousand civilians— over half of them Jews—in and around the city. Hangings were common in the burned-out centre of the city—something that could hardly escape the notice of anyone there. Sepp Dietrich was condemned to death in absentia.[6]

But for now, resting after victory, the Leibstandarte men basked in the sun of the Russian spring. According to one soldier,

> We pitched tents, and it's already warm outside. At the beginning of June we pulled back toward Losowa, where there was a fabulous lake. Here we played sports, rode horseback, and did a little bit of military duty. We built our commander a hut by the lake where he could relax. I was in the company troop ... The couriers did some training. It wouldn't be long until we'd again have a mission. We were happy that at least the sun was shining again. Everyone always talked about when our next mission would come and you couldn't get away from it.[7]

After the Easter celebration days the Leibstandarte men were assembled to Klenewoje. For a few short weeks there was thorough training for the new recruits and for officers as well. At the beginning of May Himmler himself showed up to observe the gunnery training for the new Panzer regiment. The men had collected a number of already knocked-out Russian tanks and anti-tank guns and set them up on the shooting range. Himmler nodded with satisfaction as the steel Soviet carcasses were shot up once more.

On 28 May 1943, on the occasion of Dietrich's birthday, the members of the Leibstandarte said goodbye to their long-time leader who was moving up to lead an entire SS Panzer corps. All the officers gathered for carefully orchestrated group photos, and the suave Wisch and other senior officers sat that afternoon with Dietrich at his table over bottles of wine. Even though Dietrich would remain for the next month, the symbolic transfer of the division was now done. 'Obersepp', as the officers called him, was certainly no military genius, yet his men loved the burly Bavarian. 'The man had extraordinary charisma,' Rudolf Lehmann offered. Dietrich referred to members of the Leibstandarte as 'my boys' and always reminded his combat leaders at the beginning of an operation to 'Bring my boys back'. On 6 June 1943 Dietrich handed over the reins of the Leibstandarte to Standartenführer Theodor Wisch. Peiper's old friend, Albert Frey, took over SS Panzer Grenadier Regiment 2.[8]

There was entertainment. Enterprising members of the division managed to get the Ukrainian theatre in Kharkov operating to stage several performances of Bizet's *Carmen*. For Peiper the springtime break presented other opportunities. It was perhaps during this break that the audacious commander persuaded a divisional reconnaissance pilot to give him a quick flying lesson. Off they went soaring above the steppes. After landing, with typical SS officer cockiness, Peiper announced he would try a solo flight by himself. For that he invited his chief medical officer to come along. The officer looked at him in complete disbelief. 'But you can't fly!' he stammered, 'and why do you need me to go with you?'

'Simple,' Peiper smiled as he ushered him towards the plane. 'If I do it successfully, then I've got you as a witness that I am now a qualified pilot.' What?

'If I don't', Peiper concluded sardonically, 'well, it will be very handy to have a qualified doctor right at hand.'[9] At that they took off, coming back minutes later to a successful landing. Peiper grinned broadly as he emerged from the Storch. His medical officer was shaking.

With such tales, word of Peiper's fame as an SS daredevil spread across the Nazi landscape. One only had to glance at the headlines of *Das Schwartz Korps* on 15 April 1943:

'Knight's Cross for Sturmbannführer Peiper'

There was a photo of the dashing SS leader with the black Knight's Cross dangling from his neck. The Führer personally made the award, the caption read. Peiper's good fortune did not come solely from luck. 'Orders and instruction,' the article concluded, 'did not come from hesitant deliberation, but from a character which united heart, mind and hand.'[10]

By the end of April 1943 the Leibstandarte was again at a strength of over twenty-one thousand men.[11] By this time SS volunteers holding proper SS racial perspectives were no longer available in sufficient numbers to replace casualty losses. Increasingly often now the gaps were filled with men who didn't fulfil the expectations of their fanatical superiors. Nevertheless, most of the men who entered the Waffen SS in 1943 were youngsters at the time Hitler assumed power and came of age under the influence of National Socialism. At schooling through the HJ (Hitler Youth) and the *Reichsarbeitsdienst* programme (civilian work service), they were 'indoctrinated in the spirit of National Socialism, and were prepared to go to war at an impressionable age'.[12] A large portion of the personnel replacements in early 1943 were diverted to the SS from the Luftwaffe, lacking not only a desire to join the Waffen SS but also any infantry training whatsoever.[13]

Many of these men, though, had already logged long years of military service, so the military life was familiar to them. During this period desertion became a problem in the SS for the first time, and problems with the replacement personnel continued.[14] To begin with, the Reconnaissance Battalion received five totally green NCOs and thirty-three enlisted men, and from the hospital came three Unterführer (NCOs) and seven enlisted soldiers in addition to 192 enlisted personnel from the Replacement Batallion.[15] Soon disciplinary problems arose. Troops guilty of minor infractions such as 'The Racket with Two Cows' and unauthorized use of a motorcycle received the same punishment as six SS men convicted of raping a Russian woman: twenty-one days detention, a mild sentence imposed by Gustav Knittel.[16]

At about the same time Albert Frey received a thousand recruits from the Alsace region for his Grenadier Regiment. 'The men arrived in one group,' he said. 'They came from Alsace-Lorraine. A number of them had never spoken German. Others learned our language but only imperfectly. None of them were volunteers.'[17] The men required intensive training in weapons and equipment, but particularly they needed to be integrated into the unit. Heinz von Westernhagen, the commander of the assault gun battalion, wrote in the middle of April 1943: 'I suppose we will stay here for some time, as the gaps are too large and we must not only fill them, but also weld the units together again before we take on a mission.'[18]

In addition to military training, the officers pushed intensive *weltanschauungsunterricht* (ideological training) on new recruits who were sworn into the SS.[19] Such training took on increasing importance after 1943, when non-volunteer replacements were assigned to SS units. This dilution threatened the 'elite' political conviction of the SS units, and ideological conformity to SS standards was now given a large emphasis.[20]

On 24 February 1943 Himmler had issued an SS directive in response to the crisis on the Eastern Front: the war with the Russians had demonstrated that victory would come only to troops who 'were not only militarily competent, but also convinced and fervent believers of our Weltanschauung [world view] … The longer the war lasts, the more we must educate all of our leaders, non-commissioned leaders, and men to be yet more fanatic and convincing proponents of the Nazi ideology, according to the ideas of our Führer Adolf Hitler.'[21] In the middle of May 1943 the SS Main Office released practical instructions to implement Himmler's ideological education of the troops: 'In recognition of the immense value of ideological-political training during the war, and the future challenge of endowing our troops with unbendable will to bear weapons for the preservation of the people, all means—including in special actions—should be used to educate the troops.'

As a result of Himmler's order, Waffen SS commanders were held responsible for the ideological education of their troops. 'As the first line of instruction', their leadership style would stand as an example.

The scheduled classes were given the same importance as weapons and field training, as in lessons, because 'ideological theory is the backbone of the attitude of the men.' It was also emphasized that at every opportunity, even at the front line and in combat, breaks must be used for the men as lessons 'for brief ideological instruction at the enemy gates'.

In particular, the platoon leaders and officers had key duties in this task. 'Ideological and political teaching can take place in the outposts even right up to the attack 'to encourage the degree of fanaticism in the men necessary to annihilate the enemy ... Instruction will take place right up to the trenches'. The goal was to develop politicized soldiers who were solid in their world view and fanatic warriors for Hitler's ideas.[22] Sport and celebration were eyed as key elements to cement loyalty, and the sport and swimming festivals organized in Peiper's battalion served this purpose directly. The experienced SS leaders determined the standards and methods by which the replacement army and Luftwaffe troops were assimilated. At times, though, in spite of all efforts, the outcome was dismal. For example, on 9 June 1943, thirty-six men labelled 'totally unfit for service' were culled and marched back to Berlin for return to the Luftwaffe.[23]

Meanwhile, Peiper accumulated medals for his accumulating experience. On 6 May, he received the German Cross in Gold, which Sepp Dietrich had requested in March, and so Hitler's latest SS hero was given leave to go home in June 1943. Although living conditions in Berlin remained civil—Sigurd could still see the latest fashions on display at the Kurfürstendamm and the philharmonic continued its concert schedule unabated—the edges were fraying.[24] The deportations of the city's remaining Jews was in full swing during that spring, and the many neatly uniformed soldiers seen on the streets increasingly included those maimed, on crutches or otherwise bandaged. In spite of the city's well-known *Ordungsliebe*—passion for order without drama—a certain tension not previously seen arose on its streets. Berlin was worried.

Air raid drills were commonplace, and it seemed certain that the Allied bombing campaign could hardly continue to neglect Hitler's power centre. That Peiper and his family still had preferred status was clear by ledger notes at Rudi Brandt's Berlin office on Prinz Albrechtstrasse. Brandt was Himmler's office manager. By this time in Berlin many foodstuffs other than bread and potatoes—particularly real coffee beans, butter, sugar and eggs—were in impossibly short supply. However, based on an inside decree by Himmler that May, Frau Peiper and thirty other privileged families were to receive special allocations of prized victuals.[25] Thus, Peiper would eat well during his short leave before returning to Russia. When would it be time to get his family out of Berlin? Sigurd and her two children were still safe, but for how long?

By the time Peiper returned later in the month, the hot Ukrainian summer was in full blossom. The ground that had been mud before was now a parched dusty grassland, better for tank and SPW going if the command could be rehabilitated. The Leibstandarte, at over 22,200 men, was now at full strength.[26] Training went on, although fuel was hoarded for a coming operation, and driving time with the new vehicles was limited. This perhaps bothered Peiper most of all. For his fast-moving operations, seasoned drivers were more important than gun loaders.

While Peiper worried about training, Hitler and his generals pondered the next move in the Russian chess game. The obvious target was the enemy salient bulging westward into the German lines between Belgorod and Orel. Projecting like a boil on the Eastern Front, the 160km-wide zone almost begged to be lanced off. Code-named 'Zitadelle' by Hitler, the plan had much to argue for it. Since the fall of Kharkov the Soviets had poured tanks, troops and artillery into the region, looking to use it as a springboard for a summer offensive of their own. Who would go first?

Von Manstein opined that the Kursk salient was ripe for the taking in late April. Under his plan the Wehrmacht would simultaneously slash its way from the north and the south, closing its armoured pincers near Kursk. Chopping off the salient would bag a huge concentration of Soviet forces and leave open the way for the holy grail of an advance on Moscow some 380km to the north. The opportunity required quick action before Stalin realized the danger.

And so the magnetic attraction of Zitadelle proved its undoing. The allure of the Kursk salient was equally clear to the Soviet planners. Beyond concentrating armies, they intended to build up a colossal series of criss-crossing trenches, minefields, *Pakfront* positions and tank traps.[27] Such a devil's labyrinth, they reckoned, would waste the German Panzers that would be thrown at them.

Indeed, the Soviets had accurately divined German intentions. Located on the southern side of the salient and essayed to spearhead the attack, the Leibstandarte was to converge on the Russian town of Kursk with the German Panzer forces descending from the north. If it worked, at least two Russian armies would be destroyed. In the meantime, intelligence clearly showed a massive build-up of armour and troops on both sides of the fence. Operation Zitadelle evolved into the largest fully anticipated battle in history.

Experienced with battles of attrition in the First World War, Hitler was familiar with this type of warfare, which promised enormous losses in exchange for little captured real estate. 'Every time I think of this attack,' he confided to General Guderian on 10 May, 'my stomach turns over.' What else was there to do? Guderian suggested that Hitler's physical reaction was correct: forget Zitadelle and prepare a more effective defence. However, solely to defend was to abandon the initiative to the hated Russians. 'We are in the position,' commented General Friedrich von Mellenthin, 'of a man who has seized a wolf by the ears and dare not let him go.'

For Hitler, procrastination became a weekly event, blaming the delays on poor weather, the need to get more reinforcements, to procure the promised Tiger tanks and, ultimately, to find some way to win what amounted to a zero-sum game.[28] 'We have to succeed this time!' he blustered to his generals on 1 July, 'and for this reason we have to wait for the latest heavy and super-heavy tanks.' Yet Hitler seemed strangely unsure of himself, looking to Hoth and von Manstein for reassurance. There was none. Von Manstein had insisted the attack be mounted no later than the beginning of May. That was now eight weeks past.

The need for success in Zitadelle was more than obvious to Jochen Peiper. During his furlough to Germany that June he made one of his numerous visits to his former boss, Heinrich Himmler. There was plenty of bad news from just about everywhere. 'The framework is creaking,' Peiper confided to one of those under his command.[29] There was more than just bad news about the war. Although details are unknown, Peiper seems to have learned directly about the *Vernichtungslager*—the extermination camps—now murdering millions of Jews in Poland.[30] When he returned to Kharkov that June, he again met with Otto Dinse, his faithful battalion adjutant who had fought with him through thick and thin in Russia. Dinse sensed that something was bothering his commander. What was it?

Peiper told Dinse of the murder factories—horrible places, he said, where thousands were being gassed and burned with assembly-line efficiency. This was not altogether surprising to Dinse. He had plenty of experience with the racial war in Łódź (Litzmanstadt). The former adjutant of the Bremen police chief worked with the UWZ (Central Resettlement Office) in the SS Sonderkommando to transport thousands of Jews from Łódź to Lublin, ostensibly to make room for the ethnic Germans to relocate there. In fact, the mission eventually became the responsibility of Adolf Eichmann as part of the overall effort to move the Jews, first to Lublin and then later to extermination camps.[31] That process was deadly efficient: on 28 April 1943 the SS police leader in Lublin, Sturmbannführer Hermann Hofle, reported that the 'recorded arrivals' at

Lublin, Belzec, Sobibor and Treblinka who were a part of Einsatz Reinhard totalled 1.27 million persons.[32]

But now, in Russia, Dinse heard directly from Peiper on the progression of the policy he had witnessed at Łódź: the extermination camps.

'We had better win this war,' Peiper confided, 'or we'll be in deep trouble.'[33]

Chapter 8

Zitadelle

'The whole art of war consists in getting at what is on the other side of the hill.'

—The Duke of Wellington

At Hitler's *Wolfsschanze* headquarters the German leader saw the tense standoff in Russia much the same way as Jochen Peiper. During one visit armaments minister Albert Speer lunched in silence with Hitler—'an hour of almost complete torture'—punctuated only by Hitler's praise for his new vegetarian cook and the usual outburst against the general staff. But then afterwards Speer attended a military conference with Hitler along with generals and adjutants: Wilhelm Keitel, Alfred Jodl, Walter Warlimont and Nicolaus von Below. In spite of the food, the mood was oppressive.

Someone opened the windows of the briefing room to let in fresh air. At one point Hitler quietly stepped over to the open window and peered out while the others stood behind him. The room was silent, and Hitler seemed deep in thought. 'Gentlemen,' he announced quietly but emphatically, 'the bridges behind us are burned.' What did that mean? Speer felt a cold shiver cross the length of his spine. The Final Solution?

'I remember very clearly that I had a dreadful foreboding, a sudden sense of something awesome.' But before he could dwell on his baleful premonition, the discussion moved on. Once again they treaded the recondite options for a military solution to the mess in the East.[1]

Winning that war would not be possible without preparation to win Zitadelle. Although Peiper's men continued their training with their SPWs and new infantry guns, time was clearly aiding the enemy in a disproportionate fashion. By the end of June all Soviet preparations were complete, with three initial defensive belts which had hundreds of tanks and Katyusha rocket launchers bunched up in the zone. For the Germans the whole thing was looking like a death ride. As if to

Zitadelle and the Battle for Prochorowka
4–12 July 1943

contradict the prospects, Hitler carefully instructed the Waffen SS leaders that the usual willingness to sacrifice should be moderated with Zitadelle: losses should be minimized.

On 28 June the *Aufmarsch*—the concentration march—began for Operation Zitadelle. Two days later superiors briefed all the regimental and battalion commanders on the tremendous attack about to take place. Theodor Wisch would be in charge of the division for the first time. Peiper's III Battalion would fight alongside the Panzer regiment. Even with a heavy cloudburst that turned the road to Koruscha into a mud slick, all units slipped and skidded into place. On 2 July Peiper briefed all the subordinates. He didn't tell them what he had told Dinse, but winning, they all understood, was plenty important.

Back at *Wolfsschanze* on 1 July a tense scene unfolded over afternoon tea. Hitler's generals tried to talk him out of Zitadelle. For once their reasons were not lack of preparation but rather too much of it. The right time to launch the attack had passed weeks before, they insisted. All the new Panther and Tiger tanks, the elaborate sand-table exercises, and special training would be for nothing. Aerial reconnaissance showed that the Russians were more than ready, and, courtesy of Hitler's vacillation, hundreds of T-34 tanks and thousands of guns had moved into the salient. Hitler countered that the added enemy strength simply buoyed the prize. Now there were six armies—fourty per cent of the Russian infantry and seventy-five per cent of its armour—packed in the battle zone. If they were encircled and destroyed, that would be decisive. It could be a repeat of the vast destruction wrought on the Russians before at Kiev and Vyazma earlier in the war. But Hitler slipped around the obvious question: Could that still be done in the summer of 1943?

On the Russian side the uncertainty was great. That the Soviet high command embraced the importance of the contest was never in doubt. The decisive character of the coming battle had all the trappings of a modern-day battle of Kulikovo—the historic clash in 1380 in which Prince Dmitri Donskoi ousted the oppressive Tartars. Mindful of such, Stalin was beside himself with worry that Hitler's great attack might begin in May before he was ready. A Soviet spy ring in Switzerland had forecast the great German attack would begin that month, but recurring postponement made that whole mass of intelligence suspect. The Russians were receiving information from the super-secret Allied ULTRA decrypts of German radio transmissions being decoded in England. That made clear the postponements of the assault for insertion of the new super-heavy Tiger tanks and even gave the German code name for the offensive. There were some false leads as well. Message decrypts from the

Japanese ambassador in Berlin, Hiroshi Oshima, seemed to indicate that Zitadelle was now forsaken.[2]

For the Soviets, being wrong would be costly. The prime strategy for Marshal Georgy Zhukov was resoundingly simple. As he saw it, the most effective method of dealing with the ominous build-up of the German military might in the East was to lie back and wait for the enemy to impale themselves on carefully prepared defences. Knowing where the Germans would attack made the perfect opportunity. Consequently, the Russian army had spent the entire spring and early summer laboriously fabricating lethal belts of fortifications—a hellish gauntlet of mines, tank traps, anti-tank gun blinds and dug-in tanks. Russian soldiers planted three thousand anti-tank and antipersonnel mines per kilometre of defensive front between the belts; the whole thing was a perdition of gun emplacements, fortifications and trenches gouged out of the earth and erected at enormous cost. As Zhukov saw it, after their enemy wasted themselves on the deadly prairie fortress before Kursk, the Soviet army would rise and launch a massive counteroffensive. With the enemy weakened and then hammered back, this plan, he told Stalin, would vanquish the invaders once and for all from Mother Russia. What if the Japanese ambassador was right and the Germans didn't attack? Then what?

Oshima was at least partly right. Uncharacteristically, Hitler was unsure of himself. Guderian suggested that Hitler heed his intuition and drop the whole thing. Yet following a recommendation from the general staff was an anathema to Hitler. Embracing the plan, he vowed total confidence in Generalfeldmarschal Walter Model, who would lead the Ninth Army in the northern front. Hermann Hoth, who looked on disapprovingly, would lead the stronger southern blow with an armada of seven hundred tanks, including the three SS divisions with Peiper and the Leibstandarte. Counting both the north and south wings of the German attack, there were as many tanks committed to Zitadelle as participated in the entire invasion of Russia. Zitadelle would be the largest set-piece battle ever fought. As such, it would be a battle totally unlike the free-wheeling cavalry raids of Peiper's heyday with his Blowtorch Battalion in February and March. There would be no sudden night attack to punch 20km into enemy territory with a destructive joy ride. Opposite of Kursk, there were minefields, anti-tank ditches and *Pakfronts* 20km deep.

On the night of 2 July the Leibstandarte came to the assembly area as a reserve. Designated a spearhead reserve, they were to await the word to attack. Twenty-four hours later everyone was on full alert. Günther

126

Borchers was with the engineer battalion that would assist the forward infantry:

> We were rolling once more; at 7:30 PM our 'Mystery Tour' began, and we travelled through the night, destination unknown. Once we got to the first staging position, talk about the mission was allowed. The engineers were to be attached to the individual Infantry Company in the front. We were now to fight with flame-throwers and that was a sure ticket to heaven for us. We also had to get to get within 25 metres of the Russians for the flame-throwers to work. We might as well have made out our will.[3]

SS Sturmbannführer Peiper was ordered with his III Battalion to the Panzer group of the division. The main objective: to break through and reach a bridgehead over the Psel River. For the job, the Leibstandarte possessed some 145 tanks and assault guns.[4]

One of these tanks was Panzer No. 705. From that mount, the day before, all Obersturmführer Ralf Tiemann could see was a great expanse of grassy slopes stretching into the distance from the edge of the Mk IV gun's blunt muzzle brake. The steppes of the Ukraine were like a yellow sea—an ocean shimmering in the heat of the July 1943 sun. Nearby were flowers blending into a seemingly endless swathe of golden fields ending at the horizon that hid the enemy, who could not be far behind it. His tanks concentrated on the grassy fields in secrecy. At least so he thought.

Then, on the night of 4 July, the Russians captured a German prisoner on the southern front just before them. The captive swore that the German offensive would begin at dawn the next day. Nikolai F. Vatutin, the pudgy general commanding the opposing Voronezh sector, believed the report. Without hesitation he ordered his artillery to immediately begin a pre-emptive artillery barrage to disrupt the Germans. General Zhukov obtained similar intelligence on the northern front, and he then ordered his artillery and aircraft to blast the Germans apart without delay. Before dawn he heard a 'terrible rumbling' of rockets, shells and guns that grew into a clamour so loud and diabolical that Zhukov recalled it as a 'symphony from hell'.[5]

Great masses of the Katyusha rockets—'Stalin's Organs'—screamed into the German assembly points, suddenly exploding in smoke and flame. Despite losses and initial confusion, the calculated nature of the fire suggested disturbing developments. The Russians seemed to be waiting. Zitadelle was evolving into a suicide run in which the

Leibstandarte would charge right into the lion's mouth. Still, orders were orders. Particularly when a *dienstlicher Befehl*—direct order—came right from the Führer.

The attack sprung in the dark summer night. At 0130 hours Max Hansen and Albert Frey sent their grenadiers rushing forward in a stealthy night advance. This surprised no one; the advance ran head on into the Russian strength. Fierce hand-to-hand combat took place along a series of low hills at the front before the village of Bykowka. For all the hot and dry weather in the Ukraine over the previous weeks, there was thunder and lightning in the night. The flashes in the distance grew near with thunder into a coruscating brilliance that illuminated the vast grassland before them. Later it began to rain—to add to the misery and dread. The men sat around smoking in their foxholes and their tents, nervously worrying about what the next day would bring. It rained all night while terrible infantry battles eddied through the network of Soviet trenches before Bykowka.

Morning brought great clouds of fire and smoke on the horizon as German guns blasted Bykowka into submission. The smoke drifted into a blue sky studded with puffy cumulus clouds. There was a tremendous racket. Meanwhile, Peiper's battalion with the Panzer regiment was held in reserve—they would not be committed until the known line of Russian anti-tank guns had been neutralized. Then, at daybreak, a swarm of Stuka dive bombers fell on the enemy line, furiously blasting the ground for twenty minutes. As soon as the last bomb fell, the SS infantry surged forward into a hell of barbed wire, bunkers, mines and trenches. When the first gully-like anti-tank ditch was seized and blasted, no one suspected that the enemy had arrayed the Ukrainian countryside ahead into one gigantic hornets' nest of fortifications.

At 0300 furious fire from all the heavy weapons started. The artillery regiment, the Nebelwerfer Brigade, the mortars and Stuka bombers trampled for an hour on the Russian fortifications. For the Russians it must have been hell. We had never experienced such heavy fire. The heavens were black with the smoke of detonated grenades and the smoke from the Nebelwerfer. The sun didn't have the power to penetrate the fog even once. The first Russian position was in our hands now. One truck ran over a mine and flew into the air, and a Russian Pak fired at it, too. Our expectations were not too high and sure enough, now we had to rip every metre of ground from the Russians in hard fighting. They fought tenaciously from their bunkers and didn't give themselves up to be prisoners. We took fire from our flanks and rear. A lot of German planes were in the area and joined in with the ground fighting. The Russians also had strong air support concentrated in the area. Their soldiers were elite troops from Stalingrad, with some Mongolians and Siberians too. Our Stukas and attack aircraft—there were hundreds—zeroed in on the Russian positions, without regard to danger from the Russian flak and fighters. Fire roared over our heads— both ours and theirs. Many planes crashed, and only a few were high enough that the crew could bail out and be rescued. We took the first Russian tank obstacle and blew it up, and then our Panzers could join in the fight. There were no patches of empty ground. Everywhere was a bunker, a dug-in Panzer, or a minefield, for example. We cleared the roads through the minefields so the tanks and battle vehicles could follow. The sun parched us and our canteens were emptied quickly, and the springs were dry.[6]

Peiper paced nervously, waiting for his armour to be committed. At last the order came, sending Peiper's halftracks rumbling forward with the Panzers. It was 1430 hours on Monday, 5 July. There were so many tanks in the massive phalanx that it resembled a parade formation.

The idea was to quickly advance to take a bridgehead across the Psel River. Kursk, the key to the encirclement of six Russian armies, lay just 60km beyond. Yet as darkness fell on Monday night the tank group ran into a massive *Pakfront* of Russian anti-tank guns near Jakowlewo. That ended the day; there would be no Peiper-style attempt to breach the line in the darkness.

In the meantime the rest of the 2nd Regiment collapsed the enemy resistance before Bykowka, and the Panzer group received orders to blast its way through the second enemy line east of Jakowlewo and establish the promised bridgehead. After penetrating the first line of trenches and machine gun nests, the German infantry found itself assailed by waves of Russian troops and T-34 tanks. Their opponents were the Russian elite 6th Guards Tank Army. The new heavy Tigers moved up to provide protection, although a curtain of Soviet artillery damaged two of the heavy tanks badly enough to make them immobile. The first day of fierce fighting ended in a tangle of barbed wire and minefields. Peiper had barely been in action, but the Leibstandarte infantry paid dearly for the short advance of the tank group. Ninety-seven were dead, and some 522 officers and men were wounded.[7] In Peiper's war there had never been a day as bloody as that.

Not that things looked much better from the Russian side. At the headquarters of General Vatutin, Nikita Khrushchev, Stalin's energetic political overseer, nervously conferred with the military leader of the Voronezh front. Things were shaky and trending worse. He realized, he told Vatutin, this was where the Kursk battle would be decided. They had to maintain their nerve: 'The next two or three days will be terrible. Either we hold or the Germans take Kursk. They are putting everything on one card. It's a matter of life and death for them. We must ensure that they break their necks.'[8]

German predawn patrols on 6 July showed that the squat hills south of Jakowlewo were crawling with Russian troops and tanks. So dense was the concentration that any shot fired was likely to find a target. Fierce fighting erupted again, with the Leibstandarte grenadiers clearing the enemy trench line near Jakowlewo. Intent on setting things moving, the new divisional commander, Theodor Wisch, personally led the Panzer group, including Peiper and his SPWs. They were to break through to Teterewino and the Psel River beyond.

As they advanced, two columns of forty T-34s emerged out of the yellow dust on their left flank, spiralling gunshot into the German column. There was the crack of enemy fire and resounding explosions as the rounds struck close by. The ground shook as the German tank guns responded. The Panzer group quickly defeated the enemy thrust, leaving seven armoured hulks smoking on the grassland. As the others turned to retreat to Olchowka, they were hunted down by Stukas mounting anti-tank guns that hung in the air like Teutonic wasps. Dark clouds of smoke rose from the parched plain and drifted into the summer sky. According to Günther Borchers, who was fighting under Peiper:

> The Russians came now with huge mass-produced tanks—sometimes around 200 of them. Our tanks knocked many of them out, but the Russians just kept coming back with new tanks. Where did they get them all? We reached the highway between Kursk and Belgorod. The fighting just never let up. They kept throwing new soldiers, tanks, and weapons at us. Fallen Russians lay all over the place. They had really fought bravely to their death.[9]

By 1630 hours the Blowtorch Battalion seemed to be coming into its own. Peiper signalled his men to gather up after the breakthrough at Lutschki. They were going to make a dash towards Teterewino. If they made it, the inertia might just take them to the Psel River. Like at Belgorod, Peiper ordered his SPWs to attack at full speed in a wide formation. To Erhard Gührs, they rushed into deep trouble:

> Suddenly, everything goes wrong. There are mines all over the roads. There are anti-tank guns and tanks behind a tank trench on the ridge

in front of us. Four of our Panzers hit mines. The Luftwaffe air support officer travelling with us in his Schützenpanzerwagen flew up into the air after his vehicle explodes! We will not reach the ridge. But Teterewino is soon in our hands. But can we stay there?[10]

Several Mk IV Panzers of the 7th Company lay broken and crippled on mines before the village, but racing ahead at dusk Peiper and Gührs made it into Teterewino. In the night was the unmistakable sound of tank motors—and not German ones. They set up defence in the village and hunkered down for the night. They did not have to wait long. By 0130 hours Obersturmführer Georg Preuss reported that six Russian T-34s were slamming shells into his position, and the 13th Company counted even more. Close-in fighting raged all night. Morning saw five of the Russian tanks crippled and smoking before the village; prisoners told Peiper that the T-34s had rushed out of Moscow four days before. Later in the night three Russian tanks covered with Russian infantry bolted out of the darkness and into the streets of Teterewino. By then some Tigers had reached Peiper and shot down all three Russian tanks at point-blank range.

The next morning started out quietly enough, if hot, but calamity soon returned. Serious bombing runs on Peiper's battalion destroyed several vehicles and left many dead and wounded. Off to the left of the battalion a large Soviet tank assault struck the line, to be turned back when SS Sturmbannführer Christian Tychsen shot down thirty tanks. But soon reconnaissance revealed that thirty-five enemy T-34s were massed on the ridge just across from Peiper. Erhard Gührs saw Martin Gross and Peiper confer on what to do about this dangerous development. The plan: attack before they can. 'Gross advanced with his tanks,' Gührs wrote in his diary, 'and shoots down 16 tanks without losses.' In any case, the Leibstandarte losses for the day were serious: 84 killed, 384 wounded and 19 missing.[11] Before dawn a pack of Russian T-34s counterattacked the route over which the German tanks had advanced. The assaults were only turned back after heavy fighting and close Stuka bomber support—things were getting plenty hot all over the congested battlefield. Wisch decided it was now or never to reach the Psel River and Kursk beyond.

Preceded by strong Luftwaffe close support, at 0600 hours on 8 July the tank group attacked in the direction of the Panzer *Rollbahn* (assigned rolling road) towards the small rail town of Prochorowka. Supported by the Panzers, Peiper's SPWs sped across the rolling grassy hills in a spread out formation, sending plumes of dust skyward. His men seemed eager to challenge anything that would come forth. They didn't have to wait long. Erhard Guehrs wrote,

It is already noon when it starts. In my vehicle there is already SS reporter King. We are driving with the 2nd wave behind the tanks. First village is taken and now it is [a] big mix-up. In front of us there is no further going ahead. To the left are the Russians. Right is the former attack direction. There are Russians there too. Behind us the Russians are breaking into the village with 35 tanks. Poor infantry. Our Peiper battalion lies behind our tanks, which cannot go forward. It is a big mess. We are leaving the vehicles and we are singing 'Comrades we have seen the world'. This strange and easy mood is started again by Commander Peiper. It is so fatalistic as to be comical. Behind us the situation is cleared by itself. Two Tigers which were stuck in Teterewino with track-drive problems are now shooting down all enemy tanks which break through. Terrific fighting by broken down tanks. This is easily written, but it was an unbelievable thing. Peiper is taking over the command of the battle group because Commander Schönberger is called to the division staff headquarters. Peiper orders at once the attack with our mixed battalion of tanks and SPWs on Rickson. I have a pretty bad feeling about it. I am shaving my face before battle. Why? I don't know.[12]

Less than an hour passed before more than thirty Russian tanks charging at them out of the north assailed the Panzer group. T-34s were charging everywhere, the dust was choking and visibility went to zero. Peiper and the SS tankers swept into the tumult of jousting steel chariots at high noon. It was a tank battle fought a point-blank range in zero visibility, defying any plan.

There was no holding back Peiper. On they pushed into the yellow expanse. The further they punched along on the Teterewino to Prochorowka road, the faster they rode. The tension was palpable. Erhard Gührs was with the assault:

We are now showing the tanks how we want to do it. Moving out from behind the ridge, we are accelerating at full speed with the tanks driving as fast as they can. Peiper drives us forward on the microphone. It is like a wild hunt. I tell my men to go as fast as they can … With this speed, we could go right over the Russian anti-tank position. The Panzer büschen are driving behind me. On our left is the 13th company 800 metres further on to the village. Explosions left and right, forward and behind. I have headphones on and give orders through the microphone. I can hardly hear the explosions. On the left, our men are putting down smoke. Only 500m to the village, it should be possible to get there. Then I see three Russian tanks coming out [of] the fog shooting wildly. One SPW is hit and I order a pullback 300 metres to a small gap. An Obstuf. from the artillery SPWs got hit point-blank. All inside are dead. I tried again to drive forward to pass the village on the right flank. The 11th Kompanie with Haupsturmführer Guhl are trying on the left side. The tanks are still far behind us. They cannot keep up with our pace. My 'Grilles' are driving to the front. We are rushing to the front and it is working. Then all of a sudden I see 15 tanks. Distance 1500 m. Our Grillen and KVKs are shooting.[13]

They wheeled to the north-west to sweep up the enemy from the heavily defended Okrabriska State Farm before descending suddenly from the north upon the strategic Hill 252.2. In an effort to silence Soviet guns and vehicles, General Hoth allocated his 4th Panzer Army artillery to start pounding the hill and rear areas while Stuka dive bombers descended in a swarm upon the Russians. In a quick rush they were on the hill just 3km south-west of Prokhorovka. But in that short Russian moment the tables turned. The enemy suddenly materialised out of the dust and shimmering heat. The lead armoured vehicle was hit and spewed smoke. Within minutes it was clear that they were encircled—with more and more enemy flocking towards them to cut them down. Would this be his Little Big Horn? Peiper, the press-celebrated magnificent SS warrior, was now encircled, with his men like Wild West cowboys fending off swarming natives. Erhard Gührs, for his part, was unfazed. 'The Russians cut us off,' he wrote in his diary. 'This doesn't bother us anymore. We feel completely superior to the Russians.'[14]

When this happened to George Armstrong Custer in another faraway hilltop grassland in another time, he had sent an immortal message to his subordinate, quickly scrawled on a tattered note and sent via galloping messenger: 'Benteen, Come Quick!' Of course, Custer and his cavalry had also felt completely superior to their Indian enemy. There were just … well … too many of them.

The modern messenger for Jochen Peiper was the short-wave transmitter. When he told his old superior, Teddi Wisch—who was now in charge of the whole division—about his predicament, he laconically reeled off his position north of Teterewino halfway to the golden prize of Prochorowka. What Peiper rattled off to the Leibstandarte headquarters is not recorded, but it may as well have been 'Teddi, come quick!' But then, with Peiper's sardonic cynicism, it was more likely a challenge: 'I am here out front … where are those assigned to follow me?'

Help came in the form of tanks from Haupsturmführer Ralf Tiemann's 7th Panzer Company, which had suffered so greatly from mines the previous day. Word of just how much trouble Peiper had managed to get into arrived from a breathless infantry messenger. Peiper was wounded, he said, and was surrounded by the enemy. Tiemann looked to the scene before him with total disbelief. The steppes ahead disappeared in a fog of gun smoke, and dust kicked up by wheeling vehicles all packed into the swirling arena before Kursk, attempting to shoot each other down. There was a wall of fire and smoke ahead, with booming, cracking explosions in the summer heat. The whole sky seemed on fire. Somewhere on the other side of that hell was Jochen Peiper. Before Tiemann lay an exploding canvas. Surely Peiper and the others of his command must be dead.

Tiemann contacted one of the few operational tanks still close by, that of Rolf Ehrhardt. Like Tiemann, Ehrhardt, the tank driver, could not believe the cascade of gunfire and destruction that raged just ahead: 'Behind us there were the smoking wrecks of the first wave of Soviet tanks. Before us was a wall which could not be pierced. There stood dozens of T-34s from the main wave which we had taken care of in a heavy and dogged battle. It was a wall of steel and fire.'[15]

In the middle of the surrealist scene Ehrhardt viewed a procession of ghostly images of Panzer grenadiers, overrun and chased by Soviet tanks loaded with clinging Russian soldiers. He heard Tiemann was on the radio: Peiper, the head of the III Battalion was wounded and surrounded. Tiemann told Ehrhardt that his tank was closest to the missing III Battalion that was just ahead … on the other side of the wall of steel and fire. Suddenly, a T-34 emerged from the blinding smoke; there was a sharp whistle on an anti-tank round and the phantom shuddered and stopped. They were going into that? Tiemann knew what he was asking: 'Drive like a son of a bitch!' he told him. 'It is your only chance.' Ehrhardt never heard the taciturn Tiemann use that kind of *Landser* language—things must be really screwed up. The platoon leader came by to confirm the order and make certain the operation went ahead, as any level-headed person would have refused. 'Start engines! Get ready for action … Driver, march!' Their Panzer lurched forward:

After a few moments, I was surrounded by smoke. I had to drive slower so as not to drive off in the wrong direction. The sights before my view slot were like scenes from a silent film: wrecks, flames, twisted and unreal figures wearing Soviet helmets. Crater upon crater. Suddenly there was a heavy hit somewhere.[16]

The world that afternoon was suffused with orange dust and black smoke—a pyre of burning tanks and death. In the hellish inferno Ehrhardt had no idea how he would find Peiper's command post. The messenger they had brought along had no idea where they were. Nor did Ehrhardt. Inside there was the din of the running gears and tracks and one muffled explosion after another. Above that there was a rattling sound like rocks hitting a steel drum—small arms fire ricocheting off their Panzer. Inside the steel Panzer was like a *backofen*—the air became stifling, dust laden and hot. Sweat coursed over his uniform as Ehrhardt drove along. They were driving right though the enemy line.

Ehrhardt's platoon leader was on the radio, warning the others to stay back. Being furthest along, he signalled that he had no idea where he was going, but he would go it alone. The last they heard from him was his unembellished report of being hit several times. When the radio fell silent, they knew he was dead. Ehrhardt knew they were right in the middle of the enemy. The only helmets they could see were Russian ones bobbing in the gloom. In the smoke and dust there was not a single *schützenpanzerwagen*, just Russian soldiers, running pell-mell across his narrow vision. As if an apparition of doom, a T-34 loomed out of the dust, scarcely 100m away. Like Wild West gunslingers, it was who could get off the first shot.

Bang! The loud metallic resonance left Ehrhardt's ears ringing. Someone screamed. His Panzer was hit; there was a foul smell of scorched metal. The gunner was dead and the radio knocked out; the commander of their tank slumped over too, mortally wounded. Ehrhardt watched in horror as a gang of Russian soldiers attempted to rush up to seize his stricken tank. He gunned the accelerator—it still ran. Completely disoriented, he wheeled his tank about 90 degrees, the tracks chattering noisily. He held the throttle down, full speed. The enemy soldiers disappeared into the smoke and dust like a nightmarish apparition. This seemed the right direction, but Ehrhardt was still blinded; his bullet-proof vision slit was shattered. He had no choice but to stick his head outside.

Peering into the haze, he gunned the engine and churned forward. Suddenly, he emerged out of the smoke and came upon a friendly Panzer. They all headed back together. Ehrhardt ran the gauntlet once more, threading through a tank trench and bolting for friendly lines. How they made it, Ehrhardt would never be sure. On reaching friendly lines he staggered out of his Mk IV Panzer, as did the other surviving members— the radio operator and the wounded gun loader. Someone later counted three tank rounds that had punched through his Panzer's steel armour.

And what of Peiper? It seems another Panzer had reached the intrepid commander, who wasn't wounded after all. Unlike Custer, Peiper had made it out of his Little Big Horn to fight another day. Rolf Ehrhardt was simply happy to be alive.

Later that evening German Luftwaffe intelligence got word of strong Russian tank forces massing on the western flank of the Leibstandarte. This was General Vatutin's 2nd Guards Tank Corps, which had been hurried to counter the dangerous penetrations made by Hausser's SS armour. Vatutin's intent was obvious: cut off the SS tank group. Hoth's response was to turn the Leibstandarte to the left and meet the enemy tank columns head on.

The sun rose on 8 July to reveal a scorching hot summer day in the parched Russian land. From their hilltop positions the Leibstandarte officers could see at least forty Russian tanks approaching from the west near Wysselok that morning. Waves of Stuka and Henschel 129 aircraft with spouting anti-tank cannons pummelled the Russian tanks columns. The forewarned German armour trained its guns to pick off the enemy as they approached. The gunnery contest lasted for over an hour, after which the westward advance resumed. All along the line stretching from Teterewino the Russians attacked, most of the pressure falling on Albert Frey's SS Panzer Grenadier Regiment 2, which knocked out more than a dozen tanks. Meanwhile, one of the crippled Tigers turned out to be completely unapproachable for the enemy: a single Mk VI knocked out twenty-two T-34s. At the close of the day the Leibstandarte reported having 'eliminated 88 enemy tanks' against a loss of thirty-two men killed, ninety-nine wounded and six missing.[17] The enemy faltered. And the next day the Leibstandarte, with the Totenkopf Division on its left, was at last able to reach the Psel River, the final obstacle before Kursk.

But four days of uninterrupted fighting had sapped the strength of Peiper's men and the others in the tank group. Twenty-three Panzers were lost, and the exhausted infantry rested for the day as they waited for the bridges across the Psel to be completed. With that they would make the big attack they hoped would seal a German victory.

The Russians, in the meantime, thought the German silence and quietude meant they had won the battle. Was Hitler pulling back?

Chapter 9

'The Tigers are Burning'

'There is less danger from enemy guns the closer to them one gets.'
—Peter the Great

With the reverses in the first week of fighting in the East, could Hitler's great summer offensive be won? The Leibstandarte, Hitler's own fanatic palace guard fighting division, would soon be thrown anew into the cataclysmic fight with the Soviets.

At midnight on 10 July 1943 Peiper and his armoured vehicles concentrated in Teterewino. The SPW weapons carriers bristled with guns and Panzer grenadiers. On Peiper's command they were ready to renew the decisive advance of the Panzer group on Kursk.

They couldn't know it, but during the predawn the SS Totenkopf Division to their distant side had failed to dislodge the enemy from the north side of the Psel River and push their way across. That had been an essential part of the operation. The other two battalions of the SS Panzer Grenadier Regiment 2 attempted to assist by throwing back the Russians astride the Teterewino–Prochorowka road. This they did, although while coming under a punishing Russian artillery bombardment. In the afternoon drenching thunderstorms swept the area, leaving all the soldiers dripping in their camouflage smocks. As the roads returned to their mud-like status, the infantry of Rudi Sandig, aided by fire from Tiger tanks and assault guns, managed to capture the nearby strategic hill position and destroy another fifty-three enemy tanks. Peiper waited the entire day for the big breakthrough that never came. Even so, the enemy continued to take tremendous losses; Hausser thought they were at the breaking point.

Karl Wortmann, a gunner with the flak battalion, jotted a telling entry into his diary:

The day was gradually giving way to evening. The march route in front of us was still heavily occupied by other units. The air was thick with swirling clouds of dust. I could not have watched the columns much longer. I looked instead for the last resting place of our comrades, which was said to be somewhere nearby. A little bit off the march route, I found a simple graveyard ... One wooden cross as simple as the next. The names on the crosses were mostly unknown to the other men who stopped by to read them. But they meant something to me. The men had died only days ago at the beginning of the attack. Their 3.7 cm gun took a direct hit at close range ... A memory came back to me clearly. In my mind, I could see the men now beneath me. Oberscharführer Georg Weidner, now resting under the second mound, had been my gun commander since 1940 ... But the demands of war had put a lot of time between then and now. The war had grown harder and more brutal ... I stood sunk in my thoughts for a long time.[1]

Wortmann stared at the dangling German helmets stuck atop the simple white crosses in the roadside wheat field as a crew of a nearby flak gun looked on. Lost in his own pain, he likely thought nothing of the Russians on the other side, whose suffering the German invaders had made so dear in defending their homeland—Soviet losses at Kursk were astronomically high.

If both sides were keenly aware of the cost, they also understood that the shattering battle was at its deciding point. The next day's effort on 11 July would be the Herculean surge that would either take Peiper and the Leibstandarte to a big victory or deny Hitler's aims.

The Germans planned to surprise the enemy with a night assault, but that was not to be. The day got off to a sluggish start. Delayed by the disintegrating roads brought on by recent afternoon rains, the first and second battalions of SS Panzer Grenadier Regiment 2 marched forward towards Prochorowka at 0500 hours. Within an hour and a half they were caught in a terrific Russian artillery barrage, paced by a pack of T-34s sallying from the woods near Jamki. The enemy counterattacks were so continuous that a flock of Stukas—including those of tank-busting ace Hans-Ulrich Rudel—swooped down to eliminate the enemy. But that did not go unchallenged. Buzzing Russian Sturmovik fighter-bombers spiralled in the blue umbrella above the Panzer regiment headquarters. The sky was peppered with black smudges of nonstop German anti-aircraft fire.

The Germans brought up rockets, artillery and Tiger tanks. By 1000 hours the II Battalion under Rudolf Sandig had penetrated to the enemy hill position and smashed across the belt of anti-tank trenches. The engineer battalion under Obersturmführer Taubert hurried forward and made crossing sites over the trenches and cleared mines. Fifteen minutes later orders arrived for Peiper and his grenadiers to seize Hill 252.2, a nondescript grassy rise just to the left of the main road to Prochorowka. Hardly a hill, the place was the last major patch of elevated terrain before reaching their objective.

Scarcely 3.2km away, the Germans schemed. Their faces black with dust and smoke, a camouflage-capped Peiper briefly reviewed the assault plan with Erhard Gührs and his young adjutant, Werner Wolff. They pointed and swept their hands across a spread-out map. Peiper was unshaven, and all looked drawn and tense. They smoked cigarettes to still their nerves. Peiper told everyone they would wade into the enemy in the usual style: full speed—all guns blazing.

But unlike his preferred approach, this attack would not come at night; instead, this assault would come fully expected and in full daylight.

Just after noon Peiper and his battle group threw themselves forward in an all-out charge. Soon they overtook the tank trench and crashed into the enemy bastion at Hill 252.2. As they surged ahead, Rudolf von Ribbentrop's 6th Panzer Company provided dedicated tank fire. They were almost there—just 4km more. From both sides of the hill tank guns barked in rapid succession. But unlike before, the Russians did not back down. The dusty plain offered little cover when a hoard of Soviet infantry rushed forward with such speed and fury that they were only turned back by German soldiers firing MG 42s off the shoulders of machine gun loaders, kneeling in the grass.

Somehow, by 1300 hours the Panzer group churned forward and drove home an assault that wrested the hilltop from the enemy. 'I would gladly take you and your company into our bunch!' Peiper shouted to von Ribbentrop.[2] The Russians streamed away like a receding tide, leaving behind the carnage of broken bodies and machines. Victory?

But unknown to Peiper, the Russians were bringing in massive reinforcements—two entire tank corps. Their aim was simple but definite: halt the advance of the SS armour. And so, thirty minutes after capturing the grassy hill, a large Russian tank wedge slammed into the lines of the SS Regiment 1 just to the south. This was repulsed with great difficulty, but the danger was hardly averted. Within an hour Peiper and the Panzer group were throwing back more tank attacks. Further advance was impossible, and the way towards Prochorowka seemed studded with Russian anti-tank guns, backed by packs of T-34s. Losses soared. Rings of smoke rose eerily from the horizon, indicating the explosive death of another tank. Flame-tinged mushroom clouds signalled where others blazed. Although the SS division claimed they took out twenty-one Soviet tanks that day and captured 135 prisoners, the overall tank strength of their own division now dipped to just seventy tanks and assault guns; another twenty-one of the division's veterans were dead and 203 wounded.[3]

On 12 July both sides started the day again intent on victory. The SS tankers expected to shake the crumbling enemy resistance, cross the Psel, dash for Kursk and cement the Russian fate. The SS Totenkopf Division was finally across that river and driving to the north, while the 2 SS Das Reich Division was strung out along a 10km front south of Prochorowka. Only the SS Leibstandarte was actually west of the town.

Meanwhile, reinforcing Soviet tanks clattered onto the field from the Eastern Steppes. One of the commanders, General Pavel A. Rotmistrov, already had experience fighting off German Panzer assaults aimed to relieve Stalingrad the previous winter. Stalin had personally phoned Rotmistrov on 6 July—his birthday—and sent him off on a punishing three-day, 370km forced march to Prochorowka. Even though his tank crews were parched and exhausted from the day-and-night march, Rotmistrov hurried out from the village to set up a headquarters. He located his vantage point on a hilltop orchard overlooking the rolling grassland to the west of the town.

Knowing he would face the heavy Tigers, Rotmistrov conceived a bold tactic to engage his armour: he would rush the tanks at full speed to achieve a close-in gun battle where the greater T-34 manoeuvrability would be emphasized over the Tigers' thick armour and long-range guns. He planned to charge at the enemy at first light, depending on arriving Soviet reinforcements to carry the day.[4] The next morning Rotmistrov looked out from his hilltop onto an endless grain field stretching below him. The entire landscape shone golden orange from the filtered light of the rising sun. Off in the distance was a woodland where he knew German tanks were concentrating. From that vicinity intelligence reports the night before reported a growling din of engines. Early that morning came the code word for the Russian advance: 'Steel-steel!'

'Papa' Hausser planned a full-scale attack in the other direction. Unaware of the arrival of the enemy reserves, the SS Panzer general looked to strike early and then plough into the enemy with three newly arrived Panzer divisions. As the entirety of his vaunted II SS Panzer Corps had no more than 273 tanks, Hausser depended on the arrival of the three Panzer divisions of Kempf's III Panzer Corps to redress the balance within the planned assault.[5] His attack would also launch at daybreak. Once more Peiper and the armour of the Leibstandarte would lead the way for the Germans, perched as they were, west of Prochorowka. At 0600 hours Peiper rose and prepared to issue orders. A skirmish line of infantry from SS Panzer Grenadier Regiment 2 had already begun to move forward to screen their path; soon they would charge off. '*Hals-und Beinbruch*!'—'Break your neck and legs!'[6]

But the Russians attacked before Peiper could get started. Across a narrow neck of Russian steppe a colossal pack of steel Soviet war wagons emerged from hiding and then thundered towards them, cloaked in gigantic dust clouds. Peiper and von Ribbentrop's 6th Panzer Company were just waking up on the reverse side of Hill 252.2 when grenadiers at the base of their position began firing off purple flares. That was a warning for enemy tanks.

Seeing the flares, Peiper and his men grabbed their weapons. There was a thundering sound from below, mingled with metallic creaks, as if a thousand metal horses were galloping down from the Prochorowka road. What could be seen? The yellow cloud of gunpowder, dust and diesel fumes were so dense and acrid that their eyes watered. And out of this ugly and malicious looking cloud came the metallic horses. At first they were vague grey outlines within the wall of dust. That changed. Soon fully visible, they could be seen hurtling forward—heading straight for Peiper's group at breakneck speed. Peiper estimated there were 150 tanks as he watched the beasts breast their security line and cross over the top of the first trench line. Soon they would be at their position on the reverse side of the hill.

The Soviets were attacking with 222 tanks: headed right for Peiper came the 29th Tank Corps.[7] Von Ribbentrop's Panzer company had only seven battle-worthy Mk IVs, and the whole division had just sixty-seven tanks. The Russians were firing with everything they had. Entire segments of the German line disappeared in an avalanche of explosions and smoke. SS Hauptsturmführer Siegfried Wandt, in charge of 13th Company, was badly wounded. Werner Wolff, Peiper's adjutant, quickly rallied his shaken men and organized a defensive front to engage the tanks and the following Russian infantry. But the Russian tanks rushed forward so quickly that they ran right through Peiper's positions, suddenly coming upon an anti-tank ditch that they themselves had created prior to the battle.

The foolhardy Russian tanks turned about, frenetically milling before the tank moat—shooting, firing and clattering about near Peiper's position. In a show of fool's courage, Wolff charged one of the T-34s with a halftrack mounting only a puny 37mm gun. Wolff could not know that he had set upon the tank of the general leading the attack. He drew alongside, pumping rounds into the rear of the Russian T-34 until it halted. Ignoring machine gunfire, Wolff then jumped on board the tank and wrestled its emerging commander in hand-to-hand combat. He killed the Soviet general with his own dagger, as recorded by the SS war correspondent:[8]

> It is thundering closer again. It sounds like a madly galloping herd of wild horses or destructively charging crazed buffaloes. The ground shakes under the stomping. Smoke and steam have grown so dense that the eyes tear and the lungs hurt with every breath. Horrid and malicious is the poisonous yellow cloud, this steaming and stinking breath of the modern god of war. Out of it grows the uncertain contours of the approaching tanks going at high speed.[9]

Now the Russian tanks were headed straight for Peiper's SPW. Frantically arming grenades, he shouted for his men to make ready. There was cursing; the Russian tanks were moving so fast that the usual tactic of slapping an anti-tank mine onto them was impossible. One tank slowed as it reached the Russian anti-tank ditch. Peiper sprang from the ground, jumped atop the lumbering T-34 and threw open its turret hatch. He dropped two grenades inside and sprang from the tank to fall prone in the dry grass. There was a muffled explosion and a hollow metallic ring as the T-34 stopped. There was little time to think. Another Russian tank clattered up behind the first. Peiper calmly shouldered a Karabiner 98k with rifle grenade. As he held the trigger, his blinking Knight's Cross shone out from his camouflage jacket. This behemoth charged ahead as it reached the ditch just across from him—just 3m away. Peiper loosed the grenade into the side of the lumbering tank near its weak point between the chassis and turret.

There was a loud thud, then an explosion and fire, yet the tank was moving forward at such speed that it clattered on another 20m before shuttering, belching smoke and stopping. There were cheers. Peiper grinned as he put down his weapons. His teeth were shining from his sunburned and powder-darkened face, and he announced, 'This should do for the close-combat badge, boys!'[10]

There was little time to relish the moment. Out of the yellowish-white smoke appeared shadowy shapes in the tall grass—Russian infantry. Close by, Werner Wolff fired away at the apparitions with a machine gun. However, one Russian infantryman was able to close within 30m—a jammed machine pistol of another SS man had been unable to cut him down. Then suddenly there echoed the roar of an exploding hand grenade. Amid the German lines came shouts and groans. An MG 42 belched again in a long rip, then quiet.

Out of the smoke Peiper appeared with a bottle of cognac. A quick swig lifted spirits in the tank ditch, but Peiper put on a serious face. 'Don't get caught!' He pointed to his Luger on his belt and told them, 'The last round is for yourself!': better to die by one's own hand than let the Russians butcher you. Then Werner Wolff appeared with a belt of machine gun rounds laced around his neck. He had 'put away the dog who threw the hand grenade'. Just outside the foxhole a company commander was howling the Panzer song into the smoke and noise of battle.[11] '*Wir sind Panzergrenadiere auf den Ketten liegt unser Glück*'— 'We are Panzer grenadiers, on our tracks rest our luck.' Erhard Gührs, with the heavy SPW Company, had been sleeping soundly:

> During the night we took a ridge and threw out the Russians. We went into our foxholes. Giving out orders for guards. But by 7 AM, they attacked right in the middle of our position. Nearly everyone was sleeping when suddenly they attacked with airplanes and countless tanks with infantry riding on them. It was hell. They were around us, on top of us and between us. We were fighting man against man. We were jumping out of our foxholes with anti-tank weapons out of our SPWs. We are jumping on our SPW and facing the enemy everywhere. We fought man-to-man, jumping out of our foxholes to slap our magnetic hollow charge explosives on the enemy tanks, leaping on our Schützenpanzerwagen to take on an enemy vehicle or man we spotted … not one Russian tank got away. 148 tanks lay destroyed on the battlefield. It was only for two hours, but it was hell.[12]

But of the victors, many men of Peiper's battalion lay wounded or exhausted from the nihilistic battle. Dead and dying, Russian and German—all lay strewn about the hillslope in a gruesome scene. Presently Peiper reappeared. 'Let's go, children,' he said, as if joking. 'A Panzer will bring you to the rear.' The wounded were bundled up and moved away in a halftrack.

Some of the casualties were personal, including Peiper's old SS machine gunner comrade, Ernst Klink. He and Peiper went back a while. Now his leg was shattered, with great loss of blood; Peiper personally saw that the son of Gertrud Scholtz-Klink—the *Reichfrauenführerin*— was speedily loaded onto a Fieseler Storch and sent off to a field hospital.[13]

But upon arriving at the hospital, the war was near. Klink received life-giving plasma, but even the battalion surgeon there would be wounded in the fighting. Outside the battle roared on in an unearthly clamour.

The world had never seen a tank battle like this. An enormous contest of hurtling metal chariots resolved in chaos. The crush of tanks—sometimes only a few metres apart—was unprecedented. Squeezing 850 tanks into an area of only 5 square kilometres created a bizarre situation in which each commander lost control of the battle.[14] Maintaining formation was impossible. Like the clash of mounted knights in medieval times, the tank columns bearing down at full speed ran head on into each other, so dense in numbers that the battlefield became a wild melee of careening machines, driving and firing in all directions. They were like a giant stampede of metallic rhinos, charging each other on a Russian veldt, clanking, swerving and belching cannon shot.

Other desperate battles eddied about Peiper, but eventually the danger to the SPWs subsided as the Russians turned back. Some thirty Russian tanks penetrated the III Battalion positions, but not one made it back. Those that pushed beyond Peiper were hunted down by the Panzers of Tiemann's 7th Company beyond. SS Unterscharführer Hans Siptrott destroyed six T-34s by himself, and Rudolf von Ribbentrop, in charge of 6th Panzer Company, took out fourteen.

Tanks faced each other at ranges more appropriate to high-noon gun battles—firing so close that armour and calibres mattered less than being first on the draw. In this the vaunted Tigers were finally at a disadvantage. From the fields hideous sounds rang out of metal shot slamming into steel, the ammunition often piercing before detonating, then sending turrets splintering off into the air. In every direction were twisted coffins of burning metal. It was impossible to tell who had the upper hand. Armageddon in the East was fought like a demolition derby in which the last moving tank won. And amid the dust and smoke it was impossible to tell who that would be.

The sound of a tank apocalypse was like a wall of noise—a sonic background of gunfire—a crackling din at all distances. The entire earth trembled with the hellish crescendo of bursting shells, screaming planes, grinding tracks and exploding tanks. The massive thunder continued for eight hours amid a stifling heat. Each five-man Panzer crew attempted to kill off an enemy so numerous that the prospects for any individual tank crew approached suicide. The tankers who survived a crippled Panzer would be virtually doomed—forced to escape across minefields, raked by high-velocity tank rounds, machine gunfire and exploding shells and bombs.

In the air over the carnage, a gigantic dogfight raged in which aircraft hung like alien wasps, attempting to shoot each other down or to prey on the enemy shrouded in dust clouds below. There was one wave of planes after another, with machines periodically hurtling down to explode on the wide expanse of the Donets grain fields. By the afternoon something unprecedented transpired: the Russians gained the upper hand in the air. In response, German flak guns turned skyward.

Meanwhile, the Russian strength on the ground seemed inexorable: the more tanks the Germans shot down, the more other T-34s rose to challenge the surviving Panzer crews. Said one German tanker:

> [W]e found ourselves taking on a seemingly inexhaustible mass of enemy armour—never have I received such an overwhelming impression of Russian strength and numbers as on that day. The clouds of dust made it difficult to get help from the Luftwaffe, and soon many of the T-34s had broken past our screen and were streaming like rats all over the old battlefield.[15]

Each tank fought a lone battle in single combat in which defeat was to become another of the numerous burning hulks flaming across the steppe lands. Hours witnessed an enormous armoured brawl, where golden Donets wheat fields were churned up by spinning tank tracks and bullets and anti-tank fire shredded groves of farm fruit trees. The atmosphere was a confused hell of tanks and guns in which everything exploded at once, infused by the smell of burning cordite, oily diesel fuel and gasoline. The landscape was grotesquely covered with the mangled or burned bodies of men who lost their lives fighting alongside the armoured juggernauts. The sky darkened with a pall of smoke; hundreds of crippled tanks blazed on the steppes like torches. In the afternoon a violent thunderstorm swept again over the prairie before Prochorowka— the peals of thunder indistinguishable from the blasts of gunfire. The sudden rain drenched the agony in a short downpour as if to cool the charred carcasses of men and machine.

At one point a marauding group of Russian tanks penetrated the thin screen of the reconnaissance battalion to reach the Leibstandarte artillery guns, which fired over open sights to stop the Soviet vehicles.

By 0900 hours the enemy was repulsed, with Peiper's men alone having cut down fifteen Russian tanks. The Russian armour seemed to mill in confusion after the clash before the tank ditch—their effective command perhaps hampered by the fact that the T-34s only had a crew of four. Unlike the German tank commanders, their harried Russian counterparts also doubled as the crew gunner. It was an awkward arrangement that, along with their ineffective radio communication, made for a failing coordination.

Despite this local success, just a half-dozen kilometres to the south another massive Russian armoured blow challenged SS Regiment 1 with all its resources to resist the iron tide. Scarcely twenty minutes later another Russian tank assault came barrelling up the Prochorowka road, again aimed at Peiper and the Company. On the gently rolling hill 241.6, Peiper hastily met with Oberführer Wisch and Albert Frey to improvise a riposte. They agreed that the thirty-three remaining tanks at the disposal of the Panzer regiment might best be used to smack the advancing enemy from two sides after drawing them into a trap. That morning the Leibstandarte's 'attack spearhead' counted no fewer than three hundred enemy tanks at ranges where periscopes and binoculars were no longer necessary. The German gunners had a clear field of vision, while the Soviet advance was nearly blinded by battlefield dust. The very first fusillade from the German gunners left nineteen Russian tanks burning. By day's end the Leibstandarte claimed that one hundred of the steel enemy had been destroyed.[16]

In some instances Soviet tanks rammed SPWs. 'I had never experienced war like that,' Ralf Tiemann wrote home, 'in combat against enemy tanks outnumbering us by a factor of ten':

> It was a furious battle ... Our regiment destroyed 62 enemy tanks in this one day. My company, which made first contact with the enemy, destroyed 20 by itself. Until today, they had only destroyed 43 total ... My panzer was shot to pieces, but I got out in time; only the radio operator was wounded. Now my good old Panzer 705 is back in the repair shop. I am writing you this letter shortly before a new battle ... Around us is the vast expanse of the steppe with the hidden Balkas [ravines]. A wind always blows the clouds away so the sun can shine between the rain showers for a few seconds.[17]

That night Obergruppenführer Hausser paced inside Dietrich's field headquarters. Even behind closed doors they could hear the guns pounding. Despite losing another forty-eight men killed and 321 wounded, he insisted that 192 Soviet tanks had been destroyed that day—a figure so fantastic that he had to vouch for its veracity for the evening report to Hitler's headquarters.[18] They thought the Russians were being bled white and did not know that the Soviets were equally optimistic. Georgi Zhukov, the Soviet leader opposite Peiper's forces, said, 'The morale of his troops had been shaken by the long battles with the 1st Tank Army and the 6th Guards and 7th Guards Armies ... the fighting was particularly fierce in the area around Prochorowka where the 5th Guards Tank Army under General P.A. Rotmistrow had an enormous success.'[19] Certainly there were many in the German camp who would argue with that pronouncement, but the Prochorowka head-bashing contest looked impossible to win. Aerial reconnaissance showed the Russians so strong in front of Prochorowka that General Hoth called for an envelopment of the enemy bastion with a turn to the north of that stubborn village.

Consequently, the orders for 13 July were for Peiper and the rest of the division to advance on the line of knobby crests north-east of the near-unpronounceable village of Swch-Oktjabrskij while the Totenkopf Division wheeled to the north. In fact, at daybreak on 13 July the Russians had emerged from the hills and made another desperate bid to capture Hill 252.2. They were turned back, but the initiative seemed to be slipping from German hands. To counter, Peiper and the rest of the Panzer group set off at 1000 hours in a full-speed assault attacking along the railway that led to the Oktjabrskij State Farm. Peiper's column quickly reached their objective, only to run into a deep tank ditch and a massive *Pakfront* reinforced by dug-in T-34s overlooking the ridge line. Even amid losses, they held on. At 1240 hours a powerful Russian counterattack, spiked by a swarm of tanks from the Russian 29th Tanks Corps, drove over the main German defensive line and were only turned back by concentrated artillery fire on top of the SS positions.[20] At sunset Peiper was still there.

Even as nightfall came, the battlefield east of Prochorowka was never without light. An eerie scene was illuminated by a fearsome spectacle: a blackness interrupted with swirling flames and sparks emanating from shattered metallic carcasses of tanks and planes destroyed over the previous two days. Occasionally ammunition or fuel tanks exploded with loud concussion and spouting fireworks. The blazing points of light spread to the horizon.

As the tanks burned, an evening briefing began at Hitler's East Prussian headquarters between the Führer and Field Marshalls von Manstein and von Kluge, in charge of the army groups to the north and south of the great effort. News came of ominous developments in both the East and West. Just three days before, the American and British forces began the invasion of Sicily—an exceedingly dangerous development for Germany's less-than stalwart Italian allies. Would the Italian fascist leader, Benito Mussolini, soon collapse? If that happened, with Italy fallen and Africa lost, the entire door to Germany would be totally open in the south. But the war had come to Germany in any case. Within the Reich borders the British and American bombings of German cities reached a new level with the firebombing of Hamburg. Thousands of the city's citizens died in a single night.

Back in Russia, on 12 July Hermann Hoth saw no further promise in continuing the Kursk advance from the north—the Russians were simply too strong. Intent on a breakthrough, General Model had flung a thousand tanks in his 9th Panzer Army into a 5km-wide corridor. Although pushed back, the Russian defences did not shatter, and a thicket of mines, *Pakfronts* and anti-tank trenches slowed the German advance. Model halted just south of Ponyri. Even worse, the Russian armies to Model's north attacked boldly into his flank towards Orel. This cancelled the entire advance on Kursk from the north. Even so, von Manstein, in the south, did not agree with the order to end Zitadelle.[21] Strangely, it would be the ever-offensive-minded Adolf Hitler who would lose his nerve. Wary of developments in the West, he decided to break off the attack. The Leibstandarte Adolf Hitler would be hurried to Italy. In Hitler's logic their presence would give the Italians a good ideological dose and reason to stay the Axis course.

Meanwhile, in Moscow, Stalin finally divulged information on the great battle taking place in Central Russia. His report claimed that 586 German tanks had been destroyed in the fighting on 9 July alone. Hundreds more destroyed German armoured vehicles were reported as felled over the following week. Even if the numbers were wildly exaggerated, they communicated that the Germans were taking a beating. Most telling was the title of the Russian battlefield report: 'The Tigers are burning.'[22]

Dietrich's exhausted command of the Leibstandarte Adolf Hitler welcomed a respite on 14 July, but the spell also raised concern: it smelled of defeat. They had given the Russians everything they had, and still the enemy glared at them from Prochorowka. That morning the Russians heaped artillery fire on the SS heads and probed their positions. The Totenkopf Division to their left threw back fierce enemy assaults. Guenther Borchers with Peiper's troop wrote,

> Now we had some rest. We dug ourselves in, but it wasn't very peaceful because fighter planes and tanks were fighting all around us. It was good that the Stukas were there and dropped bombs on the tanks. We blew up a mill in our position so the Russians couldn't use it to shoot from. Two T-34s broke through into our position, and a Nebelwerfer Battery shot some salvos at them as they recklessly drove on farther. They shot an aide station and an ambulance, but then a light machine gun man took care of them. Both tanks burned immediately. Russian weapons lay all over.[23]

The next day the Leibstandarte pulled out of the line. Heinz von Westernhagen, who had fought beside Peiper leading the assault gun battalion, wrote home to emphasize the nature of their enemy. 'Our men naturally don't fight like animals,' he penned from the Kursk battlefield, 'but like lions and without pardon.'[24] SS *Härte*—toughness of heart—take no prisoners. A recently declassified document leads credence to the involvement of Peiper's battalion in atrocities in Russia.[25]

For a time it looked as if the Leibstandarte would make a quick attempt to smash the enemy salient west of Kursk. Yet the resumption of a huge Russian summer offensive made that objective impertinent. On 17 July, the Leibstandarte pulled back to assemble in Teterewino after the Russians launched a surprise attack. SS Oberscharführer Hans Siptrott led a Mk IV Panzer to catch the enemy in their flank and rapidly shot down six T-34s. That event, which Siptrott's commander would later call 'a shining defensive success', was little more than a parting gesture.[26]

A day later the Leibstandarte went to Belgorod, thinking they might fight there. But just as soon as they arrived, they were sent back to the train station in Stalino. Orders told them to turn over their remaining tanks to Totenkopf and entrain immediately for Innsbruck, Austria, where they would receive new Panthers. The Italians had just overthrown Benito Mussolini, and 'the worst rumours were floating around'. The Leibstandarte was going to Italy.[27]

The world had never seen as cataclysmic a tank battle as that at Kursk. Counting both sides, some six thousand tanks and four thousand planes had locked into the deadly combat before the city. The Russians claimed to have destroyed twenty-nine hundred German tanks, but that number, even if grossly inflated, did speak of tremendous losses.[28] The final great German attack on the Eastern Front was hardly a Blitzkrieg or even a battle of movement; it became a vast set-piece conflict resolved like the First World War, with prepared positions, trenches and tanks. Even if more than six Soviet tanks were destroyed for each German one, the battlefield was a graveyard to the last great Panzer force:

[A] few weeks later, I travelled through the fair Ukrainian countryside ... I could see how the area north of Belgorod had been turned into a hideous desert, in which every tree and bush had been smashed by shell fire. Hundreds of burned-out tanks and wrecked planes still littered the battlefield, and even several miles away from it the air was filled with the stench of thousands of half-buried Russian and German corpses.[29]

Zitadelle was a German strategic failure. Everyone knew that much. More aware than most was Sepp Dietrich. Having emerged from the debacle at Kursk to take over the forming I SS Panzer Corps in Belgium,

Dietrich departed, deeply convinced that the war in the East could no longer be won. At Kharkov his division had dealt a knock-out blow to an enemy who came back to create one line after another of anti-tank guns. During the pitched battle at Kursk he witnessed how the Russians had absorbed their best punch—and one in which the Leibstandarte claimed five hundred tanks. And still the Russians came. Was it not true that Soviet factories were spitting out T-34s twice as quickly as German assembly lines could produce tanks?[30] And 'their tanks were better,' Dietrich concluded. 'They were less complicated and easier to manoeuvre. Our tanks were much too complicated and sensitive—they seemed to have been made by a Swiss watchmaker.' Peiper, however, was astonished—negatively—by the Russian soldier:

> On account of the innumerable different races, it is impossible for me to analyse the man as such. Generally, one could only note that his cruelty increased with the square of the distance from the Reich border. More fitting, one should not say 'the Russian' but rather 'the Bolshevist.' … Besides his familiar attachment to nihilism, two souls live in the breast of the Russian soldier: the infantile good-naturedness of the 'simple fellow' alternates with the animal-like cruelty of the Asiatic … The ability to keep going even on very little and his capacity for suffering surpasses our European comprehension. His instinctive connection with nature as well as his unused nerves make him especially dangerous at night and during inclement weather. The darker the night, the heavier the rain, and the stronger the snowstorm, the more infallible an attack from the Russian can be expected … The Russian has beaten us with the inexhaustible power of his human reservoir …[31]

Returning from the Eastern Front, Dietrich made an ill-advised semi-public proclamation to Alfred Rosenberg of his view of prospects for the war. Himmler reacted quickly: 'It is said that you no longer believe that we can be victorious over the Russians.' That bit of blasphemy was unacceptable, even for a favourite paladin. Himmler suggested that Dietrich set the record straight: 'Certainly, your opinion about the combat effectiveness of the Russians was misunderstood.' He went on to say, 'I myself know well how you think of the war in Russia. We fully agree that it is not easy. However, it is certain for us that the Russians can be vanquished in the future.'[32]

But for Dietrich, and likely for Jochen Peiper as well, certainty fell to the other side of the equation. By the summer of 1943 Germany could no longer realistically hope to win the war in the East. Nevertheless, for Jochen Peiper there remained the overwhelming faith in the SS, even if they were losing the war in Russia. In his opinion the Leibstandarte remained completely superior:

> The Russian losses are, for our calculations, so colossal, and yet it would be wrong to think that this happened in a senseless sacrifice. On the contrary, here again one can recognize a utility scheme for manpower based on a brutal and ice-cold suitability … From the perspective of the vanquished, the Russian appears today to many like a superhuman. That this is not correct, however, nobody knows better than the 'old' divisions of the Waffen SS. We were never affected by the disintegration and psychoses described, but we learned to beat the opponent at his own game. There was no method of fighting in which we were not superior to the Russian, and there was no attack in which we did not 'drive them off in pairs', be it during a snowstorm or during the night.[33]

Peiper was partly right. A sober analysis of the battle of Prochorowka reveals the Germans destroyed at least six times as many Russian tanks as they lost.[34] Moreover, losses to the Soviet Army were catastrophic—over quarter of a million killed, wounded or captured against roughly fifty thousand losses to the Wehrmacht.[35] Even so, after winning the battle of attrition at Prochorowka, Germany failed the contest of trapping the Russian army in one fell swoop. A decisive victory eluded them. Anything else was defeat.

Yet, soon the Leibstandarte were headed again by rail away from Russia, bound for Italy. 'Once again a week in a train,' wrote home Ralf Tiemann, 'a week of sun and nothing to do … We stood in the cars in shorts and watched old and new landscapes go by … Everything was deeply peaceful—summer—it is barely believable for us after the past few days.'[36]

Jochen Peiper breathed a deep sigh, speaking in hushed confidence to the commander of the first battalion of the Panzer Grenadier Regiment 2. The Americans had just landed at Sicily, he told SS Haupsturmführer Hans Röhwer. Did he know what that meant? Röhwer shook his head.

'Herr Röhwer,' Jochen Peiper whispered, 'the war is lost.'[37]

Chapter 10

Italy

'Italia! O Italia! thou who hast the fatal gift of beauty.'[1]

Domenico Favole was a big fish in a small Italian town. If most famous as a well-travelled entrepreneur in tiny Boves, Favole was also known as a tough self-made Italian businessman.

Born in Fossano on the Northern Italian plain in 1906, he had moved to the tiny Piedmontese town of Boves in 1922 and struck it rich in the burgeoning silk industry. The years during Mussolini's ascent and assumption to power had been very good for the demand of high-quality clothing. The little Roman town of Boves, he thought, was an ideal place for a business. He set up a factory there, just off the main square of the Piazza Italia, employing over 170 people—many of them women, as he thought them better at the work, with their dedication, careful hands and attention to detail. In any case, the Italian war stripped away the menfolk; they had gone along with the Germans to fight and die in Africa and Russia.

Boves was a sleepy northern Italian town. The tiny enclave had emerged from obscurity in Roman times. Wedged in the verdant foot-hills, this small village was called Bovesium, named for 'bulls'. Later the settlement was partly abandoned due to the Saracen invasion and, in 1396, became part of the expansive holdings of the Savoy family. This lasted until 1800, when Napoleon took control of the region. Even in modern times the French influence was still lingering in Boves and nearby Cuneo from the emperor's interlude.[2]

Perhaps the French influence worked another way, for the people of the Piedmontese region were known as a more emotionally restrained Italian populace than their more effusive neighbours to the south. The stuccoed homes in the village were frayed around the edges in typical Mediterranean fashion. The painted wooden shutters were often in poor repair, and the wrought-iron balconies looked like most needed new paint. The beauty was undeniable—each facade was coloured in a rainbow of earth tones suggesting all the colours of pomodoro—soft unripe greens, both light and deep reds and even sun-dried-tomato browns. Red, white and pink geraniums spilled out of window boxes facing the town square.

The noisy streets were arrayed in scallop patterns of cobble stones. The place bustled with activity—bikes and carts and the occasional car or motorbike. If a small place, the cafés were ever busy with espresso drinkers and tasters of the native grape. Conversations were loud and hands ever animated. Anyone knowing the locals could not be surprised, for even if the northern Italians were known as austere in comparison to those in Rome, they were still totally unlike the Germans. Many there considered their wartime allies emotionally stunted: critical, negative and humourless—so un-Italian.

To be sure, the campaign with Germans from 1940 onwards was not particularly good for the Italians—at least that was the view from the people in the street. If most thought the standard of living was worse, the demand for silk-wear remained strong. Favole's business had never been better. Yet by 1943, even the most amblyopic could see Mussolini's empire teetering with the freefall of German fortunes.

Everything came to a head on 25 July in the summer of 1943. That was the Sunday when Mussolini fell from power.[3] The very next day the handsome and charismatic Duccio Galimberti—already a legend in Cuneo—loudly hailed the people from the main square. He stood proudly before a microphone thrust before him on the balcony, shoulder to shoulder with other prominent townspeople. The Piazza Vittorio Emanuele II was the same place where, on 20 May 1939, Mussolini had triumphantly proclaimed the land for fascism. Galimberti was a rebel. 'Mussolini is finished,' he cried out. 'The fascist party is done.' He went on declare, 'Now it is time to liberate our Italy … Yes, the war goes on till the flight of the last German, till the last trace of the Fascist regime disappears, till the victory of the Italian people who revile the Mussolini tyranny!'[4]

From the podium he called on idealistic able-bodied Italian youth to revolt against the fascists: '*Viva l'Italia!*'

Domenico Favole was there, but being middle aged, there were few stars in his eyes. Having travelled all over Europe and even ventured to the Olympic Games in Los Angeles in 1932, he was a realist. Although he may have disapproved of *Il Duce*, Mussolini had, after all, been good for business, and Favole was a business man. Even so, the tumult of the summer of 1943 threw everything into total confusion—always bad for any market. But if a hard-nosed entrepreneur, Favole was also devoutly

Italian. He took solace in that at least the Piedmontese way of life— a casual social atmosphere built around friends, pasta and wine—was not interrupted. The rich surrounding agricultural lands allowed that; the tomatoes were good and the mushrooms plentiful. And one could still get a good espresso—an important aspect for productivity. Although focused on the money to be made, Favole had the usual Italian corporate-paternal instinct: he took care of his workers, and they took care of him. The Germans? Well, they were still good business. But with the bedlam in the summer of 1943, who knew what would come next?[5]

Bouncing along on the train from Russia to Italy, Jochen Peiper's thoughts likely wandered to the battles won and lost—an unending blur of days and nights with the fighting and the dead. After the cathartic conflict of Operation Zitadelle that summer, Hitler's vow to rule the world rung ever more hollow. The Germans were winning battles in Russia and losing the war. And there was the historic precedent. For Peiper 1943 might as well have been 1915 all over again. 'The Italians!' they swore. Different Kaiser, same problem.

What Hitler had called the 'Pact of Steel'—the alliance between Italy and the Reich—was now in shambles. 'We made a mistake in our estimation of the military efficiency and political reliability of Fascist Italy,' Hitler claimed to his staff. The German leader complained loudly to Alfred Jodl, his chief of staff: 'Even Mussolini could not make anything out of the Italians,' he sneered, 'but Italians.'[6]

Now *Il Duce* was unseated, under arrest by his own countrymen. The new Italian government, under Marshal Pietro Badoglio, was undecided as to with whom they would side. The aims of his army were more uncertain still. Would it take up arms against the Americans landing on its beaches or join them against their former allies?

Hitler and his namesake command looked to have a say in their decision. On 10 July 1943 the Americans landed at Sicily, and Mussolini was arrested on 25 July. Week by week the situation deteriorated in Italy. On the last day of August Sepp Dietrich met in Munich with Generalfeld-marschal Erwin Rommel, who was to take over the defence of Italy—it seemed likely to collapse at any moment. In particular, the German leader worried that the Italians might suddenly turn on them and seize the passes through the Alps. To avoid that catastrophe, the Leibstandarte was to take over the defence between the Brenner Pass and the city of Verona. Their exhausted division would be bolstered both by an expansive draft of replacements as well as a new group of Tiger and Panther tanks just forming at the Sennelager tank training grounds. Still, there were other reasons why the Leibstandarte had been chosen for Italy.

In January 1943 the Italians refused to cooperate with Himmler's scheme for rounding up the Jews living in the occupied zone of France under their control.[7] In March they blocked similar plans from deporting Jews from Italy. This moved German foreign minister Joachim von Ribbentrop to complain to Benito Mussolini that 'Italian military circles … lack a proper understanding of the Jewish question'.[8] This naiveté seemed to extend to German army military circles as well; there was more on the agenda than Rommel seemed to know or wanted to know.

In attendance at the Munich meeting at Generalfeldmarschal Rommel's headquarters on the last day of July was SS Obergruppenführer Karl Wolff and Dr Wilhelm Harster, who had news for Rommel about other objectives for operations in the frontiers of his Army Group B. The only representative of a German ground force unit was Theodor Wisch in charge of the Leibstandarte Adolf Hitler. Why was he there? That was quickly told. Wolff and Harster were looking to coordinate the response of the SD and Sipo—the security police—to how the Jewish question would be handled in Northern Italy.[9] For that they would use Hitler's own bodyguard division to provide security for the police to round up the Jews. The 24th Panzer Division would be along for the other important task: to provide backbone in case the Italian armies decided to surrender.[10] So rather than being sent to Salerno to fight the Americans, the Leibstandarte was to send a political message to their former ally and begin Himmler's delayed vision of a *judenfrei* Italy. Rommel, for his part, seemed shocked by the news of the measures for 'internal security of Italy' that would be part of the assignment for Wisch's division with the secret police, but Wolff made it clear that this new mission came from Hitler himself.

That much was true. On 6 September Wolff was personally invited to meet Hitler at the *Wolfsschanze* to discuss the situation in Italy.[11] The German leader wanted to make sure he understood the need to end 'the unbearable situation in Italy, one way or another'. While all SS resources were to endeavour to rescue Mussolini, his vacuum of power was to be used to transform Italy to a more Germanic vision: most sensitive was that Wolff was to strip the Vatican of all power—even destroying it if necessary. The secret police were to begin to round up the Jews who had been taking refuge in Italy after fleeing France.[12] 'The SD should put together for you a list of the most dangerous persons,' Hitler told Wolff. 'There will be an uproar in the world, but that will soon die down.'[13] On 10 September Hitler himself appointed Wolff to a new post to make things happen: Special Advisor for Police Matters with the Italian Government.

From the beginning Dr Harster's SD and security police needed the logistical and security support of the Leibstandarte in the early going, particularly given the fact that the Italian forces were on the cusp of capitulating or even switching allegiances. In any case, Hitler's Own was there for the very beginning of the *Endlösung* in Italy—a situation not by chance. The assigned SD and Gestapo were given the same Leibstandarte Adolf Hitler cuff titles, and some were even sent the divisional staff.[14] The SD would first be directly assigned to the Leibstandarte to start the process of rounding up Jews, first in Northern Italy, and then other SS forces would operate more systematically in Rome. In Milan the Leibstandarte would take on SS Obersturmführer Walter Rauff of the RSHA (Reich Security Main Office), infamous for having designed gassing vans to murder Jews in Russia.[15] Meanwhile, SS Hauptsturmführer Theodor Dannecker, who had functioned ruthlessly in Adolf Eichmann's office for the *Endlösung*, would be in charge of transport for the evacuation. Evacuation to where? For that, Harster had explicit orders: Auschwitz.[16] On 9 September, Karl Wolff and Dr Harster travelled to Italy in preparation for the action.

Back in Berlin in early September 1943, Heinrich Himmler remained obsessed with the need to free Mussolini. After frustration with General Kurt Student to use an air corps to effect *Il Duce's* release, Himmler directed that all available SS and police forces be used for this objective. However, with that emphasis settled, he ordered Wolff to begin the ground work—particularly in Rome—to effect the delayed deportation of the Italian Jews. The sweep was to begin immediately after Mussolini was freed; with Mussolini as a puppet of a German occupation, there would be no further way to resist Himmler's policy of racial extermination.[17]

However, for the average Leibstandarte man there was little knowledge of the big picture. What they knew was where they were—and that was not Russia. When compared with the Eastern Front, the assignment was a holiday. Italy beckoned with its cool lush hills, flourishing green valleys and tangerine-bright Mediterranean sun. Even after a week Peiper and the rest were still cleaning Russian dust from their teeth. They passed through Poland and then Germany. There were crowds at the stops to cheer them—it hardly seemed a war lost. They cleaned weapons, retold stories; there was plenty of time to rest. Finally the train clacked through the snow-capped mountains of Austria.

On 1 August Peiper, with his SPW battalion, arrived at Innsbruck to unload from the flatcars. The alpine air was cool and thin. From there they would be under their own power grinding up and down the Alps. Four days later he rolled with his wheeled vehicles to the Italian city of Trient and then down into the Po Valley to assume security for the region around the city of Cuneo. There he held a meeting with his men to describe the coming operation: they would buttress the crumbling Italian army or else disarm them. It sounded easy. On the contrary, news from back home showed that the war had already crossed the Reich borders.

In 1942 Allied bombers began to blast away at Hitler's Reich. The first raids had been small, but the second half of 1943 saw a billowing cascade of bombs falling from Allied planes into Germany. On the night of 27 July a fleet of British bombers struck Hamburg, dropping more than 2,000 tons of incendiaries that consumed the city in a raging firestorm. A 'lake of fire' spread over a two-square-mile area at the centre of the city. Over the next five days some forty thousand people in Hamburg were incinerated.[18] The citizens of every city in Germany wondered whether they would be next. What the Germans had visited on London in 1940 now came back in larger circle.

In Peiper's hometown of Berlin the prescience of blazing Hamburg created a palpable fear. Indeed, in spring 1943 a number of neighbouring homes in Berlin's central district had been bombed. Most believed that the capital city would be next. There was a rumour that the real death toll in Hamburg was 150,000—it was actually only a quarter of that, but that was horrific enough. Panic swept Berlin. Nightly air raid sirens wailed— mostly false alarms, but more and more evenings were spent in the cellar.[19] Finally, at the end of July, Joseph Goebbels, the Reich propaganda minister and Gauleiter of Berlin, called for all women and children to leave town. That prompted Sigurd Peiper and her family to join the mass exodus and look for a safer location. Now pregnant with her third child, she wrote on 25 August to her old office friend Rudi Brandt after having moved out of Berlin to the farmhouse of her sister-in-law. Word had already got out about the bombing of the city two days before:

> I write to you to ask for a favour—I want to give my congratulations to our high chief and his promotion to the head of the interior ministry. This big new promotion will bring a bright light too on you and your work ... Where did your wife and your boy evacuate to? ... I am sitting here at the table writing you at night in the shine of the kerosene lamp. There is a phone, but it's mostly dead ... I feel pretty good and the kids too. At the moment, I enjoy a lazy life with my children.[20]

Rudi wrote back to Sigurd on 28 August 1943 to send tardy birthday greetings and to assure her that Himmler and the others were fine. 'The tasks of our chief become even greater. The Reichsführer SS is very optimistic for this heavy work like he has done it every time before ... I've recently gotten a promotion, which is good even though my wife and kids have had to leave Berlin to Schneidemühle … During the last air attack on Berlin, I was here, but there was no damage to our bunker office.'[21]

As before, being well connected had advantages. Peiper's former boss, Heinrich Himmler, had his highly publicized family idyll, Haus Lindenfycht, at Gemund on the shores of Lake Tegernsee. Why not locate there? It was safe and beautiful, with the aura of a Germanic fairy tale. It was one of those pure Bavarian alpine lakes, a favourite haunt of kings and nobles. The place was nestled in the scenic valley, surrounded by the spectacular views of the towering Alps.[22]

For lofty members of the SS a steely blue glacial lake was clearly the place to be. Karl Wolff, Himmler's right-hand man, now in Italy, had also built a house on the Tegernsee and was raising his children there.[23] In the same neighbourhood lived the family of Werner Grothmann, the current adjutant to the Reichsführer SS. Even Sigurd's widowed friend from Kiel, Lina Heydrich, had taken up residence in the valley.[24] The mayor appropriately touted it as 'the first address in fine living', and main street had been renamed 'Adolf Hitlerstrasse'. And at the entrance to wartime Rottach-Egern was an altogether telling proclamation: 'This is a Jew-free village'.[25]

Not surprisingly, given the number of members of National Socialist upper crust living there, the place was known throughout Hitler's Germany as *Lago di bonzo*—the Lake of the Bosses.[26] So, with Himmler's assistance, Peiper moved his family to the two-storey Gottshaberhof Villa at 183½ Wolfgrubstrasse in Rottach-Egern. There they would be far away from the bombs and close to the power centre of Himmler's SS. By 7 November 1943, Sigurd and her children had completed the move, but the news was not all good.[27] From nearby Tegernsee, Himmler's own 14-year-old daughter, Gudrun, registered neighbourhood doubts in her diary. No longer did her idolized father bring brightly coloured tulips and fruit from Holland:

> [T]he fights are indescribably heavy. We were in the east before Stalingrad and now we are behind Kiev … And the terrible terrorist raids from the air. Unfortunately, many Germans no longer believe in victory, but we must triumph. Pappi [father] is doing so much to contribute to our effort.[28]

What Gudrun Himmler did not know was that 'Pappi's' contribution to the effort was methodically eliminating Jews from Europe. In October

in Posen, Poland, Himmler candidly addressed an assembled group of
SS leaders:

> I also want to refer here to a very difficult matter. We can now talk very
> openly about this among ourselves, and yet we will never discuss this
> publicly ... I am now referring to the evacuation of the Jews, to the
> extermination of the Jewish people. This is something that is easily said:
> 'The Jewish people will be exterminated,' says every Party member,
> 'this is very obvious, it is in our program—elimination of the Jews,
> extermination, will do.' And then they turn up, the brave 80 million
> Germans, and each one has a decent Jew. It is of course obvious that
> the others are swine, but this particular one is a splendid Jew.

Several in the audience laughed nervously, and Himmler's voice was
strangely nasal. But now the man peering from behind wire-rimmed
glasses slowed his delivery and fished for words—'But of all those who
talk this way, none had observed it, none had endured it.' What did
that mean?

> Most of you here know what it means when 100 corpses lie next to
> each other, when 500 lie there or when 1,000 are lined up. To have
> endured this and at the same time to have remained a decent person—
> with exceptions due to human weakness—had made us tough. This is
> an honour roll in our history which has never been and will never be
> put in writing ... We have the moral right, we had the duty to our people
> to do it, to kill this people who would kill us.[29]

Himmler had long espoused a code of silence when it came to talk of
dark things. As if borrowing a page from the Sicilian mafia, he excluded
stenographers and tape recorders from sensitive discussions. Typically
the audience was limited to those who needed to know. Yet this time,
Himmler violated his own rule. A reel-to-reel recorder etched his words
onto oversized red-oxide magnetic tape; he even arranged a sound check
to make certain all was in order. For three long hours he spewed a litany
of details of an officially sanctioned genocide. Why would he speak of this
now? Well, naturally, he still believed the Germans would prevail in the
conflict—that was nature's law, he said. In actuality, the real reason was
to cement devotion. The calamitous events of recent months suggested
the need to improve the resolve within Himmler's SS. His generals
needed to pursue this war without a hint of pity. In recounting terrible
deeds that the regime sanctioned, he, like Brutus, washed the hands of
Caesar's lieutenants in a trail of blood.

Of this damning speech Peiper may have known nothing. But word of it spread like wildfire among higher-up SS officers.[30] That night Himmler's Posen audience indulged in a drunken revelry the likes of which was seldom seen in that staid organization. With such things disclosed, anesthetization seemed in order. The SS officers would be drawn into the *blutkitt*—the blood cement—where all shared in the collective guilt if the war were not won. Peiper had long ago told those at Himmler's headquarters that SS men not wanting contact with this Hades were best to move to the front. Still, Peiper maintained his relationship.

On each of Peiper's visits back to Germany Himmler always seemed willing to keep him in the loop of the deepening depths of SS depravity. Meanwhile, in a letter in late summer, Himmler indulged his penchant for racial purity, complaining to Sepp Dietrich that too many illegitimate children were being born to men of the Leibstandarte in Russia.[31]

Yet, Italy was a long way from either Russia or Himmler's collective perdition. Dietrich would respond with alacrity weeks later that his Leibstandarte was now in Italy, so the complaint about mass infidelity in Russia was moot. What statistical evidence did he have? Peiper and his battalion spent the next five days journeying through Northern Italy amid a spectacular mountain backdrop. The weather was perfect for the drive, and everyone seemed in good spirits—only the halftrack drivers worried of the hairpin mountain roads. As Peiper's column geared through the mountainous countryside of southern Tyrol, they were greeted by enthusiastic Austrians—the most welcome of which were the girls who seemed to crowd and coo around every vehicle. 'Again and again,' remembered one, 'the trucks were stopped so they could hand us delicious fruit.'[32]

> We were greeted all over by the locals with flowers, fruit, and wine. Everywhere they stood on the street and waved to us. The streets there were very narrow and it was very hot. We travelled through Bozen [Bolzano] toward Trient [Trento]. There, we met up with our company again. We ate a lot of grapes grown for wine and tomato salad, and also some exceptional ice cream.[33]

Men and equipment came quickly. On 10 August, the long-promised Mk V Panzer tanks for the first Panzer battalion arrived at the Italian rail station of Reggio Emilia. New Mk IVs were already there, and three days later Peiper's men laden in halftracks reached Trient and the outskirts of Verona. There they waited, ready to support the Bavarians and Austrians of 44th Infantry Division if help were needed. Days passed without crisis—or even military concern.

A week later they debouched into Reggio-Emilia, north-west of Bologna. The SS men basked in the prospects: a little Barbera wine at sidewalk cafés, a bowl of steaming agnolotti, followed by a walk in the warm Mediterranean sun. Upon arrival in Reggio Emilia on 19 August, Peiper and his troop took off their hats and strode through the city streets. As they marched, they belted out 'Erika' in strident baritones. Proud Germans, singing about the little flower. Crews filmed their procession, while the curious clogged the streets. Italian kids in shorts and knee socks rode bikes alongside.[34]

> *Auf der Heide blüht ein kleines Blümelein*
> *Und das heißt: Erika …*
> (In a moor a small flower grows
> And it is called heather.)[35]

Everyone was smiling as they sang. Paul Guhl and Werner Wolff flanked Peiper. Their marching song even blared over German radio and was featured in the wartime newsreels back home. The Italian weeks passed like a Ligurian summer holiday.

> We were situated in the area of Reggio in a vineyard. In the evenings I was often with an Italian family, where we drank wine and made music. It was quite cosy. We always went on late into the evenings, and I had to make tracks through the streets to get back for taps at 2200. Sometimes we went to the bars with our comrades and came back drunk to our home base. In the meantime I received another motorcycle. We made frequent excursions to Arno and reconnoitred the bridges on the road from Florenz to Pisa. We stood watch next to the Itacker [derogatory term for Italian soldiers]. There's quite a difference between them with their weapons in their arms and us with our weapons on our shoulder. Then the revolt happened in Italy. We immediately occupied the electrical works, the train station, and all other important buildings. Yes, and then we still had to disarm the Italian soldiers in their own barracks![36]

On 28 August Peiper's men threw a party with the usual Waffen SS sporting competitions. Young Werner Wolff showed his prowess at both boxing and fencing. Peiper even arranged for some of his men to fly sightseeing tours in confiscated Italian aircraft.

> From the Reich, we passed Glaciers and fields
> To a land that is short of Peiper's forests

But there are large gardens with wine
into them we go instead of into the forests.
We gain a lot of strength in our bones,
Because we sniff vitamins from morning till night.
'In the land of red oranges,' we sing, 'we have appeared.'
And Italy's sun shines its heat
Onto our blowtorches, just to tease.[37]

The war of autumn of 1943 seemed casual. It was warm that September. Peiper's SS men took the opportunity to don the seldom-seen tropical SS uniform: shorts with turned-down socks over their shoes. They could show off well-toned legs and get a suntan—fuel for vanity, and there was plenty of that in the Leibstandarte.

SS men ate the fragrant cheese pizza. They drank the thick Barolo wine, and sipped pungent espresso. They took snapshots to send back home. The landscape was altogether more enticing than Russia, and the green hills of the Piemonte were not even the highlight. For, even if difficult to approach, the Italian women had a magnetic beauty—olive skin and shapely bodies. They could send deprived young German soldiers into a priapic delirium.

If not Italian idyllic, it was close. Still, the real job kept encroaching on the fun. Peiper and his battalion were to disarm the Italians and put down any rumoured Communist uprising. In particular they were to make certain that the regular army forces of the Italian Fourth Army did not make contact with the 'partisans' operating in Turin. Finally, there was a troubling rumour that the Americans might try to land nearby. Yet the closer one looked, the clearer it became that the Fourth Army was disbanding—or at least not organized.[38]

To Peiper's sensibilities the faltering Italians made a poor impression. Just as they had proven poor allies for Germany at the beginning of the First World War, their spirits flagged with the recent blows to Hitler's war fortunes.[39] To the Waffen SS the Italians were quickly becoming *Untermenschen*, like their other enemies in the war. The fact that they were disloyal was the worst. Still, Peiper claimed the Italian Fourth Army still had many weapons, and he was particularly worried about the prospect of having to fight renegades in the mountains.

Even an army general like Field Marshal Erwin Rommel had suspicions. 'We can imagine only too well what the Italians have up their sleeve,' Rommel noted in his diary, 'a quick jump over onto the other side, lock, stock and barrel.' In any case, he appeared delighted to have

Sepp Dietrich's old crack division, to whom Hitler had granted carte blanche for the operation: 'He's fully prepared to play hell with the Italians to make them dance to his tune.'[40]

Peiper and Otto Dinse made their headquarters at the big prefect building in the Piedmontese town of Cuneo. For living quarters they took over a private home on the fashionable Viale Angeli. They were nice digs, with no comparison to Russia. No straw and mud—there were real beds, warm and cosy. Shortly after their arrival they were met by the prim and proper Italian commander Costantino Salvi of the provincial government, who surrendered the town. He would try to maintain civilian order, he said. The fabled Communist revolt looked to be just another rumour.[41]

Then it happened.

Chapter 11

'Dancing on the Volcano'

'It's good to trust others, but not to do so is much better.'
—Benito Mussolini

On the evening of Wednesday, 8 September 1943 the Italians were quitting the Second World War—at least as an Axis Power.

For Jochen Peiper, Hitler's dedicated SS officer warrior, it was a stark reminder of the tragedy of the failed Italian alliance in the Kaiser's war. History was now repeated once more and extending to foreboding German military reverses in the summer of 1943.

In Italy, from 1925 onwards, Benito Mussolini had fashioned a fascist government, styling himself as *Il Duce*, an iron-fisted charismatic leader. Embarking on an expansive military conquest in Africa, Mussolini promised the people of Italy a return to the greatness of the Roman Empire. The Greater Mediterranean would be their *Mare Nostrum*, he said, declaring that 'the twentieth century will be a century of Italian power'. He created a powerful navy to control the Mediterranean Sea and planned a large modern army as well, but a decade of imperial expansion to secure North and East Africa had nearly exhausted his poorly equipped forces.

Still, it was natural that Mussolini and Hitler combined forces, given their mutual ambitions in Europe and Africa. In January 1936, *Il Duce* had declared an Axis with Hitler's Germany, culminating in the Pact of Steel in 1939, which bound together Fascist Italy and National Socialist Germany in a full military alliance. The Italian armies under Mussolini then fought in Eastern Africa, North Africa and Greece in an effort for coordinated Axis conquest. Yet in Africa and Greece, the British and Commonwealth forces severely punished Mussolini's troops, so much so that German divisions had to bail them out.

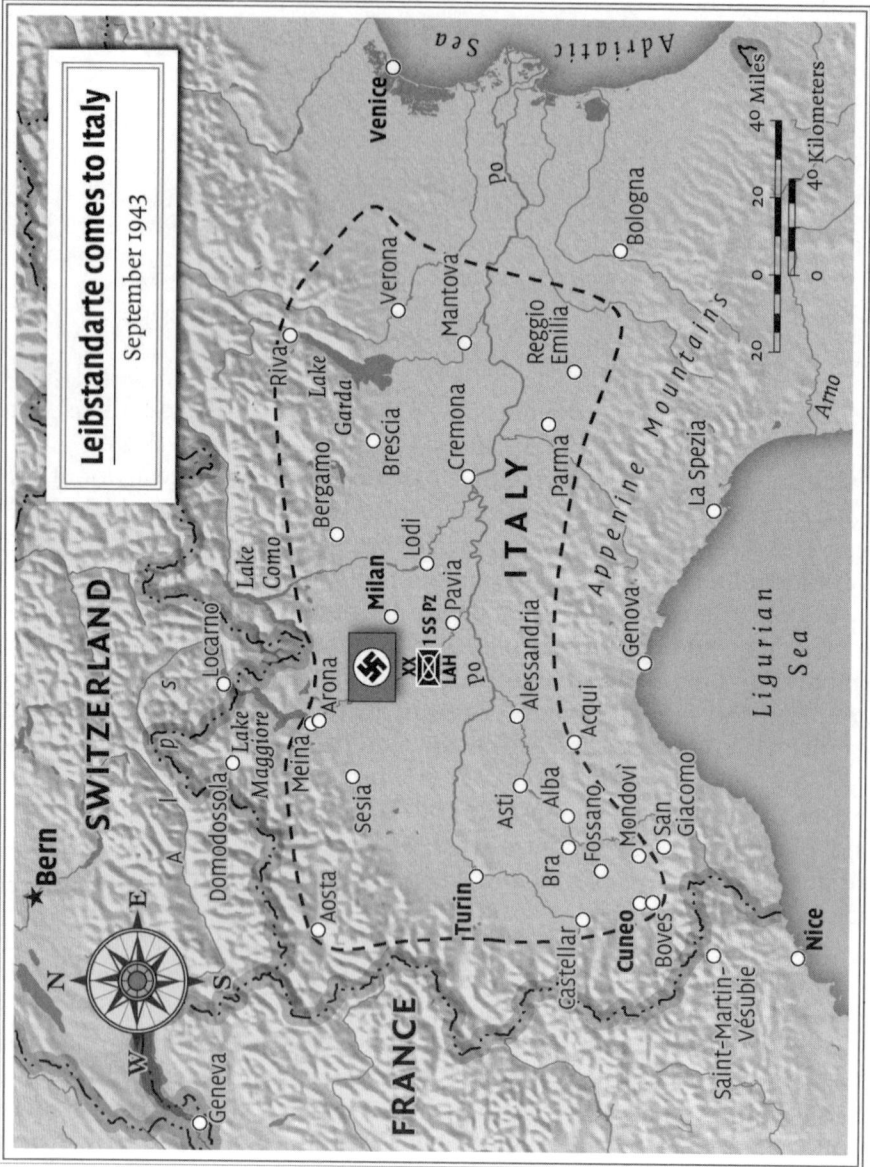

Leibstandarte comes to Italy
September 1943

Although *Mussolini* had volunteered over two hundred thousand soldiers for the massive campaign in the Soviet Union, the Italian showing alongside German forces had been poor. The conventional wisdom of Hitler's fighting men at the front said a thousand German infantry were the equal of ten thousand Italians. Not only were Mussolini's forces poorly outfitted, but many claimed that Italian determination seemed low as well. Every Italian tank carried with it a white flag at the ready, venturing a popular joke making the rounds among German soldiery.[1] But was that true? In any case, the capitulation in Tunisia in 1943 was a huge disaster—with many Italian captives. And in the East the *Armata Italiana* in Russia suffered heavy losses at Stalingrad and elsewhere— nearly half of those fighting with the Hitler's legions there were killed or captive, most to be never seen again.

Even worse for Mussolini's reputation at home, German troops had entered Italy to bolster their sagging military fortunes. As if to cap the failed alliance, that preparation was not enough, for in July 1943 the Allies invaded Sicily and brought the war to Italy's doorstep. By August they had seized the island and largely destroyed the Italian Sixth Army. In the meantime, a furious Allied bombing of Rome on 19 July 1943 deeply soured Italian enthusiasm for continuing the conflict. Not so differently from the First World War, the Italian alliance with Germany not only faltered but seemed likely to defect to the Allied side.

With the shaky alliance teetering with declining German fortunes in Russia, Peiper and his trusted command from the Leibstandarte Adolf Hitler, 1st SS Panzer Grenadier Division, arrived in Northern Italy: the Brenner Pass must be held or risk another debacle. Moreover, the command bearing Hitler's own name was to make sure the defecting Italians laid down arms as soon as official word came of surrender.

At the top, *Il Duce* was out. Even after twenty years of uninterrupted reign, on 25 July 1943 Mussolini himself had been unceremoniously arrested after King Victorio Emmanuel III had dismissed him in Rome. He was then spirited away to a remote region in the Albruzzo Mountains. General Pietro Badoglio assumed power in Italy with an antifascist government. However, to what allegiance would the fickle officers and the soldiers of the Italian army side?

Yet, apart from that responsibility to Germany, upon arrival from the Tyrolian heights Peiper's SS troopers in Italy saw their occupation of the area south of Milan as an armed vacation. Now, relaxing and enjoying the September daytime sunshine, most of Hitler's namesake SS division toyed with vanity or recovered from the trauma of what they had just experienced in Russia. In the meantime a full contingent of the latest

German tanks had arrived at Milan to turn their command into a full Panzer division. There was almost a celebratory atmosphere, even with the uncertain Italian allegiance.

Later that Wednesday night of 8 September some of Peiper's men passed time in an Italian bar, listening to music and enjoying a glass of *Stravecchia*—the fiery local brandy. The day was still warm. Then 'the music stopped and there was a speech by Marshal Badoglio, the Italian head of the new government. In seconds, the Italians were on the tables yelling: *"Viva, Viva Badoglio!"'*[2]

The Italians would no longer fight. On signal Hitler's headquarters flashed the operative code word: *'Fall Achse'*—'Operation Axis'. Within the plans for Fall Achse, Generalfeldmarschal Albert Kesselring declared all of Italy a war zone. Rommel's Army Group B, with eight divisions, was to manage the abolition of the Italian army.

In the streets of Northern Italy arose a 'little revolution'. Many were happy that Mussolini was gone, but there was also apprehension and even scorn that the cowardly King Emanuele had deserted his people—flown from Rome to Brindisi in the early morning hours of 9 September. The Italian Fourth Army had long been allegiant to the king and Badoglio. What now? Many Italian soldiers thought of themselves as rebels; later they would call themselves partisans. They fled to the forested hills to hide and scheme.

'Finito!' many of the relieved Italians cried in the streets. However, those of the Leibstandarte saw it quite differently: they were not amused. 'War is not finito!' one called back. 'Tomorrow we are going on with the war.'[3]

Within the hour the Panzer regiment took possession of the airport at Reggio-Emilia. Rumours ran wild. One said Allied forces would land to seize the airport that night. Two tanks and a Kübelwagen packed with grenadiers raced to the landing strip. An SS man fired off his machine pistol into the air, and eight Italian soldiers hurried out to surrender at the airport. Meanwhile, Peiper and his halftracks spent 9 September disarming the entire town of Reggio.[4] The Italian soldiers there seemed relieved, passing over their rifles and walking back home. Many were smiling.

On 10 September Peiper watched as Italian soldiers at the barracks of Alessandria laid down their weapons. There were large stacks. The same happened on the following days at the flat-land agricultural towns of Asti, Alba, Bra, Fossano and Mondovi. On 14 September, Peiper took prisoner a general of the Italian Fourth Army, Brigadier General Elligio

Rosso, later claiming that, as evidence, there were still strong armed Italian units in the area south-west of Cuneo. These were the Italian armies who had spent months defending the mountain passes on the French border but now seemed eager to disband. Peiper briefly exchanged gunfire with what he saw as bandits, but it was pretty tame stuff. In fact, the Italian Fourth Army was evaporating like a morning mist over the vineyards— quickly ceasing to exist.

On 14 September the armoured halftracks and self-propelled guns of Peiper's battalion reached Cuneo and, after brief negotiations, took three generals, seventy-nine officers and 254 soldiers prisoner.[5] Antonio Bassignano remembered how Peiper's vehicles rolled into town with two vehicles pointing their cannons at his office. Their appearance was intimidating, but there was no fighting in Cuneo.[6] If the war in the Italian Piemonte seemed over, elsewhere in Italy events proved more gripping. At Salerno, seeking to capitalize on the confusion, American forces struggled on the beaches against fierce German counterattack.

On 13 September Benito Mussolini, who had been imprisoned in the Abruzzo Mountains, was rescued in a spectacular German commando operation.[7] Troops led by the bombastic SS Hauptsturmführer Otto Skorzeny staged the improbable feat—a well-planned raid so dramatic Hollywood might well have scripted it. Mussolini was held captive at the Grand Sasso—an Italian mountaintop ski resort at 2,100m. That should have made his prison inviolate. Nonetheless, in the silence of the late summer afternoon a hundred German paratroopers in wooden gliders boldly descended on the Grand Sasso in broad daylight. Bursting forth from their wooden DFS 230 aircraft, they rapidly over-came the Italian captors—so surprised was the surrendering Italian colonel that he toasted the tall Austrian with a goblet of wine: 'For the victors!'[8]

Within minutes Skorzeny located Mussolini and freed him with a greeting. 'Duce, the Führer has sent me as a token of his loyal friendship!' he shouted. Another frail Fieseler Storch aircraft then landed. In a harrowing take-off, with Skorzeny along, the tiny aircraft with *Il Duce* stuffed inside plummeted off the mountain precipice after the runway ended, only gaining speed through freefall to eventually climb away. Skorzeny himself was shocked to survive, but soon *Il Duce* was delivered to safety, and then later both men flew back to meet Hitler at his headquarters in East Prussia.

So released, Mussolini was to set up a new Italian Socialist Republic from the resort area around Lake Garda. However, in late 1943, the Italian fascist leader was so unpopular with his countrymen that he was assigned a reconnaissance company from the Leibstandarte for protection. Even now, the Leibstandarte Adolf Hitler still drew the missions dictated by Hitler's personal whim: Teddi Wisch was asked to send an escort from his engineer battalion to help Mussolini's wife move to Lake Garda, while another contingent under Himmler's old adjutant, Karl Wolff, was to discreetly locate a villa for Mussolini's mistress a few kilometres away.[9]

Moving down into the Piedmontese section of Italy, Peiper's half-tracked infantry battalion was spread out as an occupation force: his staff and 13th and 14th Companies were in Cuneo under Ehrhard Gührs and Otto Dinse. The 11th Company under Obersturmführer Hans Schmidt was in Mondovi, and Fassano and the 12th Company under Obersturmführer Georg Preuss was in Borgo San Dalmazzo. The worry was to run into the reactionary bands of the Italian army. However, the move was uneventful; there was no resistance. Instead, lots of curious Italian women peered from balconies with kids leaning from street corners to see the German tanks. The skies were clear, and the biggest risk was sunburn. While fodder for the scrapbook, such intrigue was hardly war.

The first ominous news came at 1130 hours on 16 September, when Peiper learned that the barracks at Cuneo were empty, as the Italian soldiers had set off to the hills rather than surrender. He was even more worried to learn that a cache of weapons there had been recently plundered. On the afternoon of 18 September, a stiffly formal Italian lieutenant colonel suddenly appeared at Peiper's headquarters in town with surprising news. The officer said he was the appointed emissary of the Italian Fourth Army. More to the point, he conveyed a threatening message: the Germans must leave Cuneo in the next twenty-four hours or they would be destroyed to a man. Peiper chaffed—such stuff must be nipped in the bud.[10]

The one island of Italian resistance was at the foot of Monte Bisalta near the parish of Boves. Nestled amid the green mountains of Northern Italy, the Piedmontese village of seven thousand was nothing much—the place was famous for its prize bulls and beef—hence the name. Its houses' whitewashed walls and red-tile roofs were nested in a pine-green valley 6.5km south of Cuneo. Even in war, food in the region was plentiful, and farmers gauged this mess nearly over. At the town centre, the Piazza Italia, they met at the Caffe Cernaia to gossip about the war. Italy's second misadventure with Germany appeared near an end. Many in the region were ready to give their uncertain partners in two failed wars a swift kick—good riddance.

Jochen Peiper sensed trouble. In Northern Italy the town of Cuneo was known as 'the wedge'. Built on a high tableland straddling two rivers, the city of fifty thousand had always been a place of military significance. Indeed, it was one bastion Napoleon never conquered, becoming famous as the city of the seven sieges. Even now the place was filled with seventeenth-century barracks, and the conscripts from the region were famous as Alpini—mountain troops. Just like Napoleon had torn down the walls of Cuneo when he first took possession, Peiper too saw this region as a place of latent danger.

As a first order of business, Peiper ordered a sheaf of leaflets printed. Serious reprisals, he warned, would befall anyone aiding the hold-out partisans continuing the fight for the Italian Fourth Army. Luftwaffe planes disgorged the hand bills, which fluttered like butterflies from the skies south of Cuneo.

Domenico Favole was in Cuneo on business when the Germans came motoring across the big bridge into town at noon on 12 September. Everyone knew they would come. And there they were, jockeying an anaemic-looking Italian tank, painted with the German cross, into the crowded Vittorio Emanuele II square in the middle of the city.[11] The sprawling weekend market was completely disrupted as a German convoy pushed aside vegetable stands and merchants. Soon Germans popped out of brand-new Italian cars—some of the appropriated were stylish convertibles. It did not take him long to size up the new Germans. Silver SS lightning bolts adorned their collars, and 'Adolf Hitler' was embroidered on the sleeve stripe of each armband.

From his vantage Favole noticed that everyone seemed to be responding to a young, slender German commander in a carefully pressed uniform. There was also a Northern Italian soldier, obviously now with the Waffen SS, who seemed to have the challenging job of barking out all German statements in the native tongue.[12] Favole overheard their commander ask directions to the Prefetto—Prefect building—in Cuneo. There Peiper got together with General Costantino Salvi, the recently self-designated fascist *governatore* of the province who professed the aim to fully cooperate with the Germans 'so they will enter the town peacefully and in respect for Italian public powers'. Salvi spoke fluent German and offered to help Peiper draft a series of warnings. The first was to direct all the local officials and important business people to go to the Prefettura for a meeting.

The Germans soon settled into the big government building on the Via Roma. The mayor, Antonio Bassignano, and his council sat in the big room, surrounded by murals celebrating the violent past of the city. Favole

171

was there as well. Soon they were addressed by a self-assured young German officer who gave a jarring speech.[13] Standing in the ornately baroque Prefect building, Peiper announced an immediate nightly curfew in Cuneo from eight o'clock at night until six in the morning. He sternly informed everyone that it was his job to disarm the Italian armies still in the region. As such, he demanded that all Italian soldiers must come to surrender their weapons and end the habit of simply putting on civilian clothes and going home. Firearms were to be dropped off at a barracks in town. Italian soldiers were to report to the barracks in town. The mayor and his members said they would see that the word got out.

When Peiper left the Prefect building before dark, Cuneo's face showed an unsubtle change. As always, there was the red, white and green flag of Italy fluttering at a 45-degree angle above the entrance. But now it was joined by the red, white and black of the Nazi *Hakenkreuz*. The curfew, Salvi announced, would go into immediate effect. Peiper departed with Otto Dinse to their upscale home on the fashionable Viale Angeli. Their balcony looked out to the south to the twin peaks of Mount Bisalta and Boves below it. Peiper retired that evening, snug in the knowledge that his banners were now nailed up all over Cuneo:

> Soldiers of the 4th Army will immediately present themselves for complete disarmament at the casern of the 4th Alpine Artillery Regiment in Cuneo. Those not complying with this order will be classified as deserters and will be punished according to the laws of war.
> —The German Commander[14]

Such a notice should suffice. The missing Italian soldiers would report to Otto Dinse.

But the next day nothing happened. No soldiers came to surrender. The designated barracks remained empty and ghost-like. Not a single gun appeared for deposit.[15] Even the mayor made himself scarce, and no one came to even speak with the Germans at the Prefect. All the while soldiers looking to sell or trade their guns frequently approached those living in Cuneo. Other Italian soldiers did as Peiper had forbade—they simply donned civilian garb and stamped home. But thinking of the defiant partisan hero Duccio Galimberti—many took their guns and headed off to the hills to the south before the Valle Vermenagna. Peiper and Dinse sat puzzled in Cuneo.

According to the residents of Boves, an irate Jochen Peiper came to the village of Boves with a fresh ultimatum on the morning of 16 September after the lack of response to his posted request for disarmament. That much we know is true, for Domenico Favole clearly remembered that Saturday. Now there was a new notice:

Italiani!

After the infamous attack against the new Italian governor, *Il Duce*, without precedence and incomprehensible disloyalty, you have betrayed your German allies. In southern Italy some of the divisions of the forces and unity of the Navy have turned arms against their loyal German comrades, even trampling the memory and sacrifice of fallen Italian sons in this war.

The German armed forces found it necessary to quickly disarm the Italian troops and hold them as prisoners of war in holding camps until it is possible to stabilize their new position. Some isolated units and remaining detachments have disbanded, blindly inspired by subversive propaganda. They have fled to the mountains where they devise acts of terror against the population and ally with the resistance, refusing to present themselves at the holding camps. These soldiers have forsaken the civilian population which they have dragged into calamity. They are no longer considered legitimate troops, but live outside of any sort of legitimacy and consequently will be annihilated down to the last man. Any civilians that harbour these partisans will be met with the most severe punishment.

Italians! The Duce is in power again!

Italy's greatest son appeals to the old and trusted fascists to join him once again in the continued fight against England, their mortal enemy, in order to erase the shame of their betrayal. Italians who continue to pursue honour and dignity will accept our invitation to join us and present themselves immediately to the German military authority of Cuneo.

All soldiers of the Italian army must present themselves without delay to the Commandant, in uniform, and with their arms. Any failure to do so would be considered an attack according to the laws of war and those guilty will be transferred to detention camps in Germany.

—The Commander of the Troop of the Province of Cuneo

General PEIPER

Cuneo, 16 September 1943[16]

General Peiper? The real SS Major Peiper wanted to find the mayor of Boves to have a chat.[17] He crossed the big bridge astride the Gesso River and motored into Boves. Arriving along the Corso Trieste along with Otto Dinse, he went straight ahead to the mayor's office in the tower by the

Caffe Roma downtown. He wanted to see Alessandro Gastinelli, the *podestá* supposedly loyal to Mussolini. But he was nowhere to be found. Hearing of the simmering troubles from Cuneo, Gastinelli had fled to Peveragno just to the east.

Peiper aimed to warn Gastinelli not to help the resistance. It was hot that afternoon, and Peiper was decked out in rolled-up short sleeves, with his trousers stuffed in his jack boots. His angular tanned face gleamed in the heat and frustration. With Mayor Gastinelli unavailable, Peiper summoned the most senior official available at the town hall. That brought forth the local land surveyor at the office, Nino Daneile. He knew nothing about administration of the town, Daneile explained; he was in charge of land surveys. Never mind, said Peiper, who demanded a local map. Where were the rebels hiding? Daneile shrugged.

Undaunted, Peiper and Dinse demanded to see the person in charge. Who was next in line after Alessandro Gastinelli? Next to appear from the back room was the mayor's clerk, Cavalier De Carolis, who emerged from an office and seemed to shrink as he approached the Germans standing there. Peiper warned De Carolis of the grave consequences to civilians that would result in the event of any armed uprising. Dinse could see the young clerk was nervous.[18] There was a specific threat—perhaps the definition of 'severe punishment'. The boy passed out after Dinse read him the demands. Teresa Gastinelli's mother—Alessandro's wife— had her run to the bar to fetch some cognac to resuscitate De Carolis. Even when revived, De Carolis stood shaking.

Domenico Favole rose on Saturday, 16 September just like any other day. The September summer sun shone on the dark green hills above Boves as he walked from his home the few steps to the courtyard of his silk factory. It was half past eight. There in the courtyard he was surprised to see two German soldiers in shorts standing with the city clerk. The clerk was shouting loudly that all the male workers of the factory had to go immediately to the Piazza Italia. 'Where was the mayor?' Favole thought, but by the clerk's tone he knew something was seriously wrong. His words had that edge and loudness in Italian that can only mean trouble. 'Come with me,' he told the eight men at his factory. He sent the women workers home.

From the dark-yellow walls of his factory he walked the short distance to the plaza. There in the main square over 300 hundred men from the town were lining up under a cloud-dotted blue sky. Ominously they stood across from the fountain in the Piazza Italia, with its cannon-studded monument commemorating the 224 from the village who had died in the First World War.[19] The Germans were standing before them. Favole recognized the Italian SS man and Peiper, who he had seen in Cuneo the previous Tuesday.

It was warm that afternoon. Several of the Germans were standing about at the Caffé Roma drinking carbonated lemonade drinks. Teresa Gastinelli nervously brought out the sodas, her mother reminding her not to charge the Germans. Someone whispered to Favole that they had been rousing Italian men from their homes since early morning. The senior German officer and others under him were at the Albergo Cernaia across the way, drinking coffee at the wicker tables and chairs. One officer was supervising the line-up. It was Peiper, Favole realized.

Eventually the line of nervous Italian men standing by the monument became still and hesitant. Peiper got up and stood before them, clearing his throat. 'The German army is allied with the Italian army. There is no reason that Italians will become our enemies!' It was strangely quiet in the square as Peiper spoke. To Favole the fear seemed almost palpable. 'All you men will go and convince the others in the hills to return to Cuneo to surrender.' They must go off to the mountains and inform brothers, sons and husbands to lay down arms. 'If you do that and the soldiers surrender,' he said, 'nothing will happen.' Otherwise, Peiper said, he would destroy the town.[20] Even his dire message, translated from German to Italian, had a certain cheerfulness—a dispassionate Prussian tone that somehow intrigued Favole. This German commander, he thought, seemed so young.

The crowd of men from Boves began to disperse, but Favole had a question. By that time Peiper and the other German officers had retired to the wicker tables at the Cernaia for cigarettes and more coffee. Domenico Favole confidently strode over to their table. They were arguing in loud voices, about what Favole did not know. They looked surprised to see an Italian approach their circle, but the visitor nodded his head ever so slightly, pulled out a chair and seated himself. 'Excuse me,' Favole said, introducing himself, 'but I run the silk factory here in town. We produce clothing for Germany.' Peiper looked dismayed—what was the meaning of this guy?

Unable to speak Italian, he began to speak French and even a little English. Favole spoke a little of each too. It was an awkward, halting communication. Even so, he soon had the message across that he wanted his male workers back to reopen his silk factory. Peiper stormed. 'I can't understand why you Italians don't want to fight. You should stay and fight,' he said angrily. 'I fought with the Italians in Russia, and now see what is happening.' Favole changed the subject; he was tempted to talk politics with the German but thought better of it. He was not asking about

175

loyalty, he told the German boss; he merely wanted to open his factory. Peiper complained something loudly to him in German that Favole couldn't understand. It was just before noon.

Presently a German motorcycle with a sidecar zoomed up. Favole got in, its driver clearly indicating they were to go to Favole's workplace. As the factory was less than 200m away, they were soon at its gates. Favole called his factory manager to join them. Together they gave the German a quick tour of the assembly line, which had obviously been shut down in the middle of production. Back at Favole's desk the German quickly scribbled permission for his factory to resume operation. That was all Favole cared about; by three that afternoon, after the long Italian lunch hours, he could resume production. He forgot about Peiper and the Germans. Now life could get back to normal. Meanwhile, Peiper went back to Cuneo and waited for the Italian soldiers to surrender.

The reaction was just like before – nothing.

At nightfall a disgruntled Peiper left Boves with his men. Had he given up? The German morning report was laconic: 'In the area of Boves-Chiusa, south of Cuneo, disarming of resisting Italian units is still proceeding ... The leader of these troops, General Pesenti, escaped when the LSSAH intervened ... numerous camps of escaping troops are being transported away.'[21]

On the morning of 19 September, the flaxen-haired Otto Dinse sent two of his NCOs, Kurt Butenhoff and Klaus Wieczorek, from the motor pool off in a Kübelwagen on a mission to look for some replacement parts in a depot that the Italians had abandoned.[22]

When Dinse's two German men approached the market square of Boves, they were set upon by a truck packed with Italian soldiers and adorned with a fluttering Italian flag. Two Italians on the hood of the truck waved their weapons. 'Halt!'[23] Without a word the two SS men surrendered. Soon they were blindfolded and spirited off to the mountains south of the town and locked into the tower at the school of San Giacomo. Inside the church an effigy of San Giacomo, the sad-faced patron saint of pilgrims, almost appeared to preside over the proceedings while the Italian renegade soldiers dug into the hills around the mountain chapel. The fountain, with its fabled healing waters, bubbled outside the tower where the German soldiers were hidden.

The locals claimed Peiper had provoked the townspeople into taking his men captive by offering them as bait. He did this, they said, so he could use that as a pretence to fire on the town. But Dinse found the accusation ridiculous: 'Peiper's nature was to never sacrifice a man unnecessarily.'[24]

In the meantime, in Boves, those hearing of the rebel seizure gasped in dread. 'Fly away!' cried the owner of the Caffé Roma to her 15-year-old daughter. She was to leave town with her brother. 'Those stupid boys!'[25]

One of these 'boys' was Natale Macario, a native of Boves who was only 20 years old but eager to leave the Cuneo Regiment and join the partisans. Impugning the demands of Peiper, he fled to the hills to reach the others at San Giacomo on 17 September. There, he found himself shocked at their pathetic weaponry. News spread quickly of the two German hostages, but that could only stir the hornets. To fight the Germans, they had only mouldy firearms with few bullets. There was a single cannon with a single shell.[26]

Back in Boves two Italian policemen rushed up to tell the German officer that his two officers were being held hostage in the mountains south of Boves. Dinse quickly passed the word along to his commander. That was completely unacceptable, Peiper said.

Dinse's staff car and another halftrack rattled through the town; he was off to find his missing men. Even focused ahead, he couldn't help but notice the peculiar silence. Boves was like a ghost town. The windows were shuttered and the streets empty. A quiet Italian village? Very strange. Dinse recalled the Italian policeman's refusal to come along. As his little column passed south beyond the town, the climbing mountain road drew between two narrow tree-covered slopes about a kilometre beyond the municipal limits. Unlike the deserted streets of Boves, the steep green hills to the left and right teemed with movement. They rode up to the Tetti Marro just before the little mountain brook and bridge across the Sergent Valley. Dinse pressed binoculars to his eyes. 'A trap … Stop!' he cried. That seemed to be the signal—sudden gunfire.

Dinse yelled for SS Sturmmann Willi Steinmetz to jump from their heavy car and set up a machine gun. He would provide covering fire as they turned around—there was barely enough room to do that. Bullets whizzed, rattled and ricocheted about the vehicle, and the firing grew. Two men of Dinse's group were wounded. Steinmetz, cradling the machine gun, suddenly collapsed, felled by a rifle shot through the head. Dinse was soon on the radio as his men flung smoke grenades to cover their turnabout. An Italian rebel, Domenico Burlando, also fell nearby in the exchange of gunfire.

Peiper's radio crackled. Dinse spoke plainly but quickly, emphasizing his words over the gunfire popping and snapping over the headset. 'I am in a fight with the Italians … I have one killed.' They had been ambushed, he continued, just outside of town. Now they were taking well-aimed fire from both sides of the narrow valley. Dinse said he could use some help. Peiper knew Dinse well: stocky, wiry and tough, he was always understated. That meant he was in big trouble.

The radio blared once again. Dinse said, he had wounded. It was just the sort of thing Peiper hated—losses for little reason. And with that, the stories of what happened at Boves on 19 September 1943 diverge down two irreconcilable paths.[27]

According to the Italians, Peiper showed up in the early afternoon at the Piazza Italia. There was no resistance in Boves, but the Italian witnesses remembered the town being sealed off. The SS commander directed several armoured halftracks to park at the main entrances to the village. Not finding the mayor, Peiper demanded that the local priest, Don Giuseppe Bernardi and an industrial businessman, Antonio Vassallo, go to San Giacomo to demand freedom for his men. The priest, a fine-featured and quiet man clothed in a clerical robe, asked for Peiper's written assurance that if that were done, there would be no action against the town.

Multiple Italian witnesses remembered the same dialogue from Peiper. Seemingly low on patience, he answered the priest with great arrogance: 'The word of honour of one German soldier is worth more than a thousand Italians.'[28] If they succeeded in freeing his men safely, he would spare Boves.

Otherwise, Peiper warned, he would destroy the town.

Chapter 12

Boves

'War begun, hell unchained.'
—Italian Proverb

Soon after Peiper's grave ultimatum to the Italians in Boves, German self-propelled artillery, 'Grille', with 150mm infantry guns mounted on an old Czech tank chassis, began to assemble near the hamlet of Tettmarro. Presently the guns began to fire on the Italian soldiers in the hills—at least where they thought the soldiers were.

Natale Macario was among the rebels. The Germans were shelling the nearby village of Castellar, and in return the village fired its single cannon shell—with no effect at all. While off trying to locate some ammunition to bolster the limited rebel supply, Macario heard the shooting at the Sergent Bridge. What was happening? He had no idea, but the longer he wondered, the more German shells seemed to fall around him.

By 1400 hours Bernardi and Vassallo had fashioned a truce signal out of a broomstick and a white flag. Shortly thereafter the Germans forced Bernardi and Vassallo onto a halftrack to accompany them to the Colla Valley and San Giacomo; Luciano Aldo Dalmasso came along by car. At San Giacomo they were able to convince the Italian soldiers to give up the German captives. Peiper arranged for the priest and Vassallo to be moved to the hills, where they could witness the spectacle of the furiously burning town.

Hoping to heal relations with the Germans, Dalmasso sent for his son, Vittorio Luigi, to help drive back the captured German car that had been taken from the captives. Successful in their mission, Don Bernardi. Vassallo, and both prisoners motored back to Boves after 1500 hours, at which point Dalmasso and his son left. But despite their assistance, the Germans held Bernardi and Vassallo near the memorial at the town centre. And now, they said, Peiper had ordered reprisals.

Later the townspeople charged that Peiper had Vassallo and Bernardi moved down into a building near the town hall, where they were shot in the legs until they fell. Petrol was then poured over the two and they were set ablaze. The next day their charred bodies were found buried in the blackened wreckage of the burned-out house across from the main square at No. 4 Corosu Trieste.[1] Forensic examination showed that the two men had been shot. The dentist identified them as Vassallo and Don Bernardi, the priest.

The Germans began shooting soon after the first SS armoured vehicles appeared in town. By that time most of the inhabitants had fled, but others stayed behind—the old, the ill or the handicapped. According to the Italians, the SS men smashed the doors of houses, sloshed gasoline inside and threw in grenades. Soon the market town burned furiously. Some waited to run until threatened by flames, when they were then shot down while trying to escape. One of the worst incidents involved the young assistant parish priest, Mario Ghibaudo, who had assisted an old woman to flee the flame-engulfed town before stopping to render absolution to a slain elderly man, only to then be shot himself after SS men caught up with him. Another was that of Giovanni Battista Dutto, a 71-year-old grandfather who ran back to his burning house to save his grandson. Emerging from the flames with the crib under one arm, Dutto was shot in the back by a nearby SS sentry. One man, Giacomo Dalmasso, was shot in the neck but survived to become a troublesome witness.[2] One woman, 87-year-old Bo Caterina, died in her burning home rather than leave. The Italians claimed that a total of 350 houses were burned, with twenty-three inhabitants killed.[3] However, the number of burned houses was eventually found to have been somewhat less. Even so, as the SS left at dusk, numerous buildings in the town were engulfed in flames. When Peiper returned to Cuneo he forbade the local fire brigade to go to Boves.

There was even an Italian accusation levelled at Peiper that pre-dated the events at Boves. Supposedly, on 16 to 18 September 1943, Peiper's troops orchestrated the rounding up of Jews who had taken refuge in the region around Cuneo. On 18 September the SS arrested more than 350 Jews in the area.[4] Afterwards the collected Jews were sent to a recently installed German concentration camp for Italian Jews near Borgo San Dalmazzo. Peiper categorically denied any involvement in the arrest of the Jews, even though his unit was the only SS unit in the Cuneo area during that time. Moreover, the 11th Company under Georg Preuss was in the area of Borgo San Dalmazzo, where the concentration camp was set up. Even Peiper admitted as much but claimed that the Italians were holding the Jews captive there.

There was a declaration warning that all 'foreigners' had to report to the Caserne Degli Alpini in Borgo San Dalmazzo or else face being shot. The commander, SS Hauptsturmführer Müller, signed the announcement.[5]

Who were the people being collected at the concentration camp at Borgo San Dalmazzo? All were Jewish. Two of them were Walter Marx and his mother, Johanna. A Jewish refugee from Heilbronn, in May of 1940 his family was ordered by the Germans to leave Luxembourg City for the unoccupied part of France, where they looked to remain in Montpellier until they could immigrate to the United States. That hope ended in 1942, when the French police began cooperating with the German SS in deporting the Jews.

The orders for this had come from on top. On 5 April 1942, Peiper's former boss, Heinrich Himmler, discussed French occupation policy with Hitler over dinner. He declared that 'the best way of settling the French problem would be to carry off every year a certain number of racially healthy children, chosen amongst France's Germanic population, settling the children in German boarding schools'. Hitler responded that the attempts at Germanisation were unimportant to him; culling out the less desirable elements were more important. Six weeks earlier, on 22 February, Hitler had instructed Himmler, 'We shall regain our health only by eliminating the Jew.'[6]

Walter Marx and his family were on the sharp end of Hitler and Himmler's policies. For money, a French woman had agreed to hide the family in the upper floor of her apartment in Montpellier. This was successful for several weeks until one day, in spite of precautions, the French police knocked on the door and demanded to look inside.[7]

The Marx family were sent to the French police station straight off and then released for a time—as Walter's father had special protection, being a member of the Association of Jews in France. Yet that protection waned in November 1942, when the Americans landed in North Africa and the Germans occupied all of France. After that point the Germans began accelerating deportation of the Jews. In February 1943 the French police arrested Walter's father, Ludwig, along with some two thousand Jewish adult males and transported them to Drancy, the large assembly camp near Paris. For the thousands assembled there, their next stop would be the elimination camps. Ludwig Marx was sent to Majdanek in Poland. Although Walter and his mother did not know it, his father was gassed two days after arriving at the camp.

Walter and his mother learned that Jews appeared to be safe in the Italian-occupied area of France around Nice. After the arrest of his father, they decided to flee there, arriving in April 1943 and finding four hundred other Jews seeking safe haven, where they were provided with vacant apartments. They stayed in Saint-Martin-Vésubie, a village wedged high up in the French Alps, close to the Italian border, which eventually housed a thousand Jews who hoped to survive in relative peace.[8] For Walter the place 'was like paradise'. This went on for about five months, although Walter's mother was very stressed from futile efforts to find out what might have happened to her husband. In the summer of 1943 a Jewish refugee showed up at St Martin with a wild story. The dishevelled man claimed to have escaped from Auschwitz just weeks earlier. 'They're burning Jews at this camp!' he insisted at the community centre. 'We didn't believe him,' Marx admitted. 'We thought he was crazy.'[9]

Then, on 8 September 1943, when Italy capitulated to the Allies, the German agents appeared in Nice. Panic set in with the little group. Where to go? Johanna, Walter's mother, spoke with Italian soldiers headed back home. 'Come back with us,' they reasoned. 'By the time we get home the Americans will be there.' Walter and his mother hastily loaded backpacks with food and clothing. 'When Italy signed an armistice with the Allies, the Italian soldiers packed up and retreated across the mountains back to Italy and we followed them expecting to find the Allies on our arrival there.'[10]

The Vésubie Valley is connected to Cuneo by two alpine passes, via winding rocky paths reaching 2,400m. Using these scree-strewn alpine passes, hundreds of Jews, including Walter and his mother, left St Martin on 11 September in search of safety, taking the view that the capitulation of Italian forces made Italy a safe haven for them. Walter and his 43-year-old mother left with hundreds of others. The Jewish refugees began to climb up the Alps in a journey some called a 'biblical exodus'. Without special equipment or provisions, the mountainous climb was exhausting (Walter ditched one suitcase along the way), although the retreating Italian soldiers were kind to the Jewish refugees. Still, after two days the haggard group of Jews debouched into the Gesso Valley, reaching the little Northern Italian village of Borgo San Dalmazzo at the extreme north-western edge of Italy.

Not knowing where to take refuge, they eventually found accommodation in a small hotel, the 'Cavallo Rosso'. It was there, for the first time, that Walter met Maddalena Giraudo, known by her friends as Nella. She was the pretty 23-year-old daughter of the hotel owner, and the two soon became fast friends. As the Italian army had deserted, maybe here Walter and his mother would be safe until war's end.

It was not to be. Although the village of five thousand was filled with sympathetic Italians, Borgo San Dalmazzo soon capitulated at the hands of German troops occupying Italy. On the misty Saturday morning of 18 September, the Germans occupying the area issued a decree. Signed by SS Hauptsturmführer Müller, the 'Comando Germanico', it warned all foreigners to present themselves at the 'Caserna degli Alpini' before 1800 hours that night or else they would be shot together with the people who hid them.[11]

Walter and his mother, along with some 350 other Jews, appeared at the designated location, which had been turned into a makeshift concentration camp, and SS men immediately arrested them.[12] Each prisoner was numbered; Walter was given 225, and his mother was number 226. Although Walter did not know it, the SS men were from the Leibstandarte Adolf Hitler and the battalion of Jochen Peiper.[13] In the distance to the east that day was smoke. Later word came that the Germans had burned one of the villages, Boves, just 4km away.

The SS contingent overseeing the camp was from the 12th Panzer Grenadier Company led by SS Obersturmführer Georg Preuss under Jochen Peiper. The SS men seized the group of Jews, loaded them into trucks and moved them into the makeshift concentration camp at Borgo San Dalmazzo, which had formerly been an Italian military barracks. Soon there were about 350 other Jews held with them. The conditions were bad: dirty straw for a floor, old cots upon which to sleep, rats everywhere and watery soup for sustenance. Although the guards were not brutal, the SS men ordered all the adult males to work, which consisted of loading all material found in the barracks—such as weapons, ammunition, food and clothing—onto trucks to transport the booty to waiting railway cars. At the camp Walter remembered one SS man named Israel—a strange irony.[14] Walter, now a strong young man, volunteered most days as part of the work detail.

During one of these trips the loaded truck on which young Walter was riding ran out of gas, and he, together with seven or eight others, were ordered by the SS guards to push it to the nearby railway car. It was pitch dark that night, and Walter did not see the tank (it was a halftrack) on the left side of the road in the darkness. Being first on the left side, young Walter was caught between the truck and the halftrack. His companions pushed the truck into the halftrack with his body smashed between. He screamed and fainted as his right leg went numb.

Later he awoke in terrible pain while being moved to a local hospital. But his injuries were so severe that they could not treat him there, so on the following day he was moved to a larger hospital. The accident had broken the first lumbar vertebrae, with resulting nerve damage and near paralysis to his right leg.

Young Walter was in the Santa Croce hospital in Cuneo from 16 October 1943 until 30 January 1944. At first his mother was allowed to visit him three times a week under guard. Even more touching, Nella came to visit him every few days as well. While Walter was at the hospital he met another Jewish boy who had been admitted, Michel Marienberg. He had been severely beaten at Borgo San Dalmazzo by an SS guard and nearly died. Although the Germans had been rather civilized while he was at the camp, had things taken a darker turn? Walter did not know it, but the first train shipping Jews to Auschwitz had left the Borgo train station in November. One day at the hospital his mother did not come anymore. When Nella came next, Walter was struck by the painful gaze in her piercing brown eyes. She had come to tell Walter that his mother had been deported from the concentration camp at Borgo, along with 349 others on 21 November.[15] 'All the people there have been shipped away.' They had been loaded into cattle cars, she told him, and they had left in the morning. Walter wept. 'I was 17 years old,' he recalled, 'all alone in a strange land, not even speaking the language.'

Towards the end of January 1944 the director of the hospital stopped by to inform Walter that the local headquarters of the SS was inquiring as to when he would be well enough to be transported; he had told them that Walter would be well enough in a week. Yet, sensing what deportation would mean, the hospital director confided that he had made arrangements with the cardinal in Genoa to hide him. On 30 January Marx hastily left the hospital on crutches and boarded a train. But after reaching Genoa, in a bewildering episode, the cardinal refused to help, perhaps fearing that Walter might be an informant. Confused, Walter reluctantly returned to Borgo to find Nella at the hotel. The young woman put him up for two weeks confined to a hotel room, but said it was far too dangerous: the Germans were coming to the hotel all the time, and someone would sooner or later notice her frequent trips to the room bringing food.

Making the best of a bad situation, Nella arranged to transport young Walter into the mountains, where she suggested he join the Italian resistance. This he did, being given phony identification papers as Giuseppe Barale. He fought with the resistance in the Piedmontese hills above Cuneo, being wounded in one skirmish with the Germans in August 1944. He survived the war as a resistance fighter and even as an undercover interpreter for the Germans. At the end of the conflict Marx returned to France, determined to find his mother and father.

What was the fate of the train with Walter's mother going to Auschwitz? In the end over two hundred Jews were crammed into a sealed railcar and sent to the elimination camp, where they were gassed in December 1943. One woman and a few men of the convoy survived.[16] Neither of Walter's parents survived, and even his grandfather had died while confined at Theresienstadt.[17] Walter eventually immigrated to the United States in November 1946 but lost touch with Nella Giraudo, only to be reunited long after the war.[18]

Was Peiper involved in the fate of those at Borgo San Dalmazzo? A communique to the II SS Panzer Corps looked to be a smoking gun. However, French SS apologist Gilbert Gilles would later write in his memoirs that the Jews had been rounded up not by Peiper but by the Gestapo and placed in a church within sight of their train. Gilles had Peiper comforting the Jews and distributing food and provisions.[19] Later Peiper had told Charles Whiting in an interview that he had helped release a group of Jews from an Italian-run concentration camp simply because the rabbi in charge was a Berliner like himself.[20] Jochen Peiper as the good Samaritan? Hardly.

Indeed, the message from Peiper to II SS Panzer Corps on 20 September said, '216 Jews detained in Borgo San Dalmazzo. Waiting for SD.'[21] Surely the SD would not be waiting on itself. But although Gilles's story seemed totally improbable, the Italian version attributing this decision to Peiper himself seemed exaggerated as well. Within the report to II SS Panzer Corps the officer involved in rounding up the Jews was a certain SS Hauptsturmführer Müller. A member of Peiper's battalion? Peiper and Dinse claimed not. In any case, the Stuttgart proceedings could not conclusively prove Peiper's guilt in that affair, even though no other SS units were in the Cuneo area that could have rounded up the Jews.[22] Moreover, there is a document showing that after Müller, the camp at Borgo San Dalmazzo was turned over to a Lieutenant Georg Proist, a phonetic misspelling for Georg Preuss who was with Peiper.

On 28 September Peiper's men also arrested the Italian Jews of Cuneo, Saluzzo and the surrounding areas, and moved them down to the camp at Borgo San Dalmazzo. But different to the other Jews, the Italian Jews were released at the end of October and were saved from being moved to Auschwitz. However, this happened after Peiper had released the command of the area around Cuneo. The other European Jews were sent in livestock trains and deported via Drancy in France to Auschwitz.[23]

On 23 March 1966, when asked if his unit had anything to do with the arresting of Jews in the area around Cuneo and their deportation to a camp, he said,

> No, that was not our task. I learned much later that the there was a Judenlage in Borgo San Dalmazzo. Shortly after that we left Cuneo to Russia, I went with my military surgeon, I think it was Dr Breme, and I think it might have been Borgo San Dalmazzo and inspected the camp. The camp was guarded by Italian Carabineri. Then I have ordered that the Jews had to get out of there [aus dem Staub machen]. We said to the Carabineri that your job is finished now. My military surgeon then called the circumstances of the camp as a big potential illness outbreak [*seuchenherd*—typical SS term used for ghettos in the East that were then liquidated] and thus was a potential danger. Otherwise, the goings-on in the camp did not affect me, as there was another army officer, Col. Grabinger in Cuneo [who took over].[24]

This statement was totally fabricated. No one at the camp was allowed leave on their own accord; rather, they were transported to Auschwitz. Peiper would later describe his encounters with the Italian Jews at Borgo San Dalmazzo, as noted by a former Wehrmacht captain listening to him speak in 1969 at a meeting of the Knight's Cross Holders in Stuttgart:

> Peiper found a factory area surrounded by Italian soldiers. A camp with imprisoned Jews. Peiper sent the guards home. In the camp he found completely neglected people, starved and desperate. There was nothing like a camp commander. The guards simply had remained. Most of the people were Jews from Berlin. Peiper, himself from Berlin, was devastated by this experience and decided to give these people freedom. He described the scenes of gratitude—how these people got on their knees in front of him and put their arms around him.[25]

And with that point, we take up the account of 19 September from Peiper and his cohorts.

Otto Dinse said he learned from his motor sergeant of an Italian engineer depot near Boves, where they could obtain needed vehicle repair parts. His sergeant and an assistant set off in the morning in a Kübelwagen to the Italian barracks some 5km away. Reaching the marketplace in Boves, they came upon two Italian army trucks loaded with soldiers. 'Stop!' they called. 'You are now prisoners.' They soon found themselves blindfolded, driven into the mountains and locked in a tower. 'At noon, I received a phone call from the Italian police station in Boves,' Dinse remembered, 'telling me that two members of my unit had been taken prisoners by regular Italian troops.' Soon the SS captain spoke with the puzzled policeman standing in Boves at the vehicle abandoned by his missing men. Dinse asked about their whereabouts. They were a little south of the town, the policeman said. They had left in two trucks loaded with noisy Italians brandishing machine guns.[26] Dinse relayed the message to Peiper. Already irritated, Peiper ordered Dinse to go back and retrieve his men.

Dinse sought the return of the prisoners from the mayor of Boves, but the mayor was nowhere to be found. Dinse approached the local Catholic priest, but he also said he could not help because he had no contact with partisan bands sallying from the mountains. The policeman had told him that the priest 'had connections with the partisans'. It seemed clear to Dinse that the renegade Italian bands were in cahoots with the locals. That may have been a fatal error, for it was all too reminiscent of the partisans in Russia. In any case, Dinse knew he could expect little cooperation. When he asked the local *carabinieri* to go with him, he stuttered excuses. 'I did not take the entire matter seriously,' Dinse admitted.

Never mind. With a dozen men in a heavy car and halftrack, Dinse sped through the town heading south. After a kilometre, they observed concealed Italian soldiers darting about the dense woods on the left and right sides of the valley. Some appeared to be trying to work their way around to his rear along the forested hills of the Roca Rina. Just as he ordered a halt, a gunshot rang out. Dinse got Peiper on the transmitter. Peiper called for Dinse's remaining troops and Gühr's 13th Company to immediately saddle up. It would take some time for them to arrive, but Peiper told Dinse that Gühr's company would reach him shortly. Just then a hail of bullets struck as they passed the wooden Sergent Bridge to San Giacomo. They were across from several farmhouses. Where were the bullets coming from? Dinse began to try to turn around in the narrow road, ordering a machine gunner to let loose suppression fire. But the man entrusted with the heavy machine gun was soon cut down as he tried to dismount from the halftrack.

By radio Peiper gave the order to pull back to the south edge of the village until he could come with support from the rest of the battalion. Under fire, Dinse pulled back in great haste, leaving the dead soldier. He waited for more than half an hour under fire.

At this critical juncture the Italian and German versions of the story split completely.[27]

Chapter 13

The Wrong War

'War is the province of chance. In no other sphere of human activity must such a margin be left for this intruder. It increases the uncertainty of every circumstance and deranges the course of events.'

—Von Clausewitz

What was Peiper's version of the story of the otherwise damning events at Boves, Italy, in September 1943?

After one of his men was taken captive, Peiper claimed he quickly mounted a company of Panzer grenadiers into his halftracks in Cuneo. He then waved a platoon of 150mm self-propelled infantry guns—the 'Crickets', or Grille, to follow close behind. Engines roared, and soon the little column rattled towards Boves. However, as they approached the first houses, gunfire swept the road. Civilians, Peiper claimed, were firing from the windows.[1] Soon, there were more shots and even hand grenades from the surrounding hills. Machine gunfire ripped through the open top of the halftrack, banging around on its interior. In his story of the events Peiper claimed his radio operator was killed instantly, another man was wounded and rounds even burned through his tunic. He was not wounded, but Peiper hastily ordered his vehicles to pull back to the edge of town. He had to rely on hand signals; his radio was wrecked. They turned about in the smoke and roared off in disgust.

But how much of Peiper's above story was true? According to the reports of Peiper's own superiors, there was no fighting or anything worth mentioning during the September period in Northern Italy when the Boves incident occurred. 'Nothing to report,' said the war diary of Hugo's Kraas's SS Panzer Grenadier Regiment 2, of which Peiper's unit was a part, a diary that also had nothing to say between 17 and 22 September.[2] In reality, according to the *Deutsche Dienststelle*, or WASt—which maintains records of German war dead—only Steinmetz was killed that

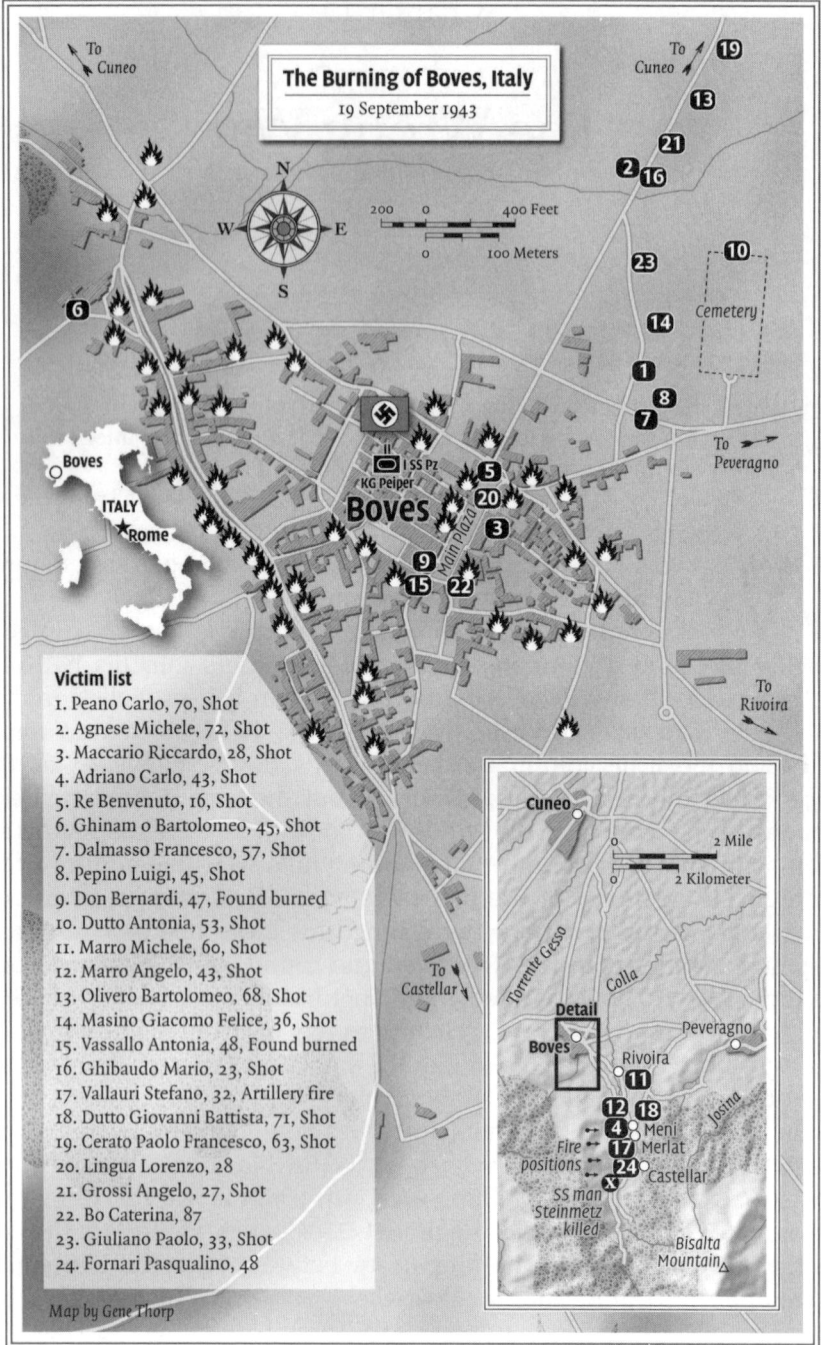

The Burning of Boves, Italy
19 September 1943

Map by Gene Thorp

Victim list

1. Peano Carlo, 70, Shot
2. Agnese Michele, 72, Shot
3. Maccario Riccardo, 28, Shot
4. Adriano Carlo, 43, Shot
5. Re Benvenuto, 16, Shot
6. Ghinam o Bartolomeo, 45, Shot
7. Dalmasso Francesco, 57, Shot
8. Pepino Luigi, 45, Shot
9. Don Bernardi, 47, Found burned
10. Dutto Antonia, 53, Shot
11. Marro Michele, 60, Shot
12. Marro Angelo, 43, Shot
13. Olivero Bartolomeo, 68, Shot
14. Masino Giacomo Felice, 36, Shot
15. Vassallo Antonia, 48, Found burned
16. Ghibaudo Mario, 23, Shot
17. Vallauri Stefano, 32, Artillery fire
18. Dutto Giovanni Battista, 71, Shot
19. Cerato Paolo Francesco, 63, Shot
20. Lingua Lorenzo, 28
21. Grossi Angelo, 27, Shot
22. Bo Caterina, 87
23. Giuliano Paolo, 33, Shot
24. Fornari Pasqualino, 48

day, and the radio operator he claimed to have been killed in Boves was to be found working for Volkswagen after the war.[3] Indeed, when other members of the battalion were interviewed by the state attorney in 1965, they gave a version of the events very different from the version Peiper, Dinse and Gührs had propounded. For instance, SS Mann Josef Schauer, member of the 14th Company, claimed there was no fighting in the village at all:

> To my knowledge I was the very first vehicle; we drove into the small village. I recall it was a certain place, probably the central marketplace. There seemed to be a village hall there and close by a church. By this time, the war was practically over. That meant I was standing with my vehicles for hours there. Other parts of our unit had driven further on to the south in the direction of the mountains. I heard only rumours of the actions. For example, it was said that heavy weapons were ordered to shoot at the resistance positions. On the contrary, in the main plaza, a lot of German vehicles stood around, but I cannot give an exact figure. To be honest, we were much more interested in looking for Italian ice cream than to be worried about the general situation. Boves itself was relatively quiet, hardly any inhabitants were seen … Sometime later, I suddenly noticed a lot of activity in the village. Then I got the news that the village had to be evacuated in order to search all the houses. After that, something must have happened, but I can no longer recall. In any case, it was told that the village had be burned down as a measure for revenge. I also have seen that some of the houses near the marketplace started burning.[4]

Then asked by the state attorney as to whether any German artillery— the *Grillen*—shelled directly into the village, Schauer, responded,

> No, I certainly know that exactly. When we drove into the village, neither side, whether German or Italian, there was no shooting. Outside of the Boves, one could hear the shooting. One also had to hear how the Grillen shot, but into Boves, the Grillen did not shoot. Nor was there machine gun into the village. In no way did the fire in Boves start by German artillery or machine gunfire. I only recall that the starting to burn down the houses was a measure for revenge for the hijacking of the SS men. If the result of the burnings were as big as drawn on that map, I can't recall.

SS Sturmann Joachim Molt was a member of platoon of Heinz Tomhardt's 13th Company. He told a story different from a combat action, claiming that SS men were looting stores:

This action started with the hijacking of two SS men by partisans. For me, it was an anti-partisan action ... We passed through a village; I know today it was Boves. But we were not shot at. Only later the Spitze received some fire ... On the way back, I passed Boves again in my armoured vehicle. While doing this, I observed that some German soldiers carried things out from the different shops. I didn't think that this was correct behaviour. Still I saw no evidence of burning in the town at that time. The village seemed to be empty for me.[5]

SS Sturmann Herbert Exner was a member of the crew of the Grille of Rottenführer Werner Wittenburg, who, according to Peiper and Dinse, was supposedly was involved in shelling Boves:

We shot with our heavy infantry guns into the mountains ... When we drove back, by no means was the village burning ... I have not seen that the village was burning ... I only recall that we shot with our Grille about three rounds. We haven't been with Grille in the village itself, but we went into firing positions at the outskirts of the village.[6]

When asked by the state attorney if they had fired their artillery into the village of Boves, he answered, 'No, there were some houses where we shot, but they were in the mountains up on the ridge.' The town had not been shelled, according to Peiper's own cannoneers?[7] It was as if they described the wrong war.

Contrary to all the stories of Peiper, Dinse, Gührs and the other SS leaders, the state attorney in 1967 wrote the following conclusion: 'By the result of the interrogation, there is no doubt that Boves was set on fire.' Still, they could not open the case because they could not prove that there was a direct order for the mayhem in the Italian town.

In fact, SS Unterscharführer Gerhard Buhr was in Cuneo, but everyone had left—or so he claimed.

When there was the mission in Boves, I drove in spite of my duty desk, I drove in my motorcycle. I drove to the village because I was curious about what was going on. I drove directly into the village. Doing this, I saw our vehicles stood around in the street and the crews were waiting by their vehicles as if bored. When I came to Boves there was no fire anywhere. When I was there I chatted with some SS guys. Everything was quiet. We smoked and had some pleasant conversations.[8]

We must contrast this with Peiper's statement supposedly explaining how civilians would be shot in the village: 'It is very natural that during the ending of such battle situations, it is always possible that there is some shooting on single running persons because there is no time to determine whether this is a combatant or not.'[9] If there were no combatants, there was no stress at the end of a combat action, and the 'unintended' killing of civilians and priests was concentrated in the area around the cemetery and the marketplace. Few seemed to have been running, and those killed appeared to have been executed with an awareness of their age and gender.

Of the twenty-four victims, twenty-three were men, and autopsies showed that only one of the Italians had died from shells or explosions near Castellar. Other than four people, all others were shot by machine pistols, rifles or pistols. Three men were shot at the marketplace; two of them were found with a hand grenade and one was a Carabinieri. Clearly the SS saw them as partisans. As a commander, Peiper was most likely informed and had called for their execution. The 87-year-old woman, in ill health, died from asphyxiation after the SS set her house on fire. In the area of the cemetery, in the north-east part of the village, eleven mostly old men were executed by small arms fire. The circumstances of the death of the eleven old Italians in the area of the cemetery could only be explained by their execution by one of Peiper's units—most likely the engineer platoon of the 14th Company under SS Hauptscharführer Wilhelm Haferstroh, an old fighter in the Leibstandarte.[10]

Meanwhile, the two hijacked soldiers, Wieczorek and Butenhoff, returned to their own unit unharmed. In 1965 Butenhoff claimed that he escaped from the Italian imprisonment on his own, but he provided no details of how he did this. As shown later, Butenhoff's statement not only contradicts other Italian statements, but also was doubted by several other Germans. For example, SS Rottenführer Werner Wittenburg, who was with Peiper's battalion, told investigators:

> The two emissaries, the priest and the mayor were sent to get the imprisoned SS men back. It was said that at first the two Italians had refused to help, but then it was made clear to them that if they continued to refuse, they would be made hostages. Then, both Italians declared to go as emissaries. In Cuneo, I got the information that the priest and the mayor, who went off as emissaries, later died. The circumstances on how that happened is not known to me, and Hscha. Fritz Nürnberger said, 'I think the imprisoned SS men were brought back by the help of Italian emissaries, because there were stories that they were brought with their eyes blindfolded.'[11]

SS man Gerhard Buhr, who had been with Leibstandarte since 1939, had a similar story:

I recall that someone sent an emissary to the partisans. As I recall, our prisoners came back by the help of the emissaries. I think I might recall that the mayor and the priest were used as emissaries. At least there was talk about that. I believe that someone had made a white flag for these persons to bring back our prisoners... I cannot say if there was some shooting at this time or not.[12]

Against this we have Dinse's denouncement: 'There was no agreement with the priest. I wanted from the priest that he would bring back both prisoners and said I would go with him if my security is guaranteed. The priest refused with the statement that he had no connection to the partisans. In my opinion, he did not want to work with me. With that our conversation was over.'[13]

The question as to whether these two men were *parlementaires*, negotiating a ceasefire, would become important in the later legal investigation since the Italian priest, Don Bernardi, and the businessman, Vasallo, were both later murdered. They had brought back the two German prisoners only to be later executed. They were shot, with their bodies later found crumpled and charred on the first floor of the burned-out house next to the marketplace. On the other side, the defence tried to discredit all Italian statements indicating that Vasallo and Bernardi were the ones who brought back the German prisoners.

Then in 1965 came Butenhoff's retraction and a modified statement:

I stick with the story and I swear to it that we were not freed from our imprisonment by any priest or other persons and brought back. If there are named any witnesses from the Italian side that claimed they rescued us, it could not be true. At the end, it was myself who would have been brought back and I wasn't. I came back on my own initiative. After my return, as far as I could see, there were no riots, either in the way that houses were burned or that civilians were shot. I think we can exclude that anything like that happened. After his return, Peiper said to me, 'We are very happy that you are now back. It is not our task to wage a partisan war and let's go home.'[14]

In fact, however, Peiper and his comrades had stressed the picture of a big battle. At Boves they claimed they had lost eight men. According to the German stories, the doctor, Freiderich, had to treat the six to eight who were wounded while under fire in the town square.[15] But was it true? If fact, in spite of the large number of SS men testifying before the investigation, no one could identify any of the half-dozen men who had been supposedly wounded. The great suspicion, to the German investigators, was that they were made up. In fact, the allegation of wounded by SS leaders in Boves had only one reason: to support the idea of a battle that never took place.

In any case, in the SS version of the events, soon they were back up in the green hills above Boves. They were safe, but it was retreat and, worse, before the Italians. Peiper seethed. Here they were—a pointless police action to oversee the orderly defection of their Allies—and now a man from his company was dead. And Italians were doing just what he had asked the mayor not to do.

He found a good position for his self-propelled artillery to set up their guns amid an opening in the trees on one side of the village. His orders showed little emotion—ice cold. Once on the high ground, Peiper helped the box-shaped gun carriages to place Boves in their cross-hairs. Dinse, Gührs and Rudolf Möhrlin stood by as shells were fed to the guns. 'Führer!' Big 15cm shells arced overhead to slam into the tile-roofed nineteenth-century houses. One after another, the buildings exploded and splintered, falling onto the cobble-stoned streets. Some caught fire, and set others alight. Peiper said it was because winds fanned the flames.[16]

Observing through binoculars, Peiper could see both 'uniformed figures running as well as those in civilian clothes' under cover of smoke from the burning houses.[17] But the civilian reference seemed hardly significant. Peiper said Boves's wooden houses easily caught fire in the battle—at least that was the German side of things. In fact, almost all of the houses had an exterior stucco finish. The houses only burned because the interior floors and wooden members of the attic were set ablaze.[18]

In any case, any view from Peiper's position was obscured by the roiling smoke from the blazing buildings. As the guns slammed shells into its streets, he ordered his halftracks to proceed in the usual fashion—full throttle. But when they reached the entrance to Boves, they found nothing but six abandoned artillery guns. Another look through binoculars to the right, and he 'spotted Italian soldiers and civilians disappearing up the mountainside'.

Soon Peiper's column was on the other side of town making contact with Dinse's beleaguered group. At about the same time, the recovery of the body of the dead SS man seemed to be the signal for the Italian gunners up in the hills. Mortar rounds began to fall about Peiper's rescue party. He was soon on the radio directing the Grille to locate the source of the fire and let them have it. Moments later, big shells slammed into the hills before them. In the midst of all the chaos Peiper spied two men waving handkerchiefs just ahead. Closer inspection revealed the two missing men of Dinse's reconnaissance party. They seemed as surprised to be picked up as Peiper's people were to find them. Their guards had run, they said, as soon as the shelling started. They escaped towards the sound of the grinding tracks of the Grille. Yet, heading back through Boves, the lead SPW of Erhard Gührs was again taken under fire in a narrow defile. Once more they had to change directions under cover of smoke grenades. After that, things finally quieted down. Peiper had the gun platoon take over the occupation of Boves while he moved back to Cuneo.

The following day Peiper spoke to General Salvi at the local prefect. Salvi 'expressed the government's deepest regret about the Boves incident'. Of course, Salvi was still a Podestá, reporting to the lame-duck regime of Mussolini. Peiper seemed pleased with the outcome:

> The following day, I sent a company to Peveragno, a town in the region where similar attacks were expected. To my satisfaction, the mayor of that town held considerable influence over his compatriots which had not yet been disarmed. He energetically denounced the segments of the town stirred up by Allied agents and promised to restore order and prevent further incidents … I am of the opinion that our action to free our encircled comrades in Boves nipped in the bud the Italian army's attack on Cuneo … our one-time intervention prevented immeasurable casualties which would have resulted.[19]

But the attack by the Italian Fourth Army was imaginary; the disbanded army did not even exist.[20] Not surprising, the immediate report to II SS Panzer Corps was monotone, saying that up to that time 147,000 Italian prisoners had been taken, but with at least a quarter more evading capture: 'In numerous towns, some of the garrisons avoided disarmament by fleeing … Near Turin, in Cuneo and south of Cuneo, there was some resistance which can now be considered broken … The communist danger is serious … There are guerrillas south of Cuneo, probably mixtures of Italian soldiers, communists and prisoners of war.'[21] Peiper sent in an unremarkable daily report that day—all routine. It made no mention of having one of his men killed, nor did he mention any larger battle.[22] Unlike Peiper's contention, there was no threatened attack on Cuneo and Turin, nor was there any such mention within the II SS Panzer Corps or higher intelligence reports in the Italian theatre represented by Generalfeldmarschal Albert Kesselring and Oberbefehlshaber Süd:

> In the area Cuneo–Boves on 19 September combat action involving partisan groups occurred. Two members of the LSSAH were abducted

by bandits. The first attempt to liberate them failed due to heavy enemy resistance. A reinforced company succeeded in liberating the men after breaking the resistance in Boves and on the road to Castellar. The male population of Boves fled into the mountains, taking small arms. During the fighting the towns of Boves and Castellar were burned down. The supply bases for the bandits were burned down. In almost every burning house munitions exploded. A few bandits were shot dead. Remnants of bandits withdrew into the mountains.[23]

From there, word of the incident filtered back to Generalfeldmarschal Erwin Rommel's headquarters. Army Group B took events seriously, estimating that as many as fifteen thousand Italian soldiers had been recruited into these communist bands—many drawn from the recently dissolved Torino and Isonzo Divisions and calling themselves the 'White Guard'.[24] Rommel issued a stern warning over Italian radio:

> Any sentimental thoughts from German soldiers towards members of the Badoglio gangs wearing the uniforms of our former comrades in arms are completely inappropriate. Any one of these fighting against German soldiers has given up any claim to our mercy and will be treated with the severity that such riffraff deserve when they turn their weapons against their friends.[25]

Peiper's experience at Boves was atypical. Elsewhere the Italians surrendered in droves; by 19 September Army Group B recorded 387,000 peacefully disarmed.[26] Somehow Peiper had managed to find war's hurricane eye.

All night on 19 September Natale Macario watched from San Giacomo as Boves burned below him. It glowed in an unworldly fashion—like embers in a distant fireplace. The town was burning. Meanwhile, German shells kept sporadically dropping around them near San Giacomo. Could Boves be any more dangerous? But most important, Macario was worried sick about his family in Boves. He ducked after another shell. Impulsively, the youth took off on foot in the darkness, avoiding the direct approach on the main road. Macario arrived to find Boves coloured orange and red by the fading flames. Locating his street, his heart dropped when he saw his house among those burned. Yet he was immeasurably relieved when he found his mother and father crouching out in the garden near their home. There were few people in town and no men. Most were hiding in the cellars, and the burning town stank of blackened straw and wood. The boy wanted to help his shaken family, but his mother insisted he return to the hills—the Germans would be back.[27]

While Macario was fleeing once more to the hills in the pre-dawn of 20 September, Domenico Favole was just returning from a business trip to Torino. He took the 407 train to Cuneo early in the morning as he always did to catch some sleep on the way. There were few riders on the train, but he thought nothing of it. Arriving, he located his parked motorbike and set off towards Boves along the path paralleling the Gesso River. He had not gone far when he came upon a large group of people on foot heading the other direction. They recognized him. 'Signore Favole! Don't go to Boves,' one cried out. 'Turn back! You'll be killed!' Favole stopped and asked what they were talking about. Their eyes blazed with fear. 'Don't you know? The Germans are killing everyone there ... Look! The town is burning.'

It was true. From where they stood in the road, they could clearly see the smudge of smoke floating from between the big green hills below Mount Bisalta. Favole said nothing but started his motorbike and sped on. Arriving at Boves, he found the entire town nearly deserted. There were two men shot dead lying in the Piazza Italia, and dozens of homes were still smouldering. His eyes burned, and it was difficult to see or breathe, but there were no Germans. He went to the house of Mayor Gastinelli on the Piazza Garibaldi to find out what had happened. The mayor's wife was there but almost beside herself in panic. 'Where is he?' Favole asked. She would barely open the door: 'He's hiding, of course!'[28]

Favole found Gastinelli in Peveragno. The mayor told him of the horror of the previous day but was not keen to return. Favole shrugged and said he was going back—his factory was there. When Favole biked back to town later that afternoon he still found almost no one, but some of the smoke had cleared. Looking about in a badly burned house on the Coroso Trieste, he found two bodies just inside, so badly burned that they 'looked like logs'. He had no idea who they were. It was only with dental records that he and everyone else learned that the carbonized forms were all that remained of Don Bernardi, the priest, and Antonio Vassallo.

The killings by Peiper's battalion were not the only murders the Leibstandarte Adolf Hitler committed in Italy that September. That the division was following through with the racial policies already announced by Karl Wolff and Dr Harster weeks before—to arrest all Jews—became ever clearer in another killing spree. The incident erupted on the western shores of Lago Maggiore on the edge of the Southern Alps on the same day Peiper was burning Boves. Between 17 and 24 September

1943, SS men of the 1st Battalion, SS Panzer Grenadier Regiment 2, (Peiper's sister battalion) arrested several Jewish families—about fifty men, women and children in the resort area of Lago Maggorie.[29] On 19 September SS leader Hauptsturmführer Hans Röhwer, who Peiper knew well, seems to have decided to murder the Jews. With its headquarters in Baveno, the 1st Battalion occupied the luxurious villas around the lake. Even before the meeting, Röhwer, with the other SS men, had gone on a drunken rampage, destroying parts of their Italian villa and raping a woman there.[30] Röhwer and his men—all fighters from the Eastern Front—knew what was expected after the briefing on 19 September.[31]

The next day members of the battalion killed fifty-four Jews in the villages around Lago Maggoire in Baveno, Meina and Arona.[32] Some victims were brutally murdered. In the basement of one home a family of three members were killed and then incinerated in the home furnace. Other victims had their hands tied before being thrown into the lake to drown. So hideous were the crimes that the local Italians in that tourist locale would demand justice after the war.

When Generalfeldmarschal Erwin Rommel was informed of the atrocity in 1943, he was deeply shocked. It was the first time he was confronted directly with the murder of the Jews. When his son Manfred told him during his next holiday that he wanted to volunteer with the SS, Rommel still remembered the incident with disgust. He forcefully forbade his son's intentions to join the SS. 'No further questions about that', he said. Not only had Peiper made sure that 'a bad reputation' was lived up to in Italy, but the entire Leibstandarte Adolf Hitler had demonstrated similar infamy.

Nor was Lago Maggoire the end of the war crimes associated with the Leibstandarte that autumn. On 13 September 1943 Himmler sent another *Juden experten*, SS Gruppenführer Odilo Globocnik—'Globus'—to Trieste in Italy to assist with the round-up of the Jews in the Adriatic Peninsula.[33] Between 2 and 11 October 1943, under Globus's direction, dozens of civilians were killed in anti-partisan actions by the battalions of SS Obersturmbannführer Albert Frey's Panzer Grenadier Regiment 1 operating around Istria.[34]

Still, near Cuneo, as autumn wore on, Boves continued as the locus of Italian resistance in north-western Italy. There had been many brave actions against the Germans at year's end.[35] On the last day of 1943 and the first three days of 1944 a large uprising of resistance fighters in Boves was put down only after the Germans torched a further five hundred houses and killed another 157 'partisans'. Those following did more damage than when Peiper was there. After the war the town was widely admired as the 'cradle of resistance' to Nazi Germany. And so, on 23 September 1961, Boves received the Gold Medal for Civil Valor. Recalling the actions of 19 September 1943, the president of the minister's cabinet, Amintore Fanfani, issued the honour directly.[36]

Was Boves a war crime? After the war Peiper protested that Boves had been 'not a massacre, but a battle'.[37] Dinse further stated that 'if civilians were killed in Boves, then this happened only in combat operations'. He claimed to know nothing of the killing of two alleged Italian parliamentarians. Yet even with the conflicting accounts, Peiper and his men did not come off guiltless. There were clear indications of atrocities committed by Peiper's command—the sort of thing that dogged the Leibstandarte over the years.[38]

In any case, Peiper and his men did not remain long in Italy after the mess at Boves. In the beginning of October the battalion was sent from Cuneo to Alessandria, where new personnel boiled out of boxcars and training resumed. Unofficially, the men of the division, like Peiper, were still on vacation—enjoying ice cream, pasta, hunting and Italian sports cars. If ever there had been worries about any combat in Italy, such had long faded. On 22 October the Leibstandarte was officially designated a Panzer division—something of a formality, as the tanks comprising a Panzer regiment had been with them now for over a month.[39] There was also time to take care of administrative stuff—proposals for combat badges and decorations. Peiper now had the close-combat badge in bronze and silver as well as the tank destruction badge for his adventures at Kursk.

Peiper took the opportunity to catch up on correspondence and write to his old family friend and Himmler's mistress, Hedwig 'Bunny' Potthast. With the threat of bombs, Hedwig had moved out from Berlin to Brückenthin, some distance from the SS clinic at Hohenlychen. There she and Himmler's son, Helge, stayed near Oswald and Eleonore Pohl at the palatial Comthurey estate. As the business administrator of the concentration camp system, Pohl was now indescribably rich. Life at Comthurey was lived as if they were Prussian nobility. The perfectly manicured yards, tree-lined lakes and herb gardens were kept in immaculate condition by more than 150 women prisoners who constantly toiled there from nearby Ravensbrück Concentration Camp. As Himmler's lover and mother of his son, Hedwig was a kept woman; an Estonian governess, Johanna Alber, helped take care of the house, and they wanted for nothing. Himmler himself would periodically visit Hedwig's quarters at the Brückenthiner Jägerhaus dressed in civilian clothes and posing as a college professor. When he came, Himmler and his mistress would often take walks on the banks of the scenic Großer Gadowsees Lake.

Meanwhile, even in war, Peiper, too, was living the *viva loca* in Italy:[40]

17 October 1943

My dear Häschen:

It is Sunday, once again! I sit in my robber-baron castle, look through the bull's-eye panes into the grey October sky, and think very dearly of you. Your last letter made me very happy, because I read in it that I had not been totally forgotten.

Time flies! Your little Helge by now runs babbling behind his Mami. I cannot yet imagine it—just like Hinrich! Why don't you send me a more recent photo. I am immensely happy about the increase of our family being under way and grateful. Let us hope that everything will turn out well!

While you at home are struggling with the present-day shortages, I am here leading the lazy life of a master. Thinking about the severely struggling comrades on the Eastern Front, one sometimes feels really bad. My most beautiful leisure-time activity is flying. I had a captured pilot instruct me for five days. Now I have already thirty glorious solo flights behind me. Besides, I am part-time owner of a wonderful horse and a racing car. Somehow, one must be able to keep your head for the long run.

Despite that, I am aiming for it. If one ever will get used to living in orderly circumstances? Occasionally, certain doubts arise! Above all, when one observes the moral conduct of comrades in high places. I am getting grey and old and am beginning to muse! How are you spending your long days? Because of K.H.'s new office, there will be even less time available than before. I am enjoying with you two this visible success, all the inspiring work. I hope he can find upright, honourable and believing co-workers, so that he will not be so alone in this immensely difficult time. I constantly think of the time, during which I was permitted to be with him! The longer the distance in time, the more one notices how much one absorbed knowledge that is giving direction for the entire life. Also in this respect, insight arrives, as one grows older! I am very happy about Sigurd's new alternative quarters. Too bad that you have now rowed physically so far from each other. I always imagined it to be so beautiful. What will become of us, nobody knows. Nothing is harder to endure than a series of good days. I think we are going to celebrate Christmas again in our second heaven.

Please write to me a small wish list. One can get quite a lot around here. The big problem is the transport, because almost all small packages are opened and plundered! Now, for today very heartfelt greetings for you. This letter, please, is just for you!

    Wishing for you and for your two men all the best and beautiful, I am always

    Your faithful Jochen.[41]

The delivery of winter clothing was a sure sign of their destination— their 'second heaven' where Peiper ventured they would spend Russian holidays. On 26 October the tanks and Peiper's halftracks were all loaded up on the trains once more. Whistles blared as they headed towards St Pölten. They were gone from Italy, never to return. For his part, Peiper would be careful to never again set foot in that land.

Back at Boves, Domenico Favole was grateful for personal blessings. Although he never forgot his meeting with Peiper on 16 September 1943, he harboured no ill feelings. Even so, he could not rid his mind of the vision of the charred body of Antonio Vassallo in the burned-out house at No. 4 Coroso Trieste. Knowing his position within the town's social strata—and the German awareness of it—he felt quite sure that had he not been in Torino, he would have died in the ashes like Vassallo. He had been unafraid of the Germans—some thought brazen. 'I saw no reason to be afraid. They were young; I had a business.' But he was not harmed, nor was anyone who had worked for him. And with hundreds of homes torched, both his own home and his silk factory were untouched in the violent upheavals in Boves either of 19 September nor later in December. So moved, he erected a large stone monument to the grace of the Mother Mary that still stands just off the Piazza Italia.

It was important, Domenico Favole pledged, that no one forget those days.[42]

Chapter 14

Panzer Leader

'If the tanks succeed, then victory follows.'
—General Heinz Guderian

Russia again. Since the Leibstandarte's exodus the previous summer, German fortunes on the Eastern Front had plummeted once more. In August the Russians had launched a powerful summer offensive, and von Manstein's Army Group South was thrown back violently. Although boasting a paper strength of forty-two divisions, many could barely count a thousand rifles, and there were not even a hundred tanks in the entire command. By September's end the Soviet advance was irresistible, and Kharkov fell once more. By mid-1944 a million Germans would have died there—as many as the British had lost in the entire First World War. Many more Russians fell. It was a bloodbath beyond comprehension.

On 1 November 1943, Soviet counterattacks reached the west bank of the Dnieper River, one at Dnepropetrovsk and the other south of Kiev. Three weeks later the Ukrainian armies, with two expanding pincers, threatened to engulf the 1st Panzer Army. Generalfeldmarschal Erich von Manstein met with Hitler and pleaded with him for the reassignment of the 1st Panzer and 1st SS Panzer Division to meet the developing crisis. Von Manstein warned that without an immediate riposte, Army Group South was doomed. Faced with impending disaster, Hitler reluctantly agreed.[1]

Meanwhile, the transfer of the new SS Panzer Division was marked by paralyzing disorder, with its tracked elements being moved by rail and the wheeled portions moving by roads. The I Battalion of the new Panzer Regiment was awaiting their new heavy tanks from the Magdeburg depot when orders arrived directly from the Führer's headquarters: the Panthers were to rush to the front, 'regardless of the state of the new

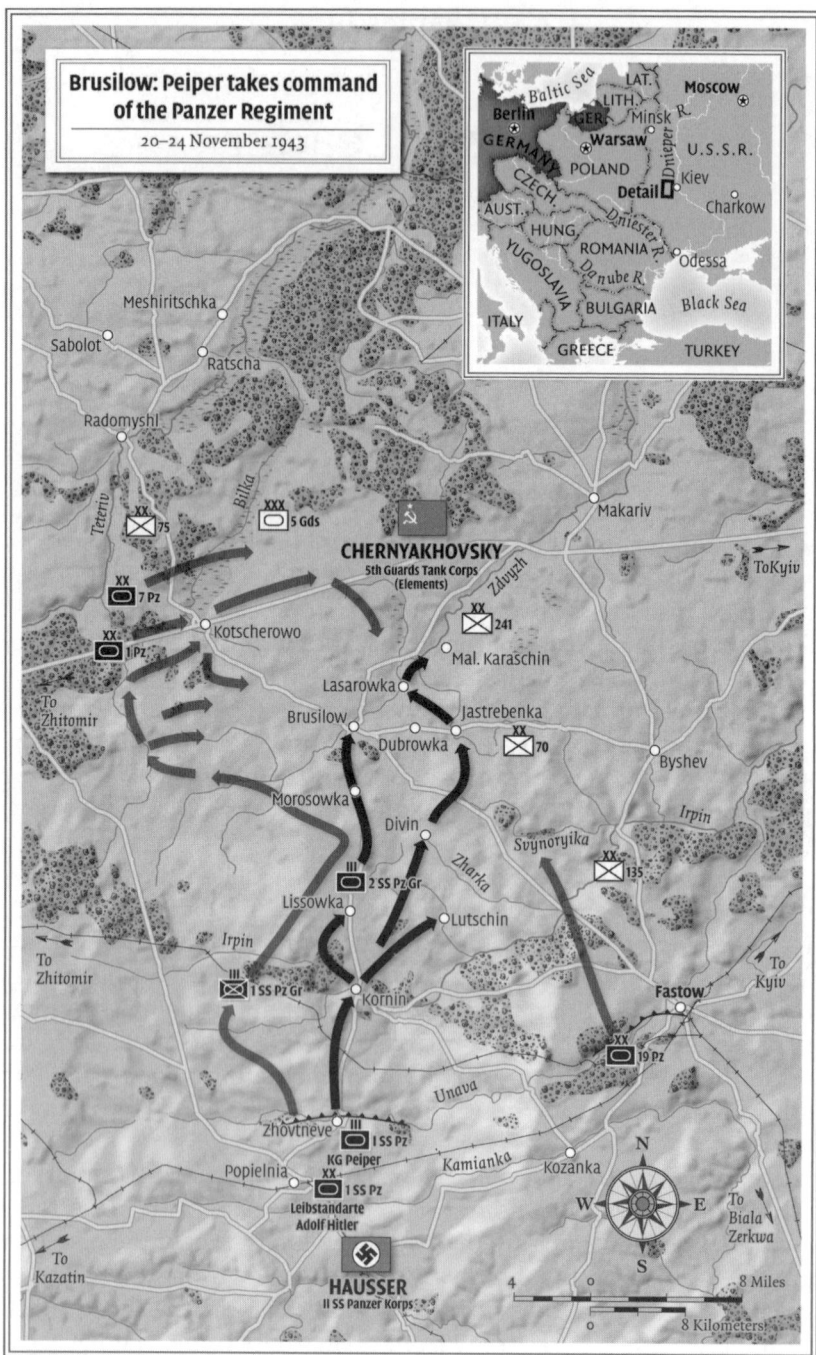

**Brusilow: Peiper takes command
of the Panzer Regiment**
20–24 November 1943

Moscow

Baltic Sea
LAT.
LITH.
Berlin
GER.
Minsk R.
GERMANY
Warsaw
U.S.S.R.
CZECH.
POLAND
Dnieper R.
Detail
Kiev
AUST.
Charkow
Dniester R.
HUNG.
ROMANIA
Danube R.
Odessa
YUGOSLAVIA
ITALY
BULGARIA
Black Sea
GREECE
TURKEY

Meshiritschka

Sabolot
Ratscha

Radomyshl

Teteriv

Billa

XX
75

XXX
5 Gds

CHERNYAKHOVSKY
5th Guards Tank Corps
(Elements)

Makariv

To Kyiv

XX
7 Pz

Kotscherowo

Zdvyzh

XX
241

XX
1 Pz

Mal. Karaschin

Lasarowka

To
Zhitomir

Brusilow

Dubrowka

Jastrebenka

Byshev

XX
70

Irpin

Morosowka

Divin

XX
135

Svynoryika

Zharka

III
2 SS Pz Gr

Lissowka

Lutschin

Irpin

To
Zhitomir

III
1 SS Pz Gr

Kornin

Fastow

To
Kyiv

XX
19 Pz

Unava

Zhovtneve

III
1 SS Pz

KG Peiper

Kamianka

Kozanka

Popielnia

XX
1 SS Pz

Leibstandarte
Adolf Hitler

N

W   E

S

To
Biala
Zerkwa

To
Kazatin

HAUSSER
II SS Panzer Korps

4   0   8 Miles

0   8 Kilometers

equipment'. Hitler's direct order said nothing about where they would end up: '[I]t contained the remarkable instruction that the battalion would probably go into action directly from the rail flat cars against Russian tanks which had broken through! ... During the voyage, rumours and gossip made it impossible to gain a clear view of the facts on our mission.'[2]

They arrived in Russia helter-skelter, with the trucks coming first. Hans Gruhle and the tanks of the Panzer regiment hastily assembled in Kazatin. The atmosphere was depressing and cold, with snow-packed roads under dark skies. Since the Russian offensives that summer a new and cruel aspect now flourished: neither side was taking prisoners. And that was not all. Himmler was quick to remind everyone that the Russian army was known to largely live off the land during its advance in a manner similar to his historical fascination, Genghis Khan. Now forced to relinquish long-held zones, Hitler ordered his generals to torch anything of value: crops, cattle, food stocks, housing, utilities and machinery—all was to be utterly destroyed. He called it 'scorched earth' and von Manstein obeyed.[3]

With miserable weather, Luftwaffe reconnaissance vanished. Somehow the Russians had secretly concentrated an entire tank army in the supposedly impassable marshland north of Kiev. On 3 November the Soviet forces of Lieutenant General Vatutin's First Ukrainian Front flattened the Nazi defences north of the Ukrainian city and, within three days, had routed its defenders. Responding to the emergency, the Leibstandarte was sent off to the 4th Panzer Army and the XLVIII Panzer Corps. But that move had scattered their resources pell-mell.

Amid the confusion, Kiev fell to the Soviets at 0400 hours on 6 November. The big man of that day was Nikita Sergeyevich Khrushchev. The stocky party chief of the Ukraine entered the city adorned in a general's uniform and was cheered from the streets as its liberator. He arrived just in time for the annual celebration of the Russian revolution. He waved from tanks of the 3rd Guard Tank Army as they clattered down the Khreshchatyk, Kiev's main boulevard. Soon the Russian tanks had taken the town of Fastow, through which all the local German supply lines ran. Precious Nazi trains and railcars fell into Russian hands. For the Germans it was a logistical disaster.[4]

The Russians relished the German catastrophe. In Moscow the eviction of the Germans from Kiev was celebrated with a gleeful fireworks display. On 7 November the Soviet Foreign Minister Vyacheslav Molotov hosted a lavish party where the vodka was so plentiful that the British ambassador fell face first onto the banquet table. The party sparkled with opulence—jewels and furs and Russian high society, with generals in weighty medal-studded uniforms. There was even a guest appearance from the great Russian classical composer Dimitri Shostakovich. Endless toasts were made to victory, with the result that an exuberant Molotov had to be supported later in the evening as he encouraged his guests to raise their glasses once more.[5]

They had reason to celebrate. The Russians were surging so rapidly on both sides of Kiev that they controlled many of the planned detraining points of Hitler's namesake Panzer division. The 1st Company of SS Panzer Grenadier Regiment 2 was shipped to the wrong place, only to have to fight while unloading; Peiper's old buddy from France, Jupp Diefenthal, was badly wounded in the melee. Other companies met with disaster, detraining right into encirclement by Russian tanks at Popielnia. T-34s covered with Soviet soldiers captured most of the 9th Company. One German hiding in a potato field watched Russian soldiers execute his comrades with shots to the back of the neck. At least three SS men shot themselves rather than be captured.[6]

By 10 November the tanks of the Panzer regiment had assembled in snow-packed Kazatin and prepared to advance on Fastow. Hans Gruhle, in charge of the heavy tanks, worried about the entire enterprise. The land was swampy, and the clay-lined ditches stood in slush and water. The sludgy roads were nearly impassable, the few stone bridges were guarded and the rickety wooden ones would hardly carry a tank. And no supply train was safe from sudden night attacks from partisans. Then there was the weather, 'a medley of fog, showers, rain and snow with the mud resembling a thick paste'. Gruhle was suspicious of the native population; many 'women, children and greybeards' were detained and interrogated.[7]

When the tank attack set out at 0600 hours on 11 November under Sturmbannführer Herbert Kuhlmann, the wheeled elements immediately sank down to their hubs. From there the tanks moved alone. At 1500 hours, the Panzers ran into Russian T-34s peering out of the fog and quickly shot them up before being stopped by a cluster of anti-tank guns and dwindling fuel supplies. Regardless, Kampfgruppe Kuhlmann attacked the next morning and routed the enemy in a wild tank shoot-out. The Panther battalion lost nine of their number to claim twenty-four of the enemy. Later, on the afternoon of 12 November, the Panzers captured Kozanka and, for the rest of the night, battled Russian tanks beyond that place. Soon Gruhle and Kampfgruppe Kuhlmann linked up the 25th Panzer Division. But there, German commanders halted the advance when word arrived that the Russians had broken through west of Kiev. The tanks were to hand over the won territory to the 25th Panzer

206

Division and swing north-west to seize and block the Zhitomir–Kiev highway.

This stroke was not unexpected. The highway from Kiev to Zhitomir was one of the few real highways in the region—more than 10m wide, paved and with excellent bridges. Accordingly, the Soviets put up a big fight near Kotscherowo to protect it for their own advance. The Germans found that the area was laced with the wooden-frame mines that were difficult to detect and left the stricken tanks crippled before Russian thickets of anti-tank guns eager to finish them off. By the time the Panzer regiment seized the highway on 18 November, they had lost sixty of the eighty Panzers with which they had started the operation.[8] Any retreat meant large losses without the possibility of salvage.[9]

General Hermann Balck, in charge of XLVIII Panzer Corps, and his chief of staff, Oberst F.W. von Mellenthin, outlined their task. The reinforced Panzer corps was to strike deep into of the flank of the 38th Soviet Army and smash their bridgehead on the west bank of the Dnieper River, where they would surround Vatutin's army. However, General Erhard Raus, the commander of the 4th Panzer Army, thought this course was foolhardy and settled instead for a more modest blow to recoup Zhitomir. Balck disagreed but was overruled.[10] The Leibstandarte would be the main assault spearhead along with the 1st Panzer Division of the army. Due to assembly problems, the division was split up, with two battle groups hurled directly into combat as they arrived.

Peiper was lost in the rail delays and did not reach the front with his battalion until late on the 14 November. Even then he announced his arrival at the Biala Zerkwa rail station with only his heavy company of halftracks. However, the gravity of the events thrust his available forces quickly into the fire. On 16 November Peiper's infantry-laden halftracks sped forward, paced by ten Tigers of the heavy 13th Company. Otto Dinse was in command as they headed across the frozen plains from Lisowka towards Brusilow. Reports had Zhitomir occupied by drunken troops of the 1st Guards Cavalry Corps, who revelled in the seized liquor stores of the 4th Panzer Army. That advantage notwithstanding, the German counterattack achieved complete surprise, and soon the Leibstandarte reached the Kiev–Zhitomir railway, with the Russian cavalry falling back in disarray towards Kiev.[11] Paced by a group of five Tigers, Lutschin was taken mid-afternoon on 17 November by Kampfgruppe Dinse, knocking out five T-34s.[12]

The stage was now prepared for the final advance on Brusilow to close the pocket. By 18 November, however, the Russians had recovered their balance. When the II Panzer Battalion advanced on Morosowka with a

Mk IV under SS Oberscharführer Hans Siptrott in the lead, the Soviets allowed the Panzer to edge the first hits before unleashing a deadly fire.[13] Characteristically, Siptrott charged recklessly forward, ignoring one blow to his tank, blasting down two anti-tank guns and running over three more by the time he routed the enemy at the entrance to the village. On 19 November Peiper was again on the move, this time punching through to the Biala Zerkwa rail station in a storm of cold rain.[14] Just in time, he relieved Otto Dinse, who had been fighting alone in that sector with his company and a few Tigers. Siptrott was busy, too: during the night of 19 November the Soviets launched a surprise attack to regain Morosowka. Upon taking Russian fire, Siptrott lofted a flare and, with the battlefield so illuminated, shot down three T-34s. So rebuked, the Russians pulled back.[15]

Attempting to capitalize on the initial progress, on 20 November the Leibstandarte launched a two-pronged assault to eradicate the Russian concentration around Brusilow. Now with his entire battalion, Peiper and the Tiger Company sloshed slowly forward, with tank trenches and quagmire hindering further progress. One German tank attempted to use a ford but was mired down to its turret; the rescue took two days' work from two 42-ton special towing vehicles. The Leibstandarte were stuck fast just west of Brusilow. And again the Soviet counterattacked in desperation from around Divin. During the action SS Obersturmbann-führer Schönberger attempted to coordinate the assault from his command post in the trenches:

> In the morning of 19 November, the 25th Panzer Division is relieving our tanks. We, too, receive a day of rest. We have a lot of work getting the tanks ready, because the Panzer regiment is supposed to go into action again. But things happened differently. Before we get ourselves ready for new action, we receive a surprise attack by a Stalin organ, as we call the Russian rocket launchers, which, mounted on trucks, have great mobility. While we remain unhurt in our slit trenches, our regimental commander Georg Schönberger was so severely wounded by a grenade splinter that he died right there.[16]

It was just after noon on 20 November. Although Peiper's attack against Brusilow sputtered to a halt in the rain and fog, Wisch immediately installed him as the new leader of the Panzer regiment.[17] Fritz Kosmehl was in the tank that carried the Panzer regiment leader:

> We are shocked. Our quiet, thoughtful commander [Schönberger] was not really well liked, but was respected for his circumspection

concerning men and material. Whom are we going to get? It is going to be Sturmbannführer Jochen Peiper, who until now commanded the rapidly advancing SPW battalion. We had a dark foreboding because the adjustment from this idea of a courageous cavalry attack to tank tactics may not proceed without serious consequences.[18]

It was a surprising move. Why had they not chosen Martin Gross, the experienced commander of the II Panzer Battalion, or a seasoned tank man like Herbert Kuhlmann of the I Battalion? The answer likely lay with Peiper's close relationship with Wisch and Wisch's perception that Schönberger had been too timid with the tanks.[19] Peiper was more than junior for the post.

Peiper, however, was also known for a flagrantly audacious style of warfare. The word *cautious* did not exist in the Peiper lexicon. 'He is a leader of captivating impetus,' Wisch emphasized as he recommended that the 28-year-old immediately be promoted to Obersturmbannführer:

He is a modest, thoughtful and energetic personality. As commander of the SPW battalion, he demonstrated intelligent thinking, and during fast, nimble advances, he exploited every opportunity to the advantage of the division. This special gift for grasping and exploiting a favourable situation, as well as his toughness during counterattack and experience in leading combat deep inside the enemy main battle line as well as behind enemy lines, make him especially suitable to be the commander of the tank regiment.[20]

The enlisted men who came under his new leadership looked askance; the old hands such as Gross and Kuhlmann were slighted. Meanwhile, in the echelons above, the chief of staff of the XLVIII Panzer Corps worried that 'it was the first time of the war that this famous division had failed to gain its objective'.[21] Von Mellenthin's concern was real— the Leibstandarte had been stopped just about everywhere. The Russians were fighting as if they knew they had the upper hand. Taking stock, Peiper found his new tank command with just nineteen Mk IVs, eleven Panthers and five Tigers. Many were shot up and others befouled in the muddy quagmire.[22] Now in the third year of the war in the East, the concentration of hundreds of Russian anti-tank guns scattered about the landscape and camouflaged in every haystack and hollow transformed the armoured battle. Ace tankers, like Michael Wittmann, professed to no longer fear T-34s. 'Tanks are important,' he said, 'but the anti-tank guns are doubly so.'[23]

Given the opportunity, Peiper immediately reorganized the tank command. Even if these horses were cold-bloods, Peiper planned a much more aggressive use of the Panzer arm: more attacks, faster assaults at full speed, more night operations and all in concert with his old halftrack battalion, now entrusted to the iron will of Paul Guhl. Would it work?

His first chance to try this out came just after noon on 23 November. The new commander led Panzer Group Peiper, including his old SPW battalion, the Mk IVs of his tank regiment and the four serviceable Tigers of the heavy company. They were pushing to close the Brusilow pocket, advancing towards the thatched roofs of Dubrowka. He put Oberscharführer Hans Siptrott, his workhorse Panzer man, in the lead Mk IV. Even as the miserable rains continued, Peiper had the tanks charge out of a forest south-west of Jastrebenka and throttle down a slope at full speed towards Lasarowka. From the tanker's hatch Siptrott and the others could see the Russians fleeing, but trouble lay beyond.

As they debouched from cover, an unseen brace of anti-tank guns shot up six Panzers, looking for a place to cross the Sdvish River. Siptrott exchanged fire, destroying one of the 7.62cm cannon just before his own tank was hit. Inside the stricken Panzer, even with two of his men wounded, Siptrott ordered the driver forward full throttle. In the middle of the road just before Dubrowka stood the last anti-tank gun. Siptrott's Mk IV roared forward, the tank now on fire and charging, with the gun crew frantically readying to shoot down the crazed tank.[24] In a confusing final moment the Russian crew fled their weapon just before Siptrott's tank crushed the gun and clattered on to open the road into the little town. The rest of the Panzers followed behind, but fifteen armored vehicles had been shot down.[25] Even Peiper's own tank had been hit.

The next day Peiper managed to form a small bridgehead at noon, but did so while sloshing through the rain and mud, running into the 'worst possible road conditions that made a concerted march movement impossible'.[26] Worse, attempting to move beyond Starizkaja, they ran into another thicket of anti-tank guns on Hill 185, with fire so intense that even Peiper called off the attack.[27] A pack of T-34s charged the bridgehead from Mal Karaschin. Six more Panzers lay smoking with down-turned guns on the snow-covered plain. The SPW battalion suffered, too. One of Peiper's cronies, Wolff, was shot through the thigh and only prevented the surgeons from amputating his right leg by threatening a stretcher bearer with his pistol.[28] 'Heavy losses to our own tanks,' penned the divisional chief of staff at the end of the day.[29]

Fritz Kosmehl and Otto Becker heard about Peiper's first disastrous actions—their own tank was out for maintenance with a damaged transmission gear. Fritz Kosmehl said,

> Already the next day we hear the news that Peiper, in the adjutant's tank stormed so far ahead that it received an anti-tank gun hit ... the driver and the radioman were seriously injured ... At first we mistakenly heard they were dead. If the transmission gear had not been damaged, we would now have a spot on the divisional honour roll plaque ... During the second attack that Peiper makes in the Ordnance officer tank, the same thing happens.[30]

Later their tank was repaired, and they were called to regimental headquarters:

> We finally had arrived at the destination ... Sturmbannführer Jochen Peiper is in an operations meeting with the battalion and company commanders. He orders us to enter. That is when we see him for the first time; he is exactly how I had imagined him. He looks incredibly young, yet one cannot discern his age from his dominating face. In the first moments, I see toughness, clear features and very penetrating eyes. I can't determine their colour. He looks up and down silently, while we are at attention. 'Who is Becker?' he asks. When my friend answers, he announces. 'Tomorrow morning at 8 o'clock, the command tank is to stand ready for combat in front of my door. In case this shouldn't happen, you can prepare yourself for the probation company! Dismissed!' We stumbled out and looked at each other with a depressed look.[31]

The next morning it was the turn of Becker and Kosmehl to go into combat with their new hell-for-leather commander, Jochen Peiper. They were clearly worried:

> When Peiper entered the tank, his demeanour was correct and charming; no questions or asides about past events. He tossed me a box of 100 cigarettes and explained: 'For everybody—and I always get a lit one!' We drove to the assembly area. On the way we met a man by himself. He immediately ordered us to stop and asked the man for name, unit, and orders. It was obvious that he did not tolerate shirking. Towards noon we arrived at the attacking company, with which we were supposed to drive. He and Ostuf. Jahn left us—and we longingly sniffed the smell of the field kitchen. Suddenly, Peiper appeared, carrying three ration kits and bringing lunch for us. We were simply perplexed,

because something like that we did not know from our old commander. When I still rode with him in an armoured reconnaissance vehicle, we did not get warm food for days on end.

Surely, Peiper won our hearts by storm; we sensed what comradeship meant to him. It had been demonstrated in the future again and again, because he did not demand more from his people than he was prepared to do himself. However, he always demanded from his non-commissioned and commissioned officers effort that went far beyond that of enlisted personnel. During our first mission, we broke through the enemy lines and operated in the Russian communications zone. We were along a railway embankment and came under mortar fire. As we tried to leave this position and Becker started the engine, it did not start. We have had heavy Morse and voice radio traffic and the battery went on strike. Peiper ordered me to get out and operate the flywheel starter by hand. Open the hatch—we rode a Mark IV—and get out. Rip the crank from its mounting, hurry to the stern of the tank, insert crank, and turn. Did that damned mass not want to get rolling? The air was full of iron and the fire intensified. Ah, the engine started and, relieved, I slid into my right front seat. 'Well done!' Peiper said and gave the order 'Tank forward!' During the new breakthrough the Russian lines we were hit by a 2cm steel-core bullet, which smashed through the side steel apron—but got stuck in the side armour at the level of my head.[32]

Even with Peiper turned back, by 24 November the Brusilow *Kessel*, or encirclement, closed with eighteen hundred Russian dead left on the field of battle, along with 152 tanks and 325 artillery pieces and anti-tank guns.[33] Still, all considered, it was a hollow victory. Many Soviet soldiers escaped encirclement by frosty night, and on 25 November the fickle Russian thermometer rose once more, leaving all stranded in a sea of mud. The Russians fortified their shaky defences west of the Dnieper River. To block the main road to Kiev, Hermann Balck ordered a surprise assault as soon as the ground froze.

That took most of a week. On 28 November Peiper and his tanks concentrated just before Radomyshl, a town of twelve thousand located some 94km west of Kiev. With him were eight Tigers of Heinz Kling's company and forty-one other Panzers. Peiper's armour concentrated in the Bulytschety Forest, straddling the Panzer rolling road to Radomyshl.[34] With the big tanks Peiper and Kling pried the enemy away from the village of Garboroff by 1000 hours and then turned south-east in the freezing rain to intercept an enemy-flanking threat.[35] They captured twenty-three trucks and twenty anti-tank guns, and killed 220 of the enemy, with no prisoners reported.[36]

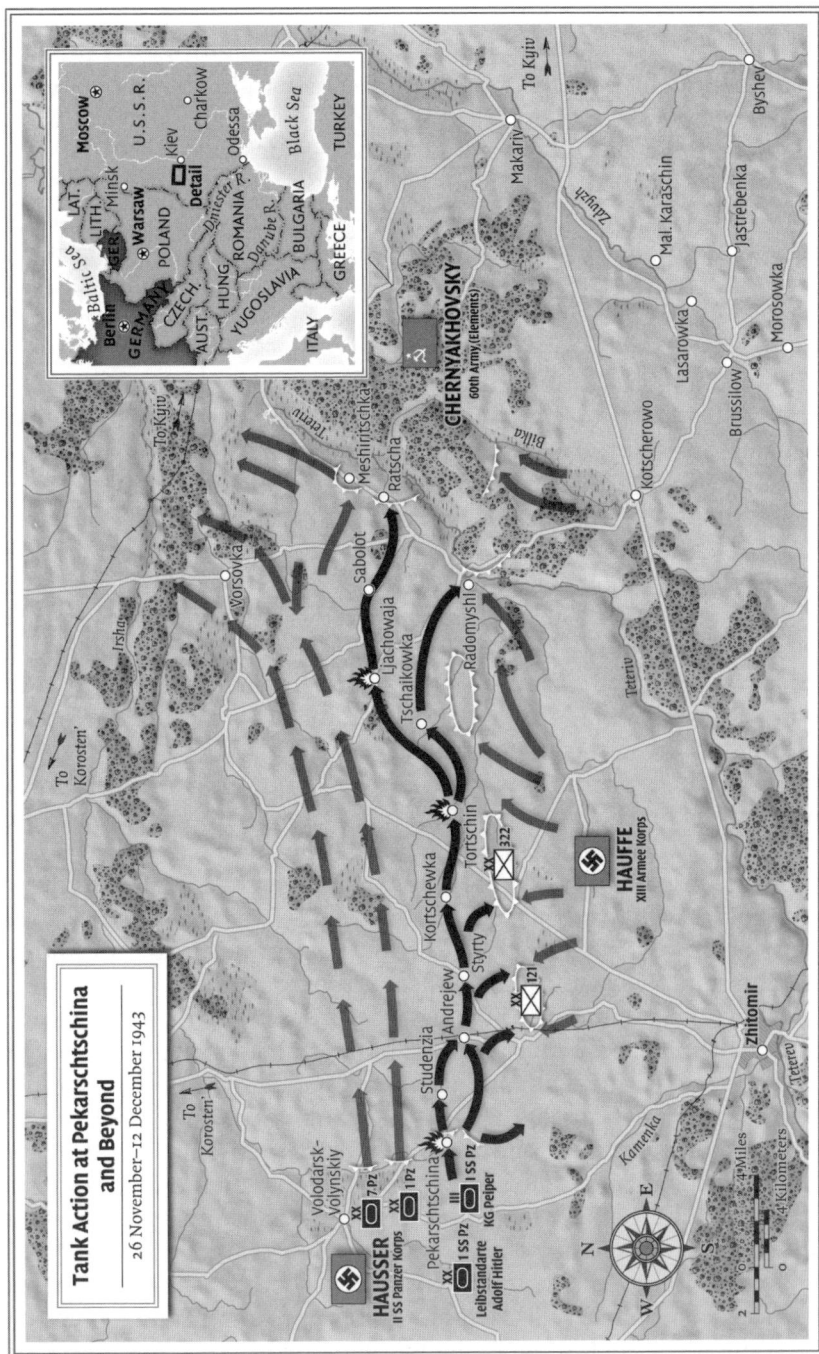

Tank Action at Pekarschtschina and Beyond

26 November–12 December 1943

Moscow

U.S.S.R.

LAT.
LITH.
Minsk
Warsaw
POLAND
Detail
Kiev
Charkow
Odessa
Black Sea
TURKEY
GREECE
BULGARIA
ROMANIA
Danube R.
Dniester R.
Dnieper R.
YUGOSLAVIA
HUNG.
AUST.
CZECH.
GERMANY
Berlin
Baltic Sea

To Kyiv

Byshe

Makariv

Mal. Karaschin

Jastrebenka

Morosowka

Lasarowka

Brussilow

Zdwizh

CHERNYAKHOVSKY
60th Army (Elements)

Kotscherowo

Bilka

Teteriv

Meshinitschka
Ratscha

Teteriv

Sabolot

Worsowka

Radomyshl

Ljachowka

Tschaikowka

To
Korosten'

Irsha

Tortschin

322

HAUFFE
XIII Armee Korps

Kortschewka

Styrty

Andrejew

[2]

Zhitomir

Studenzia

To
Korosten'

Teterev

Kamenka

Volodarsk-Volynskiy

7 Pz

1 Pz

Pekarschtschina

1 SS Pz

KG Peiper

N
W   E
S

Miles
Kilometers

1 SS Pz Korps

Leibstandarte
Adolf Hitler

HAUSSER
II SS Panzer Korps

Paul Guhl, who had taken over Peiper's old battalion, proclaimed himself an 'SPW man, body and soul'. But their former commander was still held in awe. Peiper was, said the men of his former command, 'one cool cookie'. He never raised his voice nor seemed excited. Men of the SPW battalion had a bet going: a thousand Marks to the poor sod who could make Peiper lose his temper. No one collected.[37] That SS officer was now commanding the division steel, and he intended to change the way warfare was conducted. He would ride his tanks like the *Schützenpanzerwagen* and the cavalry horses before that. He would transform these war wagons into thoroughbred chariots that would pound forward at a three-beat gait.

Who said a Panzer couldn't gallop?

The first chance to find out came on 5 December 1943. Peiper's first major operation called for him to pierce the flank of the Russian enemy opposite the XIII Army Corps. He led a battle group of his own namesake consisting of the 1st SS Panzer Regiment, his III Battalion of the SS Grenadier Regiment 2 along with engineer and reconnaissance elements. The weather had turned dry and cold—much better for his motorized forces. He assembled the troops by 1500 hours that afternoon. Orders were to gain the high ground near Styrty and reach Radomyschl in concert with 7th Panzer Division. Peiper intended to slash towards the tiny Russian village of Pekarschtschina in a night attack; SPWs would fight right alongside the tanks.

In the early morning darkness at 0230 hours on 6 December, the light frost was bright in the moonlight as Peiper's troops emerged from Studenzia. The sleepy forward traffic controller for the division reported that the dense column of armour and halftracks had roared by him in the darkness and were headed to the front. Reconnaissance revealed that the enemy was dug in at the front before him in depth and that Pekarschtschina was stoutly defended. Other feelers showed the terrain impossible for flanking the town; besides, orders said the nearby bridges must be taken intact. Peiper waved the halftracks forward to ram into the front while 'firing with his weapons and flame-throwers from the armoured personnel carriers'.[38] Full speed, all weapons.

It was still dark. The blind advance unnerved Hans Siptrott, who commanded a Panzer IV. He had been with Peiper on these forays before, but this time the roads were unknown—the maps always seemed bad in Russia—and it was impossible to see.[39] He became lost at one point, and his fright reached a state of near panic. There was plenty of reason. The Eastern battlefield was a more harsh and unforgiving place than that of only a year before when he had galloped in his tank with Peiper in the far-flung glory at Belgorod. The enemy seemed more confident, the anti-tank guns more numerous and the mines even worse. In the dark on a lost highway, surely they would run into danger. Somehow they made it.[40]

Peiper's halftracks and tanks burst out of the cold night. Even with complete surprise, there was bitter fighting. Paul Guhl was badly wounded when a Russian mortar shell struck the machine gun shield. Otto Dinse promptly replaced him in charge of the SPWs. The Russians defended bravely and died bravely by the score, but within two hours the thatched roofs of the place were roaring towers of flame as the gunfire subsided. At 0500 hours, when the sun began to rise over the frosty landscape, it was over.

At 0645 hours on 6 December, Peiper found himself before Andrejew but faced with a bevy of anti-tank guns.[41] Peiper, code-named 'Rose Leader', called on the Tiger company of the Panzer regiment under Hauptsturmführer Heinz Kling. 'Utmost dispatch requested!' he called over the radio.[42] The village was his just after daybreak. As the enemy was still confused, he ordered no pause in the advance. Proceeding east, his tank group smashed several artillery batteries and, at 1000 hours, took the high ground on both sides of Styrty. Peiper's phalanx moved so rapidly towards Kortschewka that it took the 121st Rifle Division totally by surprise, destroying its headquarters in Kiselewka. There was some localized fighting for Hill 204 just before noon, leaving 'the battle-field … covered with many dead'.[43] Tiger ace Michael Wittmann smashed three more T-34s that rose to challenge Peiper's approach. The sleepless Panzer regiment commander paused to take on supplies.

Divisional headquarters had other ideas, however. By radio the divisional adjutant, Sturmbannführer Rudolf Lehmann, encouraged Peiper to continue the advance towards Tschaikowka. To Lehmann's dismay, however, he discovered that his radio-equipped tank didn't have Peiper's call signal. Knowing Peiper well, he broadcast clearly over the air without code. 'Jochen, this is Rudi, come in please.'[44] Peiper answered, but Lehmann found the Panzer leader truculent and taking a short break. 'What are you doing?' Lehmann asked.

'We are frying potatoes!' came the sardonic response.
Lehmann chaffed: 'Are you stopping because you are tired?'
'Kiss my ass!' came the reply. 'I am attacking, over and out.'[45]

Within twenty minutes his tanks and halftracks were on the move again, firing at whatever enemy came into view. The headquarters of both the

322nd and 148th Rifle Divisions were run down and the Russians thrown into a panic. At 1430 hours Peiper seized Tortschin and its nearby railway line. At nightfall Rudi Lehmann showed up to brief Peiper on the strong enemy forces ahead. Peiper's forces were still clearing the enemy from houses and the crackle of gunfire, and the artillery's thunder was the sonic backdrop for a winter discussion. Only at night, with the petrol tanks nearly dry, did Peiper finally stop—a thrust of 30km behind enemy lines. The recorded destruction was tremendous: twenty-two artillery pieces, seventy-six anti-tank guns, forty vehicles, seventy-one horse-drawn wagons, and a total of 1,450 killed. There was no mention of any prisoners.[46]

If this was not enough, the following day, on 7 December, Peiper resumed his hell-for-leather ride, punching 10km deeper into the enemy flank. He struck for Tschaikowka, a village interdicting his supply road. Just after dark he circled the hamlet past Hill 213 to assault from the north. The fighting there was short but brutal; the enemy there were gunned down and burned out. Peiper continued on, forcing his way into the fortified town of Sabolot. The fighting there was house to house too, but by 1000 hours Peiper had the place. However, further progress proved impossible, given the anti-tank guns ahead. Peiper had punched 42km behind enemy lines and captured the staffs of four Russian divisions. The added litany of enemy losses was astounding, even when allowing for exaggeration in a field commendation: one T-34, an additional eight artillery pieces, sixty-one anti-tank guns, five vehicles, 930 enemy dead, and just three prisoners. The divisional commander, Theodor Wisch, professed to admire Peiper's leadership: 'his lightning-fast execution and exploitation of favourable opportunities helped the division to a great success'. Lightning fast.

At the headquarters of the XLVIII Panzer Corps, Oberst von Mellenthin listened as his intelligence officer relayed intercepted Russian radio traffic. A Russian general seemed particularly disinclined to accept as true that some German tank-led cavalry raid was running about hell-bent some 30km behind friendly lines—it couldn't be. 'Report at once where the enemy comes from,' commanded one of the impatient messages. 'Your report is unbelievable.'

'Ask the devil's grandmother,' came the response. 'How should I know where the enemy comes from!' To them Panzer Group Peiper was like a wild band of SS fiends who materialized out of the frigid darkness, spitting fire and death across the frozen Ukrainian prairie.[47] Erich Rumpf recalled,

Peiper was well known and, like Panzer Meyer, an extremely merciless warrior. That he as a soldier had a great knowledge and that the other

Jochen Peiper shown at Hitler's Berghof alpine headquarters along with Himmler for a visit on 29 July 1940 after the German conquest of France. (Frentz)

Peiper (right) stands with SS Gen. Karl Wolff at the Berghof, July 1940 (Frentz)

Peiper is converses with Max Wünsche, who was then Hitler's SS adjutant at his headquarters. The German leader wished to discuss the timing for a vast campaign against Soviet Russia. (Frentz)

Peiper and SS officer Max Wünschepose for Hitler's photographer, Walter Frentz, at the Berghof in July, 1940 (Frentz)

Peiper at the inspection of Dachau concentration camp in January 1941. Himmler is saluted by SS Maj. Alexander Piorkowski while Peiper looks on from just behind. SS adjutant Karl Wolff is just getting out of Himmler's Mercedes. On the right is SS Maj. Richard Glücks, the SS inspector of the concentration camps. At war's end, Glücks killed himself and Piorkowski was hanged at Landsberg prison on 22 October 1948 where Peiper was also held. (KZ Gedenkstätte Dachau)

Peiper (left) with Himmler and an other unidentified SS man in Himmler's command train, the Sonderzug Heinrich. (Thomson)

On 29 June 1941, Himmler visited Hitler at his Rastenburg headquarters, just after the opening of the massive German attack on Russia. Peiper is seen at the right edge of the photograph. Himmler is engaged in conversation with SS Gruf. Karl Wolff. Behind Peiper is one of the Hitler's adjutants, SS Obstuf. Hans Pfeiffer. (Frentz)

Peiper and Himmler arrived in Grodno, a city of 50,000 with nearly half of the population Jewish on 30 June 1941, with the SS Reichführer complaining that none of the killing teams—the *Einsatzgruppen*—had yet arrived. Photographers recorded the scene as Peiper took notes and Himmler interviewed a local peasant woman. (Witte)

On 9 July 1941, the III Battalion of the Leibstandarte and 11th Company under SS Hauptsturmführer Albert Frey (on the left) cleared the woods north of Miropol to open the tank road to Zhitomir in the Ukraine. Engagements there, along the old Stalin line, were brutal as members of a German company had been murdered near Olyka-Bronki on 3 July which set the tone for events to come. In the ensuing actions against the enemy north of Miropol, the SS camera man was careful to record the primitive appearance of those captured. (NARA)

Following Olyka, the SS men razed the hamlets north of Miropol through which they advanced. (SS Kriegsberichter Paul Augustin, 9 July 1941; NARA).

In early August 1941, Peiper (background) meets with Albert Frey (left foreground), after his release from Himmler. The location is north of Nikolajew in the Ukraine. The man standing is SS Untersturmführer Herbert Fasching with the IV Battalion. To the right rear is SS Obersturmführer Gerhard Bremer, soon awarded a Knight's Cross for fighting with Kurt Meyer's reconnaissance battalion during the early weeks of Barbarossa. (NARA)

Waffen SS columns advanced East during the opening summer weeks of Operation Barbarossa, often burning villages in their wake. (NARA)

Peiper with a host of other officers of the Leibstandarte welcomes Gen. Rudolf Schmundt, Hitler's adjutant, to Sepp Dietrich's field headquarters where he arrived by Fieseler Storch August 1941. (Lippl)

Inside Dietrich's field headquarters, August 1941. Far left: Peiper, next to him, Max Wünsche, then Dietrich and Hitler's army adjutant Gen. Rudolf Schmundt. (Lippl)

Peiper, having grown a mustache in the frigid Russian winter is seen peering through a periscope and then staring across enemy lines during the static snowbound trench warfare that took place in Taganrog along the Black Sea in December 1941. (Spezzano)

Peiper addresses the audience at a competitive SS sporting event in November 1942 in Verneuil-sur-Avre, France, west of Paris, where the Leibstandarte Adolf Hitler was being retrained and equipped. On his right is his adjutant, Otto Dinse. (Author)

Peiper and SS Brig. Gen. Theodor Wisch plan the upcoming attack to free the 320th Infanterie Division surrounded near Liman, south of Kharkov. Photos likely taken on 11 February 1943. (NARA)

Peiper and Wisch meet in the Ukrainian hamlet of Podolchow (Podol'okh) prior to the 320th Infantry Division rescue mission, 11 February 1943. (NARA)

Peiper's rescue column escorting the 320th Infanterie Division to safety after having been surrounded by the Soviet winter advance (NARA) 12-14 February 1943. (Kurt Meyer Archive)

Kurt Meyer and
Max Wünsche
discuss the bitter
winter fighting near
Kharkov in 1943.
(BA–K)

Peiper seen in his command SPW prior to an attack on 20 February 1943.
Photographed by SS Kriegsberichter Paul Augustin. (NARA)

One of the Sturmgeschütz assault guns accompanying Peiper's troop dashes across the frozen Russian step, a Soviet soldier throws up his hands in surrender only to be shot down as the assault gun continues the advance. 20 February 1943. (NARA)

Peiper salutes over the lowered coffin of SS Obstf. Lukas Westrup, killed during the fighting near Krasnograd, Ukraine, 24 February 1943. (Kurt Meyer Archive)

Elements of Battle Group Peiper moving through the village of Ljachowa, March, 1943. (BA-K)

Elements of the panzer battalion move with KampfgruppePeiper through a small Ukrainian village in March 1943 (BA-K)

Another image in the series by Johan King in March 1943 showing SS grenadiers burning their way through a Russian village. (BA–K)

Peiper's SPW battalion moves through one of the villages near Kharkov as its commander stops to light a cigarette on the burning thatch of one of the houses. Photos from SS Kriegberichter Johan King who operated with Peiper's battalion during this time. (BA–K)

commanders of the division were obeying him. Where Panzermeyer and Peiper [were seen], there would be fire and you could see by the clouds of smoke where they are. As a sign for this, his SPW had the Lötlampen. It is known that any of his soldiers who showed weakness, he would punish. Intellectually, he was over all the other leaders. He was restless and hard in battle and he was restless and hard against the weaker and the opponent.[48]

As always, Peiper was far forward, right in the thick of the fighting and so focused on the spear-point of the tank attack that the rear echelon was virtually on their own. To be sure, this posed grave risks for brazen leaders. Peiper's promotion into the boots of the dead Schönberger was one illustration. Another came in the fighting on 8 December to consolidate the territory around Sabolot, where the commander of the Mk IVs of the 7th Panzer Company, Herbert Sprunk, was killed. As always, there was someone waiting to be promoted. This time it was an intrepid younger Panzer man with a penchant for horses and drink, SS Untersturmführer Werner Sternebeck, who found that even if he had little strength, his superior, Jochen Peiper, was not about to give up such attacks.

On the night of 8 December Peiper and his tired men paused in Sabolot. The village of Ljachowaja burned brightly in the distance—a red arc in the night sky flickering and pulsing with the collapse of flaming timbers. On the outskirts of town the dug-in barrels of the abandoned enemy anti-tank guns lay splintered and twisted about, their dead crews scattered about the macabre scene. They had fired until the last moment—a dense collection of guns so deadly that Peiper had rushed the village at full speed. Exhausted, Peiper's men slept the night in their tanks or stretched out on beds of straw, covered in fur-lined parkas. Frost whitened the hulls of the tanks, while clouds of vapour floated out of their turrets telling of the sleeping warmth inside. At headquarters Peiper, the insomniac, unexpectedly popped in: 'Night attack on Krasnoborki!' he cheerfully announced to a chorus of yawns. He left to make personal briefings. Soon they were in his quarters holding up leaden eyelids. Peiper had another smoke.

At daybreak Peiper stood outside, waiting for the fog to lift. Going back in, he rousted his orderly, who was still snoring on the straw floor. There was a jolting blare of obscene noise, and the orderly awoke with a start. There, standing before him, was Jochen Peiper, grinning with a giant base tuba wrapped around his lanky form. 'The trumpet of Jericho!' he announced. 'Coffee!' Peiper nodded. When the orderly returned, he found

Peiper sitting at his chair, washed and shaven and awaiting his coffee. Caffeine was important, as some said he had slept no more than eight hours in the last week.[49]

Orders told Peiper to kick the enemy out of Meshiritschka and the hills to the north. But that was easier said than done. Peiper's devil-may-care style of warfare was running out of tanks. On 9 December Peiper only had eight Mk IVs, five Mk Vs and four Tigers.[50] Regardless, he put in an all-out attack. The armoured pack sallied through some Russian woods, being careful to watch mines. At the head was Peiper, eschewing the cover of the tanks and travelling in a heavy armoured car, binoculars at the ready and a Schmeisser machine pistol on his lap. He was still thinking like the cavalryman that he was. 'There is the enemy … Now! Lead right on the canter.'

By the end of the day they had seized the village and nearby Ratscha. Michael Wittmann had holed another six Russian tanks, but at a cost.[51] sharpshooting Russian gunners repeatedly hit one of Kling's Tigers, wounding the Panzer crew. And when the small tank group attempted to thrust further, a wall-like *Pakfront* repelled them. The crude Russian wooden mines were everywhere. Even the best attention was unable to prevent two Tigers from being impaled. The huge metal behemoths were not destroyed, but their running gear was messed up, and they were marooned until wheels could be replaced. Stubbornly, Peiper was not about to abandon the machines or their crews. 'Establish all around hedgehog defence!' he ordered as darkness approached. The little battle group, far behind enemy lines, formed a circle of metal war wagons, with Peiper's command car and Kling's Tiger at its centre. Within the steel circle were the stricken Tigers.[52]

Soon it was dark and cold. The chill inside the steel-hulled tanks was even more frigid than outdoors. The crews took turns attempting fitful sleep while one man stood guard in the top of the turret. There were a few thatched-roofed buildings inside the encampment, and up to twenty men crowded inside them to avoid the cold. But these mud huts were home to lice and fleas. And worse than that, the Soviets were just getting an inkling that the enemy had invaded their lines, so there were short encounters with patrols during the night. They could not stay here long. Then came the word that the Tigers could not be repaired. It was soon decided that the crews would wait during the day with the stricken tanks while Peiper got help. At least the cold had turned the white blanket into something over which a 50-ton war machine could tread without sinking.

The following morning the little group resumed their march, this time heading for friendly lines in light snowfall. They encountered the surprised enemy in Meshiritschka, a village teeming with anti-tank guns hurrying to change their facing. One of the Tigers had its gun muzzle blown off by an armour-piercing round, and Peiper barked at one of his halftracks to take out the offending weapon. A crackle of gunfire, the hollow thud of hand grenades, and the position was wiped out. When Peiper's little caravan reached friendly lines they were reduced to a single functioning Tiger and a few halftracks. In the meantime the reconnaissance battalion under Gustav Knittel attacked to reach the Tigers. Peiper, along with a 3-ton prime mover, followed up to reach the stricken vehicles. Soon the tanks were repaired, fuelled and waddling back to friendly lines.

There was scarcely a break. On 10 December, Peiper crashed south towards Krasnoborki with the SPW battalion. The Panzer group had just crossed the first hill south of Meshiritschka when the view ahead disappeared as a hurricane of artillery bursts ploughed up the ground. 'The enemy is strong with well-sited weapons in fortified positions,' reported the war diary.[53] Direct hits knocked out some vehicles. Then the Russian anti-tank guns took over, with fire so dense that it seemed as if there were no way to make it through the blizzard of shells. Then T-34s swept forward, ushered by yelling Russian infantry. The Panzers foundered before the anti-tank guns. Wisch, the division commander watching from the village, called off the attack in disgust. Several of the few remaining tanks splintered and burned. In a melancholic funk, the commander of the SS Panzer Grenadier Regiment 2 wrote home, 'The best I can tell you is that I am in once piece … Our strength is running out.'[54]

Wisch was more than disappointed with Peiper's handling of the tanks that day. Returning to his quarters from the snow-bound battlefield, Wisch composed a primer on how future tank attacks would be conducted. 'Attacking across a wide plain, devoid of any cover, against a fortified town demands a careful coordination of all movements.' he began. All guns must be properly sighted, and the artillery must time the bombardment so the shelling would lift just before the Panzer column—racing at highest speed—would reach the objective in one fell swoop. Grenadiers were to ride off the tank decks, and smoke shells were to be used to obscure the enemy vision of the surging tanks.[55] Good advice, but too late: Peiper had lost four of his company commanders—half of his Panzer leaders—in the first weeks of his tenure. If the material losses were severe, the casualties to leaders was shocking. The tank regiment now had only a few combat ready vehicles.

The rest were shot up, mangled or in need of big wrenches.

Chapter 15

The Oak Leaves

'A soldier will fight long and hard for a bit of coloured ribbon.'
—Napoleon

Was Jochen Peiper the best choice for the tank leader of Hitler's Own Panzer division?

Some said that the previous Leibstandarte Panzer commanders were disappointed—to put it mildly—at Peiper's appointment. Werner Poetschke and Kuhlmann were the more experienced tank hands, and one other SS officer, Martin Gross, would soon be seeking a transfer. Rumours said that Himmler and Dietrich had more to do with his selection to lead the regiment than any real experience. He was, after all, an SPW man, enamoured with fast night-time raids behind enemy lines in the heavily armed steel chariots that were the *Schützenpanzerwagen*. And tanks, for all Peiper wanted them to be similarly loose and free-wheeling, were hardly like fast stallions with a big gun.

On 14 December 1943, soon after having taken over command, Panzer Group Peiper reached the enemy line near Fedorowka alongside the 68th Infantry Division but was embattled in bitter fighting for every Russian hamlet. The thatched-roofed houses blazed brightly, turning the patchy section of snow into a brilliant patchwork of mud and fluorescent orange. Burning wood and straw smudged the air with a fog of cold stench. 'The places burned furiously from the flame-throwers,' wrote the regimental chronologer.[1] The further operation against Radomyschl ended when the Leibstandarte broke off the attack to face Russian troops approaching from the south-east.

Yet if Teddi Wisch wanted an aggressive regimental tank commander, he had found him in Jochen Peiper. As often as they could get fuel and ammunition, the Panzer group was off on another slashing adventure. Even so, every hill or depression seemed to conceal another *Pakfront*. There was a price to such aggression: more and more tanks were shot up.

Peiper had roared off on 5 December with sixty-six operational, but four days later there were only two Tigers combat ready and twelve other tanks remaining. 'If we don't get new tanks up to the front in a hurry,' Peiper worried over the radio, 'the Russians are going to light a fire under our ass.'[2]

Even Peiper's close officer comrade, Albert Frey, in charge of SS Panzer Grenadier Regiment 1, became critical of such foolhardy tank-led cavalry rides. The two faced off in a loud quarrel over who was in charge when tanks fought with the grenadiers. And everyone heard it. Peiper said he was in charge, but Frey said no, he outranked him. It was all a matter of battlefield competence, Frey opined. His grenadiers did not have tanks or SPWs, and Peiper's bold methods were too risky.[3] 'Peiper burns up his men,' Frey concluded caustically.[4] The irony was intended, and Frey prevailed. Hans Siptrott, the hard-nosed NCO who had been on the sharp end of Peiper's hell-for-leather use of tanks, saw it differently. 'I didn't realize he burned me down,' he said many years later. 'Peiper was a *Draufgänger*—a go-getter—and led his regiment accordingly.'[5]

With few tanks left to command, Peiper indulged in a bit of nostalgia for his old life back in the comfort as Himmler's adjutant. He knew the score within his own command. How would he ever survive the fighting out here? He wrote again to Hedwig Potthast, worrying that she no longer answered his letters now that she was pregnant with yet another child by Himmler.

> Regimental Command Post, 15 December 1943
>> Dear Little Sister!
>> Even though I am a little disappointed that I do not hear anything from you and that my last letter remained unanswered, I do not want to miss wishing you and your Helge everything good and beautiful from my heart for the coming Julfest.
>> During these very difficult times, it is a beautiful and calming feeling to know that you all are safely in a warm nest. When on the 24th you will be standing happily and contentedly under the Christmas tree with your loved ones, and your crown prince cheerfully will put his little arms around your neck, and when you will be listening a little into yourself, you will notice good wishes and greetings drifting from afar. They should tell you that I am remaining the same old one in faithful friendship and affection, that is
>> Your Jochen.[6]

At the front the holiday celebration seemed remote. Some of Peiper's burned machines could be brought back to life. Tank mechanics toiled round the clock, and by 19 December Peiper could count thirty-three Mk

IVs, twelve Panthers and seven Tigers.[7] New orders for the XLVIII Panzer Corps called for the Leibstandarte to cut off and surround a vulnerable-looking pocket of Russian forces near Meleni. The 7th Panzer Division was to seal the pocket from the right. The attack on 19 December made uncharacteristically slow progress, with Peiper's advance slowed by the thick underbrush and the usual string of anti-tank guns. Caught in Russian crosshairs, many tanks were lost once more. And east of Tschepowitschi a grenadier company saw twenty-five men killed in an hour by hidden Siberian marksmen who calmly picked off each victim with a rifle shot through the head.

At dawn on 20 December Peiper set off under cold and cloudy skies towards the Soviet train station at Tschepowitschi. Nearby he scattered an enemy convoy, and his orderly officer, SS Untersturmführer Arndt Fischer, captured a valuable map describing the enemy dispositions. A Tiger formed the point of the column, with other tanks clattering behind. Looking down from a forest, Peiper saw nothing save the usual huts, twisted rail tracks and a shot-up locomotive. There had to be a *Pakfront*. Scanning with binoculars, he found them. Peiper got in the first shot, but soon the guns were hurling shells back—blinking muzzle flashes 'looking like lightning coming out of the ground'. Village huts exploded as German shells crashed around them. Several dug-in Russian anti-tank guns disappeared in shell bursts, but not all. As the Panthers neared the train station, several exploded.

In response Peiper's tank waddled down the main village road, now illuminated by fiercely burning buildings. Two T-34s appeared at the opposite end of the street. Before anyone could react, a bright flame enveloped the first. Two more loud cracks: the other Russian tank suddenly splintered into a thousand pieces. Soon twenty-one Soviet tanks and assault guns were mangled, but Peiper's Panzer regiment ended the day with scarcely twenty of its own.[8]

Even with little remaining armoured strength, Jochen Peiper's reckless debut as Panzer leader of the Leibstandarte left the Soviet 16th Army battered and incapable of offensive moves. The Soviets had been dealt a crushing defeat, even if not a knockout. Oberst von Mellenthin thought General Balck's mastery of armoured operations were 'the most brilliant in my experience', and Balck himself expressly thanked the daredevil warrior from the Leibstandarte.[9] Even Peiper's previously fatalistic tank crew had grown to respect him, with one stating,

> Inside the tank, Peiper called us by our first name, but stayed with the formal sie, which we took as a sign of honour. We knew we could

depend on each other and this feeling caused us to gain limitless security. The extent to which the solidarity had grown was to be experienced by us on Christmas Eve 1943. In the meantime a lot of snow had fallen and a bitter cold had gripped the steppe and villages. The three of us from the crew of Panzer 001 sat together with other members of the regimental staff in our quarters, one of those miserable peasant houses, in which only the big stove spread comfort. Suddenly, a messenger stepped in and ordered us three immediately to the command post. We drudged through the night suspecting nothing, but hoping that no mission was awaiting us.

As we entered the large room, we saw, by brightness suddenly blinded, a large number of officers assembled in front of the Christmas tree. Peiper stepped out of this circle, saluted us with a handshake, and wished us a Merry Christmas. He thanked us for our missions and handed each one of us as a personal present, a bottle of schnapps... With his normal inaccessibility, by many around him interpreted as shyness and coldness, again his personal warmth broke through, which he—for whatever reason—hid with self-control. He always demonstrated extreme toughness towards himself and demanded it from his men, regardless of rank ... As the units shrunk because of high losses and fewer tanks were available, he rode with us in solo missions and hunkered with us in ambush positions in the freezing cold tank.[10]

At the end of 1943, even far from home, Peiper claimed to relish his assignment. 'Far in the east, in my armoured car,' he would later write home, 'I was allowed to keep watch for Germany on December 24th.'[11] And the *Schutzenpanzerwagen* were now replaced by tanks, even as Peiper longed for a distant home. 'Light a candle, roast a fir twig,' he wrote his family, 'and then shut the eyes to wander ... to a Christmas tree, the inner light of which nobody can take from you!'

What were the Christmas presents for Peiper? On the second day of Christmas a dozen new Panthers arrived along with a contingent of replacement infantry, but with dreary reminders that the war did not pause for yuletide. The new tanks were hardly off the train before Peiper and his men were being sent to the front. Near Woliza the new contingent destroyed ten T-34s before losing two of their own. However, the newly arrived infantry recoiled when hit by the Soviet armour. 'Tank shock', said one seasoned SS officer—the new replacements were not like the old hares. And there were fewer and fewer old veterans. The sobering fact was that the available divisional infantry strength on 28 December 1943 was only 1,026 officers and men. Even more fantastic were the losses: three times that number had been killed or wounded in the last sixteen days of fighting. Peiper's tank strength—despite the new Panthers had sunk to just over two dozen turrets.[12] Peiper wrote,

> The Russian is cut out for defence. The peasant, not yet touched by civilization, moves with much more confidence through the landscape and knows how to make excellent use of nature. The stamina in times of crisis and their absolute indifference towards threats from the rear and the flanks is incredible! In the fight of individual pockets of resistance, he continues with a fatalistic attitude … While the German soldier became more and more frightened of tanks, the opposite was true of the other side.[13]

Gone were the days when the Russians fled—even from blowtorches. Now they stood their ground and shuttled more anti-tank rounds into plentiful guns.

The following days were more of the same. Each time the Russians pierced the lines, the Mk IVs under Werner Sternebeck laid into them and shot them down. But a massive Soviet armoured blow at 1030 hours on the last day of the year near Perwomaiskij actually forced the Leibstandarte back. Twenty-five Russian tanks lay smashed, but when the firing was done, the Soviets owned the battlefield. On New Year's Day the Leibstandarte Adolf Hitler pulled back to a new line, with Russian tanks at their heels. The following morning the Russian tank assaults were so numerous that German gunners mistook two Mk IVs in the fog for T-34s and destroyed their own.

When the mists cleared, the SS men were repeatedly stung by Russian fighter-bombers, duly noting that not a single Luftwaffe plane crossed the sky. Fighting raged the entire day, leaving Otto Dinse, the replacement leader of the SPW battalion, badly wounded. It wasn't until dark that the Soviets were repulsed; the division was near the end of its rope. General Vatutin was riding roughshod over the 4th Panzer Army. By 3 January all the Russian territory lost since November had been won back, and the German defence crumpled and fractured to the breaking point. Another spreading Russian advance from Kirovograd was threatening to envelop the entire sector 'Stalingrad style'. At the front wide gaps appeared in the line while Soviet artillery shells rained down.

The Leibstandarte was ordered to pull back even as the Soviet forces eagerly pressed forward. On the night of 4 January the division passed to the XIII Army Corps, where Peiper's tanks were to move against the enemy who had broken through at Chutor Petrowskogo. Just about everything was in short supply. Where would petrol come from for that transfer? 'Fuel should be taken from the countryside,' came the abrupt response from the new chief of staff. Rudolf Lehmann couldn't stand that: 'Our Tigers and Panthers don't eat hay.'[14]

The Russians attacked with unusual violence. The retreat road went through the thatched village of Osadowka, which the Russians seized and held. But with some Jerrycans of petrol and a few tanks, Peiper personally led the armoured column with infantry in halftracks that burned the enemy out of there. By midnight on 7 January the retreat route was open, and on the following day Peiper halted a powerful intrusion of the division's lines. Leading a dozen tanks paced by Stukas overhead, Peiper's band engulfed thirty-one T-34s and the infantry riding atop them.[15] Some deserters and prisoners from the Soviet 7th Guards Tank Army were less than 18 years old and others old men. Were the Russians reaching the end of their seemingly inexhaustible resources?[16]

The next day Peiper and his twelve tanks were thrown headlong against a Russian penetration near Januschpol. Among them, however, were Michael Wittmann and the other Tiger sharpshooters. The Russians showed up with a mass tank attack from the 54th Guard Tank Brigade. The attacking Soviet column moved right into Wittmann's kill zone. Peering through his optical sight, Gunner Bobby Woll picked off three tanks as quickly as the crosshairs could be moved from one vehicle to another. With the Russians thrown into confusion, Peiper's few tanks counterattacked. All told, some forty Russian armoured vehicles were put out of action as the enemy threat melted. General der Panzertruppe Hermann Balck was so elated with Peiper's command performance that he saw to it that his name was praised in the daily report.[17]

But praise did not fight the war. On 13 January a strong Russian tank force steamrolled through the frozen division boundary with Kampfgruppe Künsberg of the 68th Infantry Division. Again Peiper and his tanks were called on. In the action Wittmann's Tigers charged out of the cold wind at the surprised Russian army and dispatched all thirty-seven T-34s by midafternoon.[18] Wittmann claimed his eightieth tank destroyed. Oberst Heinz von Künsberg was elated. 'My good friend Peiper sent two Tigers into my sector,' he said, and after that? 'Wittmann destroyed countless enemy tanks.'[19]

Countless was the key word. When Peiper attacked towards the Chutorysko collective farm in frozen weather on 14 January, they destroyed more T-34s. Again the Russians fled. To Peiper this seemed the signal to launch another hell-for-leather Panzer raid. So just after noon he flung his handful of tanks and the SPWs to the north-west. The tank group destroyed two Russian infantry regiments, and by the time he reached

Krassnopol the enemy was abandoning his weapons and fleeing north.[20] But the snow pack was treacherous on 15 January, and several tanks slid off the road from Januschpol. Heading further on into the dark night, Peiper halted before thickening flashes from anti-tank guns west of Molotschki. He radioed back, complaining of the gunnery of the *Pakfront* before him, reporting four Tigers stuck in a frozen swamp.[21] The next afternoon he thrust again to the east. But as soon as they ventured from Stetkowzy, a volley of anti-tank fire shot down four German tanks. The entire Panzer group fell under a smoky curtain of rocket fire. He pulled back.[22]

The following two days were mercifully quiet. During the interlude Peiper's radioman, Fritz Kosmehl, became seriously ill—even a hot vodka gargle could not open his congested throat. Kosmehl was sent to a field hospital by motorcycle, with Dresden native Horst Schumann arriving as his replacement. Schumann had a little time to get acquainted, being advised by Helmut Jahn, the gunner, to rest when there was any possibility, for Peiper's command specialty was *Nachtangriffen*—night attacks.[23]

For now there was time for slumber, an escape to forget a winter of appalling cold, snow and frozen corpses.[24] Even outnumbered, Peiper's tank guns had done their part—particularly the Tigers. From 5 December 1943 to 17 January 1944 they destroyed 146 Russian tanks. The leader was Michael Wittmann and his crew. On 18 January Peiper and Wisch held a little ceremony for him out in the snowy Russian wasteland. Peiper removed his heavy coat for the camera. Wittmann had just been credited with the destruction of his sixtieth tank. That was old hat—within weeks he claimed forty-seven more. The German tank crew, in their black uniforms, stood stiffly in front of their big whitewashed Tiger, showing concentric kill rings around its huge muzzle. Peiper, in a visored soft cap, smiled as he shook hands with the little group. Wittmann, the world's leading tank killing ace, was awarded the Knight's Cross. Handshakes and smiles in the frigid air. Still, the T-34 turkey shoot and all the Panzer raids with blackened Russian villages did little to hide an expanding sense that the war in the East had careened out of control. Peiper himself remembered,

> The moral breakdown of the German Eastern Army did not occur on account of the quality of the adversary—in this we were always superior to him—but on account of the psychological aspects ... even if we killed as many as we could (we figure an average loss of one German for every ten Russians), new masses from the unknown hinterland would gush forth ceaselessly and the practice of the enemy would be animal-like—impulsive—and disregarding the customary rules of war. The wind of the steppes of Asia blew into our faces ... 'Who is this monster?' I did not understand him, cried our soldiers and a cold sweat

broke out on their body. He started to retreat, not because the situation to his front, but of that on his right or left ... 'The Russians are coming!' ... The efficiency of our cultured human society from the West lost out against the primitive instinctive strength of the Asiatic onslaught![25]

Russia's frozen wasteland posed a war beyond guns. Against the shortage of rations came reports of food poisoning from local stocks. Soon there was an order that no men could visit Russian markets, slaughter local animals or eat Russian food. Worst of all—they were forbidden Soviet vodka. There was even sloppy discipline in maintenance crews: orders went out that uniforms and weapons must be better maintained; officers were to make special efforts to improve these matters.[26] Certainly Peiper would not tolerate an unkept appearance.

At one point a new SS officer came into Peiper's headquarters unshaven. Peiper looked pained. 'Where did you get that flea catcher on your face?' he asked. It was for warmth, he replied. That had to go. 'But I've never had lice,' the officer told him. Peiper nodded and replied, 'Obviously you have never been at the front!'[27] On another occasion a Waffen SS man spied an officer bent over and staring into a mirror propped up on the side in a snow-laden halftrack. He had no shirt on in the freezing cold, only a towel around his neck, standing in the snow in highly polished boots. Coming closer, the tank man saw the grooming officer was Peiper—never sloppy.[28]

Even an archetypal SS warrior was hard-pressed to exude optimism now. He was exhausted and uncharacteristically lethargic, suffering medical troubles that sent him by rail back to Upper Bavaria on 20 January. Herbert Kuhlmann took over command of the few tanks of the Panzer regiment on 23 January 1944.[29] But before he left, Peiper spoke to Horst Schumann, his new Morse operator, and SS Rottenführer Heini Kiel, his second radio operator. Even if Peiper was an officer—and that created a gulf even in the Waffen SS—inside the tank Schumann noted an unusual comradery. Now Peiper seemed a little worried as he passed over leadership of Panzer 055 to SS Sturmbannführer Horst Finzelberg. Overeager, Finzelberg had been an instructor with the SS Panzer Training School in Bitsch and had just come from 'Nord', the 6th SS Gebirgs Division.[30] Even though he had been wounded, he had volunteered to go back to the front. 'Oh, Finzelberg will lead you in the attack,' Peiper told them, 'but please drive as the last tank. He wants a medal and I don't want to lose my Panzer.'

If Peiper's deadpan humour was hardly reassuring, it was also uncannily accurate. For on 26 January, in a daylight attack on Napadowka, the regimental command tank was suddenly pierced by a captured 88mm gun that struck the turret from the left side. After a hideous clang, Schumann looked to see Finzelberg doubled over, killed instantly while Kiel, behind him, was beheaded by the anti-tank shell. Jahn jumped out of the tank before Becker even stopped driving. Then Schumann and Becker abandoned the stricken Mk IV and ran for it.[31] It was only weeks later when the coffin-like tank could be recovered, brought back to the Panzer workshop with the bodies of the two crewmen still grotesquely frozen inside.

Peiper, meanwhile, made his way back to Germany. Those he left at the front were keenly aware of the losses. Increasingly their ranks were filled with inexperienced troops. Who believed the war could still be won?[32] And did it even matter for Peiper, the nihilistic warrior? He was fighting for fighting's sake, in daring night-time raids, where victory followed in spite of the odds. His troop had halted the Russian 16th Army. Proof came on 27 January 1944, when Jochen Peiper got the telegram—a new decoration. He was to set off to Berlin immediately.

On this Thursday he was with Heinrich Himmler at his Hochwald headquarters from 1500 to 1800 hours just before setting off to receive the anticipated award.[33] Inside Himmler's warm and cosy receiving room with flowers, lavish SS wall tapestries and hot coffee, Russia's frozen miseries seemed far away. There were also warm handshakes from K.H, and his staff. After all, Peiper was the 377th German soldier to be decorated with the Oak Leaves to the Knight's Cross. That was something. 'In case a man falls in action,' the SS newspaper recited the week before, 'the Leibstandarte Adolf Hitler still lives, fights and proves again that whatever assignments it may get, it still carries the name of the Führer which obligates even the last man of an SS Panzer division.' The newspaper called that the 'spirit of Adolf Hitler'.[34]

On the same day of Peiper's big notification, Hitler welcomed a hundred of his most trusted military leaders to his Rastenburg headquarters. After a simple lunch in which table-side conversations were muted and non-festive, Hitler addressed his generals in a two-hour monologue. The themes were the same: the struggle of the party, the beauty of a natural existence and the need to hold out in the East. For Hitler that theme harkened back to men like Peiper. The seeds of victory, he maintained, were not simply in the loyalty of his soldiers but in their fanatical will to succeed.

> [I]f Providence should actually deny us victory in this battle of life and death, and if it is the will of the Almighty that this should end in

catastrophe for the German people, then you, my generals and admirals must gather around me with upraised swords to fight to the last drop of blood for the honour of Germany.[35]

In the middle of that tirade Field Marshal Erich von Manstein interrupted loudly: 'And so it will be Mein Führer!' Although the admonition seemed a rallying call, it struck Hitler as ambivalent—even mocking. The field marshal was dismissed.

Three days after von Manstein's faux pas came the anniversary of Hitler's 1933 takeover of power and Peiper's twenty-ninth birthday. Unlike the *Machtergreifung* of years past, the occasion featured only Hitler's distant radio address from his field headquarters in East Prussia. Peiper listened with the rest on the frigid plains of Russia.

Hitler shrilly appealed to the need to fight on with the usual rant: the enemy was the 'Jewish bacillus" and without a German victory, the Bolshevists would overrun Europe and turn it into a slave state of international Jewry.[36] His followers heard not a word of sympathy over the loss of countless husbands and sons nor a word of compassion for the wrecked cities from the devastating bomber raids. Rather than praise for the men at the front or those toiling at factories, there were threats. If the German people did not rise to victory, they would deserve total destruction. And of course, there was no mention of the great misery inflicted on Europe: millions killed in war and millions more Jews and 'racial undesirables' gassed and put to death in Himmler's Polish elimination camps.

As Hitler's voice crackled across the airwaves, the people of Peiper's old hometown of Berlin ran for cover. Air sirens announced the arrival of five hundred British bombers over the winter skies of the capital city. The fireworks on Peiper's birthday in Berlin that night displayed a spectacular harbinger for 1944, for it was not shrieking rockets hailing the twelfth year of National Socialism but rather a rain of deadly incendiary bombs that turned the Sportpalast into a raging blaze.[37] The scene of Hitler's great public speeches of 1938 was reduced to ashes.

Peiper would only later learn of the strike on Berlin, relieved that his parents, wife and family were now in Tegernsee. For now, on 30 January, he still basked in the mythic feat of earning the Oak Leaves for the most elite tank regiment in Germany. In spite of his leader's lacklustre speech on his birthday, it must have seemed a crowning moment. There was little hesitation to leave the frozen front for Rastenburg. As several of his comrades reminded him, there was no Panzer regiment left to lead. And besides, his old rival, Max Wünsche, had just come from headquarters

230

where, on Peiper's birthday, Himmler and Dietrich had crowned him with promotion to SS Obersturmbannführer. That demanded a response.

On 3 February 1944, when Peiper saw Hitler, it was after a long separation. Peiper's black Panzer uniform was pressed and his hair carefully slicked back for the occasion. The accommodation at Rastenburg looked Spartan and cold. Even during the recent holiday season Hitler had paid little attention to the usual festivities. There had been not even a single candle at *Wolfsschanze* over Christmas. Grim austerity and determination replaced '*Stille Nacht, Heilige Nacht*'. Whereas Peiper remembered Hitler as the fiery and charismatic leader from his 'asphalt soldier' days, the man who greeted him seemed pale, tubby and frail. Hitler was suffering a cold, confiding in his doctor that he had been unable to sleep since the calamitous bombing attack on Berlin.[38]

When Hitler's personal photographer, Walter Frentz, framed both men before the lacquered wood-panelled decor of the East front headquarters, the lens found Jochen Peiper diminished. Even the best lighting and make-up could not hide an unhealthy pallor. Although the Panzer uniform beamed immaculate and the grooming was perfect, the man underneath was thin and gaunt. His Adam's apple protruded from his long neck as if he had a goitre, and a drawn belt revealed his thinning waist. Hitler managed a half-smile as he clasped Peiper's hand. The newly decorated soldier looked sullen and expectant. Hitler asked Peiper to tell him of the fighting in the East. Peiper chose his words carefully. The war there was hard, he said, describing the declining conditions. Peiper knowingly paused. Hitler assured Peiper that he had Germany's confidence and admiration. So dismissed, Peiper managed a tired smile outside Hitler's headquarters for the photographers. The silvered Oak Leaves on his lapel gleamed against the cold pines surrounding the *Wolfsschanze*.

After the meeting with Hitler, Peiper journeyed the 10km to Himmler's adjoining Hochwald headquarters. Armed guards examined his papers at the barbed-wire gate and allowed Peiper to drive on into the wooded thicket that was Himmler's domain. The core of the Reichsführer SS headquarters compound was several wooden barracks, neatly ramshackled in a characteristically German fashion. The whole thing was short on charm: camouflaged carefully in the woods and surrounded by a barbed-wire fence and constantly patrolled by armed guards with dogs. In the middle of the compound stood Himmler's HQ train, puffing away under steam to run its communications and dining car. The uniformed men coming and going all looked out of place; the whole outdoor arrangement looked as if gentleman hunters with shotguns would shortly appear. When they met, Peiper found Himmler apprehensive. 'Russia is like the giant hydra of Greek myth,' the Reichsführer professed. 'If you cut off its head, seven more grow in its place.'[39] That night a dinner of three courses with wine and coffee in the dining car celebrated that his adjutant had done good. Even sporting the Oak Leaves, Peiper looked poorly.[40]

Everyone knew why. For the last two months Peiper's men had looked on as their daredevil leader chain-smoked cigarettes, gulped black coffee and shunned rest or diversion. Even his vanity suffered, with dark circles under tired eyes and a sickly yellow skin, oddly highlighting his preened features. Some said he seldom slept more than twelve hours a week. It showed; he seemed profoundly fatigued, even when impelled by a cureless drive. When asked, Jochen said he was simply suffering from the Eastern Front. Would it take a heart attack to prove him the Iron Soldier of the Waffen SS? As Himmler's own man and the Panzer leader of Hitler's personal tank regiment, he considered himself to carry a special obligation.

In Peiper's absence, 22 January saw the Leibstandarte subordinated to the XLVI Panzer Corps. Without Peiper, command of the Panzer group— there could no longer be talk of a tank regiment—fell to Herbert Kuhlmann. There was little to covet in Kuhlmann's inheritance. The entire division was reduced to the strength of a single battalion. And as if to underscore the hardship, Herbert Kuhlmann was evacuated with a heart attack on 9 March. An even harder man, Werner Poetschke, took over the leadership of the two or three Panzers still running. His adjutant knew the blond, square-jawed replacement as 'a hundred per cent soldier'.[41] Yet Russia even took a toll beyond the physical. The Leibstandarte men had been there so long that several of them had begun to mumble to themselves in Russian: How would they learn to be Germans again?[42] Heinz von Westernhagen, leading the Tiger battalion beside Peiper, pondered the question:

> After the war, I want to withdraw from just being in the military and harvest my cabbage in the East [Latvia] ... I am getting used to Russia and find it pleasing. The expansiveness of the country captivates the person and fascinates me. Already now I can imagine to remain in Russia later on ... If this war does not rip me apart, I'll hang up my soldier's uniform and become a farmer in the Baltic. Otherwise, the Devil can have me.[43]

The answer, at least for Peiper, was recuperation. It was his first time to see his family in their new Bavarian home in Rottach-Egern. For him, after Russia the romantic alpine village was like a dream. The ice-blue of Tegernsee was framed by the Bavarian Alps rising 2,000m out of the alpine valley. The villa at 177½ Wolfgrubstrasse, where Sigurd and the children lived, was covered in snow and looked like an idealized gingerbread landscape, with its ornate dark wood balcony etched against the thick white winter blanket. Jochen arrived on the third floor of the Gsottha-berhof to a warm greeting from a very pregnant wife.[44] Now he could see what he had only read about in her letters. The relief was palpable, even if the returning warrior nearly fell from illness and exhaustion.

The Peiper family could see that Daddy was ailing. For that there would be nourishment—hot food, the love of his woman and beautiful sleep in his new home. Sleep and warm soup replaced all-night tank raids fed by cigarettes and coffee. But of it all, sleep was most dear. One morning, after the nightly cure, Peiper awoke to find himself a headline in the *Völkischer Beobachter*. The article described his fabled Zhitomir exploits: 'The Oak Leaves for SS Major Peiper'.[45] The Nazi reporters said he had destroyed a hundred tanks and terrorized the enemy. That much was true. The usual prescription was a Third Reich hero welcome, but a big celebration was not his style.

Peiper quietly retired to his home to enjoy the view out through the naked beech trees towards Wallberg Mountain.[46] The surrounding peaks were cloaked in a deep snow. The peace and quiet of his new neighbourhood contrasted strangely with Russia, with its chaos, noise and death.

The upper Bavarians, accustomed to tourism and a stylish life, were friendly to the family. They greeted him knowingly in the charming local dialect, exuding respect for his privacy. And even though the local paper, the *Tegernseer Zeitung*, echoed the story of his Oak Leaves on the front page on 4 February, each issue closed with ever-longer lists of sons, fathers and brothers whose names adjoined black Maltese crosses—'*Für das Vaterland gefallen*'. Could any celebration be appropriate?[47] Although the local *Kraft durch Freude*—Strength through Joy—programme kept the movies coming to the film theatre in Rottach-Egern and trotted out sports and childhood sledding events, the levity was strained.[48] Simple food items such as butter, eggs and potatoes were in short supply. And the small close-knit community of fifteen thousand was now teeming with thousands of wounded soldiers being housed in hotels converted into hospitals. Many homes had even taken in outsiders, seeing that thousands had streamed into town, seeking refuge from the increasingly deadly air raids on Munich.

Even under dedicated care, Peiper remained exhausted and in poor health. Himmler's surgeon, Dr Karl Gebhardt, who also lived in Tegernsee, ordered that the SS icon should see a specialist.[49] Viewing the physical demise of his former adjutant, still another resident of Tegernsee, Heinrich Himmler, worried for his entire organization. Unlike Kharkov, his SS troopers had been ejected from Russia. There was no SS magic now, and the 'arrival of Himmler at the Führer HQ now seemed to chill the atmosphere'.[50] Word had it that Hitler was now making scornful remarks after he departed the *Wolfsschanze*. Soon Himmler and the SS would be in the same lot as Göring and his anaemic Luftwaffe.

Then Himmler had an idea—an epiphany he thought that suddenly revealed the source of Waffen woes. Food was the problem. Bad food was creating bad health and bad morale for his Nordic warriors. He ordered that his troopers immediately report bad cooks within the Waffen SS. That thus, within weeks the low-performing cooks in SS field kitchens were spirited away to the 'school for bad cooks'. There, in Berlin, *pas cuisine* chefs dispensed bland flavourless food, with a good meal served between, to impress on them the contrast. 'This is what you did to our fighting men,' they were told. And the predicable admonition: 'You will learn to prepare good food—or else.' And so it was—another of Himmler's outlandish ideas—'half weird, half good.'[51]

On 11 and 12 February 1944 SS doctors at Dachau's 'SS Health and Fitness Centre'—an epithet of beyond ironic contradiction—examined Jochen Peiper.[52] They pronounced him ailing from low blood pressure. That was the reason for the fainting spells. The man was also suffering nervous exhaustion—a ready Waffen SS euphemism for battle fatigue. He was ordered to take a rest. Anyone learning that Peiper went to the SS doctors in Dachau must wonder how he did not learn of the diabolical goings on at the town's infamous concentration camp. The SS health centre was just outside its electrified barbed-wire fence, amid the botanical gardens and greenhouses that fed Himmler's obsession with herbs and spices.

Just inside the stockade spread the gates of hell. In the winter of 1944, eighteen thousand inmates were incarcerated there. How did Jochen Peiper not hear of rumours of the treatment of those at the camp? Some victims were subjected to high-altitude tests and died in the agony from near vacuum. Or perhaps someone whispered of how Dr Sigmund Rascher was performing experiments with inmates immersed in icy water to see how Luftwaffe pilots might survive hypothermia in the North Sea? Himmler's driver, Franz Lucas—who was on a friendly basis with Peiper since 1938—knew of these diabolical experiments first-hand. Indeed, Lucas said that he and Himmler personally witnessed Polish prisoners at Dachau being immersed in icy water to see if they could survive for extended periods. Amazingly, after the experiments Lucas related how he and Himmler had lunch at the Dachau commissary with some of the prisoners who survived.[53]

It would be very surprising if Peiper did not know of them either. Or would he have heard of the pseudo-medical procedures where demented camp doctors injected victims with malaria or other pathogens? that very February some forty Russian students arrived at Dachau from Moosburg only to be shot upon entering the camp. And on the days when Peiper was treated in the hospital seven more prisoners died in the concentration camp.[54] Hunger and typhus epidemics were rampant; the deceased inmates were cremated.[55] That Peiper never heard of any of the terrible events at Dachau—yet being plugged into Himmler's SS hierarchy and having visited Dachau on numerous occasions—strains all credibility.

Staying home likely seemed a better choice. In this, Peiper obeyed his doctors, convalescing with his family. It was the longest time he was home during the entire war. Away from the draining conflict, there were some better days. On 7 March 1944, Peiper's second daughter, Silke, was born; there would be another engraved china candlestick holder to come from Himmler's office.[56] Even so, the failing war and his failing health sent him back to Berlin. On 2 April he was in the capital city being treated for 'nerve damage' due to shell shock.[57] Remaining in Berlin, Peiper met briefly with Hitler's propaganda minister, Joseph Goebbels, a few days later. Berlin was now a sad sight, with many of its buildings razed by bombs and its streets choked by rubble. Peiper's father's old neighbourhood in Wilhelmsdorf was now a ruin, and each night the air raid sirens wailed, sending everyone to the shelters.[58] Goebbels was intrigued to speak to what he considered a newly anointed SS hero. But Peiper was not optimistic: Did Minster Goebbels really believe the war could still be won? A nimbus of doubt descended over the conversation.[59]

More than most, Goebbels understood the disquiet. In Germany morale had begun to falter; indeed, he had written a propaganda piece to address the inevitable questions. 'Many of us will have asked ourselves more frequently over the five years that this war has gone on,' he was now writing, 'why it is so especially difficult for the German people?'[60] Difficult? Peiper sarcastically professed his opinion. With poisonous leadership in years past, the war was now scarcely winnable.

'The year 1943 was the most difficult year of the war,' Goebbels professed. The best chance was to hold the front and force a break between the Anglos and the Soviets. And to do that they must defeat the expected invasion in the west. What events would be remembered from the war a hundred years hence? Goebbels agreed that was impossible to fathom. 'Few signs,' he said, 'of the enemy's air terror would remain ten years after peace.' 'The longer the war lasts,' he concluded, 'the more fanatically we pursue it.' And even in the face of the worst, Goebbels proclaimed his Führer to be 'the man of the century'. If the propaganda minister could not dismiss Peiper's apprehension, he had still had a pat answer. 'He commands, we follow.'[61]

> The Führer sometimes asks himself in a worried sort of way whether the white man is going to be able in the long run to maintain his supremacy over the tremendous reservoir of human beings in the East ... the Führer referred to the wars of the Turks and to the conquest of Genghis Khan, which led him far into the heart of Europe ... the main burden of this fight must be borne by us. We don't know how later generations will stand up to dealing with it ... The Führer gave expression to his unshakeable conviction that the Reich will be the master of Europe ... From there the way to world domination is practically certain.[62]

Goebbels was unflappable. 'In the storms that rage around us,' he opined, 'we are prouder than ever before to be German.'

While Peiper bitterly spoke his mind to the Berlin National Socialist upper-crust, his faraway division fought a costly and futile campaign to rescue fifty-six thousand trapped Germans in the Cherkassy–Korsun pocket. The catastrophe reached a final climax on 21 March 1944, when two hundred Soviet tanks crashed through the fragmented Leibstandarte lines between Tarnopol and Proskurov. There was little to stop the enemy. The end of March saw the division nearly wiped out when subjected to entrapment, assault and then perilous escape from the Hube pocket. 'Losses can never be too high!' Adolf Hitler had remarked to Generalfeldmarschal Walter von Reichenau in 1942. 'They sow the seeds of future glory.'[63]

Certainly after the winter of 1944, if Hitler remained focused on Darwinian attrition, he would have not been disappointed. On 7 April the 1st SS Panzer Division was armoured in name only—being reduced to just two Tigers and nine assault guns. Only a small battle group under Werner Poetschke remained—just 1,305 men, the whole of the division.[64] On 14 April 1944 the divisional residue boarded trains and chugged off to the West. Transport did not take long; so emaciated was the Leibstandarte that only a few trains were needed to transport the entire lot. Four days later Wisch established the divisional headquarters at Turnhout, Belgium, where it was assigned to Dietrich's I SS Panzer Corps.

When Peiper headed back, his unit was once more being reconstituted from ashes. The Leibstandarte was already training in Beverloo, Belgium, to oppose the anticipated invasion of France. In the meantime some of the old hands in the division looked warily on the latest rebuilding effort for the Leibstandarte, and it was affecting morale. The rank-and-file now contained 'a lot of ordinary Germans', an old hare ventured. There were many *Volksdeutsche*, too—ethnic Germans, that some, like Peiper, saw as watering down the elite. There was even a notification making the rounds that French volunteers in the Waffen SS should be treated well and given an equivalent pay grade to what they had managed in 1940. 'The SS isn't what it used to be,' one concluded.[65]

Still, in the end, for Jochen Peiper there was no comprehending the failure in Russia. 'I strove hard to get some light into the mystery of the German defeat in the East,' he later wrote, 'rooted more in the psychological than on military grounds.'[66]

Now they would meet the British and American invasion on French shores. It was the non-German land that seemed to come and go in Peiper's life. He would be there this time to cast the Americans and British back into the sea. The Western Allies now seemed set on reversing the conquest of National Socialism and then bringing Hitler and his Germany to its knees.

But that objective—the very end of the Third Reich—would not come freely or willingly. Peiper remained proud of Hitler's accomplishments and his aim—to create a unified Europe, banish the communists and re-order it with Aryan masters.[67]

Militarily there were some glimmers of hope: new Luftwaffe jets, Joseph Goebbels assured that the German economy was now on a total war footing and Albert Speer's amped-up industry assured that tanks and aircraft were being churned out at a rapid rate. When Peiper saw his old SS friend, Hans Schwarz Van Berk, at Goebbel's office in Berlin, he heard more about the first of the secret weapons—a pulse jet-powered robot bomb. The war correspondent was an old friend of Peiper's, having been with Das Reich during the war and fought in Russia. Schwarz Van Berk suggested it be called the *Vergeltungswaffe-1*—Vengeance Weapon No. 1.[68] Shortened to V-1, Hitler eagerly agreed.

There still remained the issue of fighting on the ground. As Jochen Peiper saw it, to reach the Fatherland, the Allies would first need to cross France. And to do that they must face the Leibstandarte Adolf Hitler.

Would his men fight the gallant fight, or would it be like Russia?[69]

Chapter 16

Waiting for the Invasion

'It will undoubtedly happen that the enemy will make the attempt, today, tomorrow or the next day, at some time to break into this fortress of Europe.'

—Heinrich Himmler

Even amid war, spring in France seemed promising—nearly idyllic. Then, in 1944—as always—Madame Francine Vico savoured the beauty of her early season garden. There in the side courtyard of the ancient L'Abbaye d'Ardenne, her delicate white and purple crocuses would suddenly sprout out of the matted grey and yellowed ground. That sudden March eruption of green and white—the tiny snowdrops— was the much-anticipated call to spring and the herald of warmer temperatures along the Normandy coast, for the wet winter winds of the Calvados region were rainy and cold enough that any coming warmth was welcome. Since her family had located there in 1923, planting the tiny bulbs had been a comforting ritual.

The big abbey from the thirteenth century where she made her garden was a special place in regional history. Located on a long, sloping saddle of rock, the religious icon was appropriately located on the highest point around Caen, France. From its six-sided limestone towers, one could either look out to the dark blue sea just to the west or to the golden green-tinged fields to the east, boasting of beets and peas amid the golden grains. But for the spring of 1944 Vico kept her eyes to the ground and simple things.[1] With the spring snowdrops already up and gone, she planted new ones in hopes for a better spring in 1945.

Vico's garden provided a focus throughout the years of turmoil in France—years that had seen France fall to the Germans and now occupied for four years. Locals said the British and Americans would liberate them in the summer of 1943, but they never came. And now they said they would come that spring, but the snowdrops burst out of the ground and then withered, with no sign of their liberators. Would this be the summer the British and Americans might liberate them from German clutches? Would 1945 bring freedom? Squeezing her crucifix, she prayed. Save her daughters, she had no idea who might be informers to the menacing German occupation forces. One had to be careful. Indeed, she had no idea where her older son Jacques was, and she didn't ask.

In May of 1940 Jacques Vico had watched the Germans strut through Normandy, marching proudly five across and singing in baritone harmony. The youthful display was so extraordinary and in such contrast to the downtrodden, unwashed and tattered uniforms of the beaten French who walked dejectedly before them. He was ashamed. As a tear came to his eye, he reflected that French society as he knew it was destroyed. 'They are too proud,' he muttered to himself as the legions passed. 'Their strength is corrupt. We won't bow to them.' True to his promise, he joined the resistance at a time when there were more French pledging allegiance to the pro-German government of Vichy than the exiled French of Charles de Gaulle. Even though it was a desperate situation, Jacques still had hope while listening to de Gaulle in Britain promise that 'the war will become worldwide and we continue it. Tomorrow we will crush our enemies. The flame will never go out.'

His brother, Jean-Marie, his sister and even his father, Roland, were also in the resistance, but so secret was the allegiance that none of them knew of each other's actions. The gravity of the secrecy became painfully obvious on 15 December 1943, when the local Gestapo arrested Roland Vico and hauled him off to jail in Caen. Soon the slick and wily local Gestapo also apprehended Jacques's best friend, then tortured him to confession and shot him. Jacques and his brother then moved a large cache of weapons stored in the abbey just the night before the Gestapo came. Pretending to be resistance fighters themselves, French turncoats told their 15-year-old sister that they were looking for her brother, who they understood was one of them. 'One, he is not part of the resistance,' she insisted, 'and he's not here.' Then something dropped from the pocket of one of the smarmy Frenchmen. Margarite stooped down. 'Here are your German cigarettes,' she said, reaching up. The Gestapo men were furious. They arrested her mother, Francine, and took her to prison. Now both parents were gone.

Nothing was safe after that. Both brothers went underground, all the while continuing their risky jobs for the resistance. Jacques assumed a new identity, as did his brother. Both travelled on an unknown schedule, under a changing alias, depending on luck and the generosity of locals. They always moved with an eye to danger: capture, torture and worse.

In early February 1944 Francine Vico emerged from the Gestapo jail in Caen. She was weak and scared. The last she had heard, her husband, Roland, had been sent off to Mauthausen concentration camp in Austria. With horrid rumours of what went on in that place, she dared not think of his fate. And she knew nothing of her sons. They were missing, and no one knew where they were. Was her France gone for good? Even with German soldiers occupying the abbey, she planted the tiny crocus bulbs in her garden around two large stones in an oval pattern as she always did. It was a small act of tranquillity in the midst of a crazy war. Francine prayed for France; she prayed for her sons and husband.

* * *

In March of 1944 Jochen Peiper was lucky to be alive. The Waffen SS glorification of death in battle and the nearly religious exaltation of fighting had left countless comrades silent in graves stretching from the Urals to France. SS officer battle casualties soared. The number of times a man had been wounded became a bragging right within the ranks and even its leadership. Had not Himmler boasted to an audience in 1942 that nearly all the first class of fifty-four officers from the SS Junkerschule at Bad Tölz had fallen in battle?[2]

Returning from a long stay with his family in Tegernsee at the end of March, Peiper was still ailing. Thus, he shipped off to the SS hospital in Berlin, where doctors treated him for 'heavy symptoms of typhus and diphtheria'.[3] Also suffering shell shock and classified as 'unfit for duty', Peiper characteristically ignored the advice. Two days later he was off to Belgium to re-join his division, with an important stopover in Charleroi.

Belgian Rexist and SS hero Leon Degrelle had just come back from a catastrophic fight in Russia to escape encirclement from the Cherkassy pocket—fewer than half his Belgians came out of the fight alive. Hitler himself had personally presented Degrelle with the Ritterkreuz on 20 February as he was feted by the Nazi propaganda machine desperate for pan-Germanic war heroes enthusiastically embracing the struggle. 'If I had a son,' Hitler told the Belgian wistfully, 'I would want him to be just like you.'[4] In Brussels, Paris and Berlin Degrelle made rousing speeches where he posed as the embodiment of the New Europe desperately fighting to save Western civilization from the ravages of Bolshevist and American barbarians. The *Chef de Rex* fully intended to ride the Nazi coat-tails to power and assume leadership of occupied Belgium, throwing lavish parties throughout Belgium for Rexist supporters.

On 2 April 1944 the Leibstandarte Adolf Hitler, with Sepp Dietrich and Jochen Peiper in attendance, met Degrelle and the Légion Wallonie at the Grand Place of Charleroi south of Brussels. There military decorations were doled out, and a borrowed Leibstandarte motorized column 17km long sputtered through Brussels in the bright afternoon sunshine. A large crowd of sympathizers and curious onlookers gathered to witness the parade of Hitler's Belgian propaganda pantheon.[5] Degrelle, the Ardennes native of Bouillon, was thoroughly intoxicated by his reception, his arm outstretched in a Hitler salute while his children rode atop his flower-draped halftrack, describing it as:

> Trains of welcoming young girls with vibrant eyes waited for us at the boundary of Brussels. The centre of the capital was a sea of faces and flags. The panzers could hardly pass among the tens of thousands of people who had hurried to see and madly cheer our soldiers. The crowd tossed like the sea, shouting and throwing thousands of roses.[6]

Peiper, who looked on dispassionately, had concerns other than roses and champagne receptions. While in Brussels that day the local commandant chastised the SS colonel, complaining that when the Leibstandarte had passed through the city in recent weeks it had done so as an embarrassing rabble. Having gotten off the trains, they appeared more as impoverished pathetic plebeians on Russian *panje* wagons than Hitler's own proud tank regiment. Done with Degrelle and his egoistic campaign, Peiper drove on to the regimental headquarters in Hasselt, Belgium, that had been set up in a large school not far from the famous Hotel Aux trois Pistolets that served as a frequent meeting place. Peiper stashed his gear in a vacant home and headed off to the regimental flag. To his consternation, although his headquarters was bustling, he found that his Panzer regiment had not a single tank. Some of the men had jokingly taken to calling themselves *SS Panzer Division Hott*—horse drawn.[7] Peiper was not amused.

SS tank driver Manfred Thorn recalled that pistols were the only weapons they possessed as their dilapidated company moved to quarters in an old school in Genk that April. The great influx of new men was composed of totally raw recruits. This was the first time the most basic training was taking place in such a short space of time before being used on the Front, which Thorn found distinctly discouraging.[8] In spite of the company chief Werner Wolff's enthusiasm, men of the 7th Panzer

Company seemed depressed. SS Untersturmführer Kurt Sametreiter was a decorated tank man but, like everyone else, was without tanks:

> It was in Genk that I fell out of favour with Jochen Peiper and because I had the welfare of my men at heart—twice! When one thought back to Russian campaigns one thought about the bitter cold Russian winter and accompanying fleas and the unbearably hot summers— over 40° and mosquitos ... Upon receiving my first orders after arriving in Genk, I noticed more than enough exercise hours, which I decided to replace with 'mend and darn' hours out in the sun. Peiper was furious and I was placed under house-arrest being given office work for five days. Yes, the morale of the men in Genk was not the best and so I arranged a 'Revue Night' with professionals from the town. The evening was going well and a few of the officers had been invited to sit in the front row when I decided that a highlight was needed. I asked for volunteers, borrowed the costumes of the ladies from the revue and we dressed ourselves in these costumes. We pranced around the stage to hilarious laughter of all present—except one. The remaining vacant seat in the front row had now been filled—by Peiper! His eyes bored holes into me, telling me that it would be better if I disappeared from the stage, which I did in all haste. The next day, I received orders to present myself to our commander 'Teddi' Theodor Wisch, who, with a smirk on his face, told me that I had in the future to make a very large circle around Jochen Peiper, who did not want to set eyes on me. My behaviour the previous evening was not fitting for a Ritterkreuz holder![9]

Still, the surviving Panzer men from the Ukraine were encouraged by the climate and greatly reduced danger. There were even gifts from Hitler— the so-called *Führerpaketen*. The gift—of rare rations: sugar, butter, honey and marmalade—was authorized for personnel on leave, particularly those coming from the East. In quiet moments—far from the danger recently faced—some sat about, while the musically inclined, such as SS officer Günter Gaul, squeezed out singalong tunes on their accordions. As they listened and sang Lili Marlene to the strains of the beaten squeeze box, Belgium became another world.

To be sure, the steely commander was welcomed on his return by those he recognized, but there were many new faces. True, trusted men such as Heinz Kling in Waterscheid and Werner Pötschke in Houthalen were there, but his command was only a shadow of what he had left in Russia. Equipment was still pathetic, and uniforms and boots were tattered. Sloppy—for Peiper, that was worst.

The immediate task was to rebuild, train and refit. The Leibstandarte had been so shattered that there was little left.[10] An early move was to transfer two thousand men of lower rank from the 12th SS, and then replacements of every variety began to arrive. On 19 April 1944 the division—including drivers and cooks—consisted of only seventy-four hundred men with no heavy weapons.[11] Given the avalanche of replacements fed into the ranks, many of the 'young marchers' taken on had absolutely no driving or weapons experience. Some were castoffs from the Luftwaffe (always eyed with suspicion) or officers fresh out of an SS Junkerschule. Most from the cadet school only had a modicum of infantry training; indeed, in the summer 1944, fifty-seven per cent of SS officers were 20 years or younger.[12] Their numbers included Russian Hiwis and even two Englishmen, a London taxi driver and a lorry driver from the Midlands who had served with the Flak battalion in Russia.[13]

In the meantime Hitler, who always took an interest in his namesake division, ordered that tanks be shipped to the division with his decreed priority. Many would arrive, fresh from the factory, but getting them to Belgium would take some time. Peiper's old boss, Heinrich Himmler, took an interest, too. While the Leibstandarte staggered into Belgium, the Reichführer SS was busy celebrating the creation of new Waffen SS legions. The latest was the 17th SS Panzer Grenadier Division, Götz von Berlichingen—named after the Franconian Imperial Knight, mercenary and poet. On 10 April 1944, with Sepp Dietrich present, Himmler gave a rousing speech at the division activation at the town hall in Thouars, France, designed to inspire the latest Waffen SS formation:

> We have travelled a long way since the founding of the SS. In 1925 the Führer founded a new organization called the *Schutzstaffel* [Protective Column]. At the time the SS was made up of a very small minority … to guarantee that wherever the Führer went, he would always be protected … We guaranteed his body and his life. That is why we were founded and we have gone our own way, blind in our loyalty to the Reich, to the mythos of this ancient, holy, German Reich based on the ideal of a select racial and human minority.[14]

SS Sturmbannführer Hans Lingner, who had been in the same SS officer's class as Peiper—graduating at Braunschweig in April 1936—would eventually lead the 17th SS in autumn in full bravado. He agreed that his SS leaders would be focused on total effort in battle, no matter the odds. Did not fighting when the war was lost mean unnecessary bloodshed? 'We have all been brought up from the cradle,' he would later say, 'to consider Leonida's fight at Thermopylae as the highest form of sacrifice for one's people.'[15]

Himmler said the first and most hallowed name was given to the first Waffen SS battalion as it was expanded, the Leibstandarte Adolf Hitler—'the restorer of the new Germany'. That, Himmler said proudly, now was the famous 1st SS Panzer Division.

Was Himmler not paying close attention? As the Leibstandarte arrived in Belgium they took on all sorts of standard replacements—even poorly motivated ex-Luftwaffe men. Seeking some counter to the 'watering down', Peiper personally sought out previously wounded Leibstandarte veterans returning from hospitals and, perhaps goaded by his own circumstance, set off on a teletype campaign to try to even shake loose experienced Panzer officers still in the hospitals.[16] Results were substandard with the bruising SS style of leadership—there always seemed a shortage of officers and NCOs. As a result, Peiper would order each tank company to go into battle with only three officers.[17]

Material standards were atrocious as well. Side arms from Russia were 'like a pile of junk', and training in tanks was impossible—there were none. In one sense it didn't matter, for there was no gasoline. After Russia, parade marches and firing exercises seemed lame, but that was all there was to do.[18] As an emergency measure, tank crews were moved from the 12th SS Panzer Division forming in Normandy. SS Private Hartwig Kammescheidt had been moved from the Hitlerjugend Division, where he and his youthful tank men had been enjoying the sunny days in Normandy and were now dismayed to find themselves back in cold, misty Belgium. Worse, they were in the 6th Panzer Company now—supposedly with Panzer IVs not yet present. They then found themselves harassed by their company leader, SS officer Benoni Junker, who had the youths march in parade file until they threw up or fell out in exhaustion. Instead, they idolized Peiper—whom Junker seemed to undermine covertly. 'He made an excellent impression on us, reminding us of Max Wünsche.'[19]

While the men of the 6th Panzer Company were ordered around by Junker, others fared better. 'The 7th Company was better off with their young chief, [Werner] Wolf, who was completely courageous and competent,' remembered Kammescheit. Two hours of weekly ideological discourse replaced realistic training exercises with combat weapons.[20] Peiper and the old hares must have cringed. Anticipating the dodge, a divisional special order insisted the ideological training not be omitted, calling it 'just as essential as weapons or terrain studies.' Indeed, a specific schooling pamphlet entitled 'Der Dietrich'—the passkey—was part of the course work.

Anticipating the invasion, the Leibstandarte's weekly newspaper pumped up the anti-American rhetoric. To Nazi propagandists, the Americans, with the Jews from New York, were just as evil as the Bolshevists in Russia. 'The Germany that is rising has to destroy these enemies,' newspaper quoted, 'give the world conscience against capitalism and Judaism':

> The Americans have no culture and you cannot compare the American way of life to that of Northern Europe. The Americans want to lead everything in the world. They are convinced that they are the chosen people. American jazz is more popular than Wagner in Germany, American architecture has replaced the great buildings that emerged from Greece ... The American cocktail has taken over the coffee shops of Paris. They have to convince everyone that the world of tomorrow belongs to America.[21]

Worse than pointless propaganda, Peiper learned that the Tiger company upon which he had learned to depend upon so heavily in Russia was now to be detached. It would be formed as a corps battalion and would no longer fight directly under him. No more Michael Wittmann—and no Tigers. They were close by to be sure; by 30 April SS Heavy Panzer Battalion 101 would be billeted in Gournay-en-Bray. Hitler gave explicit orders at the end of April dictating that the division's rfitting was to have all preference in men, equipment and weapons. And rumours ran wild that the division would receive a heavy Tiger battalion rather than Mk IVs. But when that failed to materialize, word circulated that they would get both battalions outfitted with the heavy Panthers. Peiper himself grew anxious of that prospect as well. If they depended solely on the Panthers, he warned one of his officers, the great Allied bombing campaign might hit its critical factories and leave them with nary a tank.[22]

On 27 April Peiper motored to Louviers, north-west of Paris, to see the manoeuvres of the 12th SS Panzer Division with the other big names in Hitler's Panzer leadership such as General Heinz Guderian. Peiper's input was caustic enough: they were still awaiting even a single tank, and the physical replacements being received were not impressive. Dietrich returned back to Belgium to inspect his old division and hand out medals on 5 May in the typical outdoor forested scene preferred for such occasions. Peiper was there as Dietrich awarded him the medal for bravery in the Ukraine. He, like Dietrich, was outfitted in full regalia: Knight's cross, tank assault badge and crusher cap while shaking hands and striding about with his old fighting comrade, Albert Frey, in jodhpurs and polished boots. SS Unterschaführer Valentin Bersin, who had a reputation for crazy bravery leading a Panzer tank—'a real rowdy'—was one of the recipients.

The concern about equipment only faded when a clutch of Panzer Mk IV model Ausf. Js appeared on 10 May. Peiper's brand-new Panzer IV, sporting a metal side skirt to protect against a bazooka, had '001' smartly stencilled on its freshly painted turret. Yet even at the end of May, the continuing fuel shortages and Allied air power meant that virtually none of the new Panzer men had even driven their tanks.[23] Moreover, with the unabated fighting on the Eastern Front, there was no ammunition to spare for gun training. Instead, they practised how to use pine boughs to turn a steel Panzer into something resembling a conifer-covered hunting blind. Well and good, but how would these new men drive and fire?[24] They were still short of equipment: Peiper personally sent Rolf Reiser to bring back the thirty-eight Panthers the regiment was to draw from a depot at Mailly-le-Camp.[25] Peiper's night guard at the Leibstandarte headquarters in Hasselt was SS Unterscharführer Günter Gaul. He had fought with Peiper in Russia near Krasnopol and remembered his superior from their summer days in Vernuil, France, in 1942. Late at night, while Gaul watched over the telephones, Peiper stopped by to engage Gaul in conversation. The topics were wide ranging, but they most often featured Peiper's near obsession with training and obtaining the best equipment for his command—how else would they throw back any invasion when it came?[26]

Flirting with a defeatist attitude, Peiper now also had problems with Himmler. It seems that word had got back of his conversation with Joseph Goebbels the month before, when SS leader Peiper had been bad mouthing the upper military leadership around Hitler, suggesting that the war was already lost. Oddly, old Sepp Dietrich came to his defence: 'You know him from the time when he served as your personal adjutant. Never was there this kind of corrosive criticism that carried him away in April of this year … We need to be sincere and honest, because only this way of association with each other serves our sacred cause. This is just the way I want you to interpret and classify the [recent] sarcastic and inflammatory statement of SS-Ostubaf. Peiper.'

> Peiper is the centre piece of my whole corps. The success of the Leibstandarte Panzer Regiment is unthinkable without him. His passion, his commitment and last but not least his brilliant way of leading troops under his command makes him one of the most outstanding leaders in the entire Waffen SS, if not the entire Wehrmacht.[27]

Meanwhile, wary of American air power, the 'centre piece' of Dietrich's whole corps, Jochen Peiper, moved his headquarters to an inconspicuous location on 1 May, a children's home in a park between Hasselt and Kiewitt. On 14 May the tankers of the division assembled in a grassy field near Houthalen, where Jochen reviewed his new men, now with at least a few tanks. Werner Poetschke mustered the men. The new Panthers stood out starkly like steel-ordered monuments, while those to be decorated lined up before them. There were boxes of medals for the soldiers who had survived the fierce fighting in the East—twenty-seven men donned the Iron Cross first class, and 160 received the second-class award. Peiper presented the medals as a red and black Hakenkreuz flag fluttered in the spring air before the line of tanks. Ribbons and crosses settled on new collars.

After festivities broke up, Peiper located his Panthers at a Belgian monastery and had the Mk IV tanks and their two Panzer companies camouflaged about an old international boarding school in Genk. Peiper made the move with one eye to security—the natives were sometimes unfriendly—and the other cast upwards. Air attack and protection from it was an ever-present danger as British and American fighters prowled the spring sky. The rail bridge at Hasselt was bombed one week after another. Everybody—even tank men—were trained to fight as infantry in case the Allies decided to drop paratroopers on their heads. In the meantime, SS Obersturmführer Fritz Steipart made his quarters for the 5th Panzer Company with his heavy Panther tanks at the turreted Château de Bockrijk, and found the expansive estate grounds made security a bit easier.

Hasselt had historical significance for Peiper. The Hôtel Aux trois Pistolets was where Himmler had dropped off his young adjutant in May 1940 when he re-joined the Leibstandarte for the campaign in France. Peiper set up his bed in Kiewit, 6km north-east of the city, and invited Sigurd to join him. Soon Frau Peiper appeared on 17 April 1944, and they were together again in Belgium. It must have seemed a bit like the halcyon days in the West years before: in 1942 Jochen and Sigurd had enjoyed a lovely French summer together between the war-torn forays into Russia. Compared to the East, this was a vacation.

Ever attentive to Himmler's obsessions with marriage and the importance of siring German children, Peiper also invited the spouses of his other subordinates to join them that spring. At the end of May the NCOs put on a social, complete with a handball tournament. In that sport Jochen was an eager participant. And a short distance along the rail line was tiny Waterscheid, where his men stopped by the tavern to be plied with alcohol while local musicians improvised waltzes on the harmonica and drum. The place was packed every night until curfew, as each SS man did his best to appeal to the few women who would dance. Soon, some of the extracurricular activities got out of hand with drinking and more drinking—excessive revelry, of which Peiper always disapproved; indeed, he was simply towing the line that Himmler had expounded the previous fall.[28]

Werner Sternebeck was one of the serious party leaders. Even in Russia, although he fought tough all day, when he got to the rear he was a changed man. For him the war was something of which to make the best. A horse lover by nature, Sternebeck sometimes wore riding breeches and slung a sabre from his waist. If there was a horse to ride, he rode it, and if there was drink, he drank. If there were ladies, it was his job as a dashing SS officer to charm them. He was a dedicated eccentric—the man was known to signal his tanks to advance in Russia not by the customary pumped balled fist but rather by an angled sword held forward from the turret.

Peiper hated all that stuff—particularly from an officer. The liquor situation was clearly out of hand; even his orderly was hurt in a drunken vehicle accident—Peiper had the guilty man confined to quarters and given 'choice' assignments. When the sun rose on German hangovers, the weather was warm and the trees shone in luminescent bright green. Even a Belgian mining town in May 1944 seemed like the old days.[29]

While Peiper attempted to bring his command into shape, his friendly rival, Max Wünsche, continued to garner the limelight—now the Panzer regiment commander in the Hitlerjugend Panzer Division. Wünsche had spent the entire year preparing his youthful tankers for this engagement— constant driver and gunnery training, inspections of the Panzer workshops and even inspirational visits to the battlefields of Verdun and Belleau Wood. Peiper's competitor was poised. His mug graced the cover of *Das Schwarze Korps* on 23 March 1944, depicting Himmler shaking his hand in the presence of Dietrich and Kurt Meyer on the occasion of his recent promotion.[30]

On their mutual birthday of 20 April, Hitler always telephoned Wünsche no matter where he happened to be during the war. In 1939 he had given Max an autographed and gold-engraved copy of *Mein Kampf*, but in 1944 Max had a personal invite from Hitler himself to pay a visit to the Berghof. With Wünsche arriving by rail at Berchtesgaden, Hitler thoughtfully had a car waiting for him.[31] Soon Hitler's former adjutant found himself at a gala birthday celebration at Hitler's alpine retreat. There was also the obligatory handshake photo with Hitler as Himmler looked on. Also featured at the Führer's birthday gathering was Genobst. Hans Hube, who had just miraculously extricated the 1st Panzer Army from encirclement and certain destruction on the Russian Front. Hitler was now awarding diamonds to Oak Leaves for the defensive battle.

Just after lunch there was a massive stack of birthday presents to open. That done, Wünsche went along with Himmler and the inner circle for a demonstration of new low-slung Jagdpanzer IV tank killers. Dr Ferdinand Porsche, who had conceived the vaunted Tiger tank, was helping Hitler to design better armour to fight his war. To that aim, there was even one of the first prototypes of the hulking 72-ton Jadgtiger with its 128mm gun to show the German leader. He, along with others, looked on approvingly at the early production arrayed on a motorway near Klessheim castle. Returning back to the Berghof, there was the daily jaunt to the teahouse for *gemütliche* conversation around a crackling fire with coffee and strudel. Wünsche felt right back at home, and Hitler likely felt the same. For less than a month later, on 18 May, the Führer served as best man at Wünsche's wartime wedding, held right after the meeting in Berchtesgaden.[32] That was a highly unusual honour in Hitler's Germany.

Who could get more press? Back in Belgium, in the first week of June, Goebbels's war correspondents turned out to film Peiper's Panther battalion trundling about under the Belgian sun. Peiper's re-formed command didn't look rag-tag. It didn't look afraid.

There was Werner Pötschke—tough as nails with his new Knight's Cross. The man had been wounded eight times, and his face was scarred and grizzled. Here was an SS commander so hard that those under him learned to fear him—indeed, to avoid him.[33] Even an open collar on a uniform could earn a point mission for an enlisted man in the next attack. A microphone thrust before SS Unterscharführer Valentin Bersin sent the enthusiasm of a brash young tank leader coursing across German airwaves. The SS Leibstandarte was cocky and confident.

Unknown to Peiper, Allied code breakers had an accurate pulse on their efforts to reconstitute. While noting on 19 May that the division now had a ration strength of 17,257 men and a tank strength of eighty-six, the intercept told of being short 4,143 men and of the great need for trucks and heavy weapons.[34] So inadequate was the state of readiness that forty greenhorns from the Panzer regiment were sent off to Normandy to train with the Panzer Lehr Division. Some recruits only had a driver's licence. There was help from a small cadre of old hares—Guhl and the SPW battalion were close by, but not with the tank arm. Gerhard Nüske would serve as his adjutant and swashbuckling Werner Sternebeck as his orderly officer. Both were *'alte Panzerhasen'*.[35] Peiper handed over command of the 7th Panzer Company to his former adjutant, Werner Wolff.

Wolff had been severely wounded in Russia in November and returned to Peiper that April. Although he had no training with tanks, Peiper trusted Wolff completely. He was a well-known loner—curt, self-absorbed, and prone to act rather than seek direction. Yet this was the strapping youth who stood tall amid the hellish maelstrom of Kursk, leading, shooting, shouting and flinging hand grenades. He was after all, the SS officer who had mounted a Russian tank there and killed its commander with a knife. He was fearless, and Peiper wanted him. And so Wolff became a tank man, based not on experience but rather bravery—a fact that irked his battalion superior, SS Obersturmführer Heinz Kling. Another SS officer, Erich Rumpf, recalled,

> Peiper loved to give drastic orders and especially appreciated officers who followed his manner. His special darlings were Wolff, Preuss and Guhl. They all were officers with him with the SPW battalion. He was responsible for carrying out a ruthless combat. Not only were the orders he gave decisive, but also the knowledge of every member of his troop that their commander generally approves of a ruthless combat and that he particularly appreciates members who fight in this spirit and holds them as courageous and daring decision makers for the others. He was the unquestioned master of the regiment.[36]

Even though it was a tall order to whip the raw recruits into technically capable Panzer men, it was another to transform them into ideological soldiers who understood what National Socialism meant, Waffen SS style. While impugning Himmler's fantasies of a knightly order to serve as unflinching instruments of Hitler's will, men such as Werner Wolff viewed their status in more prosaic terms. To them the Waffen SS was a blood brotherhood in a merciless and fatalistic assault troop where personal loyalties were only peripheral to Adolf Hitler and National Socialism. The true dedication was to its charismatic leaders, men like Dietrich, Peiper or Meyer. They had to learn that special mode of Waffen SS fighting—a 'blend of determination and ruthlessness'.[37] Old SS types or young hotheads such as Wolff found the attitude of ex-Luftwaffe men gutless and reprehensible. But the division leaders aimed to show they meant business.

In early May some of the replacement troops got into serious trouble. Four young soldiers broke into a local farmhouse and stole chickens and a bicycle. Within the Waffen SS, theft was one of those egregious crimes of which there was little tolerance; indeed, there was record of a

Hitlerjugend Waffen SS man being sent to Dachau concentration camp for simply listening to a single Allied radio broadcast.[38] In any case, formal court martial proceedings took place in a grassy meadow in front of the assembled Panzer regiment on 28 May 1944. Peiper, Kuhlmann and Pötschke presided before the divisional judge, SS Sturmbannführer Markus Jochum. All four 'looters' were found guilty and summarily shot immediately after the trial before the assembled regiment. The real reason for the shooting likely had little to do with stealing chickens and everything to do with obedience from the new rag-tag replacements whom Peiper found offending.[39]

Arndt Fischer, then in charge of a platoon in the 3rd Panzer Company, was mortified. He had been training these greenhorns. 'We could barely stand it,' he recalled. 'Our operations were already suicide affairs. You could have at least given these young rascals a chance to redeem themselves in one of them!'[40] Who exactly gave the order for the execution is uncertain. However, it is a fact that after the war the Chief Prosecutor's Office of Bavaria sought to question Peiper regarding the incident.[41] 'I was present during the shootings,' Peiper said. 'There was a regular trial of the field court of the division. The men belonged to the SS Division Hitlerjugend as replacements for the SS. These people were fully trained, but sent away from their former unit. So, this was not the best *Menschenmaterial*.'[42]

Human material? Beyond that unfeeling appraisal, it is certain that Peiper approved of the proceedings: 'I can remember from the West, before the invasion, I had an incident in my regiment, where five young men who plundered and committed other things were shot. Afterwards, nobody was more upset about them having been executed than Sepp Dietrich. I admit, we thought it to have been totally correct.'[43]

Killing enemies and killing their own. Guilt and shock seemed to reach everywhere within the German war machine that summer of 1944.

Back at Hitler's headquarters the staff of generals who planned and plotted to repel the western invasion warily looked over their shoulders to the Russians' growing strength. On 5 May 1944, a group of generals assembled far south in the Bavarian Alps at the Hitler Youth training centre at Ordensburg Sonthofen. Heinrich Himmler soon addressed the group. 'Of this you can be sure,' he told the assembly. 'Had we not eliminated the Jews in Germany we would not have been able to endure the bombing.'

The Jewish question in Germany and the occupied countries has been solved. It has been solved in accordance with the struggle for the

252

survival of our people, in which the survival of our blood is at stake … We are all soldiers, whatever uniform we wear. You might like to sympathize with me and imagine how hard it was to fulfil this soldierly order that was given to me that I followed and carried out of obedience and with the utmost conviction … In this showdown with Asia, we must accustom ourselves to the ground rules and consign to oblivion the morals of past European wars which are dear and much closer to us … Even as Germans, with our deep heartfelt good-natured feeling, we cannot justify allowing hate-filled avengers to grow up so that our children and grandchildren have to settle with them, because we … were too weak or cowardly and left the children for them.[44]

The crisis of summer 1944 seemed to drive the National Socialist state further to its Freikorpian roots, a *Weltanschauung*—world view—of war and destruction. The 'success' that Himmler could point to was the Reich's terrible secret. That summer the gas chambers and crematoria in Poland grimly churned to their maximum deathly output, while the number of *Untermenschen* working and dying as slaves for the master race reached a diabolical apex. Could any real soldier welcome that? It is, then again, surprising that with the war all but lost, a similar address given to another group of generals three weeks later elicited applause when Himmler announced the 'solution' to the Jewish question. 'You know me well enough,' he announced, 'to realize that I am no bloodthirsty fellow and am not one to take amusement in whatever tough thing that I have to do.'[45] Why reveal this now? Was it an expression of pride or an admission of collapsing internal morality? Or perhaps it was to draw the generals into complicity within a regime engaged in criminal acts of historic dimension. 'The bombing,' Himmler justified, 'is in the last analysis organized by the Jews.'

Meanwhile, prospects for rebuilding Peiper's command were not hurt by the fact that the new SS corps commander and frequent divisional visitor was Sepp Dietrich. He arrived one morning at the end of May to consult Generaloberst Heinz Guderian, now the chief inspector of the Panzer troops. Guderian addressed the men at their school in Genk with a promise of many new tanks.[46] Afterwards, a luncheon was served in which Jochen Peiper and Werner Wolff sat directly across from Guderian and Dietrich. At one point Peiper turned to Dietrich: 'Wolff has been engaged for seven years,' he said staring across the table, 'and he doesn't want to get married.' Wolff's jaw dropped as Peiper smiled knowingly. Wolff, who had been carrying on as a confirmed bachelor for some time, had a hometown sweetheart. Dietrich, the hoary old soldier, didn't hesitate. He told the 21-year-old SS officer to bring his fiancée to Belgium and marry her. Soon they sent off Wolff's tank gunner to Memel to bring the girl back and make an honest man of Peiper's favourite.[47]

Meantime, just days after Guderian's promise, came word that twenty-five new Panzer IVs had arrived in Hasselt and needed picking up. Manfred Thorn and Gerhard Stiller were among the selected drivers who made their way to the train station, only to find that there was not enough gasoline for the tanks to unload off the flatcars and get them back to Genk. Only by pilfering cars did they get enough *Benzin* to move them back. For the Panzer men it was maddening.

Regardless of such confusion, the summer solstice approached. Even in the depths of the war, division orders emphasized that nothing was to interrupt the special *Sonnwendfeier* celebrations. Within the divisional orders was an exact description of how the holiday was to be celebrated in the fifth year of war—complete with poems and songs to be sung together from the *SS Liederbuch*. Company leaders were to make sure it was celebrated punctually at 2200 hours on 21 June. The key change was substitution for the roaring fire typically used for the midnight celebration: the firewood was to be assembled and the music played, but due to the Allied air power, no fires were to be lit.[48] A *Sonnwendfeier* with no big bonfire? No one seemed to think the invasion was coming— at least for now.

Meanwhile, Peiper was still focused on marrying off his single Waffen SS officers. That obsession fully extended to Kurt Meyer as well. 'With us [the SS] once he is an Obersturmführer, unless he is married, then the poor fellow can sit around for years with no promotion.' But Meyer took it one step further, with the proviso—like Himmler—that it might be useful to take on mistresses as well:

> The family is the nucleus around which a strong state is built, but the war has torn such enormous gaps among German men, woman and children, that ways must be found to prevent the drying up of healthy blood of German women. After the end of the war hundreds of thousands will be left behind without menfolk. It is impossible that hundreds of thousands of 25- to 30-year-old girls should wander around the Reich as useless 'duds' until they're 60 to 70 years old.[49]

Nor were matrimonial concerns confined only to Peiper's orbit. On 3 June 1944 another big celebration was in the offing at Hitler's mountain retreat in the Obersalzberg. Gretl Braun, the sister to Hitler's mistress Eva, would marry Himmler's adjutant to Hitler, SS Brigadeführer Hermann Fegelein. Peiper had known Fegelein since the beginning of his career, both having got their start riding horses in the early days of the SS Reitersturm. Participating in savage anti-partisan warfare in the East—and being rewarded copiously—Fegelein now came to roost at Hitler's Berghof. There, since the spring of 1944, Fegelein had been Waffen SS liaison officer between Himmler and Hitler. The SS Reichsführer was proud of Fegelein.

Having made fast friends with Party Minister Martin Bormann, the SS officer soon became a dinner table fixture at Hitler's grandiose quarters at the Berghof. 'Fegelein was the daring cavalryman type,' Hitler's secretary Traudl Junge recalled. 'He had a very large nose and wore the Knight's Cross with oak leaves and swords. No wonder he was used to women flocking around him.'[50] Soon Eva Braun's sister, Gretl, took a shine to the dashing Fegelein. Whether the attraction was genuine or careerism, the two were married in an elegant ceremony in Hitler's spectacular alpine retreat. Hitler was there amid the craggy peaks of the Obersalzberg at the Kehlsteinhaus—Martin Bormann and Peiper's old boss Himmler, too. 'I want this lovely wedding to be just like mine,' Eva Braun gushed. The SS ceremony complete, the gowned dancers swayed, and champagne flowed like a river in front of the Italian red marble fireplace in the great room. The gaiety seemed to deny there was even a war going on.

But there was, even if all the military news was mostly about the Allied seizure of Rome and Kesselring's orderly pull-back to the Apennines. All remained quiet on the coast of France. Instead of his typical obsession with military calamity, Hitler now eagerly engaged his household secretaries and adjutants in idle prattle about the future of Europe and the threat of "the Jews and Bolsheviks"—all fed by summer walks for tea and apple cake.[51] Hitler had already given his low opinion of U.S. soldiers, who his staff told him were 'eager to desert'. While his ambassador, Walther Hewel, argued that there is certainly 'some good human material there'. Hitler demurred. 'Not so much as you think,' he said—and those were mainly from the regions settled from Europe. 'America will never be the Rome of the future ... The farmers are impoverished. I have seen pictures ... they are a wretched and embittered lot of migratory trash.'[52] Hitler opined how a great culture such as in Rome is supported by the strength of agriculture, as reflected in its soldiers. As Peiper would have recognized, Hitler's conviction was nearly straight from Himmler's obsession in the SS with the peasant soldiers, the *Wehrbauern*.[53]

Days later, on the night of 5 June 1944, neither Peiper nor Hitler's OKW (Oberkommando der Wehrmacht) headquarters had the slightest idea that the decisive event of the war was upon them. Although the invasion of France had been expected for the last month, the prospects now seemed less likely. On that day the Luftwaffe meteorologist in Paris reported that no invasion would be possible for the next two weeks due to a combination of poor weather, moon phase and tides.[54] With the beach defence safe from Allied invasion, that was welcome news to Generalfeldmarschal Erwin Rommel.

Rommel, the man Peiper had known from Poland, had seen his star rise to the Nazi zenith. The German field marshal was now known all over the world for his fantastic battles in North Africa, where, from 1941 to 1942 the Desert Fox had completely outwitted his stodgy English foes in a war of bluff, surprise and audacity. At the end of 1943, Hitler gave Rommel the job to oversee the preparations for an effective coastal defence to resist Allied landings in France. It was the antithesis of the sweeping battles of movement across reaches of arid impassable terrain that he had fought in Libya. Now he would prepare to fight a static battle on a beachfront. As with everything he did, Rommel set to the task with tremendous energy, even designing a fiendish spear-like anti-parachutist obstacle for protecting behind the beaches, immediately termed 'Rommel's asparagus'.[55]

The defence along the French coastline grew stronger each day. What had been an aging series of unconnected strong points was slowly transformed into a nightmarish defensive labyrinth. This pleased Adolf Hitler, who, ever on the lookout for grandiose appellation, called the fortification network his 'Atlantic Wall'. In January 1944 he spoke admiringly of Rommel's coastal barrier—a tangle of beachfront mines, machine gun nests, concrete emplacements and barbed wire. He even anticipated the Allied landings with relish. 'They will get the thrashing of their lives!'[56] Sepp Dietrich, the head of the I SS Panzer Corps, was less enamoured with Rommel: 'He had only fought in Africa, never Russia,' Dietrich complained, 'so what did he know of war?'[57]

While professionally Rommel accorded his new assignment with all the military enthusiasm he could bring to bear, other contradictory influences were afoot. For months Claus von Stauffenberg, who had fought with Rommel at Kasserine Pass, had covertly worked with a cabal of Wehrmacht officers to end the war. A way needed to be found to halt Hitler and the madness of a regime that everyone had come to realize was practicing a not-so-secret genocide in both Russia and Poland. By the spring of 1944, a wide-ranging movement was afoot to assassinate Hitler and transfer the reins of leadership to a cabal of German generals who would find a way to end the war. In Döberitz, in late 1943, von Stauffenberg had met with another aristocratic military leader, Freiherr

Friedrich August von der Heydte. The native of Landshut was in the hospital and recovering from a miraculous escape—jumping without deploying his parachute—from a crashing Luftwaffe reconnaissance plane the previous September near Rome.[58]

The two convalescing German officers spoke soberly of the war and other events back home. Von der Heydte was now claiming that most of the Jews had been swept from Bavaria and Austria and that at least half a million Jews had been put to death in the East at places "worse than Lublin". Although von der Heydte and von Stauffenberg were both proud to be German, as they related to each other, this terrible secret could only end in disaster. What Rommel knew of the conspiracy—much less to the extent he participated—is still a matter of debate. However, one brief episode in May 1944 suggests he considered cooperating with at least one of the schemes afoot to end the war—likely a plan to arrest Hitler and seize Berlin before the invasion.[59] Moreover, General Hans Eberbach, who would soon lead Panzer Group West in France, was later heard in British captivity describing how Rommel had confided in him that he would take part in the upcoming uprising against Hitler.[60] There were others in on the scheme— even from the Luftwaffe—although none from the Waffen SS. National Socialist diehards such as Peiper or Kurt Meyer would have been horrified.

On 17 May 1944 Freiherr von der Heydte invited Erwin Rommel in France to his officers' mess at the Hotel de Ville in Pèriers. Von der Heydte had had his elite 6th Fallschirmjäger (Parachute) Regiment in France since the week before. Coming inside his mess, Rommel was pleased to note von der Heydte's men proudly wearing the black armlet with 'Afrika' embossed in white. Von der Heydte had fought with the Afrika Korps at the climactic battle of El Alamein in the summer of 1942. Unlike the nihilistic war elsewhere, Rommel's campaign in North Africa had ended with a reputation for relative chivalry for both sides in victory or defeat. Now Rommel had come into intimate knowledge of the mass killings in the East and the Final Solution. In particular he loathed the Waffen SS.[61] How could the senseless war be brought to a halt? After introductions and the end of the meal, Rommel managed to get his host off to the side. 'Heydte, are you sure of your regiment?' the field marshal asked in a low voice. The baron did not hesitate. 'Absolutely.'

Then another question: 'Are you sure of every man?'

'Completely,' he responded. The 6th Fallschirmjäger Regiment was volunteer only and hand-picked by von der Heydte. He considered it a true elite. 'If need be, would they obey you alone?' Rommel pressed.

'Me alone,' the baron replied. 'We want a lot of units like yours,' said Rommel.[62] And then Rommel had another question: 'Baron, could you send your paratroopers the other way?' He said he could—but that could only mean towards Berlin. 'Does this mean you are on the outside?' von der Heydte asked. Rommel gazed back unmoving. Holding the Atlantic Wall would still be important, Rommel counselled. He would need him. Even after the two parted, Obst von der Heydte continued to get his bearings in Normandy. This led to a conversation with General Marcks in charge of the LXXXIV Infantry Corps. Were preparations ready in Cherbourg? Marcks shook his head. 'Emplacements without guns, ammunition depots without ammunition, minefields without mines and a large number of men in uniform with hardly a soldier among them.'[63]

Doubt lingered at the top as well. For his part, Rommel's superior, Generalfeldmarschal Gerd von Rundstedt, derided the Atlantic Wall as 'a bit of cheap bluff'.[64] Although greatly improved, Rommel was unconvinced his handiwork could hold the Allies long before the beaches.[65] In any case, he firmly believed that the Anglos must be stopped at the water's edge. This would require tank reserves waiting just behind the sand dunes. 'If we don't manage to throw them back at once,' Rommel warned Hitler and Albert Speer earlier that spring, 'the invasion will succeed in spite of the Atlantic Wall.' Why? He recounted dreadful experiences under a rain of bombs while attempting to evacuate his Africa Corps from Tunis. 'The bombs were dropped in such concentrations that our best troops were demoralized. If you cannot check the bombing, all other methods will be ineffective.'[66]

Aging field marshal von Rundstedt was in charge of Obefehlschaber (OB) West—all German forces in France. Von Rundstedt was both old (66 years) and old school. The field marshal was posted at an opulent estate at Saint-Germain-en-Laye on the north-west outskirts of Paris, where he professed to live a modest lifestyle, although while enjoying good French food and wine and cigars. His personal energy on the wane, like Hitler, he seldom rose before mid-morning. Although complaining that his post was mainly one of the venerated field marshal, von Runstedt was considered something of a strategic genius—at least up until 1944. He and Rommel had an uneasy relationship, with von Runstedt deriding his upstart as unrealistic (the Atlantic Wall, he reckoned, would not hold for more than twenty-four hours) and Rommel was surprised by von Runstedt's pessimism and flagging energy (Rommel was up and active at 0600 hours). But worst of all, Rommel complained that the old field marshal had no direct experience of the dramatic changes afoot with modern warfare—particularly as affected by air power and motorized logistics.

The central conflict was that, contrary to Rommel, von Runstedt advocated holding a central Panzer reserve in the woods north of Paris.

From there they could set off en masse to confront the invasion on the beach. At the next echelon below the aristocratic Prussian general, and pre-war attaché to London, Leo Freiherr Geyr von Schweppenburg of Panzer Group West, convinced von Rundstedt that the armour would be needed to contest an expected massive airborne assault. In calling for a powerful central reserve, Geyr embraced the conventional thinking dating back to Napoleon. Geyr longed for a gigantic sweeping tank battle, Kharkov style. Let the Allies come ashore he opined. 'That was a big chance to engage the Allies in a real tank battle.' In his dreams he saw himself gloriously smashing Patton's forces as they assembled just beyond the beachhead.[67]

There would be plenty of opportunity to smash the Allies using the Waffen SS tank forces such as those under Wünsche or Peiper. Indeed, both Peiper and Wünsche had been in attendance for the meeting in Louviers, France - halfway between Paris and Normanday- from 27 to 29 April. There, Peiper, with Dietrich, Kurt Meyer and Walter Krüger, listened patiently as Geyr von Schweppenberg ironed out his central Panzer reserve strategy.[68] The Leibstandarte and the Hitlerjugend tank divisions would be a central part of the grand reserve. Fully attired in long leather overcoats, Peiper and Meyer listened as the tank experts debated the readiness of the Panzer arm. Peiper admitted to von Schweppenberg that they were in the process of an emergency retrofit after losing almost everything in Russia. But like Kurt Meyer, he assured the Panzer command that they would be ready to move from Panzer Group West when so ordered.[69]

SS Brigadeführer Fritz Kraemer, the savvy I SS Panzer Corps chief of staff who had transferred to the SS from the army, attended each of the wargames showing how things could go with the invasion. At each session, enthusiastic representatives of the Luftwaffe stressed that the Panzer divisions in France would have powerful German air force support. A squadron of reconnaissance aircraft would be assigned to each Panzer division, and just as in Russia, strong fighter-bomber support would arrive promptly when requested by radio. Given such assurances, Kraemer found himself agreeing with von Schweppenberg that 'it would be wise to concentrate the Panzer division in two or three inland groups to employ them on the fifth or sixth day of the invasion to repel the landed enemy'.[70] That would ensure maximum flexibility to smash the landings and throw the Allies back into the sea. Meanwhile, in the meetings General der Panzertruppen Walter Krüger, with the LVIII Panzer Corps, noted that his forces would soon include the 2nd SS Panzer Division to prevent any partisan uprising in the south of France. He ventured that the objective would be to move quickly enough so that, like at Dieppe, the tanks could crush the Allied invasion on the beaches.[71]

But Erwin Rommel saw Geyr's plan as arrogant fancy. He believed that Allied air power turned the conventional wisdom on its head. Movement paralysis was likely under unfriendly skies. Von Rundstedt, the aging adroit classical strategist, and Geyr, the haughty professional, knew nothing of Allied air power. From Africa, Rommel knew more of it than he wanted.

Against Rommel's judgement, Geyr and von Rundstedt maintained that even with Allied air superiority, they could rapidly move up to the threatened zones by night. Geyr, the haughty Panzer specialist, dismissed Rommel. 'I expect the landing to be successful,' Geyr said. 'We cannot really stop the guns of the Anglo-American fleet with merely a few mines.' The big danger, claimed the Baron, was the armada of Allied naval guns and not the airplanes.

Not one to underestimate himself, the baron boasted ownership of a 'stopwatch mind' (*Gedanken der Stoppuhr*) and would have the Panzers on their way in minutes. Who was right? Geyr blamed Rommel for the 'bitter controversy' and even dunned von Rundstedt for remaining aloof.[72] Hitler couldn't make up his mind.

Peiper knew both men. He travelled with Rommel early on, having served alongside the dashing officer in 1939 when the two men had escorted Hitler's train in Poland. The other, Leo Geyr von Schweppenberg, a Prussian cavalry officer, was inescapable in German armoured circles, enjoying the blessings of Panzer specialist Heinz Guderian. However, 58-year-old Geyr, obsessed with a tank-infused version of Napoleon's central position stratagem, was arrogant to a fault. And even though he had led a Panzer corps in the 1941 Battle of Moscow, the baron had not experienced the paralyzing punishment of Allied air power. In contrast, Rommel, the Desert Fox, had seen plenty of U.S. and British aircraft in his reverses at El Alamein and Kasserine Pass. But neither Peiper nor Geyr had seen the havoc Allied air power could raise. 'The war will be lost or won on the beaches,' Rommel confided to his adjutant Helmuth Lang.[73] But for now the controversy remained a professional disagreement, mostly lost amid the prospects of a storm to make an invasion all but foolhardy in the early summer weather in France.

* * *

Before dawn on Tuesday 4 June, 51-year-old Erwin Rommel awoke at his headquarters in La Roche Guyon on the Seine midway between

Normandy and Paris. As he was soon departing, he reviewed the situation with his bespectacled chief of staff, General Major Hans Speidel. The commander of Army Group B was fashionably housed in the thousand-year-old castle of the Dukes of Rochefoucald, where he coordinated the defence of France. Given the bad weather, the field marshal aimed to take advantage of the break to first drive to his Swabian home in Herrlingen. It was, after all, his wife, Lucie's, birthday on 6 June—he must be there. 'I believe we will win the defensive battle in the west if we still have time to prepare,' he had written Lucie confidently the previous week.[74] Rommel stopped in Paris to purchase some fashionable hand-made shoes for her, mindful that on the beaches along the Atlantic Wall he had overseen four million mines buried under the sand. In addition, there were a half a million personnel and tank barriers assembled to make the beaches a labyrinth of deadly traps. Was it enough?

Now, the ever-efficient Erwin Rommel planned that once Lucie's birthday candles were dim in Herrlingen, he would drive on to Berchtesgaden to meet Hitler. Although still expecting the invasion in the north, over the last week he had become increasingly worried about the deficiencies of the Normandy defences. He was particularly aggravated that the three additional line battalions of the 352nd Infantry Division had not been moved up to the beaches as he had ordered. On a hunch, he decided to persuade Hitler—against the wishes of his nemesis, Geyr von Schweppenberg—to transfer two Panzer divisions and a rocket brigade to the Calvados coast. An avid and aggressive chess player, Rommel insisted the powerful Panzer Lehr Division should be moved closer up. With this array of tanks, he would check the invasion at the beaches. Two more divisions and it would be mate. He motored off in the inclement German weather, confident the invasion would not come.[75] 'Each day, we are getting stronger,' he wrote his wife.

Others took advantage of the lull. The SS Panzer Corps commander, Sepp Dietrich, was off in Brussels to visit Teddi Wisch and get a briefing on the Leibstandarte. Finishing a meal polished off with cigars and wine, Wisch told him the reorganization still had a way to go. The division was now full strength in personnel for the Panzer grenadier regiments, but Peiper's tank regiment was still short of the promised strength, and the refurbishment of support equipment remained deficient.[76] Weapons training was particularly lacking. And when would fuel arrive to train tank drivers?

After a few drinks, Dietrich was back to disparaging Erwin Rommel's soldiering ability. 'What did he know of war?' Dietrich opined. He constantly had himself photographed by Dr Berndt, his publicity man, for the newspapers back home. All he could do was stand on a tank, baton in hand and shout 'I am the King of Africa!'[77]

Across the border, in Saint-Germain-en-Laye, a fashionable suburb of Paris, 68-year-old Generalfeldmarschal Gerd von Rundstedt did not wake until 1030 hours on 5 June. It was noon before he consulted his chief of staff, General Günther Blumentritt. Both welcomed the poor weather forecast. Bad weather meant a day off. An intelligence report after the weather report sealed it: 'imminence of invasion is not recognizable'. Von Rundstedt, the confirmed Francophile, and his son left the briefing for their favourite Parisian restaurant, the Coq Hardi in Bougival.[78] It was a relaxing day.

In the meantime Hans Speidel, in Rommel's headquarters, took the chance to host a dinner party featuring special guest Ernst Jünger, one of those writers on the Nazi approval list who once waxed poetic about death and sacrifice for Germany.[79] The big excitement was a highly secret manuscript penned by Jünger and provided to both Rommel and Speidel. The document proposed a diplomatic end to the war after Hitler's arrest. Speidel, the closet philosopher, looked forward to the discussion.

At midnight in the Norman city of Saint-Lô, the staff of the German VIII Army Corps toasted the 6 June birthday of their stern-looking commander, General Erich Marcks. The party took place late at night because Marcks was scheduled to depart with the rest of the leadership of the 7th Army to a big wargame in Rennes at first light. Toasting the quiet night before the game, they enjoyed a bottle of Chablis. 'Prost!' 'À votre santé!'

The Kriegsspiel examined the improbable prospect of an Allied landing in their backyard of Normandy. General Max Pemsel, the chief of staff of the 7th Army, worried about the initial results from the military exercise. Not only was everyone away from the front, but the wargame taught that they would need to act like lightning to throw the enemy back into the sea if there stood any chance to turn the enemy. How quickly could they get those tank divisions up to the front? Everyone aimed to streamline the chain of command and redistribute some forces as soon as they got back. Pemsel and the others went to bed dissatisfied. Luckily the weather was still bad.

On Monday, 5 June, at the Bavarian mountain perch of Berchtesgaden, Adolf Hitler had followed his nose. Having stayed up until nearly dawn the previous night, the German leader rose at eleven to spend two hours with the noon military briefing. Lunch came at 1600 hours, with a clutch of Nazi dignitaries; his mistress, Eva Braun; and his dedicated secretaries. Before the ladies, Hitler held court, excusing the meatless offering of his vegetarian repast. 'The elephant is the strongest animal,' he preached. 'He also cannot stand meat.'

After lunch the group moved to the bloom-filled summer garden for conversation and cake. Hitler, strolling along with his hat and walking stick in hand, had the ear of Joseph Goebbels. For months in his diary Goebbels had been obsessed with the invasion. 'The Führer is convinced the invasion will fail,' he had written. When it would happen, Hitler did not know, but he praised Rommel above all, noting that having been rudely ejected from Africa, he had a grudge to revenge. 'Rommel will repel it in the most brutal fashion,' Hitler predicted—with tanks on the beaches. 'He will serve the English and the Americans some hot soup!'[80]

It was a splendid alpine afternoon on 5 June, even lazy, and they soon they reached the Tea House, a round stone building nestled in the woods. Goebbels whispered to his Führer that there was now a need to put the German economy on a 'total war' footing—Rome had just fallen. Hitler calmly responded that within a few days he would unleash a devilish surprise on the British—hundreds of robot V-1 bombs would devastate London.[81] Perhaps the first salvo could be set off to arrive at rush hour. To be sure, the preparation of the Luftwaffe seemed the most worrisome question.

Drinking cups of lime-blossom tea, Hitler pronounced Britain now finished. Rommel, his vaunted warrior, had just assured him that any invasion would be promptly thrown back, just like at Dieppe. Each day that passed, he wrote to his wife, Lucie, the beach defences were growing more thorny: 'Each day, every week we get stronger ... Every day is worth a fortune.'[82] That satisfied Hitler, who seemed the picture of composure that day, taking a cat nap at 1800 hours before dinner along with Albert Speer. The military briefing then came at 2300 hours. Just before midnight on 6 June Hitler called his secretaries back to view newsreels. Afterwards there was more tea, apple cake and small talk to the music of Wagner, Lehar and Strauss. Goebbels departed at 0200 hours before Hitler retired. As he left, the night was jolted by an unusual early summer thunderstorm. The crackle of the thunder reverberated across the mountains. 'The mood,' he noted, 'was like the good old times.'[83]

While Hitler and the German high command slept, a vast armada of over five thousand ships and troop carriers—the largest amphibious invasion in history—steamed across the English Channel.[84] At the head of this great campaign was General Dwight D. Eisenhower. At 2130 hours on Sunday, 4 June, the avuncular supreme commander of the Allied forces met with the other Allied chiefs in a bare library at Southwick House. All appeared stone-faced in uniform, save the head of British forces, General Bernard Law Montgomery. The hero of El Alamein wore his customary sweater topped with a beret; very British and even chipper.

Eisenhower's news was not good—a reflection of the weather that had cancelled the operation the preceding day. Still, there was a break in the forecast—one that would bring marginally acceptable weather conditions for the invasion. Eisenhower had to make a decision. If he did not go on 6 June, he would have to wait until 19 June or even 1 July. That was too late. Thousands of troops, fully briefed and ready, had already been cooped in troop carriers for more than a day in waiting. If the operation were delayed and the multitudes returned to port, how would the great secret be kept? His intelligence sources, too, were warning of a nefarious series of secret weapons that Hitler would soon have ready. Eisenhower glanced at the faces around the room.

'We have a great force of fighter-bombers,' he said. He then turned to Montgomery as if for support. 'Do you see any reason for not going Tuesday?'

'I would say—Go!' Montgomery piped up.

Eisenhower pursed his lips and nodded. 'The question,' he continued, 'just how long can you hang out the operation on the end of a limb and let it hang there ... I'm quite positive we must give the order ... I don't like it, but there it is.'[85]

In London the rain and wind continued all night. Later, on Monday afternoon, Eisenhower was seized with doubt, going so far as to pen a note to be released to the press in case he had to abandon the beachhead. 'Our landings in the Cherbourg–Le Havre area have failed to gain a satisfactory foothold and I have withdrawn the troops ... any blame or fault attached to the attempt is mine alone.'[86] Putting away the folded note, he set off to personally meet the rugged paratroopers of the U.S. 101st Airborne Division, who would parachute into France before dawn.

Meanwhile, Hitler's intelligence services groped for information, blinded by a lack of effective Luftwaffe reconnaissance operations.[87] True, the Luftwaffe had a clever plan of a riposte with their limited stable of aircraft, *Drohende Gefahr West*. Like an elaborate confidence trick, 'Urgent Danger West' would disperse its aircraft to protect them on the ground from fighter-bomber attacks, and then, when the invasion was upon France, Luftflotte 3 would swiftly shuttle aircraft from the Fatherland and distant fronts. The plan was, then, for a sudden knock-out blow to wreck the Allies on the beaches like at Dunkirk. Still, at the beginning of June the Luftwaffe knew nothing at all of the coming invasion.

The aerial blind spot was even apparent to the German forces on the ground. The chief intelligence officer of the 12th SS Panzer Division—posted 90km from Normandy—sent an emissary to Evreux, France, in May to seek out information from the commander of the reconnaissance Ju-88 unit posted there. Disappointing news came from Luftwaffe Oberstleutnant Volprecht von Riedesel leading Kampfgeschwader 54. In recent days his air crew had been completely unsuccessful in penetrating British air space. There were standing patrols over the Channel. Surely the Allies would not go to that trouble without an imminent invasion?[88] Although the last effective reconnaissance of England at the end of May revealed nothing; a major part of the southern English coastline had avoided scrutiny.[89] Not good.

All day on 5 June scores of ships sailed from England towards the Normandy coast. It was an incredibly conspicuous movement—an entire flotilla with thousands of ships, boats and landing craft. And like Rommel, Admiral Karl Dönitz was on holiday. Dönitz, whose U-boats and patrol craft were to theoretically play a nearly sacrificial role in thwarting the invasion, was relaxing in the Black Forest. German naval patrols of the English Channel scheduled for the night of 5 June were cancelled due to the bad weather. And yet in the age of aerial reconnaissance, radio eavesdroppers and *Abwehr* agents, the German high command knew absolutely nothing of Operation Overlord until parachutists began to float into Normandy after midnight. The failure of the aerial or naval reconnaissance forces to examine the ship-ridden English Channel on the afternoon of 5 June remains one of the great, if seldom recognized, blunders of the war.[90]

Incredibly, although the German army in France had been on the very highest alert since the beginning of June, a remarkable bit of intelligence was ignored. At the beginning of 1944 the head of the intelligence service, Admiral Canaris, learned from agents of a tip-off radio message to be transmitted to the French resistance shortly before the invasion began. The message contained two lines from a poem from Paul Verlaine's 'Chanson d'Automne' that was to be transmitted forty-eight hours before the invasion began. Amazingly, on the afternoon of 5 June 1944, the intelligence section of the German 15th Army in northern France signalled Hitler's headquarters with the news that the BBC was broadcasting this puzzling bit of verse. General Alfred Jodl was personally informed of that news, but there it faded. Canaris had fallen out of favour at Hitler's headquarters; Himmler had taken his place as the head of intelligence.

And with Jodl's flippant dismissal passed a fleeting opportunity to anticipate the invasion.[91]

In any case, the Allied planners knew they had preserved the secret of D-Day. At five minutes to midnight on 5 June 1944 Generalfeldmarschal Karl Gerd von Rundstedt, in his Parisian headquarters, signalled via the German top secret communication apparatus called Enigma that there was nothing to suggest that the invasion was imminent. The message was promptly decrypted by the ULTRA code breakers at Bletchley Park, who passed on the welcome information to Eisenhower and his staff before dawn on 6 June.[92]

Less than twenty hours later any sense of German military calm in France totally vanished.

At 2200 hours on 6 June a message flashed to Jochen Peiper's tank command in Belgium:

> The Anglo-American invasion started in the early morning hours of the 6th of June in the area of Le Havre to Cherbourg ... The regiment must be prepared to take action immediately. Training is immediately suspended. All excess equipment must be discarded so that the maximum numbers of fighters and weapons can be transported quickly.[93]

The Allies were landing at Normandy.

Chapter 17

Total Sacrifice

'Twas a summer day—the sixth of June: I like to be particular in dates,
Not only of the age and year, but moon; they are a sort of post-house,
where the Fates Change horses, making history change its tune.'
—Lord Byron, *Don Juan*

By noon on 6 June 1944 German military telephones jangled and buzzed across France and the length and reach of Hitler's Reich. The invasion was on.

Several were urgent phone messages insisting that Sepp Dietrich take immediate action to bring the SS into the fray to oppose the American forces swarming on the French Channel coast. The burly SS leader had been in conference in Brussels with Leibstandarte commander Teddi Wisch when news of the landings first came, and he then hastily set off for Paris to confer with von Rundstedt. Von Rundstedt, for his part, seemed unfazed. At his headquarters he awoke to his customary breakfast before spending an hour studying the situation. He attempted to calm Dietrich. For the first time Dietrich would command a full tank corps—an assignment many thought beyond his mental capacity. Perhaps for this reason, a seasoned army officer, General Major Fritz Kraemer, was assigned to help run the show.

In any case, I SS Panzer Corps could count on an impressive array of German weaponry, including, as it did, both the 1st SS (124 tanks, tank destroyers and assault guns) and 12th SS Panzer Divisions (149 armoured vehicles) as well as the powerful Panzer Lehr Division with 217 tanks.[1] The 12th SS Hitlerjugend Division was in Acon-Evreux, less than 100km from the invasion front, but the Leibstandarte was held in reserve at Beverloo, Belgium over five times that far away. In part, the distant location was due to not only the incomplete refitting but also the conviction that the main Allied invasion would eventually strike at the Pas-de-Calais.[2]

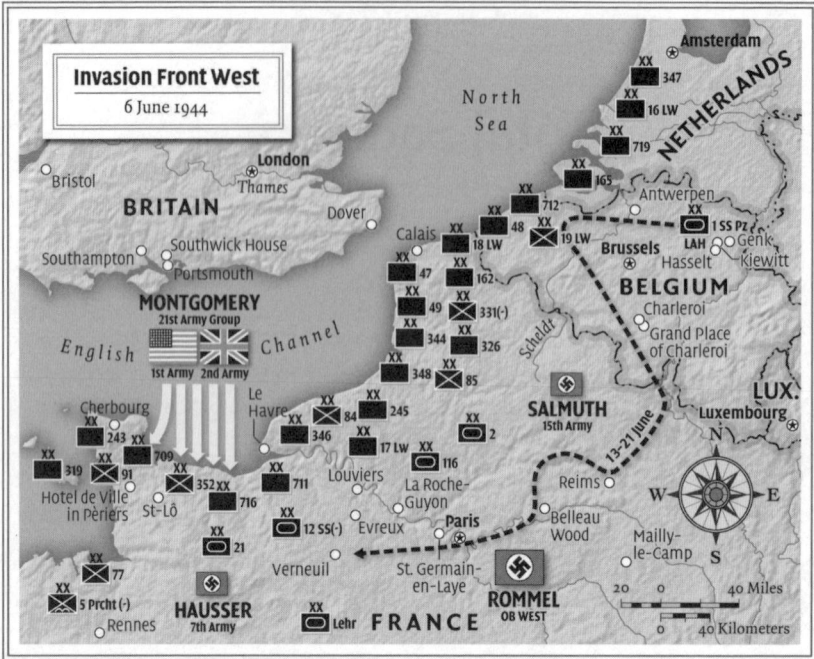

Invasion Front West
6 June 1944

North Sea

Amsterdam

347

16 LW

719

165

712

48

18 LW

19 LW

47

162

49

331(-)

344

326

348

85

84

245

346

17 LW

116

711

352

716

243

709

319

91

Hotel de Ville
in Pèriers

St-Lô

5 Prcht (-)

77

12 SS(-)

21

Lehr

NETHERLANDS

Antwerpen

1 SS PZ

LAH

Brussels

Genk
Kiewitt

Hasselt

BELGIUM

Charleroi

Grand Place
of Charleroi

LUX.

Luxembourg

SALMUTH
15th Army

Scheldt

13-21 June

Reims

Belleau
Wood

Mailly-
le-Camp

La Roche-
Guyon

Paris

Evreux

Louviers

Le Havre

Cherbourg

Verneuil

St. Germain-
en-Laye

ROMMEL
OB WEST

FRANCE

HAUSSER
7th Army

Rennes

BRITAIN

London

Thames

Bristol

Dover

Calais

Southwick House

Southampton

Portsmouth

MONTGOMERY
21st Army Group

1st Army 2nd Army

English Channel

20   0   40 Miles

0   40 Kilometers

N
W   E
S

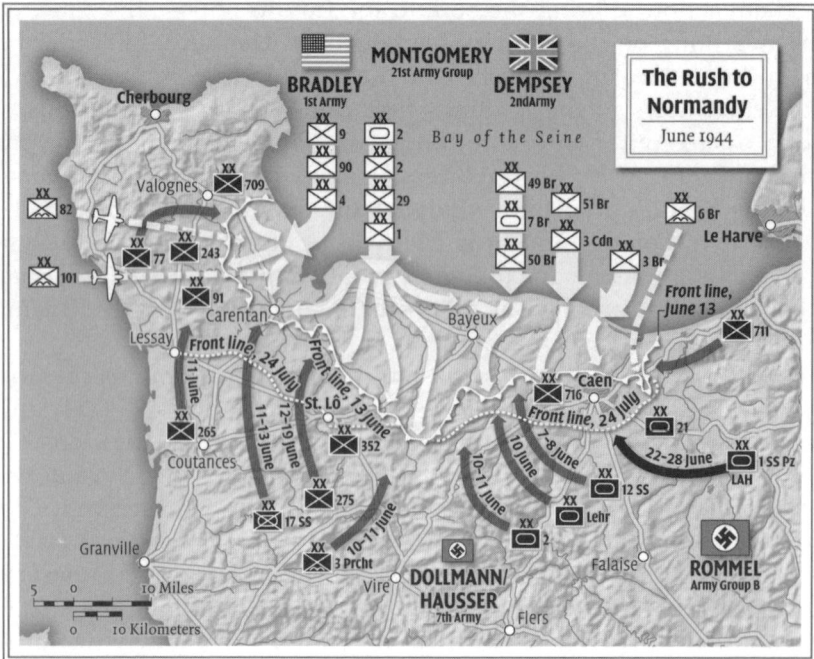

The Rush to Normandy
June 1944

MONTGOMERY
21st Army Group

BRADLEY
1st Army

DEMPSEY
2nd Army

Cherbourg

Valognes

82

709

77   243

101

91

Carentan

Lessay   Front line,
11 June

Front line,
24 July

St. Lô

11-13 June

12-19 June

Coutances

265

352

275

17 SS

3 Prcht

Granville

10-11 June

Vire

DOLLMANN/
HAUSSER
7th Army

Flers

Bay of the Seine

9

90

4

2

29

1

49 Br

7 Br

50 Br

51 Br

3 Cdn

3 Br

6 Br

Le Harve

Front line,
June 13

711

Bayeux

Caen

716

Front line, 24 July

7-8 June

10 June

10-11 June

21

12 SS

Lehr

2

Falaise

1 SS Pz
LAH

22-28 June

ROMMEL
Army Group B

5   0   10 Miles

0   10 Kilometers

Although Hitler's intuition forecast the Allies would land in Normandy, von Rundstedt and others—considering a massive weight of evidence—convinced him that this was a feint and that the real decisive landing would come in the Pas-de-Calais.[3] That was the logical choice, being the launch pad for the straight shot to the Ruhr Valley. After all, the German industrial heartland was a large strategic factor in any estimation.[4] At the same time, on 4 June von Rundstedt worried that 'the well-known ability of the enemy to bite fast makes it essential to destroy the enemy as rapidly as possible'.[5] In early May, as a concession to Rommel's worry, the 12th SS Division was moved from Belgium to Evreux, closer to the coast. That, like all other such decisions, required Hitler's agreement.

Hitler's battlefield micro-management hurt another way. He had forbidden the Panzer troops to be moved without his express permission. But given Hitler's odd hours—he did not go to bed until 0300 hours—he was still sleeping the following morning, with no one willing to wake him.[6] Von Rundstedt began pressing for release of the 12th SS Panzer and Panzer Lehr divisions at 0445 hours, but this went unheeded. Hitler snoozed as the Americans, British and Canadians bravely stormed the Normandy beaches. Bleary eyed, Hitler wandered out of his quarters in his nightdress at 1000 hours and was greeted with the news of a massive Allied invasion. The German leader seemed unsurprised, saying he had slept well, was in good spirits and was not about to let the events interrupt his daily schedule. The Allied attack, he ventured, was likely a diversion for the real operation that would come in the Pas-de-Calais. On that day Hitler was to meet Prime Minister Döme Sztójay from Hungary. The meeting was to take place at the Castle Klessheim, which had originally belonged to the Prince Archbishop of Salzburg and was now used to impress foreign dignitaries. It was a bright sunny day in early summer Alpine splendour as Hitler's procession drove to Klessheim, an hour's distance from the Berghof.

In the car Hitler seemed jubilant to have finally come to grips with the enemy in the West: 'Now we can give them a nice little packet!' he quipped to his driver. 'I can hold the Russians as long as I want.' Presently the entourage arrived at the magnificent castle. Hitler seemed invigorated as he entered. There, in a large room, across from rows of medieval armour, attendants displayed a manicured map for the midday war conference. Several pencilled red arrows pointed to the beaches at Normandy. Parachutists had been landing all over the place since 0100 hours. Allied infantry had fought their way onto the beaches at 0630 hours.

'So this is it!' he proclaimed, pointing to the map. Hitler seemed pleased. He was careful to remind his audience that Normandy was where he thought the invasion would come. He hastily drafted a fanciful order: 'The enemy is to be annihilated at the bridgehead by evening of June 6th.'[7] Within nine hours, he ventured, the beachfront must be erased. In any case, where were Rommel's tanks? Were they bearing down on the beaches? Himmler, who was also present, seemed delighted as well, even smiling. He was happy; his mistress, Hedwig Potthast, had just given birth to their second child.[8] Now focused on things military, the Reichsführer leaned forward to assure Hitler that his SS divisions were now headed to the danger zone. They would soon cut the Allies to ribbons.

Finally advised as to the goings-on at the French beaches, General-feldmarschal Rommel was on the phone shortly to address the thin-faced Generalleutnant Erich Marcks with the LXXXIV Army Corps. Rommel had been displeased with the Normandy defences when he had reviewed them the previous month, and his last-minute appeal to move the Panzer divisions forward was left undone. Unware that Marcks and his under-lings had failed to move more than two of the available ten infantry battalions of the 352nd Infantry Division to defend Omaha Beach, Rommel had sharp instructions: 'There will be no fight on land,' Rommel insisted, 'only on the beaches.'[9]

The reality was quite different. It was not until 1430 hours that von Rundstedt was able to move the 12th SS Panzer Division.[10] Orders for Kurt Meyer and the Hitlerjugend were simple, if late: immediately thrust north of Caen and throw the Allies back in the sea.[11] Against that, the British and Canadian forces under the British 21st Army Group had contrary objectives: seize the city of Caen—a vital strategic objective. As the 12th SS was still some distance off—which Rommel had warned was a mistake—what of his nearby Normandy Panzer reserve, the 21st Panzer Division?

That key division in Normandy was ostensibly led by General Lieu-tenant Edgar Feuchtinger. Yet when the invasion came, Feuchtinger was not even there. He awoke in Paris at the side of his exotic dancer mistress, with whom he had been enjoying the city's many diversions. Although he hurried back to Caen, upon arrival Feuchtinger was timid. After all, he had no experience of leading tanks—indeed, little experience with combat leadership itself. Disdained by those such as Peiper and Meyer, Feuchtinger was one of those well-connected National Socialist party members who had been assigned a cushy position in France. Feuchtinger, a bon vivant, seemed to have little heart for fighting; he had only commanded an artillery regiment in combat years before. In any case, on Tuesday, 6

June, upon returning from Paris with his woman, Feuchtinger appeared nearly paralyzed by the gravity of events. He stayed to the rear while leaving key decisions to his subordinates—notably Obst Hans von Luck. All through the morning his division sat idly about while thousands of Allied soldiers surged onto the beaches.

Although blasted from the air and naval gunfire, the division needed the corps commander, Erich Marks, to prod them into action. The 21st Panzer Division at last moved out north of Caen in the afternoon, intending to roll up the British advance from the beaches. But Hitler's morning slumber and dilatory hesitation in German high command was decisive. Arriving late, the Panzer-led fist ran afoul of the heavily gunned tanks of the Staffordshire Yeomanry heading in the opposite direction. With little to hold them in the morning, they had already left the sands of Sword Beach to move far inland alongside the 185th Regiment, British 3rd Infantry Division. The two combatants slammed into each other on Periers Ridge. Losses in the meeting engagement were heavy, and both sides dug in.

However, another German thrust moved through a gap in the British defences—for a moment the attack jeopardized the Allied lodgement at Sword Beach when armoured reconnaissance with Kampfgruppe Rauch reached as far as Luc-sur-Mer on the coast, in sight of the shoreline. However, seeing parachutes overhead in the gathering darkness, Feuchtinger lost his nerve. In reality, it was a deceptive airborne assault staged to his rear near the mouth of the Orne River, but the timid Feuchtinger, an artilleryman, was spooked, pulling back even as the Hitlerjugend Panzer Division struggled to reach the British zone.[12] Hitler had opined that the Allies would consider themselves lucky to stay on their beachhead for nine hours before Rommel's tanks swept them out to sea. Like the failed Allied Dieppe landing the year before, it would be a crushing blow to Allied morale. Midnight passed as the Allies groped their way further inland while chaos reigned in the local command of the German 7th Army.

By 0930 hours on the following morning of 7 June, the 12th SS had only reached as far as Villers-Bocage. Rather than the possibility of a pre-dawn armoured advance, the boy-soldiers set off from Dreux in broad daylight. Within minutes they were dodging bombs and wing-mounted machine guns as they attempted to thread their way down the dusty French roads. An old veteran of the Leibstandarte now with the Hitlerjugend, Obersturmführer Heinz Schmolke, moved his grenadier company out that afternoon. Quickly they were set upon by the Allied *Jabos*. He soon brought his men under the dense foliage of the Forêt des Cinglais rather than risk the buzzing fighter-bombers.[13] Like an assault of metalized locusts, the air attack was unprecedented. The U.S. air force alone operated 8,722 aircraft over German heads on D-Day. Against this, Luftflotte 3 could only count a hundred sorties launched.[14]

At the headquarters of Generaloberst Friedrich Dollmann's 7th Army in Le Mans, a message arrived that was to be read immediately to all the soldiers. It was from Hitler himself:

> Soldiers of the Western Front!
> The enemy has begun his long-awaited attack on Europe. His aim is well known to all of use ... Defence against this attack is a matter of life and death for our nation and a historical task ... Here what counts is to stand and fight or to die. Every leader, every commander of a base, an island or a fortress or a ship is honour bound to me, never to capitulate; he will continue the struggle to the last fighter, to the last shell, to the last round ... Wherever the enemy attacks he must be destroyed. He would not succeed in gaining a foothold on the coast defended by us. Victory will be ours! You are called upon to fight for it and so fulfil the legacy of our fallen comrades.
> —Adolf Hitler[15]

Under the massive air umbrella—over 14,000 sorties—the British and American armies had landed 156,000 troops, unified their beachheads and shattered the German coastal defences by the end of the first day.[16] Even so, future Allied progress looked uncertain. The Normandy terrain to the south near Bayeux was crisscrossed by bocage—small fields ringed by high hedgerows and sunken lanes. The densely overgrown banks made it impossible to see beyond a single pasture, greatly favouring the defence. Moreover, the Norman countryside was poor tank terrain.

However, to the north the region around Caen consisted of more open rolling hills covered with wheat, flax and sugar beet. Here the possession of a single rise could allow dominating fields of fire for kilometres around it. Sitting on a rise on the grain fields of Caen, the tank contest decisively favoured the Germans—the frontal hulls of the Panthers and Tigers were nearly impervious to the armour-piercing rounds from their foes, all while mounting guns that could slice through the Sherman M4A1 tanks before they even pulled into range. Further, beyond terrain, Hitler was more worried about the approach to Caen. 'At the beginning,' his chief of staff related, 'we considered the British as strong, more battle-wise and hence more dangerous than the Americans.'[17]

But could the German armour reach the tank battlefield? With the conviction that the Allies would still land at the Pas-de-Calais, the Leibstandarte continued to be held north, moving in the pre-dawn hours of 9 June from the Tourhout area to the mouth of the Schelde Estuary. The *Fremde Herre West* had intercepted an intentional leaked report on Allied strength intended for the Belgian resistance that indicated that there would be a second landing at the Pas-de-Calais the following day.[18] German intelligence was completely flummoxed.

Meanwhile, the lavishly equipped Panzer Lehr Division would not reach the invasion front until 9 June after a nightmare march in which it saw 200 of its vehicles flamed from the air. The Panzer Lehr Division stalled at Thury-Harcourt, 160km from Caen.[19] Its commander, General Fritz Bayerlein, an old *Afrika Korps* veteran, had been given the special mission to defeat the invasion with an elite tank force. 'You alone must hurl the enemy back into the Channel,' General Guderian had told him earlier that spring. 'Your goal is not the coast. It is the sea.'[20] Now Bayerlein sarcastically described his march route from Vire as a '*Jabo Rennstrecke*—a fighter-bomber race course!'[21] He was only able to move his tanks at night and became terribly disorganized in the move towards Caen. Against that, an urgent telephone call from Rommel with Army Group B called for an assault by the I SS Panzer Corps no later than 1600 hours. The redoubtable Kurt Meyer and Max Wünsche— Peiper's old unspoken rival—would lead the assault.

Kurt Meyer had set up his headquarters in the towering stone ruins of the Ancienne Abbaye Ardenne just south-west of Caen. Meyer was determined to put on a good show with his new command. Short, arrogant and sporting a boxer's nose, Meyer epitomized the image of the fanatical German SS officer willing to fight to the death for Hitler and National Socialism. Seemingly impervious to pain and abuse—he claimed to have had twenty-five bones broken in his body—Kurt Meyer was a brave and skilful foe.

Over the spring, he drilled the 17- and 18-year-old Hitler youth under his command into tough soldiers, moulded in his own fanatical style. Based on his combat years with the Leibstandarte, Meyer eschewed parade drills or traditional marksmanship as taught at the *SS Junkerschule*; instead, he preferred physical toughening through sport and field exercises with live ammunition. In place of ceremony and marching drills, Meyer emphasized visual camouflage, noise discipline and night combat. 'They went to war, superbly trained,' said Meyer. He claimed to be constantly reminded of the youth of his charge: growing boys needed additional rations. Appropriately, his quartermaster issued his underage trainees candy rather than cigarettes to supplement rations. But if derided as the 'Baby Division', Meyer was intensely proud of them, imbued, as he claimed, 'with a belief in the rightness and justice of the German cause'.[22]

His grenadiers would need every bit of their training on Wednesday, 7 June 1944. Knowing the air activity, Meyer had traded in his fat Kfz 15 command car for a nimble off-road VW Kubelwagen. Even then, they had difficulty reaching the castle, for the small vehicle was chased from ditch to ditch by roving Allied fighters; Meyer made a mental note to travel by motorcycle from then on. Upon reaching the Abbey, Meyer met briefly with Max Wünsche. As befitting readiness for battle, Wünsche was in his camouflage uniform but otherwise perfectly groomed and appointed. He held his chin high as he told Meyer about the tank situation. Panzermeyer frowned—there was no glare to match his own. He was pleased that Wünsche and his Panthers were on hand but disappointed to learn that the other tank battalion was hung up. The reconnaissance battalion, under brawny Gerhard Bremer, was bushwhacked as well, nailed by air attack and sent scurrying for cover. Watching the uninterrupted aerial circus overhead, he hid along the Caen–Lisieux road.[23]

For a mascot's luck, Meyer gave his German shepherd a few pats before ascending the long steps of the church tower. The monastery was an old ruin surrounded by a large orchard ringed by dilapidated stone walls. Reaching its apex, the view to the west spread out as if a spectacular Norman mosaic. An expanse of golden grain fields stretched towards the coast. There were flashes over the blue horizon. 'If only we could eliminate that damned naval gunfire,' Meyer thought to himself. 'Heavy shells were roaring over our heads like express trains.'

> I climbed the tower to have a look … What a surprise! The terrain as far as the coast was spread before me like a sand table. There was intense activity over the coast. Ship after ship bobbed on the water; countless barrage balloons protected this armada from air attack. The measure was unnecessary; the Luftwaffe appeared not to exist anymore … Enemy tank formations were forming up west of Douvres. The whole expanse looked like an anthill. And what was going on behind us— smoking rubble, empty roads and burning vehicles. The Caen–Falaise road was straight as an arrow for kilometres on end, but there wasn't a single indicator of German combat power. It was waiting under cover somewhere.[24]

Just then fighter-bombers attacked the monastery, forcing everyone to duck but doing no real damage. Meyer scowled. Recovering, he pressed field binoculars to his eyes and couldn't believe what he saw. Not 200m away a Canadian tank stuttered to a halt atop a shallow rise. The hatch popped open, and its commander peered out towards nearby Carpiquet airfield. He calmly lit a cigarette, waiting for other tanks to pull up.

Meyer was flabbergasted. He quickly got on the radio and, in a calm voice, told his men to hold their fire. The Canadians were coming up alongside. Orders said to wait for the 21st Panzer Division to begin the attack, but this was an opportunity. Wünsche called the 21st Panzer on the radio, whispering instinctively. The Canadian tanks revved up and toiled eastward towards Franqueville. There was a hush.

Meyer whispered urgently into the radio to Wünsche waiting in the orchard below. Over the radio Meyer heard his voice: '*Achtung! Panzer Marsch!*' Suddenly the right side of the orchard exploded in a stampede of muzzle flashes and cracks so closely spaced they sounded like monstrous firecrackers. The lead Canadian tank exploded; others were burning, with crews bailing out. The thunder of guns roared across the fields. Now a German tank was hit, flames blasting out of its hatches. The German tanks surged ahead into the flank of the enemy advancing on the little village of Buron on the left and Cambes to the right. Meyer took off to lead from the front, zipping along on a BMW motorcycle.

Meyer sputtered and wove across the pock-marked landscape, constantly encouraging his grenadiers to make ready and taunting fighter-bombers attempting to give chase. But even though dodging like a jack rabbit, they almost got him. Thrown off his machine by a rain of shells, Meyer took cover with an equally shocked Canadian soldier in a bomb crater. Both kept their heads down as shrapnel whizzed through the air. And then, hearing a nearby German motor, Meyer jumped out to grab a ride. For a mad hour it looked as if Max Wünsche's Panthers might break through to the beaches. Yet when the artillery and anti-tank fire swept his steel wedge in the Canadian line, losses mounted as the tank thrust foundered in shelling and confusion. Meyer pulled back at dusk.[25] Soon he was back to his headquarters, where some 150 Canadian prisoners were milling around in the orchard. Meyer claimed to pay little attention to them, dismayed, as he was, to learn that the tanks of the 21st Panzer Division had not budged from Couvre Chef while other Canadian forces jabbed at his right flank. Buron was under such a massive bombardment that it disappeared before Meyer in smoke and explosion.

Thoroughly contemptuous of his enemies, Meyer would later admit that his command had frequently taken no prisoners in the conflict in Russia.[26] Now in France, near Authie, Meyer's men shot on the spot captured Canadians of the North Nova Scotia Highlanders. Local villagers claimed thirty-seven killed, and a war crimes investigation agreed that twenty-three had been disarmed and then shot in cold blood. But the greater barbarity came when some bodies were dragged into the streets to be smashed gruesomely under grinding tank treads.[27] Others, at first more fortunate, trudged onto German headquarters at the Abbey. There they were interrogated in an enclosure in its open courtyard. SS Sturmann Jan Jesionek claimed that Meyer was exceedingly angry that day.

'What shall we do with these prisoners? They only eat our rations.' Jesionek recalled someone asking. 'In the future, no prisoners are to be taken.'

Meyer then turned to another officer present and whispered instructions that Jesionek could not make out.[28] A short time later each prisoner was taken, one by one, up three stone steps to a nearby garden wall and dispatched with pistol shots to the head. Jesionek remembered some of the men shaking hands with each other before being led away.

Two other German witnesses said they heard Meyer repeat, 'My regiment takes no prisoners.'[29] Regardless of whether he said it, there was plenty of killing. In all there was a total of 134 murdered Canadian prisoners of war with many French witnesses.[30] More than a dozen were killed in the woods behind the Chateau d'Audrieu by Gerd Bremer's men and more on the following day, amounting to twenty-six in total. Bremer's presence was identified by French witnesses who observed his Knight's Cross, which could have only been the brutish commander of the 12th SS Reconnaissance Battalion.

Nearby, an SS battle group commanded by Obersturmführer Karl Heinz Milius of Meyer's regiment captured several dozen Canadian prisoners near Burnon on 7 June. Many were shot down after surrendering. Later atrocities at Les Menil Patry and Haut du Bosq featured the cold-hearted opium addict in charge of SS Panzer Grenadier Regiment 26, Wilhelm Mohnke.[31] From that time forward the engagements between the 12th SS Division and the Canadians took on a special savagery.[32] The Canadians called the 12th SS the 'Murder Division', and the Germans claimed that the Canadians weren't taking prisoners either. Even Jochen Peiper claimed to be a witness: 'I myself experienced that Canadians murdered some of our men,' he said, 'with "commando methods", namely by self-strangulation.'[33]

In any case, the Ardenne Abbey episode was hardly a bright spot for Dietrich's Waffen SS debut in Normandy. That was already difficult. His chief of staff, Fritz Kraemer, attempted to move their headquarters to Rouen and quickly got a taste of Allied air power:

> [T]here were burning vehicles of all kinds on the road. No Flak or air forces were available for defence against [the] enemy fighter planes so they were able to attack as though carrying out training exercises.

Air attacks had a paralyzing effect on some of our drivers. German
soldiers were not accustomed to this type of attack.[34]

'Our dreams of a strong Luftwaffe did not materialize,' Kraemer noted
ruefully, observing that so numerous were the American fighter-bombers
that they sometimes gave chase to individual German soldiers. Under
the rainstorm of aerial bombs, rockets and machine gun fire, Kraemer
and Dietrich met with Fritz Witt, the commander of Hitlerjugend, on the
road to their new headquarters. Caen—the historical city where William
the Conqueror had begun his journey of conquest across the English
Channel—was now a sea of flames. Witt told Dietrich that his ordered
counterattack could not be achieved due to the Allied *Jabos*: 'It was nearly
impossible to move on the road by daylight. Troops and equipment could
only be brought up at night.'[35] SS Panzer Grenadier Regiment 25 now
approached north-west of Caen; the rest of the division was hiding and
assiduously avoiding the roads that had become a shooting gallery for
Allied planes. 'The air,' commented one SS trooper, 'had a high iron
content.'[36]

On the Falaise–Caen road Meyer drove through a stream of French
refugees, watching as his last platoon and a civilian bus was shot up
with rockets and bombs. A Schwimmwagen lifted off the road in an
ugly blast. 'The woods attracted us like magnets,' Meyer recalled. 'More
and more fighter planes were above us.'[37] Meyer reached Fritz Witt,
the 12th SS commander. As they spoke, the sky buzzed with so many
planes that to Meyer it looked like *Parteitag Geschwader*. The swooping
Allied fighter-bombers looked like the old Luftwaffe dress parades from
the Nuremberg party days.

Dietrich and Kraemer went on to the headquarters of the 21st Panzer
Division at Saint-Pierre-sur-Dives, some 30km south-east of Caen. They
arrived to learn that Commander Feuchtinger was in the field with the
716th Infantry Division but had foolishly failed to take a radio with him—a
mistake Fritz Kraemer commented was 'tantamount to travelling without
one's head'.[38] The missing officer was at the headquarters of General
Lieutenant Wilhelm Richter getting a briefing on the desperate situation
before the invasion beaches. In the meantime, Kurt Meyer groped his
way through the darkness to meet them, his 'hellish trip' illuminated by
burning trucks. Later, Dietrich was able to raise Feuchtinger on a field
telephone, but only well enough to discover that he was not effectively
in control of his division. He had launched an attack towards the beaches
as ordered, but this was halted just east of Lion-sur-Mer. He did know
that the British were already as far inland as Ranville, for his troops there

reported repelling their advance. So much for the 21st Panzer attack to roll up the invasion beach.[39]

By nightfall General Richter knew his battered 716th Infantry Division was on the verge of collapse. When Meyer and Feuchtinger showed up at his underground headquarters, they were met with a depressing scene. Threading through the bunker passageways, the two passed by multitudes of groaning German wounded. At the briefing Richter told them that he no longer had effective contact with his combat formations. Just then, one of his regimental commanders called on a field telephone, informing Richter that the enemy was on the roof of his bunker. It would be his last transmission. Even the unflappable Meyer concluded that the 716th 'was destroyed in the truest sense of the word'. It ceased to exist in only twenty-four hours.

Jolted by the bedlam near the front, Dietrich and Kraemer returned to their headquarters, pleading with General Friedrich Dollmann, head of the 7th Army, for the release of the Panzer Lehr Division. At midnight Kurt Meyer showed up at the headquarters of the 21st Panzer Division. While Feuchtinger, the timid artillery commander, complained that a counterattack would be impossible until Lehr arrived, Panzermeyer arrogantly dismissed his judgement. The British before them, he said, were 'little fish' who would 'soon be driven back into the sea'.[40] They were to launch a coordinated attack at first light.

But morning saw a hail of artillery falling on the assembly areas of the German divisions. Meyer was short on fuel for his tanks, and the inexperienced Feuchtinger appeared shaken by the cataclysmic developments. Undaunted, Max Wünsche's tanks and Meyer's grenadiers punched to the west but were soon turned back. Feuchtinger said Canadian anti-tank and artillery fire halted them, while a chagrined Meyer claimed it was Feuchtinger's lack of nerve and unwillingness to share in the 21st Panzer's petrol stocks. The 'little fish' had thrown back Panzermeyer.[41]

While the Allies fought in a ferocious contest with the 7th Army for the beaches of Normandy, many German divisions sat about inactive, lining the long French coast and waiting for the 'real' invasion at Pas-de-Calais. One of these included Peiper with the Leibstandarte SS Adolf Hitler. On Tuesday, 6 June the long-anticipated code word flashed to the headquarters of the 1st SS Panzer Division.

Code name: Blücher—the Allied invasion in the West.

As word trickled down from Peiper to his company commanders and men, there was one whisper after another: 'Invasion! They're coming!'

On 9 June the division was told to move to a new assembly area near Ghent, on the warning that the Allies might try to seize the Scheldt Estuary.

By that time the II Panzer Battalion had thirty-three Mk IVs, although they were still short of strength for the heavy Panthers. Rolf Reiser was sent again to Mailly-le-Camp East of Paris, where he was to bring back thirty-eight Mk Vs, only to find he must wait because sabotage by rail explosives in Maubege had delayed the shipment. Still, when these arrived and were cloaked in a forest near Barbery, the divisional heavy tank strength rose sharply.

In any case, the Allied subterfuge seemed complete. German intelligence believed the second invasion to the north of Normandy could be expected on 10 June and that they must be prepared to repulse it.[42] Peiper's men were relieved to finally be moving. 'The invasion of the continent is in full swing,' an SS Sturmmann wrote to his parents. 'We are breathing easier ... we can still hope we can be there in time to give our enemies a blow from which they won't recover.'[43]

In inky blackness Peiper's tanks ground slowly along the pavement from Hasselt—16km per hour was a good march rate. They were still out when the morning sun rose high, and the dark steel Panzers baked with oven-like interior conditions inside. Transmissions overheated. With inexperienced tank drivers, tanks ran into each other, and commanders had to take over the yokes to prevent more accidents. Dead tired, they halted at the end of 10 June near the town of Ursel, just east of the Schedlt Estuary and south of Antwerp. A small party of soldiers with radios posted themselves in a windmill at the south-west edge of town. The tanks were carefully parked under trees, behind houses and in the shadows.[44]

While Peiper and the 1st SS dallied, the 'schoolboy' division caught the limelight. Max Wünsche—who before the invasion had attracted the SS photographers as he stood ramrod straight in the turret of his Panther tank, headphones pressed closely to his ears and hair perfectly coiffured— was now in combat garb. But Max lived for the photographers; in the din of battle on 9 June the *Kriegsberichter* snapped Wünsche and the foreign minister's son, Rudolf Ribbentrop, both bandaged and battle scarred as they later darted around the battlefield in a motorcycle with a sidecar: they were fighting wounded. The Hitler Youth division looked big that summer in the calamitous battles for Normandy. They displayed the SS braggadocio—the *unerschütterliche kampfkraft*—the unshakeable will to fight. All the time Meyer, dashing around on his motorcycle, and Wünsche, driving the tanks, gathered glory amid bloody sacrifice.

In the meantime, Jochen Peiper and his tanks idled inland near the north Belgian coast. They waited for the real invasion, which the general staff remained convinced would come at the Pas-de-Calais. Even if on alert, Peiper and his men mostly watched the windmills turn near Ursel.

Back at the front, on 9 June the special central tank reserve, Panzer Group West, awkwardly jockeyed its armoured divisions for what was to be a knock-out blow, although while it was assailed constantly by Allied aircraft.[45] General Geyr von Schweppenberg was to have attacked the beachheads by the morning of the second or, at the latest, third days, but punished constantly from the air, he was still not ready. Each day was spent hiding from fighter-bombers under trees, bushes and building eaves—hardly strategic. A bombing on 9 June against the tank regiment of the 21st Panzer Division put several tanks *hors de combat* arising from the damage to vehicles being buried in mud. Then at dusk at 2030 hours on the following day, 10 June, a savage air attack flattened von Schweppenberg's field headquarters 20km south-east of Caen. Although wounded, Geyr survived, but the strike killed seventeen of his staff, rendering Panzer Group West nugatory.[46] Although the precision air attack took place at dusk, no one suspected that German radio intercepts had provided code breakers the precise coordinates of Geyr's poorly concealed headquarters.[47] Geyr, meanwhile, was completely disheartened, resigning his command; General Hans Eberbach would be assigned to take over.

As command improvisation, Dietrich was assigned directly to Dollmann's 7th Army, and the planned German counter-blow was delayed for twenty-four critical hours. Meanwhile, von Rundstedt communicated with OKW and Hitler admitted as much that Rommel had been right. With the tanks remote from the beaches, one Panzer platoon after another was torched on the road, not even being able to fire a single shot.

In the meantime, British Field Marshal Montgomery also endeavoured to increase his strength, making use of two of his most experienced formations, the 51st Highland Division and the 7th Armoured. The Scottish elite took the task of moving beyond the 6th Airborne's positions east of the Orne River, while the 7th Armoured planned to strike Caen from the north-east. Strength would clash with strength.[48]

On 10 June the British 7th Armoured Division flung itself into the line west of Caen to enlarge the penetration made by the 50th Infantry Division. The intended target was the flank of the Panzer Lehr Division. Although the British achieved little penetration of the stubborn German line, a gap developed between the villages of Caumont and Villers-Bocage. Noting this lapse on 13 June, the 7th Armoured hurled a column of tanks at the enemy. At first they seemed on the verge of success, entering Villers-Bocage well behind the positions of Bayerlein's Panzer Lehr. Perhaps they could encircle the German armour.

What the British did not know was that recent orders commanded the SS Heavy Panzer Battalion 101 down to Caen to join the fight. This included SS Obersturmführer Michael Wittmann, the world's leading tank ace. As it happened, the British armour rattled forward just as Wittmann's 2nd Panzer Company entered Villers-Bocage with four Tigers and one Mk IV. Wittmann himself ran into a pack of British Cromwell tanks at the edge of the village, shooting down four in as many minutes. Wittmann then sped up to join the other Tigers, clattering parallel along the entire British column, slamming one shell after another into the helpless 22nd Armoured Brigade at point-blank range.

In all, Wittmann knocked out a further twenty-seven British tanks and as many halftracks and other vehicles—all in the space of thirty minutes. It was arguably the most spectacular armoured feat of the war. However, as if to underscore the difference of the tank fight in Russia and that in the West, by the time the victorious Tigers returned to pass through Villers-Bocage, British tanks and anti-tank guns were lying in wait. Firing broadside, they holed all five, striking where their armour was vulnerable. Even so, Wittmann and all the Panzer crews escaped, knowing they had averted the threat to turn the German flank. Wittmann, to whom Peiper had presented the Knight's Cross in Russia the previous winter, now wore the Swords to the Knight's Cross. What did Peiper think? 'He was not an impressive personality,' the SS colonel later recalled, 'but he could see really well; his anticipation of enemy tank movements was almost prophetic.'

> Once, I was with him at the front in Russia. 'Can I shoot?' he asked. 'No, why? There are no targets.' 'Yes,' he told me, 'I will shoot.' He could see tanks very far away. Boom-boom-boom—three shots. Soon there were smoke rings in the distance and he had hit three tanks. He had the eyes of an eagle.[49]

Never one to miss the opportunity, Himmler's propaganda machine trebled the feat, dubbing Wittmann the 'Tank Killer'.[50] Meanwhile, the adjutant of SS Heavy Panzer Battalion 101, Unstersturmführer Eduard Kalinowsky, wrote to his wife in Frankfurt with deep misgivings, but a determination to stick it out with the Tiger battalion. They had just suffered a powerful fighter-bomber attack in the woods, killing several and incapacitating several Tigers. 'It is very hard for the soldiers here,' he told her, 'for the English and the Americans employ an enormous quantity of material, there is almost no end to their air attacks. But these, too, have finally abated in recent days and now it's our turn to give them proper hell.'[51]

While Peiper and the Leibstandarte waited for employment, their sister division, the 2nd SS Panzer Division (Das Reich), had orders to proceed to Normandy. Its commander, Heinz Lammerding, had an intolerant reputation when it came to partisans. Peiper had come to know the man during his time with Himmler. The long-faced Lammerding, scarred and sour in appearance, had spent years fighting with the Totenkopf Division, to the glowing admiration of Theodor Eicke at a time when his brutish command comprised some of the most loathsome thugs in the entire SS.[52] After graduating from that assignment, Lammerding became chief of staff to General Erich von dem Bach-Zelewski during his murderous partisan 'cleaning operations' in the Pripet Marshes in Russia in 1943. So pleased had Himmler been with the slaughter that he awarded Lammerding command of the 2nd SS Panzer Division, Das Reich.

When Lammerding arrived in France in April 1944 he found his new command so fought out after the Cherkassy debacle that only a few grizzled SS veterans remained. A large draft of Alsatian conscripts of questionable fervour brought the division up to strength.[53] Since its arrival in France in April 1944, the division had been plagued with attacks from partisans in the Toulouse region. In mid-May some thousand *franc-tireurs* suddenly descended on the railhead at Figeac and kidnaped some German soldiers. And there had been other altercations in Caussade, with bridges exploding when someone attempted to cross.[54]

Receiving orders to proceed to Normandy, the division took six days to move 150km from Montauban to Brive-la-Gaillarde. While the armour moved in fits by rail, the rest of the division moved sluggardly through Limoges, constantly harassed by the French resistance. Dozens of SS men died in ambushes. Most of the German garrison in Tulle had been overcome and killed.[55] Lammerding saw to it in a division order on 9 June that vengeance would be doled out: any house from where shots were fired at Germans 'would be burned to the ground, and to atone for each killed SS men, ten guerrillas would be put to death.[56] Yet the final straw may have come when Sturmbannführer Helmut Kämpfe, the head of the I Battalion, 4 SS Grenadier Regiment, disappeared near the village of Gueret. Brutal reprisals began—ones that Hitler himself now sanctioned: 'The continuing increase in acts of terror and sabotage in the occupied territories are being committed by organized bands … The troops and every single member of the Armed Forces, SS and Police, when they catch terrorists and saboteurs in the act, are immediately to kill them on the spot.'[57]

The most grotesque result was a public display on 9 June designed to quell the fervour of the *résistants*. Nearly a hundred male citizens of Tulle were marched to the Place de Souillac and grotesquely hanged from trees, lampposts and balconies. French witnesses said Lammerding himself watched the victims strung up as he sipped wine at a roadside café. After the war, predictably, he claimed to have left before those acts of unspeakable savagery.[58]

Worse was to come. On 10 June 1944 a Das Reich SS company rounded up all the men, women and children of Oradour-sur-Glane in south-western France and brutally murdered most of the seven hundred inhabitants. Many were shot, while others were burned alive in the church.[59] Ostensibly the justification for the murders stemmed from the actions of the French resistance in the region.[60] And while the Allies were inclined to see the maquis as brave resistance fighters helping to liberate their native land, the Russian-tested soldiery of the Waffen SS saw them as partisans to be rooted out and eliminated. There is scant evidence that the maquisards were active in Oradour; indeed, the reasons the small village became the focal point of the savage reprisal have never been satisfactorily explained.[61]

Lammerding made an immediate effort to suppress news of the atrocity, but its size and horrible circumstance precluded effective damage control. Word spread quickly across France and even within the ranks of the German Army. Upon hearing of it, Field Marshal Rommel demanded that those responsible should be court martialled. Even Allied code breakers surmised that something unusual was up when the SS division signalled on 12 June of carrying out 'limited operations against partisans'.[62] 'Limited operations' such as Tulle and Oradour could only be understood within the context of the Russian experience, went the SS exculpatory explanations. In the midst of training, the Leibstandarte issued an order forbidding such actions and encouraged instructions for proper 'behaviour towards the French civilians':

> So far, the French population in the area of action are mostly friendly and helpful. Recently our troops have committed a number of incidents such as murder, rape and unauthorized seizure of French property. Such behaviour drives the civilians into the hands of the terrorists. Decent German soldiers will have to pay for that with their blood. This is to be made clear to all soldiers. In the future, such violations will be curbed or otherwise severely punished.[63]

Back in Belgium, Peiper and his tanks waited for the big attack on the northern coast while the war swirled just below them. There were plenty of signs that something was wrong. The Belgian partisans sprang into action as BBC radio broadcast a string of incoherent references to flowers and scented herbs—seemingly code words to arouse the guerrillas before the big invasion of Calais. Word had it that a large mass of British ships and landing craft had been sighted opposite Boulogne, and the Allied air forces began to bomb the German defences on the coast there. All the while a blizzard of radio transmissions described preparations of eleven divisions of the fictitious 1st U.S. Army Group, led by the missing U.S. General George Patton.

Little did the *Abwehr* the German military intelligence service, suspect the complete hoodwink of their intelligence by 'Fortitude', the spectacular Allied counterintelligence operation designed to keep the Germans focused on the certainty that the Calais landing was looming, even though it was nothing more than a feint.[64] But in early June Hitler was deeply suspicious, recalling his intuition eight weeks earlier that Normandy was the place. 'The way the British are dishing this up to us strikes me as absurd theatre,' he told Alfred Jodl. 'I can't help feeling that the whole thing will turn out to be a shameless charade.'[65] On 12 June Hitler may have begun to realize he had been taken in by Allied deceptions, ordering that the 1st SS Panzer Division be assigned to Normandy under the I SS Panzer Corps, while the long-awaited vengeance weapons, the V-1 buzz bomb, be unleashed against England the following day.[66] He claimed these weapons 'would decide the war' and bring about the collapse of the English.

Now at mid-month, Field Marshal Rommel telephoned Alfred Jodl at Hitler's headquarters to emphasize the looming crisis: 'I suggest you send some gentlemen from OKW to come and have a look for themselves.' After he hung up he penned a short note to his wife, Lucie. 'The enemy's air superiority has a grave effect on our movements,' he jotted in frustration. 'The invasion is quite likely to start [at] other places, too. There's simply no answer for it.'[67] The next day capped the situation. He had stopped by to monitor the progress of big-headed Geyr von Schweppenburg's grand Panzer assault to take place at Caen, only to watch the entire affair unravel under a torment of air and naval bombardment: 'They're lying about like firing targets.'[68]

On 12 June word came that the Allied forces had seized Carentan in bloody fighting in spite of Rommel's charge to von der Heydte and the 6th Fallschirmjäger (Parachute) Regiment to hold it fast. Carentan was the key to the entire Cherbourg peninsula. In the meantime, from his mountaintop vantage at the Berghof, Hitler informed von Rundstedt that he would soon have the 9th SS and 10th SS Panzer Divisions that he had ordered from Russia to France with all possible haste.[69] That news was less than reassuring—it was taking days to move a German division a few score kilometres. On that Monday the one-legged corps commander in Normandy, General Erich Marcks, motored off to inspect the crumbling situation, only to be killed when an air attack flattened his command car. The only good news concerned the commitment of the 8th and 9th Nebelwerfer brigades, whose fire seemed to have halted the U.S. advance wherever the rocket artillery was massed.

Cagey Gerd von Rundstedt weighed in with a pessimistic assessment. The Anglo-Americans had substantially reinforced their 100km-wide lodgement on the Calvados coast, and von Rundstedt looked askance at the unused strength in the Pas-de-Calais. Given the near paralysis of German movement, he might have second-guessed his judgement on the central Panzer reserve, but there was no changing that now. He quickly composed the assessment and insisted it be sent to Hitler straight away. 'I must point out,' he began, 'that given the disproportionate material, a situation might develop that forces us to make some fundamental decisions.'[70] What did that mean?

The answer lay in a recent meeting of Rommel's chief of staff, Hans Speidel with General Blumentritt, his opposite in Rundstedt's office. Speidel whispered that a circle of men were forming to convince Hitler to make a separate peace in the west. How they would do that was not discussed. Something larger was afoot. Rommel still worried about a larger second invasion that was to come. The general staff intelligence officer, Oberst Alexis von Roenne, insisted that the Patton army was still to launch the main invasion in Calais. The bulk of the powerful German 15th Army was to stay where they were.

If the Allied firepower remained immense, their warships off the coast constituted a special danger. While German intelligence officers ridiculed Geyr's claim that the vessels could fire only a score kilometres inland, the commander of Panzer Group West knew otherwise. 'Gentlemen, just stand here for a while,' he challenged, 'and you'll find out how far they can fire!'[71]

Proof came on 14 June 1944. From the Bay of the Seine the battleships HMS *Ramilles* and *Nelson* gunned huge 15in shells 30km inland that fell almost without warning. So it was on that Wednesday, while the 12th SS Hitlerjugend division commander, Fritz Witt, and his orderly played cards in their idle time, their headquarters was flattened by 'an unlucky hit'. Pierced by shrapnel, Witt died instantly.[72] Kurt Meyer replaced him.

In the meantime, Dietrich reported that in the fighting near Tilly he was only able to prevent the collapse of the flank of the Panzer Lehr

Division by throwing in communications personnel, tank crews and drivers with no vehicles. It might still be possible to throw the British back into the sea—but only with two good Panzer and three good infantry divisions along with effective support from the Luftwaffe. The latter request seemed particularly far-fetched.[73] On 16 June Dietrich personally complained to Erwin Rommel: 'I am being bled white and I am getting nowhere!'

'You must attack,' Rommel countered.

'With what?' Dietrich threw up his hands. 'We haven't enough troops. We need another eight or ten divisions in the next day or two or we're finished. If the 15th Army wasn't sitting on its ass in Northern France and Belgium, we could get some help.'[74]

Rommel had no answer, but von Rundstedt sided with Dietrich. He lobbied Hitler for a free hand to strip fifteen infantry divisions from the south of France to allow him to replace the armour that had been rushed up to hold the line. 'To concentrate enough tanks for a decisive blow,' Rundstedt maintained, 'it is imperative that infantry be available to replace the armour.' Yet this too was denied, as it would give up the line south of the Loire River. While the fear of a second landing died hard with von Rundstedt and OB West, it achieved near immortality in Hitler's map room.

Hitler had the final say. It was his decision that Dietrich attack immediately. As if to underscore Sepp's appraisal, Rommel's attempt to drive and personally speak with Dietrich and Geyr was frustrated by a blue French sky teeming with Allied fighter-bombers. Rommel claimed he had to stop and dive for cover thirty times.[75]

While Kurt Meyer and the other Germans on the Normandy front were getting a thorough thrashing, the soldiers of the Leibstandarte Adolf Hitler were still polishing their weapons. One civilized distraction came when Werner Wolff's gunner returned with Helga, Wolff's hometown sweetheart. Since they had left from Memel, the invasion had begun, but given the Leibstandarte's recent inactivity, it seemed appropriate that the show go on. On 16 June Wolff married his 19-year-old bride in Knesselare near Ghent. The 'invasion wedding' was held in the twenty-room Chateau de St Joris ten Distel in the dense forests east of the town.

The estate was an expansive collection of manicured gardens and seventeenth-century architecture that attested to local 'blue blood' opulence. Amid the Flemish-speaking region of Belgium, the Comte de van Pottelberghe and his family spoke French and lived the finer life. Even so, the war made a wealthy existence less comfortable. The baron's family had been chased out of the main chateau to the servants' quarters when the SS occupied the estate early that summer. The prospect of war was frightening enough—the baron had lost a leg in the First World War. Although the baroness found the German soldiers scary—'they were dirty and rough'—they piqued the prepubescent curiosity of Jean, her 12-year-old daughter. Even if they broke antique furniture, the uniformed foreigners carried themselves well: big, masculine and suggesting dangerous adventure. They were polite enough to the young girl, particularly one strapping German youth intent on wooing her governess. Germans kept coming and going across the estate's moated wrought-iron gate. She scarcely noticed anymore.[76]

The weather that Friday was sunny and cool just inland of the Belgian coast. Breezes from the west skidded puffy white clouds across the blue. A few violins from the music corps provided accompaniment. Flowers spelled out 'good luck' on Wolff's path as he and his bride walked past manicured gardens, pools and lily pads. Wolff, displaying a closely cropped haircut, strode confidently in his black Panzer uniform, Helga's left arm locked in his. She wore a simple white dress and carried a bouquet of white roses. Capped SS Panzer men of the 7th Company looked expectantly as they made their way to the altar.

When they reached the shuttered chateau they saw a giant black SS banner with the characteristic silver lightning bolt runes floating above the entrance. Draped from the highest point of the roof was the red, white and black Nazi flag. Passing inside, an honour guard escorted the couple to a white-linen-covered table. At the table sat the judge advocate and Peiper off to one side; Wolff and his bride sat on the other. Flowers were arrayed on the table to form half a Hagall rune surrounding the wedding plate, and a candle burned at either end of the table, the SS ceremonial encouragement for fertility.[77] Wolff and his bride signed the documents.

At that moment Jochen Peiper stood and stepped forward to be the first to clench Wolff's hand in congratulations. There was applause, after which Peiper presided as toastmaster with a short banquet speech. In his remarks Peiper's love of classical literature and his airs of education were on display. At one point he urged the other officers not yet married to follow Wolff's example. 'His exhortation struck us as rather peculiar,' said one. 'The oldest gentlemen present, the division judge, was a bachelor.'[78]

At the reception dinner the newlyweds sat at their gaily decorated table. Save the bride, everyone seated was a Waffen SS officer in a black uniform. Helga was struck by Peiper's boyish appearance. The regimental commander sat across from Paul Guhl and Benoni Junker. As they dined,

Peiper asked every man seated how many children they had sired.[79] He looked serious. It was an awkward moment. One couple had two, some had one and others had no children at all. 'Gentlemen, I fear for your prospects for promotion,' Peiper smiled 'I have three!' Everyone laughed. Outwardly it was a joke, but the sentiment might as well have come from Peiper's old superior, Himmler.[80]

Later that night it was a big *Hochzeitstrubel*—a honeymoon party. 'That was a good excuse for a lot of drinking,' Hans Siptrott recalled.[81] Soon most of the guests were roaring drunk. 'Totally blue evening,' Junker scrawled in his diary, but unlike most times, that seemed to be acceptable with the regimental commander. 'Peiper was really big and in a good mood today.'[82]

While Peiper married off Werner Wolff that Friday, his ultimate superior, Adolf Hitler, flew out to France not far away. On Saturday, 17 June 1944 Hitler, Keitel, Jodl and their staff flew from Berchtesgaden to Metz by Focke-Wulf Condor and there boarded an armour-plated car for the drive to Margival, France. Nearby was the location of Wolfs-schlucht 2, a bunkerised field headquarters just north of Soissons. The place had been designed to direct the now-forgotten 1940 invasion of England. Now the tables were turned. Here in France he met with both Rommel and von Rundstedt, both victorious in this same land four years earlier.

Upon arrival at the field headquarters Hitler looked tired and dist-racted, sitting awkwardly on a stool while fiddling with his glasses during von Rundstedt's gloomy recounting of the disastrous first ten days on the invasion front. While Rommel nodded in agreement, von Rundstedt concluded that it was now virtually impossible to expel the Allies from France.[83] Hitler interrupted to complain about leadership, but von Rundstedt seemed unimpressed. Rommel, for his part, seemed to apologize that the critical battle for the beaches was lost. He held his tongue rather than complaining about everyone having followed Geyr's failed Panzer reserve strategy.

Even so, the meeting of former conquerors 'was a thoroughly unplea-sant reunion', recalled Nicolaus von Below, the Führer's Luftwaffe adjutant.[84] Hitler was the only one seated, playing nervously with pencils and his eyeglasses, while Rommel, grim and taciturn, described the degenerating situation in Normandy. The five beachheads of the Allied invasion had burst open, and the Americans were now fanning out across the French countryside into the Cotentin Peninsula.[85] In ten days the American, British and Canadians had landed more than half a million men and enormous amounts of weapons and materiel.

Hitler's right-hand strategist, Jodl, took notes at the meeting, jotting down points the two field marshals deemed critical. Number one on Rommel's list and heavily underscored was 'enemy air superiority'.[86] Von Rundstedt nodded, adding that he did not have the resources to eject the Allies from France. Hitler seemed to grow more agitated as the litany went on and interrupted frequently. The field marshal must be exaggerating, he said. 'You demand our confidence,' Rommel blustered, 'but you don't trust us yourself.'

As the discussion grew more heated, Rommel suggested that Hitler come to the front himself to see the battle he described as 'one terrible bloodletting'. He patiently described his strategy of a limited withdrawal outside of the range of the big naval guns where the assembled Panzer divisions would be used for a massive counterstroke against Montgomery's 21st Army Group.[87]

Hitler clung to his policy of 'holding fast tenaciously to every square foot of soil'. Changing the subject, he raptly described the recent V-1 campaign—where, on 15 June, some 244 pilotless jet bombs zoomed off to London. A total of seventy-three of the *Vergeltlungswaffen*—the vengeance weapons—exploded there before dawn. He thought they would turn the tide of the war. 'We only have to keep our nerve,' he said. 'Hold in the East, strike in the West.' If they could defeat the invasion, he charged, the English would sue for a separate peace under the mounting threat of the V-weapon bombardment. Beyond that he claimed 'masses of turbo-jet aircraft would soon chase English and American aircraft from the skies'. That was a fantasy as the jets were just entering production. However, Rommel, who had been urging the earliest possible attack with the robot bombs, at last found something to encourage.[88] His generals, agog at the new technology, suggested moving the V-1 targets from London to the Allied beachheads, where the battle for the Atlantic Wall appeared otherwise lost. That was impossible, General Lieutenant Erich Heinemann warned, confessing that 'unpredictable scattering' meant the weapons typically missed the planned targets by 15 to 18km.

Hitler nervously ate from a plate heaped with rice and vegetables after someone had tasted his food. The stew lunch had to be relocated inside a bunker because of the threat of an air raid. Following the meal, Rommel asked for a private conversation with Hitler.[89] Their discussion grew uncomfortable once more; the field marshal suggested the front could not be held much longer; Hitler should look for a political solution. Hitler, however, bade Rommel pay attention to the invasion front and leave the war to him. They left the dispute unresolved. Returning to the Obersalzberg that evening, Hitler bitterly remarked that, 'Rommel has lost his nerve. He has become a pessimist like the rest. These days only optimists can achieve anything.'[90]

At about the same time, Peiper's frustrating period of complacency in Belgium finally ended. The day before, on 13 June, Hitler ordered the Leibstandarte south to join Dietrich and his embattled corps in Normandy.[91] But it would be two days before most of the tanks and vehicles reached entraining points south-west of Paris.[92] Two days later the Germans got a big break from the weather. A huge storm—the worst in forty years—swept the Norman coast. Not only did it suspend Allied air power for three days, but the winds were so savage that great damage was done to the artificial harbours and port preparations made to supply the Allied forces.[93] Eight hundred Allied ships were damaged or sank. Only at the end of the month did the Allied supply capacity return to an acceptable level. Watching the scene, Montgomery worried. 'This weather is still the very devil. A gale all day yesterday, the same today. Nothing can be unloaded … I need to resume the offensive with a bang.'[94]

All this seemed to play into Hitler's plan to launch a withering tank attack on the Allied lodgement. As the big storm howled outside, Panzer Group West worked feverishly to bring about the big slam. It would use four SS Panzer divisions, including the Leibstandarte as the spearhead. A subsidiary operation by the army's 2nd Panzer and Panzer Lehr divisions would strike the British east of Caen to pin them down. Then the main blow would fall between Bretteville l'Orgueilleuse and south of Balleroy with the objective 'to eliminate the American III Army Corps' and roll up the invasion. As envisioned, the Leibstandarte would fight on the right flank, ultimately reaching the beaches near Bernières-sur-Mer along the Plateau-du-Calvados.[95]

As German planners eagerly drew out the attack plans with flaring marks to the beaches, Peiper and his tanks were nowhere close to their circled assembly point at Montigny. The big Panthers prowled though the streets of Eeklo to load on the train station in Maldgedem and then move towards Normandy. On Monday, 19 June 1944 Peiper's tank regiment concentrated in the area around Verneuil in France—right back where they had been two years before.[96] The tanks were spaced out on the flat cars to prevent a domino-like catastrophe. Frequent stops gathered camouflage—the Panthers looked like squat pine trees moving by rail. Still, even if escaping direct bombardment, the Allied bombing interdiction was crippling deployment. Paul Hausser reported to Panzer Group West on Thursday morning, bringing the unwelcome news that damage to the French rail system made it impossible to bring up the tanks up quickly. The Leibstandarte had to unload in the Rheims–Chalon area, nearly 500km from the fighting.[97]

Peiper and the regimental staff went by command car via secondary roads from Dreux-Evreux to L'aigle. Driving by night and parking deep in French woods by day, the German tanks slowly drew closer to Normandy. Groups of Peiper's men stayed in French homes. The locals seemed obliging enough, and some had a cache of cider or the sweet calvados— every soldier's weakness.

By 15 June Peiper's tank regiment boasted twenty-nine Panther and sixty-two Mk IV tanks combat ready—yet how to get them to the battlefront? It took the Leibstandarte two weeks to complete its move to Normandy. So much for Geyr von Schweppenburg's one-night march to the beaches. The Allied fighter-bombers were not the only problem; once unloaded from their flatcars, any tanks with mechanical problems had to be left behind; the workshop companies had no spare parts. The Panthers were still having more trouble than the lighter Mk IVs, particularly with their fire-prone Maybach engines.[98]

Even as late as July, nine repaired Panthers led by Friedrich Christ clanked noisily down the Champs Élysées before curious Parisians in a very public move towards the front.[99] Meanwhile, most of the tanks moved from Eeklo and Genk to the train station at Malgedem, where they disembarked south-west of Rouen to then motor to the front. Even that was not without issue, as two train cars were derailed when the French resistance struck with track explosives near Maubege. The heavy Panthers were delayed once more.

In the meantime the fuel situation also often became acute. Although the fuel tanks of all vehicles were filled just after unloading, obtaining further petrol always posed a problem.[100] Still, the Panzer men could tell they were drawing close when they reached Argentan at the end of June to find it smouldering from a recent air attack. So warned, they threaded through Falaise to slip from view into the dense green of the Forêt de Cinglais. There they camped on moss-feathered ground under the dappled beech, maple and spreading oak while Panzer mechanics struggled to make all the tree-branch-covered tanks ready for employment. Still waiting, Peiper's men gawked at the constancy of the Allied planes but poked fun at their commander's obsession with forest hideouts:

> Whenever the boss sees a forest, he puts us down.
> He seems to be the grandson of Hermann Löns.
> And when we get near a beautiful pine forest,
> everyone says: 'That must be a Peiper Forest!'

In the Reich, we would love to have a girl to talk with
The firs have broken our hopes.
Who needs a real featherbed!
Forest earth is quite nice.[101]

So as Peiper and his forest dwellers drew swords for the great battle in the West, the Soviets opened their long-dreaded summer offensive on 22 June—three years to the day after the Germans had invaded in 1941. Hitler himself had predicted the date but not the objective. Again, German intelligence was confused, for *Abwehr* operatives believed the Russians would assail Army Group North in the Ukraine; instead, they launched a massive Barbarossa-style pincers attack called Operation Bagration to devour Army Group Center.[102] In scarcely a week the Russians gobbled up twenty-five German divisions and three hundred thousand men in a disaster soon termed the 'destruction of Army Group Centre'. By mid-July the Soviets had pounded their way 320km to the west and the border of East Prussia.

In the West a much bigger problem for Hitler's planned sweep to the sea was a fresh offensive launched by the British. On 25 June Field Marshal Montgomery unleashed Operation Epsom, a bold attack designed to wrest the rubble of Caen from the enemy. The entire affair toppled German plans—accentuated by the fact that both Rommel and von Rundstedt were away on that day—flying off to Hitler's mountain headquarters to get another dose of his attitude. The port of Cherbourg fell on 26 June. For that, Hitler opined, heads must roll. He demanded that stocky General Friedrich Dollmann, in charge of the failed 7th Army, be immediately court martialled. Both Rommel and von Rundstedt were immediately called to Berchtesgaden on 29 June. They left as a drenching rain pelted the Norman coast. Both arrived at 1800 hours after driving all day. If Hitler was truculent and inflexible, the German leader found his match in the two men summoned. Von Rundstedt refused to bring charges against Dollmann, only to learn that the general had just taken his own life. Hitler claimed it was a heart attack, but the truth was soon widely known. Dollmann's replacement would be Obergruppenführer Paul Hausser; SS Gruppenführer Willi Bittrich would take over II SS Panzer Corps.[103]

Unfortunately for Field Marshal Montgomery, the 9th SS and 10th SS Panzer divisions had just begun to arrive from Poland and were immediately fed into the line as the British attacked between Carpiquet and Rauray. Meanwhile, Sepp Dietrich sternly warned Panzer Group West that Caen could not be long held without the commitment of the forces designed for the big attack. Both I SS and II SS Panzer Corps were immediately made available to Dietrich—a concession tacitly indicating the end of the imagined grand armoured advance to the beaches.[104] In any case, Epsom ran headlong into the increasing German strength and foundered with bloody losses. Hitler complained to Paul Hausser that even the SS had failed him. 'I explained,' Hausser would later say, 'that I couldn't make up for the failure of the Navy and the Luftwaffe.'[105]

> I requested the creation of reserves by withdrawal of the Panzer divisions. This necessitated shortening the front lines, a tactical retreat and withdrawal out of range of the enemy fleet. This plan was not approved. Absolute holding of the present positions was demanded ... Even though mobile operations in Normandy were impossible in view of the limitations of the area and our numerically limited forces, this procedure was nonetheless stupid.[106]

With Hitler there was no arguing. On 28 June Rommel stopped by to visit Dietrich and the I SS Panzer Corps. Although both commanders drew hearty smiles for photographers, their candid discussion spoke of deep worry.[107] The 12th SS Panzer Division was nearly at the end of its resources. As an emergency measure, part of the SS Panzer Grenadier Regiment 1 under Albert Frey was hurriedly fed into the line to stiffen the waning strength of Kurt Meyer's troops. Deprived of adequate artillery support, Frey's grenadiers took a beating. In the premature commitment, Max Hansen, the commander of the II Battalion, was wounded for the ninth time.

Although they shelved the big strike to the Calvados coast, SS Obergruppenführer Paul Hausser intended to immediately use the II SS Panzer Corps to flatten the British advance south of Caen. Max Wünsche and the Hitlerjugend Panzer Regiment was to seize Hill 112 and to prevent the British from punching through to the bridges over the Orne River. On the afternoon of Wednesday, 28 June Wünsche eagerly launched thirty tanks forward under a noisy curtain of rocket fire from the 7th Nebelwerfer Brigade.[108] Within hours some sixty-one British tanks had been destroyed and the village of Gavrus recaptured. But this too was rendered void as artillery and naval guns soon rocked the advancing German columns.

The following day the British 11th Armoured Division recaptured Hill 112, but then lost it once more when attacked by both the 9th SS and 10th SS Panzer divisions. A hellish bombardment assailed the German counterattack; tank and manpower losses soared. Hill 112 evoked a lunar landscape—pocked by smoking craters, burning machines and lifeless bodies. On the last day of June General Fritz Kraemer, at Dietrich's headquarters, suggested the misadventure be cancelled.[109] At least the

SS divisions should be pulled out of the range of the pummelling British naval guns. Out of the other side of its mouth I SS Panzer Corps recommended Max Wünsche for the Oak Leaves to the Knights Cross for the same action—another addition to his Christmas tree of medals. After all, as Meyer recounted in his commendation, the vain Panzer leader had destroyed 219 Allied tanks.[110] Awards amid calamity.

The tense desperation of the German circumstance did not come through the Nazi press. When Sepp Dietrich was interviewed at his headquarters near Caen on 1 July, he bragged to war reporter Günther Weber in his rich Bavarian brogue, 'We have blocked the invasion army's way to Paris,' he said. That was about the best gloss possible. When asked about the Hitlerjugend Division, he towed the company line. 'The boys go at it,' he said in the earthy vocabulary of the foxhole and beer cellar. 'They know no rest. With their good blood and full of enthusiasm they defend each dugout.' Dietrich went on about how 17-year-olds were now driving the heaviest German tanks, although now assisted also by older soldiers from the previous war. It was a roundabout manner of acknowledging Germany's growing manpower shortage.[111] With the unproductive close of Montgomery's Operation Epsom and the failed German counterattack to the coast, the struggle took on airs of a conflict not unlike the Great War. Casualties and deaths measured combat misery, as little territory changed hands.

At German supreme headquarters came grudging admissions of fading prospects. On the ground, Hitler opined his SS troops had gone soft, blaming the French women, good food and plentiful booze. To address the air debacle, he called in Reichsmarschall Hermann Göring to demand that some way be found to re-establish air superiority. That seemed impossible. To compensate, he demanded that the aerial robot bomb bombardment be stepped up—that, and renewed attack by submarines against the invasion fleet supplying the Anglos. There was even the suggestion from Hitler's fanatical female test pilot, Hanna Reitsch, to Hitler at the Berghof on 28 February 1944 that Hitler Youth suicide teams could fly newly developed Fieseler 103R jet-powered suicide bombers. Such piloted V-1 buzz bombs would cripple Allied shipping, she blustered. The idea for *Totaleinsatz*— total sacrifice—had originated with Otto Skorzeny in a page borrowed from the Kamikaze pilots of Japan. A special *Leonidas Squadron* was being set up as a part of the super secret Luftwaffe unit, KG 200. Hearing of it, Hitler demurred. 'It is not in keeping with the German character,' he opined, but he nevertheless authorized her to further develop the idea.[112]

Sacrifice or not, since arriving in Normandy, the 1st SS Panzer Division could not find a way to get at their enemy in single combat; instead, they crouched in their dappled camouflage uniforms under the trees of the Forêt de Cinglais, west of Caen, playing cards to the song of the forest wren. Otherwise they retold stale stories or hummed the popular summer song 'Süsse kleine Schaffnerin'—'Sweet Little Lady Conductor'. Such pastimes hardly seemed worthy of their fighting reputation. Knowingly, Peiper called them all together and told each to keep their guard.

'Achtung Tiefflieger!' From their hidden forest lair they watched as the British and American air forces buzzed overhead. When Peiper's men did move in daylight, it was always with an eye pointed upward. 'It was bad in the West,' remembered a gunner with the heavy Tiger battalion. 'You could not take a shit without being attacked by fighter-bombers.'[113] As a result, the dark ocher German tanks were so heavily camouflaged that they looked like giant woolly mammoths moving down the road, only covered in tree boughs rather than fur. Even individual grenadiers took to arranging foliage so that each helmeted man looked like zealous arborists. There was unbridled disdain for their weapon-laden enemy. Heinz von Westernhagen, the leader of Peiper's Tiger battalion, was badly wounded, but he felt encouraged that his brother Rolf would now fight under his command. 'The Americans with their enormous quantities of materiel,' he decried, 'are nothing more than chewing gum Indians!'

> I am completely deaf in my left ear, after I had been stuck in five horrific bomb attacks. We slowly had become specialists in that—once I took cover under one of our tanks after which 2000-kilogram bombs hit directly in front, three metres to the left, and twelve metres behind. The explosion flashes almost burned our throats and lungs. It really is not a noble behaviour of these brothers—but we shall take our revenge.[114]

But their enemy above remained exceedingly dangerous. On 2 July a spindly little American Piper Cub observation plane appeared over Wisch's divisional headquarters. Hearing a large-calibre gun in the distance, Wisch yelled, 'That's meant for us!' and jumped for cover. The shell howled in, exploding on top of his command post and killing his orderly and driver.[115]

Although Kurt Meyer grimly held onto the ruins of Caen, the strategic situation around them fell apart. Von Rundstedt requested that a staged withdrawal begin from Normandy to pull back beyond the 30km range of the giant naval guns. To lend weight to that was a telegram from Geyr von Schweppenburg indicating that his 'Panzer group is in favour of a flexible and elastic battle plan'; that, too, meant pulling back the Panzer divisions. Hitler refused: 'The present positions are to be held.' He was still arguing that the real invasion would yet come at the Pas-de-Calais so that the muscular 15th Army must remain where it was. Rommel's own intelligence drearily noted that thirty divisions had landed at Normandy but claimed that another sixty-seven were waiting in England.[116] That estimate was wrong, but it did cool Hitler's ardour for an immediate counterattack to retake Cherbourg.[117]

Back in Paris, von Rundstedt stood unbowed. As an aging icon of the German military Prussian aristocracy, he had had quite enough from the German leader he derisively called 'that Corporal'. With more questions from Berchtesgaden regarding his conduct of the battle, his response was icy. 'If you doubt what we are doing,' he acidly relayed to Keitel, 'get up here and take over this shambles yourself.'[118] That was near insubordination. Later, on 1 July, there was a heated exchange when Keitel challenged the field marshal's opinion on future moves. 'Make peace, you fools!' von Rundstedt stammered in a moment of exasperation. 'What else can you do?'[119] He clicked down the receiver. The polite notice of von Rundstedt's dismissal came on 3 July, officially citing the old field marshal's failing health.

On 5 July his replacement, Günther von Kluge, strode into Rommel's headquarters in La Roche Guyon teeming with optimism. Recovering from a serious automobile accident, the leathery East Front veteran had spent recent weeks demonstrating the proper attitude at Berchtesgaden. The 61-year-old der Kluge Hans—the Clever Hans—had been obedient to Hitler's wishes in Russia. Now, under Hitler's spell, he was steeped in the fancied magic of the V-1 flying bomb and how it would transform the war in the West. Hitler believed von Kluge had the proper fire. Almost as soon as von Kluge arrived, an argument developed. The upstart accused Rommel of unfounded fear for the enemy's materiel superiority.

Rommel saw a cure for von Kluge's delusional optimism. He sent the new field marshal off to the front. On 12 July von Kluge returned, having been often chased by *Jabos* from tree to tree. Sobered by what he had seen, von Kluge expressed an all but formal apology to Rommel.[120] Communicating with Hitler's headquarters in East Prussia, von Kluge was characteristically blunt; reinforcements arriving at the front without weapons from Brittany were even more dispiriting. 'Now they are sending me troops,' he complained, 'with nothing more than a walking stick.'[121]

'I am no pessimist,' von Kluge insisted, 'but in my view, the situation could not be more grim.'

Chapter 18

Normandy

'You will observe the Rules of Battle, of course?' the White Knight remarked, putting his helmet on too. 'I always do,' said the Red Knight, and they began banging away at each other with such a fury that Alice got behind a tree to be out of the way of the blows.[1]

The chaotic situation for the German army in Normandy was matched only by Allied military frustration in France. Intent on advancing south and turning west towards Paris, the Americans were stuck in the hedgerows around Saint-Lô and slowed to a crawl due to the closed terrain and unforgiving German resistance. 'Our army lacks discipline,' wrote one troubled observer for the theatre historian following the U.S. Army after D-Day:

As to hedgerow fighting ... at the present rate, the German can cripple us ... I continue to be amazed at the fortitude of the weakened, ratty type of soldier we have met. Old men, boys, impressed *Volksdeutsche*, but I defy any Prussian Grenadier to be more effective from a pillbox with a machine gun. Our casualties are all out of proportion to the result. Compare in the La Haye du Puits report, the gains against the figures of what's left of the 315th. Officer casualties are particularly high. The German fire, which seems to come from nowhere or everywhere at once, pins the men down, particularly when there is always a hedgerow or ditch to dive into. Then it is necessary for an officer to get up and yell at the men to get up and advance. The men do get up and follow their officers, but it results in high officer casualties.[2]

The German enemy saw little to cheer them either, and just beyond the beaches Sepp Dietrich, the leader of the SS forces, saw every reason to agree with von Kluge and his earlier pessimistic assessment. Regardless of what Hitler bade, there was no way to push the Allied forces back to the beaches. The British and Canadians concentrated before Caen, where

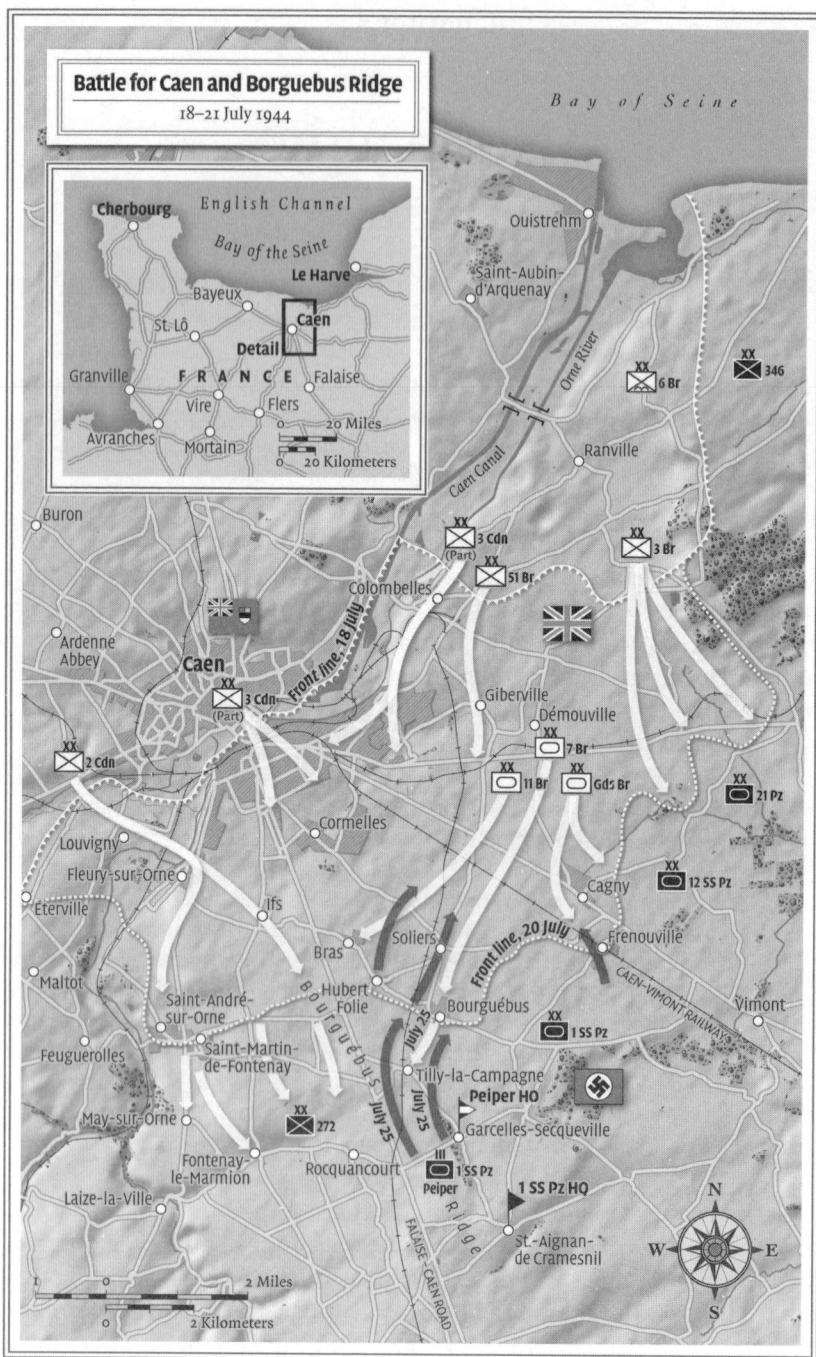

Battle for Caen and Borguebus Ridge
18–21 July 1944

the rolling fields promised better tank going. But the magnet of the royal armour just seemed to attract the most stalwart of the strong and fanatical SS tank forces.

Knowing that Caen would become an epicentre for Allied naval shells and bombs, Dietrich petitioned his superiors on Thursday, 6 July to begin evacuating civilians from the city. It began immediately with diehard Frenchmen now terrified and eager to leave. Their departure was fortunate, for the following day the Allied air forces pounded the city to smithereens.[3] That night a first wave of heavies dropped more than six thousand bombs, and between 0900 and 1000 hours the following morning 450 aircraft of the British Bomber Command struck the city in a devastating cataclysm.[4] Ironically, the massive destruction of this ancient and one-time beautiful city did little to assist Montgomery's attacking columns. When they moved out the following day, streets were closed by rubble, craters and scree piles from ruined buildings. The bombing was at once a controversy. A British-sponsored study was unable to find any evidence of destroyed German guns or tanks in the bombed-out city and concluded that no military targets were hit. It was a pointless devastation.[5]

On the American side the supreme commander, Dwight D. Eisenhower, was beside himself with anger. Montgomery's failure at Caen seemed the clearest example yet of the price of his caution and deliberate concept of battle. The participating Allied air chiefs were livid: 'Ike said yesterday that with 7,000 tons of bombs dropped in the most elaborate bombing of enemy front line positions ever accomplished only seven miles were gained—can we afford a thousand tons of bombs per mile?'[6]

While the British poked through Caen's smoking ruins, the tattered remnants of Meyer's 12th SS Panzer Division pulled back across the Orne River and then on to the suburbs of Vaucelles.[7] There they dug in, knowing that they were backed up by the fresh 1 SS Panzer Division now finally in position.[8] On 4 July the Canadian 8th Infantry brigade had attacked to recapture Carpiquet airfield to the west of Caen; however, the stubborn Hitlerjugend defenders, along with 88mm guns and a *nebelwerfer* brigade, turned the Canadian advance zone into a killing ground, with 'no prisoners being taken by either side'.

Albert Frey's SS Panzer Grenadier Regiment 1 was thrown in to conclude the battle for the Germans. The fighting there saw horrific scenes of single combat. At some point, around dawn on 5 July, the French Canadians of the Régiment de la Chaudiére went berserk and began slitting the throats of any SS men—wounded or dead—that they could find. Only threats by pistol-wielding officers were able to end the killings.[9] One SS Leibstandarte grenadier taken captive revealed that 'if the people here know what we have done to their PW we shouldn't live much longer … [The PW] were first interrogated a bit … they would [then] let him go and then fire fifty rounds with the MG when he was ten paces away, and that would be the end of him. Our CO always used to say, "What am I to do with the swine? We haven't got enough to eat ourselves."'[10]

To the south of the stubborn fight near Caen by the I SS Panzer Corps another pivotal struggle took place for possession of the Cotentin Peninsula. Straddling the peninsula, Carantan, with its nexus of roads, blocked American expansion from the Omaha and Utah bridgeheads. Oberst August Freiherr von der Heydte was fighting there with his 6th Fallschirmager Regiment to deny Carentan to the Americans seeking to break out beyond the beachheads. In early July elements of the arriving 2nd SS Panzer Division under SS Brigadeführer Heinz Lammerding moved in to help repulse assaults from the U.S. 83rd Infantry Division. In the see-saw battle for Sainteny from 7 to 9 July, von der Heydte's men took a number of American prisoners, including two U.S. doctors who unselfishly treated his own wounded. As the fighting progressed, von der Heydte needed to evacuate the doctors back via the 2nd SS covering his rear. 'Please give them especially good treatment,' the baron requested. 'Afterwards I found out both had been shot.' He demanded to personally speak to the division commander. 'Well, one of them was certainly a Jew,' Lammerding scoffed. 'He looked Jewish and the other one also.'[11] Von der Heydte was disgusted—one of his major officers had been taken prisoner, and he had planned to propose an exchange.

Meanwhile, back at Caen on Sunday, 9 July, the British clashed with Meyer's sacrificial Waffen SS rear-guard in the blasted-out suburbs. Fifty hard-nosed SS youths—all that remained of the combat strength of the I Battalion of SS Panzer Grenadier Regiment 26—blasted away from a stone farmhouse on the outskirts of Carpiquet airfield. In the meantime the remnants of the III Battalion fought on in the village of Buron as the 3rd Canadian Division advanced to the gates of Meyer's command post at the Ardennes Monastery. There the 3rd Panzer Company, under Rudolf von Ribbentrop, counterattacked boldly but lost three tanks. The son of Hitler's foreign minister was determined to prove himself in true SS fashion. When another British tank thrust aimed directly for the monastery, von Ribbentrop struck again. Like a medieval jouster, the Knight's Cross holder led his Panthers straight into the British armour. When the British turned back at dusk, von Ribbentrop's quarry, a platoon of shot-up Shermans, blazed and smoked only 100m away.[12]

Having taken over to lead the German armour in Normandy, General Eberbach was not yet discouraged. The air situation, he agreed, was fully menacing, but there were some advantages:

> Until now, the enemy advance has mostly been cautious and frontal, with heavy commitment of material, which must seriously burden his supply service ... German tanks, considering the armouring and armament, are superior to the English and American ones ... [Also] the morale of our troops is still comparatively good.[13]

'The terrain is favourable for defence,' Eberbach concluded, if the armour could be moved into the better locations. Peiper was also on the move. On 10 July, 7th Panzer Company moved up to the village of Bully across the Orne River. Reaching their assigned location, they dug foxholes into rock—a hand-blistering activity made more enthusiastic by the gusts of artillery fire sweeping the ground. Peiper installed his headquarters in a large French country home nearby, peering through a scissors scope at the collecting enemy tank formations just to the west. There was little else to do other than watch; except for the lone 7th Company, Peiper's tanks were to remain in reserve. Peiper and the tank regiment idled through July's dog days. Sitting without fighting in the heat and under radio silence, the only action they saw was when one trooper after another was killed by one of the giant naval guns, while others were wounded by the unrelenting fighter-bombers.

On 15 July the 272nd Infantry Division relieved the Leibstandarte at last. Peiper and a score of his tanks moved into shady positions under dense stands of linden trees south of a beautiful nearby chateau. He and Max Hansen located their battle headquarters at the end of a beech-tree-lined avenue in a seventeenth-century chateau in Garcelles.[14] The headquarters was opulent: Louis XVI furniture, hardwood bookcased library, all drizzled with priceless paintings and antiques—the trappings of Norman aristocracy. The Countess Alice de St Quentin had reluctantly vacated the place four days before when the German police ordered all the locals out as refugees.

The chateau had not been chosen for beauty—although that was fine enough—but rather its stout stone construction. The estate possessed many windows looking out towards Tilly and the beaches from whence danger would come. Peiper's youthful tank crew—Schumann, Kosmehl and Becker, who proudly called themselves the *trois mousquetaires*—sunned themselves in idle moments when circumstances didn't threaten. Otherwise, they went about carefully adjusting the leafy camouflage on Panzer 001 and reporting back frequently to their boss in the cellar.

Yet, as the sounds of battle drew near, the new German occupants prepared the chateau and the castle grounds for confrontation. Lattice-work windows were knocked out for fields of fire and unimpeded obser-vation. Just behind the chateau under the Linden trees, Peiper's men cleared the ground near their tanks, snaking field telephone wires from the basement to the various positions. From the upstairs dormer windows, Peiper could gain a clear view of the Norman battlefield to the west, particularly the critical crossroads village before him: Tilly-la-Campagne. To his judgement, heavier Tigers or Panthers would be of lower value in this terrain—visibility from the tank slit was only 100m or so. Always the cavalryman, Peiper was partial to the faster and more agile Mk IVs. Besides, he had already learned that the Mk IV gun could readily dispatch Allied Shermans.[15]

Peiper's troops yearned for rain and mist to cloak a possible German lance of retribution westward, but the blue skies only sprouted puffy white tufts of cumulus. Peiper's men dug deep pits under the foliage-covered Panthers to protect against the huge naval shells still screaming into the Garcelles. His adjutant, Werner Wolff, paced his quarters; the sitting around was driving him crazy. Why were they, the finest Panzer men in the German army, allowed to lie here idle and flaccid? There was a battle to be fought, and Hitler's own were not in it.

On 16 July the 2nd platoon of Peiper's 5th Panzer Company was assigned to the 9th SS Hohenstaufen Panzer Division. Its leader, SS Brigadeführer Sylvester Stadler, immediately put the tanks into an impulsive thrust towards the north section of the infamous Hill 112. Gusts of drumfire swept the shattered rise, now so shot up that only ugly stumps remained where trees had once stood. Under a blazing July sun the tanks lurched forward. Devoid of cover, all four war wagons were shot down. Each Mk IV, in turn, sparked or spouted a bright yellow flame when hit, with the Panzer men bolting out of each hatch to escape a fiery death. Soon the blackened hulks lay silently burning. The wounded were moved to the rear; the dead were left lying until night.[16] The unlucky platoon commander, SS Untersturmführer Günter Pflughaupt, was taken prisoner near Esquay, although his interrogators found him unhelpful and 'extremely secure'.[17] Still, Pflughaupt remained confident that the Allied invasion could be thrown back. 'About eight days ago,' he told his interrogators, 'we received a telegram from the Reichsführer [Himmler] to the effect that no attack is to be launched yet.' There was a meeting with the Leibstandarte division commander, he said, and a secret weapon would shortly be brought out. 'The Führer needs 4–6 weeks for mounting the reprisal weapon, which can fire accurately so as to eliminate the [enemy] artillery, and that we must hold out that long and then we could go over to the attack.'[18] Once the enemy artillery was swept away the English would retreat.

Several of the Panzer men taken prisoner in the failed attack on Hill 112 claimed that the British threatened to execute them before they were saved when others intervened. Tempers flared on the German side as well. Peiper had followed the action from his command post at Feuguerolles. Shortly he was briefed by SS Sturmann Heinz Hänze, who described the defeat of the tanks on loan from the Leibstandarte in the engagement near Hill 112.[19] Hearing of the calamity, Peiper rushed to the divisional headquarters of Hohenstaufen at the Brobeuf farm one kilometre south-west of St Honorine. He stomped beyond the doorway in anger; he planned to court martial Pflughaupt, he said. Such an idiotic operation! That proved impossible—the object of his fury was now a prisoner of the English.

Yet nothing could bring back the tanks or their crews. Soon Peiper left to return to the castle at Garcelles-Secqueville. There he and his men watched as Hill 112 disappeared under a torrent of bombs. They waited all the next day. Werner Wolff, nervously shuttling about Caen in an amphibious car, trying to determine where to commit his tanks, barely escaped a sky swarming with bomb-dropping wasps.

Against his better judgement, Erwin Rommel, too, was driving all over the French countryside persuading his commanders to give their all. In his view, the war was lost, and he now seemed unafraid to let the Führer know it. On 15 July Rommel cabled OKW with a grave report of the German losses in France: some 97,000 men and 2,160 officers had been lost in the last five weeks. Equipment losses were also crippling—at least 225 German tanks were gone. He urged Hitler to 'draw the appropriate conclusions from this situation without delay'.[20] It was an ultimatum.

On 17 July Rommel called on Sepp Dietrich and the I SS Panzer Corps with his orderly, Helmuth Lang. As requested, Kurt Meyer was there. Rommel asked for his summary. 'The British offensive south of Caen can be expected in the near future,' Meyer said. 'Our units will fight, and the soldiers will continue to die in their positions, but they will not prevent the British tanks from rolling over their bodies and marching onto Paris.' Meyer's stated willingness to sacrifice German youth under him did not even raise an eyebrow. But then Meyer got around to complaints about the air situation. 'Herr Feldmarschall, give us an air umbrella. Give us some fighter units! We are not afraid of the enemy ground forces. But we are powerless against the massed air forces.' To Rommel the circumstances must have looked like an El Alamein déjà vu—as well as to Montgomery across the line.

'Whom do you think you're talking to?' Rommel snapped. 'Do you think I move around the countryside with my eyes closed?'

'Something has to happen!' the Desert Fox warned. He was excited. 'The war in the West has to end! But what will happen in the East?'[21] Meyer, who usually glared, now looked sheepish. Dietrich changed the subject to ask the German commander to strengthen his beleaguered forces.

'Impossible,' Rommel waved his hand—there were only six thousand replacements for the entire army group.

'Then the situation is hopeless,' Dietrich sighed. Could Rommel petition Hitler for more troops? 'You stand close to Hitler's throne,' Dietrich complained. 'You could attain more than I in demanding anything.' Dietrich said that he had already confronted Hitler on this issue, 'but the Führer never goes to the front; he never believes me.'

Rommel then turned to Dietrich with a surprising question. 'Would you always carry out my orders, even if they contradict the Führer's orders?'

Dietrich thrust out his stubby arm. 'You're the chief, Herr Feldmarschall. I obey only you—whatever you are intending.' They shook hands.

'That satisfies me,' Rommel nodded. 'I would like to talk to you privately in your quarters.' The two disappeared. Although curious, Lang would not hear. When they emerged, matters appeared settled.

'Avoid the main road,' Dietrich said, suggesting the Schwabian trade in his big staff car for a Kübelwagen—they were less a *Jabos* magnet. Meyer wanted to propose a speedy BMW motorcycle, but he kept his mouth shut.

Rommel climbed back into his command car and asked Daniel, his driver, to head off back to La Roche Guyon. At first Rommel was silent, seemingly lost in thought. As they passed beyond the perimeter of the I SS Panzer Corps headquarters, he suddenly spoke up. 'I've won Dietrich over,' he pronounced.[22] It was 1600 hours on Monday, 17 July 1944.

On the road the two passed the ugly blackened carcasses of burned-out German trucks and swarms of fleeing French refugees. Some of them waved. Then, at 1800 hours, just after the car passed Livarot, two low-flying Spitfires roared down in pursuit of the hurtling car. Rommel's driver stomped on the gas pedal to reach the cover of a poplar grove up ahead. But just then the machine gun opened up. Looking over his shoulder, Rommel could see the flashes from the wing-mounted guns as bullets tore into his Horch automobile. The impact splattered the commander with glass and metal shards as the car careened off the road and overturned. Rommel was thrown out. His driver was dead. At first, local Frenchmen on the scene thought the field marshal was gone too, but he was actually in a coma with a badly fractured skull. They treated his wounds near the village of Sainte-Foy-de-Montgomery, their attention likely saving his life.[23] Army Group B was deprived of its commander—one many Germans believed was their most capable military mind.

Unknowing of his old foe's predicament-ironically in a village bearing his name-Field Marshal Montgomery fawned over his new Operation Goodwood. That plan had much in common with the failed offensive the British commander had run before; the main difference was its cheery name. 'Goodwood' sounded more like a warm-up to the master's golf tournament than the tank slam-fest it was to become. The objective of the new offensive was simple: the British would assail the line so that the SS armour would be pinned down and unable to move to the south, where Patton and his Third Army were planning a breakout. In a sense, Goodwood was a sucker punch for the knockout blow to come from Patton's Operation Cobra. Montgomery aimed to draw the German armour into a grinding battle of attrition. He was, after all, the architect of El Alamein.

On 18 July the British commander launched the new offensive after a three-hour First World War–style artillery bombardment. And Even this was reinforced by an all-out carpet bombing by the Royal Air Force, when more than a thousand bombers pounded the German positions early in the morning, followed by medium bombers from the U.S. 9th Air Force and finally Liberators from the U.S. 8th Air Force. There were so many of the four-engined bombers that they completely filled the sky. After that shattering blow—bomb loads totalling 3,400 tons—three naval guns off shore began pounding the German positions of the 16th Luftwaffe Field and the 21st Panzer divisions. Eventually the flood of steel enveloped Peiper's positions. Some of those cowering in foxholes went mad. Entire sections of the line disappeared. A machine gunner with the 7th Company of the Leibstandarte said,

> On 18 July at dawn we were in a wood near Secqueville ... we went back to our individual foxholes—it is exaggerated to call them that. After digging a furrow in the field at a depth of about a foot, we hit rock and even with picks could not dig deeper ... Suddenly we recognized the rumble of planes. At high altitude appeared innumerable four-engined planes. We had never seen so many ... The attack is coming at us. My gunner number two and I squeeze together in our hole, our faces up against each other, our legs folded together. We see the wall of fire and dust coming at us ... We are knocked upside down and then comes a second wave. Hopeless, we see the cloud of smoke breaking

up with arrival of new bombs on us ... When all is gone, my knees start to shake. I can't stop them from shaking. Shaking, we emerge from our hole. The small wood has disappeared. My second gunner is wounded ... Within a radius of 6–7 yards there are countless craters.[24]

The new commander of Panzer Group West, General Hans Eberbach, was convinced the big attack was the Allied attempt to totally collapse the German line. Borrowing an old trick from Russia, savvy old Sepp Dietrich placed his ear to the ground to hear the rumbling gallop of British armour headed his way across the Orne River. Sensing the pivotal battle, he at last committed Peiper and the rest of the 1 SS to the fighting.[25] One charge would run into the other.

At 0800 hours a powerful phalanx of fifty British tanks of the 11th Armoured Division emerged boldly from Colombelles just north of Caen. By that time Peiper's Panthers had wormed their way into covered positions on the commanding rise between Bras and Bourguébus, while other assault guns had taken up hull-down positions on the ridge 50m above the Caen plain. Meanwhile, the surrounding German defences had been bolstered by seventy-eight 88mm flak guns, a dozen more 128mm guns, 272 rocket launchers and nearly two hundred field guns.

Peiper's tanks looked down their barrels as the British armour advanced nakedly across the grain fields towards them. Their guns poked out from underneath trees and beside houses and in the sunken lanes behind hedges and assorted shrubbery. Improbably, the British tanks had nearly 3km to cross with little cover. As the tankers drove forward the first volley of German fire from the reverse slope created such terrible losses that the British tank commander of the British Fife and Forfar Yeomanry could scarcely believe it, stating, 'I saw Sherman after Sherman go up in flames and it got to such a pitch that I thought in another few minutes there would be nothing left of the regiment.'[26] The armoured carcasses blazed before Bourguébus Ridge. 'This mass of armour was lying only a stone's throw from my own tanks.' Even in Russia, Teddi Wisch had never seen anything like it: 'With my own eyes I saw forty tanks go up in flames during the evening engagement. At dawn the next morning, we went into action again and we must have destroyed another forty tanks. My own losses were twelve Panthers and one light tank.'[27]

It was at that point that the Leibstandarte, along with the 21st Panzer Division, slashed ahead. Peiper could only assemble forty-six tanks and assault guns for the riposte, but they formed an effective two-pronged strike, hitting the British armour north of the Caen–Vimont railway.[28] By 1000 hours the column had punched through to the narrow stone-lined streets of Bras and the railway to the north of Bourguébus. Out of the woods south of Garcelles the 2nd Panzer Company under Hans Malkomes attacked towards the enemy, pushing towards the Bourguébus Ridge. Undertaking a personal reconnaissance, Malkomes spied a dense pack of tanks milling about near Soliers. Although greatly outnumbered, he barked for his Panzer leaders to advance and fire. The British 29th Tank Brigade was in an uneven gunnery contest with the German Panthers, which were also on higher ground. Twenty vehicles were shot down rapidly, and Malkomes, although wounded in both eyes, followed their fleeing tracks down into Soliers.

Meanwhile, the British countered with an attack of their own. But they advanced only to learn that the German armour had pulled back to lure them into the kill zone of the 88mm anti-tank guns of the III Flak Corps. High-velocity solid shot clanged into the British tanks, and explosions blossomed in the dry farmland from crippled Sherman and Cromwell tanks belching flame. 'Out of the great array of armour that moved forward to battle that morning,' recorded the historian for the 23rd Hussars, one hundred and six tanks now lay crippled or out of action in the cornfields.'[29] Sensing victory, the Germans counterattacked once more, forcing the British 11th Armoured to retire from the battlefield, leaving 186 tanks behind. When the powerful Guards Armoured Division raced forward to steady the catastrophe, they soon lost nine Sherman tanks and called a halt to any further advance.

It was an amazing display of German tank gunnery honed from similar battles on the Eastern Front. Yet, if unequal, Goodwood sapped German strength. At the day's end Dietrich's I SS Panzer Corps could only count eighty tanks of their own. Struggling German tank recovery crews towed damaged armour back into the Forêt de Cinglais to hastily effect repairs so as to return damaged vehicles to service.[30] But the German tank gunnery had smashed the British effort. Operation Goodwood was as good as finished.

One hour before midnight, Generalfeldmarschal von Kluge phoned up General Jodl at Hitler's headquarters. Von Kluge dismissed the Führer's planned sweep to the sea. Peiper and 1st SS Panzer Division had put in a strong counterattack at nightfall between Hubert Folie and Frenouville, he said; the Luftwaffe even put in an appearance. But the counterstroke ultimately failed.[31]

After a Wednesday morning of quiet foreboding, the weary 12th SS Panzer Division—moved into the line onto Peiper's right. Finally, it was murky and raining that 19 July, and the 2nd Tactical Air Force could not put up the usual assistance. Still, the British 11th Armoured

Division took a hand at Bras and wiped out a Leibstandarte SS grenadier battalion in hand-to-hand fighting. Then the British 7th Armoured Division slugged their way into Soliers, and for a short time in the early afternoon, the British and Canadians, employing at least seventy tanks, cleared the northern slope of the Bourguébus Ridge, firing at the Leibstandarte assault gun battalion at point-blank range. The British captured the hill only to lose it almost at once to a violent Leibstandarte counterattack.[32]

But the Allies were unrelenting. On the following day, 20 July, the Canadian II Corps attacked once more. Although the 1 SS was forced to give up much of Caen and the high ground to its east, the British found Goodwood's advance costly, now having lost a total of more than 400 tanks and suffering 5,537 casualties. And still they faced a continuous German line east of the ruins.[33]

There was a large price for stalling their enemy. Since the invasion began, the German armies in Normandy had suffered 111,000 casualties, with only 10,000 replacements; front-line rifle strength dipped by sixty per cent in the Hitlerjugend Division. In fact, so desperate was the manpower shortage that Dietrich decried 'how little help with replacements we are getting from the SS main office'. Indeed, even the Leibstandarte Adolf Hitler now had Poles in the division who didn't even speak German.[34] Karl Wolff, Peiper's former haughty superior in Himmler's office, lamented the decline of SS physical standards—referring to such a Slavic influx as 'undesirable Mongols'.[35] Moreover, replacements normally assigned to the 9th Panzer Division were now switched to serve in the Leibstandarte—the assignments changed so quickly that some of the green troops went into battle still wearing Wehrmacht uniforms.[36] Eberbach suggested that someone from Hitler's command centre come out to view the carnage: 'The front feels left in the lurch!'[37]

At Peiper's headquarters in Garcelles, the hits got closer. The Canadians knew the German commanders were located there and responded with gust artillery fire at any sign of movement. At a critical juncture Peiper's old comrade, SS Obersturmbannführer Albert Frey, stealthily rushed outside the chateau to reach Karl Rettlinger, the commander of an assault gun battalion. Rettlinger had to get armour up to the front to help support his Panzer grenadiers. They were under intense attack from the Canadians, Frey told Rettlinger. He, in turn, told Frey that his very own assault gun had been shot out from under him the day before. Just then, a blast of artillery fire enveloped the estate grounds, severely wounding Frey, and they joined the battle yet again. Although the Canadians were eventually turned back, Peiper received orders to counterattack the following day to ensure their halt. It was disappointing not to count on more reinforcements—all had long since given up ideas of a roll-up of the enemy to the beaches.

There was plenty of opposing disappointment on the Allied side. On 20 July Eisenhower met Montgomery to profess his profound dissatisfaction with Goodwood. British Air Marshal Sir Arthur Tedder called for Montgomery's dismissal, as did even Churchill himself.[38] But then Montgomery had another offensive—this one cheerily named Operation Spring—that was to tear wide open where the front had merely been cracked: the embattled line near Bourguébus Ridge, where the Leibstandarte assault guns had almost been eliminated. Montgomery would commit the valiant Canadian forces to blast open the hole, and they were to do it while Patton's Third Army broke out at Saint-Lô. If that could be done, they would unhinge the entire German front. To Allied planners it was clear that if they were to make progress at enveloping the enemy, then they would have to move on Falaise. And the tiny village of Tilly-la-Campagne was smack in the middle of the route.

Unfortunately for Montgomery, the rest of Peiper's tank regiment moved up into the breach. Observing complete radio silence, Werner Wolff's 7th Panzer Company left Bully-sur-l'Orne in the early hours of 18 July, bringing twenty-five tanks into Tilly-la-Campagne. Manfred Thorn, a 19-year-old tank driver in Panzer No. 734, was in one of the five Mk IVs:

> We moved into a totally evacuated village without any idea of what to expect. All the houses were intact, with green fields and meadows surrounding the village. Our platoon came to a halt on the easterly side in an orchard, with our tanks facing north to Bourguébus a kilometre away and clothed in the early morning mist. I selected a spot for my tank about 30 yards from the last house and camouflaged it well. We could hear the sounds of battle a long way off, but in Tilly everything was quiet.[39]

The Mk IV Panzers were so smothered with tree branches that they looked like Christmas trees. So cloaked, the Panzer men waited in their lairs for anyone to dare pass by. According to Manfred Thorn:

> Every now and then a stray shell whistled into the village, making us run for the shelter of our tanks. With time this increased and the accuracy improved! It improved so much that we asked for permission to move closer to the houses to give us some better cover ... In between times, the orchard had become a garden of stumps, and the blast from the shells had destroyed our camouflage. We had better protection

from the house, and a wild vine climbing the side of the house was torn down and covered my tank beautifully ... A friend of mine chose the next house, driving in at 6 o'clock ... and edged his gun barrel through the kitchen window ... A century's old stone wall of about 5 feet high surrounded the house, and we had a blind corner which practically hid me from view ... Our infantry before us had little or no protection from this artillery fire, and the tactic was an hour-long bombardment. On 22nd July this lasted two hours, and that was just the beginning. We nearly suffocated inside the tank from the smoke and the heat reaching 110°F or more. An oncoming smokescreen always warned us of the approaching enemy, who attacked as soon as the firing stopped. This bombardment destroyed Tilly and our water supply for drinking. We had to turn to cider reserves, of which there were plenty in the cellars, to quench our thirst ... To say the least, these three-hour bombardments were unnerving, and we looked forward to the evening. It had become a habit of the other side to have an evening fire pause presumably for an evening meal. We too! While our meal wagon could only enter Tilly under cover of darkness, we always ate in the middle of the night at 11 o'clock.[40]

On 21 July, after a three-hour artillery pounding, the Canadian 3rd Division, supported by ten tanks, began to roll up German lines into the village. After breaking through the German infantry line, the Canadians poured into the village. Although the Panzers were up to their tracks in the rubble, when the enemy attempted to circle around to the southeast, Wolff pulled his tank out from under cover and began to fire, exhorting his men to throw back the enemy. The Nova Scotia Highlanders reported heavy losses from an enemy who 'shouted and threw grenades like wild men'.[41] House-to-house fighting ended when the Canadians pulled back after losing nine tanks. Wolff and his men held on grimly.[42] For the action, Wolff received a battle commendation penned by Peiper himself.

While Thorn and the 7th Company dug in their tanks around Tilly, Jochen Peiper attempted to coordinate his tank counterattack from his first-floor headquarters in the castle at Garcelles. SS Untersturmführer Rolf Reiser, from the Panzer battalion headquarters, was sent to the nearby command post of Obersturmbannführer Max Wünsche of the 12th SS Panzer Division to help coordinate operations. The artillery fire on the surrounding area was so dense that telephone lines were constantly being shot out. Radio communication was out of the question. Their clever enemy rapidly triangulated transmissions, with an avalanche of shells to follow.

Old-fashioned messengers became the preferred method of communication. Reiser was returning to Peiper with news from Panzermeyer and Wünsche when all hell broke loose. There was a droning sound overhead, and everyone craned their necks to look up the castle walls to the blue French sky. The sky glistened with what looked to be silver minnows in a blue stream. But the minnows were big Allied bombers high up. Grain-like particles descended from them that grew with each passing second. Moments later explosions began to blast the far street into dust and orange noise.

Peiper and Reiser had their Panzer tanks parked just outside the castle. Soon the shell bursts thundered closer. 'Under the tanks!' someone shouted from above. Without hesitation the men threw themselves out of a lower window in the castle and then crawled on hands and knees under the hulking tanks. The bombs roared outside, and windows splintered and crashed. The ground shook horribly. Reiser instinctively pulled his hands over his ears and held his head close to Peiper. There was a momentary halt in the bomb bursts, and before it started again, Peiper looked at Reiser as both huddled under the tank. He shouted above the noise: 'I think they're trying to finish us off here!' After another burst faded, Peiper looked up once more. 'Herr Reiser,' he said, with sarcasm, 'I think we're going to win this war just like the last one.'[43]

Higher-ups had similar doubts. While Peiper struggled in Normandy, a group of German army officers and civilians plotted to kill Adolf Hitler. Hoping to make peace with the Allies, they made their move on 20 July at the Führer's OKW headquarters east of Rastenburg. Hitler had returned to his East Prussian command post on 13 July to lend personal support to the crumbling defence facing Russia. Army Group Mitte had disintegrated under Soviet blows. Even the stalwart defensive mind of General Walter Model had become discouraged. Increasingly Hitler believed that only his physical presence would check the cancer of defeatism. He arrived on 15 July to a meeting with Heinrich Himmler at *Wolfsschanze*, where the SS Reichsführer warned sternly of the possibility of a surprise Russian airborne assault on his headquarters. The Soviets were now only 130km away.[44] The mosquitos weren't the only vicious predators in the Görlitz swamp.

Word then arrived that Rommel had been badly wounded in Normandy on 17 July. Hitler had already been in a foul humour, yet that was only the half of it. On 18 July he had been poring over maps, reviewing the crumbling situation at the front while an annoying housefly buzzed about his ears. Present in the bunker was his SS adjutant Fritz Darges— the man who had accompanied Peiper with Hitler in the madcap driving adventure in the wake of the wild successful invasion of Poland in 1939. Now the crushing Soviet advance of summer 1944 was booting them out of that country; indeed, on that very day the armies of the Soviet 1st Belorussian Front had knifed all the way to Lublin, south-east of Warsaw.

Hitler swatted repeatedly at the fly, with some of his underlings quietly snickering as he missed. When asked to help, adjutant Darges demurred. Given that the perpetrator was a flying insect, he ventured, Nicolaus von Below, the Führer's Luftwaffe adjutant, should be the one to assist. Hitler was not amused and immediately ordered Darges out of the room and sent him forthwith to the Russian Front.[45] By 20 August Darges would be fighting there to stave off the Soviet advance into Warsaw, where he and Peiper had once presided with Hitler in triumph. Darges would lead the 5th SS Panzer Regiment to blunt the Soviet tank relief columns so the savage German anti-partisan forces could exterminate the brave Polish uprising in Warsaw.[46] What happened there was a horror beyond imagination. Hearing of the uprising, Himmler had orders for his Waffen SS in Warsaw: 'Every inhabitant to be killed ... no prisoners taken ... every single house to be blown up and burned.'[47]

The big move came back at *Wolfsschanze* on 20 July when Oberst Claus Schenk von Stauffenberg, a senior officer from the reserve army, flew in from Berlin, ostensibly to discuss replacement troops. Von Stauffenberg hardly looked a conspirator. Although a Schwabian aristocrat, the man presented a freakish appearance. He wore a patch over one eye and was missing one arm—all that from fighting with the 10th Panzer Division in North Africa. Even the hand of his good arm was missing two fingers. Although von Stauffenberg had enthusiastically supported Hitler at first, he turned against him in the spring of 1942 when he learned that SS men were executing Ukrainian Jews en masse.[48] To Hitler's inner circle he presented little threat. Von Stauffenberg seemed a stalwart supporter of his chief, General Friedrich Fromm, appearing enthusiastic for Himmler's effort to raise a new people's infantry army—the *Volksgrenadiere*.

Several other attempts to kill Hitler had already failed.[49] Still, convinced that Hitler's unholy regime must end, von Stauffenberg was determined to see it through. After breakfasting at the officers' mess, the one-eyed colonel armed his briefcase bomb in the lavatory. Von Stauffenberg then made his way to Hitler's midday military briefing in the *Lagebaracke*, where Keitel perfunctorily introduced the one-eyed officer. He was likely disappointed to see that both Göring and Himmler were absent—a previous attempt had been cancelled for that reason.[50] However, the need to end Hitler's reign seems to have exceeded the need to eliminate the other two.

Göring, in another building not far away, was arguing over delays in mounting an aerial attack on Soviet power plants. Himmler was at his nearby headquarters at Hochwald on the Maursee Lake, where his Finnish masseur, Felix Kersten, gave him a much-needed treatment—his nerves were a mess. Himmler told Kersten how discord between the Americans and Russians seemed the only real prospect for Germany. Kersten said nothing; after all, that hardly seemed realistic. Kersten then went for a long walk in the quiet woods, well away from the idling train.[51]

At noon, Hitler's war conference began. It was muggy and nearly airless at the *Wolfsschanze*. For relief the casement windows of the 12m-long grey concrete conference building were swung open to catch any breeze. The briefing took place punctuated by East Prussian forest sounds and smells—wafting pine fragrance and chirping birds.

During the meeting Count von Stauffenberg carefully slipped a bulging tan leather briefcase under the heavy oak conference table while Hitler listened to a description of the East Front situation. At a half-past noon von Stauffenberg reached down with his one good arm and silently broke an acid capsule in the briefcase. No one noticed. The fuse would take ten minutes to melt. Hitler bent over the table, examining a map, supported by both arms. On a shallow pretence von Stauffenberg quietly excused himself, walking without hurry under the dappled forest light. In less than a minute he reached the double-barbed-wire perimeter and sentry gate at the western entrance.[52] They let him through. From there he motored along the cobble-stoned road on to Rastenburg airfield. Waiting there was an aircraft that would fly him to his fellow conspirators in Berlin. At 1242 hours the acid ate though the wire holding the firing pin.

The Görlitz Forest was jarred by a loud concussion. The conference building's open windows blew away, belching smoke and thunder. Alarms sounded, and SS guards swarmed over the complex. They ran about the woods, searching for an invisible enemy. The conference room was black with choking fumes. Inside were sounds of falling debris and groans. General Walter Warlimont, Jodl's chief of staff, was there:

> In a flash the map room became a scene of stampede and destruction. At one moment there was to be seen a set of men and things which together formed a focal point of world events; the next there was nothing but wounded men groaning, the acrid smell of burning and charred fragments of maps and papers fluttering in the wind. I staggered up

and jumped through a window. As my mind cleared, my thoughts turned to my colleagues. The most urgently in need of help was Colonel Brandt, a staff officer highly thought of by everybody and once a world-famous show rider; he had a leg shattered and was vainly trying to heave himself up to a window to get away from the scene of horror. Most of us collected outside in front of the hut, pale and shaken; those who were apparently unwounded supported their comrades until the ambulances arrived.[53]

Warlimont went back inside to help. The male stenographer was dead on the floor, and 'there were small flames all around, papers and maps were lying about'. He saw that the roof had been lifted, and the centre of the table was blown out. He left, dazed and concerned that perhaps the bomb had come from the foreign construction workers—a second might go off.

In the distance, just before boarding his plane at the Rastenburg Flugplatz, von Stauffenberg heard a distant boom, just like a peal of Prussian thunder on a hot July day. He stepped aboard the plane, confident that Adolf Hitler was dead.

A phone rang shrilly in Himmler's train. An excited voice told him that an attempt had been made on the Führer's life. The next minute Himmler and his bodyguard, Josef Kiermaier, bounced across the Prussian countryside in their Mercedes, swerving erratically over the 20km of uneven roads. Himmler arrived at Hitler's headquarters at 1315 hours.

Someone had moved von Stauffenberg's briefcase, unwittingly shielding Hitler from the direct blast. The conference stenographer, Heinrich Berger, along with Generals Günther Korten and Rudolf Schmundt and Colonel Heinz Brandt were horribly wounded and would shortly die. But only moments after the blast Hitler, supported by Keitel, emerged stumbling and dazed from the shattered building. 'They're bombing us!' Hitler shouted. His trousers were smoking ribbons and his right arm was badly bruised. He teetered in shock, but the Führer of the Third Reich was very much alive.

Heinz Linge, Hitler's panic-stricken SS valet, rushed to his side. 'Linge, someone has tried to kill me,' Hitler mumbled as the SS officer bodily supported him back to his Gästehaus quarters.[54] In less than a minute the doctors arrived. Hitler's personal physician, Dr Hans Karl von Hasselbach, bandaged his wounds. 'Now, I have those fellows!' he nodded with glee. Delirious? Dr Theo Morrel took Hitler's pulse and administered an injection. 'It's really nothing,' Hitler gushed. 'I'm invulnerable.' And then he grinned, his eyes shining with adrenaline. 'I'm immortal!'[55]

'After my miraculous escape from death today I am more than ever convinced that it is my fate to bring our common enterprise to a success-ful conclusion.'[56]

Keitel hustled about in agitation, shaking hands with everyone he met—sometimes several times. 'The Führer lives and now, you'll see!' Jodl angrily paced outside of Hitler's quarters—his own balding head bleeding from wounds inflicted by a falling chandelier. He cursed the *Wolfsschanze* reconstruction programme. One of the workers, he thought, had planted the bomb.[57]

As the shock and epiphany of delirium wore off, Hitler's anger blossomed. 'He was wild and sprung like a beast at everybody who might have had any connection with the thing.'[58] When Himmler arrived, he immediately sealed off the complex with SS guards. He then phoned Gestapo headquarters and commanded a posse of police investigators to depart for Rastenburg at once. Telephone communications were shut down until 1530 hours, when a vague message reached Berlin that there had been an assassination attempt but that Hitler lived. General Fromm, whom the conspirators would name as the commander-in-chief, made a frenzied effort to cancel Operation Valkyrie, much to the dismay of the fellow conspirators in Berlin. Remer's men placed Fromm under arrest. In the meantime Himmler traced the origin of the bomb to the missing von Stauffenberg and ordered the count arrested. Hitler's would-be assassin landed in Berlin at 1545 hours.

Even narrowly escaping death, Hitler demanded adherence to his planned schedule. He changed into a new uniform and had a vegetarian lunch with his secretaries. It rained briefly that afternoon just before Himmler accompanied him to meet Benito Mussolini, who was arriving at the Rastenburg train station. Mussolini looked doubly surprised to see Hitler bandaged but beaming. Providence, Hitler boasted to the deposed Italian dictator, had seen fit to spare him for the future of Germany. With Himmler still in attendance, the two dictators stared in amazement at the completely wrecked conference room. Later Hitler and *Il Duce* convened for an uncomfortable social over tea. It was the last time they would see each other.

And what of Peiper's old superior, Himmler? Did he not control Walter Schellenberg and the *Abwehr*, whose job it was to counter plots such as these? The head of the SS had been on the invitation list to the conference that day but declined, ostensibly due to other business. Yet not only did the SS Reichsführer know of the plot to kill Hitler, but he looked the other way and waited in the wings to take power. Should it succeed, he ventured, he would make peace with the Western allies while turning the German and even Japanese armies against Stalin. He even naively ventured that the British and Americans would likely cheer him on, leaking that news to the chief of the Office of Strategic Services.[59] With that fairy tale untested, Himmler was the first offering to help with the investigation when the plot failed.[60] Hitler, now bandaged, looked directly into his eyes. 'You have full power—seize it!'

'Mein Führer,' Himmler replied knowingly, 'you can leave it to me.'

Himmler jumped in his car and sped back to Birkenwald. His bodyguard, Kiermaier, awakened Kersten from a lazy summer nap, excitedly telling him of the assassination attempt. Himmler's masseur hurried to his master's villa, finding him in his study, sifting through papers. 'Now my hour has come,' Himmler mumbled to Kersten while destroying one page after another. 'I'll round up that reactionary gang … By preserving the Führer, Providence has given us a sign. I am flying immediately to Berlin.'[61] What were the papers Himmler destroyed? Kersten never knew.[62]

By the time Himmler reached Berlin, Joseph Goebbels had moved to crush the coup d'état. He placed the commander of the Berlin Guards Regiment, Oberst Otto Remer, on the phone to Hitler. Hearing his master's voice, Remer, already a fanatical Nazi, agreed to only follow his orders or those of Himmler. Remer was to put down any effort by the army to take control of Berlin. Help came from an SS commando unit, naturally under the command of Otto Skorzeny. By way of radio, at 1830 hours Hitler spoke to Germany, announcing both the attempt on his life and a miraculous survival. The next day he flashed a special order:

> Soldiers of the Army!
>
> A small circle of officers without conscience attempted to murder me and the staff of the Wehrmacht leadership in order to assume power of the country. Providence has seen to it that this crime did not succeed. The immediate forceful intervention by faithful soldiers and officers of the homeland extinguished the clique of traitors; in a few hours they were arrested. I did not expect anything else. Despite that, I know you will, as until now, fight with exemplary obedience and courage until in the end victory will be ours.
> —Adolf Hitler[63]

Retribution followed. Von Stauffenberg and his adjutant were executed in Berlin later that evening.[64] Hitler's chief of staff, Alfred Jodl, survived, but was bandaged and in shock. 'The 20th of July was the blackest day that German history has seen up to now,' he warned his military staff.[65] How far did it go? Himmler set up a court of inquiry in Berlin. Soon scores of army officers were found out in the wide-ranging plot. Fromm and many others were shortly executed or handed a pistol. Even the convalescing Rommel was implicated, taking his own life in the fall of 1944 rather than be disgraced in a trial. By 1 August Himmler introduced the *Sippenhaftung*—not only the arrest of conspirators but also of their families. 'This man is a traitor, the blood is bad,' Peiper's former superior declared. 'There is bad blood in them and it will be eradicated.'

Although rumours claimed that Hausser and Dietrich would have sided with the army had the plot succeeded, that seemed naive. Both men owed their career to Hitler and his ideological organization. In truth, not a single SS officer was implicated in the wide-ranging conspiracy.[66] Even so, on 24 July 1944 Dietrich found it appropriate to recertify his loyalty:

> On 23 July 1944, the Corps reported the destruction of 1,100 tanks, shooting down 110 aircraft and capturing 70 officers and 1,924 prisoners. The success was attained by the Corps that fought at the focal points of the battle at the Calvados Coast. The hard combat was typified by the strong material and air superiority of the enemy …
>
> Now, a new battle is looming. It is going to be extremely difficult, because the enemy has gathered his available tank forces for forcing a breakthrough. In this fighting too, the Corps is going to stand like an iron wall! The divisions, combat proven on the battlefields of Europe and welded together into a blood brotherhood, will stand firm … This fight is about Germany … We shall prove ourselves worthy of our comrades, who died for the greatness of our people.
>
> Long live the Führer!
—SS Obergruppenführer Dietrich[67]

An immediate impact of the attempt on the German leader's life at the fighting front was the Hitler salute. From that time forward the Wehrmacht forbade the traditional cocked hand of the German army salute; all salutes would be with the outstretched arm—'Heil Hitler!' Himmler, in turn, had now been installed as the new head of the Replacement Army and phoned Sepp Dietrich, whom he lamely ordered to be ready to bring the Leibstandarte to Paris—unaware that it was currently in a crushing tank battle with the British 11th Armoured Division west of Caen. Himmler's naivety did not inspire the confidence of regular army men, who sometimes derogatorily referred to the SS Reichsführer as the *Unterweltsmarshall*—the marshal of the underworld.[68]

While the political intrigue played out in Berlin, the Normandy fighting raged on. In the last days of July the Canadians zeroed in on Peiper's headquarters in the Garcelles castle, shelling the stone chateau whenever a messenger ran forth. Periodically artillery spotter planes would swoop overhead—even dropping smoke to guide the Allied artillery fire. The chateau slowly cracked and splintered into a smoking ruin as Peiper's tank and SPW troops held grimly onto Tilly-la-Campagne and Verrières. One veteran after another fell to shrapnel. Peiper could only think of the maddening loss of opportunity: the only time they had been able to use their magnificent metal sword in the attack was on 18 July, when the Panzer battalion surged forward until fighter-bombers stopped them. Now all they could do was try to stop an enemy that preferred to bomb and blast the German line to win battles. Like the others, Peiper's command Panzer IV—number 001—sat immobile on the castle grounds. Panzers as pillboxes—how could they display the Waffen SS courage in single combat? According to Fritz Kosmehl:

The regimental command post was housed for an extended period of time in a chateau. A wide avenue, stretching for kilometres, led to the castle. We had buried the tanks of the commander and the adjutant left and right at the first trees of the avenue. That was necessary, because an enemy battery could fire directly into the castle and did fire on everything that moved in front of it. Panzer 001 took over Morse radio traffic and Panzer 002 voice. When we had to shuttle between the castle and the command post with radio messages, we made a sport out of taking the first few steps very casually, like strolling, ignoring the danger. Not until we heard the discharge did we put on a spurt. Our signal officer reprimanded us for that repeatedly, while Peiper tolerated it with amusement.

The artillery rounds demolished the little castle systematically—floor by floor. That did not matter much to the command post and our quarters. First, we were on the rear side on the ground floor. We did not let the artillery fire disturb us. Instead, we rummaged around the upper floors. There I found in a room, made rather airy by artillery hits, lace underwear in a wardrobe, which once may have belonged to a baroness. Our headquarters company was far away; we did not get there and I could not get myself fresh underwear. I decided to put on a silk chemise with lace ruffles instead of my dirty shirt, tucking the protruding lace under the lapels of my tanker uniform. I felt better.

Back down in the room with messengers, drivers, and radio operators, I soon had forgotten my costume. When I was called to the command post for picking up an outgoing radio message, I no longer thought of it. After my sharp salute, it got curiously silent among the officers present, they stared at me silently, until our signal officer screamed at me: 'Do you want to go to a masked ball?' First I did not understand him at all, but as I saw the amused smile of Peiper and the now grinning

318

faces of the other officers, I got the message and, fast as lightning, stuffed the lace away …

Another time our driver Otto and I rummaged around the castle and discovered fire extinguishers. To find out if they still worked, we immediately put two to work and fought a marvellous foam battle. Suddenly, Peiper stood in the middle of the room—we froze. But he grabbed a third fire extinguisher from the wall and now things really got rolling. Was that the severe commander with the reputation of being unapproachable? No, he once could let himself go and play the mischievous boy.[69]

On 25 July, the 3rd Canadian Division attacked Tilly-la-Campagne with renewed fury. The Canadians put down a smokescreen so dense that the wheat fields disappeared in a grey haze. Then came artillery, thick and fast, only ending when Canadian troops and tanks were right on top of the German positions. The Panther battalion lost several vehicles in Verrières and pulled back. At the end of the day Obersturmführer Erich Rumpf and the 9th Panzer Pioneer Company counterattacked with a few Panthers and retook the village, only to be halted by artillery shells and British rocket-firing Typhoon fighter-bombers.[70]

The second Panzer battalion and the halftracks of the SPW battalion endured the same bombardment. First the Canadians pounded the hills and hedges before Tilly with pre-dawn artillery fire. The grenadiers cowered in their holes, and the tankers hunkered down underneath their steel machines. Then the Canadian tanks roared up from the north-west. Yet, with the sun just rising, the Canadians tankers were looking into bright shafts of light, while the Panzers had a potentially perfect view. Manfred Thorn was out with his loader trying to snatch a bite to eat:

We filled our mess tins and then ran through bomb craters right across Tilly to our Panzers. Our instincts didn't let us down. Our commandant, Rottenführer Rattke, yelled out to us from the turret: 'Where have you been? Three Canadian tanks are 30 metres away in the field!' Our Panzer stood well camouflaged right next to the wall of a house, and in front of it was a 1.5-metre-high stone wall. The three Canadian tanks hadn't noticed us yet. A shot from our main gun would surely have brought our deaths. The loader and I took our positions immediately. The radioman called a message to the company leader: 'Enemy tanks, coming from Bourguébous towards our position.[71]

Thorn immediately fired up the engine of his tank and pulled the Panzer back in reverse. He set out across an easterly ravine to work his way behind the Canadian tanks: 'With extreme care, we drove upon the three enemy tanks which we could already see … At a distance of about 20 metres the No. 1 gunner opened fire on the first tank. It burned immediately. The second and third tank each received a hit. The crews got out.'

In five minutes one Canadian tank after another shuddered and came to a halt. One exploded in an ugly flame in front of the German positions. The unprotected grenadiers suffered many casualties, but the Panzers dominated the fields before Tilly. So disappointed was the Canadian high command with the result of the day's actions—139 casualties and many tanks lost—that they sacked the commander of the 3rd Division's 9th Brigade. Tilly was deemed 'a tough nut'.[72] There had been nothing worse since the failed Canadian landing at Dieppe.

Manfred Thorn was apprehensive as they worked their way right into the middle of the enemy position. Although they kept a sharp eye for infantry, there were no guarantees. After the last tank caught fire, a loud racket erupted on top of their Mk IV. 'Don't open up your hatches!' Thorn roared at his crew. 'The Tommies are on the wagon!' There was more noise, and Thorn prepared to do some wild driving to throw them off. 'It's Obersturmführer Wolff,' a voice called. 'Open up!' That was their youthful SS company leader. Thorn was worried—they had driven off without orders. But that didn't seem an issue. 'Well done!' Wolff said, poking his head inside. He handed them a bottle of cognac.[73] 'Keep it up!'

To be sure, the Waffen SS men with the 12th SS Hitlerjugend Division were already in plenty of trouble associated with the widely reported killing of many Canadian prisoners taken on 7 June 1944. Interrogated members said that SS Untersturmführer Waldenberger gave the orders to shoot the Canadians. Implicated within this negative intrigue was Bernard Siebken, Peiper's old comrade from palmier days in France 1940. Witnesses said he had ordered all prisoners shot.[74] Intimately involved in all of this, too, was Wilhelm Mohnke, still thoroughly hooked on opiates and an SS junkie. The divisional doctor, Dr Schuett, provided Mohnke with morphine injections.[75] One witness, Withold Stangenberg, described Mohnke on 14 June 1944:

> Two corporals brought three English or Canadian POWs to the battle headquarters of SS Panzer Grenadier Regiment 26 for interrogation …
> The regimental commander, Mohnke, conducted the interrogation in the presence of Hstuf. Kaiser and other SS officers whom I did not know. I watched the proceedings from about 80–100 yards. The interrogation

lasted about 15–20 minutes. During that time, Mohnke shouted and gesticulated all the time. Then the British PWs were searched and everything was taken from them, including their identity disks. Then the two corporals took them about 500–600 yards away towards the British lines towards a meadow where one of the corporals shot them in the back with his MP. Mohnke and Kaiser were watching the shooting. The corporal emptied an entire magazine into the three POWs and then ran back to Mohnke. The bodies were not buried.[76]

By mid-July the Leibstandarte had forged a contemptuous opinion of their Western opponents. The British soldiers defended more stoutly, they said, while the Americans depended on enormous firepower to win. Derided SS reporters on the ground said, 'The American infantry defence is only hard so long as they know there is artillery support.'[77] The chaos of Normandy was relative. Peiper concluded, 'In spite of the comparatively higher losses, the German soldier compared the Western Front to a place of internal recreation, and always felt he was superior to the Russian soldier.'[78]

Both the British and the Americans interrogators in Normandy noted that few SS men were taken alive relative to German Army counterparts. Still, with a great number of *Volksdeutsche* in their ranks, there were some deserters, even in the Leibstandarte. A horrific story of how this was handled came from an Alsatian drafted into the division who was spotted trying to desert with French refugees. Returned, his commander then ordered members of his own company to beat the deserter to death. His broken body was later thrown into a bomb crater, but he somehow survived to tell the story. His SS Hauptsturmführer declared this as a good example to others of *kameradenerziehung*—education in comradeship.[79]

There were even guidelines for the proper treatment of prisoners— as if this were something needing emphasis. 'If you take prisoners,' the admonition went, 'you are not allowed to take money from them.' Another distinction was clear to Arndt Fischer. 'In the West, you could assume that you could become a prisoner if you were shot down,' he said. 'That was not the case in Russia.'[80]

While Peiper's command drew near the clash in France, reports began to accumulate of his troops' questionable actions in Russia—and the evidence came from the testimony of captured prisoners of the Waffen SS. Untersturmführer Karl-Walter Becker of the 12th SS Panzer Division was wounded in the early fighting in Normandy and found himself recovering in a Waffen SS hospital in Bretenil in the middle of July. There Becker met his old comrade, Unterscharführer Helmut Feldvoss, from his days with the III Battalion of the 2 Panzer Grenadier Regiment of the

Leibstandarte. Later Becker would be taken captive. Peiper was not yet on Western Allied intelligence radar screens, but Feldvoss and Becker had some details beyond 'scorched earth':

> During the retreat of the Leibstandarte in the spring of 1943, the III Battalion of the 2nd Regiment distinguished itself by burning down everything in its way. For this purpose they used soldering-lamps [blowtorches], which are part of the standard equipment of every armoured SPW ... In recognition of this fact, the battalion received as a visible tactical emblem the 'burning blowtorch'. The commander at that time, Sturmbannführer Peiper, had as adjutant Untersturmführer Wolff. Wolff personally murdered several hundred Russians; some were shot, others were run over by SPWs.[81]

Who was this Peiper and his adjutant, Werner Wolff?

Chapter 19

Operation Lüttich

'War … is harmful, not only to the conquered but to the conqueror.'
—William the Conqueror

Located 25km inland from the English Channel, the city of Caen had long been a centre of commerce in the Calvados region. Founded in AD 912, the city became famous for its architecture that would grace Normandy and eventually trace back to William the Conqueror, who, after his audacious invasion of England, was buried at the Abbaye-aux-Hommes in Caen.

The city had been home to conflict throughout its long history. In the Hundred Years' War King Edward III of England stormed the city on 26 July 1346, razing its buildings and killing three thousand of its citizens. The English armies burned much of the merchants' quarter, and only the castle of Caen held out, despite a vigorous siege. A few days later the English armies left, marching east on to victory at the Battle of Crécy. Caen was then captured by Henry V in 1417, with civilians killed and punished for being the first city to put up any resistance to his invasion of France. Henry V was convinced that Caen was the key to conquest and dominion of the Norman coast.

More than five hundred years later, on 30 July 1944, British Field Marshal Montgomery agreed, as the Caen sector was still the central pivot in Normandy. Despite having destroyed seventy per cent of the city with bombs and shells, the Germans in France still stubbornly held out beyond its ruins. In particular, Montgomery decreed that the German enemy near Tilly-la-Campagne must be destroyed. Knowing that the Leibstandarte held that sector, he planned to throw in all reserves to break the Germans—even if it meant heavy losses.

General Guy Simonds, leading the Canadian II Corps, meanwhile, believed the way to deal with the savvy SS tankers was to attack them

Operation Lüttich and the Counteroffensive to Mortain
6–11 August 1944

FRONT LINES
Aug. 8
Allies
German
Aug. 9
Allies
German

COLLINS
VII Corps

St.-Michel-de-Montjoie

To Avranches

Front line, Aug. 9

Cherancé-le-Roussel

Sée River
Le Mesnil Tôve

Bouanne R.

Attack of RAF Typhoons

Juvigny-le-Tertre

CCB   3

HOBBS

Fontenay

N
W   E
S

1/2   0   1 Mile
0   1 Kilometer

XX   4
3   39
XX   9
39
3   119
XX   30
1   119
XX   35

116 Pz
84
2 Pz (-)
2 Pz
KG Schacke
1 SS Pz Rn
Knittel
117
Bellefontaine
1 SS Pz
KG Kuhlmann
St. Barthélemy
1 SS Pz
117
117
2 SS/4 Pz Gr. "DF"
l'Abbaye Blanche
Hill 314
120
Mortain
2 SS Pz
Romagny
2 SS Pz Rn
17 SS Pz Rn
2 SS Pz (-)
120
St.-Clément-Rancoudray

Vengeons
To Vire
1 SS
KG Schiller
Sourdeval

HAUSSER
7th Army

HAISLIP
XV Corps

English Channel
Bay of the Seine
Cherbourg
Le Harve
Bayeux
Caen
St. Lô
FRANCE
Granville
Vire
Falaise
Detail
Flers
Avranches
Mortain
0   20 Miles
0   20 Kilometers

at night. The first move came on the evening of 31 July, when sporadic shellfire that had quickened to a deafening two-hour punishment paused, and a brigade of the Canadian 2nd Division emerged from a smokescreen and swept up to a few farm buildings on the outskirts of that village. It was a fierce, confused battle cloaked in fog and smoke.[1]

While Peiper and the 1st SS fought Montgomery to a standstill on the grain fields east of Caen, General George S. Patton, the swaggering U.S. Third Army commander, stood ready to change everything on the opposite side of the Calvados coast. 'Drive!'—that was the word on 25 July, signalling that Operation Cobra had begun. Over the two preceding days concentrated carpet bombing had all but destroyed the Panzer Lehr Division.[2] Shortly afterwards the Americans overwhelmed the frail German line. By Sunday, 30 July the U.S. 4th Armoured Division knifed its way to Avranches, and on the following Monday they seized Pontaubault and its critical bridgehead across the Sélune River. The 17th SS Panzer Grenadier Division in particular was smashed near Roncey. 'The men had been full of pep and vinegar' when the division was formed and mustered over 18,000 men, but six weeks later the newest SS division was fully beleaguered from the hedgerow fighting, reporting a strength of only 8,500. 'The airplane is winning the war for the Americans,' SS Hauptsturmführer Wilhelm Alvatter ventured.[3]

The door was kicked open by month's end, and Patton's Third Army roared east past Avranches, spreading into Brittany and threatening to encircle the entire German line. Opposite him, Generalfeldmarschal von Kluge recognized the negative trajectory, ordering an immediate counterattack from the 77th Infantry Division to reseize Pontaubault and its bridge. The morning of Monday, 31 July dawned in fog and drizzle. At first the German blow seemed to carry. Pontaubault fell, and the surprised American infantry fell back to the bridge. Then, at noon, the skies cleared, and it was the same old story: fighter-bombers blasted the infantry into knots of grey-clad figures cowering under trees. Still, the U.S. 30th Infantry Division suffered in close-in fighting so severely that at dusk both sides called a temporary truce so their dead and wounded could be retrieved.[4] Then, after the breakthrough, the biggest delay for the U.S. 4th and 6th Armoured Divisions was not German resistance, which crumbled before them, but handling the expanding mass of prisoners. 'Send them to the rear disarmed without guards.' The advance was not to be halted—that became standing orders.[5]

At his headquarters in Normandy, the previously optimistic Generalfeldmarschal Günther von Kluge was racked with doubt. On the final day of the month his chief of staff, General Günther von Blumentritt, phoned him in Le Mans at the 7th Army command post. So disastrous were recent events—Patton was poised to plunge south of Avranches—that von Kluge found himself controlling not only Army Group B and OB West but now the leaderless LXXXIV Army Corps as well. Messengers dashed in and out with the latest news of a crushing Allied advance. 'It's a crazy situation here!' he shouted into the phone. Von Kluge said Jodl and Walter Warlimont from Hitler's headquarters should come to the front to see what things were like. 'These people are totally disconnected. You cannot imagine how things are around here!' Without anti-tank weapons, he warned, the dam would burst on the left wing.

'It's a gigantic mess [*Riesensaurei*] around here!' Blumentritt relayed news that Hitler's headquarters was asking if a line of barrier positions had been constructed to contain the dangerous American penetration.

'One can only laugh out loud!' von Kluge railed. 'Don't they read any of our reports? They seem to be living on the moon!' Von Kluge hung up. He was off to oversee the counterstroke to be launched at Mortain. There was an ominous tone to his voice.[6] 'Patton', he muttered.

In the meantime, on 1 August, General Warlimont had arrived at General Eberbach's headquarters to get a closer view of things and to lecture the German leaders, hoping to give them some ginger to turn things around. Eberbach was unimpressed: 'A wave of optimism flowed from him. Among other things, he hinted at the arrival of a large number of aeroplanes and of reinforcement of tanks and men to arrive very soon.'[7]

What did Eberbach think of the planned counterattack of the 7th Army to Avranches? 'Hopeless,' he replied, 'because the enemy air forces would soon stop it if not crush it.' Eberbach also detailed how German ground forces were too weak. 'In the case of a breakthrough it would be difficult to hold the extended front with our forces and the supply of four Panzer divisions though the narrow attack zone solely during night-time hours.' With the Allied air power during the day, anything else would be foolhardy.

'You're looking too darkly at the situation,' Warlimont counselled. 'What would you suggest?'

'Pull back to the Seine,' Eberbach was quick to reply.

At that, Warlimont demurred, 'That's politically unbearable,' he concluded. The conversation was over.

To any sensible German leader, the time had come to pull back to the Seine. Instead of that pragmatic course, Adolf Hitler dictated that the situation would be best restored by a bold counterattack on the neck of Patton's dangerous penetration. Certainly it was true that cutting off the U.S. Third Army spearheads would rectify the situation. Still, Montgomery's hammer blows were transparent—clearly designed to keep the attack-worthy SS armour pinned before Caen. In the waning hours of Wednesday, 2 August, von Kluge put in a call to Alfred Jodl. Hitler had reckoned that four Panzer divisions would be necessary to cut off Patton. Where could they be found?[8]

From his headquarters Hitler dismissed Patton's Operation Cobra. 'That is nothing but the shameless daring of a few tanks,' he shrugged to Generaloberst Heinz Guderian. Frowning at the red flags on the map of Western France, the German general reminded Hitler that it was with a few such 'daring tanks' that Guderian had cut through the Maginot Line in France in 1940, an advance that eventually surged to the Atlantic coastline. 'A tank commander who doesn't lead recklessly can never be successful,' he grumbled to Hitler. 'Fate gives him just a few hours to do his stuff.'[9]

Before Caen the grinding fight continued, with Peiper unaware of the flood of American armour pouring deep into France. The next night the Canadian 4th Armoured Division took a hand. Although driven for cover by fierce mortar shelling, a few troops managed to worm their way into Tilly and destroy two German tanks with handheld PIAT anti-tank weapons.[10] A further attack from the rail line west of the village ran into fierce resistance—two of three assisting tanks were shot down, and the Canadians pulled back. When that effort failed, the Allies dropped a shellfire hurricane on Tilly. SS tanker Manfred Thorn was there:

[W]e overheard plans made by the Canadians to plaster the remaining ruins of Tilly from the air and mentally said goodbye to family and friends. It started at 4 o'clock with thousands of shells hitting us all at once and suddenly the Lightning [fighter-bombers] joined in the fight from the air … Every man who took part in holding this unimportant village could never forget its name. The one remaining wall of my house toppled over on my tank No. 734 and we had to shovel her free. One of our tanks from the 4th platoon was badly hit and plating landed in the lap of the driver, cutting off both his legs. He begged his comrades to shoot him … It was a wonder that no more than 15 of our tanks were destroyed in this action. All around us were craters big enough to put a tank into. We thought the end had come. We sat in our tanks in deafening noise, each with our own thoughts, not daring to take our eyes off the area from which the enemy would come … we were still fighting the next day.[11]

Similar blows on 1 August were also beaten back—each time with heavy Canadian casualties. The Calgary Highlanders lost 178 men, and the

Lincoln and Welland Regiment took a further fifty-eight casualties the following day. The Canadian troopers could only grudgingly acknowledge the 'extraordinary tenacity' of their enemy.[12]

As it always seemed, the hard-boiled Panzer veteran Hans Siptrott was in the thick of the fighting. The artillery drumfire had gone on for six hours. Siptrott's No. 712 was hit so often, it was virtually disabled. A track was torn off, the turret no longer traversed, and its machine gun had been blown off. The Panzer IV's 75mm cannon would not even fire. On that August morning the Canadian infantry surrounded his impotent beast and began to do away with it—a well-placed rocket into the exposed hull or a flaming petrol bomb would take care of it. Yet as the infantry closed in, Siptrott emerged from the tank and lobbed hand grenades and blasted away with a submachine gun. The infantry backed off just long enough for Werner Wolff to counterattack in Panzer No. 701 to reach the position and rescue Siptrott and his crew. Like a cat with nine lives, Hans had survived, an action so desperate and foolhardy that Peiper put Siptrott in for the German Cross in Gold.[13] Even as an NCO, Siptrott got the coveted *Spiegelei*—fried egg, sunny-side up.

Peiper saw the position of Tilly just before his Garcelles outpost as the key to the division's defence. Lose it and they would need to pull back. Werner Wolff, leading the 7th Panzer Company, had his headquarters in a farmhouse in town. Those under his command feared Peiper's protégé, whom one subordinate characterized as 'a red-hot SS officer who was a fanatical leader, though a good soldier'.[14] Peiper was so impressed by Werner Wolff's bravado that he put the youth in for the Honour Roll of the German army. Describing his actions: 'Once again, SS Obersturmführer Wolff eliminated the enemy,' Peiper's commendation read, 'by leading a daring counterattack in his own tank without any type of support in a fight which lasted an hour and a half.'[15]

The battle for Tilly spun out of German control. Observing radio silence, there was no method of effective communication, and using runners in the artillery fire storm was to condemn such men. With everyone hunkered down, flares might not be seen. Werner Wolff, new to the command of tanks, did not even need to master mobile tactics; his Panzers at Tilly fought as steel bunkers, nearly immobile and shelled continuously. The tankers holed up inside were nearly deaf. Even at midnight the hamlet of Garcelles glowed an ugly orange-red from the fires burning after the avalanche of artillery fire.

Wolff was plenty frustrated. He was an ardent Waffen SS man, holding complete contempt for his winning enemy. His youthful appearance betrayed a hard demeanour. When not fighting, he read German classical literature—a predilection he shared with Peiper. In particular, he was impassioned by the poet Friedrich Hölderlin. For him the final lines of the poem, *'Tod fürs Vaterland'*—Death for the Fatherland—held a special place:[16]

> The messengers of victory descend:
> The battle is ours!
> Live high above, Oh Fatherland,
> And do not count the dead!
> For you, Oh Dearest
> Not one too many fell. Dear Fatherland!

Waffen SS contempt for the enemy had repercussions. At the end of the battle on 1 August, Wolff's troops took some fifteen Canadians prisoner; Unterscharführer Rolf Ehrhardt and another SS man named Schrader brought them to his headquarters.[17] Many of the soldiers were wounded and under the care of Unterscharführer Josef Frank, the company medical orderly. Ten of the walking wounded were later taken to battalion headquarters, leaving behind the five more seriously wounded. Allegedly there was no means to evacuate them to the rear:

> The five who were not fit to walk had been lodged in the headquarters of the company. I was present when at about 2000 hours Obersturmführer Wolff gave the verbal order to Rottenführer Gust to shoot these five prisoners, but Gust was successful in disobeying this order by telling Obersturmführer Wolff that he had already talked with the Canadians before and didn't think he could accept the responsibility. Wolff said to me, 'Frank, you will do it.' Present when the order was given were SS Rottenführer Wesenberg and Sturmmann Seika, and we entered the room where the prisoners were lying, and I said to the first one, 'Boy come hospital.' We then took the man to a house opposite the company headquarters, a house that was badly damaged. We brought him to the ruins. I then told them to look through a hole in the wall and I then took my revolver from my pocket and shot him in the back of the neck. The prisoner was unaware of his death. I made sure that he was dead by feeling his pulse and looking into the white of his eyes. In the meantime, Wesenberg and Seika were busy bringing the second prisoner over. The same was repeated, and likewise the third. The fourth prisoner was brought in as I had trouble with my pistol. Wesenberg gave me a hand checking it. After he was present, I then shot number four. Seika went back to fetch number five. We brought him to the shooting place, Seika left and the fifth one escaped. All four

prisoners were severely injured when I shot them, unarmed, and didn't make an attempt to escape. After the shooting of each prisoner, I took his body to the next room. I only fired one shot at each man, and I shot him in the neck. I made sure that he was dead. All prisoners when seated were unaware of their deaths. I reported to Obersturmführer Wolff together with Wesenberg that his order had been carried out in the case of the four prisoners and Wesenberg reported the escape of number five. Wolff gave the order to Wesenberg to find number five as soon as possible. I accompanied Wesenberg and later we found a body in a bomb crater and Wesenberg shot this man.[18]

When Wesenberg and Frank returned to Wolff it was dark, and he was dubious of their claim to have killed the fifth prisoner. He ordered each to verify the identity of the killed man at daylight. In the meantime Oberscharführer Willi Bolze captured a wounded Canadian that same afternoon but, unsure what to do with him, gave him water and left him at the crossroads. Upon learning of this, Wolff was displeased. 'Shoot him,' Wolff suggested, but Bolze refused and returned to his tank and complained to the members of his crew about the incident. Meanwhile, Wolff ordered his tank driver, Rolf Ehrhardt, to team with Wesenberg and search for the abandoned prisoner. Later Ehrhardt and Wesenberg reported that the dead prisoner in the crater was not the one missing.[19] Wolff told Erhardt not to come back until the missing prisoner was dead. The following morning Wesenberg and Ehrhardt approached SS Sturmmann Georg Fleps about the whereabouts of the prisoner Bolze had discovered the previous day, explaining they needed to 'bump him off'.[20]

Bolze appeared and escorted Wesenberg and Ehrhardt to the house where he had last seen the Canadian prisoner hobbling towards its entrance. Soon they found the Canadian man hiding behind some furniture in a hallway.[21] Ehrhardt recognized him. He and Bolze left the house as Wesenberg entered. They had just gone a short distance when they heard several pistol shots. Ehrhardt asked whether the prisoner was dead. Wesenberg simply said, 'Three head shots.'

Bolze found the entire affair revolting. 'It is disgusting to shoot POWs,' he said.

'What can we do?' Ehrhardt shrugged. 'It is an order from Obersturmführer Wolff who told us we not dare come back otherwise.' But later Ehrhardt returned to his tank to tell his radio operator that, 'I could understand the necessity of killing an enemy in an attack, but not under circumstances like that.'[22] Bolze returned to his tank crew and ruefully informed Fleps that they had found the prisoner and killed him.[23]

Back at the front, Jochen Peiper's health was a mess. Like everyone else, he was sleeping little, smoking a lot and eating poorly. But beyond that, Peiper suffered jaundice—likely from hepatitis—along with low blood pressure and fainting spells, a fact widely known among Waffen SS leaders in Normandy. The rumor was that the Panzer leader was no longer combat-worthy.[24] Several of Peiper's comrades recalled that he had a heart attack and was evacuated.[25]

The truth was that ailing Peiper was wounded in the fighting with the Canadians on 2 August.[26] That seemed a more glamorous fate than a heart attack—and it was true. The 5th Panzer Company had just repulsed the Canadians at Rocquancourt, taking many prisoners terrified of their prospects of being captured by the Waffen SS.[27] During a conference in the basement of the blasted-out chateau at Garcelles, Peiper's tank crew and others were discussing the bitter fight when a sharp salvo of shells enveloped them. Everyone ducked as shrapnel splintered a basement window. One army officer was severely wounded in the head, but Peiper was hit too. A hot metal shard had entered his left thigh and lodged near his sciatic nerve. But there was more: Peiper was near the end of his mental resources. He was evacuated to the rear.

So on 2 August 1944, in the midst of the nihilistic fighting for Tilly, Peiper was evacuated to SS Feldlazarett 501, the I SS Panzer Corps hospital in Sées on the Orne River some 70km south-east of Garcelles. At 'Der Menschenkenner', as it was called by its head, Dr Erwin Babel, the medical staff with their Ukrainian nurses tended to Peiper's wounds.[28] More than the shrapnel was his debilitating combat fatigue and hepatitis, yet he did not stay, as communications indicated the front was headed their way. By 6 August he was assigned back in Germany at a reserve hospital in Upper Bavaria near Lake Tegernsee—at least on paper. However, with the calamity at the front, he hastened to the headquarters of the 1st SS Panzer Regiment, now under Kuhlmann and re-forming north of Paris. He decamped to the beautifully castled town of Chantilly, staying until the last week of August to see how his command had made out in the disastrous battles.

Only when the front split asunder and orders came to move the tank regiment—or what was left of it—back to Germany did he finally move back to Tegernsee to try to recover his strength close to Sigurd and the children.[29] Peiper's young daughter, Elke, remembered her father returning briefly to Rottach that May of 1944 and taking her and her young brother into the surrounding woods for a rare outing together.[30] The tree saplings in the glacial valley were budding in late spring, but

331

Elke's memory of Papa was fleeting—he was soon back with his field command.

While Peiper went down in fighting and fatigue, Heinrich Himmler, his old boss, was off making speeches:

> The meaning of the war is the historical affirmation of the Greater German Reich before the world ... it would be a sufficient justification for a six-year war when one considers that Frederick the Great fought a Seven Years' War in a much more hopeless situation ... The meaning of the war is the mastering and ordering of the continent called Europe to which we have given culture and life.[31]

Nazi propagandist Schwarz van Berk dutifully took down the pointless bombast, even if some now spoke of Himmler as living in *Wolken-Kuckucksheim*—cloud cuckoo land.[32] And as if to underscore that view, while the German forces in France risked total destruction, the Reichsführer instructed Oswald Pohl to see if large quantities of Vichy Wasser and Perrier could be preserved for his SS.[33]

Far away from Himmler's dream, the fighting continued without Peiper. The rain of artillery was unrelenting, and near Caen, Tilly was a smoking pile of cratered ruins. The Waffen SS was still there on 5 August when the Canadians attacked once more. It was only the following day that the village was given up, and this when the 1st SS Panzer Division departed after relief by the 89th Infantry Division, which had been in Normandy only a matter of days.[34] The rumour was that the Leibstandarte would take part in a big Panzer attack near Saint-Lô—anything to leave the dust and death of Tilly. Thorn recalled wearily, 'We were finally released from this Hell.'[35] When the Panzer regiment pulled out, so short was the bomber-ravaged transport that more than a dozen soldiers crowded atop each operating tank, truck or car.

In the meantime the audacious U.S. Lieutenant General George S. Patton expanded the Pontaubault bridgehead over the Sélune River. Quite at odds with Hitler's derision of Patton's operation, across the single bridge span he fed seven divisions and one hundred thousand men in seventy-two hours. Waving tanks forward, Patton told his armour to forget their flanks. 'The objective is ahead!' Rennes fell on 4 August as a pack of Sherman tanks and American infantry swung left to envelope the SS divisions east of Caen.

Hitler seemed unfazed by the ruptured front. Instead, he conceived a bold plan code-named Operation Lüttich (Liège), where a decisive attack would smash towards Avranches, punching 30km to the coast and casting the Allies back into the sea. On the surface, it was a sensible plan. 'We must strike like lightning,' Hitler implored his staff. 'When we reach the sea, the American spearheads will be cut off.'[36] Hitler did not know that on 3 August ULTRA intercepts of his communications with his field commands clearly revealed his planned intentions down to the various commanders and formations involved.[37] Surprise was gone.

Just forty-five minutes before midnight on 2 August, von Kluge rang up Hitler's headquarters. Jodl answered. The Avranches counterattack must be launched at once, von Kluge insisted. Didn't he and Hitler know that Patton was now gallivanting around their rear? 'Don't worry about the enemy breakthrough on the west flank,' Jodl countered. 'The stronger their forces advance beyond there, the more decisive will be the counterattack of our strong tank forces!'[38]

'Strong tank forces' were to forge a 15km wedge tipped by the Leibstandarte and the 2nd Panzer Division. Three other Panzer divisions were to assist, fighting under the banner of the XLVII Panzerkorps.[39] Von Kluge wanted to launch the attack at midnight on 7 August to jump-start the move across the high ground between the Sée and Sélune rivers before the *Jabos* could show up. Yet, even moving as quickly as possible, the Leibstandarte was not in position. A portion of the division had to be left behind to help the infantry division hold the British off at Vire and the Canadians at Tilly; only the Panzer battalion and the reconnaissance battalion could proceed immediately. The 2nd Panzer Division moved off by itself at midnight, with the Leibstandarte to join on arrival. Herbert Kuhlmann, now in charge of the Panzer regiment, had about sixty tanks that were to dash forward and seize the strategic hilltop near Mortain and then smash on to the west, cutting off Patton—just like in Russia. But the French skies were not those over Kharkov.

The armoured cars and SPWs of the reconnaissance battalion under Gustav Knittel were at first cloaked by mist in the morning advance and hit a gap in the U.S. line, quickly rolling through Bellefontaine and Le Mesnil-Tôve towards Juvigny, moving along with elements of the 2nd Panzer Division. However, the stronger Leibstandarte tank thrust under Kuhlmann was channelled down a single road leading west from Saint-Barthélemy and ran afoul of elements of the 117th Infantry Regiment of the U.S. 30th Division. The larger German problem was the opposition overhead. So vulnerable was the advance that as the road-bound tank column was approaching Bourlopin, British rocket-firing Typhoons of 83rd Group, 2nd Tactical Air Force, assailed it ferociously.

The tree-level fighter-bombers were 'swarming like bees', and several lead vehicles were hit—one tank was even destroyed by a crashing Typhoon.

Jupp Diefenthal, commanding Peiper's old III Battalion, lost his hearing when a bomb detonated right beside his SPW and Kuhlmann's own Panzer was hit and set afire.[40] With choking smoke, visibility ebbed to zero as vehicles burned and traffic jammed. The advance of the 1st SS tank column halted. Kuhlmann and his tank crew sought refuge in hedges and ditches, as did the other grenadiers in the flaming column. Any assistance of the Leibstandarte to the 2nd Panzer Division advance was dashed. SS commander Paul Hausser commented,

> The continuous employment of chains of fighter-bomber flights prevented traffic of even individual passenger cars on main roads. Keeping time schedules was impossible. Supply of ammunition and gasoline was stopped almost entirely by destruction of bridges and attacks on trains and supply columns. Trains could only move at night ... The lack of gasoline was most serious.[41]

Oberst Reinhard with the XLVII Panzer Corps was so disgusted by the air assault on 7 August that he angrily contacted the Luftwaffe liaison, who assured him that all available fighter planes had been dispatched to the battle zone. 'Not one German plane has been seen,' he complained. 'The Leibstandarte also reports that [enemy] fighter-bomber attacks of such calibre have never before been experienced. The attack of Leibstandarte has been stopped. Five of their tanks are out of action.'[42] The obsessively professional commander of the 2nd Panzer Division, General der Panzertruppen Heinrich Freiherr von Lüttwitz, was fighting alongside the Leibstandarte. The aristocratic von Lüttwitz scornfully reported seeing exactly six Luftwaffe aircraft over the last week—against the hundreds now assailing his tank columns. *Unglaublich*—unbelievable.

Still, with the Normandy battle seemingly lost, the will to fight had not faded. Arndt Fischer was wounded in the attack and, like Peiper, had been sent back to a field hospital north of Paris. Although peppered with shell splinters all along his left side, Fischer did not want to go home as his hospitalization neared its end. As soon as they would release the young 21-year-old veteran, he left in a Volkswagen for the front.[43] It would be the first time the Leibstandarte would fight the U.S. Army. 'I knew my duty belonged with my comrades at the front.'

At mid-afternoon on 5 August, Alfred Jodl phoned von Kluge. How were preparations for Lüttich progressing? Only half of the Leibstandarte would be available, von Kluge replied, but at least the tanks were arriving.[44] Hitler responded by promising a reserve of heavy tanks from Mailly le Camp and some Panzer IVs and armoured cars from the arriving

11th Panzer Division. More to the point, he wanted a new commander for the XLVII Panzer Corps, Eberbach from the 5th Panzer Army—recently created by simply renaming Panzer Group West. Von Kluge was disconcerted; it was late to be getting reinforcements for an attack that was to start in five hours, much less to be changing commanders. Clearly Hitler wanted a massive counteroffensive of army size. But in von Kluge's desperate assessment, that was impossible. Allied air power would detect the concentration and smash it before it crossed the start line. Somehow von Kluge convinced the German leader to launch the limited counterattack immediately; to do otherwise was to invite the Allied air fleet.

Hitler agreed reluctantly, dispatching an observer to Normandy to ensure that the operation was pursued with the proper fanaticism, stating, 'The decision in the Battle of France, depends on the success of the [Avranches] attack ... The command in the West has a unique opportunity ... to completely change the situation.' At his nervous headquarters, Hitler turned to a general who was present, looking for a nod of agreement that Operation Lüttich would 'throw the enemy into the sea'.[45] At the front von Kluge was seized with doubt and more, given that the evening before the attack was to start the Leibstandarte and its tank regiment, upon which much hope was pinned for the planned counterattack, had only just reached Flers—some distance from the jump-off point; in particular, the 116th Panzer Division on the northern flank seemed unprepared for the offensive.

In the warm August night the vehicles and tanks of the 1st SS Panzer Division had rolled 80km across jammed roads to reach the assembly. Hausser exhorted them: 'The Führer has ordered us to break through to the coast,' he said laconically. 'Only one thing matters: unflagging determination and a firm will to win!'[46]

Before dawn on 7 August the three Panzer divisions of the XLVII Panzer Corps, less the Leibstandarte, which was moving out from east of Mortain, struck the American lines.[47] Shielded by darkness and then by a thick morning fog, the attacking Panzer divisions advanced a third of the distance to Avranches by noon—some 10km. Arriving late, the Leibstandarte was fed into the line going directly from a road march into the assault. At first the morning mist cloaked the battlefield, and Wisch and his division punched 7km west towards Juvigny. Gustav Knittel and his Panzer reconnaissance battalion raced to Le Mesnil-Tôve with the Panzer battalion clanking forward to Saint-Barthélemy. At 1245 hours the air operations officer with 1st SS Panzer Division was signalling the Luftwaffe that extremely strong fighter-bomber activity was bringing the attack to a standstill. Commitment of available German fighter forces to the area Saint-Barthélemy–Juvigny–Romagny was requested urgently. Ironically, the Luftwaffe soon responded that, despite great efforts, most sorties ordered to the area had been intercepted in air battles stretching all the way back to the dispatching airfields.[48] Still, somehow twenty Fw 190 fighters showed up to bomb and strafe the positions of the U.S. 3rd Armoured Division artillery near Mortain.[49] Yet that was hardly enough. The 2nd SS Panzer and 17th SS Panzer Grenadier divisions battered their way into the town of Mortain itself against the U.S. 30th Infantry Division, but were then hammered by the Allied fighter-bombers that otherwise ruled the skies before the German advance.

There were few roads in the advance zone of Peiper's newly handed over 1st SS Panzer Regiment. 'Our tanks stood on an asphalt road and we were not moving forward,' remembered one nervous infantryman riding on the armour. 'They must think we're in Russia, where you can get away with big assemblies of Panzers like this.' However, by mid-morning the mists lifted to reveal the German columns only 10km from the coast, but jammed in rush-hour formation and naked before Allied air power.[50] 'We all cursed Hermann's [Göring's] Luftwaffe.' Remembered one Panzer man: 'Black clouds of smoke climbed into the sky everywhere marking dead tanks.'[51] Halftracks and trucks were shot, burned and wrecked. When the SS flak opened up, they managed to shoot down one of the marauding fighter-bombers, only to have the plane impale itself on the lead Panzer in the armoured column. As the tank and aircraft burned furiously in a sunken lane, the way forward was blocked. Next came anti-tank fire. It took hours to sort out the mess. 'We were so strongly blasted with rockets and bombs,' remembered one of Knittel's crew, 'that those surviving are blind and deaf and amazed to be alive.'[52]

Although some post-war accounts have mistakenly placed Peiper at the scene, Fischer remembered clearly that it was Herbert Kuhlmann leading the Panzer regiment—a Panzer man who had ably demonstrated his bravery at Kharkov and in the Tcherkassy Pocket. After the war, Dietrich's chief of staff, Fritz Kraemer, blamed the outcome of the disastrous counterattack on 7 August on the tardy arrival of Leibstandarte armour. 'If Peiper had been there,' he claimed, 'this would not have happened.'[53] Arndt Fischer disagreed. 'I was in the attack,' he said. 'There was no way of getting through. There was only one road.' When the fog lifted, the bombers were everywhere. 'It was like hunting rabbits … they hunted down each tank.'[54]

Fischer had reason to remember 7 August clearly; he was shot down twice in his tank in a single day. Driving at the point, his Panzer's front

336

drive sprocket was blown off in one exchange. So immobilized, his gunner blasted away the offending anti-tank gun but was forced to turn back. 'Once, my tank was hit at a distance of fifty metres from an American anti-tank gun. I got out on a captured American tractor [prime mover] that I drove back to our command post. There I picked up the adjutant officer's tank and moved up again.'

Werner Poetschke shouted over the radio, 'Fischer, you're further up than me!' But being out front was hardly safe. 'They came down on us like hornets,' he remembered.[55] An Allied fighter bombed Fischer's second Panther, and shell splinters wounded him. The other Panzers managed to get past Saint-Barthélemy, but there they stopped. Dozens of the British Typhoons loosened their rockets on the German column as if on practice runs.

Herbert Kuhlmann found it impossible to get the attack moving after that. The road was a flaming mass of exploding vehicles with Waffen SS men hiding as best as they could in the hedges. Hans Malkomes was wounded again for the fifth time. Jupp Diefenthal was nearly killed. Paul Zwigart was driving his command SPW when the world seemed to explode. His nerves, he claimed, were never the same afterwards:

> The Allied bombers attacked us overwhelmingly and there was a full hit on my SPW. I left my SPW and headed to take refuge in the command bunker. The bombs hit us. A comrade was killed. I was buried alive in rubble. Another comrade dug me out and took me to the medical train. I was just there for two or three days when I received notice to return.[56]

Obersturmfüher Hans Schmidt took Diefenthal's place. In the explosion-filled chaos, Zwigart found his new commander talking darkly of retribution: 'Presumably we face nigger troops. If this is true, naturally we take no prisoners of war. We will give it to those half-monkeys.'[57]

It proved impossible to get close to the enemy to take them captive or not. 'Come and fight, you cowards!' Peiper would later say of it all. 'Put on your uniform, mount your tank and let's do battle.'[58] But there was no such chivalrous battle in Normandy. Dozens of Panzer men died, and most of the tanks were damaged or destroyed. On top of the air attacks was an aerial-directed artillery bombardment that shredded the Panzer grenadiers around Saint-Barthélemy. According to a captured Leibstandarte medical officer, the grenadier companies were so blasted by shells and bombs that Kampfstärke—battle strength—plummeted to fewer than fifty men.[59] The tank regiment commander of the 2nd Panzer

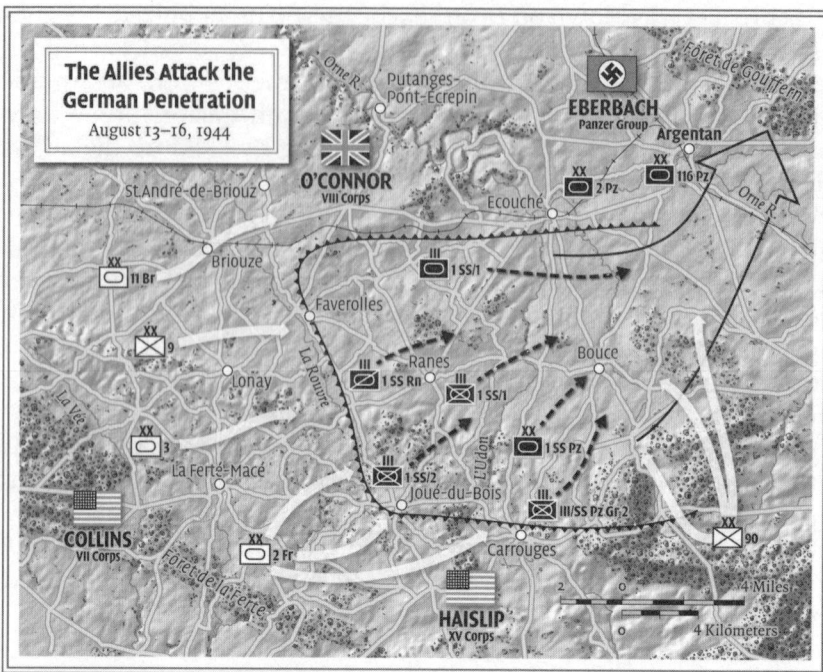

The Allies Attack the German Penetration
August 13–16, 1944

O'CONNOR
VIII Corps

EBERBACH
Panzer Group

Argentan

Forêt de Gouffern

Orne R.

Putanges-
Pont-Ecrepin

Ecouché

2 Pz

116 Pz

St.André-de-Briouz

Briouze

11 Br

Faverolles

1 SS/1

9

Ranes

Bouce

La Roume

1 SS Rn

1 SS/1

Lonay

3

L'Udon

1 SS Pz

La Ferté-Macé

1 SS/2
Joué-du-Bois

III/SS Pz Gr 2

COLLINS
VII Corps

Forêt de la Ferté

2 Fr

Carrouges

90

La Vée

HAISLIP
XV Corps

2   0
4 Miles
4 Kilometers

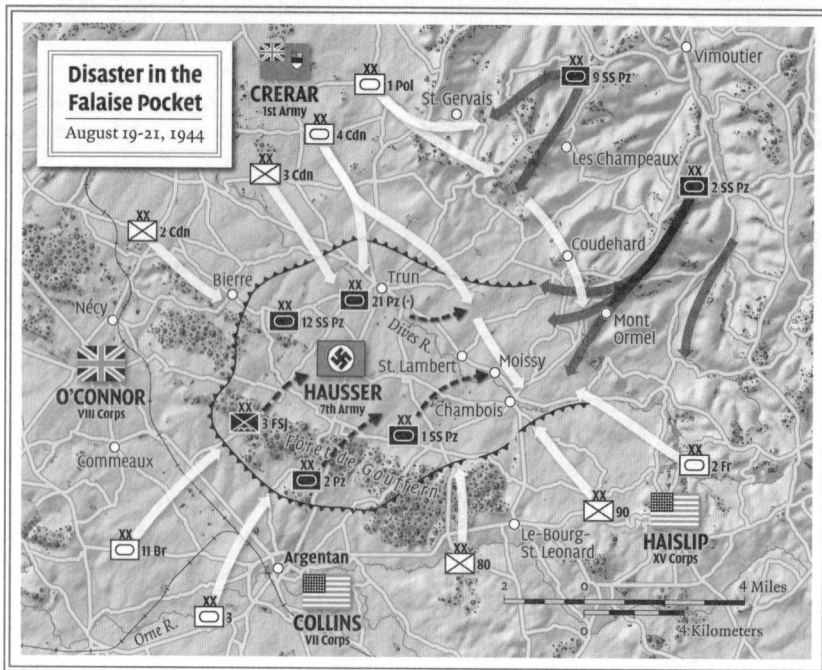

Disaster in the Falaise Pocket
August 19-21, 1944

CRERAR
–1st Army

1 Pol

St. Gervais

9 SS Pz

Vimoutier

4 Cdn

3 Cdn

Les Champeaux

2 SS Pz

2 Cdn

Bierre

Coudehard

Nécy

Trun

21 Pz (-)

12 SS Pz

Dives R.

Mont
Ormel

O'CONNOR
VIII Corps

HAUSSER
7th Army

St. Lambert

Moissy

3 FSJ

Chambois

1 SS Pz

Forêt de Gouffern

2 Fr

2 Pz

90

Commeaux

11 Br

80

Le-Bourg-
St. Leonard

HAISLIP
XV Corps

Argentan

3

COLLINS
VII Corps

Orne R.

2   0
4 Miles
4 Kilometers

Division was killed, and the leader of the 10th Company of the SPW battalion, Georg Preuss, learned that his runner died while attempting to bring him that grim news. The III SPW Battalion was locked in desperate battle with the Americans for possession of Saint-Barthélemy, its combat strength reduced to only a score of men hugging the ground as the fighter-bombers charged anything that moved. Later that night Peiper's old cohort, Erhard Gührs, was severely wounded when his foxhole took a direct hit. His seventh wound of the war nearly cost him his left arm, but the man sitting next to him disappeared in the blast.

At higher-up German headquarters, von Kluge was nearly apoplectic in addressing the 7th Army commander:

> There is really no doubt, inasmuch as every commanding officer is aware of the importance of the operation. Each man must give his very best. If we have not advanced considerably by this evening, the operation will have been a failure. Alencon must be held if the troops are to be fed. Defence there must be such that the enemy cannot advance further. I'm putting the SS Leibstandarte at your disposal.[60]

In the meantime, the 2nd SS Panzer Division wrested Mortain from the U.S. 30th Infantry Division in fierce combat where the Americans counterattacked, but the German unit was unable to reach the 1st SS Panzer Division to close the trap. The next day, 8 August, the Leibstandarte attacked again, reaching Bellefontaine and Juvigny, but that was high tide. The Americans then launched a powerful strike on Saint-Barthélemy. As usual, the Germans counterattacked the counterattack, roaring off towards the Americans north-west of Mortain at dawn on Tuesday, 8 August.

Nevertheless, so nearly suicidal was it to run the gauntlet of American anti-tank fire that experienced Panzer commanders of the 6th Company left their tank hatches cracked open for rapid escape. They would never have done that in Russia, for the Soviets were fond of jumping onto tanks and dropping grenades down any open port. But here the tank battles were more like medieval jousting events; both sides often even allowed dehorsed tankers to scamper back to friendly lines rather than machine gun them down, as would be the mode in the East. Despite that, losses were very heavy.

Although von Kluge had little enthusiasm for Lüttich from the beginning, Hitler decreed that it must continue—blaming the field marshal for a poorly coordinated start.[61] Von Kluge's fear fully blossomed on the evening of 7 August. General Montgomery launched Operation

Totalize—an astonishingly apt metaphor—for an offensive designed to yield a knockout punch to the stubborn SS forces south of Caen. The assault was to be led by a sudden surge of mechanized armoured infantry at night. To precede the advance, a vast aerial swarm of 1,019 aircraft from RAF Bomber Command struck a massive carpet-bombing blow before the armoured halftracks and tanks clanked forward in the darkness.

This time von Kluge estimated there were six hundred enemy tanks—in fact, there were fourteen hundred tanks, halftracks and assault vehicles in all in seven British and Canadian divisions. Although the disorganization in the Allied ranks from a night advance was profound, the Germans were stunned, and the lines pierced in several places. The newly arrived German 89th Infantry Division was thrown into near panic, and the nearby 272nd Infantry Division similarly pushed to the verge of collapse.[62] Kurt Meyer sputtered off to personally give the division commander a stronger backbone. Arriving, however, he found that its leader knew nothing. All communication was severed. As a result, Meyer set off himself but was caught in the aerial bombardment:

> I got out of my car and my knees were trembling, the sweat poured down my face and my clothes were soaked with perspiration. It was not that I was particularly anxious for myself because my experiences of the last five years had inured me against fear of death, but I realized that if I failed now and I did not deploy my division correctly, the Allies would be through to Falaise, and the German armies in the West completely trapped. I knew how weak my division was and the double task which confronted me gave me at that time some of the worst moments I had ever had in my life.[63]

Meyer watched in disbelief that morning as a rabble of German soldiers bolted down the road to the east, shells exploding in ugly bursts just to the west. Soon the 89th Infantry Division would cease to exist, and the enemy would sweep into his SS division's exposed flank. Meyer emerged from the rubble and, even amid the shelling, posted himself in the middle of the road before the fleeing soldiers. He calmly lit a cigar as if he had just finished dinner. As the disorderly contingent looked to walk past him, Meyer puffed away: 'Are you going to leave me alone to cope with the enemy?' The soldiers paused, looking at Meyer as if he were crazed. And then, just as quickly, they stopped, gripped their guns and headed back to fight.

The immediate crisis averted, the redoubtable SS officer commandeered a pack of Tiger tanks from the 101st SS Panzer Battalion and sent them off to aid Max Wünsche, who had just appeared. A typical SS warrior,

Wünsche was delighted to order a counterattack against the Canadian 4th Infantry Division—odds be damned. The ensuing clash of armour did not send the Canadians reeling, but it clearly took the wheels off Operation Totalize. A clutch of 88mm guns and the usual timidity held Montgomery to a scant 5km penetration. Soon part of the 10th Infantry Division arrived to stabilize things momentarily. There could be no talk of transferring the 12th SS Hitlerjugend to the Avranches offensive—there was scarcely more than a single combat-worthy battle group.[64]

One of the losses while fighting Totalize was SS Hauptsturmführer Michael Wittmann, the most famous tank ace in Hitler's army. On 8 August Germany's 'tank killer' fell in battle just west of the Falaise–Caen road while contesting the Allied tank columns. He and his crew died instantly when their Tiger I took a direct hit. His tank exploded violently, the turret splintering off through the air to auger into a French pasture. In his career Wittmann had destroyed 138 enemy tanks, but now he was gone. Peiper eulogized him: '[W]e have lost a great soldier, who was suddenly called away from us by unavoidable Providence after a meteoric rise to the zenith of his reputation.'[65] Although hardly compensation, the sacrifice of the Tigers may have made the difference as, somehow, Kurt Meyer in Potigny found himself still holding the line at the end of the day.

In the meantime, at the opposite end of the battlefield on that same day, 8 August, and pointed to Avranches on the coast, the Leibstandarte tank regiment was at last able to capture Bellefontaine and Juvigny just north of Mortain. Yet they could only hold those objectives temporarily. American reinforcements grew too strong, and the Leibstandarte changed over to defensive positions.

Each day the German position in France grew more impossible. In von Kluge's despondent report to 5th Panzer Army, he confided tersely, 'I foresee that the failure of this attack can lead to the collapse of the entire Normandy front.' He warned, 'but the order [from Hitler] is absolute so that it must be obeyed.'[66]

General Heinrich 'Hans' Eberbach was near panic: 'I look to tomorrow with a heavy heart.'

Chapter 20

Falaise to the Seine

'The hardest thing of all is for a soldier to retreat.'
—Duke of Wellington

As the Western Front splintered into a rout for German forces in France in early August 1944, Jochen Peiper was not even there. Yet most of his old comrades in his war were still fighting: Kurt Meyer, Max Wünsche, Teddi Wisch, Sepp Dietrich and, of course, the NCOs and enlisted men who were part of the Panzer Regiment Peiper.

Instead, Peiper, the shell-shocked Waffen SS tank commander, was evacuated hurriedly. His exit came just as U.S. General George Patton's Operation Cobra ripped open the German front and threatened a far-reaching disaster for von Rundstedt's Oberbefehlschaber (OB) West. An American version of an archetypal dashing tank commander, Patton's Third Army then crashed through German positions west of Le Mans by 11 August—just 130km from Paris, capturing the surprised former headquarters of the German 7th Army. Patton then wheeled north towards Argentan and threatened to close the neck of the pocket by meeting the Canadians fighting near Falaise. Patton complained most of all about having to wait for the British to catch up. Pursued with a cavalryman's aggressiveness, Patton was sure that such a daring lunge would trap the mass of Hitler's armies in Normandy—a Stalingrad-like event in the West.

Falaise itself was another old town of ten thousand souls in Normandy, famous for its striking round, turreted castle from the eleventh century built upon a rocky outcrop overlooking the River Ante. At its gate stood a huge bronze statue to celebrate the birthplace of William the Conqueror, the Norman king, rearing on his powerful horse. For nearly a thousand years it had been famous most as the birthplace of William, but in the geography of the situation Patton saw the opportunity for a turning point in the war with Hitler in France. There he might bag the entire German

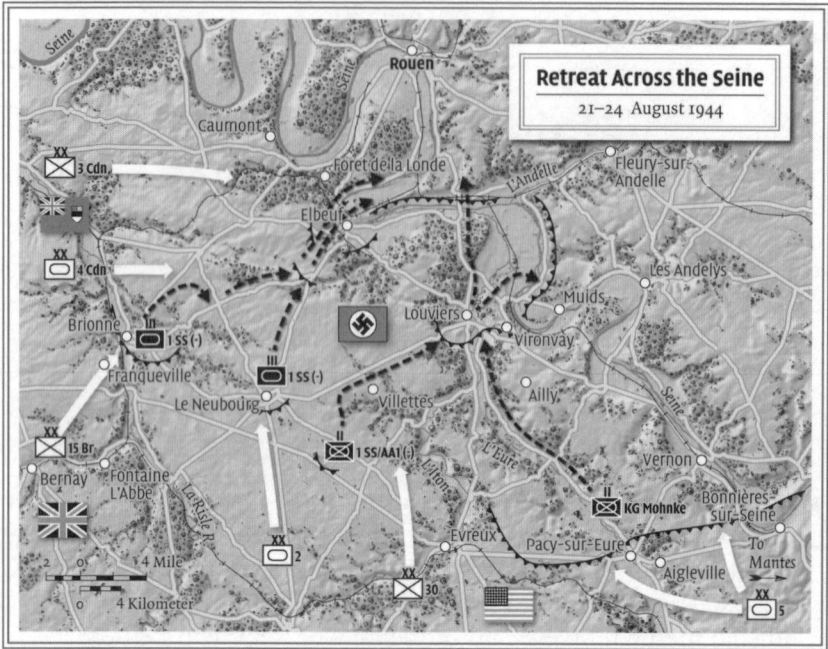

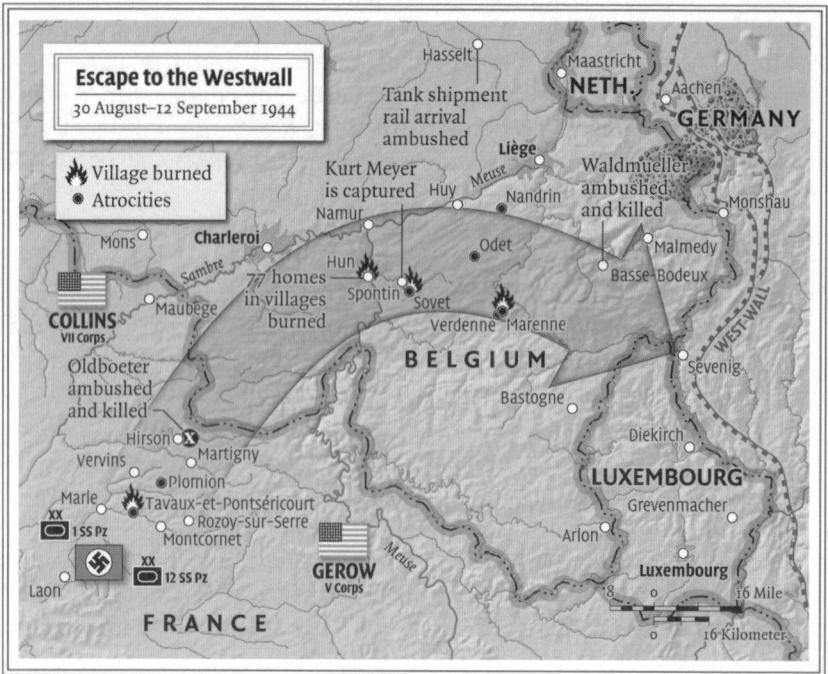

army in the West. The American commander of the Allied Supreme Forces, General Dwight D. Eisenhower, agreed that such an immense military catastrophe for Hitler in the West could end the war before Christmas. That was a major prize.

But Hitler, recovering from the attempt on his life, was unmoved, convinced that his survival portended his vital authority to save another German war that seemed to be lost. Rather than directing an escape from this snare, the German leader ordered von Kluge to launch yet another counterattack towards Avranches, this time under Eberbach and nourished with more tanks and equipment. Sepp Dietrich, who had provisional charge of the 5th Panzer Army, was aghast, complaining that the Canadians could not be held much longer. Eberbach agreed, recommending that von Kluge find a way to call off this disastrous operation.[1]

When the commander of the 272nd Infantry Division suggested that Dietrich might take this up with Hitler, he demurred. The events of 20 July had altered the prospects—even for the favoured. True, he had personally received the coveted Oak Leaves with Sword and Diamonds from Hitler on 6 August, but that was no guarantee. Hitler had barely feigned a smile during the meeting, and the shorter Dietrich looked pudgy and pensive. 'If I want to get shot,' Dietrich told the infantry division commander, 'that's the way to do it!'[2]

Hitler was more insistent than ever that the operation go forward, allocating two SS Panzer divisions, the 9th and 10th, as well as the battered 21st Panzer Division. This time they would strike out from Domfront towards Saint-Hilaire and then Avranches—65km to cover rather than the 40km in the original operation. On paper the night attack would begin on 11 August. Even so, as that Friday approached, the prospects looked quite impossible. Eberbach informed Hitler that the operation could not be launched until 20 August due to the need for promised equipment and favourable moonlight conditions. Hitler objected immediately. The new attack was to come off on 14 August at the latest. Yet on that Monday there were only 353 combat-ready grenadiers and twenty-nine tanks in the Leibstandarte, the strongest of the three divisions in Panzer Group Eberbach.[3]

On 14 August the Leibstandarte was attacked all day, but even the SS was no exception to the spreading chaos. 'The 1st SS Panzer Division had never fought so miserably,' Eberbach recalled. 'The fighting morale of German troops cracked. I openly told this to Generalfeldmarschal Model on 18 August in a meeting at Fontaine l'Abbé ... The morale of the German troops in the west suffered at that time a blow from which they may not recover.'[4]

German tank strength facing Avranches became quickly irrelevant. While Kurt Meyer's 12th SS Panzer Division holding the high ground was able to turn back the 4th Canadian Armoured Division on 9 and 10 August with heavy tank losses before Hill 195, Meyer now had fewer than a thousand exhausted grenadiers still fighting. Only the arrival of the 85th Infantry Division prevented the German line from collapsing right away.

However, Kurt Meyer knew his troops could not hold out much longer. 'We were at the end of our tether,' he recalled. The renewal of the Canadian assault and that of the 1st Polish Armoured Division towards Falaise on 14 August (Operation Tractable) smashed into his tattered Hitlerjugend Division and the infantry divisions on its flanks. SS General Major Fritz Kraemer, now leading the SS Panzer Corps, prevailed upon a mass of Luftwaffe flak guns to stem the tide near the Laison River. Even with that finger in the dyke, other leaks spouted. He put in a desperate call to Sepp Dietrich. Especially menacing, he told him, was the U.S. XV Corps's sudden turn north from Le Mans towards Alençon. Should the jaws come together, all the German Panzer forces would be trapped. Hitler's ill-advised advance south towards Avranches was a German move from the door to deep inside the trap. Dietrich arrived speedily to consult with a shaken Kraemer: 'If the front held ... is not withdrawn immediately and if every effort is not made to move the forces toward the east and out of threatened encirclement, the army group will have to write off both armies ... immediate measures are necessary before it is too late.'[5]

Dietrich was soon on the phone with von Kluge, appealing for the 21st Panzer Division to reinforce the crumbling defence before Falaise.[6]

At the front, on 11 August Werner Wolff ordered his 7th Panzer Company of Peiper's Panzer regiment to conduct a delaying action from Tilly. But without effective communication Wolff did not call on his still-strong tank company to head for Carrouges, where it could have held off the Americans bent on entrapping the entire division. By the time Wolff ordered the company forward, it was too late. Most of the II Panzer Battalion was outflanked and trapped along with the rest, but some of the old Panzer men managed to get out. According to Manfred Thorn:

On the night of the 13th we made a motorized march in the darkness over Falaise in a southerly direction towards Rânes. The next day, the 14th, at midday when I continued my march I had to report that my tank had a brake failure. My comrade Heinrich Theye also had a brake failure. The rest of the company went on their way. We repaired the brakes and were taking a break when an American bomber attacked a lorry on a nearby road and so too close for comfort we moved our position, which was a bad mistake. A short distance away we found Sepp Armberger and the 8th company, who told us that we found ourselves in a small pocket surrounded by Americans. He sent us both back to where we had made our pause within the last hour and Gerd Leppin our tank commander wanted to make a reconnaissance. After leaving the tank we heard a cry for help from him, but could not see him or the reason for his cry. I decided to move for a better view and we received a direct hit. We bailed out under fire, having to leave our radio operator, who I decided had died instantly from very bad wounds. A short time after that Heinrich also received a direct hit and American tanks were heard coming in our direction. Armberger waded through a small lake with a Panzerfaust and destroyed both of the tanks. During the night we went on foot to reach Faverolles the next day. It was Sunday and we could hear the service coming from the small church—so close to the Front? There, to our surprise, we found our company who had not reached Mortain. A messenger ran into the church to say that the Americans were close on our heels and so we left, once more on foot towards Trun. It was the 15th of August.[7]

As Thorn left on foot for Trun with a group of others, there were rumors from SS troopers in the tank regiment who had not seen each other in weeks. 'The news went around,' Thorn remembered, 'that Jochen Peiper had been taken into hospital with a heart attack.'

At the top, aides reported to Hitler that, 'SS Gruppenführer Hausser no longer believes the attack against Avranches is possible.'[8] That, of course, was an understatement. The entire 7th Army was in dire risk of encirclement. On 12 August, the 1st SS Panzer Regiment concentrated in Carrouges with just thirty tanks and so little fuel that several tanks had to be blown up lest they fall to the enemy. The following day the Leibstandarte, along with the 2nd Panzer Division, arrived in Argentan to attempt to hold back the Americans. Five SS, six army Panzer and eight infantry divisions were ensnared between the U.S. Third and the Canadian 1st Armies. There was only one small loop in the noose near Falaise. The 12th SS Panzer Division—now only fifteen tanks and 500 exhausted infantry—fought savagely to hold open the narrow escape corridor.[9]

In the meantime the 2nd SS and 9th SS divisions streamed through, then turned to attack the U.S. forces struggling to close off the escape route. All the while the sky was filled with buzzing fighter-bombers pouring rockets, bombs and machine gun fire into the fleeing German columns. The remaining escape route was now only 2km wide. Grenadiers hunkered down under splintered trees, blasted houses or hedges while exposed horse-drawn artillery and supply columns were blasted savagely. Thousands of horses were brutally cut down, and in the summer heat their tragic bloated bodies, strewn among dead grenadiers and burning trucks, made for scenes of unimaginable stench and carnage.

Hitler seemed oblivious to the developing apocalypse. Instead, he focused on what he saw as the failure of von Kluge to mount an effective counterattack at Avranches. The field marshal who had come to Normandy with such expectation from Hitler was a mental wreck.[10] Capping it off was his experience on 15 August, when Allied aircraft hunted him down and he spent most of the day crouching in a gully. His command car was wrecked along with both radio transmitters, placing him totally out of contact. Von Kluge then became lost in the night chaos of German traffic and did not show up at headquarters until midnight on 15–16 August.

Hitler, who now was naturally suspicious of all German army officers, thought von Kluge was trying to negotiate surrender. When he did return to his headquarters that Tuesday night, von Kluge learned that he had been relieved of command, to be replaced by Generalfeldmarschal Walter Model from the Eastern Front. Hitler was sickened by his situation maps on Tuesday, 15 August, made doubly insulting by the knowledge that it was Napoleon's birthday. He quickly bounded to a new paranoia: missing Generalfeldmarschal von Kluge was seeking an armistice with the Western Allies. In the meantime the Allies finally opened a new front, landing four divisions in the south of France under the U.S. Seventh Army and immediately advancing north up the Rhône Valley. 'August 15', Hitler would later claim, 'was the worst day of my life.'[11]

Many German soldiers in Normandy could say the same of that week— at least those who survived. For, the following day, the 2nd Canadian Division overwhelmed Meyer's 12th SS Panzer Division trying to hold open the neck of the pocket near Falaise–Chambois. A fatalistic contingent of sixty members of the Hitler Youth well illustrated the desperate nature of the fighting when they held out in an embattled Falaise school for three days and fought—so sacrificially that only four were captured.[12] On 16 August the Canadians stormed into Falaise itself, although the battle with Meyer's nihilistic SS youths continued for two more days. The walls of the ancient castle, birthplace of William the Conqueror, was only pocked by rounds to take out German snipers, but the rest of the town was nothing but rubble and ruin.

Meanwhile, the U.S. Army captured members of the Leibstandarte's SS Panzer Grenadier Regiment 2 who had been fighting in the Rânes and Joué-du-Bois area, south of Falaise, which reported heavy losses from the artillery drumfire on Saint-Barthélemy the week before, such that its companies had a combat strength of only twenty-five to fifty men each and that many of the Leibstandarte's tanks were now gone—only thirty-five were available. Still, even though losses were high, morale in the division's remainder fighting in the Falaise pocket remained surprisingly high.[13]

On the morning of 16 August, General Georg Keppler took over command of the I SS Panzer Corps, as Sepp Dietrich was now placed in charge of the 5th Panzer Army, arriving to the Falaise chaos at Les Autels-Saint-Bazile, some 12km north-east of Trun. SS Brigadeführer Fritz Kraemer briefed Keppler on the grim situation. A strong American and Canadian tank assault was pounding for Trun, clearly looking to encircle the entire lot of the German forces before Normandy. As the Allied tank columns thrust west of Couroy, the II SS Panzer Corps under General Wilhelm Bittrich received emergency orders to open an escape route through Vimoutiers. 'I had no further doubt,' Keppler remembered in his second day in command, 'that the main intention of the enemy in this combat sector was the closing of the Falaise pocket.'[14] Keppler rushed a few available assault guns to the Leibstandarte on the left. In the meantime General Eberbach reported flagging physical stamina; the Panzer troops were hungry, with many not having had rations in two days.[15]

On Thursday, 17 August, panic seized the Germans forces near the encirclement. An American pilot zooming overhead in a P-47 reported a teeming mass of enemy troops—bumper to bumper—rushing east on every road between Argentan and Falaise. 'It looks like the entire German Army,' he exclaimed.[16] Lack of fuel meant that the roads even beyond the dense columns were dotted with abandoned trucks and other transport. The stampede east to Falaise had begun. 'Every assault gun was covered with infantrymen,' a gunner remembered. 'Everyone wanted to get out of that pocket.'[17] The divisional command of the Leibstandarte vaporized; no one knew what was going on. Late on Friday afternoon the trapdoor shut when the Americans and Canadians met at Trun. The village itself resembled Armageddon. All to the south was burning devastation, dead horses and human corpses—a scene littered with all forms of wreckage. Werner Wolff, Peiper's favoured protégé, was seriously wounded while attempting to save Leibstandarte's 7th Panzer Company from total encirclement. And just then Generalfeldmarschal Model had arrived at the thankless command of a disaster.[18]

Werner Poetschke was among the few not wounded and took over what little remained of the Panzer regiment. On 17 August Poetschke sent out Rolf Reiser to attempt to reach Chantilly, where his command was to regroup. Reiser hiked on foot with his ordnance officer, Untersturmführer Hermann Kahl. 'There were so many American aeroplanes, you couldn't get anywhere on a vehicle. So we each put on knapsacks and ran on foot carrying food because it was impossible to make it in a Volkswagen.' Even then, Reiser's backpacking party was set upon by Allied fighter-bombers. He dropped to the ground as the bombs exploded around him. Feeling a warm sticky fluid on his back, Reiser feared the worst: pierced by shrapnel, canned food in his knapsack oozed onto his back. 'It probably saved my life.'[19]

Sturmmann Ernst Kufner of the Leibstandarte kept his Tiger covered with branches and nestled under trees or against hedges:

> With the arrival of dawn, the tank had to be camouflaged at the side of the road. Combat vehicles which thought they could continue driving down the road became easy prey for the fighter-bombers. The enemy aircraft were in the air from dawn until late in the evening and kept the road under constant surveillance. They never failed to find badly camouflaged vehicles by the road.[20]

The mass of German troops was now compressed into a narrow killing zone and brought under stultifying artillery fire. Save for a swathe of wooded valley between the Orne and Dives river valleys, the single remaining escape route offered no cover. Artillery observers and Allied aircraft eyed all movements. Fog provided a morning cloak, but on the afternoon of 18 August and the following day the Allies rained down an explosive fountain of guns and bombs.

Gerhard Stiller was at the helm of his Panzer IV No. 711 headed from Saint-André-de-Briouze towards an escape across the Orne at the bridge at Putanges-Pont-Écrepin. His tank clanked east with infantry clinging to his deck:

> We slowly began to meet traffic jams and it became worse and worse. The Military Police were present and made sure that we had right of way but even so it was chaos at the junction of the D15 and three kilometres before Putanges. Destroyed vehicles clogged the road, and men trying to clear the road were hindered by the oncoming mass of moving vehicles and troops on foot, some carrying their wounded comrade on their back. The moving vehicles took them on board when there was room. There were burning vehicles, dead horses from a horse-drawn Wehrmacht supply unit having been attacked by pursuit bombers. Everything on two or four wheels or legs was headed in one direction—the Orne.[21]

On the evening of 19 August, division commander Wisch managed to raise Gustav Knittel on the radio. 'Where can the division cross the Dives River?' Knittel worked by candlelight in a straw-floored French barn as shells boomed outside—the sky arced with ominous heat lightning. 'Our crossing stands or falls with the fate of Saint-Lambert,' Knittel declared. With that, he sent his armoured vehicles bolting down the tarmac. 'It is necessary to fight to open that route,' he told his company chiefs, 'and hold it open.'[22] The division acknowledged receipt of the first part of the message but had to break off—they were under direct attack by Allied tanks.

Knittel's men forced their own horse-drawn vehicles off the jammed road at gunpoint. Up ahead, near the crossing at Saint-Lambert, Canadian tanks blasted away at the path, now so filled with burning vehicles that it resembled a long swathe of flame. All around were hideous scenes: the dead and dying strewn about dismembered, and countless horses wounded and running free amid howling artillery fire. Knittel's driver, Leopold Eigenberger, had been killed, but Jupp Steinbuechel took over, and they drove on at full speed with the dead man tied to the hood.

On 19 and 20 August, under the partial cloak of rain, drizzle and mist, the fragmented battle groups of the Leibstandarte launched a desperate bid to escape the Falaise *Kessel*. SS Obersturmführer Josef 'Sepp' Armberger of the 8th Panzer Grenadier Company personally knocked out four Sherman tanks with a cache of Panzerfausts, although he was cut down while stalking another.[23] His sacrifice was for naught, Livarot was lost as Allied pressure increased all along the front.

Because the II SS Panzer Corps radio had been blasted, General Eberbach took to the roads clogged with burning vehicles to communicate with General Bittrich directly.[24] Bittrich reported that they had little fuel and ammunition, but even with only twenty tanks he launched an assault across the one remaining road of advance so packed with burned-out vehicles that tanks had to clear a lane before they could move forward. Somehow more than two thousand SS grenadiers broke the encirclement south of Les Champeaux and Coudehard. The total number who escaped was much greater, although most were without tanks guns, radio and more.

Meanwhile, Manfred Thorn managed to break out on foot to snag an operable tank (No. 702) in Vimoutiers and, amazingly, found fuel.

> On the 20th during the night a massive breakout was planned. The 7th left with a part of the Tank Regiment and other parts of the division to break out of the Falaise Pocket from the assembly point at Tournay. We fought our way through Mont Ormel, Surdeval and Chambrois.

Our next station was Vimoutiers, always looking for driveable vehicles under way. Hundreds were abandoned because there were no supplies of *Benzin*. The stream of vehicles, men and horses made it a slow journey. A tank drove slowly by and stopped just ahead of us on the road. I then heard my name and Karl Suttner appeared. He was driving Wolf's 702 and needed a second driver—me! It was the only driveable tank of the regiment left. We also took [Georg] Fleps on board. Later Arnold from Siptrott's tank. I was thankful that Suttner had asked me to assist him with the driving of Wolff's tank because then I would have had to walk to the Seine. We left Trun under bombardment along congested roads, everyone on two and on four legs or wheels/tracks. Vehicles of every type were abandoned and we had not seen a benzin (gasoline) transport anywhere. We did not begin to worry about benzin until we had reached the outskirts of Evreux, where by luck we noticed a Wehrmacht fuel truck parked at a countryside tavern. I still had my cigarette ration undistributed in my breadbag. (I did not smoke and so typically saved my ration for comrades.) After stopping I walked to the cab of the fuel truck where the driver still sat and asked him about conditions to the Seine if he knew. I offered him a cigarette. He had none himself and so I gave him a couple. During a short conversation I asked him who was in charge of the transport—rank, unit and name. I thanked him and wrote this information on a piece of paper and walked into the tavern, giving the piece of paper to the owner, who loudly asked for the said officer. He was very surprised at being asked for by name. After asking a couple of questions I told him that we had been told to report to the Wehrmacht for supplies and there were 200-litre canisters loaded on their vehicle. I needed 200 litres and was given it—without problems, but had to sign for it. This lasted us until we reached Monschau in Belgium. We then headed for the Seine over Orbec, Bernay and Elbeuf, where we took the ferry. The journey back to Germany was nerve-wracking. A Mark IV needed 400 litres of benzin for every 100 kilometres. Our commander had informed us in Tournay of an acute problem with *Benzin*. Our supply roads were under continual bombardment. We were told 'lay your hands on benzin as and where you can and before you decide to destroy your vehicle—we need them. The Wehrmacht will help us where they can.' They did, but usually with one 200-litre canister—for 50 kilometres. It was a lucky day when a Wehrmacht transporter with a fresh load could let you have 400 litres—two canisters.[25]

Few were as lucky as Thorn to escape unscathed. Worried that he might accidently drive over the swarms of German soldiers in their path, Thorn's comrade, Gerhard Stiller, was badly wounded when he stuck his head out of the cupola of his tank. In the cauldron of battle the division commander Theodor Wisch was also badly wounded, shot through the thigh, although the 2nd Panzer Division refused to assist in the chaos at a regimental aid post.[26] His SS officers were only able to avoid his capture by putting him away on a speeding halftrack packed with wounded. Nearby, Peiper's SS enthusiastic mentor from Braunschweig, SS General Paul Hausser, fought a desperate battle. With a submachine gun slung over his shoulder, Hausser personally led a breakout attempt until he was seriously wounded by shrapnel from artillery drumfire. Like Wisch, he rode out of the encirclement on the back of a Leibstandarte halftrack.[27] In the meantime the chief of staff of the 7th Army, General Major Rudolf von Gersdorff, organized some 1,500 desperate soldiers from every assortment of unit around a few Tiger tanks into an ad hoc battle group.[28] Led by the Tigers, the battle group shot down nearly a dozen British Churchill tanks that were holding the encirclement shut near Saint-Lambert until the frantic German group was able to reach elements of the 2nd SS Panzer Division attempting to crack open the *kessel* from the outside.

By the time Falaise was over, the Allies had netted thousands of shell-shocked German prisoners and counted more than ten thousand corpses on the bloodied summer fields.[29] Only about half the German armies trapped in the Falaise pocket escaped. Moreover, the Falaise was a killing ground for experienced Leibstandarte leaders. On the same day Hausser and Wisch were wounded, Knight's Cross holder SS Sturmbannführer Hans Becker (I Battalion, SS Panzer Grenadier Regiment 2) and SS Sturmbannführer Heinrich Heimann (1st SS Panzerjäger [Anti-tank] Battalion) were killed in action.

The Leibstandarte tanks were also trapped, with the Panzer crews racing from one tree to the next in the sweltering heat as fighter-bombers chased each one. Even Herbert Kuhlmann, Peiper's replacement, was one of the hunted. Inside Kuhlmann's tank was Peiper's former tank crew—Otto Becker, Fritz Kosmehl and Horst Schumann—who, that French summer, continued to refer to themselves chummily as '*des trois mousquetaires*'. Their Panther attempted to join several Mark IVs that had just broken out of the encirclement near Chambois. Kuhlmann spotted an American anti-tank gun and quickly called for camouflage smoke. 'At that moment, we were hit from behind,' SS Untersharführer Fritz Kosmehl recalled. 'The round came through the engine.' A face full of splinters blinded Peiper's old radio operator. The Panzer burst into flame, with the escape hatch blocked. Kuhlmann and Peiper's driver,

Otto Becker, and voice radioman Horst Schumann managed to get out. They narrowly escaped the burning tank, convinced that Kosmehl was gone, trapped inside a flaming steel coffin.

Somehow Kosmehl felt his way while inside the stricken Panzer, choking and groping to find a hammer and slugging open the hatch. Emerging outside, he realized he couldn't see and crawled along in total blindness. Still, even though having taken a back full of shrapnel, Kuhlmann managed to get the disoriented man to a nearby SPW. Just minutes later the SPW exploded. Amazingly, Kuhlmann somehow led the group out of encirclement on foot. Not only was the Panzer regiment leaderless; it had also virtually ceased to exist.[30] Casualties included Sturmbannführer Heinz Kling, the II Battalion commander; Otto Dinse, in charge of the SPW Battalion; and the commander of Peiper's old 11th Company, Obersturmführer Heinz Tomhardt.

Disasters loomed at the upper echelon as well. Stunned at his dismissal, the hard-nosed von Kluge prepared to report directly to Hitler to atone for his inaction. He penned a final confession and gave the letter to be delivered. 'It's all up with me,' he announced. Von Kluge bade his adjutant to come with him on the return ride across France. That afternoon they lunched under the shade of a tree near Clermont-en-Argonne. After handing over the carefully prepared letter, von Kluge bit down on a potassium cyanide capsule.[31]

Dietrich delivered the letter. Upon reading the dead man's parting words, Hitler seethed. If his successor, Walter Model, was unable 'to master the situation', the note read, then circumstances demanded a decision—facing the facts. 'Should the new weapons in which you place so much hope, especially those of the Luftwaffe, not bring success— then, My Führer, make up your mind to end the war. The German people have borne such untold suffering that it is time to put an end to this horror.'[32]

While Hitler considered a dead field marshal's advice, the impact of artillery and bombs on the surrounded troops in the Falaise added to the carnage of smashed vehicles, abandoned tanks and masses of dead horses obscenely swollen in the summer heat.[33] On 22 August the U.S. V Corps estimated that all the Allied forces reducing the Falaise pocket— American, French and Canadian—had taken thirty thousand prisoners. This sum included 332 prisoners from the Leibstandarte captured by the U.S. 90th Division attacking from the south.[34] On the north side of the encirclement, the Germans fought desperately against the British and Canadians squeezing the salient. Frequently the civilians and ordinary German soldiers paid for the actions of the SS.

Near Livarot a group of Waffen SS men stopped at a large farmhouse and asked for milk, but the young women there told them there was none. The SS men moved on a few hundred metres away and rested in a ditch. Not long afterwards a scouting party of Canadian soldiers appeared on jeeps with the young girls dashing out to cut flowers for their liberators. After the Canadian patrol moved on, the SS band suddenly returned to the farm and exacted vengeance with submachine guns and grenades. Six young women died. Soon thereafter members of the local French resistance appeared with prisoners taken from straggling soldiers of the regular army. 'We took the same number of German prisoners as there had been victims at the farm at Le Mesnil-Bacley, a member of the local Resistance wrote later, 'and made them dig their own graves … And once they were finished, they were publicly executed.'[35]

When Sepp Dietrich ordered his commanders to count heads on 21 August, he learned that Kurt Meyer's division possessed only 300 exhausted grenadiers, ten tanks and no artillery. The 1st SS Panzer Division had alternately fled and cowered through the Fôret de Gouffern the previous day, running an unimaginable gauntlet of artillery, tank fire and bomb from buzzing aircraft as they dashed towards Moissy–Chambois. Thoroughly wrecked, Hitler's own division was momentarily too disorganized to even respond to Dietrich's request.[36] There was no let-up, for, while Hitler finally consented to pull the German line back to the Seine River, Patton's racing troops were nearly there already. Much of the Nazi defence degenerated into a frenzied rout. Survivors, individuals or small groups fled to Germany.[37] Yet Hitler had other ideas, decreeing that the remaining forces fight in front of the Seine River and counterattack to 'maintain contact between the 5th Panzer Army and Paris'.[38]

In the meantime, Joseph Goebbels listened to Hitler at Rastenberg condemning Hermann Göring for the shortcomings of the German air force and particularly for the technical failure of the Heinkel 177. The supposed miracle heavy bomber was now routinely exploding upon take-off. How were the Allies able to bomb his armies at will in Normandy while the Luftwaffe was unable to respond? Hitler demanded an audience with his legendary blond bombing expert, Werner Baumbach. Goebbels lamented the reality of the Western Front. 'The Americans are now showing off to us the same blitzkrieg tactics that we demonstrated to the French and British in 1940.'[39] This time it was lightning war in reverse.

Meanwhile, at the front, having extricated themselves from the chaos of the Falaise pocket, on 20 August Sepp Dietrich had inherited command of the 5th Panzer Army after Eberbach took over command of the thoroughly blasted 7th Army. Hitler's orders to fight before the Seine were effectively ignored by Dietrich, who was then chastised by Generalfeldmarschal Model. Dietrich was incensed, offering to give up his command. 'I am not a schoolboy you can pull up by my ears.'[40] In the field, danger of a second encirclement increased daily, he told Hans Spiedel. The U.S. 5th Armoured Division launched a series of attacks from the Seine bridgehead near Mantes.

In the meantime, battered elements of the Leibstandarte held the area around Le Neubourg, with orders to delay the enemy and then cross the Seine near Elbeuf to assemble in Fleury-sur-Andelle on the other side. At first, on 22 August, parachute flares dropped by the Americans eerily lit up the roads by night. The transfer of the command post of the 1st SS Panzer Division from Capelles-les-Grandes to Villettes could only be accomplished after the sun went down because of the Allied fighter-bombers, which seemed to be everywhere. General Lieutenant Alfred Gause, Dietrich's chief of staff, minced no words. 'Hold under all circumstances,' he warned the LXXXI Army Corps charged with slowing down the American tanks that seemed to be seen on every road. 'Otherwise nobody gets across the Seine River anymore.' At the time the 7th and 5th Panzer Army elements had been frantically crossing the big river in the vicinity of Rouen with the help of two dozen ferries.[41] Great quantities of men and equipment arduously crossed at night when the *Jabos* were away, but the wastage of weapons and accoutrements on the south bank was enormous—it was littered with horse-drawn caissons, impressed French cars and even oversized artillery pieces. Even without the constant fire of fighter-bombers, SS officers arriving at the river found the scene one of absolute chaos. The wait for the ferries was so long that wounded men were being awkwardly rowed across the river on boats and anything that would float.

As U.S. forces pushed within 10km of Elbeuf, Model managed a frantic counterattack comprising remnants of the 116th Panzer Division grandiosely listed as Panzer Group Schwerin, elements of the 2nd SS Panzer Division and remainders of the 21st Panzer Division. The German assault punished the Allied advance, and Schwerin's tanks momentarily cast the Americans out of Elbeuf. There 4,000 German soldiers and nearly 2,000 motor vehicles crossed on the night of 24–25 August, organized by General Lieutenant Feuchtinger, who had received the unwelcome assignment of overseeing the amphibious operation to move the defeated German army across the Seine.[42]

Meanwhile, isolated Waffen SS contingents were determined to keep up the fight wherever they stood. A particularly fanatical fighting element was Kampfgruppe Mohnke, formed around elements of the 12th SS Panzer Division returning from leave near Ailly. They combined with combat remnants of the 17th SS Panzer Grenadier Division and the flak troops from Leibstandarte. Along with Mohnke's troops, which were subordinate to the inexperienced and newly arrived 17th Luftwaffe Feld Division, was another battle group formed around Leibstandarte survivors from Falaise. Kampfgruppe Wahl-Kranke fought a series of sharp hit-and-run actions from 20 to 24 August with the U.S. 5th Armoured Division south of Rouen.[43]

Mohnke set up a blocking position near Vironvay-le-Hamelet, just west of Louviers and bolstered by nearly a dozen tanks. The SS battle groups—several hundred strong each and freely brandishing anti-tank weapons, armour and a number of self-propelled artillery pieces—were ostensibly holding open a way for retreating SS forces across the Seine River at Muids, Vernon and Bonnièrres-sur-Seine.

Although badly outnumbered, they were still strong enough to engage in a quasi SS guerrilla campaign. With German combat power melting, French resistance was operating out in the open. Indeed, that same day the resistance reported having captured nine German soldiers in Pacy-sur-Eure who were being held in the bakery for delivery to the Americans. 'German infantry returned to Aigleville last night,' reported the 5th Armoured Division intelligence officer, 'and killed twenty-one civilians. Civilians are afraid it will happen in Pacy next.'[44] When the 5th Armoured arrived at Pacy and Aigleville on 21 August, the marauding SS infantry was gone—reportedly hiding in the woods and deep grain fields northwest of the town. Meanwhile, a group of mixed 12th SS and Leibstandarte soldiers showed up to the north in Louviers the following day with still another south in the village of Ivry-la-Bataille, where they were 'very aggressive and killing civilians who cannot answer questions'.[45]

All that was true. In a dispatch to Dietrich, Wilhelm Mohnke proudly claimed his command had destroyed forty-five Sherman tanks but then offhandedly related that during the actions his command had liquidated forty-one French 'terrorists'.[46]

While this went on, the fragments of Peiper's 1st SS Panzer Regiment, now tankless, collected at a separate headquarters location north of Paris. 'The Panzer regiment was in 18–20 August in the area of Chambois, Saint Lambert, with Kuhlmann in command after Peiper had become ill,' Hans Gruhle recalled after the war. 'By the 20th of August, we were north of Paris under Poetschke who inspired the repair crews to bring some Mk Vs back to life … We had three more, which were then lost before the Seine.'[47] Around the same time the Canadian forces and the U.S. 90th

Infantry Division reported linking up near Chambois and entrapping at least 12,000 of the enemy—many of them SS forces.

Benoni Junker, having recovered in Paris, had re-joined the division to jot in his diary on 30 August that the replacement staff had arrived, with a discussion with Werner Poetschke in the I Panzer Battalion, which again had no tanks but plenty of ambition. 'Poetschke is totally crazy and out of control.' Junker wrote.[48] In the meantime, Hitler chillingly ordered that any uprising against the German occupation in Paris be ruthlessly put down 'as with Warsaw'.[49] Although Paris had been amazingly quiet since the invasion, on 12 August a mass exodus of German forces in Paris began.

General Dietrich von Choltitz was left to defend the city with 'many armed sales clerks', and Junker-class officers aghast that the war had descended on the Place de la Concorde. Von Choltitz was the Hollywood cliché of a German general: monocled, fat, overly confident—and comfortable in the good life of Paris, although ready to condemn others. 'Having enjoyed for years a luxurious and easy life in the playground of the world, Paris, these officers were in no way willing to spend a night outside in some rain.' Cast out of their elegant 1835 palace, the Le Meurice, with ornate Louis XVI suites offering every amenity, these officers were hardly enthusiastic to join the shooting war. These masters were the *Herrenmenschen*, with little heart for battle, that Peiper and other SS leaders derisively called 'etappen schweine'—rear-area pigs.[50] Now, as the Americans approached, Choltitz complained that many Luftwaffe units assigned to his Parisian defence eagerly fled, leaving countless weapons behind— and worse. 'Throughout the whole of France, the damned Luftwaffe has taken away whole trainloads of the most beautiful antique furniture from private houses!' Choltitz railed. 'It's an incredible disgrace ... this stealing because the poor unfortunate people have been conquered.'[51]

Regardless of such excuses, not even Waffen SS officers in Paris seemed above its charms. 'All there were well satisfied with their assignments and living extremely well and only fearing that they might at some time be moved from their happy home to a less desirable post.' This fear arose from the general order that had gone out that all officers who had served in France for two years were to be exchanged with officers currently serving on the Russian Front. 'To make themselves indispensable, the officers in Paris were adept at supplying the head office in Berlin with black market goods unobtainable in Germany. As an example, the Leibstandarte Adolf Hitler had an office in the Rue General Aubert whose sole purpose was to buy up scarce black market goods (millions of francs in value) and send them in freight cards back to Germany.'[52] Others close by were swept up by the sudden American advance. SS

Sturmann Max Ketterer had been a replacement to the Leibstandarte at Sées, sent to the division before being captured in the whirlwind fall of the French city on 23 August.[53]

In the meantime, in the real shooting war in France, the SS bands made their move to escape beyond the Falaise trap. Taking advantage of a rainstorm that grounded the Allied fighter-bombers, the tattered remains of the Leibstandarte funnelled across the Seine River near Rouen north of Muids, closely pursued by American armour. 'We arrived at the ferry across the Seine at Elbeuf,' remembered the driver for SS Sturmbann-führer Hugo Ullerich, escorting the flak troops of the Leibstandarte. 'There was complete confusion on the road approaching it. Everyone and everything wanted to cross the river.'[54] Traffic jammed up. A big problem was providing berths for transport across the river for the hulking Tiger tanks of Heavy SS Panzer Battalion 101. Although many troopers escaped across on ferries and rafts, the west bank of the great river was cluttered with the littered refuse of an army in flight. There was no chance of an effective defence. 'The Seine crossing,' Dietrich noted ruefully, 'was almost as big a disaster as the Falaise pocket.'[55]

There were seventy bridges across the Seine in the region of Paris alone; orders to destroy them all ignored the German need for a headlong rush to the border ahead of Allied forces. All the while the Leibstandarte was virtually leaderless; the artillery commander functioned in an emergency capacity until Wilhelm Mohnke took over on 30 August. With Hausser wounded, Sepp Dietrich took over the detritus of the 7th Army fleeing to cross the Seine.

'*Tous aux barricades!*' On 19 August the Free French resistance (FFI) forces in Paris brazenly began firing on any German forces still left behind as the Allied forces closed in on the City of Light. Over the next four days chaos reigned as German attempts to quell the uprising were put down by determined FFI resistance fighters lobbing incendiary Molotov cocktails onto tanks that showed themselves. On the humid evening of 24 August, General von Choltitz knew it was over. He and his officers were discussing their fate while floating on champagne in his fashionable office at the opulent Le Meurice. Then the bells began ringing. At first they droned hesitantly, but soon the bells reached a resounding roar. Von Choltitz immediately phoned General Lieutenant Hans Speidel, the Army Group B chief of staff, and, upon reaching him, held the receiver outstretched to the oversized casement window. Speidel knew immediately what the bells told: Paris was back with the Allies.

In the early Friday afternoon of 25 August, Adolf Hitler, at his East Prussia headquarters, became suspicious. There was no further information on von Choltitz and the defence of the French capital. 'Jodl!' he shouted to his senior OKW staff officer. *'Brennt Paris?'*—Is Paris Burning? Jodl did not answer. 'Is Paris burning right now, Jodl?' Hitler again demanded. As his military chief had no information, Hitler said Generalfeldmarschal Model should receive the same question. Paris, he insisted, 'must be reduced to a pile of ruins'.[56]

Hitler could not have been pleased with what he learned later. On that Friday, in spite of Hitler's orders to lay torch to the French capital, Paris was liberated in an extravagant display both by General Philippe Leclerc's French 2nd Armoured Division and the U.S. 4th Infantry. The well-trimmed troops marched in sartorial dress under the Arc de Triumph.[57] Even with sporadic gunfire that momentarily sent revellers scurrying, wildly enthusiastic French crowds chanted the 'Marseillais' while every manner of spirits flowed. Then, with dramatic flourish, General Charles de Gaulle rode triumphantly through the Arc de Triumph.

Three days after the liberation of Paris, Generalfeldmarschal Model decreed that a single combat unit for action be formed out of the ruinous gaggle of the three fleeing SS Panzer divisions. Even that was a hamstrung proposition—there were few tanks and little fuel. Racing for the German border, the elements of the Leibstandarte and Hitlerjugend were only temporarily 'merged' into Kampfverband Meyer in the area of Marle–Montcornet, although they did not retreat north in the form of a single unit. The Kampfverband was named after Kurt Meyer, the commanding officer of the Hitlerjugend division, as the Leibstandarte was still leaderless. When the remnants of the Hitlerjugend and Leibstandarte retreated to the French border, Mohnke was still in command of his own battle group, fighting a delaying action on the borders of the Seine River. When elements of the Hitlerjugend redirected to the area of Hirson on 27 August, Mohnke and his battle group remained behind and would only link up in the Hirson area two days later.

On 27 August the vanquished Leibstandarte and Hitlerjugend—without Kampfgruppe Mohnke and Kampfgruppe Waldmüller—received orders to assemble in the Laon–Marle region. The first elements of Milius's SS Panzer Grenadier Regiment 25 reached the area of Martigny, south-east of Hirson, via Mons-en-Chaussée on 28 August, while others were still fighting on the east bank of the Seine. Kampfgruppe Mohnke (II Battalion, SS Panzer Grenadier Regiment 25 and II Battalion, SS Panzer Grenadier Regiment 26) most likely arrived in the Hirson area on 30 August. Kampfgruppe Waldmüller (I/25) had by then already taken new positions near Montcornet.

Meanwhile, on 29 August, having been routed from its holding position near Muids by the British 15th Scottish Division, Kampfgruppe Mohnke fought a delaying action, holding up the Canadians at the Forêt de la Londe south of Rouen. Soon thrown back, Mohnke and his team fled 95km east to the Beauvais area before dashing north of Paris towards Hirson.[58] On 28 August Eberbach ordered the creation of a series of Kampfgruppen from the escaping detritus of SS tank divisions who had passed the gauntlet at Falaise. Kampfverband Meyer, with elements of the 1st SS Panzer Division (Sperrgruppe Ullerich) and Kampfgruppe Hitlerjugend (Kampfgruppen Waldmüller and Olboeter), were sent to the area of Marle–Montcornet. The beleaguered SS battle groups, including Kampfverband Meyer, were ordered to secure the back-stop positions near Laon, although limited fuel supplies led to an improvised line from Marle to Rozoy-sur-Serre. The Allies were right behind.

On the last day of August, by advancing through the night, the British Guards Armoured Division seized Amiens and undamaged bridges across the Somme River before overrunning the 5th Panzer Army headquarters at Saleux. Ill-starred General der Panzertruppe Hans Eberbach fell into British hands, and the British tanks narrowly missed snatching Sepp Dietrich. The Allied armour was uncontested, Model worried to General Blumentritt at OB West headquarters: not only was there no real front, but worse: 'There are no forces left with which to oppose them.'[59] By the end of the month the Leibstandarte group would be assigned to Wilhelm Mohnke, who was transferred to the 1st SS after SS Sturmbannführer Wisch was badly wounded during the Falaise debacle.

The Seine having been breached, on 28 August Generalfeldmarschal Walter Model, now in charge of the chaos on the Western Front, ordered at least a single strong combat-ready unit be cobbled together from the detritus of the 1st SS, 2nd SS and 12th SS Panzer Divisions, with the intention to fight a delaying action through eastern France as surviving forces pulled back through Belgium to Germany. 'We received a radio message from the division,' recalled SS Sturmbannführer Hugo Ullerich, 'ordering us to put together a Kampfgruppe … Our mission was to stop or at least delay the American advance around Vervins and La Capelle.'[60] In the meantime a captured orderly from the XLVII Panzer Corps, commanding the failed Operation Lüttich, announced that they 'no longer controlled any units', instead being assigned to collect stragglers near Laon.[61]

Amid all the confusion brought on by Hitler's meddling at the lowest level, the German tank factories were still sending Panthers, Jagdpanzers and even Tigers to the Hitlerjugend Division at Reims and I SS Panzer Corps at Soissons from Paderborn. The heavy tanks arrived only to find no fuel available and total chaos at the unloading depots.[62] Most of the fuel-starved vehicles were abandoned, never reaching Kampfgruppe Jurgensen, which had been on the rail destination orders from Paderborn. Similarly, seven new Panzer tanks arrived with the Hitlerjugend division in the area south of Hirson on 29 August. All were fed into Kampfgruppe Berlin, which fought together with Kampfgruppen Waldmüller and Olboeter. Confronted by vastly superior American numbers, all the vehicles were promptly lost.

Meanwhile, days before, Peiper's 1st SS Panzer Regiment—or what was left of it—was assembling in the area around Compiègne while the two Panzer grenadier regiments were aiming to come together around Vervins.[63] Manfred Thorn was still driving the sole surviving Mk IV, No. 702, from the Falaise pocket. He and his crew, SS men Georg Fleps and Otto Arnold, stopped in Clermont, north of Paris, exhausted and in need of sleep. Thorn remembered,

> It was about five days out from the pocket. We had to make an over-night stop, looking for a suitable place to park the tank under scrutiny from a young Frenchman. He offered them his garage but the drive-way was too narrow. He still insisted that they could park on the road outside of his house. He was a little too insistent. We left him to find a mansion-house with a park and they then slept in the foyer of the house, leaving a guard (either Arnold or Fleps) to guard the tank. Suddenly in the middle of the night, we were woken with shots at one o'clock. The guard had a graze on his arm but nothing more serious. They fired a couple of rounds into the park with an MG and the rest of the night was peaceful. Either French Resistance or Communists were responsible … After an angry row at the train station, we were able to load our tank on a train in Compiègne bound for Metz.[64]

The Leibstandarte—or the fragmented pieces of it—were officially transferred to the II SS Panzerkorps under SS Gruppenführer Wilhelm Bittrich. Acting as if these were still divisions, Hitler, in typical illogical whimsy, ordered the 'mobile concentration' to attack towards Reims.

'There is no real front,' Patton's Third Army reported laconically from the south. Its lead tanks were advancing into a vacuum but then sputtering out of gas. Patton himself was nearly ebullient. 'We jumped seventy miles today and took Sens, Montereau, and Melun so fast the bridges were not blown,' Patton wrote to his wife on 21 August. In his diary he was more pointed: 'We can be in Germany in ten days.'[65]

The U.S. First Army found the same vacuum before it, its enemy now 'no longer a cohesive force, but a number of fugitive battle groups' gripped by a 'desperate planless flight'.[66] With the 5th Panzer Army headquarters captured, 'The troops were really on their own,' and an unending series of disaster messages flooded Model's headquarters. There can no longer be any discussion of a 'planned retreat', one said. 'The enemy tanks can move in any direction at will.'[67] The Allies thought that with the right strike—a sudden thrust deep into Germany—it might finish off the Third Reich. What would stop them? 'End the war in '44!' American GIs yelled from the back of trucks barrelling down the dusty roads in France. Along the northern reaches of the Meuse River the U.S. 3rd Armoured captured Huy and then Liège, delayed not by the fleeing Germans but by the masses of Belgian refugees on the roads. 'Once again,' the tankers related laconically, 'cognac, champagne and pretty girls.'[68] Passing down the wide cobble-stoned avenues, squealing femmes ran out bearing flowers, bottles of wine and even ice cream. Was this how the war would end?

Even General Eisenhower, with his Midwest tendency to the ordinary, welled with optimism. He started a conversation with Generals Montgomery, Bradley and Patton of the prospects of being home for Christmas. The main friction slowing the columns racing for Germany was the voracious rate at which gasoline was being burned—103,000 gallons per day for just the lead 3rd Armoured Division of VII Corps. Against that, at the end of August Patton's Third Army was only receiving 32,000 gallons a day—hardly enough to move. As it was, the U.S. forces, not including the new group moving from the south of France, were burning 800,000 gallons of gasoline each day, not to mention 34 pounds of food, ammunition, medical and other logistical supplies for every soldier on the continent.

'Damn it, Brad,' Patton complained to General Omar Bradley, in charge of the 12th Army Group. 'Give me 400,000 gallons of gasoline and I'll put you inside Germany in two days.'[69] That gasoline was not to be had, coming as it was over the overextended Red Ball Express. The 132 American truck companies of that famed improvisation comprised 6,000 vehicles. The whole operation necessitated a fatigue-ridden three-day round trip from the beachhead to the frontline. It was a logistical nightmare, limited by the speed of 2.5-ton GMCs hauling thousands of 5-gallon fuel cans.[70] As it was, with the delivery trucks consuming gasoline themselves on the way, only 2 gallons were delivered for every 3 gallons hitting the road from the beachhead.

However, on the other side of the fence, von Kluge's replacement, Generalfeldmarschal Model, prepared to encourage his forces to stop and defend from the German border. Known as a lion of defence, he addressed German forces from Louvain on 3 September, mindful that he had just been vanquished from the battlefields of France. He challenged his forces on the Western Front to vociferously defend the Homeland. 'Soldiers of the Western Army: We have lost a battle,' he admitted, 'but we will still win this war!'

> With the enemy advance and the withdrawal of a front, a great stream of troops has been set in motion. Several hundred thousand troops are moving backwards, Army, Luftwaffe and tank units. Troops must reassemble and form new strong points or lines according to orders that are received … So while closely packed columns turn off the road to sort themselves out, others push on … As your new commander in chief, I direct this call to your honour as soldiers.[71]

In his closing message, Model decried the need for time for Germany to field additional troops in the West as well as new weapons. 'Soldiers, we must gain this time for the Führer!' Amid the chaos at the front, rumours swirled. First, a premature rumour in Brussels that Hitler was dead; then another that Himmler had killed himself.[72]

Neither were true.

Chapter 21

Escape to the Westwall

Now at the end of August 1944, while ailing Jochen Peiper made his way to a Rottach hospital, the vanquished German army was fleeing from France. *Heim ins Reich*—it was every SS trooper for himself in the flight back to the border as the nature of the 'tooth and claw' battle for the French countryside came into sharp focus. Resistance members rose brazenly after years of hiding, brandishing arms to hunt and ambush the running enemy across familiar terrain and backroads. To be sure, there was a certain cynicism in response to the sheer numbers from ordinary Frenchmen. 'The explosive growth of the FFI is incredible,' wrote one French local. 'All the village boys who chased girls and danced on Saturday night appear with a brassard and a submachine gun.'[1]

In any case, the American and British regulars embraced the French resistance, the FFI, and later the *Armée Blanche* of Belgium. They provided intelligence and more. Termed *Terroristen* or *Partisane* by the Germans, the guerrilla bands harassed the retreating German columns at every turn. Experienced German battle leaders cautioned to use only the most savvy, battle-tested couriers and drivers. Reasons for the warnings were not difficult to come by. For instance, on 22 July, on the reinforcement route from Charleville to Hirson the resistance ambushed a German convoy of four-ton trucks, destroying all vehicles while seizing or destroying fuel, ammunition and weapons and killing drivers. During the flight to the Seine, Panzer Group Eberbach reported innumerable flat tyres from nails doused on roads by the French resistance. On 6 August an agent reported that a dozen trains carrying Tiger tanks departing Mailly-le-Camp had been held up because of thorough sabotage. Captured German prisoners confessed that 'we are more afraid of the terrorists than the enemy'.[2] In a preliminary account, Belgian resistance reported that between 3 and 24 August some 415 sabotage actions, including nine destroyed bridges, fifty-three train derailments and countless telephone wires cut. In fights on 23 and 24 August alone the resistance claimed fifty-one Germans killed in ambushes.[3] Meanwhile, covert resistance teams and secret agents with special espionage missions to harass the German retreat parachuted nightly into various parts of France and Belgium.

Taking Leibstandarte remnants under his wing, SS leader Hugo Ullerich set to work on 29 August organizing elements around his anti-aircraft battalion near Marle. At first he was pleased to locate two recently arrived Tiger tanks, but he was chagrined to learn they had almost no fuel; one had to be abandoned and put to the torch. As Ullerich collected elements of the reconnaissance battalion, the artillery regiment and some infantry stragglers, he found that the Americans had already bypassed his blockade to the south. Stopping the enemy? 'With such meagre forces, that was simply not possible.' So fast were the Americans advancing that part of the Kampfgruppe Ullerich commenced to march east in the wake of the Americans, moving solely at night to evade capture as they slipped past Amiens.

'The third and last night,' remembered Ernst Buchta, a driver with the Flak Battalion, 'the deeply sunken road we were on left us no choice but to drive through a little village ... We saw all the houses decorated with the Tricolour and the Stars and Stripes ... When the people inside heard our column approaching, they streamed out of the doors. Frenchmen and Americans shouted, 'Vive la France!' and 'Vive America!' They thought we were Americans. We opened fire with everything we had ... Under rifle fire from left and right we roared through the village. With the accelerator on the floor, we made it through.'[4]

Dutifully following orders, Kampfverband Meyer (SS Brigadeführer Kurt Meyer) approached Marle–Montcornet with a plan to set up road-blocks. On 30 August, a reconnaissance party of SS soldiers in trucks and Schwimmwagens arrived at the village of Tavaux-et-Pontséricourt. To thwart the approaching VII Corps, U.S. First Army, the squad of SS engineers prepared to dynamite the willow-draped bridge across the La Serre River. But suddenly a dozen armed French resistance fighters descended on the SS party setting the charges. One SS man was killed near the river and another fled. In the ensuing firefight one SS officer was mortally wounded before the French resistance fighters could be dispersed.[5] With retaliation virtually certain, the maquis moved their men and weapons into hiding in the thick deciduous woods of Saint-Pierre-du-Val, some 5km north of town.

For sure, the reconnaissance elements with the 12th SS Division had a fearful reputation. After capture near Brouillet on 31 August, SS Unterscharführer (Sergeant) Sepp Engshuber, with Heavy SS Panzer Battalion 101, later told of SS Major Gerhard Bremer's involvement in war crimes in Normandy. Bremer was an old hare of the Waffen SS, having joined the SS Regiment Germania when aged 19. Transferred to the Leibstandarte on the eve of the war, the stocky native of Saarbrücken distinguished himself in Poland, France and the Balkans, and was one of the earliest Waffen SS recipients of the Knight's Cross for exploits in Russia. Leading the motorcycle company, Bremer was seldom seen without the Ritterkreuzträger dangling from his neck and had a reputation for reckless nihilistic battle similar to the other fanatic members of the Leibstandarte reconnaissance arm.[6] Wehrmacht General der Panzertruppen Heinz Eberbach had come to closely know the Waffen SS leaders in Normandy and classified Witt, Meyer and Wünsche as idealists, but he confessed that he placed both Mohnke and Bremer in the 'bullies and brawlers' category.[7]

Engshuber reported personal knowledge of Bremer's involvement earlier in the campaign for the shooting of nineteen Canadian prisoners, members of the Canadian Royal Winnipeg Rifles, killed near the Château d'Audrieu (Putot-en-Bessin) in June. As Engshuber described him, Bremer 'never smiled, is bestial' and possessed 'an uncontrollable temper'. While pleasing Kurt Meyer, Bremer was not popular with many under him, having even beaten one of his own officers. Engshuber said Bremer's brutality was chronic, and when transferred to the Hitlerjugend in June 1943, he had been involved in other atrocities with the Leibstandarte, killing Russian prisoners at Taganrog in 1941.[8] Yet in 1944, such Waffen SS men remained predisposed to violence. As in Russia, there was great contempt for civilians and the 'laws of warfare.'

In the early afternoon of 31 August, two Tiger tanks and more SS men appeared in the streets of Tavaux. These included troopers both of the 12th SS (I Battalion/SS Panzer Grenadier Regiment 25) and also Sperrgruppe Ullerich, the 450-man battle group built from the remnants of the Leibstandarte and now under provisional command of the leader of the divisional flak battalion, SS Sturmbannführer Hugo Ullerich.[9] Brutal reprisals began at once, with twenty civilians shot down in the streets and many of the hapless victims set on fire. The youngest of those executed was a 2-year-old boy; the oldest was over 70. The wife of FFI leader Pierre Maujean, Mme Odette Maujean, was brutally beaten, then doused in gasoline and burned alive before her children. When the oldest of her children, a 9-year-old, refused to tell their father's location, they were all locked in a cellar and the house set on fire. Fortunately, horrified neighbours rescued the children as the SS men fled the village.

Similar to what had taken place at Boves, some eighty-six of the houses in the town were systematically burned. The following day the village was liberated by the U.S. 9th Infantry Division and the 3rd Armoured Division. The savage SS troops were gone, having set up a tank-backed roadblock across the La Serre River north of Montcornet.[10] The violence in that region had been confined to Tavaux and Montcornet. On that same day, 31 August, stragglers from the 12th SS, I Battalion, SS Panzer Grenadier Regiment 25, shot fourteen Frenchmen and burned thirty-six houses in the village of Plomion just east of Vervins. SS prisoners taken nearby claimed that SS Sturmbannführer Hans Waldmüller had ordered the shootings; having seen his camouflage-clad troopers come under sniper fire, the SS major ordered a reprisal.[11]

In the meantime, with the traffic-jammed retreat routes of the SS men watched menacingly from the air, Generalfeldmarschal Model ordered that marches were best carried out during the evening or with heavy camouflage. As it was, U.S. intelligence reported that German columns seen from French airspace resembled 'walking greenhouses'. Even horses were crowned with leafy saplings.[12] The following day, on 1 September, a hodgepodge of Leibstandarte troops under Peiper's old comrade, Jupp Diefenthal, reached the vicinity of Charleroi, Belgium, soon to be assigned to somehow screen the yawning gap between the German 7th Army and 1st Army.[13] In the meantime prisoners from the Leibstandarte were swept up by the U.S. 3rd Armoured Division in Buironfosse, France, and later by the 9th Infantry Division east of the Belgian village of Flavion.[14] The assembly included the surviving shell-shocked detritus from the Falaise debacle as well as indifferent Luftwaffe conscripts from disbanded searchlight battalions. That evening elements of the flak soldiers and SS Panzer Grenadier Regiment 2 were sent south from Maubege to block the American advance near Avesne-sur-Helpe.[15]

In the meantime much of the remainder of the 12th SS Division was brought under the leadership of SS Obersturmbannführer Karl Heinz Milius (Kampfgruppe Milius), which was attached to the 2nd SS Panzer Division moving through the Ardennes. The rest of the division—the 600 men of Bremer's 12th SS Panzer Reconnaissance Battalion and other elements—withdrew towards the German border via Liège.

The war between the French and Belgian resistance and the SS men flared to a merciless level. Although exact identifications of the SS units could not be made, on 6 September civilians from the village of Nadrin claimed that SS men (likely elements of Kampfgruppe Rink) 'killed seven civilians when civilians shot a German officer in the head'. Three or four houses were set afire.[16] In spite of the disaster in Normandy, SS fanaticism remained strong. When members of the SS bands were captured at the beginning of September, their interrogators reported 'very high morale'.[17]

Indeed, after SS Unterscharführer Joseph Andlinger of 4th Company, SS Panzer Grenadier Regiment 4, was taken prisoner on 1 September 1944, he was thoroughly contemptuous of his captors and assured them that, 'Hitler will still win the war.' They must, he claimed, as Germany was the sole brake on Bolshevism.

Still, the elements of the Leibstandarte were scattered, with many lost and straggling; the dragnet of prisoners of the 1st SS were identified in Flavion between Phillipeville and Dinant in Belgium not far from the Meuse River. As late as 17 September Leibstandarte men such as runner Wilhelm Fiesser, with the 4th Company, SS Panzer Grenadier Regiment 2, were being taken captive. They were amazed at the quantity of American weapons while revealing a stark racial outlook. 'Even Negros have machine pistols,' he blustered, 'while I only have a K.98 rifle.' Having been wounded in Normandy, Fiesser escaped from a hospital in liberated Paris only to be captured while attempting to slip across the Meuse River near Dinant.[18]

Remainders of the 12th SS Panzer Division were in a foul mood: over the preceding days two of its more experienced battalion officers had been killed by the resistance, and Kurt Meyer was still moving with the command: on 2 September Hauptsturmführer Heinz Schrott was ambushed near Trélon north of Hirson. While leading a column with ten SPWs and three tanks, Sturmbannführer Erich Olboeter was blown up that same night east of Hirson. Resistance fighters pulled a mine across the road before Olboeter's speeding command car near Montorieux. His legs blown off, the highly decorated officer died at a field hospital in Charleville-Mézières hours later. And then on 10 September, Sturmbannführer Hans Waldmüller, a Knight's Cross holder like Olboeter, was killed in the Ardennes by Belgian maquisards between Werbomont and Stavelot.[19] As he sped through the conifers just west of Basse Bodeux, members of the Belgian resistance pulled a cable across the road. Waldmüller, his adjutant, and the driver were sent sprawling. His adjutant was shot in the head; Waldmüller was butchered with a knife. On 6 September the 12th SS came out with an official policy: terrorists were to be met with 'the hardest punishment', with even relatives of hidden terrorists to be shot or hanged.[20]

According to Meyer, by 30 August Kampfgruppe Mohnke had joined his troop north of Hirson near Anor, France, and two days later the mixed band of SS troops had reached Yvoir–Houx on the border of Belgium along the Meuse River.[21] There the German retreat stopped, now ordered by SS Gruppenführer Georg Keppler with the I SS Panzer Corps to defend the natural barrier; the 90km stretch from Namur to Charleville.[22] On the east bank of the forested gorges of the Meuse the SS troops dug in and prepared to give sharp battle to the American 9th Infantry Division attempting to breast the strategic river. On 1 September, elements of the Leibstandarte took over the defence of Charleroi along the north bank of the Meuse from a battalion of the 347th Infantry Division. Meanwhile, the I SS Panzer Corps moved to the Ardennes near Soy to coordinate the defence of the Meuse River. To the south they allocated elements of the 12th SS Panzer Division from Lustin to Dinant and the 2nd SS assigned to the sector south of Dinant to Givet.

The Meuse River—50m wide with steep banks and a strong current—was a formidable obstacle. The 9th Infantry teams were repeatedly repulsed by SPWs spouting streams of machine gun bullets, rockets and even flame-throwers from SS troops on the east bank. The Meuse crossings in the U.S. 9th Infantry Division sector near Rivière failed, with many American soldiers being captured by Bernard Siebken's men. Attempts further south near Blaimont were countered by heavy counterattacks emanating from the 2nd SS Panzer Division, which thrust forward a SPW battalion of the SS Panzer Grenadier Regiment 4 ('Der Führer'), equipped with flame-throwing vehicles. Amid the fighting the SS men seemed determined to quash any uprising by civilian resistance: some 300 showed up in Givet to loot the town. On 4 September civilians told intelligence operatives with the U.S. 9th Infantry Division of atrocities days before on the west bank of the Meuse.

Three kilometres south of Vireux, along the Meuse, the U.S. 4th Cavalry Group managed to ford the river while learning that, in nearby Anheé, elements of the 12th SS Hitlerjugend had killed thirteen and torched fifty-eight houses.[23] Similarly, in the tiny villages of Arbre, Profondeville and Hun, the enemy actions were 'characterized by wanton destruction of houses and property and the murder of civilians'.[24] During the night of 4–5 September, German patrols infiltrated the west bank of the Meuse River, murdering at least twenty-two civilians and setting fire to more than seventy-seven houses in the villages of Godinne, Rivière, Rouillon, Hun and Anhée. These war crimes resulted from a direct order given by SS Panzer Grenadier Regiment 25 in the evening of 4 September. Its war diary records that 'all houses on the west bank are to be torched and people showing up on the west bank of the Meuse River are to be shot'. Similar orders were also found in the war diary of SS Panzer Artillery Regiment 12, hinting that these orders originated from the divisional staff. These war crimes were most likely committed by men of I Battalion/SS Panzer Grenadier Regiment 25 whilst holding the line between Godinne and Houx.

Much of this may have been in reaction to the sudden eruption of Belgian resistance. This even led to strange encounters, for instance, in Namur, where the *Armée Blanche* took to the streets to fight it out with

German-sympathetic Rexists in the Meuse River town. The 9th Infantry Division, having lost five assault boats to a failed crossing attempt, identified the 26th Regiment of 12th SS Panzer Division, Hitlerjugend as involved in repeated civilian atrocities.[25] Eventually, on 6 September, the U.S. 3rd Armoured, delayed by flagging fuel deliveries, forced a crossing near Namur after smashing the German 347th Infantry Division. This was timely in that the U.S. 9th Infantry had fought its way to the east bank, near Houx and Bouvignes-sur-Meuse, only to see the advance lodgement temporarily surrounded. The east bank position had been subjected to a withering assault such that 200 men were lost near Blaimont. Eventually the position stabilized when the U.S. 3rd Armoured Division arrived with prisoners seized from the Leibstandarte, 2nd SS and 12th SS divisions. Members of the resistance reported to the U.S. VII Corps that on that same day fighting ended in Dinant and the SS troops had begun to pull out towards Spontin.

Not only were the SS men brutal to French and Belgian civilians at any sign of less than total cooperation, but they were also threatening ordinary Wehrmacht men at pistol point who looked to flee or even to abandon the positions facing the 9th Infantry Division along the Meuse River. They would 'fight to the last man' or else be shot, reported members from the Landeschutzen Battalion 234 and the Sicherrungs Battalion 1029, which later managed to surrender. Relations between the SS and the regular German army forces were strained at best.[26] The SS men even prevented wounded men from being evacuated while the river line was being defended—no one was allowed to pull back.

Almost inevitably, wherever the Leibstandarte and the Hitlerjugend division moved during their flight to the German border, more civilian shootings took place. Even to the rear this continued, with resistance fighters hiding in woods west of Namur, in an appeal to the liberating U.S. Army forces, reporting 'Germans killing all civilians as well as resistance members'.[27]

On 4 September Peiper's old command, the III Battalion/SS Panzer Grenadier Regiment 2, under Jupp Diefenthal, were ordered to assemble in the Ardennes. On 5 September they were in the area of Marche–Hotton and then moved into the region around Marche-en-Famenne. Later elements moved to Saint-Hubert by 8 September and then to Dochamps the following day, with their numbers amounting to three tattered companies, some anti-aircraft guns and one company of self-propelled halftracks. Not coincidentally, a series of brutal war crimes transpired in the Belgian Ardennes wherever Kampfgruppe Diefenthal moved— particularly elements under the command of SS Untersturmführer Hubert

Dickgreber. In Verdenne, not far from Marche, nine civilians were killed. In Sovet, Belgium, just west of Ciney, eighteen people, including two women, were gunned down, and the village priest Vicar Breusart was shot before multiple houses were set afire.[28]

In Marenne two were shot and twenty-eight houses burned, and in Marche-en-Famenne another Belgian citizen was killed and a café there set ablaze.[29] On 4 September, in nearby Odet, south of Huy on the Meuse, three civilians were shot down, with horrified witnesses recalling seeing 'Leibstandarte Adolf Hitler' on the uniform cuff of the perpetrators. Further shootings in nearby Navaugle and Herstal in the vicinity of Liège in Belgium shadowed the movements of elements of the Leibstandarte motoring to the east.[30]

Another small battle group from the Leibstandarte, Kampfgruppe Rink (SS Hauptsturmführer Herbert Rink), fought a delaying action with the U.S. armies as the Americans advanced across the Meuse River into the Belgian Ardennes near Ohey and Modave towards the German border.[31] As the Americans seized Huy, the remaining elements of the 12th SS Panzer Reconnaissance Battalion were committed near Ohey on 4 September with a few tanks to delay the enemy. Meanwhile, the I SS Panzer Corps headquarters pulled back to Erzee after Belgian resistance fighters shot down one of the corps command staff members when they brazenly ambushed German columns on the Ardennes roads. The Germans quickly surmised that the Belgian resistance was even more deadly to the unwary than the French were. Remembered one SS leader: 'The Maquis had armed itself more strongly, even with heavy weapons, and thus represented a great danger for the supply service of the 2nd SS Panzer Division across the Ardennes. It also nearly paralyzed all the traffic of single vehicles.'[32]

On 8 September, Kampfgruppe Rink was near Ouffet and pulling back to the German border in a series of sporadic delaying actions with American forces in pursuit.[33] According to captured German prisoners, the entire 1st SS Panzer Division was reduced to less than the strength of a single regiment, with elements scattered over the rear areas of Belgium.[34] General Georg Keppler revealed that the I SS Panzer Corps reserves consisted of '800 men and one tank to cover a front of 70 kilometres'.

Peiper's old command, the Leibstandarte tank regiment, had already pulled back, although they maintained a rear group of tankless Panzer men, assembled in Hasselt, Belgium. There they were attached to the 116th Panzer Division, with both divisions awaiting tanks in shipment. 'The sixth year of war,' Benoni Junker wondered aloud in his diary, 'the whole thing seems really crappy, but my personal situation is good.'

He had been sent to Liège to collect tanks the previous days but arrived to find frustration. 'No tanks—no nothing at all … only two amazing majors also waiting for tanks.'[35]

The attempt to pick up tanks for the 1st SS Panzer Division came to nothing; the U.S. 3rd Armoured's Combat Command R caught Junker and the others of the Leibstandarte 6th Panzer Company flat-footed near Rocourt on the evening of 7–8 September—destroying at least five delivered Mk IV tanks in an amateurish spectacle. Junker had been caught by surprise upon waking after dozing from a drinking bout. He fled from the scene but would come under critical scrutiny from the leadership of the 116th Panzer Division. Three days later Junker joined the 1st SS Panzer Regiment assembling in Germany, first passing through Aachen and Düren to reach the town of Lohmar, where the fractured pieces were assembling.

On 4 September Antwerp fell, but not its port, and the Allied armies pressed ahead at a dizzying pace—similar in speed and territory to the old Leibstandarte advances in Russia; it was blitzkrieg in reverse. An intelligence officer with the U.S. First Army recalled the scene:

> Many 7th Army formations escaped from the pocket and fled, not in good order, to the German frontier. As it was 300 odd miles away, following them was fun. We drove through the lovely French countryside in the August sun and pitched tents for stands of two or three nights in the kitchen gardens of some beautiful chateau … Not long after the Second Battle of Mons on September 2nd, the 250,000th prisoner of war was about to pass through one of the First Army POW cages. A member of our section suggested a formal ceremony at which the lucky German would be given a War Bond. Of course it was not held, but it is cited as evidence of the buoyancy with which we were infected.[36]

The Americans reached the German frontier bordering Belgium and Luxembourg. And it was also on Monday, 4 September that the Leibstandarte SS Adolf Hitler was ordered back to Germany for 'total rest and relaxation'—at least eventually. As they motored east, stragglers from multiple SS formations were still concentrating in Couvins.[37] There were few left to look forward to such a respite and there was clear evidence of lapsing morale. Similarly, one battle group of the 12th SS left the Meuse River town of Huy on 6 September with three Tiger tanks and 250 men, heading east for Germany, while another section of the Hitlerjugend Division, Kampfgruppe Milius, headed south to join the Leibstandarte in the Ardennes.[38]

In the meantime, the 116th Panzer Division, the newly minted Panzer Brigade 105 and the remainders of the 89th and 347th Infantry divisions, were assigned to screen the retreat with troops from Das Reich, who were maintaining a fighting presence in the Ardennes. On that same day, 6 September, the U.S. VII Corps in the vicinity reported a surge in those surrendering—7,000 prisoners from a conglomerised amalgam of the German Army. Two days later, on 9 September, the U.S. 3rd Armoured alone reported taking 317 prisoners from sixty different enemy formations, even though they were marooned for a day for want of gasoline.[39] And yet it was clear in France that fewer SS men were surrendering compared to Wehrmacht soldiers retreating from Falaise in dejection. On the contrary, many of the SS men were preferring to fight to the death along the way, corresponding to Himmler's 1941 edict: there should no such thing as a 'captive SS man'.[40]

There were exceptions. SS Sergeant Karl Heinz Beckert, with Kampfgruppe Olböter of the 12th SS, captured on 31 August, admitted 'disappointment after disappointment' to his interrogators, saying, 'Our secret weapons seem to make an appearance only in the home town newspapers.'[41] Nevertheless, periodically the threat of such weapons looked real. From the invasion front, V-1 flying bombs were roaring over the advancing Allied tank columns, spitting a red-orange fire that thundered in the days and glowed noisily in the night. Some fell harmlessly as duds, but others growled on towards their targets. There was more to add to Allied intelligence worries that there might be something to the Hitlerian secret weapons braggadocio: beginning on 1 September increasing numbers of German fighters appeared over the Allied spearheads near Liège, including a pair of the new Me 262 jet fighters.

The secret weapons? The real advent of futuristic robot war was exemplified by the A-4 rocket developed by Werner von Braun at Pennemünde. Courtesy of Himmler's use of concentration camp labour for underground manufacture, the A-4 rocket programme was awarded to the Reichsführer to come under SS control. At the end of August, Himmler ordered SS Obergruppenführer Hans Kammler, his secretive and coldly efficient engineering head of Department D, to begin deploying and firing the advanced rocket. At 1843 hours on 8 September the first pair of ballistic missiles descended on London, screaming down from 90km above the Earth and slamming into the British capital at supersonic speed. One of the two-ton warheads exploded in an unoccupied section in London, but the other detonated at Staveley Road, killing three in an instant. On the following day another rocket hit Maisons-Alfort on the outskirts of Paris on 9 September. Nine were killed and thirty-one more wounded.[42]

In all, more than thirty-one hundred of the new vengeance weapons (now termed *Vergeltungswaffe* 2, or V-2) would be fired at the Allies— half of them assigned to strike London. Whereas the V-1 jet-powered robot bomb could be shot down, for the massive V-2 rocket there was no defence and very little warning after the double crack of its sonic boom.[43] If this fabled surprise was real, could there be other Hitler *Wunderwaffen*?

Yet on the ground, the German forces were still falling back pell-mell to the border while American armour moved ahead in lurching motions, slowed by an inadequate gasoline supply. On 7 September, Generalfeldmarschal Model and von Rundstedt met in Stadtkyll just across the German border in the Eifel east of Malmédy and agreed that the main threat was coming from the U.S. First Army moving through the Ardennes and from Liège towards Aachen.[44] Perhaps the Waffen SS units could slow the advance for units to reach the Westwall? On 10 September intercepted radio communication of the SS Panzer Grenadier Regiment 4 of Das Reich revealed to Allied forces that elements of the 1st SS Panzer Division—a rear-guard of Kampfgruppe Diefenthal—were pulling back to Dochamps after being overmatched by U.S. tanks sallying forth from the Ardennes village of Hotton astride the Ourthe River.[45]

Other combat elements were called on to continued sacrifice with the German 7th Army. When Obersturmführer Herbert Rink reached the German border on 12 September with orders to stop the Americans in the Ardennes, he was shocked to find the vaunted Westwall in terrible condition. Rather than a foreboding defensive line the Allies called 'The Siegfried Line', they instead discovered damp, mouldering bunkers in dilapidated condition without telephone communications.

> There were no barbed-wire barriers. No fields of fire. Everything was overgrown and run down for years. Some of the bunkers were being used for storage of the harvest ... Our machine guns and anti-tank weapons did not even fit into the gun emplacements. Yet at any moment the enemy could arrive and the battle could begin ... It was lucky of us that the U.S. First Army had so many supply problems.[46]

Hitler ordered civilians to take up shovels along the Westwall. As Himmler had been given overall command of the defence of the Homeland zone, Peiper's former superior immediately ordered the local Gauleiters along the western German border to mobilize the young men of the Hitler Jugend, the girls of the *Bund Deutscher Mädel* and even the Reich Labour Service to immediately begin emergency efforts to improve the obsolete fortification. Soon massive ditches and entrenchments were under construction—even if improperly located or ill advised.[47]

Meanwhile, after the Falaise debacle, thousands of German soldiers were now in captivity. In Russia, Jochen Peiper had advocated death rather than surrender. 'Save the last cartridge for yourself, boys!' he would say.[48] But here in the west things differed from the official call to sacrifice: 'Each German soldier is expected to prefer death with a weapon in his hand to becoming a prisoner.'[49] Such orders notwithstanding, the Falaise debacle saw an unusual number of Leibstandarte men taken prisoner. With near encirclement, it was surrender or death. Attrition cost the 12th SS Panzer Division half its strength—some 9,000 officers and men—and the Leibstandarte lost at least a third, escaping with only thirty-five tanks.[50] At the end of September 1944 neither division had more than a dozen tanks altogether. The wastage of SS officers was even more; taken captive were none other than Max Wünsche and Kurt Meyer.

On Sunday, 20 August Wünsche and two other regimental officers—Georg Isecke, along with his adjutant, Fritz Freitag; and the *regimental doctor*, Rudolf Stiawa—were cut off in the confusion far behind Allied lines. On 21 August they stumbled into an Allied command post and received fire, scattering them. In the confusion Dr Stiawa was separated from them and captured. Even though Wünsche was wounded, the small group hid by day and skulked in the darkness by night, gnawing on raw beets to appease their hunger. On the second day the group lost Isecke, who was captured by American soldiers after a wrong turn. Wünsche and Freitag sought refuge in a wrecked truck, supposedly pilfering a pile of Luftwaffe uniforms. Mindful of the enemy attitude towards the *Schutzstafel*, both shed their tattered Waffen SS uniforms and, with the available replacement garb, became Luftwaffe. On the morning of 22 August the men commandeered a German halftrack, boldly driving through the village of Saint-Lambert in broad daylight. When they came up to a Canadian military policeman, Wünsche laid on the horn and pressed the accelerator; the MP waved them on. Eyes wide driving on, they knew that kind of luck couldn't last; the two abandoned the vehicle and set off on foot.

On the night of 23, August Wünsche, Freitag and another Wehrmacht man they had come upon hid in a hedgerow thicket across from the road in the castled village of Coudehard. As daylight faded, the fugitives dined on tins of pork and, after a puff on a cache of discovered cigars, fell fast asleep. They were awakened the following morning by British infantry brandishing machine guns. Despite their uniform subterfuge, the Brits quickly identified Wünsche as the tank regiment commander of the 12th SS Panzer.[51]

After being held in a wire cage for a day, the SS officer was conveyed on 26 August some 40km from the headquarters of British Field Marshal Montgomery. Within the tented village he saw Montgomery dismount a command car wearing his trademark black beret. There he was told that German prisoners of war would be treated fairly according to the Geneva Convention, 'but not the Waffen SS'. Montgomery glared into Wünsche's blue eyes. 'They will be treated for what they are—political garbage.'[52] Without a chance to respond, Wünsche was spirited away to England on a British destroyer. On 9 September, near London, English officers interrogated him, looking to fathom morale in the Waffen SS. 'Prisoner is a confirmed Nazi,' the officer concluded, 'but has a rather "Jekyll and Hyde" personality.' He offered no opinions, impressing his captors with 'the evasiveness of his answers'.

> Prisoner tends to be shocked and hurt by suggestions that the SS should be considered as a force apart from the Army. He is convinced of the loyalty of the SS to the National Socialist faith and to the Führer ... Whereas the higher SS officers are good Nazis, PW emphasizes that they are all 'professional soldiers'. ... He tries to ingratiate himself by maintaining that he is, above all, a soldier.[53]

In the end Wünsche was defiant. 'The Waffen SS is loyal to Hitler and to the Nazi movement,' Wünsche said, 'because it is necessary for a soldier to know what he is fighting for.' Adolf Hitler reciprocated his concern. 'These days there is only bad news,' Reishsleiter Martin Bormann wrote to his wife. 'The day before yesterday we had the report that Wünsche, who commanded a tank regiment in the Leibstandarte [sic], is missing. Either he was badly injured or captured by the British ... Let us hope he was captured.'[54] Indeed, so disturbed was Hitler when learning of his captivity that he approached the Allies for a prisoner exchange to return the Führer's favourite. Nothing came of it. Although the U.S. War Department entertained the idea, the British who held the 'vain and uncooperative' Wünsche steadfastly refused any deal.[55]

While his rival was conveyed to a PoW cage in England, Jochen Peiper learned of the cataclysmic developments from visitors to his sunny room in Lake Tegern's Bayernhof Hotel. He was there by the end of August. Tourism long gone, the Bayernhof had been converted to a reserve hospital. Sigurd had travelled there daily by bicycle, and later in the month Jochen went on a brief leave to stay with his family in Rottach-Egern. There was a hike in the cool green hills above Lake Tegernsee, for which the whole family and the neighbours went along. But Peiper seemed distant. He and his wife had private talks under the shade of the big birch tree facing the Waldberg in the backyard.[56] They talked, but Peiper's mind was fixed on the total collapse in France:

> When I think about the invasion, I get totally sick. What a sad connection between indifference and stupidity, between neglect and leadership failings on *all* levels. And how easily can one dismiss it with the placement of dagger Number 2: 'the Führer has ordered ...' There was nothing that we did not do wrong and there was, God knows, no shortage of marshals and medal-studded generals. It is really hard to understand—all that after such long professional experience—their professionals versus our amateurs![57]

Peiper did not stay home long. Training was a good distraction from depression; he was obsessed with the losses at Normandy. 'We Germans were really naive,' Peiper scolded. 'The *Götterdivision*—God's own Division, the Leibstandarte Adolf Hitler—itself was shot down by artillery and bombs. Hitler himself had never been in other countries than Germany and Austria and had no idea about materiel production there.'

Peiper then echoed many of the Germans in Normandy: 'We were shouting at the front lines. "Fight, you American cowards!" Instead there was a three-hour bombardment by their artillery.'[58] General Hans Eberbach, who was in charge of the counteroffensive at Avranches, of which the Leibstandarte and 2nd Panzer Division led the way, was also critical. In Normandy, he had complained, the Leibstandarte fought 'worse than ever before'.[59] Regardless, SS Brigadeführer Fritz Kraemer of the I SS Panzer Corps remained amazed that during the critical first week of September that the Americans did not attempt to advance in force from the German border in the Ardennes. 'All soldiers reckoned with a breakthrough up to the Rhine to take place at any time. No fighting would have been necessary. The way was absolutely free!' Kraemer could not know that it was logistics and a shortage of fuel and ammunition that explained the Allied hesitation the first days in September. 'Reminiscent of World War I,' he recalled, 'we talked of the West Wall miracle.'[60] And sure enough, within two weeks the German forces along the Siegfried Line began to collect and reorganize while additional divisions arrived from other fronts.

As autumn approached, Peiper, although ailing, took time to visit the nearby SS officer's school in Bad Tölz, where SS Sturmbannführer Hans Kempin was overseeing wartime reserve officers training for close-in tank fighting.[61] With live ammunition, Panzer grenadier trainees assaulted old T-34s that Paul Hausser had hauled back from Kharkov. That spectacle provided a less than reassuring wartime backdrop to the conversation. Yes, Fritz Witt was dead and Max Wünsche was missing, they mused, but what of Panzermeyer?

He was still out there. In a series of chaotic death-ridden scenes, the commander of the 12th SS escaped from Falaise. Yet in fleeing to the Meuse River in Belgium, where SS dregs tried to make a stand, Kurt Meyer found himself a fugitive behind enemy lines. Ingloriously hiding for a day in a chicken coup near Namur, members of the Belgian resistance took him captive on 6 September.

To his interrogators Meyer saw the Normandy battles as 'magnificent in the finest Wagnerian tradition'—and himself as a National Socialist Siegfried.[62] 'You will hear a lot against Adolf Hitler in this camp,' Meyer proclaimed, 'but you'll never hear it from me. As far as I am concerned, he was, and still is, the greatest thing that ever happened for Germany.'[63]

* * *

In March 1945 the Germans were gone from the Abbaye d'Ardennes. Although the place was wrecked by shelling, Madame Francine Vico was grateful that her sons were alive. Jean-Marie was home, and son Jacques was on leave from the French Leclerc Division—perhaps her husband still lived, too. France was again French. Winter had passed, and there was the promise of warmth and peace. She walked up to the little park behind the abbey to see if the snowdrops were up that she always looked forward to each spring. What she saw in the garden surprised her. The tiny white crocuses were popping up through the grass and scattered all over. There was no oval pattern around the two ornamental stones; obviously the bulbs had been disturbed. Perhaps the Germans had buried some papers—or maybe even treasure. With her son, Jean-Marie got a shovel and began digging where the ground had been turned up around the snowdrops. What they found shocked them: there was a jaw bone—a skull—a human skull ....

Although horrified, the two Vico boys soon discovered five shallow graves scattered around the garden and nearby. They marked the sad places with simple wooden crosses. By the time the Canadian Graves unit had finished the grisly excavation detail, they found bodies of some nineteen Canadian soldiers who had been shot by Kurt Meyer's men at the Abbaye d'Ardennes.[64]

Meyer was in deep. A SHAEF court of inquiry concluded that the 12th SS Panzer Division had given secret orders that prisoners should be shot, as 'it was understood throughout the division that a policy of denying quarter or executing prisoners after interrogation was openly approved'.[65] The Allies claimed that a total of sixty-four unarmed soldiers were killed as a result. Kurt Meyer was brought before a Canadian military court in late 1945.[66] In his final oral defence he signalled trouble:

> I am convinced that in the Division there were elements, who, due to the year-long battles, due to five years of war, had in a certain effect become brutalized … I take every responsibility for what in the framework of the tactical possibilities, I ordered. But the situation was basically an unnatural one … I wish to assure the court that I gave no order to annihilate defenceless people.[67]

The prosecution attempted to get Panzermeyer to admit that he was aware the executions had taken place on the doorstep of his headquarters. This went nowhere. In a test of courtroom intimidation, Meyer stared down both damning Waffen SS witnesses and the prosecutor. Even Max Wünsche, the commander of the 12th SS Panzer Regiment, stepped up to the witness dock on Meyer's behalf. Decked out in a beige-coloured tunic with dark slacks and a chest of medals, Wünsche looked to be the perfect Hollywood Nazi, as he too glared at the prosecution. Vain and contemptuous, Max said he heard nothing about any shootings on 8 June.

Eventually the weight of the evidence capsized Meyer's arrogance. At the judge's table sat Brigadier General Harry Foster, head of the Canadian 7th Brigade, whose men Meyer's troops had executed:

> There was an irony to this whole distasteful affair. Not because of what happened to my men—that was inexcusable. But then again war itself is inexcusable. What struck me as I sat in my comfortable chair looking down on this hard-nosed Nazi was that not one of us sitting on the bench, with the exception of Bredin, could claim clean hands in the matter of war crimes … It hadn't all been one-sided. Our troops did some pretty dreadful things to the Germans. Didn't that make all of us who were commanding officers just a guilty as Meyer? I remember thinking at the time: you poor arrogant bastard. Except for an accident of birth and background our positions might have been reversed. In which case I would now be standing before you asking for justice at this meeting of the generals.[68]

When sentenced to death, Meyer bowed awkwardly before the court. It was 28 December 1945.[69]

Others did not make it that far. Given Oradour, Tulle and similar savagery, members of the Waffen SS were at special risk in France and Belgium. Word of the deaths by ambush of Erich Olboeter and Hans Waldmüller the first week in September 1944 made the rounds of the I SS Panzer Corps—and a mental note made about the partisans in the Ardennes.[70] As the German border grew closer, so did enemy resolve. By 10 September the Germans were deep in the Ardennes, with a vindictive band of 150 pausing to burn and pillage Nonceveux just east of Aywaille in Belgium. Something of a guerrilla war continued after a group of men from the Armée Blanche harassed the guardians of several fuelless German tanks and heavy guns who were hiding in Monceau after getting that far.[71] On that same date the 83rd Reconnaissance Battalion of the 3rd Armoured Division was repulsed by a clutch of German tanks of Panzer Brigade 105, firing from hull-down positions south-east of Limbourg. Other U.S. Army elements attempting to thread their way through the hilly Ardennes were thwarted by minefields and blown bridges across the Ourthe River.

For some Ardennais villages, the threat was imminent. When the Americans closed in to liberate the village of La Gleize, Belgium, in early September, all those remaining of the three hundred souls in the village were petrified with fear. The headquarters of the 12th SS's Kampfgruppe Milus arrived there, and the surly troopers in the village seemed bent on vengeance; between sixty and seventy civilians were rounded up and forced into the cellar of Arthur George behind the eleventh-century church. One of these forced to the cellar was 17-year-old Gerard Gregoire.

The Hitlerjugend men in charge seemed to want to execute them all—news had already spread about what the SS were doing in some villages in France. The man proposing their execution railed that two SS men of the Hitlerjugend Division had been recently executed by Belgian partisans near Haute Bodeux; the SS rumour was that the Belgians who did the deed were from La Gleize.[72] Now they would all die too. Fortunately a German officer with a cooler head arrived, ordering, 'Don't kill all these people!' The two soldiers had an argument, but the one wishing to execute everyone finally departed. When the Germans left and the Americans liberated the village on 12 September, Gerard Gregoire thought the war was over in La Gleize, Belgium, in the Ardennes.[73]

By the first week in September 1944 the Allies were gripped by infectious optimism and wild rumours. 'One thing is certain,' Allied intelligence wondered aloud. 'The enemy has lost the war and the defeat of the 7th Army and Panzer Gruppe West will hasten its end ...' Would it have been more profitable for the Allies if Hitler's bomb had been better? ... Or ought the Allies to feel grateful that he has lived on to continue his strategic blunders?'[74] In Brussels crowds erupted in a madly wild celebratory display when the Guards Armoured Division liberated the capital on 3 September. Amid the carnival atmosphere, a virulent rumour swept the city that Hitler was dead. This turned out to be wrong. Others claimed that the Germans seemed defeated and would soon capitulate. 'There is every reason to believe it,' the BBC commentators opined on the night of 6 September. Even the taciturn head of the U.S. First Army, General Courtney Hodges, told his chief of staff that 'given ten days of good weather ... the war might well be over as [far as] organized resistance is concerned'.[75] Yet Hodges remained worried that 'during the last week that the supply of gasoline remains a major problem'.

The logistical limitation had another manifestation: command jealousy. Both Montgomery, in charge of the British 21st Army Group, and Patton, commanding the U.S. Third Army, demanded that Eisenhower provide them with the priority in gasoline and ammunition. For a time Montgomery got his way with a bold plan for a parachute operation using both British and U.S. airborne divisions to seize multiple bridges across Holland that would lead across the Rhine River and strike directly into the heart of the Rhineland. Strongly reinforced, the British field marshal fancied himself advancing on Berlin by the end of the month. In retrospect, Operation Market Garden was foolhardy given that the drop zones were also the assembly areas of the 9th SS and 10th SS Panzer divisions—Montgomery's promise to end the war before autumn faltered in ferocious fighting. It proved impossible to capture and hold not only the length of 'Hell's Highway' from Eindhoven but also the bridge across the Rhine River at Arnhem. During the ten days of the battle the British 1st Airborne Division lost 1,300 killed, 1,700 wounded and 3,800 captured. At the end the proud division ceased to exist.[76]

Even after giving up on Market Garden, there was simply not enough fuel or ammunition to support a powerful Allied broad-front offensive into the heart of Germany. Along the border at the Westwall, which the Allies called the Siegfried Line, the U.S. and British offensive effort sputtered to a stop on 10 September, with Patton fighting in the Lorraine and the U.S. First Army attempting to pry open the 'Dragon's Teeth' in the Huertgen Forest and the Eifel.[77] It became a battle for hillside pillboxes and bunkers across difficult terrain. And there was no more assistance from the French and Belgian resistance. 'The population of Malmédy and Eupen are not friendly like France,' noted the First Army intelligence officers, 'but no incidents yet.' The 28th Infantry Division patrolling uneasily along the Ardennes Westwall line in Germany near Sevenig was even less sure. For several days prisoners had been captured from the 2nd SS Division, and vehicles of the Leibstandarte Adolf Hitler had been spotted west of Bastogne. Most of the 1st SS had now crossed back across the German border for emergency refitting.

In the meantime, as the summer faded, the weather in the Eifel area along the Westwall turned cool, foggy and overcast. Now there were no more cheering crowds bearing flowers or shouts of 'Vive l'Amérique' in the German-speaking Belgian villages or those just across the border. As in Sevenig, in the German Eifel the local populace appeared brooding and sullen, even with white flags hanging in the windows. Ominously, on 15 September, an opportunistic German sniper had taken to sporadically firing on anyone brazenly walking down the streets on the western part of the village. As if to cap that off, on 16 September the division chaplain was returning from Kesfeld when he came upon two civilians wearing Swastika armbands and brandishing a Nazi flag. What were they doing with that, the chaplain wanted to know? 'Hitler is coming!' the youths stammered loudly before wrenching away the Hakenkreuz and dashing off.[78]

If Market Garden was a failure, there was little to encourage the other side. The frayed remnants of the Leibstandarte SS Adolf Hitler scattered back to the German border: *'Heim ins Reich'*—Home to Germany. On 5 September, a request by OB West for a division status report for Leibstandarte came back with only the news that a frayed battle group was marching through the Belgian Ardennes towards Marche and heading east.

Meanwhile, Hitler and his inner circle pondered the accumulating devastation. Nearly 300,000 German men had been lost in France, with more than half of those now prisoners. Fully 2,000 tanks and armoured vehicles were now roadside steel junk stretching from Normandy to the Ardennes. Eisenhower's operatives, still considering how to most rapidly end the war, were congratulating themselves on obliterating eleven enemy armoured divisions, of which the Leibstandarte was one. To General Fritz Bayerlein, who had led the once-powerful Panzer Lehr Division, it was a 'battle of annihilation' without comparison and fully worse than Tannenberg in the First World War.[79] At the beginning of September Hitler professed himself unworried about the situation—the Americans were outrunning their supplies, and even as his armed legions were in ribbons, he relished the potential of a counterattack near Reims.[80] To buy time, he declared, the Westwall along the German border must be held at all costs.

Yet at the end of August, Generalfeldmarschal Model, who was now acting as the supreme field commander in the West—OB West as well as Army Group B—approached Hitler and his household military office, the OKW, with a thoroughly discouraging assessment. The trajectory at the beginning of September reflected a rapidly worsening position, he related. The real strength in the west was a chimera of the full-strength numbers of Hitler's tabulation. Most divisions were at regimental strength, with few heavy weapons. The main the refugees reaching the German border were bringing only a rifle or pistol. Moreover, Hitler's obsessive *idée fixe* 'stand and hold' order was unrealistic without big changes on the Western Front.[81] Model asked to be provided with three divisions to cover a massive defensive gap in the Belfort area, flak artillery be moved from Germany to the west and three Panzer divisions to be transferred from the Eastern Front without delay.

Model's sudden pessimism after Falaise was met with consternation from Hitler, who then relieved him of the OB West supreme command. The German leader adroitly awarded that figurehead position to aging Generalfeldmarschal Gerd von Rundstedt, who had a public reputation as a great strategist. Beyond that, Himmler, in his new role as head of the replacement army, was given domain over the chaos of the rear areas in the Western Front. 'Heinrich H. drove to the West Wall yesterday,' Reichsleiter Martin Bormann wrote to his wife on 3 September. 'He is tackling his task of Commander in Chief of the Reserve Army with magnificent energy.' What exactly did that mean?

In fact, Peiper's old boss, the SS Reichsführer, was moving about and giving the word that the deluge of stragglers and deserters would be halted or else. By train and field car, Peiper's old boss criss-crossed the southern zone on the Western Front between Mulhouse and Trier, claiming to speak to 'thousands of soldiers'. Many were disheartened or on the run, and Himmler, with his new authority, swiftly threatened 'brutal measures' for officers shirking their duty.[82] With such coercion— even fear for one's family—scenes of German panic and flight faded as autumn drew near.

On the ground in Belgium, the situation fully illustrated Model's pragmatic concerns. On 1 September a member of the Leibstandarte's 2nd Battery, 1st SS Flak Battalion, captured days before near Vervins, said that of 300 men, there were only half left, and most heavy weapons were missing. Worse, he reported that in recent days members of the Leibstandarte attempting to reach Germany were sometimes forced to appropriate fuel from Wehrmacht units at gunpoint, leading to disputes over rank and even fist fights. 'If the V-2 or other drastic measures do not appear soon,' he had overheard from superiors, 'then we are faced with surrender "en masse".'[83] When the 7th Panzer Company collected itself in Siegburg east of Aachen that September, Manfred Thorn drove back the sole surviving tank—aghast at the prospects.[84]

To be sure, there were three weeks of training at the Wietzendorf Troop training centre. Without tanks, the new men did parade marches in twelve-man rows—something that seemed silly to old hands such as Thorn. New recruits arrived in droves without any experience whatsoever. New tank drivers had never even sat in a tank before, not to mention received training for radio or weapons use. 'Horst Pilarcek was then made our Panzer Commander,' Thorn recalled, 'and he had come from the Luftwaffe!'[85] The tanks would not arrive for weeks. Where was Peiper? The rumor making the rounds was that he was still out with a heart attack.

Despite the ethos of the Waffen SS, human flesh was no match for steel. The fate of SS Unterscharführer Achim Redecker was like that of many others. The strapping blond wrote the poem about Peiper and his blowtorch battalion before he fell near Carrouges on 14 August.

> In the light of the blowtorch we dream,
> About the homeland—and peace!
> Just a dream![86]

Like the SS, the German paratroops, the Fallschirmjäger, saw themselves as an elite—unwilling to give up easily. On 4 September 1944 General Lieutenant Rüdiger von Heyking, the aristocratic Prussian commander of 6th Fallschirmjäger Division, was captured in the encirclement near Mons, Belgium. Upon interrogation by the U.S. First Army, he surprised his interpreter by quickly admitting that the war was lost. If so, the question came, why the stubborn resistance? 'Alles andere nur nicht Bolschevismus in Deutschland'—anything but communism in Germany— Von Heyking warned. 'The fear of Russia will keep Germany fighting until the bitter end.'[87]

As if to verify that view, Himmler was now raising a huge final cull of semi-able-bodied men in Germany—the twenty-sixth wave of reinforcements. With an aim to quickly raise twenty-five new divisions,

Hitler would then bestow the honorific Volksgrenadiers, or People's Infantry, on new divisions in the five hundred series. Quietly, the army leaders were referring to the formations of Himmler's replacement army as the *Götterdämmerrung* Divisions. Convalescents of moderately wounded soldiers were to be emptied from hospitals, while older and younger German men were to be called up. Also, readily drafted were Luftwaffe bomber pilots with no Heinkels and Navy sailors with no battleships.

Lastly, there were *Ohren und Magen abteilung*—stomach and ear battalions—formed of men with hearing and chronic digestive disorders intended to populate the margins of Himmler's replacement army— all this clear evidence of the scrap at the bottom of the barrel. 'Hitler and Himmler's last-ditch effort against extinction,' offered German officers to interrogators in September 1944.[88] For Peiper, to see his old boss raising desperate legions such as these could hardly have been inspiring. The SS replacements, a supposedly better amalgam of Alsatians, Hungarians and East Europeans—the *Volksdeutsche*—would bring warm bodies to replace the tremendous losses of summer, albeit with suspect allegiances.

These conscripts were exactly contrary to the old vision of the Waffen SS as a politically unified and well-armed elite. The Volksgrenadiers would likely be the physically marginalized dregs of German manhood, with scant prospects for effective military training and indifferent motivation. Peiper had already made his feelings known about the falling quality of replacements seen in the Leibstandarte. 'Not the best *Menschenmaterial*,' he warned just before summer 1944.[89] And the People's Infantry were so much the worse.

Sensing the malaise, Hitler was now downcast, disappointed that four years after having captured France in an astonishing victory in 1940, his forces were now forced to relinquish the former lands of conquest. Yet similar to his resolve after Stalingrad, Hitler, at the very apex of National Socialist leadership, seemed to suddenly find a second wind of resolve when it was clear there was no further prospect of resistance west of the German border. On 19 August, amid the calamity of Falaise and its disasters, Alfred Jodl, on Hitler's inner staff known as OKW, recorded surprising optimism in his conversation with Hitler that Saturday: 'The Führer discussed the equipment and manpower position with the Chief of OKW, Chief Army staff [General Walter Buhle] and [Albert] Speer. Prepare to take the offensive in November when the enemy air forces can't operate. Main point: some 25 divisions must be moved to the West in the next one to two months.'[90]

386

'In the West we're experiencing critical setbacks,' Goebbels recorded in his diary on 23 August, 'but the Führer hopes to regain the offensive there in a favourable weather situation ...' Goebbels ventured that this might come 'around November'. Now, unlike in the conquest of France, 'favourable weather' meant poor flying conditions and not the sunny halcyon days of May 1940. 'It is important now,' Goebbels declared, 'to do everything in our power to overcome the present crisis.'[91] Given the catastrophic situation in the west, that appeared a major question, as Hitler's health seemed poor. 'We must focus on our leader's psychological well-being and keep him in top form given his indispensable role in our war leadership.'

Hitler believed fate was on his side, remaining focused on himself as the anointed German leader of modern times. 'I am grateful to Providence that I stayed alive,' he said, referring to the failed 20 July assassination attempt. 'We will fight, if necessary at the Rhine. It makes absolutely no difference,' he announced at his East Prussian headquarters on the last day of August 1944. 'We will wage this struggle under all circumstance until, as Frederick the Great said, one of our damned enemies gets tired of continuing to fight.'[92]

Regardless of Hitler's convictions, morale at home appeared precarious, as Dr Karl Gebhardt from the SS medical compound at Hohenlychen north of Berlin wrote to Himmler in early September after a short tour of the Western Front. Addressing his old friend, the SS doctor reported the citizens of Trier just east of the Ardennes were upset regarding the many rumours making the rounds, and he had witnessed the ordered evacuation of the Eupen–Malmédy region, which had turned into a panicked rout as the population from the formerly annexed zone of Belgium attempted to reach Germany before the Americans arrived.[93]

Recuperating in Tegernsee, Jochen Peiper had missed the Falaise killing ground and the calamitous retreat to the German border. Unfazed, Kurt Meyer gushed Waffen SS pride. 'The German soldier's performance in Normandy,' he bragged, 'will forever be immortalized in the history books.' Besides, Meyer would later relate in conversation, 'If the Bolshevists succeed in conquering Germany, then it means the end of our people.'[94] Nor was Peiper inclined to optimism. Now, more than ever, the war appeared to spiral to an ugly Wagnerian end. Had Hitler's calamitous reverses altered his personal sense of duty?

Recuperating from a bout of hepatitis, Peiper continued to rest in the converted Tegernsee hotel that was now a long-term recovery hospital. Each day Sigurd Peiper pedalled her bicycle the 6km distance from

Rottach to visit Jochen and bring him food.[95] Although ailing with an ashen pallor, her man seemed resolute. Even with a slim chance to end the Second World War favourably, Peiper longed to return to his armoured SS warriors and fight once more. Where would Hitler point them?

'Where we were standing was Germany,' Peiper declared proudly, 'and as far as my tank gun reached was my kingdom!'

Chapter 22

P.O. Box 1142

On 16 December 1944 Jochen Peiper would fight again, this time in Belgium, commanding the prime armoured spearhead during Hitler's final major offensive of the war. For the Allies, the Ardennes Offensive became known as the Battle of the Bulge, but for Peiper, operation Wacht Am Rhein resulted in deep personal condemnation for his part in an atrocity soon widely known as the 'Malmédy Massacre'. This was a complex battlefield event in which eighty-four American soldiers were shot down on 17 December 1944 after surrendering to Kampfgruppe Peiper.[1] While the precursors for the SS excesses in the Ardennes were repeatedly established by Peiper's *Lötlampen*—or Blowtorch—command earlier in the war, the high-profile prisoner-shooting incident near Malmédy, Belgium, before Christmas 1944 would beleaguer the SS leader for his remaining days.

Peiper did not suspect that condemnatory fate in January 1945 when the German Ardennes Offensive was over and Hitler's last great gamble was turned back. Moreover, he did not know that top-secret surveillance of German prisoners taken in the Ardennes—known as 'P.O. Box 1142'— was solidifying his post-war fate. How did this come about?

Oddly for such a top-secret installation, Fort Hunt was hardly in a remote, out-of-the-way site; indeed, it was located in northern Virginia, just 30km south of Washington, D.C., and its verdant, tree-dotted green pastures had formerly been part of George Washington's farmlands. The U.S. Army post itself had been established during the Spanish–American War as an artillery site designed to help guard the Potomac River. Long obsolete in 1942, it was nevertheless hastily transformed when the Army and Navy decided to use it as a joint maximum secrecy interrogation facility. The resulting tightly guarded compound of eighty-seven unimpressive buildings and barracks bustling with activity was so secret that many higher-ups in U.S. Army circles didn't even know it existed. Few in the U.S. Army or even the British War Office knew such prominent prisoners were there; indeed, rumour had it that the White House itself knew nothing of it. So secret was the work at Fort Hunt that it did not exist on any manifest of holding places for German prisoners in the United States. It was known solely to U.S. military intelligence and the Organization of Strategic Services by its mundane cover name: P.O. Box 1142.[2]

The mission of P.O. Box 1142 demanded the skills of fluent German interpreters who, upon being hired, were given a nickel and told to call a telephone number from the drug store in Old Town Alexandria in Virginia. As in a clandestine spy thriller, prospective recruits were then picked up at the pharmacy front and driven in a staff car to the location. At first, most of those interrogated at Fort Hunt were U-boat men, but as the U.S. forces liberated North Africa, Italy and France, many of the prisoners came from other posts in Hitler's Reich. Prominent German prisoners moved there included rocket scientist Werner von Braun (and a coterie of others in Operation Paperclip) as well as Hitler's spymaster, Reinhard Gehlen.[3] Another was Dr Heinz Max Schlicke, who had been working on infrared fuses that could be used to trigger atomic bombs as well as aeronautical developments known today as 'stealth technology'.

By the end of the war more than 375,000 German PoWs had been brought to the United States and placed in rural camps all over the country. Many of those arriving at 1142 had until recently been picking apples in Virginia, harvesting cotton in Mississippi or cultivating potatoes in Idaho. In particular, many of the members of Kampfgruppe Peiper who had fought in the Ardennes had been shipped to the large PoW centre at Fort Knox, Kentucky, where they worked on farms in Henry County, cutting corn or tilling tobacco.

Many were more or less harmless soldiers of the Reich, swept up in the war and taken captive. But not all the prisoners were blameless: some had first-hand knowledge of German war crimes. So secret was the mission that the facility operated in contradiction to the Geneva Convention. The Red Cross was not notified when any of the 3,451 German prisoners were transferred there. Still, even though these prisoners likely had information of great importance to the interrogations, no torture was used, and most of the interrogations at Fort Hunt were cordial, even friendly affairs. 'Yes, we threatened them with being sent back to Russia,' John Gunther Dean, one of the interrogators, recalled, 'but there was no other harm of any kind.'[4]

Inside the camp there were fake Red Cross workers to help persuade prisoners to talk and an imposter Russian officer, Major Iwanowski, who appeared to frighten those who were uncooperative. But in the main, the idea was to spoil the prisoners to loosen tongues. Thus, P.O. Box 1142 was more like a vacation resort than an interrogation centre: there were books, cigarettes, even alcohol and, during exercise hours, softball and a pool for swimming in summer. Indeed, many prisoners marvelled at the food quality at Fort Hunt and shared favourable impressions of the various PoW camps they had been brought from across America. Cards were popular, and although gambling was forbidden, games of various types were provided to each cell to help pass the time. Some of the most important German rocket scientists were even taken into Washington, D.C., to go shopping in front of deeply suspicious shopkeepers.[5] But beyond wondering why they were being treated so well, why were they there in the first place?

Colonel John L. Walker, the post commander from 1943 to 1945, could tell no one the real nature of his mission. Meanwhile, the residents of Fairfax County near the camp watched with long curiosity as olive drab Army school buses with blacked-out windows roared towards the guard gate night and day. What was going on? They could have hardly have imagined that inside the buses were German soldiers, officers, scientists and engineers from Pine Grove Furnace in Pennsylvania. Debouching the buses to reside at the series of wooden barracks, those there had no idea where they were or why.

But the intelligence superiors at Fort Hunt knew what they were doing. The operation there was called MIS-Y and focused on covert listening to key German prisoners talking to each other.

Prisoners were often interrogated in a conventional fashion about what the United States and British intelligence wanted to know, but with two or three housed in each cell, most could hardly suspect that the rooms were discreetly bugged to record their conversations. Even though some noted that their fellow cellmates seemed either from a similar unit or oddly selected to conjure up tell-all adventures, they could not find anything in scouring their simple rooms that might suggest that each word they said or even mumbled was being recorded in a central facility teeming with a fleet of interpreters, translators and stenographers. The super-sensitive microphone—which could hear anything more than a bare whisper—was like a huge electrical ear built into the ceiling itself, with eavesdroppers working in shifts and listening-in twenty-four hours a day. Indeed, every square inch of the camp was bugged—the rooms, mess hall, even some of the trees.

With little ceremony, U-boat commanders, pilots, engineers, ordinary soldiers and Waffen SS men captured in the fighting in 1944–1945 were often moved rapidly across the Atlantic from Europe and placed in prison cells where they were situated with other prisoners, unaware that the walls had ears. Most of the eavesdroppers yawned as the enemy cellmates discussed one boring tale after the next—the food, the superiority of German soldiers versus their American counterparts, petty squabbling and complaints about subordinates or superiors. And there was always loneliness, girls and sex to chew over.

Once in a while the prisoners spoke of other things: the performance of German arms and weapons, the locations of weapons development centres, tactical planning and even secret matters. As the operation was listening to captured German rocket scientists and Luftwaffe engineers, the stakes were high. At times even the speculation held sway: a prime Luftwaffe designer argued fervently with his Luftwaffe pilot cellmate over whether the six-engined Messerschmidt 264 or Junkers 390 offered better potential to bomb America.

However, furtive and whispered discussions came up surprisingly frequently in the room surveillances: war crimes. These taped conversations ended up being of great importance to U.S. and British intelligence operatives.

After the bodies were recovered in the snowy field near Baugnez in January 1945 and the stunned and frozen survivors interviewed, General Dwight D. Eisenhower, the head of the Allied forces in Europe identified that the enemy unit responsible was a heavily armoured Waffen SS force known as Kampfgruppe Peiper, led by the charismatic Panzer leader Jochen Peiper.

Moreover, in the heavy fighting to stop and eventually bottle up Peiper's men, nearly a dozen of his force was captured, including some who seemed to have been somewhere near the Malmédy crossroads. Many of these SS men were in Allied hospitals, but some were captured and sent to PoW camps in the United States.

Given the great reaction to the shooting incident as a war crime, orders from the War Department went out to P.O. Box 1142 in December 1945 to help with the high-priority investigation. The idea was to have all the men who had been captured from the Leibstandarte Adolf Hitler in the Ardennes moved quickly to Fort Hunt for interrogation and covert eavesdropping. Several prisoners were immediately available. SS Rottenführer Wilhelm Reichert from the 2nd Battalion, Leibstandarte artillery regiment, had been captured in Stavelot on 24 December 1944, but when interrogated on 8 March 1945 he claimed he knew nothing about the happenings at Malmédy. The same was true of SS Mann Peter Lantschner, who had been with SS Panzer Grenadier Regiment 2 and was taken prisoner the same day; he impressed his interrogators as too dense to yield much information.[6]

Yet the interrogations at P.O. Box 1142 of two Leibstandarte men, Max Ketterer and Georg Blunder, made intelligence men at Fort Hunt eager to speak with more of those from the 1st SS Panzer Regiment. SS Sturmmann Max Ketterer had been captured near Paris on 23 August 1944 after having joined the Waffen SS the preceding April. A former waiter at the Hotel Regina in Munich, during this training near Unna in Westphalia with the SS training regiment Germania, his brutal company commander Untersturmführer Krueger had told him that 'we must learn quickly the fastest ways to kill. The more Americans and English killed, the sooner the war would be over. There were to be no prisoners made.' Ketterer told his cellmate that the training was inhumane, and recruits were beaten for the smallest infractions (two Czech SS recruits committed suicide, he told interrogators) and he was relieved to take the oath as a Waffen SS man on 28 May 1944 and assigned to the Leibstandarte Adolf Hitler. While 'on a drunk' at the end of training, Krueger bragged to the young men with grotesque and gruesome accounts of the fighting in Russia. 'After the SS troops in the Caucasus had taken a few towns, they encountered a procession of several hundred refugees. They shot these people, women, children and old men, down with machine guns, because there was no food for them.' Ketterer then proceeded to relate a series of second-hand tales—orgies of burning, killing and perversion so grotesque and macabre that the interrogators were hesitant to believe him.[7]

The other Leibstandarte man, Georg Blunder, put to surveillance on 20 January 1945, had an unusual story. Having two parents in the United States, he grew up in Chicago before leaving Lane Technical High School to go to Germany in 1938. Speaking English fluently with an American accent, Blunder volunteered for the Waffen SS in 1940 and was sent in October 1940 to Metz to train as an interpreter with the Leibstandarte Adolf Hitler. He was an SS veteran, having been with the Leibstandarte continuously in Greece, then in every other campaign in Russia, Italy and France before becoming a prisoner in the Falaise pocket on 20 August 1944. Given his ability with languages, Blunder was the key English interpreter with the division.

While his interview with U.S. Army interrogators at first seemed less than remarkable, his surveillance in his cell with cellmate Lieutenant Friedrich Doell from 22 to 24 January 1945 raised interest. Blunder bragged about Rudolf von Ribbentropp in his tank regiment, his able superior Rudolf Lehmann as well as Michael Wittmann, the tank ace. 'Dietrich is a great guy!' he blustered. But in further conversations Blunder revealed

393

intimate knowledge of the killings in Russia. 'With the Jews [in Russia] I knew no names … but that whole thing is a mess.' He then described how Sonderkommando 10a followed in the wake of the Leibstandarte in Russia and killed many. He claimed he was not directly involved—'Those guys were dyed in the wool Nazis'—but it was common knowledge that many civilians were being killed. 'There was a Sonderkommando 10a that accompanied the division in Russia. These were the men who committed all the atrocities such as rounding up the Jews, undressing them, killing them and burying them in mass graves.'[8]

Although those interviews gleaned little relative to Malmédy, it was the interrogation of an SS replacement machine gunner with the Leibstandarte engineers that blew the case open. Unlike other young SS men from the Leibstandarte, Heinz Peupelmann had been with the unit since May 1941 and had fought at all fronts. He fought with Peiper at Kiev and had been wounded at Uman before being wounded once more at Kursk and then again at Uman. He was back with the Leibstandarte in Normandy and managed to escape to Lichterfelde after the great retreat in August. Recovering from wounds, he was assigned back to the division before the Ardennes, was given a Sturmgewehr 44 assault rifle in Zülpich and was assigned as part of a thirty-six-man assault troop from the 1st SS Ersatz Battalion. He then participated in the offensive as a replacement. Peupelmann had been taken prisoner near Bastogne on 30 December 1944 and, given the Malmédy incident, was rushed over to the United States weeks later.

When he was brought to P.O. Box 1142 to Room 22B, his interviewers from 26 April 1944 found the 22-year-old native of Niedercunnersdorf worried and scared. Monitoring his personal discussions with his cellmate Unteroffizer Franz Kern, Army intelligence heard Peupelmann relate that although he had never shot any American prisoners, for several months during the war he had been stationed at the Gross-Rosen KZ, run by the Totenkopf Division, where he witnessed horrid things—so terrible that he trembled while trying to relate them to Kern.

But it was Peupelmann's identification of Peiper and his reputation in Russia that eventually piqued the interrogators' attention at Fort Hunt. Although Peupelmann had no contact with Peiper in the Ardennes and knew nothing of Malmédy, he did know Peiper from the fighting in the East. 'SS Obersturmführer Peiper, the commander of the 1st Regiment of the LSSAH in Russia ordered that no prisoners would be taken,' he told his cellmate. 'Rather than transporting them, they would be shot.'[9]

At first the information from Peupelmann and the other Leibstandarte men recuperating in U.S. Army hospitals was lost in the mass of evidence gleaned from P.O. Box 1142. In early January 1945 that was understandable, as Jochen Peiper did not figure prominently on American radar. However, after the bodies of the eighty-four shot American soldiers were recovered from the snowy field at Baugnez mid-month, news of the event soon changed his importance. At some point someone noticed the connection between what Peupelmann declared about Peiper and prisoners in Russia, in addition to the findings of the embryonic Malmédy investigation in Europe.[10] Lieutenant Colonel John S. Vorhees of the U.S. Army ordered that every artifice to aid the Malmédy investigation be undertaken. Although the Supreme Headquarters Allied Expeditionary Forces (SHAEF) head, General Dwight D. Eisenhower, had established CROWCASS (the Central Registry of War Crimes Subjects) in May 1945, the task was how to get those apprehended to confess their deeds.

Meanwhile, on 22 May 1945, Peiper himself was taken prisoner only a few kilometres from his home in Schliersee. However, in the spreading chaos after Hitler's death, Peiper was lost amid the multitudes of German captives in large PoW camps around Nuremberg. Although he was actively sought by the Americans (designated 'GI Enemy No. 1'), Peiper was not identified until 21 August 1945. Found out, he was quickly transferred to the interrogation camp of the US Third Army in Freising. While Peiper seemed eager to talk about the war, it proved impossible to get any information out of him about Malmedy. Realistically, Peiper was fully aware that of his dangerous situation. After all, his former SS mentor, Heinrich Himmler, had swallowed cyanide and ended his life on 23 May 1945, rather than talk after being taken captive by the British.

By autumn the accumulating evidence had convinced the investigators with the 7708th War Crimes Group that perhaps with covert surveillance P.O. Box 1142 might blow open the Malmédy case. Generally most Leibstandarte men they had acquired from camps such as Ebensee in Austria were highly security conscious—even paranoid. Second-hand information indicated that the SS men in captivity were repeating and agreeing upon fabricated stories that absolved Peiper.

How would they break the case and learn what Peiper's men were telling each other in secrecy? The hope was that by locating witnesses to the atrocity, covert surveillance at P.O. Box 1142 might help crack open the investigation of the Malmédy massacre as to who had been responsible for the shootings. At first representatives from P.O. Box 1142 interviewed many SS men in camps at Fort Atterbury in Indiana, Fort Knox in Kentucky and Fort Ord in Colorado to see if they could have been with the units suspected with the Kampfgruppe Peiper.[11] Meanwhile, with the war's end, the operation at P.O. Box 1142 was winding down, although the translation section of the facility was now using former SS men to provide insight into terminology and operations.[12]

Sometimes even likely prospects brought to Alexandria, Virginia—such as SS enlisted man Anton Harsch, a Yugoslavian mechanic with the 12th SS Panzer Grenadier Company—seemed to have only vague recollections. Harsch had been with the Waffen SS since 1943, had been wounded fighting with the 2nd SS Panzer Division in August 1943 and, after rehabilitating at Görlitz, was assigned to SS Panzer Grenadier Regiment 2 in January 1944. He had then transferred to Belgium, where he had trained with other recruits before the fighting in Normandy. Like many others, he escaped with the rabble fleeing France in August and retrained with the Kampfgruppe Peiper in the autumn of 1944. Harsch had been captured in La Gleize, Belgium, on 24 December and was eventually sent to Camp Forrest in Tennessee before being transferred to Fort Hunt in early 1946.

Harsch told interrogators he had passed by the Malmédy crossroads to see some sixty American prisoners standing in a field and some abandoned U.S. Army ambulances nearby. But that was all. His memories of the crossroads were vague—or were they? Those eavesdropping on his conversation with Heinz Kluge, his cellmate also from the Leibstandarte in Room 18A, heard him worry about why they had been brought to Fort Hunt. He was, he confessed, 'too nervous to eat'.

Another Leibstandarte man, SS Rottenführer Ewald Hoffmann with the 1st SS Panzer Reconnaissance Battalion, heard his company chief, SS Obersturmführer Fritz Reuss, talk on 22 December 1944 after they had passed the dead Americans, who had obviously been executed along the path of their advance. 'These dogs,' Reuss scowled, 'rather than taking prisoners, bump all of them off.'[13] Around Christmas 1944 many Belgian locals had been killed in tiny villages around Stavelot, and one of the Leibstandarte men, Helmut Grimberg of 2nd Company, SS Panzer Grenadier Regiment 1, who had been captured in Ardennes, was overheard telling his cellmate Heeke on 14 February 1946 that although he had done nothing, 'we heard orders that civilians should be bumped off'.[14]

However, the group assembled at P.O. Box 1142 included several men who seemed to have been near the crossroads near Malmédy at the time the shootings took place: Helmuth Haas, Heinz Kapperman, Lothar Hartig, Fritz Wesch, Wolfgang Schleif and Willi Braun.

Willi Braun had been a member of Hitler Jugend from 1935 to 1944 and was then incorporated into the Leibstandarte Adolf Hitler on 20 February 1944, before being moved to a position as machine gunner in SS Obersturmführer Heinz Tomhardt's 11th Company of the III Battalion, which was Peiper's old command, at the time under Jupp Diefenthal.

The SS Sturmann had been moved from Fort Ord in Colorado to Room 19 at Fort Hunt. However, his interrogators learned that he had passed the Malmédy crossroads in a halftrack, but, like Harsch, when he passed, the American prisoners there were still alive:

> Between 1100 and 1200 hours, we came out on a highway towards Stavelot. After passing the crossroads and entering the highway I saw at a distance of about 400 metres from this crossroads about 50 American prisoners of war standing in a group to the right of the road. These prisoners were unarmed and were holding their hands on top of their helmets. So far as I can remember, these prisoners were not being watched ... About 450 metres from the crossroads I saw seven or eight American trucks halted at the right side of the road. For reasons unknown to me, the entire company had to halt on this main highway for two or three minutes ... The American PWs I must emphasize especially, were still alive at the time we went by them ... Only later in captivity did I learn that these prisoners of war had been shot.[15]

SS Private Braun produced a detailed sketch of the crossroads for his interrogators, and the details encouraged his interrogators to keep looking.

Helmuth Haas had been part of the 9th SS Panzer Pioneer Company, which had also passed by the crossroads. He had been with the company under Rumpf since June 1944 and had been taken prisoner near Stavelot, Belgium, on 24 December 1944. Haas had been shipped from Fort Knox to Fort Hunt in February 1946, but in making a statement to interrogators, the occupant of 23A was tight-lipped. An earlier interrogation at Fort Knox revealed that after autumn training near Luebecke in Westphalia, Haas's platoon had travelled south on bicycles on about 10 December to Tondorf to rendezvous with the 1st SS Panzer Regiment. As if looking to avoid incrimination, he claimed that while the 1st and 2nd platoons of the 9th Panzer Pioneer Company had halftracks, he and the other member of the 3rd platoon had to ride atop tanks, only to have his particular tank break down. He somehow made his way to Stavelot around 20 December but claimed never to have been around the crossroads.[16] Was Haas lying?

His interrogators seemed to think so, as an interrogation of SS enlisted man Herbert Haeusgen soon contradicted his story. Haeusgen had also been with the 3rd platoon of the 9th Panzer Engineer Company and claimed that before reaching the village of Stavelot on the night of 19 December he recalled 'passing a field located near a road where he saw the bodies of at least 30–40 Americans'. Haeusgen also implicated another man, Otto Burckhardt, who had confided to him of having seen the dead Americans in the field as well. 'This must have been murder,' Haeusgen confessed, 'because there were too many bodies in the field to believe they had been killed in the course of a battle.' Later several Waffen SS witnesses from Kampfgruppe Peiper would place Haas on the scene as well as being an active participant in the shootings, albeit a fortunate one that escaped the trial dragnet.[17]

Lothar Hartig had recently been transferred to P.O. Box 1142 from Camp Forrest in Tennessee. Hartig, held in 21A with Willi Braun and Heinz Kappermann, had also been with the 12th SS Panzer Grenadier Company, but unlike Harsch, who had been in the same unit, had plenty to tell:

> The night from the 16th–17th of December was spent by us on the halftrack. On the morning of the 17th of December we continued to move and reached the asphalt highway which, if my memory serves right, led to Malmédy in the afternoon. Around 1300 to 1400 hours on the same day we reached a road crossing which was blocked by a tank. We were therefore forced to turn off across a meadow before reaching the crossroad in order to reach the main road leading to Saint Vith. To the right of the crossing I saw a burning building and immediately after crossing the meadow, and reaching the main road I saw at approximately at 15 metres distance from the road behind a barbed wire fence approximately 50 to 60 shot American soldiers who were laying [sic] in all directions.

'All of the bodies appeared lifeless', Hartig related. There appeared to be no other German soldiers around, although as they were proceeding down the road towards Ligneuville, 'we saw an additional 10 shot American soldiers laying sporadically along the road'. On the other side of the road Hartig observed a line of abandoned American trucks and jeeps. Shocked by the scene of tangled and twisted American bodies by the road, he and his company did not hesitate and drove along quickly to catch up with the advance elements of Kampfgruppe Peiper.

The next morning Hartig was still with the 12th SS Panzer Grenadier Company when American aircraft attacked it near Cheneux, Belgium, as Peiper thrust his heavily armoured column towards Werbomont and the Meuse River just beyond. Although taking refuge in a house, Hartig was wounded and then evacuated to La Gleize, where Peiper's battle group was eventually surrounded. When Peiper abandoned La Gleize on 24 December, Hartig was made prisoner. Meanwhile, back in their room of 21A, the three SS men—Hartig, Braun and Kappermann—all witnesses to what happened at Malmédy, seemed fully aware of the trouble they might be in and the need to keep quiet. They occupied themselves with endless card playing, discussions of the merits of American food and idle discussions of romantic conquests. Still, at one point one remarked to another, 'We are like prisoners in jail.'[18]

Although Hartig's account had blown the investigation open, of those held, it was SS man Heinz Kappermann who turned out to be the singing bird on Malmédy for the U.S. Army intelligence. Born in 1926 as the son of a farmer, Kappermann was from Blockwinkel, Bremen, having joined the Waffen SS in October 1943. After training with the 2nd SS Engineer Training Battalion near Prague, he was transferred to the Leibstandarte in May 1944 in Belgium. Kappermann then fought with the division until August before escaping the debacle in France. He trained once more with the 1st SS Panzer Regiment in the autumn. He had been a machine gunner with the 9th Panzer Engineer Company under SS Obersturmführer Erich Rumpf during the Ardennes offensive. On 17 December 1944 Kappermann found himself serving as a radio operator in one of the SPWs. He was wounded near Stavelot on 21 December, but not before he passed the fateful Malmédy crossroads on 17 December.

Kappermann was assigned to the penal platoon of the 9th Panzer Engineer Company, knowing of its unsavoury reputation: 'From my experience in the German Army, I know that unpleasant or painful assignments were given almost exclusively to the *Strafgruppen*—or penal squads.' As part of the 1st Squad of the 1st Platoon under SS Untersturmführer Günther Hering, Kappermann claimed it was common knowledge that prisoners would be shot. 'Shortly before we came out on the highway [near Baugnez] with our halftrack, the section leader, Oberscharführer [Rudolf Dörr] Doehr, jumped out of the vehicle to take an American prisoner who came out of a small wood to give himself up ... while we were halted on the highway Doehr appeared at the vehicle and said as he climbed back in, "I went away from the prisoners because I heard that they are all to be shot, and I do not want anything to do with that."' They drove on to Ligeneuville before any shooting took place. However, later, on the night of 18–19 December, Kappermann ran into his comrade from the 2nd squad, machine gunner Fred Till. What about those prisoners at the crossroads? 'The Americans had been shot,' Till told him flatly.[19]

Kappermann not only made a detailed statement to Captain Herman L. Halle of P.O. Box 1142, but on 26 February he also produced a detailed drawing that was soon forwarded, along with his statement, to the investigators of the Malmédy incident with the 7708th War Crimes Group in Wiesbaden, Germany:

> I drove as the radio operator in a halftrack along secondary roads in the fields proceeding from the previous combat action to reach the connecting road with the main highway to Stavelot ... Shortly before the road reached the main highway to Stavelot we had to turn off across a meadow, since our road was blocked by a German tank (see sketch and map). This tank was firing to the north on targets unknown to me. As we turned back into the main road I was able to see out of my radio operator's porthole between 40 and 50 American soldiers standing not far from the crossroads. I estimate that these soldiers here were between 10 and 15 metres from the edge of the road. The prisoners were unarmed, had their helmets on and were holding their hands folded over their helmets. I remember that 7 or 8 German Mark IV and Mark V tanks were proceeding along the highway from Stavelot in front of us ... Followed by the second vehicle of the 1st squad we drove along the highway to Ligneuville and passed about 14–15 American trucks. Almost all of these had their American drivers with them, although they were being guarded by a German soldier. About 700 or 800 metres past the road crossing our two vehicles had to stop since a firefight was in progress in front of us.[20]

The following month two additional Leibstandarte witnesses were brought to P.O. Box 1142, SS enlisted men Fritz Wesch and Wolfgang Schleif. When interviewed, Schleif, previously with the 10th Panzer Grenadier Company, described a scene near Malmédy nearly identical to that of Willi Braun's description. He had seen the mass of prisoners standing there at the crossroads but passed by before the terrible things that came next. However, Fritz Wesch had seen more.

Wesch had been with the 12th SS Panzer Grenadier Company, 2nd platoon, where he rode on an SPW as a 75mm cannon gunner. He corroborated Hartig's story of seeing the American soldiers lifeless in the field at Baugnez. '[I]t must have been around 1500–1600 [hours]. I saw approximately 35 to 40 American soldiers lying on the ground behind a low barbed wire fence. These soldiers had no weapons and I assumed they were dead.'[21] On 25 February 1946 Wesch told interrogators that Peiper, the battle group leader, was up ahead with the Panzer regiment when they came across the massacre scene at Baugnez: 'In this field I saw from 30 to 35 bodies of American soldiers. I had no way of knowing that these soldiers had been murdered. However, the fact that they were all piled up in a disorderly fashion, one on top of another, was evidence to me that these prisoners had been shot.'[22]

By the time nearly a thousand SS men from the Leibstandarte were concentrated near Ludwigsburg, Germany, at Interment Enclosure No. 78 in December 1945, the surveillance of enlisted men from Peiper's command at the top-secret facility at P.O. Box 1142 had largely filtered the puzzle pieces for the case against the Kampfgruppe Peiper. This was all the more important as the U.S. Army prime investigator, Dwight Fanton, worried that the SS men in their custody were fabricating agreed-upon stories in confinement. The push was to pin responsibility on SS Sturmbannführer Werner Poetschke, who had been killed before war's end. Although Peiper was kept in solitary confinement at Zuffenhausen, he somehow got out word to his troop not to talk about the Malmédy incident.[23] Yet regardless of Peiper's instruction from captivity, the combined story from enlisted men such as Peupelmann, Kappermann, Hartig, Wesch and Braun had now affixed a developing case against the Kampfgruppe Peiper.

Although it was a top-secret source and one not revealed to the public, the surveillance at the old facility at Fort Hunt, Virginia, dramatically increased confidence within the U.S. War Department that the Army investigation in Germany essentially had the accusations correct against Peiper's battle group. More specifically, Rumpf's 9th SS Panzer Engineer Company seemed strongly implicated in the shooting.

At Fort Hunt the interrogations of the Malmédy suspects was the last official use of P.O. Box 1142. Soon after the interrogation and surveillance of Fritz Wesch and Wolfgang Schleif was complete, the facilities at Fort Hunt were closed, mothballed and purposefully abandoned. Operatives incinerated sheafs of papers from the MIS-X mission and the many participants were sworn to lifelong secrecy. Declared surplus in November 1946, the Army Corps of Engineers demolished many of the Fort Hunt temporary barracks and buildings. In January 1948 the grounds were ploughed and the expunged property returned to the U.S. National Park Service.

The top-secret mission of P.O. Box 1142 was largely forgotten. With little evidence of its former importance to the duty of investigating the Malmédy massacre, Fort Hunt became a bucolic National Park that few suspect of a secret past. It's reputation today: a popular summer picnic spot south of Washington, D.C.[24]

Epilogue

'History is a set of lies agreed upon.'
—Napoleon

In the summer of 1945 the devastating Second World War in Europe was over at last. Yet, having vanquished the German military, senior officers in the U.S. Army intelligence now longed to interview their enemy. How had Allied forces been so stymied by the enemy in Normandy? And then how had confident Allied generals been so shocked by the enemy power in the Battle of the Bulge? No one could forget how a rampaging armoured advance by an SS battle group under SS Colonel Joachim Peiper had forced the U.S. First Army to hurriedly evacuate its comfortable headquarters lest it be captured. That had happened just before Christmas 1944.

And that same tank-heavy battle group—charging ahead under the moniker Kampfgruppe Peiper—seemed implicated in the shooting of eighty-four surrendered U.S. soldiers. Americans at home, reeling from the grisly images from the liberated concentration and liquidation camps, were outraged. It was as if the ethos of Hitler and National Socialism was somehow manifested at American kitchen tables by the shooting of defenceless American youths at Malmédy.

In the meantime, on 20 August 1945, Jochen Peiper surfaced at Langwasser, a massive PoW enclosure near Nuremberg.[1] Discovered in a routine, but massive collection of index cards from its fifteen thousand prisoners, Peiper was quickly evacuated to Freising, Germany, for interrogation. There they questioned him about the incident near Malmédy, Belgium. Not surprisingly, Allied prosecutors then convening at Nuremberg that summer looked to declare the Waffen SS a criminal organization.

Peiper's first interrogation came from Major Edmund L. King, who submitted a terse preliminary report on Friday, 25 August 1945. The SS colonel provided various details on his career, but King was unimpressed. 'Peiper appears to lie continuously,' he wrote. 'He is very arrogant and tries to give the appearance of a correct professional soldier.' He went on: 'During the winter offensive, Peiper led the spearhead in the Ardennes ... Peiper admits that his unit captured 150 U.S. soldiers near Malmédy who were shot, but denies having given such orders ... He is a typical SS officer and cannot be trusted.'[2]

The interrogations at Freising were exhaustive.[3] Later Peiper would claim that investigator Dwight Fanton had once held him in the interrogation chair for eight hours.[4] During those days, Peiper would compose a long, rambling description of the military operation in the Ardennes. The SS colonel went through one interrogation after another, spending most of 25 and 26 August writing his detailed opus.

Columbia law student Paul C. Guth spoke to Peiper at the end of the month. The two participants' memories of the interrogation could only agree on topics but not on substance. According to Peiper, Guth told him he had a favourable picture of the SS officer as a Panzer leader and fair soldier.[5] Peiper further claimed that Guth told him that although he admired the SS colonel, he would have his head:

> By the means of newspapers and radio your name has become known as the No. 1 war criminal. You are the most hated man in America— G.I. enemy No. 1—and the public demands your head. I am ordered to find out something against you and I have to be successful and I hope you will not envy me about it [sic: hold it against me]. We assume that you are prepared to take full responsibility for your regiment ... I readily believe that you did not issue the order for the massacre. However, how much do you want to bet that I can find three, four or perhaps five soldiers who, due to certain promises, will testify that they themselves heard you give the order! You yourself know how the German people disintegrated after this total collapse.[6]

Guth's memory of their first meeting contrasted sharply. When Peiper was brought to his office for interrogation, he recalled, the prisoner was less than cooperative, while he himself was correct and polite. Guth had more than a year's experience from Columbia law school with this sort of situation. 'I knew he was part of the Malmédy incident,' Guth recalled, 'but my charge was to get information from his position as Himmler's adjutant. I wanted information on the organization of the Waffen SS.' On this topic Peiper was helpful, constantly maintaining that he was 'purely a soldier'. Guth was unimpressed: 'That was the line of all of them.'

As if a mantra, Peiper referred to himself endlessly as a *nur soldat*—'a pure soldier'—and claimed himself responsible for any of Himmler's moral restraint. Given what was being found at the concentration camps, that protestation alone raised eyebrows. Guth said nothing about 'GI-enemy No. 1'—although that moniker might have fit. Meanwhile, Major Dwight Fanton and Lieutenant Binder from the War Crimes Division showed up at the military intelligence interrogation centre at Freising, anxious to see Peiper as well. Fanton interrogated him in lengthy sessions on 25 and 26 August 1945:

> He was a very difficult witness. He understood English perfectly, but insisted on being interrogated in German to allow himself more time for a response. I didn't speak German; but could understand it fairly well. He was fluent in English. He spoke English with an Oxford accent. He was a very personable individual. You could not help but admire him as a person. But on the other side, he was a dedicated Nazi. I interviewed him early on in August of 1945 and then saw him later during the trial. He never changed at all. I saw him on and off over a year. He gave us a lot of valuable information. I don't think he thought it was important. Peiper gave me a great deal of valuable information about the composition of his march column at the scene of the crime. He also verified the identity of certain of his officers and men who had been mentioned by prisoners of war interrogated by the inspector general and supplied information which proved to be useful in apprehending them. He admitted knowledge of the Malmédy massacre and stated that his division commander, Mohnke, had ordered him to investigate this crime which the American government had reported to the German government through Geneva.[7]

Mohnke ordering the investigation of war crimes? The fox was ordering an inquiry into the demise of the chickens. Peiper said his 'investigation proved negative'. Yet this bit of subterfuge stopped nothing. The U.S. Army Historical Section also wanted a piece of the action. A detailed interview came on Friday, 7 September 1945 when Major Kenneth W. Hechler interviewed Peiper about the military aspects of the attack in the Ardennes as part of the U.S. Army beginning its research programme so as to understand just how this major counteroffensive had so stunned the Allies nine months before:

> Oberst Peiper is a very arrogant, typical SS man, thoroughly imbued with the Nazi philosophy. He is very proud of his regiment and division and is inclined to make derogatory remarks about other units ...

As soon as it became apparent that our conversation would be confined to military tactics and not his war crimes he opened up.[8]

During the interview Hechler and his interpreter exchanged remarks to each other regarding Peiper's possible complicity in the Malmédy massacre while agreeing that they were not to ask about that specifically— all the while totally unaware that Peiper understood every word.

The first indication that we had that Colonel Peiper spoke English was on page 8 of the oral interview where, in perfect English, Colonel Peiper says 'I am sorry' when informed that he came within 300 yards of a 3-million-gallon gasoline dump at Spa. This so astounded both the interpreter and myself that we sat with our jaws hanging open for a full half minute ... On several occasions he turned heatedly to the interpreter and corrected his interpretation in perfect English.

Hechler found him 'assertive and belligerent ... an arrogant and archetypal Nazi'.[9]

At about the same time, Karl Wolff, Himmler's former protégé and Peiper's old office superior from 1939 to 1940, was now in prison in England, unaware that microphones were eavesdropping in on his conversations with cellmates. 'Now that Bolshevism is knocking on our door, and we are despised and hated by the whole world, something must be done to set Germany back on its feet.'

We are quite helpless at the moment ... We must wait until the hatred against the SS has died down a bit and they have stopped showing those photographs and films. Public opinion is against us at the moment ... In two or three years all the political prisoners will have been released and we shall go home.[10]

Kurt 'Panzer' Meyer was also in British custody and in big trouble— under investigation for war crimes. As with Wolff, hidden microphones were listening in as he chatted with others in his cell. In mid-February 1945 the SS officer scolded a defeated German army general in captivity with him. 'I wish a lot of the officers here could command my division,' he complained, 'so that they might learn some inkling of self-sacrifice and fanaticism ... They would be deeply and profoundly ashamed.' And on another occasion a few weeks earlier he was praising Adolf Hitler in near messianic terms for inspiring a 'tremendous awakening in the German people'.[11] Meyer freely vented his disdain for his enemies:

If an American Regimental commander realizes an attack is impossible he breaks it off. Englishmen and Germans do the same, but the Russians don't He rushes into the [impossible] attack with his men. Another reason the Russians attack is that they have no soul and nothing else they care for. You can do what you like with them. If it weren't for a dread of Bolshevism, the fight in the west, the whole war would have been over long ago. The fighting in the west is entirely different from that in the east. In the west, it is quite impossible to feel mutual hatred, but you can hate men coming from the remotest steppes.[12]

'It is a pity that our allies are Japan and yours are the Russians,' said Meyer. 'Why don't you join us in fighting the Reds?' That would also become Jochen Peiper's impassioned plea to Major Hal D. McCown, the U.S. officer he captured in the Ardennes.[13] Strangely, agreement with Peiper's perspective would later come from none other than the flamboyant head of the U.S. Third Army, General George S. Patton. And unknown to Peiper, the British were considering just such an attack, calling the Soviets a 'threat to Western civilization'.[14]

Indeed, on 22 May 1945, the British War Office thrust a thick sheaf of papers before the eyes of Winston Churchill. They were 'top secret', and only recently declassified, at the time the entire matter exuded deep intrigue. For, in the last weeks of the war, the British pondered a plan that Peiper might have endorsed: Operation Unthinkable.[15] Unthinkable would have sent the British armies in an attack against the Soviet forces on 1 July 1945, with the intention to quickly draw in the U.S. forces before they could be transferred to the Pacific campaign against the Japanese.

The idea was to evict the Russians from Germany—with the use of at least ten selected reconstituted German divisions. Otherwise it might be possible that the hulking Soviet armies could engulf all of Western Europe. While Himmler's involvement in any such planning remains unclear, his pathetic attempt to contact the Western Allies in the closing days of the war remains classified. Although Operation Unthinkable was not pursued—largely due to the military risks of angering the massive Soviet war machine—it showed that Peiper's Ardennes diatribe to McCown was not without similar consideration by those above him on the other side. Never mind prospects for offensive success, Churchill worried that the Soviets would seize all of Europe—stopped uneasily by the Channel: 'Pray have a study made of how then we would defend our Island.'[16] He would speak of the gravity with the Queen.

In the meantime, Russian Marshal Georgy Zhukov, of whom Patton only had disparaging things to say, was complaining in the summer of

1945 that the U.S. Third Army was slow in disbanding German SS units in Bavaria. When asked, General George S. Patton did not dispute the fact; instead, he negotiated to maintain two SS Panzer divisions to add to his U.S. Third Army. They could be useful, he confided to General Joseph T. McNarney, in preparing to fight the Russians. And who would lead them? Kurt 'Panzer' Meyer, of course. Meyer's offer flabbergasted interrogators:

> Germany fought this war for the preservation of Western culture and civilization. The menace of the East was always appreciated by the Führer and his one object was to save Europe from the menace of Bolshevism ... So seriously do I believe in this menace that I have spoken to the many young SS officers who are in this camp with me. They have all agreed with me that this Eastern danger must be dealt with first ... I am therefore prepared to offer the Allies my services and those of other SS officers in Allied hands, in helping them fight the Japanese. The peoples of the East want to sweep away all of Western culture as we know it, and set up in its place their half-developed animal-like existence...
>
> My proposition is that I be given permission to recruit one SS division of about 23,000 men from amongst the German POWs. This formation will be named the SS Division Europa and it is to be equipped with German weapons and equipment. I will have no difficulty in raising the men for such a unit to take part in the struggle against the East. We will then show you how Germans can fight.[17]

McNarney, the deputy U.S. military governor of Germany, was stunned. 'Why do you care what those goddamned bolshies think?' blustered Patton.

'We're going to have to fight them sooner or later,' Patton replied. 'Why not now while our army is intact and we can kick the Red Army back into Russia?'[18]

McNarney was too shocked to respond. With German help, Patton insisted, they could be in Moscow in thirty days. 'We can do it with my Germans,' he said. 'They hate those red bastards.' Patton, who had a low opinion of the Russians, dug a deeper hole for himself. 'Their officers, with few exceptions,' he added, 'give the appearance of recently civilized Mongolian bandits.'[19] There was swift retribution for such reckless talk: Eisenhower sacked Patton on 2 October 1945.[20]

Then, Peiper's old comrade, Kurt Meyer, was sentenced to death in December 1945. Peiper received his sentence of death by hanging seven months later, on Tuesday, 16 July 1946 in the infamous trial at Dachau.

Peiper (left) shown on one of the muddy streets of Kharkov with SS leader Fritz Witt after capturing the Ukrainian city in a sudden counter-blow from Hausser's SS Panzerkorps. Standing behind Witt is Heinz von Westernhagen. (BA-K)

Peiper shown with his adjutant Otto Dinse interrogating a captured enemy priest during his advance during the winter fighting. (Spezzano; NARA)

Peiper consults with SS leader Georg Bormann from the mount of his SPW during the Kharkov operation. (Author)

Peiper shares a schnapps with his comrade Heinz von Westernhagen during the winter fighting in February 1943. At the time, von Westernhagen was in charge of the assault guns that often supported Peiper's SPW mounted III Battalion. (Westemeier)

Peiper newly commanding the panzer regiment consults with divisional leader Teddi Wisch about the armored advance having just seized a bridge over the Msha River near Federowka, Dec 1943. (Author)

Peiper seen during the tumultuous armored battle of Operation Zitadelle near Kursk, July 1943. (Westemeier)

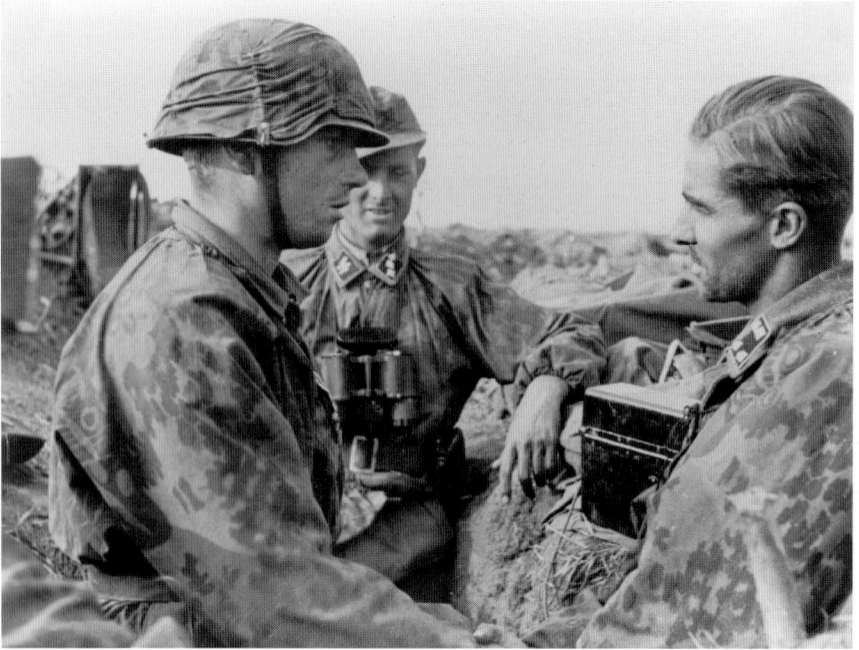

Peiper congratulates an SS grenadier receiving the Iron Cross 2nd class after the heavy fighting before Prochorowka. Peiper's adjutant, Werner Wolff, looks on approvingly. (Westemeier)

SS officers Kurt "Panzer" Meyer (left) and Max Wünsche (right) in summer of 1943. Both men would fight for years with the Leibstandarte before being moved to the 12th SS Hitler Jugend Panzer Division in early 1944. (Kurt Meyer archive)

Reggio Emilia, 9 September 1943. Left to right, SS officers Paul Guhl, Jochen Peiper and Werner Wolff sing their way marching through the Italian town NW of Bologna in early September 1943 as they begin the process of disarming Italian soldiers who had just capitulated. (Author)

Peiper's self-propelled (Grille) artillery shells the hill above Boves on 19 September 1943. (Instituto Storico della Resistenza)

Peiper's self-propelled artillery shells the hills above the tiny town of Boves on 19 September 1943. In second photo, Peiper observes the fire with binoculars while his adjutant, SS. Capt. Otto Dinse looks on. (Instituto Storico della Resistenza)

Dozens of homes in the village of Boves, Italy were burned to the ground on 19 September 1943. The village priest and mayor as well as twenty-one others in the town were executed. (BA-K)

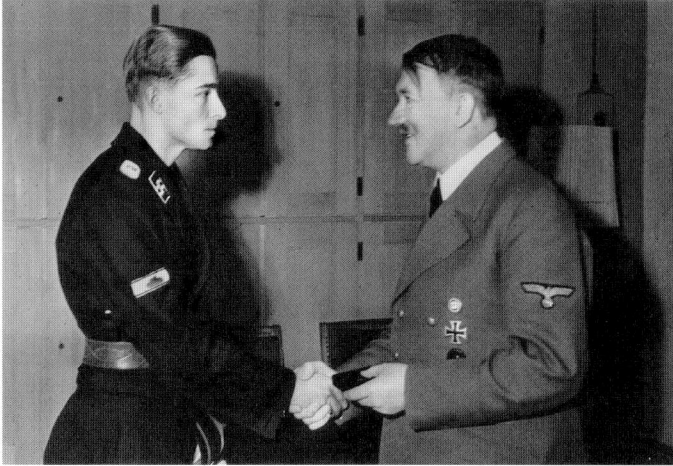

Peiper is received by Adolf Hitler at his Wolfsschanze headquarters in East Prussia on 27 January 1944. Hitler conferred on Peiper the Oaks Leaves to the Knight's Cross. (Hoffmann)

Peiper pictured outside of Wolfsschanze after receiving the Oak Leaves to the Knight's Cross, January 1944. (Hoffmann)

Peiper shown in January 1944 before leaving the Eastern Front (Weingartner)

Peiper congratulating
the tank crew of Tiger
ace Michael Wittmann
on 18 January 1944 after
Wittmann and his crew
had destroyed eighty-eight
enemy armored vehicles.
(Westemeier)

Peiper's portrait taken
after his promotion to SS
Obersturmbannführer
on 30 January 1944.
(Westemeier)

At Hasselt in Belgium in spring 1944 during training exercises for new Leibstandarte recruits, Peiper addresses Obstuf. Albert Frey. (Westemeier)

During training for meeting the invasion during May 1944, Genobst. Heinz Guderian (left) visited the tank regiment of the Leibstandarte at Genk, Belgium. Peiper (center) meets Sepp Dietrich and SS Hstuf. Heinz Kling (right) who was in charge of the Panzer Regiment's II Battalion. (Westemeier)

Peiper and divisional commander Teddi Wisch awards SS Hstuf. Werner Poetschke with the Knight's Cross on 4 June 1944 before moving to Normandy. (Author)

In May 1944, Peiper is shown standing 2nd from left in a briefing with Gen der Panzertgruppe Walter Krüger in which the deployment of tanks to oppose the invasion was discussed. In second image, Sepp Dietrich can be seen speaking with those assembled. (NARA)

German Operation Lüttich counteroffensive: a devastated SPW from the 2nd SS Panzer Division and dead SS panzer grenadier, lost in the fighting near the village of Mortain, August 1944. (BA-K)

The bodies of American soldiers shot down after surrendering are uncovered by graves registration and physician teams of the Inspector General of the U.S. First Army, on 14 January 1945. (NARA)

Peiper pictured during the failed 6 SS Panzer Army *Operation Frühlingser-wachen* offensive in Hungary in February 1945. (Westemeier)

German PWs from Europe are unloaded from an unmarked bus at Ft. Hunt, known as the highly secret P.O. Box 1142 facility in Virginia. Housed in bunkhouses, intelligence operatives eavesdropped on the PW's conversations with particular emphasis to SS men that may have been witnesses to the Malmedy incident; mid–1945. (Mark Churms, U.S. National Park Service)

Members of the *Kampfgruppe Peiper* assembled outside their Dachau quarters and present for the Malmedy Massacre trial in May 1946. Officers are in the left column with Fritz Kraemer and Joseph Diefenthal at the rear of the line. On the front right are enlisted men; in the front missing a leg is SS Sturmann Friedel Kies. Smiling, fifth behind Kies, is Georg Fleps who admitted firing the first shots at the crossroads. Front and center is Valentin Bersin for whom the U.S. Army war crimes investigation was named and considered by Peiper as bravely foolhardy. (NARA)

Peiper is questioned by Lt. Col. Burton Ellis during the Malmedy trial on 22 June 1946. (NARA)

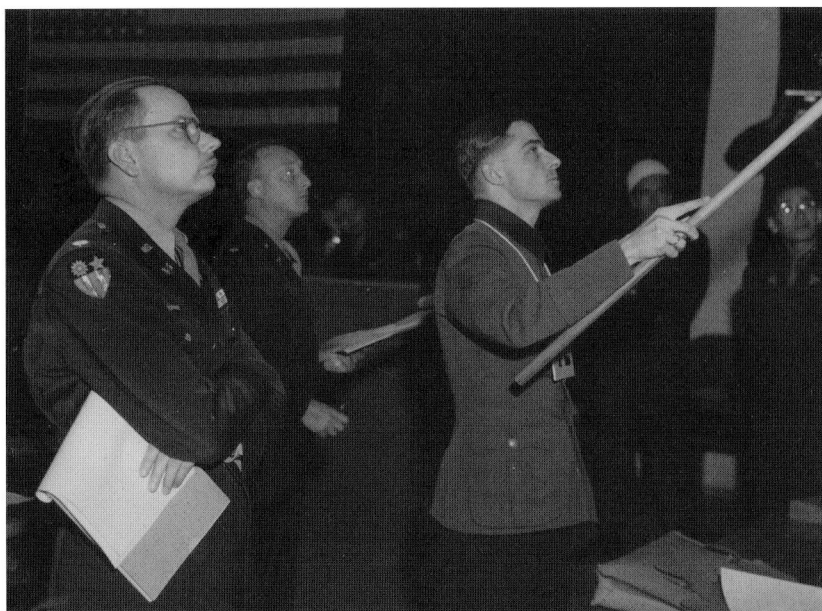

Using a detailed map and wooden pointer, Peiper instructs the audience in the Dachau courtroom about his military operation in the Ardennes while the Malmedy trial prosecutor, Lt. Col. Burton Ellis, looks on. (NARA)

Peiper (right) is shown during the Malmedy trial while SS Gen. Hermann Priess makes a point with Dr. Eugen Leer, their German defense attorney (NARA)

Peiper stands with Col. Willis Everett (center), his U.S. Army defense attorney just before sentencing. On the left is Everett legal assistant Capt. Ben N. Narvid (NARA)

Wearing identification placard No. 42, Jochen Peiper is sentenced to death on July 12, 1946 in the Dachau courtroom as his defense attorney, Willis Everett, looks on. (NARA)

Peiper shown in June 1955. Peiper was being treated for phlebitis at a U.S. Army hospital in Augsburg and had just received visitation from his uncle at Landsberg the week before (Author)

Peiper as he appeared at Landsberg before his release. WCPL is War Crimes Prison Nr. 99 (NARA)

Landsberg Prison as it appeared late 1945 (NARA)

He was guilty, the verdict read, of having led the unit that shot down eighty-four American prisoners on 17 December 1944.[21] The following day a short column of guarded trucks brought Jochen Peiper and the others from Dachau to the big complex of spired prison buildings at Landsberg, the town on the Lech River in south-western Bavaria, Germany, known for its well-preserved medieval town walls with original towers, including the turreted Bayertor gateway. More recently it had been the place where Adolf Hitler had been held prisoner in 1924 and composed his infamous *Mein Kampf*. Now, War Criminal Prison No. 1 would be the stop—perhaps the final one—for SS men found guilty in the ongoing trials.

It was a hot day, and Benoni Junker, one of Peiper's officers, remembered the olive drab Ford trucks broiling in the sun before they were crammed inside for transport:

> On a morning of a bright shining summer day we were driving through the country. We were not in a hurry to reach our point of destination, but the driver, who was separated from us by a green wall of steel, pushed full throttle that the car hunted so fast through the bends in the road that the cargo was thrown again and again against the wall. We were the cargo. A bunch of close together and sweating human beings ... Two guards had machine pistols on their knees. Through the posts I could see the dust-covered country streets. Trees and shrubs had turned field grey from the dust. Where I could see a small piece of the earth, there it was dried and cracked and grey. The sun was shining, but I was only looking through the dust which was billowing up by our vehicle ... Some of the men in the cab behind me were loud and jovial. One told jokes and the others were laughing hysterically in spite of the possibility that we had no ability to move. The sweat was on our faces and we were all hungry. But the laughing sound sounded tinny and unreal. After a while, it became silent in the car and we only heard the sound of the engine. The heat became unbearable and one man threw up. A second and third followed. The ones next to them tried in vain to get away from them. The guards who were seated at the open door watched us [and] looked away in disgust ... It was about 80–90 kilometres per hour on the road. A speed which you will only find very rarely at which you will only pass the dead bodies to a funeral. Because in a certain way our green box was a coffin. A high judge had decreed that we had to be transformed from life to death by hanging.[22]

Like Junker, Jochen Peiper was checked in, measured and weighed: 1.8m, 62kg, blond, blue eyes. His stated occupation: professional soldier.[23] Flash bulbs recorded his stony look. For Peiper, like the other forty-three Malmédy condemned, War Criminal Prison No. 1 looked to be the final stop. Peiper was fatalistic, as seemed appropriate enough. Rudi Lehmann wrote from Landsberg Prison:

> Even though I always have considered myself a favoured child of old Father Mars and had premonitions that the future would hold great plans for me, I did not expect that our last get-together at Simantarneo [the advance in Hungary in March 1945] would have been such a dramatic stage success ... In the meantime, I gained a marvellous distance from all these things.
>
> Now, I look for hours backward through a telescope at the rotating madhouse from my command post searching for the microbe that causes human stupidity. Indeed, after the strenuous escapades of our 1000-year Paladin [Hitler], I had an exceptionally good recovery and have the opinion that my life, that so often hung on a thread, might as well some day dangle from a rope ... There is not much more to be said of my Weltanschauung which has a 27 cubic metre foundation, as one easily runs into danger flirting with thoughts of one's situation.
>
> In this case the difference between obvious deportment and insanity would be very slight ... I was glad to hear a little more about the molten-down circle of old fellow travellers. Even as none [of them] writes anymore and all will have their own problems, my thoughts often are with them in gratitude and with many good wishes for them. When the stormy waves will have calmed down and come to a standstill, one lifts oneself from the bottom and ends up holding in one's hands precious memories, old names and faces.
>
> Somehow, one does not get away from these things ... Hoping to have obligated you to properly compose my obituary, I firmly shake your hand in old friendship.[24]

Peiper would have been hanged at Landsberg with the parade of weekly executions in 1949 were it not for the efforts from his defending attorney, Willis Everett. Alarmed at U.S. Army irregularities in the investigation, he sought to bring attention to the case through a Senate investigation. The long investigation at Capitol Hill featured a withering cross-examination of Burton Ellis and the prosecution by the coarse and demagogic Senator Joseph McCarthy. If completely controversial, the Senate investigation had one undeniable effect: the executions halted at least temporarily at Landsberg's gallows.

As of mid-January 1950 there were only six Malmédy men still in the Red Jackets—which denoted Germans at Landberg that remained under threat of execution.[25] Peiper, one of them, was very aware of the affidavit of Colonel Charles J. Perry entered into the Senate record on 1 June 1949. Although Perry found Peiper clean, neat, with well-combed hair and in physical health, he didn't like him. 'He was a typical Nazi, arrogant, and well educated. He spoke perfect English. He was hostile to Americans.' Perry tried to get Peiper to talk about Skorzeny and then Malmédy, but Peiper was saying nothing about either.

'The war is over,' Peiper said. 'You have won. You interpret the Hague and the Geneva Convention since you are the conquerors.'

Perry seemed a little surprised but let Peiper continue.[26]

> So far as the conditions at crossroads below Malmédy are concerned, I had been with my regiment. I was their regimental commander. I was their father. They came to me with their troubles. One of my boys told me that your air force had destroyed not only his town, but 17 of his close relatives … they were killed by your American bombs. Now, when these boys came face to face with the Americans who destroyed their families, I could not say it was wrong that they shoot.[27]

Perry wondered aloud to Peiper of the German Luftwaffe bombing of civilian targets in England. 'Peiper,' he began, 'what about Coventry?'

'The destruction of Coventry is an infamous British lie.' Peiper said, staring back. 'Nothing like that ever happened.' Perry looked to drop it, but Peiper's hackles were up. 'When my boys who have lost their families are confronted with your American killers, if it is violation they shoot them down, then you can say we violated international law. But had circumstances been otherwise, there would have been no violation.'

In Peiper's mind there was no crime, just the spoils of American juristic righteousness. 'During war, he who has might … is right' went the commonly invoked German saying. But Peiper was still behind bars. He would remain there for six more years, his condemned-to-death status only altered in 1951, with the Malmedy men's defence attorney, Willis Everett, clumsily attempting to take the case to the Supreme Court. Peiper, however, knew Everett had saved his life.

But the real birthday deliverance came from General Thomas T. Handy, in charge of the U.S. European Command, one day after the beginning of Peiper's thirty-sixth year. 'I have decided to commute the death sentence imposed on six war criminals convicted in the Malmédy case to terms of life imprisonment,' he announced on the last day of January 1951. 'The offences are connected with a confused, mobile and desperate combat action.'

> The commutation of the death sentences does not mean that there is any doubt whatsoever that each was guilty of the offences charged. No one who has actually read the record of the trial can question the

fact that 142 unarmed American soldiers who had surrendered were grouped in a field at the Malmédy crossroads and then machine gunned ... The leader of the combat group which perpetrated these crimes was Joachim Peiper. His protagonists represent him as a most forceful, inspiring leader who was the active moving spirit ... Many petitions submitted in his behalf have been based solely on the statement that as a fine officer and soldier, he could not have been guilty of the crimes charged. I am convinced that Peiper was a remarkable leader; that he was the moving spirit of the armoured unit which spearheaded the desperate attempt of the Battle of the Bulge ... I am likewise convinced that Peiper was the motivating spirit of the terror-spreading, killing prisoners of war procedure of his spearhead ... Any unprejudiced observer will be convinced that the killings of prisoners of war which took place in so many different localities could not have taken place without his knowledge and consent ... and without his driving personality behind them.[28]

Even as Handy commuted Peiper's sentence, he also went out of his way to confirm him guilty.

Secretly, however, Handy voiced to his superiors that anything other than a mass trial would not likely have sentenced Peiper to death in the first place. For the evidence produced did not indicate that Peiper had ever actually shot an American prisoner, although he had presided in situations where this took place.[29] Although abominable, Handy said, the nefarious killings under Peiper's command stood in contrast to the 'deliberate' mass murder by Himmler's infidels presiding over the concentration camps—that was the best logic he could bring to an unhappy decision. Even so, by any measure Handy's decision was a clear victory for the Malmédy men. Peiper was still jubilant days later:

My dear Colonel Everett,

We have received a great victory and next to God it is you to whom our blessings flow. In all the long and dark years you have been a beacon flame for the forlorn souls of the Malmédy boys, the voice and the conscience of good America and yours in the present success against the well-known overwhelming odds. May I, therefore Colonel, express the everlasting gratitude of the red-jacket team (retired) as well as of all the families concerned.

Henceforth in Germany, your name will stand for honesty, justice and democracy. Despite the life terms and new distortions of facts, I rest that you read of General Handy's release. We are convinced that the common cause of our nation will overcome the forces of evil in the end. The battle is won and the fight goes on, Colonel!

Hoping to meet you in a not too distant future, I shake your hands beyond time and space. While my jubilant wife, Diefenthal and Junker join me in best wishes, I am and remain very sincerely yours.[30]

At their home on Bergstrasse in Sinzheim, Elke Peiper, Jochen's daughter, arrived home in the fading winter afternoon, her face reddened by the frozen trek. On the curving tree-lined street snow still covered the ground from the storm that came from Baden-Württemburg days before. That Wednesday, the 10-year-old girl found her mother, Sigurd, waiting at the door. She was 'beside herself in excitement.' 'Mutti, what is it?'

'*Papi ist heute begnadigt worden!*' Sigurd called out—'Daddy was pardoned today!'

Elke dropped her school backpack. 'Suddenly, I realized for the first time that he would not be hanged after all and that someday he would come home to us.'[31] After years of doubt and fear, that evening there was quiet celebration.

Someday. If Peiper was no longer under a death sentence, he was still imprisoned, and his prospects of getting out anytime soon didn't look hopeful. Although his sentence was commuted, it was to life imprisonment. Peiper saw his cup as half empty. One spring night he awoke from a disturbing dream in which his old divisional chief of staff, Rudolf Lehmann, was chiding him for not writing back. Peiper knew Lehmann well; indeed, they had the same birthday, born exactly one year apart. Rudi was the 'old man'—he had joined the Leibstandarte in 1933, and it was this long-faced divisional adjutant who Peiper had reported to over the radio throughout his long escapades in Russia. Now, after 'the great collapse', the Heidelberg native told him that those on the outside were now looking at Jochen Peiper as a martyr. Peiper responded acidly in a letter, written in the vernacular of Greek tragedy:

Was it the spring storm or the greasy food? No matter. Last night we two had a familiar conversation. I woke drenched in perspiration with my hair on end and your question in my ear: 'Do you really no longer care?' I hope you will forgive me. The gait of a prisoner is pickled with multiple regulations—which, as you know, I always obey—and one sinks into regimentation and follows the leaders deeper into the swamp. I think that every day one must again fight for inner space and distance oneself from the poisoning miasma everywhere ... Often one no longer draws the sword but merely throws it into the face of the charging masses—silently and without expression. But I don't want to lecture you on prisoner psychology or confinement psychosis. You know it well enough. Rather, I want to describe the importance

413

for us to have a connection to the outside. My latent flirting with the role of a martyr demands new resonance and self-confirmation. Just as the old Savonarola would not have had any fun in the bonfire [of the vanities] without applauding spectators, Homo Landsbergensis feels the same being locked up ... I myself crouch like a Hyronymus [sic] in his shell, keep myself busy with Lao-tsu and my disease and dreamlike cloud mountains created by [the guards'] air-improving cigars.[32]

If Lehmann was attentive, Peiper denounced most of the rest, as he saw himself forgotten. In particular, he was dismayed by his old Waffen SS cohort: 'Has Herr Wünsche made any noises?' he asked with disdain—Wünsche was out scot-free. 'There are quite a number of former friends who lightly drive about the landscape in the Mercedes and do not know they are permitted to write me,' Peiper wrote bitterly. 'There is a whole world between a Mercedes and a writing hand!' He went on to say, 'There is nothing to report about myself. I live as a hermit with my books and with the bacteria which is poisoning my blood. What can one do? Not even the healthiest body can endure such abuse over the long run.'[33]

Kurt Meyer, meanwhile, was held in Canada and then later in Germany, but by 1954 the Cold War was altering American sensibilities in Europe. As Meyer and Peiper had predicted, Soviet Russia had become the big threat to the continent, and the political environment changed with each passing month.

Indeed, on 7 September 1954 Panzermeyer left Werl Prison—exactly ten years to the day from when he was captured in a Belgian chicken coup after the debacle at the end of the Normandy fighting. The British quietly moved Meyer from a small side door to a hotel in town to avoid an unwelcome pre-dawn gathering of SS Kameraden. Yet even that ruse did not work, as he was greeted at the prison gates by his wife, representatives of the German Red Cross and members of HIAG—the welfare organization of former SS men. That a prated SS icon had been released soon blossomed into just what the British were intending to avoid. From the hotel Heinz Trapp, a comrade with the Leibstandarte Adolf Hitler spirited Meyer to the small village of Niederkrüchen and to his family.

Arriving there, Meyer was greeted wildly by scores of SS veterans lining the road with torches while drums pounded welcome. They drove through a triumphal arch customary for festivities in the Rhineland. And there, beyond that gate, stood the only survivor of Meyer's command tank, Albert Andres. He eagerly shook Meyer's hand with his one remaining arm.[34] A big party ensued—there were flowers and a huge

414

cake with the words 'Free at Last'. The Auto-Union factory in Düsseldorf even gave him a red convertible for use in his first weeks of freedom. He would soon oversee the operations of a brewery in Hagen, he told everyone. There were laughs from the audience. But before that, 'the first thing I am going to do,' Meyer announced elatedly, 'is to go on a four-week vacation to Bad Pyrmont.'

* * *

On a warm August day in 1957 Jean-Marie Vico was not too surprised to learn that a German visitor wanted to visit the Abbaye d'Ardenne near Caen. That happened from time to time, as visitors from all over Europe came to see where the terrible events of 7 June 1944 had taken place in Normandy. Still, on this summer day Jean-Marie was thunderstruck to learn that the stocky, well-dressed man at the door was none other than Kurt Meyer.[35] His mother, Francine Vico, was so agitated by the news that she went into hiding and refused to come out. After what they had found in her garden, 'How could he come?' she cried.

With some reluctance, Jean-Marie agreed to see him. The boy who had discovered the Canadian bodies in the garden accompanied Meyer for a walk through the abbey grounds. During the tour Meyer was proper and polite, but Jean-Marie boiled inside at thoughts of the untruths at his trial—the gall of this man! As they walked up the steps into the garden where the eighteen bodies had been found, he could no longer contain himself. 'Look, many years have passed,' Jean-Marie stammered. 'You are a free man. Everyone knows the iron discipline of the SS troops. It is hard to imagine that you would not have known about the execution of the Canadian prisoners.' He looked Meyer in the eyes and spoke of the trial. 'What you said was a lie and you know it well!'[36]

Meyer stared back, unmoved. 'I had learned from a guard at the entrance of the courtyard an execution had taken place,' he explained to Vico. He countered that he had sent the Unterscharführer who had done the shooting of the Canadians to an impossible defensive position north-west of Authie the following day where he had been killed. He told Vico that act had 'done justice' to the situation.

Yet Jean-Marie Vico knew better. He knew the Germans were not defending anywhere near Authie the following day; he knew Unterscharführer Bornhoft, whom he believed Meyer referred to, had, in fact, only been killed much later in the war.[37] He confronted Meyer: 'Why did you lie at your trial?'

Meyer did not look away but instead gazed stonily back at Vico, as if he still held the high ground. 'I could not, for reasons of honour, admit to an enemy court that my men had done such things.'

The meeting was over. 'I would suggest that you tell the truth when you write your memoirs.' Jean-Marie Vico motioned Kurt Meyer to the thick wooden doors at the entrance. Vico was happy to see him go.

Since the final curtain in 1945, veterans of the Waffen SS sought to distance themselves from the atrocities committed in the name of National Socialism. Realistically, could a military force, created in the ideological mould as the elite standard bearer of Nazism, ever succeed in such a venture? When Meyer got around to writing his autobiographic manifesto the following year, unlike the neo-Nazi revisionists, he did not deny that war crimes had taken place nor that the Waffen SS was culpable. But he also did not admit any guilt for the actions at the abbey. He always seemed aware of the sympathies of his audience—he was slick. Indeed, Meyer was wildly popular with old SS men. When he showed up for the 1958 meeting, 15,000 admirers cheered:

> Things happened during the war which were a disgrace to the German nation. The former soldiers of the Waffen SS are man enough to know that there were war crimes and to detest them as such. It would be silly to reject all the events with which we were charged by our former enemies as propaganda inventions ... They obviously made propaganda out of them ... They were the victors, after all, and we had no rights as the losers. But crimes did happen. It is irrelevant to discuss the number of victims; the fact that it happened is incriminating enough ... We must stand united to fight for the freedom of our comrades convicted of war crimes and put an end to the slander. Those in prison cannot defend themselves. Those who lie in countless graves no longer have a voice.[38]

The same year Meyer was released, Peiper was still incarcerated amid continual legal appeals—largely because of this condemnation for the eighty-four Americans shot down by troopers under his command near Malmédy, Belgium, on 17 December 1944.[39] Meyer's long-expressed appeals for sympathy for the Waffen SS in the early years after his release did little for Peiper, who remained at Landsberg.

Ten years after Malmédy, in 1954, there was a flurry of releases—twenty in all—from Landsberg—most of them enlisted men convicted of having shot at Baugnez, including even a number of NCOs and officers.[40] On 16 April Waffen SS old-timer, August Tonk, was released. Tonk, who had never confessed at Schwäbisch Hall, had been something of a leader of the lower ranks of the Malmédy men in Landsberg. Now, rather than a tank, he was soon driving trucks for Deutsche Werft in Hamburg. Even SS officer Erich Rumpf, who had never denied being at the Malmédy crossroads when the shooting happened, was released on the first day of October. Hans Siptrott, who had commanded Panzer No. 731 and was implicated at Baugnez, was released on 30 April 1954. Fleps, who had supposedly fired the first shot at the crossroads, had been released the preceding December.[41] Even Dr Kurt Sickel, who had confessed to ordering the death of a frostbitten American at Petit-Thier at the end of 1945, was released in May 1954.

Despite the continuing media assault on the combined appeals board for those incarcerated at War Criminal Prison No. 1, General W.H. Hoge again denied Peiper's clemency request on 20 December 1954. Peiper's leg was ailing once more and he had been in the hospital for a week when the decision came. It was depressing. Still, Peiper stood by his recent application. The Malmédy massacre, he insisted, was not a deliberate act of 'Nazi hordes running amok' but rather an 'ill-fated occurrence in the heat of battle.'[42]

The clemency reviewer, Brigadier General George W. Gardes, was unmoved. He believed there had been an order to shoot prisoners in December 1944. Nor did Peiper's do-gooder prison record or the respect for its director foster exculpatory favour. 'It is possible that Peiper's guilt may also have stemmed from the desperate situation in which his command became involved and not altogether from criminal intent,' the board acknowledged, for 'testimony at the trial indicates that some prisoners of war taken by Peiper's troops were treated properly.' Then the real reason for denial: 'Peiper has never admitted any wrongdoing nor shown any evidence of repentance ... and he does not suffer any remorse.'[43] Such was true: Peiper was unbowed. Gardes didn't like him, and Peiper returned the sentiment.

Still, there were clear signs from the parole process of the Malmédy group that the prohibition against the men associating with old comrades post-release was failing in spectacular fashion. After leaving Landsberg, August Tonk had been caught with two other Malmédy men in attending the birthday party of Günther Weiss just weeks after being released.[44] And after 30-year-old Max Reider was released on 30 August 1954, he found himself welcomed as something of a hero when he returned to the village of Rott am Inn. The mayor gave him a personal gift of 20 Deutsche Marks, two suits and a basket of flowers. The reason? 'The area of the parolee's home is filled with Nazi sympathizers,' his supervising officer worried.

Intellectual distraction was Peiper's chief weapon. In 1955 he worked in the prison book bindery, where he was able to peruse the expanding library collection.[45] Books were his best friends; he read to pass the time. And he read voraciously. Philosophy dominated his reading list, courtesy of mail from his blind tanker friend, Fritz Kosmehl. So introduced, Peiper was enraptured with the writings of Spanish existentialist José Ortega y Gasset, whom he thought to be 'the clearest thinker of the modern day'. Indeed, there was much with which to identify. One of Gasset's root metaphors saw life as a shipwreck—stressing the human need for action and innovation in order to survive. Fascism and Bolshevism were symptoms of the usurpation of power by the masses, according to Gasset.

> Under fascism, there appears for the first time in Europe a type of man who does not want to give reasons to be right, but simply shows himself resolved to impose his opinions. This is a new thing—the right to not be reasonable … When all these things are lacking there is no culture; there is in the strictest sense of the word, barbarism.

Peiper, the would-be philosopher, now needed glasses for reading, and grey patches gathered on his shaft of bronzed hair, but, he said, 'the most important thing is that my soldier's heart remains young'.[46]

> Some of us were killed in action, and now others turn their backs on their homeland. We old veterans remain here in prison, think back and look inward … On the whole, Time is racing … Really enjoy your children. Sooner than one expects, they change. I can already see it in mine. They are growing up and striving for independence before I have even had the opportunity to be with them … The circle is closing. Don't let your inner richness be choked by the waste gas of the economic miracle.

The silver hairs were on his side. As if orchestrated by a phlegmatic political clock, all the other Malmédy men were leaving Landsberg. On 16 June 1955, Jupp Diefenthal, Peiper's cell neighbour for ten years (who had been at the crossroads with Peiper), was freed. Also paroled was Paul Ochmann, accused of savage shootings in Ligneuville, and two others.[47] That left only Sepp Dietrich, Georg Preuss, Hubert Huber and Jochen Peiper.[48] Diefenthal did not forget those he left behind, specifically calling for spiritual intervention. 'We pray daily to the Lord for help.' He hoped Everett would lay on his magic hands. A sense of frustration crept in.[49]

'For me,' Peiper concluded, 'in a certain sense time has stopped.'

Two weeks later he sent a letter to Franz Reisner, one of his old tank commanders. A veteran of the savage fighting near Tilly-la-Campagne in Normandy ten years before, Reisner had recently written to him in prison. At the moment the world was in amazement and alarm at the German World Cup victory the summer before in 1954. Was West Germany on the rise?

> Normally I am only able to write to my relatives, but in your case I make an exception, by asking for an exemption. Your loyal lines have to be answered and at least an old tank commander from Tilly is not a kind of nobody like a politician or manager. About our now very little Nachkommando [here at Landsberg], let's not tell too much about it—and also not about the political situation.
>
> The truth is a fiction of time as is also the problem of the war criminals which nowadays seems mainly a function of bi-national treaties. Has injustice reached a special point? It causes one a bad conscience—even refuse to even think about it. The former comrades have enough to do for themselves. The Pharisees service our moral questions and for the masses of people who enrich themselves in the Federal Republic, we are a kind of obstacle where our being throws a shadow on the ordinary ongoing life. Lies about our merits on the battlefield now become complaints about our merits on the soccer field. If we would have at least the right song book [any party rather than the NSDAP] in our pockets, Germany's population would have spontaneously asked for our release.
>
> But at the moment, it is more likely that Landsberg will be a garrison town. What bothers me most is that we are more obliged to the general spirit of the time, for the happenings here are only a small problem. That is less difficult than the destiny which has separated me for more than a decade from my duties in my family. This is the only thing which still has some meaning for me. We do have a boy of 13 and two girls of 11 and 15 years. The way my wife brings them through will always remain a warning that one has to swim hard through the muddy water.
>
> I cannot follow your friendly invitation because there is not yet any forecast about the end of my deal here. But I can promise you that also in the future that I will try my best to not bring any disgrace to my anständige old tank commanders—the living and the dead. Farewell and again thank you.[50] Please give greetings to the rest.
>
> In comradeship and more, I am your,
> Jochen Peiper[51]

Peiper closed the letter by telling his comrade that he could not say all he wanted, given the censors. He remained loyal: 'the radio is messed up,' he said, 'but the transmitter here is still on the old frequency'.

For former SS men still held at Landsberg, events remained discouraging, in particular for Dietrich, whose wife was now looking for a divorce as soon as he was released.[52] His release was controversial; indeed, Anthony McAuliffe—the celebrated American hero who responded 'Nuts!' to a German request for surrender at Bastogne during the Battle of the Bulge—was forced to sign his release papers. However, the way in which the U.S. Defense Department handled the affair would lead the famous general to retire from the Army. Under the Bonn Conventions he could no longer reject any recommended parole approved by a unanimous Mixed Clemency Board decision. So constrained, it appeared that McAuliffe himself approved Sepp Dietrich's release.

The State Department said the responsibility rested with McAuliffe. McAuliffe was angry: both he and his predecessor, General Hoge, had already denied Dietrich's release once. Now his hands were tied, and the State Department was simply throwing him to the media dogs as the fall guy; he resigned from the Army within months.[53] The damage done; old Sepp Dietrich, one of Hitler's favourite original street toughs, was free. Here, back in West Germany, was the man who had shaped the Leibstandarte that carried Hitler's name.

On a cloudy Saturday afternoon, 22 October 1955, a big black limousine pulled up in front of the stone prison. A squat burly man emerged from the prison entrance to board the idling car. It was 63-year-old Sepp Dietrich, now released and chauffeured off in style to Ludwigsburg and freedom. There was a spate of complaints by veterans' organizations in the newspapers, and the American member on the Mixed Board clemency review committee was sacked.[54]

There would have been an even greater uproar had they known that Dietrich was released to be whisked off to a private champagne holiday reception. The controversy soon faded, leaving only three Malmédy men still in captivity. Yet, Peiper's appeal miscarried once more that autumn. With the denial coming just before Christmas, Colonel E.C. Moore, the prison director, wrote on his behalf:

> [I]nmate still feels a moral responsibility for the actions of his men, but further feels that his time of incarceration has more than atoned for the responsibility he had ... [He] took the denial of his second application in stride. He stated, 'I am eligible to apply again and will do so immediately.' The general attitude and morale of this inmate is commendable, and it is the Director's personal opinion that he sincerely regrets his aggressiveness which brought on the incident that caused his conviction ... This man is absolutely trustworthy and reliable ... further clemency is recommended.[55]

It was not to be. It was General Anthony C. McAuliffe again, who denied Peiper's succeeding clemency application on 7 April 1955. Next time, at mid-summer, Colonel Moore was even more emphatic: 'It is strongly recommended that a reduction [in his sentence] be made.' Yet again, McAuliffe denied the next request on 19 October 1955. He remembered Peiper and Malmédy—personally. Adroit legal manoeuvring continued on the outside courtesy of Peiper's potential sponsor, Dr Theodor Knapp. Hoping to sway opinion, a telegram arrived on 25 October 1955 from Dr August Hartmann indicating that, effective immediately, he was keeping a furnished room vacant for Peiper in Feurbach. Another communique from Dr Ferdinand Porsche was even more welcoming: 'We will employ Mr. Joachim Peiper upon his release.'

When the acting U.S. Parole Officer, Paul J. Gernert, visited Peiper in Landsberg in the autumn of 1955, 'he displayed bitterness at the same time he wanted to be friendly'. The sour attitude came after Peiper learned that American prisoners were eligible for parole after serving ten years, whereas the limit was changed to fifteen years in the case of German war criminals. 'Doesn't the Federal Republic [of Germany] think it necessary to influence the friendly U.S. Army not to treat German prisoners worse than their own?'[56] There was also the issue of an attorney by the name of Simpson who had expressed an interest in writing the German version of the Malmédy incident. This, Gernert warned, would be trouble, as Peiper was already known 'as a martyr in the Malmédy case'. Knapp, in turn, contacted Simpson and warned him 'under no circumstances to contact the applicant while on parole'.[57]

Aside from Gernert's worries, an investigation into his proposed workplace sponsor, Dr Albert Prinzing, revealed that the managing director of Porsche would be totally unsatisfactory because he was a former SS Hauptsturmführer in Heydrich's *Sicherheitdienst*—his dreaded security service. 'It is requested that he find a new one who is absolutely free from any ties to the Hitler regime or the SS, especially so in view of the subject's personality.'[58] Peiper needed character witnesses.

In November 1955 Anni Brohl wrote a glowing recommendation for Peiper. Brohl had been good friends with Peiper before the war, and since her son Karl-Heinz had been killed in France in May 1940, she and Peiper maintained a steady correspondence. Brohl's sister, Viktoria von Veldheim, knew Peiper even better, having met him at posh balls and other glitzy pre-war Nazi regalia.[59] After the war Brohl also remained a close friend to the Peiper family, helping Sigurd to look after their three children and praising Peiper to prison officials as 'an irreproachable man in character and manner of living'.

But those sorts of endorsements oozed out everywhere from German culture. It was now hard to find anyone who had been a devout National Socialist in Germany, much less those who might have seen war crimes as Genghis Khan's military brilliance. In any case, testimony of high character was hardly convincing to the Mixed Board reviewing the cases; indeed, Peiper was known to the staff at Landsberg as being bitter, arrogant and unrepentant. Even so, not being released for Christmas 1955 was another let-down. Luckily, Fritz Kosmehl, his old blind tank driver, had sent Peiper a book—his favourite diversion:

> Your compassionate gift let me forget the grey presence during the Christmas days. For days I was whisked away from my cell ... Yet, I am becoming largely depressed ... I see in this the overall symptom of the situation in Germany ... Sometimes I suspect that this cart can only get back on the right track after it has turned over completely.[60]

Judged by the victors, Peiper had fallen from the lofty height of fabled SS war hero to *Vorbestrafter*—with a criminal record.

It would be another year—just before Christmas 1956—before he would be released. Putting his best foot forward, he presented himself as Jochen Peiper, 'the pure soldier'. Even so, the former SS colonel derided his homeland's economic miracle even as he entered the work force:

> I am moved by the moral sell-out of Germany, more than by the senseless jogging on the treadmill of one's own slavery. One cannot yet tell if we will survive the catastrophe of 1945. Export index and gross domestic product are hardly decisive for life, but key instead are national dignity and morality. I do not give a rip for a subsistence in which we trade an uncomfortable past for an imaginary future.[61]

But the winds of the Cold War were blowing ever stronger in settling the fate of German war criminals still held. The Soviet Union invaded Hungary in October, with Austria promptly overrun by refugees fleeing Russian tanks. On 17 November Soviet leader General Nikita Khrushchev told Western diplomats, 'We will bury you.' What would be next?

Instead of the hangman's noose, a long crusade by sympathizers, the church and other SS men had left Peiper imprisoned instead for ten years at Landsberg Prison. In the closing days of 1956 Peiper's sentence was at last finally commuted. Orders received from on high, the commanding U.S. officer at War Criminal Prison No. 1, Major Daniel W. Stubbs, signed the paperwork for his pre-Christmas release on the afternoon of 22 December 1956. The event was quiet, low key and without fanfare. Stubbs noted that on strict U.S. Army orders, Peiper's release was secret and not to be made public until Christmas Day—the reaction in the States was certain to be scathing. At the door, Peiper shook hands with, Lt. Deforest Barton, the U.S. Army parole officer at Landsberg. Barton turned him over to Helmut Meng, who would escort him to his new place of work and residence in Stuttgart.

At 1400 hours that Saturday—the second darkest day of the year-Jochen Peiper and Helmut Meng, walked through the big steel-and-glass door from Landsberg. After a decade, Peiper was outside its ancient walls, finally free. Outside it was frigid early winter—5 degrees below freezing, with flurries from the recent snowstorm. Flakes swirled thickly from the sky. Outside the larches lining the walk from the prison gate stood leafless and starkly skeletal in the winter gloom. Treading down frozen *Spöttingerstrasse*, the path leading along the wide Lech River was blanketed in white.

Did Peiper ponder his fate? Porsche Automotive would be his post-release employer. Ironically, it was Dr Ferdinand Porsche who had built some of the Tiger tanks that Hitler's Panzer armies had used for the destructive assault on Europe. Taking a final gaze back at Landsberg, the low grey clouds seemed to float just above the turreted prison. The snow was still streaming down. Reaching the three-story brick train station. Meng and Peiper silently boarded a rail car, bound for Stuttgart.[62]

Inside the train, slowly clattering north, there was time for thought. What would be this new life?

Acknowledgements

Historical research spanning two decades necessarily depends on many institutions and individuals. *Peiper's War* owes a great deal to the many who helped me.

I was greatly assisted by Dr Jens Westemeier, whose PhD dissertation on Peiper at the University of Potsdam towers over supposition and myth. Jens was instrumental in making many contacts and interviews and was always helpful and provided great insight into the veracity of sources. Indeed, we did ten years of research in parallel and developed a friendship over that time. One day, perhaps, we shall write of the hunt itself.

One person to whom I owe an exceptionally heavy debt is my very professional Austrian interpreter, Helmut Thiess. More than a professor with an interest in languages, Helmut became a close friend, only to die tragically in the midst of the long research. Helmut performed a very difficult job in assisting me during three trips to Germany with many interviews as well as the translation of hundreds of pages of key documents relative to my story. I miss his warm wit and wise counsel and like to think he would be proud of what he helped me create.

Neill Thomson, an enthusiast on Jochen Peiper's life, was always gracious in assisting with various documents and matters important to the puzzle. In Holland Mike Smeets was helpful with the many titbits and interviews he has collected over the years. For interpretation for interviews and translation of French documents and correspondence, I am indebted to Angela Ackerman, Fiona Hackett and my daughter, Sarah.

Although the Peiper family has long suffered the curious, Hinrich Peiper was helpful with two interviews and clarification in a long correspondence on a number of points. In the end our relationship matured, largely as both of us came to terms with the realities of his father's past. Such a reckoning is difficult for any son, and I am impressed by his candour at the end of my work. On the other side, Peiper's eldest daughter, Elke, provided a useful, if reluctant, review of the translation of some very important wartime letters. I appreciate her help. Other close friends of the family, Ms Bettina Wieselmann and Dr Uta Müller, provided key insight. Others who knew the Peipers provided additional information, although the author respected their wishes to keep matters confidential. Luckily an author can know what they know.

In Germany Colonel Eckart Klink provided important access to his father's papers containing a voluminous correspondence with Jochen Peiper. The journalist Harvey T. Rowe, formerly with *Quick* magazine, shared documents collected in his own research into the Peiper affair. In Vienna Heinz Stutterecker, who knew Peiper in the 1970s in Stuttgart and Traves, spoke with me about his first-hand conversations with him in those days.

In Belgium I was assisted by Stephan Cazenave with photographic images from April 1944 relative to his own research on the Hitlerjugend Division. Simon Vosters, another historian, assisted with information piecing together the chaotic retreat to the German border in September 1944.

Within my project it became important to carefully evaluate crucial handwritten letters from Peiper to Hedwig Potthast by careful transcription of old script into German and then accurate English translation that considered nuances of period language. Thanks to Ann Shields and Edith and Sarah Ulbert for their layered and diligent attention in this process. Patrick Uschkereit provided similar assistance for other documents.

The hospitality of tiny Boves, Italy, was touching during our extended interviews in the summer of 2002. Thanks to Dr Daniela Silvestrin and particularly Laura Cavallera, our incomparable guide to the Piedmontese region. In Cuneo Michele Calandri, Marco Ruzzi and the Insituto Storico della Resistenza in Cuneo e Provincia were instrumental in helping me reach a balanced perspective regarding the events of 19 September 1943. Also, thanks to a specialist on German war crimes in Italy, who helped greatly with this episode, Carlo Gentile.

At the U.S. National Archives I had much help. Richard Boylan and the late John E. Taylor at the U.S. National Archives have been instrumental in helping me over a decade to wade through the mountain of documents and papers dealing with the Malmédy trial, Peiper and the multitude of records involved. Jim Kelling and Niels Cordes assisted with long hours reviewing microfilm records. Richard Raiber helped with archival sources on Peiper's trip with Himmler to Danzig. Other thanks to Patricia Spayd, an industrious historian in her own right, for her unselfish willingness to help at NARA as well as sharing work in one research trip to Germany. At the U.S. Holocaust Memorial Museum I am indebted to Dr Jürgen Matthäus and also Judith Cohen and Nancy Hartman for their help with documentary and photographic archives revealing more about Himmler and Peiper's travels and motives than I would otherwise have discovered.

Spending many weeks in Washington, I am indebted to the staff at the Tabard Inn—my home away from home. There I always felt welcome each evening after long hours with old documents. Simple acts of kindness combined with the revelry from regulars—wonderful.

Thanks to the late John Toland and his daughter Tamiko for making all of his private papers and taped interviews available to me at both the Franklin D. Roosevelt Library and the Library of Congress. In Hyde Park I was ably assisted by Karen Burtis, and at the Library of Congress I had assistance from Ronald E. Cogan, Jeff Flannery and Bryan Cornell. Linda Wheeler guided me through the NSDAP Hauptarchiv at the Hoover Institution at Stanford University, where we unearthed critical letters that Peiper wrote to Himmler's mistress during wartime; we located the originals at the BA-Koblenz. Thanks also to Nancy Richards at George Washington University for assistance with the important William R. Perl papers.

In the United Kingdom I had the considerable assistance of Vivienne Bales and Bruno Derrick, the other capable staff at the Public Records Office, now the National Archives (TNA) at Kew Gardens. Special thanks to Carl Shilleto for his assistance and friendship. In recent years Lee Richards, with his very helpful ACRE research service, has helped me obtain documents. Also there the late Charles Whiting made a number of documents and letters available to me from his association with Peiper and was kind enough to cover his recollections at his home in York. Similarly, General Michael Reynolds, the late author of his own important account of the Kampfgruppe Peiper, always lent a hand when asked. Stephan Cazenave was helpful with a series of photographs documenting Peiper's time in April 1944 before the invasion in France.

The late John S.D. Eisenhower graciously made available his personal papers at the Eisenhower library as well as agreeing to a pleasurable afternoon interview covering his father's remembrances on the Malmédy episode. At the Eisenhower Library in Abilene, Kansas, James Leyerzapf helped me wade through the collections there.

At the Institut für Zeitgeschite in Munich I was ably assisted by Eva Rimmele and Petra Mörtl. And at the Bundesarchiv-Koblenz I was guided through important personal papers by Gregor Pickro and photographic collections by Frau Ruhl. Similar help was rendered by Dr Günther Montfort and Carina Notzke at the Bundesarchiv-Freiburg and by Dr Heinz-Luger Borgert at the Bundesarchiv Ludwigsburg. In Mallersdor, noted Third Reich scholar Anton Joachimsthaler transcribed handwritten German documents written in the old script and suggested profitable research avenues.

From the side of the trial prosecution, the late Burton Ellis consented to an interview and made all of his personal papers and documents available for the work before his passing. Similarly from the defence, Willis Everett III made material available from his late father's papers.

Of particular note also must be Dr James Weingartner at the University of Southern Illinois, the author of the best single work on the trial: *Crossroads of Death*. Jim always shared from the Everett Papers and other resources to support my own project. Similarly, Dr Richard Breitman at the American University helped locate rare materials from Peiper's involvement in war crimes on the Eastern Front declassified under the Nazi War Crimes Disclosure Act of 1999.

Dr Sönke Neitze at the University of Potsdam was central in suggesting interrogations of SS personalities processed by British intelligence at the National Archives in Kew, which he became of aware of in his own research. Similarly, Dr Felix Römer provided aides for NARA records for 1st SS and 12th SS personnel's covertly taped conversations at Fort Hunt from his own research for his 2012 book, *Kameraden: Die Wehrmacht von innen*. Many thanks for their assistance and entrance to these records, which have been quite revealing.

In Germany many old veterans faced me candidly, even when our views did not match. Although a number of veterans were hesitant to speak, others were forthcoming: Hans Siptrott, Arndt Fischer, Rolf Reiser, Paul Fröhlich, Erhard Gührs, Ralf Tiemann and Manfred Thorn. In particular, Fritz Kosmehl graced me with his insight from his lengthy correspondence and meetings with Peiper after the war. I am also grateful to him for much archival material. The late Werner Ackermann consented to three extensive interviews concerning his experiences in the tank regiment of the Leibstandarte and particularly regarding key insights relative to the Malmédy incident and the post-war cover-up. I also acknowledge several unmentioned who were willing to speak only the condition of anonymity. Appreciation also to the late Hubert Meyer for allowing me access to the otherwise closed HIAG archives at BA-MA Freiburg. These made a pivotal difference in my research. Also, Kurt Meyer Jr allowed me to review his father's archives as well as consenting to an interview.

ACKNOWLEDGEMENTS

I made a special effort to present each side of the story. As such, there is certain to be material in the book that will affront both camps. To this I remain unapologetic; the story of this personality has long suffered from biased coverage. Still, please know that I approached the story with as much objectivity as I could muster and let facts speak for themselves.

Within the project I also benefitted from helpful readers. First and foremost would be Ann Hamilton Shields, who helped review the writing with critical commentary throughout. But more than this, during my last three years of work Ann really became the project research assistant in Germany and contributed hundreds of selfless hours with her husband, Mo. Equally important to *Peiper's War* has been the invaluable assistance of Carol Byrne, particularly bringing thorough research to controversial events near Kharkov in the Ukraine in 1943. Gene Thorp professionally rendered the many maps for the new book—a big undertaking.

I appreciate my literary agent, Katherine Fausset, also with Curtis Brown, who has always helped in a professional and conscientious manner. Given the laggard pace of my research and writing, I appreciate her patience.

Josephine Moore provided careful editing of the early manuscript. At *Frontline Books*, I also appreciate Martin Mace and Lisa Hoosan as well as Paul Middleton, my copy editor.

At home my family endured my years of work with Peiper and the war. Lisa served as my devoted companion for numerous European jaunts dedicated to interviews. My daughter, Sarah, a formidable writer in her own right, cheerily helped with questions of literary judgment. And my son, Wade, distracted me with sport and other facets of history and life. That means a lot.

—Danny S. Parker
Cocoa Beach, August 2019

Notes

Chapter 1: The Goths are Riding Again

1. Heinrich Himmler, 'Und wieder reiten die Goten', SS Leitheft Jg.7/ Nr. 9B, *The Waränger*, p. 2.
2. Richard J. Evans, *The Third Reich in Power* (London: Penguin, 2005), pp. 87–90.
3. The 1 March 1941 visit to Auschwitz and associated itinerary is detailed by Peter Witte, Michael Wildt, Martina Voigt, Dieter Pohl, Peter Klein/Christian, Gerlach, Christoph Dieckmann, and Andrej Angrick, *Der Dienstkalender Heinrich Himmlers 1941/42* (Hamburg: Hans Christians Verlag, 1999), p. 123.
4. B.F. Müllenheim-Rechberg, *Schlachtshiff Bismarck* (Würzburg: Verlagshaus Würzburg GmBh, 2005). The opinion of the German weather forecasters that the winter of 1941–1942 would likely be mild in Europe turned out to be completely erroneous. H. Lejenäs, 'The Severe Weather in Europe 1941–42', *Bulletin of the American Meteorological Society*, 1989.
5. Jens Westemeier, interview with Otto Dinse, 28 May 1994. For Peiper's lifelong impressions of Himmler, see Walter Harzer to Peter Strassner, 31 July 1976, BA-MA, HIAG Archives, B-438, V/320.
6. Volker Riess, *Die Anfänge der Vernichtung 'lebensunwerten Lebens' in den Reichsgauen Danzig-Westpreussen und Wartheland 1939/40* (Berlin, Frankfurt am Main: Peter Lang, 1995), pp. 304–308. Also see Testimony of Jochen Peiper, 8 April 1946, William R. Perl Papers, George Washington Library, Box 6, Folder 6. 'I was present with the RFSS during the gassing of about twenty persons. There, the insane fell asleep without any fighting. The process may have taken ten to twelve minutes.'
7. 'Vernehmung von Col. Joachim Peiper—Interrogation of Joachim Peiper', Landsberg/Lech, 17 April 1947. NA RG-238, M-1019, Roll

52, Frames 185–189. The account of Rudolf Höss contradicts Peiper's contention that he was not privy to conversations of Himmler with his subordinates.

8. 'Structure and Planning in the East', BA-K, Bild R49-0 022, 20 March 1941. Peiper can be seen standing to the rear of the exhibition and looking on as Himmler and the others study a detailed scale model of Himmler's anticipated farming communities. For Himmler's aims that Auschwitz and its surroundings become a model SS community in the East, see Peter Longerich, *Heinrich Himmler* (Oxford: Oxford University Press, 2012), p. 480.

9. 'The assumption of making living space [*Lebensraum*] did not work out, because the number of settlers did not correspond to the capacity of the place. The population fled to the east. I drove through the area where one could not find any people around anywhere.' 'Vernehmung von Col. Joachim Peiper'.

10. Rudolf Höss testimony on 14 May 1946, NARA, RG-238, NO-1210.

11. Peiper to Stephen Sanders in June 1945: 'All the Jews are bad and the Poles are worse … We have just cleansed our society and moved these people into camps and now you let them loose!'

12. Philip W. *Blood, Hitler's Bandit Hunters: The SS and the Nazi Occupation of Europe (Washington, DC: Potomac Books, 2006), p. 40.

13. Rudolf Höss, *Commandant of Auschwitz: The Autobiography of Rudolf Höss* (New York: World Publishing, 1960), p. 205. Höss specifically mentions Peiper, noting that it was Himmler's typical custom to have his adjutant be present for discussions. Richard Breitman isolates the timing of the Höss meeting with Himmler to be 13–15 July 1941: *Architect of Genocide: Himmler and the Final Solution* (New York: A.A. Knopf, 1991), pp. 294–295. Noted scholars Christopher Browning and Jurgen Matthäus make a convincing argument that the decision to develop elimination camps in Poland was an improvisation emerging from the chain of events arising from Operation Barbarossa: *The Origins of the Final Solution* (Lincoln: University of Nebraska Press, 2004), pp. 213–214. According to Höss's contradictory account, experiments at Auschwitz using Zyklon B (a crystalline form of deadly hydrogen cyanide gas) were performed in late summer. More contemporary investigation shows that 575 sick prisoners from the euthanasia centre at Sonnenstein were gassed at Auschwitz in late July (Browning and Matthäus, *Origins of the Final* Solution, p. 357).

14. 'Being a professional soldier with all my heart, I was simply not interested in politics.' Peiper to Modification Board, 5 October 1950, NARA, RG 549, 'War Crimes Cases Tried'.

15. Jochen Peiper's early life is only summarized here. For a complete account, see Danny S. Parker, *Hitler's Warrior* (Cambridge, MA: DaCapo Press, 2014), pp. 3–50.

16. Witness to the shooting near Bromberg: 'Vernehmung von Colonel Joachim Peiper'. For Peiper's description of the event to Ernst Schaefer, see Declaration of Dr Ernst Schäfer to Lloyd M. Rausch, Freising, Germany, 16 August 1945.

17. Parker, *Hitler's Warrior*, pp. 58–59.

18. For the nature of Horst's death, see Parker, *Hitler's Warrior*, pp. 72–73.

19. 'Experiences of Joachim Peiper in the Russian Theater of War, 1941–1945', Landsberg Prison, December 1946 (hereafter 'Peiper: Russian Theater'), as cited in Joseph H. Williams, *Captor-Captive* (Jacksonville, FL: Girtman Press, 1986), pp. 228–236. Peiper prepared the document for Williams while he was commandant of Landsberg Prison.

20. With territories having been annexed by Germany in 1938, the remainder of Czechoslovakia was taken over in May 1939. Under Hitler, Brno was known in German as Brünn.

21. Jochen Peiper, 'Brief Review and Reflections about the Battle in the Russian Theater of Operations,' 7 April 1946. Burton Ellis Papers (hereafter 'Brief Review'). A copy of both the original German hand-written document and an English translation are in the author's possession. This fifty-four-page essay was composed in Schwäbisch Hall while Peiper was awaiting the Malmédy proceedings, perhaps in the hope that such cooperation might help with the eventual courtroom proceedings. The early 1941 expansion of the Leibstandarte was accomplished by adding a fourth battalion—this time the guard battalion from Berlin.

22. The unit's on-paper organization for the invasion of Russia: 'SS Division Leibstandarte SS Adolf Hitler: zum Sonderbefehl vom 12.6.1941', NARA, T-354, R617, F000988-990.

23. Erich Kern, *Der Grosse Rausch* (Zürich: Thomas Verlag, 1948), p. 20. *The Great Frenzy* was written by ex-SS Untersturmführer Erich Kernmayr, alias Kern, an Austrian NSDAP hardcore reporter from Vienna. As an enthusiastic NSDAP and SS member, Kern convinced Gauleiter Josef Buerckel to allow him to pursue his job as a Nazi journalist while operating in field units of the Waffen SS. His served as an SS Rottenführer in Das Reich in early 1941, then in Russia in the summer and autumn of 1941 as a member of the 4th Battalion of the 1st SS Division Leibstandarte SS Adolf Hitler, as described in *Der Grosse Rausch*. Later in the book he lamented the German failure in Russia, arguing that a National Socialist victory would have

brought culture to the uncivilized people there. Kernmayr continued his career as a Waffen SS soldier–journalist serving in 5th SS Wiking as well as the 14th SS and 15th SS Grenadier divisions. After the war Kernmayr was an extreme right-wing editor for *National Zeitung*, press chief of the SS veterans' organization and a prolific author. He remained a zealous anti-Semite and glorifier of Germany under National Socialism. He died in 1991.

24. 'Über die Angehörigen des Stabsquartieres "Heinrich"', NA RG242, T-175, R129, 2655634–35. Peiper was among the staff of thirty who directly attended to Himmler in his mobile headquarters.

25. Ernst Rode, 'The Sphere of Duties of the Command Staff of the RFSS and their Collaboration with OKW and OKH', NARA, RG-338, FMS, MS B-629, 18 July 1947. 'Himmler, who together with Ribbentrop and Lammers, occupied the special train Heinrich had joined up with the Führer HQ at the beginning of the Russian campaign and established himself in a small forest directly north of Grosgarten along the Angerburg–Loetzen road. He called his HQ Field Command Post of the Reich Commander in Chief of the SS. His staff there consisted of only a small part of his personal staff which had remained in Berlin and was limited to one Adjutant [Peiper], who, at the same time was special missions officer in matters of the Waffen SS, one Police Office in matters of the Uniformed Regular Police and Security Police, and his private secretary, who at the same time maintained contact with all other major departments of the SS. Himmler did not have a command staff, nor did he maintain a chief of staff. He had direct control in all matters … During the first months of the war, the RFSS command staff was limited to the task of supervising and organizing the three SS brigades, scheduled to reinforce the military police, and their training for combat against partisans … through experience gained over a long period of time, the Police had come to the realization that specially trained troops were necessary to combat the partisans.'

26. See 'Schematische Nachrichtenskizze der wichtigsten Nachrichten-verbingungen nach vorn und rückwärts des Kdo. Stabes RFSS', *Kriegstagebuch des Kommandostabes Reichsführer SS, Tätigkeitsberichte der 1. und 2. SS-Infanterie-Brigade, der SS Kavallerie Brigade und von Sonderkommands der SS* (Wien: Europa Verlag, 1965), p. xi.

27. 'All officers will have to rid themselves of obsolete ideologies. I know that the necessity for such means waging a war is beyond the comprehension of you generals, but I … insist absolutely that my orders be executed without contradiction. The [Soviet] commissars are the bearers of ideology directly opposed to National Socialism.

Therefore, the commissars will be liquidated ... German soldiers found guilty of breaking international law ... will be excused. Russia has not participated in the Hague convention and has no rights under it.' Hitler's speech to his assembled generals on 30 March 1941, Halder affidavit of 22 November 1945, NCA, vol. 8, pp. 645–646.

28. 'Bericht über den Verlauf der Pripjet-Aktion vom 27.7-11.8. 1941' (p. 219 in original source), as quoted in *Unsere Ehre heisst Treue: Kriegstagebuch des Kommandostabes Reichsführer SS, Tätigkeitsberichte der 1. und 2. SS-Infanterie-Brigade, der SS Kavallerie Brigade und von Sonderkommandos der SS* (Wien: Europa Verlag, 1965), p. viii. See also BDC file of Gustav Lombard, NA A 3343 SSO-275A. Mentioning Lombard specifically, Hermann Fegelein would conclude in a report on 8 August that thus far 'in the Pripet action 10,412 plunderers and civilian soldiers shot'. Their own casualties: four wounded. NA, RG242, T-175, R129, 2655958.

29. Helmut Krausnick and Hans-Heinrich Wilhelm, *Die Truppe des Weltanschauungskrieges:Die Einsatzgruppen der Sicherheitspolizei und SD* (Stuttgart: Deutsches Verlag Anstalt, 1981), p. 540. Dr Otto Bradfisch, commander of Einsatzkommando 8, excused his personal responsibility for mass murder by saying that 'Himmler expressed [and] emphasized that these orders were based on Adolf Hitler's tasks and that a task of Adolf Hitler is a law.' Bradfisch had been present in Minsk in August 1941 when Himmler and Grothmann personally witnessed killings. Bradfisch Testimony, Staatsanwaltschaft München I, 13 June 1958, BA-L, Trial of Karl Wolff, 10a Js 39/60, C-Band, Ludwigsburg.

30. Himmler's comments were in connection to the elimination of the Polish intelligentsia and made to a group of assembled generals in Koblenz in March 1940. Helmut Krausnick, 'Hitler und die Morde in Polen', *Vierteljahrshefte für Zeitgeschichte*, #11, 1963, p. 196.

31. 'They fought to the last drop ... ': Hans Behrend, interview with author, 19 May 1996. 'They had never been a free people. Their politics were based on pressure, and Russian soldiers always fought from under pressure. Behind them were the political officers.' See also James Lucas and Matthew Cooper, *Hitler's Elite: Leibstandarte SS* (London: MacDonald's & Janes, 1975), p. 86. Data on divisional losses in the opening stages of Operation Barbarossa are found in period records: National Archives, *Kriegstagebuch der LSSAH*, July 1941, Microfilm: T-354, Roll 611.

32. An entire book has been devoted to this pivotal decision: R. Stolfi, *Hitler's Panzers East* (Norman: University of Oklahoma Press, 1992).

In a flawed thesis, discounting the Russian ability to carry on the fight from the Urals, Stolfi opines that reinforcing the advance on Moscow would have captured that city by the end of August 1941, leading to the downfall of the Soviet Union by that November. Hitler, in the meantime, was obsessed with the south: 'The Ukraine and then the Volga Basin will one day be the granary for Europe ... The Ukrainian peasant has no notion of duty ... The Russia *Lebensraum* is our India. Like the English, we shall rule this empire with a handful of men.' Norman Cameron and R.H. Stevens, eds., *Hitler's Table Talk: 1941–1944* (London: Weidenfeld & Nicolson, 1953), p. 33.

33. 'The long activity under conditions well known to you,' Peiper complained in a letter explaining his decision to leave to Himmler's mistress. Letter Jochen Peiper to Hedwig Potthast, 23 September 1941. BA-K, Nachlass Heinrich Himmler, Bestand Nr. 1126, Folder 39. Thanks to Katrin Himmler for helping to locate the originals at Koblenz and assisting with the transcriptions. Peiper had been in Berlin just prior to this time; the last date we are certain he was with Himmler at Hochwald prior to his return home was 24 July 1941, when he was in a conference with Himmler until near midnight. The birth of Hinrich Peiper on 14 April 1942 would indicate that Peiper's son must have been conceived in late July 1941. Patrick Agte (*Michael Wittmann and the Tiger Commanders of the Leibstandarte* [Winnipeg: J.J. Fedorowicz, 1996], p. 46) interviewed Werner Grothmann on 23 June 1995, and Grothmann told him Peiper left Himmler for Russia from a Berlin airfield in early August. Peiper's initial tenure with the divisional staff of the Leibstandarte in Russia is less certain, but a letter to Grothmann dated 4 August (NA RG 22, T-175, R 112, Frame 2636816) tells his replacement that 'I am in the field.' It is likely that Peiper left for Russia at the same time Himmler returned to East Prussia—5 August 1941. (Source: Peter Witte, Michael Wildt, Martina Voigt, Dieter Pohl, Peter Klein, Christian Gerlach, Christian Dieckmann, and Andrej Angrick, eds., *Himmler Dienstkalender* [Hamburg: Christians Verlag, 1999], pp. 188–190.)

34. In July 1933 Wünsche had joined the SS and in 1935 graduated from SS Junkerschule at Bad Tölz (Peiper had trained at the SS school at Braunschweig) as an SS Untersturmführer. Afterwards Wünsche was assigned to the Leibstandarte Adolf Hitler as a platoon leader. In October 1938 Wünsche had been posted as an orderly officer for Hitler. In that role Wünsche joined the Führerbegleitkommando, providing personal security for Hitler in Poland. By January 1940 he was again posted to the Leibstandarte, leading a platoon in a

436

motorcycle company under the command of Kurt Meyer during the Battle for France. In December 1940 he became an adjutant to the head of the Leibstandarte, Sepp Dietrich, where he remained for the invasion of the Balkans in spring 1941 and the invasion of the Soviet Union in the summer of 1941.

35. Photo of Peiper in steel helmet near Cherson on 19 August 1941. Jens Westemeier, *Himmler's Krieger: Joachim Peiper Waffen SS und Kriegsverbrechen* (PhD dissertation, University of Potsdam, 2009), p. 296.

36. For Peiper's command in Cherson see Rudolf Lehmann and Ralf Tiemann, *Die Leibstandarte* (Osnabrück: Munin Verlag, 1983), vol. II, p. 83. For Kurt Meyer's description of the action, see Kurt Meyer, *Grenadiers* (Munich: Schild Verlag, 1957), p. 104; and James Weingartner's objective account: *Hitler's Guard: The Story of the Leibstandarte SS Adolf Hitler, 1933–1945* (Nashville, TN: Battery Press, 1989), pp. 69–70. Combat actions are described in the divisional record: 'Bericht über den Einsatz der LSSAH vom 8.8–22.9.41', NA T-354, R213, F860-876. During this time the LSSAH destroyed ninety-two enemy tanks and captured 10,668 Russian officers and men.

37. 'Der Schnelle', or the 'Fast'. Meyer developed a reputation for speed during the opening month of Barbarossa.

38. It is interesting to note that beginning in September 1941, after leaving Himmler's services, Peiper received a secret payment (*geheimszahlung*) of 366 Reichsmarks from the Waffen SS central office that was paid twice a year—the equivalent of another complete monthly salary. This can be seen in Peiper's Berlin Document Centre (BDC) file, NA, RG-242, A3343-SSO-368A. Exactly what this was for is unknown, but it could have been to supplement his soldier's salary after leaving Himmler's side.

39. Jochen Peiper, Letter to Hedwig Potthast, 23 September 1941, NSDAP Hauptarchiv, Himmler Collection, Microfilm Roll No. 99, Hoover Institution, Stanford University. Originals can be found in Nachlass Heinrich Himmler, Bestand N-1126, Folder 39, BA-K. In the letter 'Somebody' clearly refers to Himmler. The heavy pressure Peiper says he endured during his three years as head of the SS likely refers to the conundrum brought about by the death of his brother, Horst, earlier that summer likely due to intimidation (or worse) from Theodor Eicke, Himmler's head of the concentration camps, now the head of the Totenkopf Division for which Horst Peiper was assigned. However, the letter seems to indicate that Peiper expects the war in Russia to be over soon, and if he survives, he will place himself 'unconditionally available' once more to Himmler's office, just as

he'd done after the campaign in France. However, the letter itself also seems to have considerable romantic overtones, and I reproduce it here for German readers to make their own interpretation:

Mein liebes Häschen! Hatte immer gehofft, Du würdest mir einmal einen kurzen Gruß in unsere trostlosen Steppe schicken. Leider scheinst Du mich ganz vergessen zu haben. Bei uns Sehnsucht. Ich bin glücklich diesen für unser Volk so notwendigen Krieg mitmachen zu dürfen und froh Euch geborgen zu Hause.

Ich fühle immer wieder wie gut es mir tut noch einmal herausgekommen zu sein Ich bin nicht. Die lange Tätigkeit unter den Dir hinlänglich bekannten Verhältnissen hatte in mir einen ungeheuren Druck angestaut, welcher einmal nach einem Ventil und auch einen zeitlichen Abstand verlangte.—Trotzdem merke ich schon heute, daß man nicht mehr von dem Stall loskommt in welchem man drei Jahre lang die Nüstern gebläht und die Ohren gespitzt hat.

Sollte ich meinen Pelz unversehrt nach Hause bringen, was hier übrigens garnicht so einfach ist, stehe ich bedingungslos wie immer zur Verfügung.

Dir wünsche ich für heute wie immer alles Gute, bitte Dich den Jemand von mir sehr herzlich zu grüßen und bin.

—Dein getreues Brüderlein.

40. Witte et al., *Der Dienstkalender Heinrich Himmlers 1941/42*, Himmler's day calendar, 17 September 1941, p. 213. The entry could be in Peiper's writing, although even with close examination this remains speculative, particularly when comparing it to the handwriting of the Potthast letter above. Comparing handwriting samples, I believe it is not Peiper's handwriting. Original document copy from Moscow Archives, USHMM Archives, Himmler Itineraries: 1997.A.0328. Himmler's complex of buildings and train station was also often referred to as Hegewald, a code name that was officially instituted on 15 July 1942. NA RG242, T-175, R129, F265574.

41. German Police Decodes, 11 October 1941, PRO file HW 1.1/135. See also HW 16/6, Pt. 1, Kew, London.

42. Jürgen Matthäus, 'Controlled Escalation: Himmler's Men in the Summer of 1941 and the Holocaust in Occupied Soviet Territories', *Holocaust and Genocide Studies* 21, No. 2 (Autumn 2007), p. 219.

43. Martin Cüppers, *Wegbereiter der Shoah: Die Kommandostab Reichsführer SS und die Judenvernichtung 1939–1945* (Darmstadt: Wissenschaftliche Buchgesellschaft, 2005), pp. 179–180. Sator left the Waffen SS in 1942, moving to the police in Wilhelmshaven and Bremen. After the war he went back to his birthplace of Würzburg, where he retired as the prosperous owner of a printing house.

44. In considering various sources, Oxford scholar Alan Bullock set the number at 14.5 million dead as a result of Stalin's 'dekulakization famine'. Of these, some 5 million died within the Ukraine itself—a figure approaching one-quarter of the rural population. Alan Bullock, *Hitler and Stalin* (New York: Knopf, 1992), pp. 269–277; also, more recently, Timothy Snyder, *Bloodlands: Europe Between Hitler and Stalin* (New York: Basic Books, 2010). The relevance of the number is underscored by an estimate from Robert Conquest that noted that the peasant deaths in the Ukraine during this time was higher than the total deaths for all countries in the First World War. Robert Conquest, *Harvest of Sorrow* (London: Oxford University Press, 1986), ch. 16.
45. Kern, *Der Grosse Rausch*, pp. 74–77.
46. See Richard Overy, *Russia's War* (London: Putnam, 1997), pp. 82–83.
47. See Norman Rich, *Hitler's War Aims* (New York: W.W. Norton & Co., 1974), pp. 373–375.
48. 'Ideas Concerning the Treatment of Peoples of Alien Races in the East', RFSS, Special Train, 20 May 1940, NA RG 338, Box 4, 'English Summaries and Translations Relating to War Crimes: Communications File', 290/59/18/2-5.
    Himmler wrote,

    > only if we dissolve this purée of nationalities of 15 million people, shall we be able to carry out the racial sifting which must be the basis of our intentions to fish out of this purée the racially valuable to take them to Germany to assimilate them there … I imagine in 4 or 5 years, the meaning of the word Kaschub, for instance, must become unfamiliar to everyone, because a Kaschub nationality will cease to exist. I hope the conception of the Jews will be completely obliterated by the possibility of an extensive emigration of Jews to Africa or to another colony. It must also be possible to completely obliterate the racial conceptions of Ukrainians.

    Both Hitler and Himmler considered the document sensitive: 'The Führer read over the eight pages and found them to be very good and appropriate … but it is never to be mentioned either in the form of an extract or of a reference.'
49. Himmler to Koch, see Eberhard Taubert, *Die Deutsche Ostpolitik*, p. 12, as cited by Alexander Dallin, *German Rule in Russia, 1941–45: A Study of Occupation Policies* (London: Macmillian, 1957), p. 127.
50. Ihor Kamenetsky, *Hitler's Occupation of Ukraine, 1941–1944: A Study of Totalitarian Imperialism* (Milwaukee: Marquette University Press,

1956), p. 35. For details of Koch's disastrous policy in the Ukraine, see Norman Rich, *Hitler's War Aims* (New York: W.W. Norton & Co., 1974), pp. 372–282.

51. For Koch's extremism and SS complaints, see 'The Trial of German Major War Criminals: Proceedings of the International Miltary Tribunal (IMT) sitting at Nuremberg, Germany', October 1946, vol. 25, pp. 331–342; ND 294-PS. See also Heinz Höhne, *The Order of the Death's Head: The Story of Hitler's SS* (London: Penguin Books, 2001), pp. 418–419. Koch was a 'monumentally stupid' and venal ruler who tooled about the Ukraine in a horse-drawn carriage while swaggering a riding crop—a petty emperor. So did he turn the Russians against Hitler? A widely told German joke of the time recounted that 'Stalin, in awarding a medal for supreme service to the Soviet state, regretted that the man who deserved it most [Koch] was not yet in a position to receive it personally.'

52. For Hermann Göring's disparaging assessment of the Ukrainians to Hans Herwarth von Bittenfeld, Germany and the Occupation of Russia, see Dallin, *German Rule in Russia*, p. 123. Herwarth was a specialist for Russian affairs at the German foreign office.

53. Peiper, 'Brief Review'.

54. For 'slaughtered like beasts ...': Lehmann and Tiemann, *Die Leibstandarte*, vol. II, p. 15. According to a dozen survivors of the massacre, the victims were taken to the field just off the main road to Klewan, forced to undress and relieved of all valuables as well of most of their clothing. The prisoners were then fired upon by machine guns and automatic weapons. A few managed to escape, fleeing to the nearby forest. Were the Soviets not taking any prisoners? Fernschreiben vom 8. Juli 1941 an A.O.K. 6 (Armeeoberkommando): 'Nach Meldung des III.A.K. (Army Corps) sind am 30. Juni 150 deutsche Soldaten der 25. I.D.Mot. in russischer Gefangenschaft ermordet worden. Weitere Meldungen Liège n in zwei anderen Fällen vor. Berichte werden nachgereicht.' Panzergruppe 1, Ic, BA-MA, Tagesmeldungen des A.O. K. 6, 15623/14. See also Erwin Boehm, *Geschichte der 25. Division* (Kameradenhilfswerk: Stuttgart, 1983).

55. Meyer, *Grenadiers*, pp. 75–76. The excerpt here is translated from the original German.

Although Sepp Dietrich supposedly forbade retribution after the Russian atrocities at Olyka, SS Kriegsberichter Paul Augustin, following in the wake of the advance of the Leibstandarte in July of 1941, recorded scenes of a seemingly pitiless advance in the Ukraine with racial overtones. In later frames in his photographic sequence (see photo insert) he documented Albert Frey's 11th Company moving through the forests north of Miropol on 9 July capturing many of the enemy, with images chosen to emphasize the primitive appearance of Soviet soldiery. In particular, one photograph shows houses being burned and a soldiers or local fleeing under machine gun fire in the woods along the road between Miropol and Chervoni Khatki. The source is NARA: RG 242-JRP-Box 1, Von Ribbentrop Collection of Photographs by SS Photographers: Paul Augustin. Locations verified by Rudolf Lehmann, *Leibstandarte im Bild*, Munin-Verlag, 1983, p. 124 as well as the signs photographed by Augustin, but understandably never reproduced.

56. In an ironic twist, in 1899 Russia's Czar Nicholas II had instigated the Hague conferences, which led to the Geneva Convention. Yet Nicholas was executed after the Bolshevik Revolution, and Soviet Russia never ratified the agreement on the laws of war.

57. Erich Kern (alias Erich Kernmayr), *The Dance of Death* (London: Collins, 1951), previously published in German as *Der Grosse Rausch*. As this incident constituted a potential blemish on the Leibstandarte record during the war, Rudolf Lehmann, the unit historian, made a concerted effort to discount the story. His repudiation was based primarily on the lack of Bundesarchiv records of the executions or orders to perform them. Yet Erich Kernmayr was hardly an SS detractor. He had assisted Otto Skorzeny in Budapest after his stint with the Leibstandarte and later worked as an informant to the U.S. Counterintelligence Corps operating out of Salzburg—all with the intent to pass on intelligence information to help usurp Soviet influence in post-1945 Austria. See Richard Breitman, N.J.W. Goda, T. Naftali and R. Wolfe, *U.S. Intelligence and the Nazis* (Cambridge, MA: Cambridge University Press, 2005), p. 276. Hardly a Nazi turncoat after the war, Kernmayer became a leading post-war pro-Nazi propagandist for the right-wing monthly *Nation Europa*. Wellington Long, *The New Nazis of Germany* (Philadelphia: Chilton Books, 1968). Most importantly, in the letter to Hubert Meyer, 10 May 1979, Lehmann discussed the supposed shooting of four thousand Russians by members of IV Battalion (Anhalt) in August 1941. 'I have made no progress with Kernmayer in changing his mind,' Lehmann advised Meyer, 'and he said that he stood next to where the shooting of 4,000 took place.' BA-MA, RS7/ v.509.

58. For records of the atrocity at Greigowo, see 'Nikolajew, den 19.August 1941: OKW: "Kriegsverbrechen der russischen Wehrmacht 1941"', NA RG-242, T-77, Roll 1492, F080-086. The report of Dr Heinrich

Schaffert of the 16th Panzer Division shows that the actual number murdered on 15 August was forty-one soldiers, including one Hungarian. The executed German soldiers were unarmed when discovered, with many killed in a circle. 'The majority of the bodies had shattered faces and heads. They had been beaten with heavy sharp-edged instruments … Many had broken arms. Apparently, the victims raised their arms in front of their heads against the blows … some showed signs of shooting from a short distance … Pay books and dog tags were strewn about. Most were from the II Battalion of Infantry Regiment 79 … They were butchered in a beastly manner.'

59. Heinz von Westernhagen to family, 26 August 1941. Westernhagen was at the time in an assault gun battalion of the Leibstandarte. Dörte von Westernhagen, *Die Kinder der Täter* (Munich: Deutscher Taschenbuch Verlag, 1991), p. 43.

60. Nuremberg statement of Erwin Bingel, NO-5301, as cited by Breitman, *Architect of Genocide*, p. 174.

61. Jochen Peiper, 'Kommentar zum Buch Massacre at Malmédy von Charles Whiting', September 1971, translated by Helmut Thiess, comments on p. 26, manuscript courtesy of James Weingartner.

62. Affidavit of Theodor Wisch, 13 November 1947, National Archives, RG 549, Entry 143, War Crimes Cases Tried," Malmedy, United States vs. Valentin Bersin et al., Case 6-24, (Hereafter RG-549, Case 6-24), Box 15.

63. *The Trial of German Major War Criminals: Proceedings of the International Military Tribunal at Nuremburg* (London, Germany: HMSO, 1946–1951), vol. VII, p. 59. Hitler's orders against the partisans were signed by Keitel and dated 16 December 1942.

64. Max Wünsche to Charles Messenger, 19 February 1986. Cited in Charles Messenger, *Hitler's Gladiator: The Life and Wars of Panzer Army Commander Sepp Dietrich* (London: Brassey's, 1988), p. 101.

65. Alexander Werth, *Russia at War* (New York: Carroll & Graf, 1964), p. 717. A semi-official Russian history of the partisans claims that the insurgents killed some five hundred thousand Germans during the war, including forty-seven generals and Hitler's high commissioner, Wilhelm Kube, who had a partisan time bomb placed under his bed by his beautiful Belorussian girlfriend. German soldiers always lived in fear of this frustrating enemy. At least a million of the Russian partisans were killed—many hanged after brutal torture—during the German punitive expeditions against them. Many more villagers are thought to have been put to death in their

supposed collaboration with them. See also John A. Armstrong, ed., *Soviet Partisans in World War II* (Madison: University of Wisconsin, 1964).

66. Testimony of Joachim Peiper to State Prosecutor Filipiak, 1 Js 12/65 (RSHA)-E16, 19 January 1967, Stuttgart.

67. With typical efficiency, German authorities conducted detailed autopsies and inquiries into the incident. See 'Dietrich to Himmler', 3 April 1942, NA, T-175, R108, F2631518-25.

68. Erich von Manstein, *Lost Victories* (London: Methuen, 1958), p. 180. Von Manstein mentions that on 28 June his command came across three wounded officers and thirty men who had been overrun the previous day in a field hospital. All had been killed and mutilated after being captured (p. 45). For the report from Heeresgruppe Süd, see 'Erstmeldungen der unterstellten Truppen: Panzergruppe I, Ia/Ic', NA, T-313, R10, F7236715.

69. 'OKW: 'Kriegsverbrechen der russichen Wehrmacht 1941', NA RG-242, T-77, Roll 1493, F002-0177.

70. 'Notes on German Atrocities: Interrogation of Generalmajor Walter Brüns', DIC (MIS)/CI-24, 24 April 1945, NA RG 407, 270/52/19 3–4, Box 2620A. Brüns had approached an SS official named Altemeyer to complain of his removal of all the skilled Jewish workers he was employing in his bridge-building assignments. Altemeyer informed him that he was acting on a *Führerbefehl* (Hitler order) that he was to execute all Jewish women and children around Riga and deport all Jewish males to an undisclosed location. During this time Brüns witnessed the executions, which he then reported to higher army headquarters—a fact that later resulted in his temporary dismissal from command. During the months of November and December 1941 Einsatzgruppe A reported 27,800 Jews liquidated near Riga.

71. Omar Bartov, *The Eastern Front 1941–1945: German Troops and the Barbarisation of Warfare* (London: Oxford/Macmillan, 1986).

72. Gerald Reitlinger, *The SS: The Alibi of a Nation* (London: Heinemann, 1956), p. 185. For Waffen SS personnel in the Einsatzgruppen, see George H. Stein, *The Waffen SS* (Ithaca, NY: Cornell University Press, 1966), pp. 263–264; and Höhne, *The Order of the Death's Head*, p. 358. More recently there is also Andrej Angrick, *Besatzungspolitik und Massenmord: Die Einsatzgruppe D in der südlichen Sowjetunion 1941–1943* (Hamburger Edition, 2003).

73. For the pogroms at Cherson and Nikolayjew, see Nuremberg Documents, NO-3148 and 3406. For the January 1942 report, NO-3258: 'The operational areas of the commandos, particularly in the smaller

villages were purged of Jews ... Sum total: 79,276.' For Himmler's 4 October visit to Cherson and Nikolayjew and his inspection of Police Battalion 311: 'Programm für die Reise des Reichsführer SS vom 30 Sept. bis 5.Oktober 1941,' NA, RG 242, R 112, 2637715-17. See also Ohlendorf's testimony from 3 January 1946, IMT, vol. 4, p. 318. There Himmler also met Otto Ohlendorf, in charge of Einsatzgruppe D, and Sturmbannführer Paul Zapp, who was the commander of Einsatzkommando 11a. Together they had recently liquidated more than eight thousand Jews in the region in a series of brutal mass shootings. For background on the Leibstandarte involvement, see Westemeier, *Himmlers Krieger*, p. 203.

74. Peiper's war correspondent friend, Hans Schwarz van Berk, characterized Himmler as seeking to develop loyalty in the SS through shared guilt. '[He] was the creator of the *Verbrechenspaket* which implicated all in mutual guilt; police commissars sent to Poland to kill Jews, doctors sent to KZs to experiment on prisoners.' Hans Schwarz van Berk, 15 November 1963, IfZ 1846, Akt. 3835/67.

75. USHMM, Himmler Photo Albums, Photograph 60466: Himmler speaks with Wolff while walking along an unpaved road with Peiper in the background. The photograph was taken by Franz Friedrich Bauer on Himmler's birthday, likely in East Prussia at Hochwald. Peiper is seen in the background just over Himmler's left shoulder. The photo mounting by Bauer is clearly dated 7 October 1941.

76. 'He gave all his attention to the Waffen SS, in whose conduct in battle he continuously tried to intervene.' Ernst Rode, 'The Sphere of Duties of the Command Staff of the RFSS and their Collaboration with OKW and OKH,' NARA, RG-338, FMS, MS B-629, 18 July 1947.

77. Höhne, *The Order of the Death's Head*, p. 361.

78. Felix Kersten, *The Kersten Memoirs: 1940–1945* (New York: Howard Fertig Publishers, 1994), 11 November 1941. Although the *Kersten Memoirs* need to be taken critically on controversial subjects, I believe that many facets recounted square well with Himmler's sensibilities from other sources. Although the original Swedish diaries are not available, I posit that many entries reflect the time and place where Kersen wrote of his encounters rather than the specific dates and places. Werner Grothmann commenting on his superior: 'Heinrich Himmler cannot ask of history that his fate be considered tragic, because to a large measure it was due to inadequacy and weakness. He did not have enough strength to stand up for big decisions ... His intentions ideologically were honourable ... but in decisions

there was a lack of judgement which he neglected in favour of mystical motivation ... How often the magic words, "The Führer has ordered" was a cover for his own inadequacy.' Werner Grothmann, 'Zur Person Himmler's', Dachau, 1946, Toland Papers, Box 46. On the same topic Gitta Sereny corresponded with Hitler's secretary, Christa Schroeder, in 1977 while looking into David Irving's claim that Hitler did not know of the Holocaust. Schroeder wrote to Sereny: 'Of course Hitler knew! Not only knew, it was all his ideas and his orders ... I clearly remember one day in 1941 ... I don't think I will ever forget Himmler's face when he came out after one of his long "under four eyes" conferences with Hitler. He sat down heavily in the chair on the other side of the desk and buried his face in his hands, his elbows on the desk. "My God, my God," he said, "what I am expected to do." Later, much later ... when we found out what had been done, I was sure that was the day that Hitler told him that the Jews had to be killed.'

79. Regarding the Himmler–Heydrich conversation, see Witte et al., *Der Dienstkalender Heinrich Himmlers 1941/42*, p. 278. 'Arrest of Dr Jekelius. Son of Molotov, Jew transport from Berlin. No Liquidation'. In fact, Himmler's order arrived too late. The train had arrived in Riga on 30 November, at which point SS police Chief Friedrich Jeckeln had detrained the thousand Berlin Jews along with fifteen times that many driven out of the Riga ghetto, forced them to dig trenches and shot them into pits. Breitman, *Architect of Genocide*, pp. 219–220.

80. 'Report on Interrogation of PW KP 49359 Sturmbannführer Jakob Hanreich', 19 August 1944, PWIS(H)/LDC/299, NA RG 332, Box 30, 290/56/1/5. Also see RG 498, UD 208, Box 1230. This source is extremely important, as Hanreich, an 'old fighter' from Hitler's early days, was captured in August 1944 south of Falaise in France and ventured this information well before any of the facts were widely known. Moreover, he ventured much of this information before there was any reason for coercion by his interrogators. Describing Peiper's later tenure in Russia, he said Peiper was 'particularly eager to execute the order to burn villages'.

81. SS Unterscharführer Georg Blunder, LAH, divisional radio interpreter for the division, was captured 20 August 1944; he then described the actions of Einsatzgruppen 10a, claiming the actions of these dyed-in-the-wool Nazis should not be blamed on the combat teams. Blunder spoke fluent English, his parents having been in the United States since 1928. Blunder went to Lane Technical School in Chicago

and returned to Germany in September 1938. He fought with the Leibstandarte from April 1941 onwards. File for Blunder, NARA, RG 165, Entry 179B, Box 450.

82. Angrick, *Besatzungspolitik und Massenmord*, pp. 311–315.

83. Born in 1906, Gestapo officer Heinz Otto Seetzen had become a *dutzfreunden* of Reinhard Heydrich by 1939. Later, in 1944, he became the commander of the Security Police at Minsk, where he would order the killing of more than twelve thousand individuals. After the Nazi capitulation in May 1945 Seetzen hid for a time, eventually killing himself in August 1945. See Lawrence D. Stokes, 'Heinz Seetzen-Chef des Sonderkommmmandos 10a', in Klaus Michael Mallmann and Paul Gerhard, eds., *Karrieren der Gewalt. Nationalsozialistische Täterbiographien* (Darmstadt: Wissenschaftliche Buchgesellschaft, 2004), pp. 196–206.

84. Angrick, *Besatzungspolitik und Massenmord*, p. 313. For Albert Frey's eyewitness to the shooting at Mariupol, 'Report on Interrogation of PW KP 49359 Sturmbannführer Jakob Hanreich'. Not surprisingly, after the war Frey would go to great lengths to leave Europe for Argentina—likely worried about the Taganrog–Mariupol episode being unearthed. Frey had just been awarded command of the III Battalion of the Leibstandarte on 4 October, with Peiper assuming command of his 11th Company on the same day. See Lehmann and Tiemann, *Die Leibstandarte*, vol. II, p. 122.

85. 'As far as the Kommando is concerned, proceeding in the direction of the northern Caucasus, the Jewish problem has been solved ... In Taganrog 20 Communist officials were liquidated. Ten of them were shot publicly in accordance with martial law.' See 'Operational Situation Report USSR No. 136: Activities of Einsatzgruppen A and D', Chief of the Security Police and Security Service (SD), 21 November 1941, in Yitzak Arad, Shmuel Karkwoski and Shmuel Spector, eds., *The Einsatzgruppen Reports* (New York: Macmillan, 1990).

86. IMT, vol. 21, p. 72. On 19 December 1949 a British court sentenced Erich von Manstein to eighteen years imprisonment for neglecting to protect PoWs and civilians; he was released on parole in 1953. His guilt in the Holocaust has now been documented by Oliver von Wrochem in *Erich von Mainstein: Vernichtungskrieg und Geschichtpolitik* (Paderborn: Schöningh Verlag, 2006). Best evidence suggests that, of 5.7 million Russian soldiers captured by the Germans in the Second World War, 3.3 million perished by war's end. Christian Steit, *Keine Kameraden: Die Wehrmacht und die sowjetischen Kriegsgefangenen, 1941–1945*, (Bonn: J.H.W. Dietz, 1991).

Chapter 2: On the Savage Plain

1. Johannes Hürter, *Hitlers Heerführer: Die deutschen Oberbefehlshaber im Krieg gegen die Sowjetunion 1941–42* (Munich: R. Oldenbourg Verlag, 2006). After the war the German generals would write for the U.S. Army Foreign Military Studies of their powerlessness in the advance into the Soviet Union in the summer of 1941, in particular to absolve themselves of the murderous treatment of Russian prisoners. In particular, Hürter exposes this contention as a myth, where Hitler's generals trusted the German leader to be a military genius and readily treated the Eastern Front as a special theatre of operations where the normal rules of war would not apply.

2. Albert Frey, *Ich wollte die Freiheit: Erinnerungen des Kommandeurs des 1. Panzergrenadierregiments der ehemaligen Waffen-SS* (Osnabrück: Munin Verlag, 1990), p. 204.

3. See Peiper's BDC file, 'Dienstlaufbahn: Der Reichführer SS, SS Personalhauptamt', no date. The entry clearly shows Peiper assigned to the LSSAH divisional staff on 1 October 1941 and then officially assigned in command of the 11th Company fifteen days later. His personnel file shows Peiper returning to LSSAH on 16 October 1941. Further, the memoirs of his colleague Albert Frey claim that Peiper took over the company on 4 October. Frey, *Ich wollte die Freiheit*. 'Maj. Weidenhaupt had been seriously wounded by a mine and I took over leadership of III Abteilung on 4 October and SS Captain Peiper occupied my position as leader of 11 Kp. (p. 204).

4. 'Interrogation of Lt. Alfred Lengenfeld', 21 September 1944, PWIS(H) LDC/358, NA RG 332, ETO Interrogations Reports, Box 30. Lengenfeld had been with 14 (Anti-tank) Company of LSSAH since November 1937, recalling that Meyer was 'a great athlete and an accomplished horseman and motorcycle driver'. Beyond these attributes, Lengenfeld's testimony about atrocities were later discredited. Lengenfeld was, in fact, Alfred Lenge. See next endnote.

5. 'Report on the Interrogation of 1st Lt. Alfred Lengenfeld', 21 September 1944, PoW Interrogation Section (MIS-Y) PWIS(H)/ LDC/358, RG 498, UD 228, Box 1250. Lengenfeld had been with the Leibstandarte and claimed to have refused Meyer's orders to shoot the fifty Poles near Modlin in October 1939. However, the SS man's testimony was later discredited. He was previously a member of the Leibstandarte before being moved to the Luftwaffe in February 1943, eventually fighting with the 3rd Fallschirmjäger Division, where the

Army Blanche captured him near Hasselt, Belgium, in September 1944. His real name was, in fact, Alfred Lenge, and he retracted his earlier statement in December 1944, hoping to ingratiate himself with Allied interrogators so he would be released to Germany to fight again for the Fatherland. See file NA: WO208/4295, p. 363, 'Papers recovered from Lt. Col. A.P. Scotland: Reports of atrocities in the European theatre of war'. I am grateful to Carol Bryne for helping to sort out this confusing episode.

6. Werner Haupt, *Army Group South: The Wehrmacht in Russia 1941–1945* (Atglen: Schiffer Publishing, 1998), pp. 95–101.

7. 'Fernschreiben an 1. Pz.Armee', 11 October 1941, NA RG-242, T-311, R292, F996-997.

8. In fact, the Cossacks saw the Germans as liberators from the Stalinist regime and crossed over from the Red Army to join the Germans. Many Cossacks and Ukrainians eventually ended up fighting for Hitler—formed into rapid-moving cavalry groups that were used to pursue Russian partisans. Fully two Ukrainian divisions were raised and as many as a million Russians eventually ended up fighting on the side of the Germans. S.J. Newland, *Cossacks in the German Army 1941–1945* (London: Routledge, 1991).

9. 'Additional Report on Maj. Josef Boll, OB West', U.S. First Army PWI Report, RG 338, 290/56/2/3, Box 64, 8 April 1945.

10. For diary of Canaris on 24 December 1941: David Irving, *Hitler's War* (London: Viking, 1977), p. 363. 'The Russian army communiques never report numbers of prisoners taken, but just registers laconically that "fifty officers and two thousand enlisted men were liquidated".'

11. These combat actions are summarized in Weingartner, *Hitler's Guard*, pp. 73–74. Original sources used in my account: 'Bericht über den Einsatz der LSSAH vom 22.9–18.10.1941', NA RG-242, T-175, R108, F2632263-71.

12. Account of attack on the armoured trains at Taganrog: Lehmann and Tiemann, *Die Leibstandarte*, vol. II, pp. 131–164. 'Peiper was really unhappy because of the losses in his company.' Albert Frey to Jens Westemeier, 18 February 1994.

13. Records of the SS field hospital revealed that Taganrog was secured on 17 October 1941, with some 6,387 patients treated over the following months. BA-MA, Sammlung Vorpersal, N756/107a.

14. Eberhard von Mackensen, *Vom Bug zum Kraukasus* (Neckargemünd: Kurt Vowinckel Verlag, 1967), p. 38; Kurt Meyer, *Grenadiers*, p. 145. For the 'mud season in the whole of Russia'. Dietrich to Ellis, the Ellis Papers, Schwäbisch Hall.

15. See Weingartner, *Hitler's Guard*, p. 74. Primary sources: '1. Panzerarmee Tagesmeldung' and 'Fernschreiben an 1. Panzerarmee', 28–31 October 1941, NA T-314, R185, F1242-1264. Upwards of half of the Leibstandarte combat strength was not available due to rampant dysentery; Peiper himself suffered the condition. See Peiper BDC file.

16. See 'Dietrich to Himmler: Bericht über die Kfz.-Lage der Leibstandarte SS Adolf Hitler', 13 October 1941, NA T-175, R108, 2632281-82. According to Dietrich, in mid-October only 40 per cent of the allocated transport was operational.

17. See 'Dietrich to Himmler: Bericht über die Kfz.-Lage der Leibstandarte SS Adolf Hitler', 13 October 1941, NA T-175, R108, 2632281-82.

18. Lehmann and Tiemann, *Die Leibstandarte*, vol. II, p. 175.

19. Hans Siptrott, interview with author, 15 July 2012. Siptrott was an MG 34 machine gunner with the 8th Company of the Leibstandarte Adolf Hitler.

20. Lehmann and Tiemann, *Die Leibstandarte*, vol. II, p. 164.

21. Account of SS Unterscharführer Erwin Bartmann, 'Operation Barbarossa', in Gordon Williamson, *Loyalty Is My Honor* (Osceola, WI: Motorbooks International, 1995), pp. 58–59.

22. In a surreptitiously taped conversation between a Lieutenant Schmidt and his cellmate, Faller described the fanatical fighting of the Russians in the East in the autumn of 1941. What was done with prisoners, Schmidt wanted to know? Faller: 'We killed them. Most of them were killed in this battle. They didn't surrender either ... the women fought like beasts.' Schmidt: 'What did you do with the women?' 'We shot them too.' SRM 1023, PRO: WO/208/4139, 15 November 1944.

23. For 'a tiny blacksmith shop': PRO: WO/208/3148: 7th Army Interrogation Centre, General Heinz Guderian on 14 June 1945, Scavenger Report No. 19: 'Although we penetrated it to a depth of about 1500 km, the war has barely touched that country's borders.'

24. 'Peiper: Russian Theater', pp. 230–231. 'The Donetz and heavy industrial area of Krivoi Rog fell into German hands destroyed beyond repair, while at the same time Russian workers loaded their plants and factories and rolled to the Urals ... in a relatively short time they resumed production.' Peiper's synopsis is correct; see 'The Evacuation of Industry', in Werth, *Russia at War*, pp. 213–224.

25. Lehmann and Tiemann, *Die Leibstandarte*, vol. II, p. 166.

26. For Springer's audacious capture of the Rostov rail bridge, the Kiel native would receive the Knight's Cross of the Iron Cross. See

Christopher Ailsby, *Hell on the Eastern Front: The Waffen SS in Russia* (Osceola, WI: MBI Publishing Co., 1998), pp. 36–37.

27. Albert Frey, commander of III Battalion, recalled Peiper's precarious position: 'My old 11th Company under Jochen Peiper was at the entry of the Taganrog bridge and crossed the Don in the direction of Batiesk ... with starting in darkness and during the darkness, a number of Russians were fleeing across the bridge. I feared to come into battle during the night in which the opponent could win superiority. So it came to the grotesque situation, that the left of my 11th Kp.—not many more than 30 men—hid their men in a cellar and the Russians crossed the bridge and left.' Frey, *Ich wollte die Freiheit*, p. 227. For 'Inside there was solid chaos': testimony of Hans Bäder of 14 Kompanie, as cited by Lehmann and Tiemann, *Die Leibstandarte*, vol. II, p. 166.

28. Molotov's biased description is of interest: 'The Nazi blood lust at Rostov gained wide notoriety. Having established themselves in Rostov for 10 days, the Germans murdered not only individuals and families, but in their bloody zeal annihilated scores and hundreds of residents, especially in the workers' district of the city. Near the building of the railway administration, in broad daylight, the Germans shot down 48 persons with automatic rifles ... In the Armenian cemetery they killed 200 persons.' Source: 'Note issued by V. M. Molotov, People's Commissar of Foreign Affairs of the U.S.S.R., to all ambassadors and ministers of countries with which the Soviet Union maintains diplomatic relations', Kuibyshev, 7 January 1942.

29. 'III Panzer Corps: An die Kommandeure 14.Pz. Div, 60 Div., Leibstandarte,' NA T-314, R186, F105-108. 'Not icy wind, or biting frost, insufficient winter clothing ... and the least of all the Red Army itself, was able to stop your triumphant march.'

30. Heinz von Westernhagen, 25 November 1941, Westernhagen, *Die Kinder der Täter*, p. 44.

31. 'Programm für die Reise des Reichsführer SS vom 30 Sept. bis 5 Oktober 1941', NA RG-242, T-175, R112, 2637715-17.

32. Surreptitious notes made by Dr Werner Koeppen of Hitler's dinner conversations form an important record: NA RG-242, T-84, R387, F792, guest: Himmler on 10 October 1941.

33. For the mood in Hitler's headquarters and the pivotal battle before Moscow, see David Stahel, *Kiev 1941: Hitler's Battle for Supremacy in the East* (Cambridge: Cambridge University Press, 2012), pp. 269–272.

34. For 'Russia is finished!': Walter Warlimont, *Inside Hitler's Head-quarters* (New York: Praeger, 1964), p. 194. For 'we started one month

too late', see diary entry of 25 November 1941 of Gerhard Engel, *Heeresadjutant bei Hitler 1938–1943* (Stuttgart: Deutsche Verlags Anstalt, 1974), p. 116.

35. 'In the face of the strong forces which the Russians have massed before my Army, I have decided to move back my units in an orderly fashion.' Von Kleist's controversial order: 'Panzerarmeebefehl Nr. 31', 22 November 1941, NA T-314, R166, F0110.

36. 'Information obtained from Field Marshal von Rundstedt', 10 July 1945. NA RG 407, Entry 427, Box 2620, 270/52/19/3-4/. Von Rundstedt's 'wild Nazi' assessment of von Reichenau is from the same source. 'I believe they reckoned on about 10 weeks for the entire Russian campaign … it was thought that after the first big defeats, which were expected, the Russians would give in. I didn't believe it. The winter came early; we already had ten degrees of frost and snow in November.'

37. Generalfeldmarschal von Reichenau was shocked to find himself eventually compelled to complete the withdrawal originally ordered by his sacked predecessor. The entire assignment was too much for him, and von Reichenau died suddenly from a stroke on 17 January 1942.

38. 'SS A.H. an Führerhauptquartier: Gefechtsstärken der LSSAH. am 30.11.41', 1 NA, T-314, R186, F294.

39. Halder agreed with Dietrich's assessment: the Rostov salient was not tenable. Entry for December 1: 'We have lost forces, time and von Rundstedt,' Franz Halder, *Kriegstagebuch*, vol. III (Stuttgart: Kohlhammer, 1964).

40. 'Die Schwerter für Sepp Dietrich', *Das Schwarze Korps*, 8 January 1942, Dietrich BDC file, NA, A3343 SSO-152.

41. Cameron and Stevens, *Hitler's Table Talk*, p. 168. In German: *Adolf Hitler: Monologe im Führerhauptquartier 1941–1944* (Hamburg: Albrecht Knaus, 1980).

42. 'Special Interrogation Report: Field Marshal Karl Rudolf Gerd von Rundstedt', Canadian Military Intelligence HQ, 1 Feb 1946, NA RG-407, E. 427, Box 1954P. For 'decent, but stupid', von Rundstedt, interview with Milton Shulman: Shulman, *Defeat in the West* (New York: E.P. Dutton, 1948), p. 104. Although denied by SS veterans, both post-war interviews with von Rundstedt are authentic.

43. Ulrich von Hassell, *Vom anderen Deutschland* (Frankfurt: Fischer Bücherei, 1964), pp. 218–219.

44. For Dietrich's conversation with Goebbels, see Louis Lochner, ed., *The Goebbels Diaries* (New York: Doubleday, 1948), pp. 51–52. 'The

incidents that Sepp Dietrich related to me about the Russian people in the occupied areas are simply hair-raising. They are not a people, but a conglomeration of animals ... The soldiers won't surrender as in the fashion in Western Europe, when completely surrounded they continue to fight until they are beaten to death. Bolshevism has merely accentuated this racial propensity.'

45. Kurt Meyer speaking with Wilhelm Ullersperger, GRGG 262, 18–20 February 1945, PRO: WO 208/4177. 'I have breathed in National Socialism as a religion, as my life, no matter whether it is called National Socialism ... I have realized that this is the only right life for our people ... the conditions of life and for the things that are essential for our people for the preservation of our race, our people and our culture.'

46. Jochen Peiper, 'Brief Review', 7 April 1946.

47. Heinz von Westernhagen, 25 November 1941, Westernhagen, *Die Kinder der Täter*, p. 44.

48. Hewel diary, as originally cited in Irving, *Hitler's War*, p. 362; Microform Ltd., David Irving Collection, 'Diaries and papers of Botschafter Hewel, DI-75, Group 5, Reel 16, 24 December 1941'. In reality U.S. citizens were finally waking up to the magnitude of the German design for the complete conquest of Europe—even starving England into submission. See Joseph C. Harsch, 'The Unbelievable Nazi Blueprint', *New York Times* magazine, 25 May 1941.

49. Jochen Peiper, Letter to Hedwig Potthast, 10 December 1941, NSDAP Hauptarchiv, Himmler Collection, Microfilm Roll No. 99, Hoover Institution, Stanford University.

50. See Witte et al., *Der Dienstkalender Heinrich Himmlers 1941/42*, pp. 292–296. According to Witte and colleagues, the Himmler diaries show footnote entries that appear to be in Peiper's script on various matters (need for stoves, warm clothing, etc.) on 17 and 18 December 1941. However, in examining the originals at the U.S. Holocaust Memorial Museum (Himmler Itineraries: 1997.A.0328) and being familiar with Peiper's handwriting, the author believes that although these entries are not Grothmann's, they are also not those of Peiper.

51. Himmler's conversation with Heydrich: NA RG 242, Roll 26, handwritten entries for 1 December 1941.

52. A copy of the original notes from Himmler's revealing conversation with Hitler ('Jewish Question | Eliminate as partisans') on 18 December is reproduced on p. 293 of Witte et al., *Der Dienstkalender Heinrich Himmlers 1941/42*. This telling note has become a major point in the academic discussion of when and where Hitler made his decision on

the Final Solution (*Endlösung*) to the Jewish question. As a starting point: Mark Roseman, *The Wansee Conference and the Final Solution: A Reconsideration* (New York: Holt, 2012). The famous Wannsee conference, where the orchestrated decision on the Final Solution took place, occurred within four weeks of these events:

In 1941, the Führer himself ordered the physical annihilation of the Jewish enemy. What made him go to this extreme measure, I do not know. For one thing the war in Russia was not going along in the Blitz fashion he had planned. The ruinous struggle on two fronts had begun ... Soon after the order, Gen. Heydrich called me to his office on Prinz-Albrechtstrasse. He told me about Reichsführer Himmler's order that all emigration of Jews was to be prohibited with no more exceptions ... By this time the formula 'Final Solution for the Jewish Question' had taken on a new meaning: liquidation. In this new sense, we discussed it at the special conference on Jan. 20, 1942 in the Wannsee section of Berlin. Although Himmler and Heydrich were to preside, I myself drafted Heydrich's speech to the gathering. Only a few people invited declined to attend ... After the conference, as I recall, Heydrich, [Heinrich] Müller and your humble servant sat cozily around a fireplace. I noticed for the first time that Heydrich was smoking. Not only that, but he had a cognac. Normally he touched nothing alcoholic ... We all had drinks then. We sang songs. After a while we got up on the chairs and drank a toast, then on the table and then round and round, then on the chair and the table again. Heydrich taught it to us; it was an old North German custom.

Memoirs of Adolf Eichmann, 1 November 1960, NA, Records of the Central Intelligence Agency, RG 263, File: CIA- RDP75-00149R00020050018-7, Declassified 13 June 2000.

53. Himmler flew to Taganrog on Wednesday, 24 December and then on to the Leibstandarte. See Witte et al., *Der Dienstkalender Heinrich Himmlers 1941/42*, p. 298. Unfortunately, Himmler's appointment calendar for this period does not include the usual traveller manifest: NA RG-242, T-175, R112.

54. For 'I played Santa Claus in the trench', Joachim Peiper, 'Meine lieben Eltern!', Landsberg, 26 December 1946, NA, RG 549, USAREUR War Crimes Branch, Cases Tried, 6-24, Box 60. Weather conditions from 'LAH KTB Nr. 5 for 24 December 1941', BA-MA, RS-3-1/30.

55. Lehmann and Tiemann, *Die Leibstandarte*, vol. II, pp. 195–196.

56. 'Programm für die Reise des Reichsführer SS vom 23. bis 28 December 1941', NA RG-242, T-175, R112, 2637691-92. On 23 December Himmler had flown from Rastenburg to Mariupol to visit his

Waffen SS leaders in the field. After his visit with Dietrich, Himmler continued on to visit his other SS combat units, including the 5th SS Division Wiking and the new field marshal of Army Group South, Generalfeldmarschal von Reichenau.

57. 'Report about the War Years, 1939—1945', Sepp Dietrich to Burton Ellis, Schwäbisch Hall, Ellis Papers.

58. Lehmann and Tiemann, *Die Leibstandarte*, vol. II, p. 199.

59. Affidavit of Walter Staudinger, 25 February 1948, NA, RG-549, Case 6-24, Box 51. 'I specifically remember Christmas 1941 when he spoke to Himmler in the headquarters at Nikolajewka …'.

60. 'He [Himmler] is the only man of the so-called old party members that has complete confidence of the Führer.' Secretly recorded conversation of Kurt Meyer with General Major Werner Ebeling: PRO: GRGG, 18–19 November 1944, WO 208/4364. Unlike post-war disavowal, it seems clear that officers of the Waffen SS had a very favourable view of Himmler before the Nuremberg trials.

61. On 28 December Himmler flew to Friedrichsruh and then later drove that evening to Hitler's headquarters. Peiper was not along on this trip, his place having been taken by Werner Grothmann.

62. Jochen Peiper, 'Brief Review', 7 April 1946. Looking on the growth of rear-area partisan warfare that winter, 'the front line had to be self-sufficient and looked gloomily at the thriving poison flower flourishing in the hinterlands'.

63. 'Bericht über den Ernährungs und Gesundheitszustand der Truppe!' for 27 December 1941, NA, T-175, R127, F2632259-62. Total ration strength for the LSSAH on 31 December 1941 was 9,945.

64. Jochen Peiper, Letter to Hedwig Potthast, 30 December 1941, NSDAP Hauptarchiv, Himmler Collection, Microfilm Roll No. 99, Hoover Institution, Stanford University. For Himmler's obsession with himself as King Heinrich the 1st: Gunter d'Alquen, *Reichsführer Rede zu Quedlinburg* (Magdeburg: Im Norsland Verlag, 1936). The head of SS propaganda, d'Alquen, repeated the myth: 'A thousand years ago one of the greatest Germans ever, died, but today he is so much alive, so close, that we believe to be seeing him physically in our midst.'

65. Himmler to Sigurd Peiper, 29 December 1941, 'Greetings from Jochen', Witte et al., *Der Dienstkalender Heinrich Himmlers 1941/42*, p. 299.

66. 'Meine Herzlichten Glückwünsche zum Weihnachtsfest und für das Kriegsjahr 1942, Heil Hitler!' signed personally by Himmler and distributed with the *Julleucher*. Both Sigurd and Jochen Peiper were shown on Himmler's meticulous manifest as receiving the candle holders. NA, RG-242, T-175, Roll 112.

67. Himmler's son, Helge, was born to Hedwig Potthast on 15 February 1942 in a difficult forceps delivery with the medical help of the SS Reichsführer's personal physician, Dr Karl Gebhardt (Gebhardt then became Helge's godfather). The RuSHA (Race and Resettlement Main Office) chose the boy's name for its Viking qualities—'the pure, strong, healthy one'—but the actual child was challenged by chronic physical and emotional difficulties. At the time Himmler's mistress, Häschen, was in terrible mental distress after learning that her brother, Dr Walter Potthast, had been killed on the Russian Front. Disapproving of her relationship with Himmler, Hedwig's parents broke all contact, with only her sister Thilde remaining in communication. Katrin Himmler, *Die Brüder Himmler: Eine deutsche Familiengeschichte* (Frankfurt: S. Fischer Verlag, 2005), p. 240.

68. Jochen Peiper, Letter to Hedwig Potthast, 10 January 1942, NSDAP Hauptarchiv, Himmler Collection, Microfilm Roll No. 99, Hoover Institution, Stanford University.

69. For Peiper's twenty-seventh birthday with Hugo Kraas: Agte, *Michael Wittmann and the Tiger Commanders*, p. 49. Background: Thomas Franz, *Die Eichenlaubträger 1939–1945*, vol. 1 (Osnabrück: Biblio Verlag, 1997). After the war Italian and West German authorities investigated Kraas for the murder of Jews in Italy on 25 September 1943.

70. For conditions at Sambek on 30 January 1942, see BA-MA 'Leibstandarte Adolf Hitler: KTB Nr. 5', BA-MA, RS 3-1/30.

71. Völkischer Beobachter, 1 February 1942, Munich. Copy on file at Library of Congress.

72. Episode of the flight back to the front from Albert Speer, *Inside the Third Reich* (New York: Macmillian, 1970), pp. 257–258.

73. Heinz von Westernhagen, 3 and 18 January 1942, Westernhagen, *Die Kinder der Täter*, pp. 43–45.

74. For Peiper's illness, see his personnel file: BDC, 11 February 1944 'Gesundheits und Verwendungsprüfstelle der Waffen-SS'. For the static warfare in the winter of 1942, see Lehmann and Tiemann, *Die Leibstandarte*, vol. II, pp. 201–212.

75. For Karl Wolff's secret negotiations with Stalin's representatives, see documents unearthed from Russian archives and published for the first time in Jochen von Lang, *Top Nazi: SS General Karl Wolff* (New York: Enigma Books, 2005), Appendix (original German publication in 1985). Jochen Piechocki was a wartime SS reporter in Joseph Goebbels' propaganda service who made the official radio announcement of Hitler's death on 1 May 1945. After the war he took the pen name of Jochen von Lang and served as an editor at

Stern magazine in the 1960s and 1970s, where he claimed to have uncovered the remains of Martin Bormann and Ludwig Stumpfegger under a paved Berlin street.

76. Jochen Peiper, 'Brief Review', 7 April 1946.
77. Whether Peiper received leave to attend his brother's funeral in Berlin in May is unknown. 'Petition for Pardon for my Son Joachim Peiper', Woldemar Peiper, 30 August 1946, NA RG-153, Case 6-24, Box 83.

Chapter 3: France and Back

1. 'Aufstellung des VII./LSSAH,' SS Führungshauptamt', 14 February 1942, NA T-175, R108, F2631605.
2. 'Aus einem handschriftlichen Brief des SS-Obergruppenführers Sepp Dietrich an den Reichsführer-SS', 17 December 1941, NA, Dietrich BDC file.
3. The chariot race is pictured in BA-MA, Sammlung Vorpersal, N 756/107. For other photos, see Rudolf Lehmann, *Leibstandarte im Bild* (Osnabrück: Munin Verlag, 1983), pp. 157–158. Erhard Gührs claimed to the author to recognize Peiper in one of the photos. 'That's him,' he said, 'I can tell from his figure. He loved this kind of stuff—we used to call him "pin-up boy".' Interview 16 December 2004. In spite of Gührs's claim, the author is reasonably certain Peiper was not there; however, Gustav Knittel with the reconnaissance battalion is clearly seen.
4. Ralf Tiemann had been in at the very inception of tanks in the Leibstandarte. At the beginning of January 1942 Tiemann had just been released from a field hospital in Lichterfelde when he ran across his old battalion commander, Sturmbannführer Wilhelm Mohnke. Mohnke was also convalescing after losing part of his right foot in fighting in Yugoslavia. Over a drink at the local casino Mohnke enthusiastically informed the younger SS leader that the Leibstandarte was to organize a Panzer battalion. He told Tiemann that he had chosen him as his adjutant. His job? To surreptitiously recruit the best NCOs and enlisted men for the new tank command. Tiemann had himself immediately outfitted in the black Panzer uniform and paraded about in the different crew quarters of the replacement battalion to interest the old hands. Word got out that there would soon be an SS tank unit. Within days the artifice produced a flood of eager volunteers. Yet how would they get Sepp Dietrich to agree? The opportunity came on 14 January, when Dietrich, who had just married Ursula Brenner, showed his new bride his proud command. The men of the

Leibstandarte assembled in the Leroux Building. The atmosphere was festive with laughter and champagne. Shrewdly, Mohnke used the levity of Dietrich's reception toast to announce another feather for Dietrich's soaring career: we are raising the first tank unit of the division. Already the roster was teeming with volunteers. 'To the Panzer Division Leibstandarte Adolf Hitler—Prost!' Amid the cheers and applause Dietrich could scarcely refuse. He penned his approval for the conscript. The subterfuge succeeded and soon the men and machines began organizing and training in Wildflecken. But things did not develop quickly enough for the impatient Mohnke, who, on 29 February, ran off to Berlin to 'raise hell' with Hans Jüttner, the head of the SS leadership office, over delays in delivering tanks and other allocated equipment. He became embroiled in bitter arguments with his superiors—so troubling that he was sent for psychiatric examination. Mohnke was racked with pain from his battle injury, and Tiemann did not know of his deepening reliance on opiates. He was now a total Dolatin addict—a fact acknowledged by the SS hospital staff in Berlin. Word of this got out, and he was forbidden to possess a field command. Eight weeks of detox therapy was prescribed. By the time Mohnke returned, command of the Panzer battalion was in the hands of Sturmbannführer Georg Schönberger, although the SS leader head office had recommended that Kurt Meyer would be the best leader of the tank regiment. IfZ, MA 775-1519, SS FüHA to RFSS, 13 February 1942. When Tiemann met Mohnke briefly in Würzburg he seemed a broken man. Tiemann, along with the other panzer men, moved to France to train with the rest of the division. Ralf Tiemann, interview with author, 21 October 1995; see also 'Dolatin-Sucht des SS Sturmbannführers Mohnke', 12 February 1942, NA RG 242, T-175, R108, F2631614.

5. Hans Siptrott, interview with author, 15 July 2012.
6. Witte et al., *Der Dienstkalender Heinrich Himmlers 1941/42*, p. 446. Trained as an engineer, the steely eyed Lammerding would later be charged with the civilian killings in France that took place in the mountains of Auvergne near Tulle and at Oradour-sur-Glane in the summer of 1944. The charges were unjust according to Waffen SS veterans, who maintained that the civilians—including 207 women and children—were partisans. In any case, to have Eicke's unconditional approval, as Lammerding did, required a special kind of harshness. In the autumn of 1943 Lammerding was on the staff of SS Obergruppenführer Erich von dem Bach-Zelewski, a man who was deeply implicated in the wholesale slaughter of fifteen

thousand Russian civilians. See Charles Sydnor, *Soldiers of Destruction* (Princeton, NJ: Princeton University Press, 1977), pp. 136–138 and 320. Based on his close relationship with Himmler, Lammerding would later be given command on an entire SS Panzer division. See also Lammerding's BDC file, showing qualitative evaluations by Eicke 1938 and 1939. After the war Lammerding kept a low profile as an engineer but could not stay out of trouble with the Nazi hunters.

7. It is not known whether Peiper was at the Heydrich funeral, but given his proximity to Himmler during this time it seems likely. Another of Peiper's SS officer acquaintances from meetings with Himmler, SS Gruppenführer Karl von Treuenfeld, leading the 2nd SS Infantry Brigade, was charged with capturing the assassins in Prague the day after Heydrich was mortally wounded. After an intense firefight all four participants in the Czech operation killed themselves rather than have von Treuenfeld's men take them captive. See Robert Gerwarth, *Hitler's Hangman: The Life of Heydrich* (New Haven, CT: Yale University Press, 2011).

8. Von Lang, *Top Nazi*, p. 182.

9. Letter of 11 July 1942 from Peiper in RuSHA file for Kurt Hans Hinrichsen, NA, BDC file A-3343-RS-C0383. During Peiper's visit to Himmler headquarters SS Obergruppenführer Hans-Adolf Prützmann, Kurt Knoblauch, Brigadeführer Gottfried Klingemann, Oberstgruppenführer Karl Daluege and Brigadeführer Karl Gebhardt were present for a lunch with Himmler (Dienstkalendar, 10 July 1942). For information on Kurt Hans Hinrichsen: Born 24 April 1907, his future wife was Vera Hinrichsen (nee Wentzel). Vera Hinrichsen was entering her third marriage with three children from the first marriage, three from his deceased brother. Dr. Rolf Hinrichsen had died when he went down with the rest of the crew of the Bismarck on 27 May 1941. Hans Kurt had never been before married. Vera was Catholic, and Hans Kurt was *Gottgläubig* (the SS quasi-religious designation: 'believing in God'). From his Lebenslauf in the files, Kurt-Hans Hinrichsen had been with the Reichswehr Cavalry Regiment 3 at Rathenow in 1925–1926. Then he worked at a bank in Hamburg and subsequently went to London several times. From 1928 to 1932 he had his own farm in Canada. In 1933 he worked again on a farm in Germany and then entered the SD from 1933 to 1939 and in 1939 and was sent to SS Hauptamt (Gottlob Berger). In this capacity he was involved in observing and judging potential enemies of the Reich under Dr Werner Best in the SD office: 'Letter Kurt Hans Hinrichsen to Fritz Kranefuss', 5 September 1939, NA, RG-242, T-175, Roll 57,

Frame 257148. After the outbreak of the war Hinrichsen was sent to Posen in 1939 and established in three regions for the Selbstschutz. These were among the most notorious units Himmler created under command of Ludolf von Alvensleben. These were composed of ethnic Germans of Poland and led mostly by SD leaders. Then, from May to October 1941, he fought with the SS Division Das Reich in Russia before returning to the farm of the firm Ostland GmbH in Kreis Lauster in the Warthe region of Poland.

10. Recollections of SS Hauptsturmführer Lothar Heimbach, Seetzen's aid, who was on friendly terms with Müller-John. BA-L, Heimbach to Staatsanwalt. 'I am able to remember the date exactly because it was then the birthday of my boss.' See also Stokes, 'Heinz Seetzen-Chef des Sonderkommmandos 10a'.

11. Himmler to Berger on 28 July 1942, Nuremberg Document NO 626. Of the order to exterminate the Jews, Himmler contradicted his own requirement for secrecy: 'No one can relieve me of the responsibility. I cannot allow myself (!) the luxury of discussing it with others.' Himmler had just recently witnessed some of the first gassings at Auschwitz. See Breitman, *Architect of Genocide*, pp. 236–239. It is not clear whether Peiper had already by then returned to France, but it is certain he was with Himmler at his field headquarters as late as 10 July 1942. Letter of 11 July 1942 from Peiper in RuSHA file for Kurt Hans Hinrichsen, NA, BDC file A-3343-RS-C0383.

12. For the 1964 war crimes case against Karl Wolff, see JuVSV Verfahren Lfd. Nr. 580, LG München II 640930, BGH 651026, Ludwigsburg.

13. Breitman, *Architect of Genocide*, pp. 236–239. When Auschwitz commandant Rudolf Höss was asked why he was not afraid that inmates might escape from his extermination camp and tell the world, he stoically replied, 'Our system is so terrible that nobody in the world will believe it is possible.'

14. Breitman, *Architect of Genocide*, p. 236. For the quotes of Himmler to Höss, see Jochen von Lang, ed. *Eichmann Interrogated* (New York: Farrar, Straus and Giroux, 1983), p. 83.

15. Witte et al., *Der Dienstkalender Heinrich Himmlers 1941/42*, p. 494. Those identified with Peiper in the photo are Bischoff, Hans Kammler, Rudolf Höss, Himmler, Fritz Bracht and Ernst Schmausser. However, the author's scrutiny of the photographs and others provided by the Auschwitz Archives of the same tour indicates they show Werner Grothmann, Peiper's replacement and not Peiper. Thanks to Dr Piotr Setkiewicz with the State Museum of Auschwitz-Birkenau. In any case, the fact that Peiper did not return to Verneil until 10 August

1942 convinces Himmler scholar Peter Witte that his former adjutant was still with Himmler during this time. The actual Dienstkalendar is even more vague, simply listing Auschwitz/Kattowitz for 17 and 18 July 1942 and naming those present as Gauleiter Bracht, SS Obergruppenführer Schmausser, Sturmbannführer Cäsar, Obersturmführer Vogel and Sturmbannführer Hoess. See the original Dienstkalendar copies from Moscow: USHMM, Himmler Itineraries, 1997, A.0328, Box 1.

16. Dinse, Interview with author, 21 May 1996 (hereafter Dinse interview). Otto Dinse was one of the few SS men the author interviewed who did not deny SS war crimes. 'Anyone who denies the existence of the elimination camps,' he told me in the presence of other veterans, 'he is not a comrade.'

17. 'Kriegstagebuch Nr. 6, Leibstandarte SS Adolf Hitler: Div. Befehl über den Durchmarsch durch Paris', 29 July 1942, NA, T-354, Roll 611, F0666-9; see also BA-MA, RS/3/1/31 entries for 17 to 29 July 1942. Combat strength of the freshly transported division was 11,356; ration strength was 14,256. Photos of the parade through Paris of Leibstandarte, *Völkischer Beobachter*, Nr. 214, Münnchener Ausgabe, 2 August 1942.

18. Diary of Günther Borchers, 29 July 1942, copy provided to author by Markus Lippl (hereafter Borchers's Diary). Borchers was on the engineer company of the tank regiment and rode through the streets of Paris on BMW R75 motorcycles.

19. Peiper's quarters in Verneuil were enviable: an eighteenth-century chateau in the cedar-lined municipal park just behind the Place de la Madeleine. It was formerly a private home that is today the mayor's office. For history see Josette Filleul, *Verneuil et son Canton*, vol. II (Tours: Alan Sutton, 1995).

20. 'Here in France, our new commander greeted us in a toast with champagne. Hauptsturmführer Jochen Peiper was here with his wife.' Oswald Sigmund, *Meine Ehre heisst Treue: Von der Leibstandarte ins Landsberger Kriegsverbrechergefängnis* (Essen: Heitz & Höffkes, 1992), p. 48.

21. Heinrich Springer, interview with author, 19 May 1997. Also Heinrich Springer, *Stationen eines Lebens in Krieg und Frieden* (Rosenheim: Deutsche Verlagsgesellschaft, 1996), pp. 91–98.

22. Borchers's Diary, July 1942.

23. During the occupation one Frenchman was hauled off to the concentration camps for cursing a woman who had sex with a German soldier: 'You learned to keep your mouth shut.' Jacques Bayet, Jacques

Derlon and Jean Blanchard, interview with author, Verneuil, 10 July 2002. After the war the French women who slept with the Germans had their heads shaved. The French perspective: 'They deserved it; they collaborated with their asses.'

24. Karl-Heinz Köhne, Letter, and follow-up conversation with Jens Westemeier, June 1995. Hitler himself had freely encouraged breeding by SS men with the locals. See Cameron and Stevens, *Hitler's Table Talk*, conversation with Himmler on 23 April 1942, pp. 434–435.

At Berchtesgaden we owe a great deal to the infusion of SS blood, for the local population there was of specifically poor and mixed stock ... Today thanks to the presence of a regiment of the Leibstandarte, the countryside is abounding with jolly and healthy young children. It is a practice that must be followed ... If a German soldier is expected to be ready to sacrifice his life without demur, then he is entitled to love freely and without restriction.

25. Himmler's back-and-forth exchange with Oberg and Dietrich in early 1943 is found in Helmut Heiber, ed. *Reichsführer: Briefe an und von Himmler* (Stuttgart: Deutsche Verlags-Anstalt, 1968), pp. 178–179. According to SS-Sturmbannführer Dr Greineder, Dietrich's legal affairs officer, 'In the Leibstandarte, sexual intercourse with women of other races was very frequent ... Some men more or less kept a concubine.' Helmut Krausnick, Hans Bucheim, Martin Broszat and Hans-Adolf Jacobsen, *Anatomy of the SS State* (New York: Walker and Company, 1968), p. 344.

26. Erwin Bartmann, *Für Volk and Führer: The Memoir of a Veteran of the 1st SS Panzer Division Leibstandarte Adolf Hitler* (Solihull, UK: Helion and Company, 2013), pp. 97–99.

27. 'LSSAH KTB Nr. 6', NA, T-354, Roll 611, F684.

28. Borchers's Diary, 19 August 1942. On 29 July:

At night there was always the worry that the 'Tommies' would insert some airborne saboteurs behind our lines. The training was taken on with enthusiasm, like the zeal we had in the old days. At night we often had orienteering exercises where we used compasses, maps, and diagrams to get to a designated point. The distance was usually 10–15 km and cross-country, and at the end stood the food wagon. Understandably, sometimes we couldn't 'find' our point, and instead stayed in the pub in the next village, eating there and drinking Aquavit and Calvados, wine, and champagne. In the grey dawn we went back to the Company and reported that we had finished our hike. But a few drunken comrades, who weren't able to maintain a military appearance, gave us away ... We were totally drunk when we came back at 0600 to the barracks. I reported us as back to the boss but he wanted to see the entire group of troops. I went, and got Otto Laupe too, to go to the office. We didn't see anyone there and left again. Heinz Hoot was pretty unsteady on his feet, but only Bruno Matthei was completely passed out in bed and couldn't be roused. I threw two buckets of water on him in bed but it didn't help. He still wasn't coherent.

29. 'SS Leibstandarte Adolf Hitler, KTB Nr. 2', BA-MA RS 3-1/31, Box 2.
30. 'Report on the Interrogation of Walter Schellenberger', 27 June–12 July 1946, NA, RG-498, Intelligence Records of the ETO Historical Division, UD 308, Box 1378. Schellenberg further noted that in the naïve plan to sue for peace with Britain a small piece of Holland would also be retained, as Himmler was sentimental about this region due to its 'pure-blooded Germanic population'. When flown to England for lengthy interrogation, Schellenberg was flabbergasted to see pristine London from the air—no bomb, V-1 or V-2 scars remained. 'I cannot understand,' he hissed in disbelief. 'Where is the destruction?'
31. Warlimont, *Inside Hitler's Headquarters*, p. 253.
32. Paul Krellmann to Wolfgang Vorpersal, 24 January 1976, BA-MA, Sammlung Vorpersal, N756/413. Krellmann was a Leibstandarte veteran from 1934 with the 7th and later 14th Company and served under Anhalt.
33. See BDC file for Günther Anhalt, NA, RG-242, BDC file, Roll A3343-SSO-015. Upon being relieved of command, Anhalt was hospitalized in Berlin and treated for alcoholism. As evidence in letters on 15 and 28 December 1942, Anhalt was forbidden upon Himmler's personal order from returning to the Leibstandarte—the command had been given over to Peiper. The problem had emerged earlier in the summer in June when Sepp Dietrich wrote to the SS office to complain of problems with Anhalt and Himmler sealed it. RFSS on 15 December 1942 to the SS Personal Head Office: 'Anhalt is known to me as a worthless man particularly due to his alcoholism (*auf dem Gebiet des Trunkes* …) and I forbid his relocation within the Leibstandarte. Any new assignment for Anhalt needs my explicit authorization.' Thanks to Andreas Schulz for this information within his scholarly compilation on Waffen SS personalities. The SS colonel would later recover enough to take over a command in SS Police Regiment 2, where he was implicated in war crimes, having 'fought' with SS Gruppenführer Curt von Gottberg, one of Himmler's experts on the murder campaign against Jews and the Slavs in the Ukraine

near Minsk. Anhalt was killed fighting in Berlin in the last weeks of the war.

34. 'Beförderungen in der Waffen SS: SS Hauptsturmführer Jochen Peiper', 20 September 1942, Peiper's BDC file. The application was signed both by Witt and Dietrich. Himmler's denial arrived via a teletype message from the SS main personnel office dated 18 January 1943: 'denied on 9 Nov 1942 by Reichsführer probably because of age'.

35. See Peiper's BDC file. The III Battalion was officially designated as *gepanzert* with SPW in December of 1942. On 10 December the formation was redesignated as Leibstandarte SS Panzer Grenadier Division Adolf Hitler.

36. 'Aufstellung einer schweren Panzer Kompanie für das SS Panzer-Regiment der SS Div LSSAH', 13 November 1942, NA, RG-242, T-175, R108, F2631455.

37. The former commander, SS Sturmbannführer Günther Anhalt, left his command abruptly. Peiper's decree for his men: they would be 'a unit the Führer could always rely on'. Statement by Sturmmann Erich Schöbel. Also, 'we were not thrilled': in Agte, *Michael Wittmann and the Tiger Commanders*, p. 50.

38. For Peiper's time in France see Dinse Interview; Dinse BDC file, NA RG-242, A3343-SSO-Roll 154. Dinse had been SS Abschnitt XIV in Bremen up through 1940. Then SS Hauptsturmführer Otto Dinse was with Sonderkommando in (Łódź) Litzmannstadt on 12 November 1940. A short description of the Sonderkommando task can read between the lines saying 'Brigadeführer Rosener was to inspect our business area.' He left on 15 February 1941 and joined the Leibstandarte, where he would again meet Peiper.

39. Jochen Peiper, Letter to Hedwig Potthast, 19 October 1942, NSDAP Hauptarchiv, Himmler Collection, Microfilm Roll No. 99, Hoover Institution, Stanford University. Hedwig Potthast was at this time still living in an apartment in Grunewald (33 Caspar-Theyß str., where she had moved the preceding September), the wealthy section in Berlin just west of Wilmersdorf. At that time Potthast suffered loneliness, being estranged from her family after the birth of Himmler's illegitimate son and deeply pained by the death of her brother earlier that year. For the other personalities in Himmler's office to which the letter refers: Rudi Brandt was Himmler's office manager and someone to whom Peiper and his wife had grown acquainted (BDC A3343-SSO-099); Franz Lucas was Himmler's driver (A3343-SSO-279A), Sepp Kiermaier was Himmler's bodyguard (A3343-SSO-167A) and Werner Grothmann was Peiper's replacement

as 1st adjutant (A3343-SSO-038A). Herman Dörner was another older SS officer (born in 1908; BDC File A3343-SSO-159) also on Himmler's staff, having been reassigned after serving as an SS Untersturmführer and platoon leader of the engineer company with the SS Totenkopf Division. He fought with Totenkopf in Poland and France (destroying a British tank near Simencourt near Arras on 23 May 1940) before returning to Himmler's staff in June 1940. Records of Totenkopf in France: BA-MA, NS 756/1229.

40. Dr Franz Neundorff, in Agte, *Michael Wittmann and the Tiger Commanders*, p. 53.

41. For the orchestral show at the Trocadero, see Lehmann and Tiemann, *Die Leibstandarte*, vol. II, pp. 233–234.

42. Guhl, 'Sweat saves blood': Agte, *Michael Wittmann and the Tiger Commanders*, p. 53; Guhl BDC file, NA RG-242, A3343-SSO-Roll 42A.

43. Regarding Peiper's return home, Witte et al., *Der Dienstkalender Heinrich Himmlers 1941/42*, 13 December 1942, p. 645.

44. Hitler to Himmler, 18 December 1942: 'Behind Russia stand the numberless hordes of Asia … to send wave after wave against Europe and to conquer the vast area between the Atlantic and Pacific. Germany is the advance guard against Bolshevism. America and England will have to take part in the struggle if they do not want to be destroyed themselves!' Kersten, *Memoirs*, p. 261.

45. Witte, *Der Dienstkalender Heinrich Himmlers 1941/42*, 27–28 December, pp. 656–658. Andreas Schmidt was the leader of the ethnic Transylvanian Germans from Rumania and son-in-law of Gottlob Berger. For details of the Julfest: Oberabschnitt Welt, *Die Gestaltung der Feste im Jahres und Lebenslauf in der SS familie* (Wuppertal: Völkischer Verlag Druckerei, 1940). After the war HIAG members still celebrated the Julfest; see Felix Steiner, *Die Freiwilligen: Idee und Opfergang* (Göttingen: Plesse Verlag, 1958), p. 300.

46. Borchers's Diary, 31 December 1942.

47. On New Year's Eve everyone, including Peiper, was somewhat startled at midnight when loud, clanging bells began to peal in typically peaceful Verneuil. Some mistook the clanging for a fire alert, and others just were uncertain of its source—even villagers. The following day Peiper assembled the battalion to find out who was responsible for the ruckus. It seems that members of the motorcycle reconnaissance platoon had paid the priest to allow them to ring the bells at midnight. Knowing the priest, Peiper dropped the whole thing.

48. Kriegstagebuch von 1930–1945, Erhard Gührs, personal diary provided to author (hereafter Gührs Diary).

49. Hermann Göring, Radio speech, 30 January 1943, courtesy of Jens Westemeier.

50. For the text of the Paulus Stalingrad communique to Hitler from 29 January 1943, see John Toland, *Adolf Hitler* (New York: Doubleday, 1976), p. 730. For other background on this episode, see Antony Beevor and Artemis Cooper, *Stalingrad: The Fateful Siege 1942–1943* (New York: Viking, 1999). For Hitler's perspective on Paulus and his failure: 'When the nerves break down, there is nothing but to admit that one can't handle the situation, and to shoot one's self. One can also say that the man should have shot himself just as the old commanders who threw themselves on their swords when they saw that their cause was lost. That goes without saying. Even Varus gave his slave the order: "Now kill me!"' Warlimont, *Inside Hitler's Headquarters*, p. 302.

51. By this time Himmler's SS publishing house under Gottlob Berger had carefully crafted a propaganda publication, simply titled *Der Untermensch*, a circular loaded with descriptions and photographs aiming to depict the animal-like appearance and ferocious character of the Eastern foe, 'a mixture of low and lowest humanity, truly sub-humans ... This is how the Soviet soldier looks ... Whether under the Tartars, or Peter, or Stalin, this people is born for the yoke.' NA RG-238, NO-1805. Hitler personally approved the fourth draft of the publication for wide dissemination.

52. Gührs Diary.

53. 'Kamerad, Schicksalsstunde schlägt', SS Leitheft 9, January 1943, NA, RG-242, T-611, R 44, p. 20: 'Comrade, the Fateful Hour Tolls'. Kurt Eggers was a former editor with the SS house organ, *Das Schwarze Korps*. Eggers later fought with 5th SS Division 'Wiking', where he died in action on 13 August 1943 and was martyred. Other portions of the song:

> Comrade, the Führer has said,
> The Reich must be created
> No man who doesn't risk his life can see this new world,
> Comrade, the beautiful new world is in the south and in the north
> The Reich has been conquered for this day forth.

54. Jochen Peiper, 'Brief Review', 7 April 1946. Peiper posed that, 'Had Paulus fought to the last one, as we had all expected, this sacrifice in this critical time would have proved itself to the entire army as an immense moral boost ... The army soldier thus lost to a great extent the fear of capture and ... the incentive for which he was now

prepared to fight desperately to the last breath. Needless to mention that the Waffen SS did not fall for this siren's song.'

Chapter 4: Operation Peiper

1. Literally, 'To live is to fight.'
2. Gerhard Engel, *At the Heart of the Reich: The Secret Diary of Hitler's Army Adjutant* (London: Greenhill Books, 2006), entry for 31 December 1942.
3. See David M. Glantz and Jonathan House, *When Titans Clashed* (Lawrence: University of Kansas Press, 1995), pp. 136–139 and footnotes. 'Operation Mars' had coordinated seven Soviet armies, with eighty-three divisions, 817,000 men and 2,350 tanks. Most of the tanks and nearly half the Russian armies were lost in a failed blow to surround the German armies arrayed before Moscow.
4. Recollection of Hans Behrend of the 7 Panzer Company, as cited in Ralf Tiemann, *Chronicle of the 7. Panzerkompanie Leibstandarte* (Atglen, PA: Schiffer Military History, 1998), p. 30.
5. Lehmann and Tiemann, *Die Leibstandarte*, vol. III, pp. 45–47.
6. 320th Infantry Division, KTB for February 1943, BA-MA, RH 26 /320/8. The 585th Regiment had been particularly ravaged. By 7 February its troops reported themselves down to fifty per cent of the machine gun ammunition and only sixty per cent of that for artillery with many nearly freezing wounded. Available fuel was down to 1 consumption unit (VS).
7. 'Kriegstagebuch Nr. 3 der 320 I.D.', NA, T-315, Roll 2032, F000870.
8. Borchers's Diary, 8 February 1943.
9. Source accounts of this fighting is based on the 'Kriegstagebuch Nr. 3 der 320 I.D.' as well as 'Kriegstagebuch der Armeeabteilung Lanz/Kemp für die Zeit 1.2-30.6 1943', NA, T-312, Roll 1620. For Peiper's personal perspectives see Peiper to Rudolf Lehmann, 10 April 1976, as cited by Lehmann and Tiemann, *Die Leibstandarte*, vol. III, pp. 63–64. See also James Lucas, 'Battle Group Peiper in the Mission to Rescue 320th Infantry Division, Surrounded and Cutoff South of Kharkov, February 1943', in *Battle Group Peiper* (Bradford, UK: Sphere Books Ltd., 1985), pp. 126–130. Although portions of this book represent a semi-fictionalized account of the fighting, this section is based on verifiable sources and also participant interviews conducted by Lucas.
10. For Dietrich's summary of Peiper's action and his recommendation for the German Cross in Gold, see 'Vorschlag Nr. [*sic*: missing number]

für die Verleihung des Deutschen Kreuzes in Gold', Peiper BDC File, 1943, date unintelligible (hereafter 'Vorschlag Nr.').

11. 'Josef ('Sepp') Dietrich: 7th Army Interrogation Centre', SAIC/43 11 Jun 45. WO 208/1788.

12. Dietrich's statement from the recollection of Lehmann via Lucas, Lucas, *Battle Group Peiper*, p. 16. James Lucas, the British author, was in friendly contact with the old Leibstandarte veterans in the 1970s. The name "Operation Peiper" is taken from the diary of Erhard Gührs, entry for 10 February 1943. In author's possession. See Rudolf Lehmann to Hubert Meyer, 12 June 1978, BA-MA, HIAG Records, RS 7/ v. 509.

13. 'Bericht Erhard Gührs, III gep. Btl.', Gührs Diary, February 1943.

14. 'KR. Fernschreiben An SS-Panzer Corps: Armeeabteilung Lanz, 12.2.43', NA, T-312, Roll 1620.

15. 'Spitze 320 I.D., FLiège rabwurf', NA, T-315, Roll 2033, F000091-92.

16. The 320th was just west of Ssokolowo and east of Scheludowka, near the Donets River. The village of Skirpai was just to the northeast, as shown by the original maps from the source material at the Bundesarchiv: 320th Infantry Division, KTB for February 1943, RH 26 320/8-10, BA-MA.

17. Hans Joachim Redecker, 'Die Lötlampe, 1943', Leibstandarte poem provided by anonymous source.

18. From 26 to 29 November 1812 more than ten thousand of Napoleon's French soldiers died under Russian artillery bombardment while crossing the Berezina River near Barysaw.

19. The summary of Peiper's rescue of the 320th Division is also contained in Dietrich's recommendation for the German Cross in 'Vorschlag Nr'.

20. 'Generalkommando SS Panzer Korps Fernschreiben Armee Abt. Lanz: Nachmeldung zur Tagesmeldung zum 12.2.43', T-354, R118, F3751640.

21. Jochen Peiper, 'Brief Review', 7 April 1946.

22. Dinse Interview: 'There were some terrible, cruel things that happened in that fighting. They had hanged some wounded [German] soldiers. Other terrible things were done. It was horrible.'

23. 'Report on Interrogation of PW Kp 186988 Rotenfuh. Otto Sierk, SS Vers. Kp. III/ 2 SS Pz Gren. Rgt'. 17 November 1944. NA, RG 226, Entry 109, Box 698, Folder 6160; also: PRO: WO 208/4295. Special thanks to Dr Richard Breitman for bringing my attention to this important document amid the mass of OSS material currently being declassified at the National Archives.

24. Dinse Interview.
25. Hans Lierk, Letter to Walter Krüger, 6 March 1984. After the war there were rumours that Fallschirmjäger troops helped Peiper fight out of encirclement. 'There were no Luftwaffe troops helping us to free the Herz Division,' Lierk told Krüger. 'You for sure will remember the wooden bridge over the Donez near Tjugujew during the fighting to free them.' BA-MA, RS7/ v. 372.
26. Peiper's personal recollections of the action freeing the 320th Division are taken from his own account. Peiper, Letter to Rudolf Lehmann, 10 April 1976, as cited by Lehmann and Tiemann, *Die Leibstandarte*, vol. III, pp. 63–64.
27. 'Divisionsbefehl für die Verschiebung die Div. nach Norden, 14.2.43,' 320th Infantry Division, T-315, Roll 2033, Frames 000063-64. Ironically, General Postel, promoted from the 320th Division to the XXX Army Corps, was taken prisoner by the Russian Army on 30 August 1944 after the capitulation in Romania. He was convicted as a war criminal in the Soviet Union and was sentenced to twenty-five years of hard labour in 1949. Postel died in captivity in Shakhty, Russia, on 20 September 1953.

Chapter 5: The Sword of Damocles

1. The back-and-forth conversations between Hausser and Head-quarters: 'Armee Abt. Lanz to Gen. Kdo. SS. Pz Korps', T-354, R118, F3751658. See also 'Kdo. SS Pz Korps to SS Führun gshauptamt', F3751719, Lehmann and Tiemann, *Die Leibstandarte*, vol. III, pp. 72–74.
2. In the fable Damocles traded places with the Dionysiusean king of Sicily only to be petrified with fear after learning that a sharp sword dangled over the king's bed, suspended by a single frail horsehair. Peiper saw the German field commanders in Russia as similarly inept and cowardly: 'The actual state of affairs and the true situation did not penetrate the bacchantic wall of higher headquarters and the decisions of the Führer were thus based on wrong suppositions! He grew more and more suspicious and the gap between him and his staff became more difficult to bridge.'
3. Army Group South relaying Hitler's orders that Kharkov be held: 'Fernschreiben Hr. Gr. B to SS Pz Korps', T-354, R118, F3751502.
4. It was as close as Hitler ever came to the fighting in the war. Alan Clark, *Barbarossa* (New York: William & Morrow, 1965), p. 302.
5. Gührs Diary, 19 February 1943.
6. Gührs Diary, 20 February 1943.

7. For photographic evidence of how Peiper's men chased down and shot fleeing Russian soldiers, see George Nipe and Remy Spezzano, *Platz der Leibstandarte* (Southbury, CT: RZM Imports, 2002), pp. 28–31. The photos in the sequence were taken on 20 February 1943.

8. 'Kriegstagebuch für SS Panzergrenadier Regiment 2', T-354, R118, Message received at 9:02 on 20 February 1943.

9. Joachim Peiper, interview with John Toland, 10 October 1963 (hereafter Peiper-Toland Interview).

10. 'Vorschlag Nr. für die Verleihung des Deutschen Kreuzes in Gold', Peiper BDC file, March 1943, signed by Sepp Dietrich; Gührs Diary, 22 February 1943.

11. 'Reichsführer SS gltd. SS Führungshauptamt: SS Totenkopf-Div funkt folgende Meldung', 26 February 1943. For the story of Eicke's death and the feigned condolences of many from the Waffen SS, see Sydnor, *Soldiers of Destruction*, pp. 270–276.

12. 'The air is thick enough to cut with a knife. Only four weeks ago I had a tiled bathroom, a white bed. And now I have frostbitten heels, my hide full of lice, my face eaten up by frost; and only once I slept long enough because in a barn full of straw all the techniques for waking me up were unsuccessful.' Heinz von Westernhagen, 25 February 1943, in Westernhagen, *Die Kinder der Täter*, pp. 48–49.

13. Tiemann's letter home is taken from his *Chronicle of the 7. Panzer Kompanie*, p. 41. His sentiment reflected the typical SS response to not being in the action: 'It is often painful for me to sit in the command post and not be able to take part in the battles.' The dead NCO was Oberscharführer Karl Scharna.

14. Glantz and House, 1995, p. 296. Manstein, *Lost Victories*, p. 433. Russian losses before Kharkov amounted to six tank corps, ten rifle divisions and half a dozen other brigades. Popov's losses were nearly half of the total. Ironically, it was the Soviet Sixth Army that was annihilated—the same number as the German army that had been sacrificed at Stalingrad. Meantime, the SS Panzer Corps lost nearly 44% of its strength including 160 officers and 4,300 men. While the Donets Campaign is often considered one of the last great German victories in the East, military historian, Robert Citino makes a strong case that it was rather an illustory 'brief glimpse of victory'. Robert M. Citino, *The Wehrmacht Retreats, Fighting a Lost War, 1943*, (University of Kansas, Lawrence, KS: 2012), p. 70-74.

15. Borchers's Diary, 24 February 1943.

16. 'Peiper: Russian Theater', p. 230.

Chapter 6: Kharkov

1. 'Peiper: Russian Theater', Williams, *Captor-Captive*, p. 231. 'The 'Holz-kastenmine was used to an astronomical extent. After this effort to stop the German advance there appeared, in chronological order the 'Pak' which also showed up in unprecedented quantities. These two weapons as well as 'General Winter' were responsible for the stoppage of the German military machine.'

2. Gührs Diary, 2 March 1943.

3. Oswald Siegmund, *Meine Ehre heisst Treue: Von der Leibstandarte ins Landsberger Kriegsverbrechergefängnis* (Essen: Heitz & Höffkes, 1992), p. 54. Siegmund had been an auto mechanic for three years before entering the SS in 1940. Before coming to the Leibstandarte he had been posted in Prague with an SS Totenkopfverbände (Death's Head unit): NA, RG 549, Case 6–24, Box 9. Siegmund's testimony in his own book says the blowtorches were used as weapons. The need for the weapon was clear, given the Soviet propensity for close-in combat; after all, the Hanomag factories had introduced the official version, the *Schutzenpanzerwagen* Sd Kfz 251/16, at the beginning of 1943. Its range was 30 metres. Siegmund asserted that his self-improvised copycat produced a short-range *Flammenwerfer*. BDC file, RG 242, A3343-SM-R066, F00048-56.

4. Interestingly, a historian following behind the frustrated American forces with the U.S. 79th Infantry Division in the hedgerow fighting later in 1944 in Normandy would echo Peiper's opinion of the military's use of fire: 'Fire and flame is the answer. Could we get flame-throwing tanks, backed up by plenty of flame-throwing infantryman? ... Jerry fears them above all. I believe if we started a fully equipped flame throwing division and battalion of flame-throwing tanks and burned and incinerated a huge area and everything in it, hedgerow by hedgerow and tree lane by tree lane, house and bring, hay stacks, grain fields, orchards, Jerry would have to alter his tactics.' Lieutenant Colonel C.A. Jones, 12 July 1944, Letter to Colonel G.S. Eyster from Colonel W.A. Gabor, Theatre Historian, 17 July 1944, NA, RG-498, UD 602, Historical Division, Miscellaneous Records of the Theatre Historian, Box 4061.

5. IMT, vol. 20, p. 432. After the war Paul Hausser was asked at the Nuremberg International Military Tribunal about the burning of the Russian villages of Staroverowka, Stanitschnoje and Jefremovka by men under his command during the third battle for Kharkov.

The basis of these questions appear to be from the testimony of Jakob Hanreich ('Report on Interrogation of PW KP 49359 Sturmbannführer Jakob Hanreich', 19 August 1944, PWIS(H)/LDC/299, NA RG 332, Box 30, 290/56/1/5). Hanreich had specifically named Kurt Meyer for the burning and murder of all inhabitants of Jefremowka. He also implicated Wisch's command for burning Staroverowka. However, although records show that Rudolf Sandig's II Battalion, SS Panzergrenadier Regiment 2, was credited with taking this village on 2 March, it is also recorded that Peiper's battalion was ordered there on 3 March, arriving in the afternoon and leaving later that same day. (Lehmann and Tiemann, *Die Leibstandarte*, vol. III, pp. 141–143, covers the capture of Staroverowka and Peiper's arrival the next day.) Local accounts accuse the Germans of shooting nearly seventy civilians on 2 March apparently for helping the Russian forces defend the village (http://staroverovka.ucoz.ua/publ/5-1-0-1). In the early hours of 4 March Peiper successfully captured the village of Stanitschnoje and received a battlefield commendation for his actions there, as highlighted in his personnel file. Oswald Siegmund claimed that Peiper's SPW-mounted troops used flame-throwers to burn Stanitschnoje to the ground in an assault on the morning of 4 March 1943. (Siegmund, *Meine Ehre heisst Treue*, p. 54). The day before, Peiper's battalion had attacked and captured Staroverowka, as mentioned in the Nuremberg proceedings as well as Siegmund's account. Thus, it seems naïve to dismiss the symbol of Peiper's battalion, proudly displayed on its SPWs. In the Waffen SS it was famously known as the *Lötlampen Abteilung* for burning a path wherever it moved in the East.

6.   'Abschrift Fernschreiben, KTB. Ia Anl. A: Gen Kdo. SS-Pz-Korps', T-354, R118, F3752046. Only sixty-seven tanks with eight Tigers and nineteen assault guns and sixty-five SPWs were combat ready on that date. The nature of the combat was indicated by only five prisoners taken on that date, with some six hundred enemy killed.

7.   'Report on Interrogation of PW Kp 186988 Rotenfuh. Otto Sierk, SS Vers. Kp. III/ 2 SS Pz Gren. Rgt'. 17 November 1944, RG 226, Entry 109, Box 698: 'PW confirms that the regimental order issued at the beginning of 1943 that, in case of retreat, all villages were to be evacuated and burnt.'

8.   Chief among the non-malevolent justification for the blowtorch was the poem 'Die Lötlampe', written in 1943 by Hans Joachim Redecker,

which showed the blowtorches doing everything from heating cold engines, warming cold troopers and scrambling eggs:

> The Battalion Peiper is now well known
> as the Blowtorch battalion throughout the land
> Why this name is used for us
> Will be told in the coming verses
> The tanks which well protect our lives,
> thank the torch that we use it properly.
> It warmed the oil, and then ready to jump,
> the engines started every time
> Praise for the torch and the commander.

Although blowtorches warming oil, eggs and engines may all be true, the fact remains that Oswald Siegmund explicitly claimed he personally modified the blowtorches in March 1943 to be used as weapons. Siegmund, *Meine Ehre heisst Treue.*

9. Herbert Walther, conversation with Jens Westemeier, 25 May 1994. Walther was author of *Division der Waffen SS im Einsatz* (Friedberg: Podzun-Pallas Verlag, 1993). Moreover, in a taped interview with Fritz Kosmehl on 17 December 2004 he related that even before Peiper joined the tank regiment, he and the SPW battalion was widely known to burn villages. This was the reason they were known as the *Lötlampen Abteilung*. 'I can confirm that,' he emphasised.

10. When Peiper received his commendation for the Oak Leaves on 27 December 1943 Theodor Wisch wrote of this in a telling fashion: 'Peiper took personal command of the SPW battalion and carried out a night attack on the village with unprecedented verve, such that the enemy in the trenches and the village were taken completely by surprise, and wiped out by gunnery and *flame-thrower fire* from the SPWs.' Peiper BDC file, emphasis mine. Thus, from 1943 the 1st SS Panzer Division itself acknowledged that the battalion was using flame-throwers through Wisch himself. For supporting data, see handwritten testimony of Erich Rumpf describing actions in the East, NA RG 549, Entry 143, Box 33, 'Jefremowka (Russia)'.

11. Hanreich Interrogation. Hanreich was an old fighter, born in Vienna in 1911 and active in the Nazi Party since 1933. He joined the Leibstandarte in 1940, eventually rising to the command the assault gun battalion in 1942. The SS colonel was moved to the forming Hitlerjugend Division in 1944 before his capture in Normandy later that August. NA, BDC File for Jakob Hanreich, A3343-SSO-061A.

12. In retrospect, few—perhaps most of all Jochen Peiper—could believe this naïve interpretation. There was always an imperfect memory to blame: 'I cannot say exactly if the lamps were used for setting houses on fire,' Peiper would later write to James Weingartner (Peiper to Weingartner, March 1976). 'Would you see a moral difference between setting a house on fire with a flame-thrower from a distance of 50 metres or with a torch from 30 centimetres, or massacring civilians with submachine guns from a distance of 50 metres or from a height of 50 metres from a helicopter. It is really nothing but hypocrisy to bless war and condemn its methods. There is no such thing as a neat war with clean hands.'

13. Gührs Diary, 20 February 1943.

14. Jochen Peiper, Letter to Hedwig Potthast, 24 March 1943, NSDAP Hauptarchiv, Himmler Collection, Microfilm Roll No. 99, Hoover Institution, Stanford University.

15. Statement of Paul Zwigart, 11 February 1946, NA, War Crimes Cases Tried, Case 6-24, RG-549, Box 9.

16. Gührs Diary, 3 March 1943. 'My first night with the supply troop. I can sleep endlessly.'

17. Borchers's Diary, 5 March 1943.

18. One justification: 'only in very few instances did the Russians surrender. In many cases they fought until they had nothing left, but a knife to fight with. That is why there were so very few Russian prisoners of war.' 'Testimony of Arndt Fischer to Dwight F. Fanton', 31 March 1946, RG 549, Case 6-24, Box 22.

19. See 'Secretly Taped Room Conversation of POWs Guetter—Tschitscho, Ft. Hunt', 27 June 1944, NARA, RG-165, Entry 179, Box 477.

20. For the meeting of Witt and Peiper before Kharkov, see Lehmann, *Die Leibstandarte im Bild*, p. 181.

21. SS Untersturmführer Mauer of the 2nd Company of the reconnaissance battalion: Lehmann and Tiemann, *Die Leibstandarte*, p. 155.

22. For the 'dead Russians everywhere' account of Sturmgeschützmann Krutzner, see *Wiking Ruf*, no. 7 (1955), p. 16.

23. Dinse Interview.

24. Peiper BDC file, Funkspruch an SS Sturmbannführer Jochen Peiper, 9 March 1943.

25. Word of Peiper's award was telegraphed from Himmler to Dietrich on 9 March 1943, BDC files. Evidence that Himmler maintained close communication with Sigurd Peiper during the war years is contained in a messages providing greetings from Jochen to Sigurd,

gifts for the Peiper family and even visits by Peiper's parents (see Witte et al., *Der Dienstkalender Heinrich Himmlers 1941/42*, entries for 29 December 1941 and 2 January, 23 April and 1 June 1942). There is even evidence of the allocation of black-market food stuffs from Himmler's private cache to 'Frau Peiper' and other chosen close associates. Records survive thanks to Himmler's penchant for meticulous record keeping—even when the subject was 'peas'. See entries by Erika Lorenz, 'Betr. Erbsen', RG 242, T-175, R112, F2637504, Berlin, 21 July 1942. Lorenz was known as Himmler's 'Aunty for Presents', and the office maintained a card index for gifts. Kersten, *Memoirs*, p. 122.

26. 'Wünsche declared himself ready to try to break through the Russian front to save us. Meyer implored him "be quick Max, the Battalion is at stake."' For the recollections of Rudolf von Ribbentrop, see Franz Kurowski, *Panzer Aces* (Winnipeg: J.J. Fedorowicz, 1992), p. 166.

27. In mid-February Kurt Meyer's reinforced Recon Battalion (Aufklärungsabteilung), which was part of the Angriffsgruppe SS Panzer Corps, included the following elements: 6 Panzer Regiment LAH (under Obersturmführer Astherger), 3 Artillery Regiment LAH (under Obersturmführer Haack) and 1 Panzer Regiment LAH (under Stürmbannführer Wünsche). Lehmann, *Die Leibstandarte*, p. 89.

28. On the distribution of pistols to the wounded, Meyer recalled, 'The voices of my soldiers were tearing my heart from my body … I would rather stand in a hail of fire than to have to hold another conversation like that.' Kurt Meyer, *Grenadiers*, p. 170.

29. Lehmann and Tiemann, *Die Leibstandarte*, vol. IV/1, p. 95.

30. Kurt Meyer, *Grenadiers*, p. 172.

31. Wünsche BDC file, 'DK/Gold 25.2.1943'.

32. German losses in the action were five killed and fourteen wounded. For Wünsche's exhortation 'Forward! Forward!' see Obersturmführer Isecke, as cited by Lehmann, *Die Leibstandarte*, p. 129, note 68.

33. Wünsche BDC file, citation dated 'RK 28th February 1943'.

34. Anonymous (2002) 'Special Interrogation Report: Brigadeführer Kurt Meyer Command, 12th, http://scholars.wlu.ca/cmh/vol11/iss4/6)'. 'One last point: during some of this conversation Wunsche, commander of the 12th SS Panzer Regiment, was present. Slightly younger than Meyer and decorated like a Christmas tree, he was a similar example of the system as Meyer. His ideas and general philosophy of life were stated in exactly the same terms as those of Meyer. In appearance he was approximately six feet four inches in height and broad shouldered, though by no means stout. He was

a good-looking man, blond, with eyes not unlike Meyer's and in one phase the perfect example of Aryan youth as laid down in the pages of Mein Kampf.'

35. For Hitler's conversation with Dietrich, see Lehmann and Tiemann, *Die Leibstandarte*, vol. III, p. 164. On 9 March 1942 Josef Goebbels entered in his diary: 'Sepp Dietrich is one of our best troop commanders; he is, so to speak, the Blücher of our movement ... the Führer was exceptionally happy about the way the Leibstandarte was led by Sepp Dietrich. This man has personally performed real deeds of heroism and has proved himself a great strategist in conducting his operations.' Lochner, *Goebbels Diaries*.

36. Borchers's Diary, 10 March 1943.

37. For an assessment of the Hausser vs. Hoth controversy at Kharkov, see Glantz and House, *When Titans Clashed*, p. 187, and also Karel Margry, *The Four Battles of Kharkov* (London: British International Ltd., 2001), pp. 20–27.

38. Kurt Meyer, *Grenadiers*, p. 195.

39. 'The battle was only won by assaults from house to house.' See 'Abschrift Fernschreiben: LSSAH to Gen. Kdo. SS Pz Korps', 12–13 March 1943, T-354, R118, F3752308-2314. Peiper's 13th Company alone lost thirty men in the fighting in Kharkov. For the view from the SS reconnaissance battalion, see Kurt Meyer, *Grenadiers*, pp. 201–202.

40. Borchers's Diary, 13 March 1943. According to Borchers, the surrendering Russians became suddenly civil. 'One came out with hands up; another came out playing an accordion.'

41. For Hausser's assessments of his losses, see Eddy Bauer, *Der Panzerkrieg*, vol. I (Bonn: Verlag Offene Worte, 1965), p. 242. Assisting the Leibstandarte in the operation, the Totenkopf Division had hemmed in the Russian units attempting to flee from the falling city to the east while fending off Russian attacks; the 25th Guards Rifle Division was smashed.

42. 'Sondermeldung: KTB Ia Anl. A: Aus dem Führerhauptquartier, den 14 März 1943', T-354, R118, 3752364.

43. 'Die Schwerter für Obergruppenführer Sepp Dietrich. Wie die Leibstandarte Charkow eroberte', BDC file for Dietrich, 14 March 1943.

44. For the operation of Peiper in Kharkov: Hans Siegel: 'Im Sturmgeschütz an der Spitze der Kampfgruppe Peiper zum Roten Platz nach Charkow vom 11.-13 März 1943', *Der Freiwillige* Nr. 7-8, 1994, p. 48.

45. In December 1968 there was a follow-on investigation of the Kharkov atrocities raised in 1946 at the Nuremberg trial by the German Zentralle in Ludwigsburg. About 675 members of the Leibstandarte were interrogated, including several well known to Peiper: Georg Preuss, Dr Robert Brüstle, Albert Frey, Max Hansen and Wilhelm Weidenhaupt. The former Obersturmführer Dr Rolf Schulze could be identified as the doctor who had present been at the time of the crime at Kharkov. He denied any participation and said that he did not know anything about the killing of the wounded Russian soldiers or officers—he had never even heard about it. In the interrogation the SS men generally excluded that any of the Leibstandarte men would have been able to commit such crimes. The hospital was part of the Russian defence lines, and the casualties were explained by the fighting involved. Also, it should have been known that the Russians shot their own wounded men so that they could not fall into German hands. There was no chance for the state attorney to get any further. At the end, in closing the case the state attorney said, 'It is very possible that not all the witnesses have told the truth, to protect themselves and other members of the Leibstandarte, but I can only guess that. I cannot prove it.' To ward off responsibility for their crimes, the accused Leibstandarte men excluded their own crimes, as if they did not exist, while recalling the atrocities of their enemy in detail. Then there was still another investigation in Germany that concluded in 1976. The state attorney concluded that, 'Definitely killings of Russian soldiers took place at the hospital, but there was no chance to locate those responsible and open cases against individuals.' For the massive file showing the inconclusive second investigation of the Kharkov killings, see BAL, 162/8276-8285. Landgericht Nuremberg-Fuerth, 1976.
46. For the Soviet side: I.F. Kladov et al., *The People's Verdict: A Full Report of the Proceedings of the Krasnodar and Kharkov German Atrocity Trials* (London: Hutchingson & Company, 1944).
47. Landgericht Nürnberg-Fürth [Nuremberg Court], transcript of court's judgement 27 February 1976, Az 95 Js 10 100/75. The state attorney's office in Frankfurt made the investigation, complete with extensive Soviet depositions from doctors and nurses and an exhumation report made in Kharkov in September 1943. For the denial from the Waffen SS, see Lehmann and Tiemann, *Die Leibstandarte*, vol. III, pp. 185–190.
48. Jochen Peiper, 'Brief Review', 7 April 1946. Similarly, in the document Peiper prepared for Williams (*Captor-Captive*, p. 230): 'As one travels

east, he must drop the excessive courtesy of Europe and further-
more forget the gentlemanly humane rules that were so highly
accepted and acknowledged. The Russian philosophy of war recognizes
only the will to survive or be destroyed.'

49. Lehmann and Tiemann, *Die Leibstandarte*, vol. III, p. 176.
50. Peiper-Toland Interview.
51. Rolf Moebius, 'German Heavy Armor', NARA, RG-338, Foreign
Military Studies, MS D-226.
52. Diary of Heinz Freiberg for March 1943 (hereafter Freiberg Diary),
in Tiemann, *Chronicle of the 7. Panzerkompanie*, p. 45.
53. Werner Wendt, interview with author, 21 May 1996. Born on 9 February 1921, Werner Wendt became a member of the Hitler Jugend
in 1933. Later he trained at Lichterfelde as a member of the Waffen
SS and in March 1940 came to the 2nd SS Artillery Regiment as a
cannonier in the Leibstandarte. Wendt participated in the Balkan
campaign in Yugoslavia and then the Russian campaign in 1942.
There he was transferred to the tank regiment of the Leibstandarte,
trained as a gunner on the Tiger tanks and participated in the
battle of Kharkov in 1943 with the 4th Heavy Company of the
Leibstandarte Panzer battalion. 'I moved to tanks in 1942. In
those days it looked as if the war might soon be won. There was
something very different about being with the tanks; it was much
more demanding and difficult. The Russian opponents were harder
than those before; they were ferocious and courageous. Tanks were
getting shot down all the time and burning ... The Russians would
continue to fire at you even after you shot them down and their
tanks were burning.'
54. Kurowski, *Panzer Aces*, pp. 180–181.
55. This action is summarized in Borchers's Diary for this period.
56. For Peiper's radio messages during the advance on Belgorod, see
Lehmann and Tiemann, *Die Leibstandarte*, vol. III, pp. 178–179.
57. For 'beautiful bombing run ...': Freiberg Diary, p. 46.
58. Source for the von Ribbentrop episode: Kurowski, *Panzer Aces*, p. 181.
59. 'On orders from Peiper, Obersturmführer von Ribbentrop went back
to the burning Schützenpanzerwagen after the rest of the unit had
pulled back. He was to determine whether there were wounded
grenadiers inside to be saved. He was only able to collect soldiers'
paybooks and the like; there were no more living men to be found.'
Lehmann and Tiemann, *Die Leibstandarte*, vol. III, p. 180.
60. Peter Ferdinand Koch, *Himmlers Graue Eminenz–Oswald Pohl*
(Hamburg: Verlag Facta Oblita, 1988), pp. 11–12.

61. Jochen Peiper, Letter to Hedwig Potthast, 24 March 1943, NSDAP Hauptarchiv, Himmler Collection, Microfilm Roll No. 99, Hoover Institution, Stanford University; originals at the Bundesarchiv Koblenz, 'Nachlass Heinrich Himmler: Korrespondenz Hedwig Potthast, Bestand N 1126/37'. Thanks to Gregor Pickro for help with these. This letter is extremely significant to gaining an under-standing of Peiper's view of fighting. In '*Aber auch ein schlechter Ruf verpflichtet*'—'But a bad reputation [schlechter Ruf] has its obligations'—Peiper reveals that his favourite wartime motto was taken from Nazi wartime cinematic diva Zarah Leander. The lyric is from the catchy and suggestive tune 'Yes Sir!' from the film 'zu neuen Ufern ...' Hitler loved the smoky-voiced Leander, but Himmler investigated her allegiances given her Jewish grandparents, jealously guarded Swedish citizenship, a love of Aquavit and her insistence on payment in Swedish Kroner.

62. Heinz von Westernhagen letters, 24 March–18 April 1943, Westernhagen, *Die Kinder der Täter*, p. 46.

63. Although today the favoured status of the Waffen SS is questioned, Hitler glowed effusively to others in the summer of 1943 regarding the superiority of Himmler's weaponized SS and the need to copiously equip it for future engagements: 'Besprechung des Führers mit Feldmarschall v. Kluge am 26. Juli 1943', Helmut Heiber ed., *Hitler's Lagebesprechungen*, vol. 10 (Stuttgart: Deutsche Verlags Anstalt, 1962), p. 383.

64. Lehmann and Tiemann, *Die Leibstandarte*, vol. III, p. 194.

65. 'Personelle Vorratstaktik', Gen. Kdo. SS Pz Kps. 12 April 1943, T-354, R603, F248. For the compromise of Waffen SS recruitment standards, see Bernd Wegner, *The Waffen-SS: Organization, Ideology and Function* (New York: Blackwell Publishers, 1990), pp. 305–307.

66. 'Voluntary Declaration by Hauptscharführer Alfred Kilian', 11 September 1945, PRO: WO/208/4295. Kilian was a member of the staff company of SS Panzer Grenadier Regiment 2. Lisabudowka was about 60km west of Kharkov and is shown on maps today as Lyubivka or Lyubovka.. Kilian said the order to shoot the Russian had been given by SS Hauptsturmführer Siegfried Wandt, also of the regiment staff company.

67. Röthling was captured in Normandy in the summer of 1944 and recalled how in Normandy, rather than sacrificial Russian prisoners, they had used cows to detect mines in France: SRM 643, 13 July 1944, PRO, WO 208/4138, Kew.

68. Jochen Peiper, Letter to Hedwig Potthast, 24 March 1943, NSDAP Hauptarchiv, Himmler Collection, Microfilm Roll No. 99, Hoover Institution, Stanford University.

69. An anonymous unreconstructed Leibstandarte veteran, interview with author, 20 May 1997. His viewpoint was unchanged after fifty years: 'All Russians are Asian beasts!'

70. Peiper to Weingartner, 9 April 1976. Peiper was quite correct. During the Second World War prisoners were treated in radically different ways depending on where they were taken. While only one to three per cent of American or British prisoners died in German captivity, fully fifty per cent of Soviet army prisoners died. See Rüdiger Overmans, *Das Deutsche Reich und der Zweiten Weltkrieg*, vol. 9/2 (Munich: Militärgeschlichtliches Forschungsamt, 2005), pp. 799, 820. Conversely, at least 90 per cent of German prisoners captured on the Eastern Front in 1941 soon perished, with evidence suggesting most were shot at the front soon after surrender. Christian Hartmann, *Wehrmacht in Ostkrieg: Front und militärsches Hinterland, 1941/42* (Munich: Oldenbourg Wissenschaftsverlag, 2009), pp. 542–549.

71. However, in his personal memoirs it is not surprising that Frey made no mention of this knowledge. See Frey, *Ich wollte die Freiheit*.

72. The rural village of Jefremowka/Ефремовка to which they returned is located in the Pervomaisky district of the Kharkiv Oblast. Its sister village of Semenivka lies so close to it that the casual observer would have difficulty deciding where one ended and the other began.

73. Recollection of Georg Isecke, Adjutant to Max Wünsche; Lehmann and Tiemann, *Die Leibstandarte*, vol. III, p. 104.

74. The scar-faced SS captain was likely Dr Erich Gatternig, who was with Meyer's reconnaissance battalion and had a pronounced facial scar. From the memories of Kurt Landrichter with the battalion:

'Dr Erich Gatternig—Hauptsturmführer and doctor, our battalion doctor, for what reason was he always in the frontline? Basically none, but he was always with us, close to the commander, always with a carbine in his hand. The medical tools were in his knapsack. For the companies he had two young doctors. His place is here, with Panzermeyer, with whom he established a good friendship and he knows that this is important for Panzermeyer – more important than he himself – as he likes to say. There will not be another commander like Panzermeyer soon, so he has made it his task to be guardian angel for Panzermeyer.'

(Thanks to Timo Worst for information on Gatternig and his likely identification as the culprit at Jefremowka.)

75. Translation of Rumpf statement from RG-549: 'Thereupon Hauptsturmführer Nüske went away, I suppose that he went to the command post of the commander, came back after about 30 minutes and confirmed that the order had been given by Meyer. Outraged at the behaviour of the Hauptsturmführer, he said that "he of all people had to behave like a madman" [this referred to the Hauptsturmführer] as he had no official position [or rank] and had no say within the Recon detachment [Meyer's detachment]. At the time Nüske was Obersturmführer. The expression "like mad" correctly describes the way this officer behaved and shot the woman. On the basis of this order, all the inhabitants were shot, all the cattle killed and the houses set on fire.'

76. Three-page Ukrainian document entitled Jefremowka (Yefremivka), which reports the details of the atrocity. Although this document has many detractors and does indeed have erroneous facts included, some details have been corroborated by German testimony—see note 17. For details of the children beaten to death with iron bars, see Testimony of Walter Fransee, LAH. 'Kriegsverbrechen im Osten', G.W.U. Gelman Library, William Perl Papers. Box 6 Folder 51. When taken as a prisoner after being shot down on 1 December 1943, Obserstleutnant Wilfried von Müller-Rienzburg was moved to England to Trent Park. There he told of how SS Sturmbannführer Kurt Meyer had boasted to him that when members of the Leibstandarte had taken Kharkov with only two casualties, they then destroyed an entire village, including 'women, children and old people'. SRGG 832, 13 February 1944, PRO, WO 208/4168.

77. SRM 479, 23 February 1944, WO 208/4138, British National Archives. Transcript of the overheard conversation of a German Hauptscharführer is from the 'Einsatz Kommando 3 Sicherheits Polizei', who had been captured in Italy in October 1943. This PoW related how he was told 'a fantastic story' about a 'Standartenführer Meyer'. He then detailed the method of the killing in the church, the men sent to shovel snow, the setting up of the machine gun low and the burning of those who were both alive and dead. These details match closely the local accounts. See also the account of SS Untersturmführer Krämer, whose details match almost perfectly: SRM 1079, 24 November 1944, PRO, WO 208/4139: 'An MG 42 was set up in the main aisle of the church. Then, the Russian men, women and children were made to shovel snow; then they were taken into the church,

without knowing what was happening. There were shot immediately with the MG 42 and petrol was poured on them and the whole place was set on fire.'

78. 'My wound was light, my hip was shot through the soft tissues, but my head and cheek needed a skin transplant and I was ill for a long time. It can be said that I came back from the other world, or rather from an infernal hell.' Sergey Latyshev, *Born in a Shirt* (Cherkassy: Siyach, 1991). This finding is courtesy of Carol Bryne, who has scoured Russia and the Ukraine for witnesses to these events. Another villager returning after the war was devastated to learn what had taken place: 'In my time I knew every corner of the village, every hut, and now they were left with only piles of burned and blown up huts ... We have a great grief in the village. The Germans burned one hundred and eighty people in the church, all the male population, even the elderly and teenagers were not spared ... how to live on?'

79. British National Archives, TS26/856, p. 232. Hanreich initially gave this testimony in 1944 shortly after his capture in France. Re-interrogated in Canada in 1945, he again stood by this statement. He also denied that he had been present but stated that he was in retreat to Krasnograd and had heard the story within days from 'numerous sources'. In this same testimony Hanreich also spoke about the killing of Jews by the Leibstandarte band master Muller-John in Poland, amongst other verifiable incidents.

80. Total deaths as recorded on the village memorial. Also noted were 152 villagers who had fought for the 'Motherland': eighty-three were killed, with forty-one of this number listed as missing and forty-two received known funerals. Sixty-four returned from the war.

81. During the Malmédy trial a testimony of Erich Rumpf was read out loud in which he said, 'Peiper, in his military talks, often used the phrase *"Auch ein schlechter Ruf verplichtet"* [A bad reputation has its commitments]. In what way the other officers understood "a bad reputation" isn't known to me but me personally I remember one case in Russia in which we lighted up a complete village of about 2,000 inhabitants and had to execute all on orders. This crime surely is one of the reasons/grounds for those who understand the bad reputation of the SS.' William Perl Papers, Gelman University, Affidavit of Erich Rumpf box 5/folder 24. Although Rumpf already confirmed in his other testimony that he was in Jefremowka and is no doubt recalling that episode here, he neglected to clarify in this testimony that Meyer—not Peiper—was responsible for the village massacre.

Peiper remembered this episode many years later when he sniffed, 'I remember during the trial, a "testimony" of the commanding officer of the 9th Panzer Pionier Kompanie was read, according to which we reduced a village to ashes after we had herded the people into a church à la Oradour. That referred to the Panzer Regiment to which he belonged at the time. I cannot say anything about that, because at the time I did not belong to the Panzer regiment, but to the 2nd Panzer Grenadier Regiment.' Peiper to Weingartner, March 1976.

82. Ivan Kiselev, an inhabitant of Jefremowka, was fifteen years old in February 1943. Ten members of his family were murdered that day, including his mother, his seven-year-old sister and his young four-year-old brother. He himself was also shot, but the bullet only grazed him, and he survived by feigning death. Kiseliov spent many years after the massacre looking for those responsible, garnering the help of an Italian politician. He was shown the photo of Peiper and the accusations made against him at the Malmédy trial and claimed to recognise him from these photos and was sure he had found his man. His subsequent testimony about the events that day was part of the charges against Peiper by the Italians. However, the Leibstandarte's own records corroborate the testimonies of Rumpf, Hanreich and Fransee: that it was without question Kurt Meyer who was in command that day. On 17 February1943 Peiper's battle group was fighting in the vicinity of Komarowka–Babei–Ziglerowka. 'Nahkampftage des 2.Panzer-Grenadier-Rgt LSSAH', 12 April 43, NA, RG 242, T-354, Roll 624, F0822. Source: Roger Martin, *L'affaire Peiper* (France: Editions Dagarno), p. 53. For Ivan Kiselev's details on the atrocity, see www.vecherniy.kharkov.ua/print.php?Division=history&id=3621.

83. Kurt Meyer, *Grenadiers*, pp. 172–173. When secretly taped in November 1944, Meyer revealed his core sensibililties: 'Our education has resulted in a certain amount of brutality, which is partly unconscious to us … We gained our personal strength and endurance from our faith in the purity of our ideas … from our belief in race, from our belief in a healthy, clean family life.' GRGG 226, Kurt Meyer to Hans Eberbach, 1–20 November 1944, PRO: WO 208/4364.

84. The date of Montag's wounding is detailed in his 'Verlustmeldung' document (casualty report). This document also confirms that he died three days later in Poltava. Fritz Montag was more than just a colleague of Meyer's; he was in fact a long-time friend whom Meyer had met in 1930 when he was sent to keep public order at political rallies, while a member of the police force in Schwerin. 'Meyer … [was]

impressed by Fritz Montag, who owned a small shop in Dömitz but often came to Schwerin to speak ... Meyer ... visited him frequently at home to discuss politics and listen to his storehouse of military experiences. His upright character and courteous consideration made a lasting impression.' In fact it was Montag who persuaded Meyer to join the SS three years later: 'His friend from Dömitz, Fritz Montag, had been the one responsible for Kurt and the other three party loyalists at the Police School joining the expanding SS. Montag had allied himself with the Nazis and had been appointed local SS recruiting officer. To fill its ranks, he turned to the best men in the regional SA detachments and lured them into Himmler's new elite... Montag already knew them as friends and loyal supporters of the new German Order. ... Montag encouraged Kurt to approach other friends and colleagues to join.' Tony Foster, *Meeting of Generals* (Ottawa: Methuen, 1986), pp. 102, 116–117.

85. 'Das Herz mit dem stählernen Ring', SS Leitheft, 9 January 1943, Der Reichsführer SS, SS Hauptamt Berlin, NA T-611, Roll 43. The name of the fallen SS man is not revealed, but the letter is dated 9 November 1941.

86. Speer, *Inside the Third Reich*, pp. 351–352. Although Speer's veracity should be routinely questioned, there is other substantiation of the decision not to expound an official policy to kill prisoners—even if it was a routine practice in the East. The order went out from Field Marshal Keitel that same day: 'All prisoners of war captured in the East after July 5, 1943, are to be sent to the camps of the High Command of the Armed Forces,' NA, RG 238, U.S. Evidence, Document No. 455.

87. Letter from Wilhelm Keilhaus, 4 March 1967, as cited in Höhne, *The Order of the Death's Head*, p. 469.

Chapter 7: 'We Had Better Win this War'

1. Borchers's Diary, 9 April 1943.
2. Jochen Peiper, 'Brief Review', 7 April 1946. Of Russia: 'What would you do with a woman who came riding on a tank swinging a machine pistol? There was no cruelty which would have surprised you.'
3. Rudolf von Ribbentrop, interview with Westemeier, 27 March 1993; related to author on 15 May 1997.
4. 'Peiper: Russian Theater'.
5. Himmler's address to the SS officers in Kharkov on 24 April 1943: Nuremberg Document, PS-1919b, IMT, vol. 20, p. 302. Later in the speech Himmler prepared the officers for the fact that the newly

raised SS divisions would incorporate large numbers of non-German West European volunteers. He wanted to make certain the core types would properly receive them. But how much of this could be taken seriously when Himmler waxed into one of his favourite fantasies? 'One day,' he said, closing his speech, 'we shall incorporate millions of Germans living in America!'

6. IMT, vol. 22, p. 352. Also see Bohuslav Etscher, *The Lessons of the Kharkov Trial* (London: Russian Today Society, 1944). A barber in Kharkov who lived through the German occupation told Alexander Werth: 'All those hangings made one ill for days ... And it was awful about the Jews too. They'd drive them in an endless procession through the streets, many of them pushing wheelbarrows or prams with babies inside, and they'd all weep and wail. I could understand their wanting to send the Jews away somewhere—but to kill them in this awful way, that is going a bit far, don't you think.' Werth, *Russia at War*, 'Kharkov under the Germans', pp. 612–618.

7. Borchers's Diary, 15 May 1943.

8. For Dietrich's departure, see Messenger, *Hitler's Gladiator*, pp. 117–118.

9. The story of Peiper's hair-raising solo flight is typical of his personal braggadocio. According to Charles Whiting, the apocryphal story came from Peiper himself during one of their personal conversations in the late 1960s. Letter to author, 8 August 2000.

10. 'Das Ritterkreuz für SS Sturmbannführer Peiper', *Das Schwartze Korps*, 15 April 1943.

11. Vgl. Meldungen der Verpflegungsstärke in BA-MA, RS 3-1/36, KTB LAH 1 April–3 August 1943, Situation, 30 April 1943: leaders: 618, NCOs: 3,296 and men: 18,475. The number of leaders diminished over the next two months as the new formation was raised. Ration strength on 31 May 1943: leaders: 593, NCOs: 3,343 and enlisted men: 17,351.

12. Omer Bartov, *Hitler's Army: Soldiers, Nazis and War in the Third Reich* (London: Oxford University Press, 1992), p. 167.

13. By spring 1943 some 2,500 soldiers of the Luftwaffe were transferred to the Leibstandarte. See Lehmann and Tiemann, *Die Leibstandarte*, vol. III, p. 220.

14. Compare Weingartner, *Hitler's Guard*, p. 93, with VHA, 1. SS-Pz.Div. LAH, Box 2, reports of AA 7 May 1943.

15. VHA, 1. SS-Pz.Div. LAH, Box 1, Div. to AA 10 April 1943, Zugeteilter Ersatz.

16. VHA, 1. SS-Pz.Div. LAH, Box 4, Bn. order 27 June 1943.

17. Frey, *Ich wollte die Freiheit*, p. 273. Beginning 25 August 1942 male residents in Alsace/Lorraine were inducted into Hitler's military

service. Exact numbers are unavailable, although an estimated 130,000 to 200,000 Alsace natives were drafted into the Wehrmacht and Waffen SS.

18. Heinz von Westernhagen, Letter to his older brother Harald, 18 April 1943, courtesy of Dörte von Westernhagen.
19. Weingartner, *Hitler's Guard*, p. 93.
20. Förster: 'Die weltanschauliche Erziehung', p. 110, in Jurgen Matthäus, *Ausbildungsziel Judenmord* (Frankfurt: Fischer, 2003), pp. 87–113.
21. VHA, HSSPF Russland-Süd, Box 8, FeldKdo-Stelle Hegewald, Order RFSS 24 February 1943.
22. VHA, SS-Pz.Gren.Schule Prosetschnitz, Box 1, Order SS-HA 13 March 1943; Ausarbeitung weltanschaulicher Unterricht.
23. Siegmund, *Meine Ehre heisst Treue*, p. 55.
24. Richard Bessel, ed., *Life in the Third Reich* (Oxford: Oxford University Press, 1987); Roger Moorhouse, *Berlin at War: Life and Death in Hitler's Capitol* (London: Bodley Head, 2010).
25. 'Eier, Butter, Zucker und Mehl', office ledger of Rudolf Brandt, May 1943, NA, T-175, Roll 43, Frame 2555116-7.
26. 'Generalkommando SS Panzer Corps: Zusammenstellung: LSSAH', 27 April 1943, T-354, R603, F88.
27. Increasingly, *Pakfronts* alternating with mine belts in depth and anti-tank ditches were encountered on the Eastern Front after 1942: Rolf Moebius, 'German Heavy Armor', NARA, RG-338, FMS, MS D-226.
28. 'Unternehmen Zitadelle', T-354, R603, F94. For 'my stomach turns …' and 'wolf by the ears …', see Heinz Guderian, *Panzer Leader (New York: Da Capo Press Reissue, 2001)*, pp. 246–247; F.W. von Mellenthin, *Panzer Battles* (New York: Ballantine Books, 1971), p. 277. For Enigma decrypt of Hitler on April 15, 1943, 'We must succeed rapidly …': Martin Gilbert, *The Second World War: A Complete History* (New York: Henry Holt, 1989), p. 420.
29. Peiper to Ehrhard Gührs, Gührs Diary.
30. The origin of National Socialist plans to exterminate the Jews in Europe remains an enduring academic question. On 11 November 1941 Felix Kersten, Himmler's personal masseuse, reported that his client 'was depressed', confiding in him about the terrible responsibility Hitler had given him to exterminate the Jews. See Kersten, *Memoirs*, p. 119. Others such as David Irving have denied that Hitler knew of the Final Solution on the basis of a lack of an incriminating document where the German leader acknowledges responsibility. By this logic, however, Mafia Dons would routinely prove innocent of gangland

killings, as nothing is written down and 'omerta', the code of silence, precludes confession. For a cogent summary on the topic, see Michael Shermer, 'Proving the Holocaust: The Refutation of Revisionism and the Restoration of History', *Skeptic*, vol. 2, no. 4 (June 1994). Adolf Eichmann's description of Hitler, Himmler and the Final Solution reinforces this view: 'It is not true that the Reichsführer Himmler, set down in writing anything ordering the annihilation of the Jews. Do you think he sat down to write, "My dear Eichmann, the Führer has ordered the physical annihilation of all Jews?" The truth is that Himmler never set down a line in writing on the subject. I know that he always gave his instructions orally to Pohl, who ran the concentration camps. I never received any order of the sort.' Memoirs of Adolf Eichmann, 1 November 1960, NA, Records of the Central Intelligence Agency, RG 263, File: CIA- RDP75-00149R00020050018-7, Declassified 13 June 2000.

31. BDC file for Otto Dinse, NA RG 242, A 3343-SSO, Roll 154. Dinse was in Łódź as late as the spring of 1941: Dinse, Letter to unidentified recipient, 26 March 1941. He was there until the April of 1941. In letters Dinse wrote from Łódź at that time he complained of the medical treatment his wife received from Lebensborn doctors but said nothing of the acceptability of his recent work to resettle Jews.

32. British code breakers intercepted the radio telegram of this deadly account after it was sent on 11 January 1943. Hermann Höfle was Globocnik's chief of staff at Lublin. Previously labeled Top Secret and recently declassified, the document was located by Peter Witte: PRO HW/16/23, 12 and 13/15.

33. For 'We had better win this war': Westemeier, *Himmler's Krieger*, p. 28; Dinse Interview. Peiper's comment to Dinse reflects a growing awareness of the damning implications of his previous role with Himmler. In conversation with the author, Dinse repeated his description of his encounter with Peiper in which the latter described learning of the elimination camps. He scoffed at those denying the Holocaust: 'They are not comrades.' Dinse Interview.

Chapter 8: Zitadelle

1. For 'Gentlemen, the bridges behind us are burned'. Gitta Sereny, *Albert Speer: His Battle with Truth* (New York: Knopf, 1995), p. 384. Of this moment Speer said of Hitler: 'I now think that he meant what had been done to the Jews.' That Hitler would consider gassing Jews was clearly evident in his infamous manifesto in

which he lamented not gassing Jews during the first World War: 'If at the beginning of the War, twelve or fifteen thousand of these Hebraic corrupters of our nation had been subjugated with poison gas as had to be endured in the field by hundreds of thousands of our very best German workers of all classes and professions, then the sacrifice of millions at the front would have not been in vain. On the contrary, if 12,000 scoundrels had been opportunely eliminated, perhaps a million orderly, worthwhile Germans might have been saved.' Adolf Hitler, *Mein Kampf*, vol. II (Munich: Franz Ehler, 1940), pp. 322–323.

2. See T.P. Mulligan, 'Spies, Ciphers and "Zitadelle": Intelligence and the Battle of Kursk', *Journal of Contemporary History* 22 (1987). For detailed background on Soviet preparations for the battle, see David M. Glantz and Harold S. Orenstein, eds., *The Battle for Kursk: The Soviet General Staff Study* (London: Frank Cass Publishers, 1999).

3. Borchers's Diary, 1 July 1943.

4. 'Kriegstagebuch der Abteilung Ib', 2 July 1943, T-354, R612, F13. Tank strength: Mk II: four, Pz III: twelve, Pz IV: seventy-two and Pz Vis (Tigers): eleven; eleven command tanks and thirty-one assault guns.

5. Georgi K. Zhukov, *Reminiscences and Reflections* (Moscow: Publishing House of the Press Agency, 1985), p. 183.

6. Borchers's Diary, 4 July 1943.

7. 'Kriegstagebuch der Abteilung Ib: Div. St. Qu', 5 July 1943, T-354, R612, F16. For a short overview of the Kursk battle from the perspective of Peiper's division, see Weingartner, *Hitler's Guard*, pp. 94–96.

8. Robin Cross, *Citadel: The Battle of Kursk* (New York: Sarpedon, 1993), p. 181.

9. Borchers's Diary, entry for fighting on 5 July 1943 and afterwards.

10. Gührs Diary, 6 July 1943; see also Erhard Gührs, author's interview, 16 December 2004, p. 36; Lehmann and Tiemann, *Die Leibstandarte*, vol. III, p. 217.

11. Gührs Diary, 7 July 1943; see also 'Kriegstagebuch der Abteilung Ib', 7 July 1943, T-354, R612, F17.

12. Gührs Diary, 8 July 1943.

13. Gührs Diary, 8 July 1943.

14. Gührs Diary, 8 July 1943.

15. Excerpts from Rolf Ehrhardt's account of the fighting on 7–8 July 1943: Tiemann, *Chronicle of the 7. Panzerkompanie*, pp. 55–57.

16. Tiemann, *Chronicle of the 7. Panzerkompanie*, pp. 55–57.

17. 'Kriegstagebuch der Abteilung Ib', 8 July 1943, T-354, R612, F19.

Chapter 9: 'The Tigers are Burning'

1. Diary of Karl Wortmann, 10 July 1943: Lehmann and Tiemann, *Die Leibstandarte*, vol. III, p. 231.
2. Kurowski, *Panzer Aces*, p. 193.
3. 'Kriegstagebuch der Abteilung Ib,' 11 July 1943, T-354, R612, F22.
4. Pavel Rotmistrov, 'Tanks against Tanks', in S.L. Sokolov, *Main Front: Soviet Leaders Look Back at World War II* (Lincoln, NE: Potomac Books, 1986), pp. 106–117.
5. Gotthard Heinrici and Friedrich Wilhelm Hauck, 'Zitadelle', *Wehrwissenschaftliche Rundschau* (August–October 1965), pp. 597–598. See also Ernst Klink, *Das Gesetz des Handelns: Die Operation 'Zitadelle' 1943* (Stuttgart: Schriftenreihe des Militärgeschichtlichen Forschungsamtes, Deutsche Verlags Anstalt, 1964), pp. 243–244. The anticipated reinforcement, Kempf's III Panzerkorps, comprised the 6th, 7th and 19th Panzer Divisions, including almost three hundred additional tanks.
6. Traditional German skier's greeting.
7. David M. Glantz and Jonathan M. House, *The Battle of Kursk* (Lawrence: University of Kansas Press, 1999), p. 341. The 6th Guards Tank Army had about 680 tanks total.
8. BDC file for Werner Wolff, 'Vorschlag Nr. 1 für die Nennung im Ehrenblatt des Deutschen Herres', 2 November 1944, signed by Jupp Diefenthal and Jochen Peiper, NA RG-242, SSOA-011C. Peiper described Wolff as a hero that day: 'At every focal point he stood as an upright rock in the surf.'
9. For this and other details of this fighting, with a good amount of dramatic licence, see Dr Herbert Schramm, 'Der siebenteTag', *Das Schwarze Korps*, 20 January 1944.
10. The original source for this oft-told story is an effusive account by SS war reporter Schramm, 'Der siebenteTag' (all quotes from this tale). Peiper's comment about the Nahkampfspange seems likely to be a journalist's interpretation.
11. Schramm, 'Der siebenteTag'.
12. Gührs Diary, 21 July relative to the events of 12 July 1943: 'By luck, a tank company had helped us. My company had destroyed 15 Russian tanks, but it was an expensive victory. When we left our four days, I had 16 people dead and others were wounded badly.'
13. Klink would never again see Peiper until after the war, although he was certain that his superior had saved his life that day on the Russian steppes. Surviving the war in Berlin, Klink later became a

historian at the Bundesarchiv in Freiburg and even wrote an objective account of the Kursk battle that is still considered a seminal German account: Klink, *Das Gesetz des Handelns*. For Klink's BDC file: NA, FR Seized Collection, SS Enlisted Men, A3343-SM-Roll-J017.

14. Although Soviet assessments incorrectly claim 1,200 tanks in the Prochorowka battle, the truth was that about 250 German tanks and some 600 Russian tanks were involved in the larger engagement. Glantz and Orenstein, *The Battle for Kursk*, p. 128. Another detailed count showed that 572 tanks met on the field of Prochorowka proper: David M. Glantz and Jonathan M. House, *The Battle of Kursk*, p. 152.

15. Clark, *Barbarossa*, p. 337.

16. 'Kriegstagebuch der Abteilung Ib', 11 July 1943, T-354, R612, F23.

17. Tiemann, *Chronicle of the 7. Panzerkompanie*, p. 60. The 'Balkas' were erosion gullies that threaded through the Steppe terrain that the Russians skilfully used to sometimes conceal their movements.

18. 'Kriegstagebuch der Abteilung Ib', 8 July 1943, T-354, R612, F24. For the Soviet view of the Prochorowka, see Sergi M. Shtemenko, *The Soviet General Staff at War 1941–1945* (Moscow: Progress Publishers, 1970).

19. Georgi K. Zhukov, *The Memoirs of Marshal Zhukov* (New York: Delacorte Press, 1971), pp. 460–463.

20. See Glantz and Orenstein, *The Battle for Kursk*, pp. 226–227.

21. Von Manstein to Hitler, 12 July 1943: 'Victory on the southern front of the Kursk salient is within reach. The enemy has thrown in nearly his entire strategic reserves and is badly mauled. Breaking off action now would be throwing away victory!' Steven H. Newton, *Kursk: The German View* (Cambridge, MA: DaCapo, 2002), p. 357. For a scholarly view from the Russian side: Valeriy Zamulin, *Demolishing the Myth: The Tank Battle at Prokhorovka, Kursk, July 1943: An Operational Narrative*, (Warwick, Helion, 2011).

22. Werth, *Russia at War*, p. 683. The title of the Russian report referred to the evolving defeat of Hitler's supposedly impervious Tiger tanks.

23. Borchers's Diary, 14–16 July 1943.

24. Heinz von Westernhagen to family, 15 July 1943, Westernhagen, *Die Kinder der Täter*, p. 44.

25. Paul Zwigart, an SPW driver with Peiper's battalion, claimed that another Russian village was torched and occupants shot:
    'Another case which I recall exactly during which an entire village was wiped out took place in the summer of 1943 during the feint

attack on Kursk … At that time the infantrymen of our battalion received the order 'Blowtorches ready!' I, myself, heard when the commander of the 9. Kompanie Haupsturmführer Guhl issued this order and I know that the same order was made to all companies of the battalion. I don't know any more whether on this occasion it was emphasized whether women and children as well had to be bumped off. However, in accordance with previous practice, it was apparent what it meant. I saw clearly when women with children among them came running out of the burning houses and were mowed down by our men'.

Statement of Paul Zwigart, 11 February 1946, NARA, 'War Crimes Cases Tried', Case 6-24, RG-549, Box 9.

While not surprising that there is no direct corroboration of Zwigart's claims, still another source indicates that Peiper's battalion was implicated in other civilian killings. This comes from a 'tapping' document recently declassified at the Public Records Office in London. WO 208/4138 records an overheard conversation between two German PoWs recorded from a man, Shutze, who was a member of the Leibstandarte, captured in Italy in 1943. He talks to the other PoW about crimes involving the Leibstandarte—and he specifically mentions the Blowtorch Battalion: 'They shot civilians and set fire to houses with their 'blowlamps' [sic]. A large blowlamp is painted on the sides of their vehicles. It has become sort of a badge associated with bloody crimes.' As this conversation was an overheard conversation recorded in February 1944, there can be no claim that it was a forced confession and it occurred well before Peiper became a person of interest to the Americans later that year. Thanks to Carol Byrne for locating this important document.

26. Peiper's commendation in 'Vorschlag Nr. für Verleihung des Deutschen Kreuzes in Gold', 20 October 1944, Hans Siptrott: BDC file, NA: RG-242, A3343 SSO.

27. 'Kriegstagebuch der Abteilung Ib', 8 July 1943, T-354, R612, F32-40. The Leibstandarte would pick up new tanks in Austria. See Hitler conversation with Alfred Jodl on 26 July 1943, Warlimont, *Inside Hitler's Headquarters*, pp. 356–357. 'The other morning there was to be an attack against a Russian breakthrough on the Mius. The columns were again standing on the dusty roads of Russia. The sun burned hotly in the midday sky. Then came the call. Unbelievable. The division was to pull out … prepare the Panzers to be given up … the worst rumours were floating around.' Tiemann, *Chronicle of the 7. Panzerkompanie*, p. 64.

28. The number of Russian tanks operational before the salient on 5 July was approximately 3,800; by 13 July this had been whittled down to 1,500. However, retaining the battlefield, the Russians repaired or replaced their losses; by 3 August they again possessed some 2,750 tanks. Clark, *Barbarossa*, p. 345. Overy, *Russia's War*, p. 201, sets the initial relative strength of the combatants at Kursk as Russia: 1,336,000 men, 3,444 tanks, 2,900 aircraft and 19,000 guns, and Germany: 900,000 men, 2,700 tanks, 2,000 aircraft and 10,000 guns. In the Prochorowka area the Soviets claimed to have destroyed 320 German tanks and assault guns (Soviet General Staff, 1943). However, the reality was that only about fifty-four German tanks were destroyed in the battle against some 334 Russian tanks lost from the 5th Tank Army. See N. Zetterling and A. Frankson, *Kursk 1943: A Statistical Analysis* (London: Frank Cass, 2000). A slightly different count is provided by Glantz and House, *Battle of Kursk*, pp. 274–277. However, there is general agreement that Russian tank losses were more than five times greater than their enemy.
29. Werth, *Russia at War*, p. 684.
30. Russian tank production was eleven thousand in 1943 against six thousand produced by the Germans in that year. Clark, *Barbarossa*, p. 313. Dietrich's comments about Russian versus German tanks: 'SS General Sepp Dietrich', PWB/SAIC/11 HQ 7th Army, 1 June 1945, NA, RG 332, ETO MIS-Y Sect., Box 116.
31. Jochen Peiper, 'Brief Review', 7 April 1946. Peiper's appreciation of the Russians echoed Himmler's racial opinions. 'At the same time, the simple Siberians and Kalmucks fighting in the Red Army had been warned to expect that all Western Europeans were sadistic fascists who would kill any prisoners after the most horrible tortures.' And certainly the Einsatzgruppen and killing squads made a reality of this Soviet expectation. 'Germany's nerves were exhausted by [dependence on] culture and civilization. The superior weapons which our minds developed wore out in the depth of the [Russian] land. The efficiency of the human society of the cultured West lost out against the primitive instinctive strength of the Asiatic onslaught!'
32. See Himmler, Letter to Dietrich, Feldkommandostelle, 11 August, 1943, in NA BDC file for Dietrich.
33. 'Peiper: Russian Theater', and Peiper, 'Brief Review', p. 15.
34. Zetterling and Frankson, *Kursk 1943*, pp. 107–109.
35. Hitler decisively won the attritional battle at Kursk but lost the strategic battle and surrendered the initiative in the East: Roman

Töppel, 'Die Offensive gegen Kursk 1943—Legenden, Mythen, Propaganda', MA Thesis, Dresden: Technical University, 2001.

36. Tiemann, *Chronicle of the 7. Panzerkompanie*, p. 64.

37. For Peiper's confession to Röhwer, see Agte, *Michael Wittmann and the Tiger Commanders*, p. 252. 'The framework is creaking,' Peiper told those around him. After the war Hans Röhwer was later be implicated in the killing of twenty-two Italian Jews around Lago Maggiore on 24 and 25 September 1943. BA-Ludwigsburg, Az 5 Str 218/G9; also, '1943 am Lago Maggiore: "Privater Judenmord",' *Westdeutsche Allgemeine Zeitung*, Ausgabe Nr. 154, 5 July 1968. A potentially damning perspective on Röhwer's wartime character is the 'tapping' document recently declassified at the Public Records Office in London, WO 208/4138 from the PRO, which details a covertly overheard conversation between two German PoWs recorded in England. Borack was an SS private of the Leibstandarte, captured in Italy in November 1943, who is having a conversation with Major Reinhardt, the captured chief of staff of the 344th Infantry Division. In their tapped conversation Borack described crimes involving the Leibstandarte and specifically mentions the Blowtorch Battalion. 'I drove out to fetch some food supplies and I hear screaming and wailing to the right of the road ... we went over there around the hill and into the gorge. A heavy machine gun had been placed there and another one too. And SS Haupsturmführer Röhwer, who had the German cross in Gold—the swine—was standing there watching whilst all these civilians—women and children, old men and boys, everyone were crowded into the gorge. Schwinden arrived. He couldn't stand the sight of it either.' As this conversation was overheard and recorded in February 1944, there can be no claim that it was a forced confession as it occurred well before Peiper became a person of interest to the Americans later that year.

Chapter 10: Italy

1. Lord Byron, 'Childe Harold's Pilgrimage', translation of the famous sonnet of Vincenzo da Filicaja (1642–1707). For 'We are dancing on the Volcano': Narcisse-Achille Comte de Salvandy at the fête given by Duc d'Orleans to the King of Naples (1830).

2. History of Boves from the Scuola da Pace in Boves, courtesy of Laura Cavallera.

3. For the German perspective on Italy's defection, see Albert Kesselring, 'Special Report on the Events in Italy between 25 July and 8 September 1943', NARA, RG-338, FMS, MS C-013.

4. E. Rosa, 'E Duccio parló in Patria Indipendente', 19 July 1953. See also 'Documenti Luglio-Settembre 1943', Archivio Instituto Storico Resistensza. In September Galimberti went into hiding in the Madonna del Colletto Mountains, emerging as a hero-leader of the resistance movement in the Grana Valley. Today the big square in Cuneo is known as the Piazza Galimberti.

5. Domenico Favole, interview with author, Boves, Italy, 17 July 2002 (hereafter Favole Interview).

6. Alfred Jodl, 'Answers to Questions Submitted ot Gen. Jodl', NARA, RG-338, FMS, MS A-914.

7. Saul Friedländer, *The Years of Extermination: Nazi Germany and the Jews, 1939–1945* (New York: Harper Collins, 2007), p. 553.

8. For German diplomatic conflict with the Italians over the Jewish question in early 1943, see Michael Bloch, *Ribbentrop: A Biography* (New York: Crown Publishers, 1992), p. 373.

9. BA-L, B 162/5032, Interrogation of Dr Wilhelm Harster, 22 August 1962. In September 1943 Dr Harster would be installed as chief of the security police (SD) in Italy after serving in that role in Holland, where the Jews had been deported to their annihilation over the preceding two years.

10. Carlo Gentile, 'September 1943: Documenti sull' attività della divisione "Leibstandarte Adolf Hitler" in Piemonte', in Il Presente E La Storia 47, Michele Calandri (ed.), Giugno, Cuneo, 1995.

11. For Karl Wolff's 6 September 1943 meeting with Hitler, Joachim von Ribbentrop and Ambassador Walther Hewel, see the chronology kept by his manservant, Heinz Linge: NA, RG 242, T-84, Roll 22, Linge Diaries.

12. Jewish refugees in eastern France had fled in large numbers to Italy in 1943 after learning that Mussolini was not willing to turn them over to German hands. See Daniel Carpi, *Between Mussolini and Hitler: The Jews and the Italian Authorities in France and Tunesia* (New York: Brandeis University Press, 1994).

13. Von Lang, *Top Nazi*, pp. 222–223.

14. On 17 December 1943 the chief of the SD in Italy ordered its units: 'The Leibstandarte has left the Italian theatre. I therefore, ordered that we cut off the cuff-title "Adolf Hitler" from our uniforms.' BA-Berlin Lichterfelde, R 70/Italien/ 12, p. 29. Thanks to Jens Westemeier for providing this reference.

15. After the war, although he was one of the most wanted war criminals in the world, Rauff escaped to Chile, where he voluntarily testified to German authorities at the German embassy in the investigation of Bruno Streckenbach on 28 June 1972. Asked about his role in the gassing vans: 'Regarding the annihilation of Jews in Russia I know that gas vans were used for this purpose ... Whether at that time I had doubts against the use of gas vans I cannot say. The main issue for me at the time was that the shootings were a considerable burden for the men who were in charge thereof and that this burden was taken off them through the use of the gas vans.' Rauff moved to Milan under the protection of the Leibstandarte in 1943 and ended the war in that city, being later helped by Roman Catholic Bishop Alois Hudal to escape from Europe to avoid prosecution. ZSL, II 415 AR-Z 1310/63-E32, Bl.534-549, StA Hamburg Az. 147 Js 31/67.

16. 'New Documents on the Holocaust in Italy', in Breitman et al., *U.S. Intelligence and the Nazis*, p. 82.

17. Breitman et al., *U.S. Intelligence and the Nazis*, pp. 76–83. Police attaché, SS officer Herbert Kappler in Rome would be charged with arresting the Jews there. Just after Mussolini was liberated, Kappler received a call from Himmler's office informing him of a promotion to SS Obersturmbannführer but with the immediate assignment of preparing to arrest and deport the Jews of Rome.

18. 'RAF Firestorm bombs raze Hamburg to the ground': Sharon Lucas, *World War II: Day by Day* (London: Dorling Kindersley, 2001), p. 430. Three massive raids were made over a five-day period, totalling some 8,761 tons of bombs.

19. The Allied bombers struck Berlin on 23 August 1943, but the result was quite different from that at Hamburg. The Germans had developed new night-fighter defences that rapidly crippled the British raids. Having lost many bombers, by 3 September the British had called off the attacks.

20. Sigurd Peiper to Rudi Brandt, 25 August 1943, NA, T-175, Roll 117, Frames 2641931-32.

21. Dr R. Brandt to Frau Sigurd Peiper, 28 August 1943, NA, T-175, Roll 117, Frame 2641924.

22. 'Töchter und Väter', *Stern*, no. 2 (6 January 1983), p. 60.

23. Von Lang, *Der Adjutant Karl Wolff*, p. 41.

24. Letters of Elke M., May and December 2001. The Peipers knew the Grothmann and Wolff families in Rottach-Egern, but only as acquaintances.

25. Thanks to Dr Michael Heim for the photograph showing the wartime entrance to Rottach-Egern in 1938: '*Juden betreten den Ort auf eigene Gefahr* '. Hitler had visited Rottach on 30 June 1939, to the delight of the local Kreisleiter, Herr Donninger.

26. *Bonze* was a popular wartime expression for a party member of the NSDAP who had come into a leadership position and had enriched themselves within that position.

27. Information on the Peiper family's residence in Rottach-Egern comes from its municipal office and discussion with Birgit Mitchell of the Nathan family in Rottach-Egern on 22 July 2002.

28. Diary of Gudrun Himmler, 1 November 1943, *Stern* magazine (Hamburg: Gruner +Jahr), 6 January 1983. 'If peace comes we will get a property in the East … Perhaps we will get a house on the Obersalzberg.' She was 10 years old when the war broke out. Married as Gudrun Burwitz after the war, Himmler's daughter dismissed her father's critics: 'Whatever is said about my Papi, what has been written or shall be written in the future about him—he was my father, the best father I could have and I loved him and still love him.' Gudrun Burwitz, interview with Gillich, 22 January 1974, Toland Collection, FDR Library, Box 46. Burwitz, who died on 24 May 2018, lived quietly nearby in Bad Tölz. Until she died, she was guest of honour at rousing annual meetings for old SS veterans in Schliersee.

29. Himmler's damning Posen speech of 4 October 1943 has been detailed by many scholars, e.g., IMT, PS-1919. For a particularly telling evaluation: Breitman, *Architect of Genocide*, p. 242–243; For nuances in the translation, see *Skeptic* magazine, vol. 2, no. 4, pp. 64–67.

30. Even though Karl Wolff was in Italy when Himmler's speech was given at Posen on 4 October, he was given a copy upon visiting the Reichsführer SS headquarters in East Prussia. Von Lang, *Hitler's Adjutant*, pp. 232–233. Given Peiper's close relationship to Himmler, it seems very possible he would also be given a copy of the speech— of which Himmler was very proud—when he visited Hochwald in February 1944.

31. Himmler to Dietrich, 23 July and 18 October 1943, with Dietrich's reply on 17 January 1944, T-175, Roll 24, F2529463-67

32. Rolf Ehrhardt, as quoted in Tiemann, *Chronicle of the 7. Panzer Kompanie*, p. 65.

33. Borchers's Diary, 12 August 1943.

34. For the arrival of the Leibstandarte into sunny Reggio Emilo, see 'II SS Panzerkorps', BA-MA, RS/20–21. For photos of Peiper,

Guhl and Wolff marching and singing through Reggio Emilia, see NS-Wochenschau (Weekly Newsreel), Nr. 681, 22 September 1943.

35. The song 'Erika!' by Herms Niel, 1940.

36. Borchers's Diary, 18 August 1943.

37. Redecker, 'Die Lötlampe," 1943'. *"Because we sniff vitamins from morning till night'* may not only refer only to breathing healthy forest air, but also the likelihood that soldiers of the Leibstandarte often sniffed Pervitin (methamphetamine) to enhance 24 hour march performance. See Norman Ohler, *Blitzed: Drugs in Nazi Germany*, Allen Lane, 2016.

38. An indication of how rapidly the Italian forces disbanded is given by the report of the II SS Panzer Corps from their arrival in Italy until 11 September, when they recorded 106,046 Italian soldiers surrendered. The Leibstandarte alone counted a booty of 38,591 rifles turned in during the same period. 'Gefangenen un Beute Zusammenstellung', Generalkommando II SS Panzerkorps, 12.IX,1943, BA-MA, RS 2-2/21.

39. The Triple Alliance (Germany, Austria–Hungary and Italy) was formed in 1882. However, the Italians claimed that the German declaration of offensive war against France and Russia at the beginning of the First World War freed them of its obligations under the alliance. Thus, by 1916 they had declared war on both Austria–Hungary as well as Germany.

40. David Irving, *Trail of the Fox: The Life of Field Marshal Erwin Rommel* (New York: E.P. Dutton, 1977), p. 299.

41. 'Interrogation Transcript for Otto Heinrich Dinse', State Criminal Office, Bad Würtemberg, 9 October 1964, BA Ludwigsburg, AR-Z 17/1964, 110–120 (hereafter Dinse Interrogation).

Chapter 11: 'Dancing on the Volcano'

1. For background, see Christopher Hibbert, *Mussolini: The Rise and Fall of Il Duce* (New York: St Martin's, 2008); also, R.J.B. Bosworth, *Mussolini's Italy: Life Under the Fascist Dictatorship, 1915–1945* (London: Penguin, 2006). For 'each tank carried a white flag': SRA 2615, 'Special Report Air Force', 9 June 1942, PRO: WO/208/4126. For a less biased and more measured comparison of Italian against German military effectiveness in the war, *see* James. J. Sadkovich, 'Of Myths and Men: Rommel and the Italians in North Africa', *International History Review* 13, no. 2 (1991): pp. 284–313. Poor and antiquated arms and equipment played a large role in limiting the Italian Army, although Mussolini himself alleged to Hitler that officer training was a key problem.

2. Tiemann, *Chronicle of the 7. Panzerkompanie*, p. 68. 'We collected a huge heap of weapons.'

3. Siegmund, *Meine Ehre heisst Treue*, p. 56.

4. BA-MA RS 4/1411, KTB SS Panzergrenadier Regiment 2. The entries for 9 September 1943 specifically mention Peiper and the employment of III Battalion.

5. BA-MA, RS 2-2/27, Morgenmeldulng II SS Panzerkorps, 20 September 1943. The other two generals: Brigadier General Guiseppe Andreol (2nd Infantry Division) and Brigadier General Guiseppe Capelli (4th Army).

6. Antonio Bassignano, *Cuneo agli albori del fascio e del nazifascismo* (Bertello: Borgo san Dalmazzo, Tip, 1947).

7. In September 1943 Heinrich Himmler and his occultist, Professor Kretschinger, claimed to have found Mussolini's place of captivity through the use of maps and a pendulum. Wilhelm Höttl, *The Secret Front* (Oxford, UK: Enigma Books, 1954), p. 403. This account needs to be taken with a generous grain of salt, as Höttl was a former Obersturmbannführer and was himself involved in the Holocaust of the Jews in Hungary while making himself out to be a key expert in espionage within the SS for south-east Europe.

8. For the Mussolini rescue episode, the very detailed—if self-serving— account comes from Skorzeny himself: 'My Mussolini Event 25.7.43– 12.9.43, PWI Interrogation: Otto Skorzeny', Dachau 27 July 1947, U.S. First Army G-2 Records, NA, RG-407, 101-2.13, Box 1514. Skorzeny's accomplishment paid immediate personal dividends: on the same day of the operation Hitler had Skorzeny promoted to Sturmbannführer and he received both the Iron Cross First Class and the Knight's Cross. Prior to that point Skorzeny was simply a rather average Austrian SS captain (with six weeks basic training within the replacement battalion of the Leibstandarte) but with very good connections with fellow Austrian Ernst Kaltenbrunner, who heavily promoted his career.

9. Otto Skorzeny, *Meine Kommando Unternehmen* (Munich, Universitas Verlag in F.A., Herbig Verlagsbuchhandlung GmbH, 1993); Richard Collier, *Duce! The Rise and Fall of Mussolini* (London: Collins, 1972); Lehmann and Tiemann, *Die Leibstandarte*, vol. III, pp. 284–288.

10. Story of this episode: Joachim Peiper, 'Meine Stellungnahme zum "Fall Boves"', September 1964, Zentrale Stelle der Landesjustizverwaltung, zur Aufklärung nationalsozialistischer Verbrechen, ZStL, Ludwigsburg, AR-Z 17/1964, Band I.

11. Period photographs show that the tank in the Cuneo plaza was a Carro Armato M15/42 mounting a 47mm gun. The tank had proven

completely insufficient in the fighting with Rommel in the desert but proved threatening enough against Northern Italian partisans armed only with rifles.

12. The identity of this soldier is not known, but he was likely from the Trentino Alto Adige region along the Austrian border, where everyone speaks both languages.

13. Favole Interview. Favole later learned the man was Jochen Peiper. Built in 1859 in the 'eclectic style', the Prefect was of relatively new construction in an old Italian town. Cuneo was established in 1189. See also Bassignano, *Cuneo agli albori del fascio e del nazifascismo*.

14. 'Comando Militare Germanico in Cuneo', 12 September 1943, Archivio Instituto Storico Resistensza.

15. One of those young Italian officers later remembered, 'Was it worthy for us to die in combat, we mountain natives, or would we rather choose to be imprisoned? No one could foresee how that would go. Our decision was quickly made. Peiper didn't see a single soldier answer his appeal. We directed our soldiers towards San Giacomo, out beyond Boves in a sector that was very mountainous and difficult to access.' Piero Bombelli, Nazareno Peano, Natale Macario, Bartolomeo Peano and Teresio Barale, Interviews with author, Boves, 16 July 2002.

16. For 'they will be annihilated down to the last man': 'Cosicchè esse verranno annientati fino all'ultimo uomo qual bande di partigiani'. Copy of the original sign posted by Peiper in Boves was provided to the author by Neil Thomson; translation courtesy Mark Belanian. See also 'Peiper Était Bien L'Auteur du Martyre de la Petite Ville Piémontaise de Boves', *La Montagne*, 23 July 1976.

17. Antonio Bassignano, the mayor of Cuneo who functioned as the liaison between the city government and the German SS head-quarters, insisted that the pretended rank was intentional. 'Peiper promoted himself from major to general with the purpose to create the impression that much stronger forces were at his disposal.' Office of the State Prosecutor at the Stuttgart State Court, 13 Js 161/64, BA-L, 4 February 1965.

18. Dinse Interrogation. Regarding the charges levelled at him by the mayor of Boves, Dinse declared, 'I had good relations with him. I do not understand how such stories appear.'

19. Inscription on the monument: 'To the heroes of Boves that died to give their homeland the proper boundaries while hoping for a universal peace.' The cannons were removed in 1983 when Boves was designated a 'Town of Peace'.

20. 'Nothing will happen': Favole Interview. For 'otherwise he would destroy the town': 'Peiper Était Bien L'Auteur du Martyre de la Petite Ville Piémontaise de Boves'.

21. 'Morgenmeldung: An Heeresgruppe B, 17.9.43', BA-MA, RS 2-2/21, Teil 2.

22. Later the Italians of Boves would claim that their real mission was to serve as bait for Peiper's coming retribution, 'Peiper Était Bien L'Auteur du Martyre de la Petite Ville Piémontaise de Boves'.

23. They were SS Oberscharführer Karl Wiezoreck and his assistant SS Unterscharführer Kurt Butenhoff of the 14th Company.

24. Dinse Interrogation. It must be said that Dinse's decision to send the unaccompanied NCOs into Boves was ill advised at best.

25. Testimony of Teresa Gastinelli regarding the events of 19 September 1944, 17 July 2002, Boves, courtesy of Sandro Gastinelli.

26. Natale Macario, interview with author, 16 July 2002, Boves.

27. As with all episodes of irreconcilable conflict, the writer provides both sides of the story.

28. 'Peiper Était Bien L'Auteur du Martyre de la Petite Ville Piémontaise de Boves'.

Chapter 12: Boves

1. 'Peiper Était Bien L'Auteur du Martyre de la Petite Ville Piémontaise de Boves'.

2. 'An die Staatsanwaltschaft beim Landgericht Stuttgart', Aktenzeichen: 13 Js 161/64, BA-L. Cuneo, 4 February 1965.

3. Listing of the victims: Westemeier, *Himmler's Krieger*, pp. 140–141. Source: Zst Az: 13/Js 161/64; with list of eyewitnesses.

   a. Peano Carlo, age 70, shot near the cemetery
   b. Agnese Michele, 72, shot near the cemetery
   c. Maccario Riccardo, 28, shot at the village plaza; carried a hand grenade
   d. Adriano Carlo, 43, shot at the south entrance to the village
   e. Re Benvenuto, 16, shot at the village plaza; carried a hand grenade
   f. Ghinamo Bartolomeo, 45, shot at the NW entrance to the village
   g. Dalmasso Francesco, 47, shot near the cemetery
   h. Pepino Luigi, 45, shot near the cemetery
   i. Don Benardi (priest), 47, burned to death
   j. Dutto Antonio, 53, shot near the cemetery
   k. Marro Michele, 60, shot in Rivoira by the south entrance of town
   l. Marro Angelo, 43, shot just outside the south of town

m. Olivero Bartolomeo, 68, shot near the cemetery
n. Masino Giacomo, 36, shot near the cemetery
o. Antonio Vassallo, 48, burned to death
p. Ghibaudo Mario, 23, shot near the cemetery
q. Vallauri Stefano, 32, wounded by artillery fire near Castellar, bled to death
r. Dutto Giovanni, 71, shot by pistol; bled to death north of Castellar
s. Cerato Paulo, 63, shot near the cemetery
t. Lingua Lorenzo, 28, shot in the village plaza
u. Grossi Angelo, 27, shot near the cemetery
v. Bo Caterina (female), 87, died in her burning home
w. Giuliano Paolo, 33, shot near the cemetery
x. Gornari Pasqualino, 28, found dead near La Regia after being SS prisoner for days

4. Alberto Cavaglion, *Nella Notte Stranier* (Viale Sarrea: L'Arciere, 1981).
5. For a reproduction of the announcement, see Cavaglion, *Nella Notte Stranier*, p. 68. In spite of extensive research, the identity of SS Hauptsturmführer Müller has not yet been revealed. That this could, in fact, be a cover name cannot be excluded. However, a much more likely possibility is that Müller was an SD member assigned to the Leibstandarte, as was being done for the planned exportation of the Italian Jews in September 1943. Note that the first draft of Müller's poster had the word 'Ebrei—Jews' rather than 'foreigners' (*tutti gli straniera*). The signed draft of the early poster can be seen at the Archivio Instituto Storico Resistensza in Cuneo. Thanks to Michele Calandri for providing a copy to the author.
6. H.R. Trevor Roper, ed., *Hitler's Table Talk* (New York: Enigma Books, 2000), pp. 331–332 and 401–402.
7. In charge of the deportation of the Jews in France was SS High Police Leader Carl Oberg. On orders from Reinhard Heydrich, in May 1942 he began deporting more than forty thousand Jews from France to the elimination camps. The SS had the cooperation of the Vichy Regime in France with the French police actively involved, which is still a dark chapter in French history.
8. Susan Zuccotti, *Holocaust Odysseys: The Jews of St.-Martin Vésubie and their Flight* (New Haven, CT: Yale University Press, 2007).
9. Walter Marx, interview with author, 19 March 2007.
10. Source for all information not otherwise cited in this section is from Walter Marx, interview with author, March 2007, and emailed follow-up.
11. Cavaglion, *Nella Notte Stranier*.

12. German records reveal that the prisoners detained at the mountain barracks at Borgo San Dalmazzo consisted of 119 with Polish citizenship, 56 from France, 42 from Germany, 25 from Austria, 22 Belgians, 20 Rumanians, 7 Russians, 6 Greeks, 4 Slovaks, 4 Croatians, 3 Lithuanians, 2 Turks, 2 Palestinians and single members from Holland, Algeria, Bulgaria and Switzerland. Carlo Gentile to author, 3 November 2005.

13. Records of II SS Panzer Corps, from the Bundesarchiv verifies that Peiper's battalion was actively involved in the arrests of the Jews near Cuneo. In the morning of 20 September, the corps passed on the following message to the Army Group: 'In Borgo S. Dalmazzo 216 Juden festgesetzt. SD wird erwartet—216 Jews detained in Boro San Dalmazzo. Waiting for SD,' BA-MA, Freiburg/Br., RS 2-2/21 Teil 2, Generalkommando II SS Panzerkorps, Tgb. Nr. 1087/43 gdh, Ic morning report of 20.9.1943 to Herregruppe B/Ic.' A key point: at the time of the report there were no other German troops near Cuneo aside from Peiper's battalion. That Peiper was in the vicinity of Borgo San Dalmazzo is made clear by his own account of the actions in September 1943: 'The German security forces stationed in Mondavi, Cuneo and Borgo San Dalmazzo not only reported frequent incidents with Italian soldiers and civilians, but also, by my own observations of the cooperation of the population discovered an assemblage of Italian forces along the road Mondovi–Borgo San Dalmazzo.' Peiper, 'Meine Stellungnahme zum "Fall Boves"'.' Moreover, in his testimony for the Boves investigation, Otto Dinse was even more specific: the Leibstandarte had troops in Borgo San Dalmazzo, the 12 Panzergrenadier Kompanie under SS Obersturmführer Georg Preuss. Testimony of Otto Dinse, 9 February 1966, Nachlass Robert Kempner, BA-K, N 1470/ 1171, 2–3 (hereafter Dinse Testimony).

14. This was SS Rottenführer Kurt Israel (born 23 March 1922; SS Nr 365,388), who was a halftrack driver for Paul Guhl under Peiper in the 11th Panzer Grenadier Company. He had just won the Iron Cross First Class for his fighting at Kursk in Russia.

15. Johanna Marx was deported from Borgo on Convoy 64, which on 7 December 1943 arrived at Auschwitz, where she was gassed along with 656 others. Zuccotti, *Holocaust Odysseys*, p. 137.

16. This accusation of a war crime against Peiper was written of at the end of 1976 by the Italian newspaper of Boves, *La Stampa*. The account of the Boves investigation is found in 'Vermerk: 8 AR-Z 17/64', Staatsanwalt, Ludwigsburg, 30 June 1964.

17. From Borgo San Dalmazzo 352 Jews were deported to Auschwitz, of whom no more than twelve survived. Two more were sent to Buchenwald and did not return.

18. Walter Marx: 'In September 1998 I travelled to Cuneo following an invitation from the city to participate in the festivities celebrating the 800th anniversary of the founding of the city ... [There] I delivered a speech in Borgo San Dalmazzo on the occasion of the unveiling of a monument thanking the people of the region for having assisted and saved Jewish families during World War II. It was during that speech when I mentioned the daughter of an innkeeper who had saved my life, then Nella, who was by chance in the audience, came to hug me on the podium ... We had not seen each other for 55 years. We have been very close since.' Madellena Giraudo passed away in November 2011.

19. Gilbert Gilles, *Un Ancien Waffen SS Français Reconte* (Montoire: Les Cockers, n.d.).

20. 'With that strange arrogant sense of humour of his, he [Peiper] had told the Rabbi that the Jews really owed their release to a high German official who had just arrived in the area and was a devout Nazi. Thereupon, he suggested that the Rabbi would assemble his co-religionists and go to the Nazi's house, where they could sing a few Yiddish songs to him in gratitude. The Nazi's reaction is not recorded, but the Jews remembered Peiper and testified accordingly.' Charles Whiting, *Massacre at Malmédy* (New York: Stein & Day, 1971), p. 241. Whiting insisted to the author that Peiper had personally told him this story (Whiting, interview with author, August 2001). However, this apocryphal tale must be greatly doubted. Perversely, although there were Jews from Berlin collected at Borgo San Dalmazzo, they were, in fact, sent by train to Auschwitz, where they were later gassed. The course of the train from Borgo to the elimination camp is exactly documented: Cavaglion, *Nella Notte Straniera*.

21. For the important document naming SS Lieutanant Proist (Preuss) as the successor for SS Hauptsturmführer Müller in charge of the camp at Borgo San Dalmazzo, see BAK, N1470/1175. The author also knows from his interview with Walter Marx that the SS had full responsibility for the camp there and used all the males there as workers.

22. BA-Ludwigsburg, AR-Z 17/1964, Band II. The pretrial investigation was officially terminated in March 1969.

23. For the transportation of the Jews to Auschwitz from Borgo San Dalmazzo, see the detailed accounting in Cavaglion, *Nella Notte Stranier*. Not surprisingly, after the war potentially implicated SS

veterans claimed to know nothing about the arresting of the Jews. Some made up the story that Borgo San Dalmazzo was only a materials storage area and no Jews were held there! They could only recall the good Italian food, the good hunting and the nice riding trips, but no details about the Jews. Erhard Gührs: 'Here, everything is so easy, romantic and beautiful,' he noted one week after the Boves massacre. Gührs Diary, 24 September 1943, in author's possession. When asked, Gührs claimed not to know anything about the Jews in Italy and dismissed the entire subject as 'pure propaganda'. Gührs author interview, 17 December 2004.

24. ZSL B 162/6370-6371, Peiper's statement, 23 March 1966.
25. Notes taken by Wehrmacht Hauptmann Erhard Liss of a speech given by Peiper to the Stuttgart OdR section on 28 March 1969. Liss, with 5./Sturm Regt. 195, received the Knight's Cross on 30 April 1945.
26. This section: Dinse Interrogation.
27. Source information for the two Boves scenarios are taken from the post-war Stuttgart trial. 'Beschluss vom 23.12.1968: Landgericht Stuttgart, I.gr.Strafkammer', I Ars 62/68, pp. 295-312, Zentralstelle der Landesjustizverwaltungen, Ludwigsburg.

Chapter 13: The Wrong War

1. Italian historians who have studied the events of September 1943 hotly dispute the claim that civilians fired on Peiper on 19 September. 'It is quite impossible that civilian fired guns,' Michele Calandri insisted. 'This is the great alibi of Peiper. It is false.' Instituto Storico Della Resistenza, 16 July 2002.
2. BA-MA- RS4/ 1141, KTB SS Pz-Gren. Rgt. 2, 17 September 1943, p. 5.
3. Peiper's radio operator, Heinz Dombrowski, whom he claimed had been killed in Boves, actually worked for Volkswagen in Braunschweig after the war. When this embarrassing fact was revealed within the investigation, Peiper changed his story: Testimony of Joachim Peiper on 29 November 1965, ZSL B 162/6370-6371. Uncritically, Peiper did not see fit to let Rudi Lehmann know about this error, which was then reproduced within the division chronicle, but instead left readers with the misleading impression that there had been a big battle in Boves.
4. ZSL B 162/6370-6371, Statement of Josef Schauer, 1 June 1966.
5. ZSL B 162/6370-6371, Statement of Joachim Molt, 12 July 1966.
6. ZSL B 162/6370-6371, Statement of Herbert Exner, 13 September 1965.

7. Knowledge of Peiper's burning of Boves appears to have been widespread within the 1st SS. After being captured in Normandy, Austrian SS Untersturmführer Jakob Hanreich with the Leibstandarte Sturmgeschütz Battalion was asked about war crimes of the Leibstandarte in the UK in August 1944 and related, 'In Oct 43, S of Turin III/2 Regt burnt a village. The Bn CO was Sturmbannfueher PEIPER. The inhabitants of the village have captured two members of the Bn.' Hanreich had been posted to Milan, Italy, during this time, later moving to Genoa in October 1943. PRO: WO 208/3647, TS26/856, p. 233, British National Archives, Kew.

8. ZSL B 162/6370-6371, Statement of Gerhard Buhr, 24 November 1965. Buhr had been a member of the Leibstandarte since 1939.

9. ZSL B 162/6370-6371, Statement of Joachim Peiper, 23 March 1966.

10. Born in 1916, Wilhelm Haferstroh earned the Iron Cross Second Class at Kursk but was then killed in France on 3 September 1944.

11. Nürnberger came to the Leibstandarte in August 1940 and, at the time of Boves, functioned as a motorcycle messenger in the SPW battalion. ZSL B 162/6370-6371, Statement of Fritz Nürnberger, 19 August 1965.

12. Statement of Gerhard Buhr, 24 November 1965.

13. ZSL B 162/6370-6371, Statement of Otto Dinse, 22 August 1967.

14. ZSL B 162/6370-6371, Statement of Kurt Butenhoff, 23 November 1965. The Butenhoff statement seems contrived, but with regard to Peiper's sensibilities (he could not have been happy to see the enlisted man taken prisoner), he was already known to have little patience for partisans in Russia.

15. ZSL B 162/6370-6371, Statement of Freiderich Breme, 1 October 1965.

16. This story of the shelling of Boves appears completely fabricated by post-war SS testimony. In reality, although the *Grille* were used for shelling, it was not of the town but of the surrounding mountainous area in a later stage of the events after the SS battalion had already passed through the town. However, in his own account to the Stuttgart state attorney, Peiper did claim that the guns had shelled the village—a fact not borne out by the reality that none of the buildings in Boves showed any signs of shell damage with characteristic shrapnel splinters. The author's examination of the numerous photographs of burned out houses in Boves would indicate that they burned from fires started in the lower floors, with no signs of explosions and little evidence, too, of gunfire, which would have left pockmarks on the buildings.

17. Peiper, 'Meine Stellungnahme zum 'Fall Boves'''.

18. The official German sources for the guerrilla operations in Italy: 'Anlage zum Tätigkeitsbericht der Abt. Ic, Abschlussbericht der Entwaffnungsaktion in Nord Italien', Heeresgruppe B, 19 September1943, NA RG 242, T-311, R276, F65-67. See also 'Besonderes Feindnachrichtenblatt', September 22, 1943, F84-86, and 'Stellungsnahme des Einheitsführer', T-354, R654, F363. The author personally inspected many of the vintage homes in Boves. Although wood is used in construction, the exterior is generally fire resistant—red-tile roofs with pastel-stucco walls. When the houses burned, the walls and roofs generally did not.

19. Peiper, 'Meine Stellungnahme zum "Fall Boves"'. The end of German assistant Costantino Salvi was not pleasant. Having been castigated for his part in helping the Germans, he was stripped from power. As penance, he ran an information office in Cuneo to help locate Italian prisoners being held in Germany. This, however, did not go over well with the continuing German occupation. He was arrested and deported to Germany, where he died at Flossenberg concentration camp in Germany on 17 January 1945. Bassignano, *Cuneo agli albori del fascio e nel nazifasismo*.

20. Peiper's description of the threat of the 4th Army is at variance with reports of the II SS Panzer Corps (BA-MA, RS 2-2/21, Teil 2), which makes no mention at all of any potential attack by Italian forces.

21. Generalkommando II SS Panzer Corps, 19 September 1943, BA-MA, RS 2-2/21, Teil 2.

22. The Leibstandarte report on the action is found in the Morgenmeldung for 21 September 1943 to II SS Panzer Corps, BA-MA, RS/2/2/21b.

23. 'Generalkommando IISS Panzerkorps, 21 September 1943, Ic-Morgenmeldung', BA-MA, RS 2-2/21, Teil 2. The captured heavy weaponry in the action is telling regarding the degree to which the Italian 'bandits' were armed: one 7.62cm cannon and four light machine guns.

24. 'Besonderes Feindnachrichtenblatt. Lage im Bandengebiet an der italienischen Ostgrenze und Beurteilung der Bandenlage', Oberkommando der Herresgruppe B, Ic, 22 September 1943, NA RG-242, T-311, R276, F000084.

25. 'Sonderbefehl vom Generalfeldmarschall Rommel', H.Qu. Den 23 September 1943, Oberkommando der Herresgruppe B, NA, T-311, Roll 276, F000087-88.

26. 'Abschlussbericht der Entwaffnungsaktionen in Norditalien: Oberkommando der Herresgruppe B', 19 September 1943, T-311, R276, F000065.

27. Natale Macario hid for the next four days as a partisan and then even through the long hungry winter. But at long last he returned to Cuneo, where the fascist sympathetic podestá arrested him. He left by train, destined to spend a year of hell at Auschwitz concentration camp. With barely any food and enduring back-breaking labour, he survived what many others did not. Natale Macario, interview with author, 16 July 2002.

28. All of this section: Favole Interview.

29. BA-MA., RS 2-2/21, Daily report of 17 September 1943, Leibstandarte SS Adolf Hitler to II SS Panzer Corps to Heeresgruppe B: 'Numerous Jews are being secured at Lake Maggiore.'

30. Maurice Philip Remy, *Mythos Rommel, Ullstein* (Berlin: Tachenbuch-verlag, 2002), p. 196.

31. After the war Hans Röhwer would later be implicated in the killing of twenty-two Italian Jews around Lago Maggiore on 24 and 25 September 1943. BA-Ludwigsburg, Az 5 Str 218/G9; see also '1943 am Lago Maggiore: 'Privater Judenmord', *Westdeutsche Allgemeine Zeitung*, Ausgabe Nr. 154, 5 July 1968.

32. 'Schlussbericht: 1.SS P.D. LAH', Zentrale Stelle der Landesjustiz-verwaltungen, 8-AR-Z 18/59 (Lago Maggiore), Ludwigsburg, 17 April 1964. See also Lutz Klinkhammer, *Stragi naziste in Italia. La guerra contro i civili (1943–1944)* (Rome: Donzelli, 1997), 'Eccidi sul lago Maggiore'.

33. Globocnik was principal executor of the extermination campaign against Jews in Poland: Joseph Poprzeczny, *Odilo Globocnik: Hitler's Man in the East* (London: McFarland, 2004).

34. Victims of Frey's regiment's partisan warfare in Istria: 2–11 October (thirty-seven killed near Brgndac-Pinguente), 4 October (eighteen near Nova Vas), 6–7 October (sixty at Arsa Albona), 7 October (fifty-eight at Kresini-Gimino), 9 October (thirty-one at Krmed-Rovigno), 16 October (twenty-six at Kanfanar) and 10 October (ten killed at Albrega di Parenzo). Source: Carlo Gentile, 'Stragi nazifasciste', in Victoria de Grazia and Sergio Luzzato, eds., *Dizionario del fascismo*, vol. 2 (Turin: Giulio Einaudi Editore, 2003). Based on report of the II SS Panzer Corps and the minimal casualties of the Leibstandarte units, Gentile shows that the anti-partisan warfare in October of 1943 was typical of the *Bandenkampf* style of eradication as practiced in Globocnik in Poland and by other SS units in Russia. Not surprisingly, in his post-war memoirs (p. 307), Albert Frey denied the accusations of killings in Istria, although it is telling that he himself fled to Argentina after the war.

35. Renato Aimo, *Il Prezzo Della Pace: La gente bovesana e la Resistenza 1943–45* (Cuneo: L'Arciere, 1989), pp. 56–83.
36. 'Beschluss vom 23.12.1968: Landgericht Stuttgart, I.gr.Strafkammer', I Ars 62/68, pp. 295–312, Zentralstele der Landesjustizverwaltungen, Ludwigsburg. See also Aimo, *Il Prezzo Della Pace*. Today the award received by Boves as the 'cradle of the resistance' is proudly displayed as carved in marble in the Piazza Italia. 'Citta di Boves Medaglia d'Oro al Valor Civile'.
37. Peiper to Weingartner, 13 March 1976. Dinse's denial: Dinse Interrogation.
38. German historian Gerhard Schreiber claimed that Peiper intended to give the Italians a lesson and that Boves was a typical German war crime against the newly declared *Untermenschen*. Gerhard Schreiber, *Deutsche Kriegsverbrechen in Italien* (Munich: Täter-Opfer-Strafverfolgung, 1996), pp. 128–135.
39. On 3 November 1943 the division had a ration strength of 373 officers, 2,365 NCOs and 15,639 enlisted men. 'Leibstandarte SS Adolf Hitler: Gefechts und Verpflegungsstärke, 3.11.1943', T-314, R1172, F000610. The newly authorized Panzer regiment consisted of 173 armoured vehicles (of which the following were on hand as of 23 August: thirty-one Panzer Mk IVs, sixty-six Mk Vs, fourteen Mk VIs and two Mk IIIs). Although Peiper was awarded the bronze and silver close combat badges the first week in September, he appears to have received the decoration in silver on 20 October. Peiper BDC file.
40. Dorothee Schmitz-Köster, *Kind L 364: Eline Lebensborn Familiengeschichte* (Berlin: Rowohlt, 2007), pp. 104–134.
41. Jochen Peiper, Letter to Hedwig Potthast, 17 October 1943, NSDAP Hauptarchiv, Himmler Collection, Microfilm Roll No. 99, Hoover Institution, Stanford University. The passage, 'Because of K.H's new office, there will be even less time available than before,' refers to Himmler's new appointment as Minister of the Interior on 25 August 1943: Peter Padfield, *Himmler* (New York: Henry Holt, 1991), p. 426. Days before, Himmler met with Albert Speer and his shadowy chief engineer, Heinz Kammler, after Hitler embraced a crash programme to manufacture parts for five thousand V-2 rockets in the concentration camps. Albert Speer, *The Slave State* (London: Weidenfield & Nicholson, 1981), p. 206. The reference given here regarding 'you and your two men' refers to Himmler and their son, Helge.
42. The monument on the Via Moschetti reads, 'On the day of 19 September 1943, while the crazy cruelty and barbarism cut short lives and destroyed homes, the Virgin Mary had pity on such human

misery and miraculously protected this factory.' Favole Interview. With the glut of synthetics after the war, the silk business slumped and the Boves factory closed in 1954. Favole remained an active and successful business man of sharp mental acuity even when interviewed at the age of 96.

Chapter 14: Panzer Leader

1. Mungo Melvin, *Manstein: Hitler's Greatest General*, Weidenfeld & Nicolson, London: 2010), *pp. 402–410*. In the German language, a more balanced and throrough account: Oliver von Wrochem, *Erich von Manstein: Vernichtungskrieg and Geschichtpolitik,* (Ferdinand Schöningh Verlag, Paderborn, 2006).

2. Hans Gruhle, 'The 1.SS Panzer-Regiment's Engagements Near Kiev, Russia in Winter 1943/44', prepared for Joseph Williams, 1948, manuscript in author's possession. 'On 3 November, the battalion was shipped in 16 separate trains … all attempts by the battalion to regain contact with the division were frustrated.'

3. Melvin, *Manstein*, pp. 471; von Manstein, *Lost Victories*, p. 73; and von Mellenthin, *Panzer Battles*, p. 290. In his post-war autobiography and that of subordinates, von Manstein divorced military operations of the war from his deep anti-Semitism and indirect participation in the extermination of the Jews: See Melvin, p.243. For a more complete evaluation of the overall issue of post-war whitewashing: Johannes Hürter, *Hitler Heerführer: Die deutschen Oberbefehlshaber im Krieg gegen die Sowjetunion 1941/42*, (Oldenburg, Oldenbourg Wissenschaftsverlag, 2007). Indeed, von Manstein, Hausser and those like Peiper have formed a large part of the leverage for the so-called 'myth of the Eastern Front'. See Ronald Smelser and Edward J. Davies, *The Myth of the Eastern Front: The Nazi-Soviet War in American Popular Culture.* (New York: Cambridge University Press, 2008).

4. General Hermann Hoth, one of the most experienced panzer generals on the Eastern Front, was dismissed from command of the 4th Panzer Army after the loss of Kiev.

5. Werth, *Russia at War*, p. 753. A number of foreign diplomats were carried unconscious from the drunken extravaganza. The key indicator was this: for the first time in two years Molotov was confident of ultimate Russian victory in what they would later call the 'Great Patriotic War'.

6. Testimony of Oberscharführer Söllhammer, Lehmann and Tiemann, *Die Leibstandarte*, vol. III, pp. 310–311.

7. Gruhle, 'The 1.SS Panzer-Regiment's Engagements Near Kiev, Russia in Winter 1943/44'.
8. The Panzer regiment tank strength was only four Tigers, eighteen Mk Vs and nine Mk IVs by 25 November. 'LSSAH Ia: Tagesmeldung von 25.11.1943', T-314, R1172, F 1224.
9. Against the German losses the Russians had lost about ninety tanks. Gruhle, 'The 1.SS Panzer-Regiment's Engagements Near Kiev, Russia in Winter 1943/44'.
10. Von Mellenthin, *Panzer Battles*, pp. 301–307.
11. Glantz and House, *When Titans Clashed*, p. 174.
12. BA-MA RS 4/1411, KTB SS Panzergrenadier Regiment 2.
13. For the Panzer regiment advance from Lutschin to Morosowka, see 'Tagesmeldung an Pz. A.O.K. 4, 18 November 1943' and 'Abschrift von Fernschreiben' T-314, R1172. Tank strength on that date was fourteen Mk VIs, twenty-seven Mk Vs, forty-eight Mk IVs and six Mk IIIs. The SS division claimed twenty-one T-34s destroyed and six hundred of the enemy killed, with ten prisoners.
14. BA-MA RS 4/1411, KTB SS Panzergrenadier Regiment 2, 19 November 1943.
15. Siptrott BDC file recommendation for the German Cross in Gold, NA, BDC File (file number not known), Vorschlag Nr. 469 für die Verleihung des Deutsches Kreuzes in Gold, dated 20 October 1944 and signed by Peiper on 30 December 1944. For the description of the fighting for Morosowka before Brussilov, see 'LSSAH Ia Tages-meldung', 17–23 November 1943, T-314, R1172, F001105–F001223.
16. The account of Fritz Kosmehl is taken from autobiographical material kindly provided to the author: *Kosmehl Selbstbiographie*, p. 288.
17. Tiemann, *Chronicle of the 7. Panzerkompanie*, pp. 74–75, and Gruhle, 'The 1.SS Panzer-Regiment's Engagements Near Kiev, Russia in Winter 1943/44'.
18. *Kosmehl Selbstbiographie*, p. 288. Also, in the author's interview with Arndt Fischer (15 May 1997) he indicated the same misgivings about Peiper taking over command of him and his fellow Panzer men.
19. It is clear from the personnel file of Martin Gross that he enjoyed a close relationship with and was sympathetic to the former commander, Schönberger, but Peiper was not even mentioned, as he was not a tank man. NA, BDC file for Martin Gross, A3343-SSO-036A. For Wisch's unfavourable perception of Schönberger, it is noteworthy that he was recommended for the Knight's Cross only after his death and, strangely enough, by Wisch himself. However, that the recommendation was a 'sympathy promotion' is made clear

by the fact that the award for Schönberger was made for actions that had taken place six months earlier. BDC file for Schönberger, NA, BDC File, A3343-SSO-095B.

20. 'Beförderung in der Waffen SS: Div. Gef. St., 28 November 1943', Peiper BDC file.

21. Von Mellenthin was chief of staff of XLVIII Panzer Corps. Von Mellenthin, *Panzer Battles*, p. 308.

22. 'Abschrift von Fernschreiben: 1.SS Pz. Div., Ia Tagesmeldungen, 22.11.1943', NA T-314, Roll 1172, F001126.

23. Egon Kleine and Volkmar Kühn, *Tiger die Geschichte einer legendären Waffe* (Stuttgart: Motorbuch Verlag, 1976), p. 91.

24. BDC file for Hans Siptrott, 'Vorschlag Nr. für Verleihung des Deutschen Kreuzes in Gold', 20 October 1944.

25. 'Abschrift von Fernschreiben: 1.SS Pz, 23.11.1943', NA T-314, Roll 1172, F001144-49.

26. BA-MA RS 4/1411, KTB SS Panzergrenadier Regiment 2, 24 November.

27. Tiemann, *Chronicle of the 7. Panzerkompanie*, p. 76.

28. Werner Wolff BDC file, NA Box 011C; see also Agte, *Michael Wittmann and the Tiger Commanders*, p. 250.

29. 'Abschrift von Fernschreiben: 1.SS Pz, 24.11.1943', NA T-314, Roll 1172, F001159.

30. *Kosmehl Selbstbiographie*, p. 289.

31. *Kosmehl Selbstbiographie*, p. 293.

32. Fritz Kosmehl, *Meine Begegnungen mit Joachim Peiper*, manuscript provided to author. During a visit to Traves Peiper gave Kosmehl the projectile that had struck their tank as a souvenir—ostensibly a good luck piece.

33. 'Tagesmeldung an Pz. A.O.K. 4, Ic, 24.11.1943', NA T-314, Roll 1176, F000289. A total of 626 prisoners were reported.

34. 'Abschrift von Fernschreiben: 1.SS Pz. Div. LSSAH, 28.11.43', T-314, R1172, F001307.

35. Westemeier, *Himmler's Krieger*, p. 67.

36. BA-MA RS 4/1411, KTB SS Panzergrenadier Regiment 2, 23 November. Losses of the III Battalion that day was three killed and nine wounded.

37. 'My men always said to each other: "A thousand marks to the man who disturbs the patience of the commander's mind!"' Letter Peiper to parents, Landsberg, 5 November 1946, NA, Case-6-24, RG 153, Box 83.

38. The entire account of Peiper's attack on 5 December 1943 is taken from his personal records in support of his nomination for the Oak

Leaf Cluster of the Iron Cross, dated 24 January 1944 by the divisional commander, Oberführer Theodor Wisch. National Archives, Berlin Document Centre (BDC) files. The files are arranged alphabetically; those on Peiper are extensive.

39. Hans Siptrott, interview with author, 15 July 2012.
40. Hans Siptrott, interview with author, 17 May 1997.
41. 'Tagesmeldung an Pz. A.O.K. 4', 6 December 1943, T-314, R1173, F000078.
42. Agte, *Michael Wittmann and the Tiger Commanders*, p. 135.
43. BA-MA RS 4/1411, KTB SS Panzergrenadier Regiment 2, 6 December 1943.
44. Quotations from radio conversation with Peiper cited in Lehmann and Tiemann, *Die Leibstandarte*, vol. III, p. 350.
45. Arndt Fischer disputed Peiper's profanities: 'He would not have said that': Author's interview, 15 May 1997. For 'We are frying potatoes': Dr Uta Müller, interview with author, 19 May 1999. Story as related to Benno Müller by Peiper after the war.
46. BA-MA RS 4/1411, KTB SS Panzergrenadier Regiment 2, 6–8 December 1943.
47. Von Mellenthin, *Panzer Battles*, p. 313. 'Whenever the devil is mentioned in Russian signals,' said von Mellenthin, 'one could be sure a crack-up was close at hand.'
48. 'He was further known to also punish ruthlessly every one of his own soldiers who showed any weakness. Intellectually, he surpassed the other commanders and was personally known among the highest leaders of the state. I got to know him as a man who in action valued tactical success higher than anything else, who committed himself and others ruthlessly, who punished individual weakness hard and mercilessly, the same as he was hard and merciless towards the enemy. He was a man whom you could admire as a soldier because of his success, but whom you could fear imagining him as your enemy.'

    Handwritten Testimony of Erich Rumpf describing actions in Russia: Jefremowka (Russland), NA Case 6-24, RG 549, Box 32. Thanks to Carol Byrne for the above translation of the transcribed text.
49. SS war correspondent Ernst Kurbjuhn was along for Peiper's ride and provides the glorified particulars of this episode: 'Die eisenen Särge', *Das Schwarze Korps*, 10 February 1944.
50. 'Telefonbuch Gen. Kdo XXXVIII Pz, Korps Abt Ia, 9 December 1943', Report at 17:15 PM, T-314, R1174, F000281 (hereafter Telefonbuch).
51. BA-MA RS 4/1411, KTB SS Panzergrenadier Regiment 2, 9 December 1943.

52. For the actions of 9 and 10 December 1943, see the recollection of Kling's gun loader in Agte, *Michael Wittmann and the Tiger Commanders*, p. 153; also, Lehmann and Tiemann, *Die Leibstandarte*, vol. III, pp. 353–354.
53. BA-MA RS 4/1411, KTB SS Panzergrenadier Regiment 2.
54. For Hugo Kraas writing home to his wife, see Agte, *Michael Wittmann and the Tiger Commanders*, p. 261; for the strong enemy actions, see 'Ic- Morgenmeldung vom 11.12.1943" NA T-314, Roll.1176, F000605.
55. 'Directive for Conduct of the Attack on 11.12.1943', Lehmann and Tiemann, *Die Leibstandarte*, vol. IV, p. 434.

Chapter 15: The Oak Leaves

1. BA-MA RS 4/1411, KTB SS Panzergrenadier Regiment 2, 14 December 1943, describing the fate of the villages of Medelewka and Iskra.
2. For Peiper overheard after tank losses on the radio, see Agte, *Michael Wittmann and the Tiger Commanders*, p. 261. For the tank losses: 1.SS.Pz.Div. LSSAH, Abschrift von Fernschreiben, den 4.12.43 and 10.12.43, NA T-314, Roll 1177. In comparing the losses on the two dates, it will be noted that the Germans retained the battlefield and thus hauled their shot-up hulks into repair shops, although the losses sustained by Peiper's command led to an immediate short-age of combat-ready tanks in the space of just a few days.
3. Albert Frey to Jens Westemeier, 18 February 1994, as cited in Weste-meier, *Himmler's Krieger*, p. 69. There was a 'leadership meeting' that was held at the village of Kotowka on 17 December 1943 in which these disagreements were aired. KTB SS Panzergrenadier Regiment 2.
4. '*Er hat seine Soldaten verheizt!*' Albert Frey, interview with Charles Whiting, as related to author on 19 August 2001.
5. '*Ich weiss nichts davon das er mir verheizt hat. Peiper war ein Draufgänger und hat so auch das Regiment geführt.*' Hans Siptrott statement, 21 October 2010, courtesy of Mike Smeets.
6. Jochen Peiper, Letter to Hedwig Potthast, 15 December 1943, NSDAP Hauptarchiv, Himmler Collection, Microfilm Roll #99, Hoover Institution, Stanford University.
7. Lehmann and Tiemann, *Die Leibstandarte*, vol. III, p. 363.
8. 'Die eisenen Särge'. See also Lehmann and Tiemann, *Die Leibstandarte*, vol. III, pp. 367 and 368.
9. Von Mellenthin, *Panzer Battles*, p. 318.
10. Fritz Kosmehl, 'Meine Begegnungen mit Joachim Peiper'. The 'Führerstollen' was something like a challah bread with marzipan, raisins and glazed fruit.

11. Peiper to his father, recalling various Christmas times in the war, 2 December 1946, NA, Case 6-24, RG-153, Box 83.

12. 'Einzelbefehle Versorgungslage Berichte des Gen. Kdo. XXXXVIII Pz Korps, 1 November 1943 bis 31 December 1943', NA, T-314, Roll 1176, F 1084-1092; Lehmann and Tiemann, *Die Leibstandarte*, vol. III, p. 378, Established strength was 6,566 for the two Panzer grenadier regiments: '1.SS Panzer-Div. LSSAH: Stärke der kämpfenden Truppe,' BA: RH 10/312.

13. Jochen Peiper, 'Brief Review.' 'I know positively by radio intercepts that a retreat was made impossible to Russian commanders by threats from superior commissars.'

14. Telefonbuch, NA T-314, Roll 1177; also Lehmann and Tiemann, *Die Leibstandarte*, vol. III, p. 389.

15. Telefonbuch, 8 January 1944; Ia LSSAH, 11.06 hrs.

16. Von Mellenthin, *Panzer Battles*, p. 319.

17. 'Ia, Kriegstagebuch, XXXXVIII Panzerkorps', 8 January 1944, NA T-314, Roll 1177, Operations for this period: F000258-000427.

18. Telefonbuch, 13 January 1944, 13.45 hours, NA T-314, Roll 1177.

19. Lehmann and Tiemann, *Die Leibstandarte*, vol. III, p. 401.

20. 'Abschrift von Fernschreiben: 1.SS Pz.Div. LSSAH', 15 January 1944, 1845 Uhr, NA T-314, Roll 1177. Peiper's combat-ready tank strength was five Tigers, nine Panzer Vs and five Panzer IVs. Peiper reported thirty-seven anti-tank guns and fifteen vehicles destroyed in the actions, along with 120 enemy dead and the rest running for Sherebki.

21. 'Anlage zum Kriegstagebuch Gen Kdo. XXXXVIIII Pz. Korps, Abt. Ia., Spruch Nr. 397: 15 January 1944', NA T-314, Roll 1177.

22. Telefonbuch, 17 January at 16.15 hrs, T-314, Roll 1177. Description of the actions of Peiper's tank group and the self-propelled III Battalion in January are covered in detail in KTB SS Panzergrenadier Regiment 2.

23. Horst Schumann, interview with author, 8 March 2006.

24. '1.SS Pz Div: Ia Tagesmeldung vom 21.1.44: Anlagen zum Kriegstagebuch, Gen Kdo. XXXVIII Pz Korps', NA T-314, Roll 1177. What was left of the Leibstandarte was pulled into reserve around Chmelnik, where emergency refitting began. The troops were cleaned and deloused, with tank repairs and replacement taking on a priority. By 21 January the armour situation had improved to fifty-four Panzers and twenty-three assault guns. The very complete telephone log shows German frustration over a mix-up in getting a replacement shipment of the division armour in place for use.

25. 'In the winter of 1943–1944, I experienced the destruction of Army Group South ... The German soldier possesses the highest qualities in the attack and is less suited for defence and withdrawals ... we reached a state very similar to a route ... the front-line soldier had lost his belief and hope for a successful military solution. Instead, the "Russian terror complex" emerged.' Jochen Peiper, 7 April 1946. 'Brief Review'.

26. 'Panz.Werkst.Kp.SS Panz.Rgt.1 LSSAH: Kompanie Befehl Nr. 1/44', NA, RG 242, T-354, R622, F000711, 9 February 1944.

27. Karl Paul Fröhlich, interview with author, 19 May 1997.

28. Reinhold Kyriss, interview with author, 20 May 1997.

29. 'Vorschlagsliste Nr. 2666 für die Verleihung des Ritterkreuzes des Eisernen Kreuzes: Herbert Kuhlmann' 31 January 1944, Div. Gef. St., 31 January 1944, BDC file for Kuhlmann (NA, RG-242, SS-Officers, A3343-SSO-222). During the action from 25 to 29 January 1944 Kampfgruppe Kuhlmann accounted for the destruction of 116 Russian tanks and the bulk of seven enemy divisions.

30. BDC File for Horst Finzelberg, NA, RG-242, A3343-SSO-207.

31. Horst Schumann, interview with author, 8 March 2006. Schumann was wounded in the jaw and spent several weeks in a field hospital. He would re-join Peiper's command in Belgium in the spring of 1944.

32. Jochen Peiper, 'Brief Review', 7 April 1946. For Peiper it had been the failure to end the Russian war in 1941 that cast a pall on any remaining hope. 'A peace at that time,' he surmised, 'would have provided us with a time delay of several years ... and given protection in the rear for a one-front war in the West.'

33. 'Donnerstag 27.01.1944, 15-18 Uhr Jochen Peiper', Himmler Dienstkalendar for 27 January 1944, IfZ, Munich.

34. 'Exemplary Fighting Spirit', *Das Schwarze Korps*, 13 January 1944. 'The army bulletin recently mentioned the exemplary fighting spirit of the Leibstandarte Adolf Hitler.'

35. For Hitler's speech to his generals, see Toland, *Adolf Hitler*, p. 778. On the day before, 26 January 1944, Himmler had addressed 260 high-ranking army and navy officers at Posen, Poland. As he had done in October, he admitted the diabolical: 'I can assure you that the Jewish question has been solved,' he exclaimed to thunderous applause. Six million had been killed, he said, attempting to perversely justify the heinous execution of women and children. 'I would be a weakling if I allowed hate-filled sons to grow to manhood in this battle of humans against sub-humans.' Bradley Smith and Agnes F. Peterson, *Heinrich Himmler Geheimreden 1933 bis 1945* (Frankfurt

am Main: Propyläen, 1974), p. 201. Present at the event, Lieutenant Colonel Freiherr von Gersdorff recalled Himmler mentioning that Hitler himself had given him the order for the elimination of the Jews—not surprisingly a fact not mentioned in Himmler's advance notes for his speech: NA T-175, Roll 94, Frame 614835.

36. Max Domarus, ed., *Hitler, Reden und Proklamationen 1932–1945* (Wiesbaden: Bolchazy-Carducci Publishers, 1973), 27 January 1944, pp. 2082–2086.

37. Berlin's Sportpalast was the site of two historic speeches. One was the ultimatum Hitler delivered to the Czech government on 26 September 1938 demanding the acceptance of the German occupation of the Sudetenland. And on 18 February 1943 Joseph Goebbels, speaking in the wake of the catastrophe at Stalingrad, had delivered a fiery harangue to the fifteen thousand filled seats, calling for total sacrifice. 'Do you want total war? Do you want it, if necessary, more totally radical than we could even imagine today? ... Now people, arise and storm, break loose!'

38. David Irving, *The Secret Diaries of Hitler's Doctor* (New York: Macmillan, 1983), pp. 145–146.

39. Himmler stated fears about Russia on 15 January 1944. 'His health is not good,' Felix Kersten said of his patient. 'He is depressed in mind and health.' Himmler later made the remark to his masseuse that 'militarily speaking, we must kill between 3 and 4 million Russians a year, just to stay afloat'. Kersten, *Memoirs*, pp. 129–130.

40. For the atmosphere at Himmler's headquarters in early February 1944, see Arthur Silgailis, *Latvian Legion* (San Jose, CA: R. James Bender Publishing, 1986), pp. 245–250; also, NA RG242, T-175, R129.

41. 'Testimony of Arndt Fischer to Dwight F. Fanton', 31 March 1946, RG 549, Case 6-24, Box 22.

42. Charles Whiting's interview with Gerhard Bremer of the 1 SS Panzer Reconnaissance Battalion, related to the author on 19 August 2001. Bremer, a stocky tough who had been long in the division, was later transferred to the 12th SS Panzer Division. When Whiting visited his estate facing the Mediterranean in Denia, Spain, Bremer proudly showed how his workers stood at attention for inspection in the morning arrayed with their tools. Afterwards, Bremer enthusiastically bounced Whiting around his property driving his Land Rover while cassette tapes of old SS tunes blared from his car radio. Bremer had been released from French imprisonment in 1954 and had moved to Denia which was friendly to Germans still openingly living a fascist lifestyle. Bremer died in Spain on 29 October 1989.

43. Heinz von Westernhagen, letters to family from Russia, 14 December 1942, 5 June 1943 and 14 July 1943, Westernhagen, *Die Kinder der Täter*, p. 45.
44. Today the place where Peiper and his family lived is nearby a nostalgic museum celebrating the era of horse-drawn sleighs and wagons: Kutschen, Wagen und Schlittenmuseum in Rottach-Egern.
45. 'Das Eichenlaub für SS Sturmbannführer Peiper,' *Völkischer Beobachter*, 3 February 1944.
46. The building in Rottach-Egern where his family lived was owned by the Nathan family. However, contrary to the supposition of the Peiper family, the Nathans were not Jewish. Hinrich Peiper, interview with author, 19 May 1999; Birgit Mitchell, interview with author, Rottach-Egern, 20 July 2002.
47. 'Das Eichenlaub zum Ritterkreuz', *Tegernseer Zeitung*, 4 February 1944. Handball remained popular in Tegernsee, and football (soccer) matches between north and south Bavaria were faithfully maintained. Thanks to the Mr Dessler at the Tegernseer Zeitung for allowing the author to carefully review the extant period issues for 1944.
48. At the same time clever and diabolical, the 'Strength through Joy' movement was the creation of Dr Robert Ley and was designed to provide inexpensive diversions—cruises, music, movies and sports—for civilians under the crushing oppression of wartime Germany. On 4 February 1944, when the newspaper noted Peiper's receipt of the Oak Leaves, they also announced a new film at Rottach-Egern (*Ich werde dich auf Händen tragen*), a new theatrical production in Tegernsee and a comedy in Schliersee; a local football match and special radio programmes for the weekend.
49. 'Interrogation of Karl Gebhardt', 23 July 1947, NA RG 238, M-1019, Roll 35, F298–299. Also, Roll 20, F710.
50. 'First detailed interrogation on SS Oberführer Eugen Dollmann', DSDIC/CMF/SD 57, PRO W 208/4474.
51. Dr Hellmuth Fuchs and Herbert Meyer, interview with Toland, 8 May 1971, Toland Papers, FDR Library, Box 56.
52. 'Befund der Gesundheits und Verwendungsprüfstelle der Waffen SS Dachau vom 11.02.1944', BDC, as cited by Westemeier, *Himmler's Krieger*, p. 87.
53. 'Vernehmungsniederschrift Franz Lucas', Trial of Karl Wolff, BA-L, Z-Prot. II, 10a Js 39/60, 8 November 1962. 'I can recall a visit at Dachau and at that time prisoners in flight suits were thrown into cold water and after a long time swimming, they were totally exhausted by the cold, they were fished out. The same prisoners later had lunch with

us. Then they were released from the concentration camp and were used at the front somewhere. Himmler himself spoke with these prisoners during lunchtime which have survived these tests. By rumour, these people had volunteered to take part in these tests.' Over a hundred of the test subjects died in these experiments in 1942 and 1943: George J. Annas and Michael A. Grodin, *The Nazi Doctors and the Nuremberg Code: Human Rights in Human Experimentation* (Oxford: Oxford University Press, 1992), pp. 71–73.

54. For the figures showing seven died on 11 and 12 February 1944, see SS Sterbebuch Dachau, courtesy of Albert Knoll at KZ Gedenkstätte Dachau.

55. See Martin Broszat, 'The Concentration Camps', in *Anatomy of the SS State* (New York: Walker and Company, 1965). For the Dachau experiments on concentration camp victims, see Robert J. Lifton, *The Nazi Doctors* (New York: Basic Books, 1986). Also, for Dachau in February 1944, see 'Testimony of Franz Blaha', *Trial of Major War Criminals*, vol. 5, Nuremburg, 1947, proceedings of 11 January 1946.

56. Himmler sent out china candlestick holders to SS officers within the inner circle after the birth of each child. 'Three weeks later my wife wrote: "Today I received a marvellous parcel from the Reichsführer containing a china candlestick with the name and date of birth of each child stamped on them. At the foot of each candlestick was a dedication from the Reichsführer. I asked my comrades and discovered that he had done the same for all the old SS Führer ... despite the atmosphere of hardness which he creates, he is a warm-hearted fellow."' Electronically tapped conversation between Kurt Meyer and Generalmajor Knut Eberding, C.S.D.I.C. (U.K.), G.R.G. 225, 18–19 November 1944, PRO WO. 208/6364, Kew.

57. Peiper in SS hospital in Berlin on 30 March 1944, Telegram sent on 2 April 1944, BA-MA: RS/4/1241.

58. 'To live in a frequently bombed city is not anything anyone enjoys ... [Still] we cannot help loving the city of Berlin more today than ever before, even with its heavy wounds.' Joseph Goebbels, 'Das Leben geht weiter', *Das Reich*, 16 April 1944, pp. 1–2.

59. Peiper's description of his conversation with Goebbels in April 1944 is from his uncompleted manuscript, found in Agte, *Michael Wittmann and the Tiger Commanders*, appendix, original translation by Helmut Thiess; Fedorowicz version, p. 642. The author examined the originals of the Goebbels Tagebücher at the Bundesarchiv in Koblenz (N 1118), but the diary for 1944 does not record the Peiper

meeting verbatim. The most likely date of their Berlin discussion was 1 April 1944.

60. Joseph Goebbels, 'Warum wird es uns so schwer gemacht?' *Das Reich*, 9 April 1944.

61. On 11 April Peiper met up with his division leaders, now arriving at the Hotel Kant, before continuing on to the west the following day. This from the Benoni Junker diary, courtesy of Stefan De Meyer and Timm Haasler (hereafter Junker Diary).

62. Goebbels's diary entry on Hitler's speech on 8 May 1943, Lochner, *Goebbels Diary*. Original checked for translation: Nachlass Goebbels, BA-K, N 1118/54.

63. Hugh Trevor Roper, *The Last Days of Hitler* (London: Macmillian, 1995), p. 65.

64. 'XXIV Panzerkorps: Ia, Anlagen zum KTB: Tagesmeldung an Korpsgruppe Chevallerie', 7 April 1944, NA: T-314, 930, F001081-92.

65. For 'a lot of ordinary Germans', see G-2 Records, 3rd Armoured Division, 603-2.2, Interrogation Report for 16 August 1944, Box 12255; 'Consolidated interrogation report', RG-498, UD227, PWIS(H) interrogations, Box 1249; Also, captured order from SS Gruppenführer Knoblauch: 'French Volunteers in the Waffen SS', SS Panzer Grenadier Regiment 2, 8 July 1944. In 'Annex 1 to Periodic Report No. 70', NA, FUSA, G-2 Records, RG-407, 101-2.1, Box 1392: 'SS isn't what it used to be'. 'Consolidated Report of 21 Alsatians of SS Pz Gr Reg. 4', 28 June 1944, PWIS(H)/LDC/108, RG-498, UD 228, Box 1250.

66. Jochen Peiper to Willis Everett, 7 December 1946, Everett archives.

67. Hal D. McCown, 'Observations of an American Field Officer Who Escaped from the 1st SS Panzer Division "Adolf Hitler"', RG-407, 330-2.2 G-2 Records 30th Infantry Division Box 7569: 330-2.1, Operations Reports, December 1944, 'He is completely confident of Germany's ability to whip the Allies. He spoke of Himmler's new reserve army quite at length saying that it contained so many new divisions, both armoured and otherwise, that our G-2s would all wonder where they all came from. He did his best to find out from me the success the V-1 and V-2 were having and told me that more secret weapons like those would be unloosed.'

68. Hans Schwarz Van Berk, writing in Goebbel's propaganda publication, *Das Reich*, on 17 June 1944. Ralf Georg Reuth, *Goebbels* (San Diego: Harcourt, 1990), p. 716. Born in 1902, Schwarz Van Berk was an old fighter, having joined the NSDAP in 1930. For a biographical summary, see Hans Schwarz Van Berk, 15 November 1963, IfZ 1846, Akt. 3835/67, by David Schoenbaum.

69. Hal D. McCown to Peiper, 21 December 1944, and McCown to John Toland, 5 April 1958, John S.D. Eisenhower Papers, Abilene, KS, Bitter Woods, Box 3. 'Peiper strongly defended Hitler and his program. He admitted many wrongs had been committed, but also mentioned the great good he believed Hitler was doing, specifically the elimination of the Communist menace and his Napoleonic concept of a unified and more productive Europe [with the] master race running things and elimination of undesirable persons and peoples. Peiper was a devout Nazi and was at one time the adjutant of Himmler. Peiper had a well-developed sense of humor and said he would like to take me with him to the Russian front and let me see why they had to violate all the rules of land warfare in dealing with the Russians—both soldiers and guerillas—since the Russians observed no rules themselves.'

Chapter 16: Waiting for the Invasion

1. The story of Francine Vico and family is from the author's interview with Jacques Vico as well as his tour of the Abbaye d'Ardenne near Caen on 8 July 2002.
2. 'Rede des Reichsführer SS am 23.11.1942—SS Junkerschule Tölz', NA, T-175, Records of the Reichsführer SS und Chef der Deutschen Polizei, Roll 90, F2612778-88. In his speech to the officer cadets at Bad Tölz in 1942 Himmler observed that even with an output of four hundred officers per year from the SS academies, the problem of replacements remained a serious issue.
3. The telegram from the SS hospital in Berlin describing Peiper's status on 30 March 1944 was sent to the Leibstandarte Adolf Hitler. BA-MA, RS/4/1241. 'Extensive nerve dysfunction in hands and legs, so that further treatment in a recuperation hospital is ordered … classified as currently unfit for duty.'
4. Léon Degrelle, *Campaign in Russia* (Newport Beach, VA: Institute for Historical Review, 1995), p. 262.
5. For Léon Degrelle's march through Belgium, see Martin Conway, *Collaboration in Belgium: Léon Degrelle and the Rexist Movement* (New Haven, CT: Yale University Press, 1993), pp. 244–247. For Peiper's participation in the event, see his April 1967 interview, 'L'Affaire Peiper: une interview posthume de l'ex colonel SS', *La Libre Belgique*, 19 July 1976, p. 4.
6. Degrelle, *Campaign in Russia*, p. 229.
7. Panzer Division Hott from the horse rider's word of encouragement Hottehüh!—Gee up!

8. Thorn commentary on recruits in April 1944, prepared for author, 20 February 2018.

9. Account of Kurt Sametreiter, provided by Manfred Thorn, 23 February 2018.

10. 'Generalkommando XXIV Panzerkorps, Ia, Korps Haupquartiere 7.4.1944', T-314, R730, F000709-1092. Before departing Russia their corps commander referred to the entire formation as Kamfpgruppe Leibstandarte with 'five weary panzer grenadier battalions' with a total ration strength of 1,423 men. As an example, the battle strength of the 2 SS Panzer Grenadier Regiment entering Russia on 10 November was 2,296 officers and men. However, the casualties suffered by the same regiment between that time and their departure to France (2,744) was greater than their strength. Even accounting for replacements, the regiment was virtually destroyed. 'Verlustmeldungen und Stammkarten des 2.Pz Gren. Rgt. LSSAH', T-354, R623, F000724-766. See Lehmann and Tiemann, *Die Leibstandarte,* vol. IV/1, pp. 95–96.

11. 'OB West Tagesmeldungen 19.4. 1944', BA-MA, RH 19/4/33D.

12. 'Age Groups in Pz Rgt. LSSAH'. Similarly, a routine order in the division in the spring of 1944 forbade the word 'Volksdeutsche' be used for German-speaking foreigners who were increasingly common, even in the elite Leibstandarte. T-354, R623, F000767. The order came directly from Himmler on 27 November 1943.

13. 'Special Interrogation Report of Brigadeführer Theodor Wisch, Comdr 1 SS Panzer Division "Adolf Hitler", 6 June 44–25 August 44', August 1945, U.S. First Army, PWI Interrogations, NA, RG-407, 101.1-3.2, Box 1515. The two impressed British soldiers in the Leibstandarte did not travel to Normandy when the division moved.

14. Himmler's speech to the 17th SS Panzer Grenadier Division on 10 April 1944: NA, RG-407, 3rd Armoured G-2 Records, 603-2.13, Annex 2 to Periodic Report No. 31, Box 12258.

15. 'If the whole German nation has become a nation of soldiers, then it is compelled to perish.' Referring to 1918, Lingner was not dissuaded from continued sacrifice: 'I am convinced that as a result of poverty and hunger that millions of Germans died sooner than they would have … If they die in battle, it amounts to the same thing in practice.' SRM 1121, 12 February 1945, PRO: WO 208/4140. Lingner had been captured near Zweibrücken on 10 February 1945.

16. See 'Versetzung des SS Ostuf. Rudolf Höcker' and 'Betr. Anforderung von Führer', T-354, Roll 24, F000018-20, both signed by SS Obersturmbannführer Jochen Peiper, as well as Peiper's inquiry about

the availability of SS Hauptsturmführer Richard Zimmermann from the SS hospital in Berlin.

17. 'SS Pz Regt 1, Report on Information obtained from SS Ustuf. Pflughaupt', August 1944, C.S.D.I.C. (UK) SIR 642, Combined Services Detailed Interrogation Service, RG 338, 290/56/1/1-2, Box 3 (hereafter Pflughaput Report).

18. Based on Gerhard Stiller's account (hereafter Stiller Account) in Tiemann, *Chronicle of the 7. Panzer Kompanie*, pp. 87–88.

19. Account of Hartwig Kammescheit: Stephan Cazenave, *Panzers Normandie 44: SS Panzer Regiment 1 LAH* (Bayeux, FR: Maranes Editions, 2016), p. 63.

20. '1. SS Panzer Division Leibstandarte Adolf Hitler, Divisions Sonderbefehl für die weltanschauliche Erziehung', 22 April 1944, T-354, R622, F001084-6. 'Der Dietrich' was a clever allusion to both to the passkey symbol and the moniker of the old division commander, Sepp Dietrich.

21. 'Abt. VI/LSSAH, Amerikanismus- eine Weltgefahr', May 1944, NA: RG 242, T-354, R622, F1034-39.

22. Pflughaupt Report.

23. Veterans of the Russian campaign found some of the replacement tank drivers particularly unsatisfactory. Fischer, interview with author, 15 May 1997.

24. Geyr von Schweppenburg, leading Panzergruppe West, believed that of the Panzer divisions available in June 1944, the 1st SS Panzer Division had the lowest combat efficiency: 'Discipline was a sham; the NCOs were poor. The division did not have time for thorough training before the invasion.' Leo Geyr von Schweppenburg, 'Panzer Type Divisions (Western Front)', in B-466, Panzer Group West (mid-1943–5 July 1944, NARA, RG-549, FMS.

25. SS Sturmbannführer Herbert Kuhlmann would resume responsibility for Peiper's I Battalion after his return.

26. Cazenave, *Panzers Normandie 44*, p. 21.

27. 'In the end, if we cannot express ourselves in absolute honesty to our superior officers, lies and betrayal will take away our victory.' Sepp Dietrich to Reichführer SS, I SS Panzer Corps Leibstandarte, Korps Gefechtstand, 13 May 1944, document found on auction site and copied and translated. Thanks to Patrick Uschkereit for help with this important document.

28. 'We really need to waste no words on the subject of alcohol ... With the hundreds of thousands of men we're losing in the war, we can't afford to lose still more men through addiction to alcohol and

self-destruction ... Leaders who allow their subordinates to hold drinking parties in their companies will be punished.' Himmler to his generals on 4 October 1943 at Posen (IMT, PS-1919).

29. Details of life in Hasselt: Reinhold Kyriss, interview with author, 19 May 1997.

30. In spite of Wünsche's effort to distance himself from Himmler after the war, in an interview with John Toland, he and his wife admitted that Himmler greatly admired Wünsche. Thanks to Carol Byrne for the translated conversation regarding this point in Toland's recorded interview, 10 October 1963.

31. Each year on 20 April, their mutual birthday, Hitler did something special for Max Wünsche. In 1944 he was picked up at Berchtesgaden rail station by a car sent from Hitler's Berghof. 'Interrogation of Max Wünsche: PRO WO208/3599'.

32. 'Notes on Hitler', Information obtained from Obersturmbannführer Wünsche, captured near Falaise on 24 August 1944, CSDIC(UK) SIR 905, NA, RG 226, Entry 190, Box 743, to be refiled from Nazi War Crimes Disclosure Act. Generaloberst Hube was killed in an air crash later that evening: Nicolaus von Below, *At Hitler's Side: The Memoirs of Hitler's Luftwaffe Adjutant, 1937–1945* (London: Greenhill Books, 2006), pp. 197–198. For the photo of Wünsche meeting Hitler on his birthday: *Völkischer Beobachter*, 23 April 1944.

33. Reinhold Kyriss, enlisted man of the II Panzer Battalion, interview with author, 20 May 1997. 'When he [Pötschke] came up to me, my behind was shaking. He was unpredictable.'

34. 'Inspection of the main body of the replacement personnel ... and the training capabilities of commanders and subordinate commanders show that six weeks' time must be demanded ... The division is not ready for operations ... There are deficiencies in small arms, light infantry weapons, entrenching tools, and camouflage suits ... training is thereby rendered particularly difficult ... Increased activity of the air war has interfered with the bringing up of fresh material and caused a drop in performance at motor transport parks. 1,685 members of the division are at present on courses in the Reich.' The intercepted report sought urgent replacements to non-commissioned officers, which were in very short supply. PRO: DEFE 3/170, KV 7584 and 7612 issued on 11 and 12 June 1944. Peiper's tank strength by 6 June: ninety-three Mk IVs and seventy-three Panthers.

35. Stiller Account.

36. 'Handwritten Testimony of Erich Rumpf', Case 6-24, RG 549, Box 7.

37. Steiner, *Die Freiwilligen*, p. 122.

38. 'An SS Military Crime and its Punishment: Report on Information Obtained from PW SS-Man Langer, 6th Co., SS Pz Gren. 26', CSDIC (UK) SIR 681, RG 338, 290/56/1/1-2, Box 3. Langer was captured near Caen on 27 June 1944. After his offence of listening to an enemy broadcast, he was transferred in December 1943 to the Hitlerjugend field court at Maria-ter-Heide, where he was charged with 'undermining Germany's powers of national defence' and was reminded that had he not been a youth of 19 years, he would have been shot, but being a 'miserable swine and a dirty tramp', they would send him to the 'Punishment Camp for the Waffen SS and Police' at Dachau. Langer was shocked when he arrived at Dachau to find himself in the company of Ritterkreuz recipients and others with years of experience at the front, having been sent there because of overstaying their leave by two or three days. There were 1,400 there from the Waffen SS—a number from the Leibstandarte—with most sentenced for looting. 'Shortly after my arrival, I was instructed by Oberscharführer Müller, who was in charge of my section of the camp ... Any attempt to escape would be punished by death. At that time, shootings were constantly occurring; we were required to attend each of them. Frequently ten or eleven men were shot in a week ... lesser offences were punishable by flogging and solitary confinement ... The camp was isolated by a barbed wire fence, parallel with which ran an electric fence charged with a thousand volts. Outside was a moat filled with water. Every 150 to 200 yards was a machine gun tower.' In March 1944 Langer was transferred to the punishment platoon of the 12th SS Panzer Division in Verneuil, France, where there was more physical abuse. With the invasion, Langer transferred to the front.

39. Others in the tank regiment acknowledged that the SS leadership was quite dismayed with the quality of the replacements. SS tank commander Karl Zumpe: 'Of course it wasn't easy to adapt to our discipline and high state of readiness, particularly for those coming from the Luftwaffe.' Agte, *Michael Wittmann and the Tiger Commanders*, p. 351.

40. Original source: '1.SS Panzer Division 'LSSAH,' Divisions Tagesbefehl Nr. 17: Kriegsgerichtliche Urteile'. Those executed were SS Oberschutz Anton Müller, SS Schutz Werner Wutke, SS Schutz Hugo Triebke, SS Schutz Günther Dettlaff and SS Schutz Johann Riedinger. BA-MA, RS 3-1/77. Execution for chicken theft, according to Arndt Fischer: 'This type of thing had happened before, but we were shocked at the severity of the sentence,' as cited in Westemeier, *Himmler's Krieger*, pp. 71 and 191. Also, Fischer, letter to author, 9 January 2002.

41. The date of the trial of the thieves is taken from Junker Diary. See also Rolf Reiser, interview with author, March 2006. Winston L. Field, Colonel JAGC, Deputy Judge Advocate: to Der Oberstaatsanwalt bei dem Bayerischen Landgericht regarding Case No. 7 Js 562/57,' 12 July 1956, NA: RG 549, War Crimes Tried, Landsberg: 'Stayback' files, Box 6 (290/59/17/3-4).

42. Staatsanwaltschaft Flensburg 2 Js 437/56 AR 491/66, now on file at Bundesarchiv Ludwigsburg 124 AR 491/1966. Peiper was interrogated at Landsberg on 30 July 1956 about the shooting near Beverloo, Belgium. See also 'Die Mörder sind immer noch unter uns', Neue Illustrierte, December 1955, pp. 20–22.

43. 'Wir haben es für völlig richtig gehalten, gestehe ich, ja.' Interview with Jochen Peiper, provided to author by journalist Harvey T. Rowe, who obtained the interview of Peiper from Hans Kettgen, p. 5, no date, but 1971 or 1972 based on mentioned events in the interview. Strangely, the execution of the thieving SS enlisted men appears to have taken place on Sepp Dietrich's birthday, 28 May.

44. For Himmler's speech to the generals at Sonthofen on 5 May 1944: NA: RG 242, T-175, R 92, F003476. 'This soldierly order that was given to me' does all but state that Hitler had expressly given him the charge of eliminating the Jews.

45. Himmler's second speech on 24 May 1944 to assembled generals: NA RG 242, T-195, R92, F004639.

46. 'We had a distinguished visitor at the end of May in Genk.' Account of Manfred Thorn, 23 February 2018.

47. Wolff episode, Tiemann, *Chronicle of the 7. Panzerkompanie*, pp. 100–101, and Agte, *Michael Wittmann and the Tiger Commanders*, p. 351.

48. *Politische Wochenschau*: 'Die Sonnwendfeier', June 1944, NA: RG 242, R622, F 1046-49.

49. 'If he is married and no children arrive within two years, he gets no promotion … in general a very great deal is expected of the personal effort of the SS leader and his wife.' Kurt Meyer in secretly recorded conversation with General Lieutenant Otto Elfeldt, who would later be captured near Saint-Lambert on 20 August 1944: 'Even in our generation, within the next 20 to 30 years, we must fill these gaps. If, by doing so, we overstep the limits laid down by the family ideal, it is only an exception in the national life of our people. No one has any idea how it will be done.' PRO: GRGG, 18–19 November 1944, WO 208/4364.

50. Traudl Junge, *Until the Final Hour* (New York: Arcade Publishing, 2004), pp. 123–124. See also Christa Schroeder, *Er war mein Chef*

(Coburg: Nation Europa Verlag, 1999), pp. 167–168. For details of the Gretl Braun–Fegelein wedding, see the Eva Braun photo albums at the National Archives, NA, RG-242-EB and HL. Gretl was rumoured to be promiscuous, having had a poorly concealed affair with Hitler's previous SS adjutant, Fritz Darges. In the end Darges refused her hand in marriage, much to Hitler's dismay.

51. Nicholaus von Below, *At Hitler's Side* (London: Greenhill Books, 2001), pp. 199–200.
52. 'There is no doubt that among the Anglo-Saxons, the British are the best.' Führer's Headquarters: Staff meetings, 3 March 1943, Stenographic fragment captured at Berchtesgaden, NA, RG-498, UD 304, Box 1372.
53. *Kersten, Memoirs, p. 133.*
54. The German Navy estimated that the invasion would only be possible if seas were less than eight feet, the wind was less than twenty-four knots and sea visibility greater than three miles. These conditions were not met, nor did German meteorologists know the weather conditions to the west in which Allied planners saw a break: 'Interview with Maj. Heinz Lettau', Foreign Military Studies, 5 October 1949, NA: RG 549, MS B-987.
55. The obstacles looked like *Hopfenfelderstangen*, the canted, tall wooden poles using in hop farming in Germany.
56. Irving, *Hitler's War*, p. 602.
57. 'SS Obergruppenführer Josef "Sepp" Dietrich: leader of the I.SS Panzer Corps and 6 SS Panzer Army', Intelligence Section of U.S. Historical Division, NARA, RG-498, G-2 Records Historical Division, Box 1373.
58. Friedrich August Freiherr von der Heydte, *Muss ich streben, will ich fallen* ... (Neckargemünd: Vowinckel Verlag, 1987), pp. 99–106. Also, Franz Josef Freiherr von der Heydte, interview with author, 18 March 2010. In the accident on 12 September 1943 von der Heydte had abandoned a crashing Fieseler Storch reconnaissance aircraft and survived a fall of 12 metres without a parachute! Severely injured, he would recover in a hospital over the following four months. Vonder Heydte overheard in conversation with Obst. Eberhard Wildermuth, 16–19 March 1945, TNA, WO 208/4177. Von der Heydte claims to have second-hand information that half a million people have been put to death in Czechoslovakia, that all Jews in Bavaria and Austria had been taken there including the old, infirm and "mental defectives". In reality, the largest camp there was Theresienstadt and the surrounding ghetto where an estimated

33,000 died with a further 88,000 send on to elimination camps. Lublin-Maidanek which is also mentioned saw between 78,000–235,000 gassed.

59. See 'What did Rommel Know?' in David Fraser, *Knight's Cross: A Life of Field Marshal Erwin Rommel* (New York: Harper Collins, 1993), pp. 534–552. Also in captivity, General Lieutenant Richard Schimpf, the former head of the 3rd Fallschirmjäger Division, would later claim to also have been privy to Rommel's plans, claiming they had gone all the way to a personal ultimatum. RG 338, Records of the MIS 6824 Detailed Interrogation Centre, Boxes 88–92, MIS/Y-178: 3 May 1945. 'Rommel was with me,' Schimpf was overheard telling a fellow prisoner on 3 May 1945. 'This mustn't be known and will remain strictly secret between ourselves. He wrote a letter from my place—a letter to the Führer. I saw it myself: "Immediate peace with the Western Powers—under all conditions—the war is lost."'

60. WO 208/4364, p. 537. Taped discussions of General Heinrich Eberbach overheard at Trent Park, England.

61. 'I have reason to believe that Himmler has been carrying out mass killings,' Rommel wrote to his son Manfred in late 1943. Irving, *Trail of the Fox*, p. 319.

62. Jacques Nobécourt, *Hitler's Last Gamble* (New York: Schocken Books, 1969), pp. 178–179. Von der Heydte gave a detailed account of the Ardennes operation to Nobécourt while the latter was a professor of law at the University of Würzburg. The other dialogue is from the author's interview with von der Heydte's son, who recalled memories of his father's oft-mentioned conversation with Rommel in May 1944. Franz Josef Freiherr von der Heydte, interview with author, 18 March 2010. According to von der Heydte, Rommel planned to use his regiment to help seize Gestapo headquarters in Berlin.

63. Oberst Freiherr Von der Heydte, '6th Parachute Regiment (1 May–20 August 1944)', NA, RG-549, MS B-839, Foreign Military Studies.

64. 'Information Obtained from German C-in-C West, Field Marshal von Rundstedt', MS B-823, 6 August 1945, RG 407, Entry 427, Box 2620, 270/52/19/3–4.

65. 'Special Interrogation Report Field Marshal Karl Rudolf Gerd von Rundstedt', 1 February 1946, 'Other Records Miscellaneous Intelligence and Interrogation Reports', RG 549, 290/56/3/4, Box 122. 'The Atlantic Wall ... had no depth and little surface and was an unmitigated fake. At best it might have proved an obstacle for 24 hours.'

66. Speer, *Inside the Third Reich*, p. 454.
67. 'Heinz Guderian, Leo von Geyr, and Paul Hausser', 7th Army Interrogation Centre, SAIC/X/6, 28 May 1945. Quotes are from secretly recorded conversations between the three men while they were held in captivity. RG 338, 290/56/2/4-5, Box 73.
68. For Peiper's presence at the meeting of the tank leaders in France, see photographs from spring 1944: Stephan Cazenave, *Panzerdivision Hitler Jugend: Panzer Regiment 12 Normandie 1944* (Bayeux, FR: Maranes Editions, 2015).
69. Order of Battle of Panzergruppe West on the eve of D-Day was quite powerful: LXXXVI Army Corps (346th and 711th Infantry Division, Werfer Brigade 7, Kampfgruppe Luck), and I SS Panzer Corps with 1st SS, 12th SS Panzer Divisions as well as the regular army 21st Panzer and Panzer Lehr Divisions). Although located north of the Invasion Front, the ration tank strength of the Peiper's SS Panzer Regiment 1 was formidable: thirty-eight Panthers in the five companies of I Battalion (Sturmbannführer Werner Poetschke) and firty-two Mk IVs in the five companies of II Battalion (Sturmbannführer Heinz Kling). Moreover, the anti-tank battalion (Haupsturmführer Karl Rettlinger) had another forty-four assault guns. Leibstandarte manpower strength reports in June 1944 showed 19,691 in total. Eric Lefevre, *Panzers in Normandy: Then and Now* (London: After the Battle, 1983), pp. 127–128. Immediately after the invasion took place the Leibstandarte was assigned to the LXXXIX Army Corps, moving from Beverloo to the area near Tourhout. The tank regiment concentrated in Maldegem and Eeklo in Flanders.
70. Fritz Kraemer, 'I SS Pz Corps in the West in 1944', NARA, FMS, C-024, August–September 1948.
71. See T-314, Roll 1496, Kriegstagebuch LVIII Panzerkorps, operations in Normandy, 15 April–27 July 1944, Frames 110–743.
72. 'Panzer Group West, mid-1943–5 Jul 1944', MS B-466, 'Rommel's Views', B-720 and 'Panzer Tactics in Normandy', ETHINT-13, Gen. d. Panzertruppen Geyr von Schweppenburg, NA, RG 338, Foreign Military Studies 1945–54. 'The two schools of thought represented the difference between the tactics of horse-drawn divisions of the Napoleonic age ... and that of mechanized divisions of the 20th Century.' Geyr condemned Rommel's thinking as belonging to 'the 19th Century', whereas Rommel himself derided Geyr's underestimation of the Allied air forces.
73. Rommel: 'We'll have only one chance to stop the enemy and that's while he's in the water. The first 24 hours will be decisive. For the

Allies as well as Germany, it will be the longest day.' Cornelius Ryan, *The Longest Day* (New York: Simon and Schuster, 1959), p. 27.

74. Rommel, Letter to his wife, 1 June 1944, B.H. Lidell Hart, ed., *The Rommel Papers* (London: Collins, 1953), pp. 453–456. In meetings with Goebbels in April Rommel had insisted that he needed at least until May to make successful preparation to repulse the invasion—longer, of course, would be better. Josef Goebbels, *Die Tagebücher von Joseph Goebbels, Teil II Diktate 1941–1945*, vol. 12 (Mehringer, 1995), p. 343.

75. For details of Rommel's movements from La Roche-Guyon in the forty-eight hours before D-Day, an early account has not been eclipsed: Cornelius Ryan, *The Longest Day*, (New York, Simon & Schuster, 1959); also Daniel Allen Butler, *Field Marshal: The Life and Death of Erwin Rommel*, (Philadelphia, Casemate, 2015), p. 480. On 5 June 1944, Rommel was advised by weather forecasters that the weather might be acceptable for Allied landings at Normandy on 6 June, but not at Pas de Calais where Rommel believed the invasion would come. This concern vanished, however, when the head of the German weather group, Dr. Heinz Lettau, issued another advisory claiming conditions so uncertain that the Allies would be unnerved to consider landings. Lawrence Hogben, "The Most Important Weather Forecast in the History of the World," *London Review of Books*, Vol. 16 No. 10 · 26 May 1994.

76. 'Tagesmeldung: 3.5.44', NA: T-311, Roll 24, 702083 and 702030. The Leibstandarte total strength on 3 May 1944 had been only 14,132 men. However, by 19 May, with an influx of Luftwaffe and other personnel, the roster rose to 17,257 men, with forty-one Mk Vs, forty-five Mk IVHs and forty-two assault guns. PRO: DEFE 3/170 KV 7584. By 4 June the division was still missing equipment that would make it combat ready.

77. 'Special Interrogation Report Oberstgruppenführer Josef "Sepp" Dietrich', Canadian Military HQ, Historical Section, London, 29 August 1945, NA RG 407, E427, Box 19540, WWII OPNS Reports 1940-1948, First Army, 101.2.13 1945, The Adjutant General's Office.

78. For the activities of the various echelons of the German high command on the eve of the invasion, see Ryan, *The Longest Day*, pp. 81–84.

79. Ernst Jünger was the Hitler-lauded author of *In Stahlgewitten* (*In the Storm of Steel*, 1929), with its glorification of war, larger-than-life heroes and nihilistic emphasis on *fronterlebnis* (front-line experience). However, in the early summer of 1944 Jünger had just returned to Paris after a disillusioning stint with the army on the

Eastern Front. At the time, he was completing *Der Friede* (*The Peace*), a secretly circulated opus in which he vehemently denounced Hitler and the nationalism that his writings had fostered.

80. *Aus den Tagebüchern von Joseph Goebbels seine unterredungen mit Adolf Hitler*, 18 April 1944, Band 2, January 1943–March 1945 (Passau: Sketec Verlag), p. 352.

81. Interestingly, one of the men fighting with Peiper in the West made the same observation two days before in a letter home: 'Our wonder weapons will be decisive,' he ventured. 'They're going to turn the salad around here into garbage': Heinz von Westernhagen, Letter to family, 3 June 1944, Westernhagen, *Die Kinder der Täter*, p. 44.

82. Rommel to Lucie, 6 May 1944, Hart, *Rommel Papers*.

83. Ian Kershaw, *Hitler 1936–1945 Nemesis* (New York: W.W. Norton & Co., 2000), p. 638; Irving, *Goebbels, Tagebuch*, p. 464; Recollection of Admiral Karl Jesko Puttkamer; Ryan, *The Longest Day*, p. 84.

84. Gordon A. Harrison, *Cross Channel Attack* (Washington, D.C.: Office of the Chief of Military History, U.S. Government Printing Office, 1951), p. 274.

85. Harrison, *Cross Channel Attack*, p. 274.

86. David Eisenhower, *Eisenhower at War 1943–1945* (New York: Random House, 1986), p. 252.

87. 'Von Rohden Collection: Beurteilung des Krieges: 14 August 1944', Air Historical Branch of the Air Ministry, PRO, London, Also, NA: RG 242, T-971. At the same time the Luftwaffe was blind, Allied air force planners completed a broad aerial photographic mosaic of the German defence, comprising more than four hundred aircraft in the two weeks leading up to D-Day. See Wesley Frank Craven and James L. Cate, *The Army Air Forces in World War II* (Chicago: University of Chicago Press, 1951), pp. 179–181. Hugo Sperrle's Luflotte 3 had 570 serviceable aircraft, of which about half were fighters or ground attack aircraft, which would be suitable to contest Allied air superiority. The Allied advantage was formidable: more than 10-to-1: 4,029 in the 2nd Tactical Air Force and U.S. 9th Tactical Air Force. The British home defence and U.S. Tactical Air Force assigned to the invasion had another 5,514 planes.

88. Hubert Meyer, *The History of the 12. SS Panzerdivision Hitlerjugend* (Winnipeg: J.J. Fedorowicz, 1994), p. 18. Oberleutnant Volprecht von Riedesel is mispelled and the aircraft type is erroneous in Meyer's description, who was clearly the leader of KG 54 in Evreux. Von Riedesel would be killed in action flying a Me 262 on 9 February 1945.

89. 'Marinegruppenkommando West: Seekriegsleitung/1.Abt. KTB, Der Westen', 1, 15–31 May 1944, Records and Documents Related to the Third Reich, Group 6, Reel 21, Microform Ltd., Irving Collection, London. Pre-invasion appraisal by Vice Admiral Theodor Kranke.

90. The Luftwaffe western command, Luftflotte III, possessed some five hundred aircraft. Its strongest arm was Fliegerkorps X, set for an anti-shipping role and proven in its effectiveness with its radio-controlled guided missiles in the Mediterranean campaign. Yet Generalfeldmarschal Hugo Sperrle's command really had no effective long-range daytime reconnaissance aircraft to detect the invasion fleet so as to use that potent weapon. Visual reconnaissance would have been useless on the night of 5 June, but several reconnaissance units in Luftflotte III possessed the *Hohentwiel* ship-search radar. The Luflotte III planes carrying that equipment were the Ju 290s of *Fernauflärungs Gruppe* (long-range reconnaissance) 5, and the He 177s and Fw 200s of Kampfgeschwader (bomber wing) 40 radar, which could have sighted the invasion fleet had they been aloft. However, to obscure German vision, there were two large-scale spoof invasion operations that night—Glimmer in the Calais–Boulogne area and Taxable in the Le Havre area. Evidently, Hohentwiel signals from eight separate aircraft were picked up in the Glimmer area. The Germans declared a full-scale alert there, and it seems that most of the available radar search aircraft went after the bait. Alfred Price, *The Last Year of the Luftwaffe* (London: Arms & Armour Press, 1991), p. 57; also, Dr Price, personal communication with author, 27 November 2001. Even with that limitation, a single group of German patrol boats off the French coast would have provided ample warning. Again the weather worked to a decisive disadvantage: no naval patrols went forth given the rough seas, while there is evidence that the German aerial radar reconnaissance took place, albeit in the north. Yet the bombing of the coastal areas in the Pas-de-Calais, staged to the north where the invasion was expected in the first place, looks to have deceived German intelligence. See Harrison, *Cross Channel Attack*, pp. 258–267.

91. The lines from Verlaine's poem: '*Les sanlot longs des violons de l'automne. Blessent mon coeur d'une longuer monotone*'—'The long sobs of the violins of autumn wound my heart with monotonous langour.' Ryan, *The Longest Day*, p. 31. See also Warlimont, *Inside Hitler's Headquarters*, pp. 422–423. Illuminating detail on this affair can be found from an interview with Hans Speidel, Irving, *Trail of the Fox*, pp. 362–366.

92. For the ULTRA decrypt of von Rundstedt's announcement that the invasion would not come: PRO: DEFE 3 (Defence Ministry) KV 6546. The code breakers in Hut 3 passed the reassuring message on to Allied High Command at 6:01 am on 6 June 1944 just as the Allied troops stormed the beaches.
93. 'SS Panzergrenadier Regiment 2: Tgb. Nr. 32/44 geh. Kdos', NA: RG 242, T-354, R 624, F000718, signalled by the regimental commander, Rudolf Sandig at 2220 hours.

Chapter 17: Total Sacrifice

1. German tank strengths of 1 June 1944 are taken from Eric Lefèvre, *Panzers in Normandy Then and Now* (London: After the Battle, 1983), p. 126. Peiper's tank force had forty-two Mk IVs in II Battalion and thirty-eight Panthers in I Battalion. Some forty-four assault guns in Sturmgeschütz Battalion 1 rounded out the total armoured strength.
2. 'II./Panzer Gren. Rgt 2, LAH Alarmplan!' NA: T-354, Roll 622, F001130.
3. For the far-reaching Allied intelligence diversions (Operation Fortitude)—spies, planted cryptographic messages and even fake armies to misdirect Hitler about the true location of the invasion: Anthony Cave Brown, *Bodyguard of Lies* (New York: Harper and Row, 1975).
4. Shulman, *Defeat in the West*, p. 113.
5. 'Heeresgruppe D, Kriegstagebuch Ia, 6 June 1944: Anlage 15', NA: T-354, Roll 24, F7029187.
6. Kershaw, *Hitler 1936–1945 Nemesis*, pp. 639–640.
7. For the Klessheim episode: Toland, *Adolf Hitler*, p. 785; Joachim Fest, *Hitler* (New York: Harcourt, Brace & Company, 1973), p. 705; and Warlimont, *Inside Hitler's Headquarters*, p. 427.
8. Himmler's second daughter out of their relationship, Nanette Dorothea Potthast, was born 3 June 1944. NSDAP Hauptarchiv, Hoover Institution, Stanford, Microfilm Roll No. 99. Improbably, Sepp Dietrich was made the child's godfather, as revealed in a letter from his wife, Ursel, to Himmler on 25 July 1944: 'May I ask you, dear Reichsführer, to bring the small package to your lovely little Nanette, Sepp's godchild, with our heartfelt wishes ... After the terrible attempted assassination of the Führer, a new huge burden has been put on your shoulders, with much work for you. For us it is comforting that this shop is finally cleaned up!'
9. Rommel: *'Es gibt keine Schlacht im Lande nur am Strand '*, 'G-2 Periodic Report No. 54: Interrogation of Cpl. Heinz Gerkmann, 84th Army

Corps', 2 August 1944, Records of U.S. XIX Corps, G-2 Records, RG-407, entry 427, 2.19–2.1, Box 4371. In May Rommel had reviewed the defences of Omaha Beach and found it defended too lightly, directing Major General Dietrich Kraiss to move more of his infantry battalions up to defend the beach—an order that Kraiss ignored with the tacit approval of Marcks. It was a decision that was to have disastrous consequences for Rommel's plan to turn back the Allies at the beaches.

10. 'Herresgruppe D, Kriegstagebuch Ia, 6 June 1944: Anlage 15,' NA: T-354, Roll 24, F7029187. Also described by the OB West commander: 'Special Interrogation of Field Marshal Karl Rudolf Gerd von Rundstedt', 1 February 1946, Canadian M.I. HQ Hist. Sec., 7th Army Interrogation Centre, NA: RG 549, 290/56/3/4, Box 122.

11. Kurt Meyer, *Grenadiers*, p. 219. Orders for march came at 9:30 am, with Rommel calling by telephone for an immediate counterattack at three o'clock.

12. For the failed 21st Panzer counterattack: Hans von Luck, *Panzer Commander: The Memoirs of Colonel Hans von Luck* (New York: Praeger, 1989); L.F. Ellis, *Victory in the West* (London: Her Majesty's Stationery Office, 1962), vol. I, p. 202; Terry Copp, *Fields of Fire: The Canadians in Normandy*, (Toronto: University of Toronto Press, 1998), p. 256.

13. Schmolke was taken prisoner near Caen, just north of Cristot, on 8 June at midday. RG 338: G-2 Section, MIS Records, Interrogation Reports, PWIS (H), Box 28. His opinion of his new division vs. his alma mater: 'They fought well, but lacked the experience and physique of the Leibstandarte members.'

14. Craven and Cate, *The Army Air Forces in World War II*, pp. 194–195. Allied sorties on D-Day totalled 14,000 presiding over the landing of 75,215 British and 57,500 American troops. A further 23,000 airborne had dropped behind the invasion beaches. Ellis, *Victory in the West*, vol. I, p. 223.

15. Dieter Ose, *Entscheidung im Westen, 1944: Der Oberbefehlshaber West und die Abwehr der alliierten Invasion* (Aachen: Helios, May 2013), pp. 75–76. In a message flashed to Dollmann's 7th Army on D-Day, 'The commander in chief [Hitler] … points out that the enemy beachheads are to be destroyed on the evening of June 6th since there are fears of reinforced airborne landings and further naval landings. The invasion must be cleared up before day's end.'

16. Taken by surprise, the Luftwaffe was completely outclassed by the Allied air effort. Luftflotte 3 managed only 327 sorties in response on 6 June and a further 217 missions that night. A further 173 sorties were

flown over the invasion zone the following day. Kurt Mehner, ed., *Die geheimen Tagesberichte der deutschen Wehrmachtführung im Zweiten Weltkrieg 1939–1945*, Band 10 (Osnabrück: Biblio Verlag, 1984).

17. Alfred Jodl, 'Invasion and the Normandy Campaign', NARA, RG-338, FMS, MS A-913, 2 August 1945. 'Also, Caen was the nearest way to Paris and the terrain was better south of Caen than further west.'

18. This was all part of the successful deception involved in Operation Fortitude South, in which the fictional First U.S. Army Group under General George S. Patton was to invade the Pas-de-Calais after a diversion at Normandy: See Brown, *Bodyguard of Lies*, pp. 1–10.

19. 'Heeresgruppe D, Kriegstagebuch', Frame 7029194.

20. Interview with Bayerlein: Lieutenant Samuel W. Taylor: 'As a German General Saw It', *Saturday Evening Post*, 20 October 1945.

21. 'Interrogation of Genlt. Fritz Bayerlein', 29 May 1945, Air Ministry Intelligence Summary, PRO, London. 'They enforced camouflage discipline with a will. Every vehicle was covered with tree branches and moved along hedges and the edges of woods.' One American fighter-bomber pilot recounted, 'It would have been hard to shoot at the road in any place and not hit a German car or truck.'

22. Kurt Meyer, *Grenadiers*, p. 218.

23. 'Interrogation of Sturmmann Hans Bähr', CSDIC (UK) PWIS (H), RG 338, G-2 Section, MIS-Y Section, Box 28. The 18-year-old Bähr was captured at 2 pm on 7 June. His interrogators found him stingy with information—'an insolent and confirmed Nazi'.

24. Kurt Meyer, *Grenadiers*, p. 235.

25. Feuchtinger denied Meyer's accusations: 'We were to carry out a combined operation the next morning ... We decided to drive towards Douvres and 12th SS [Division] was to take up assembly positions during the night. Artillery fire was so great that a proper coordination of the attack was impossible. Meyer did make a short spurt with some fifty tanks, but was driven back. He never reached the start line from which our combined attack was to begin. Allied anti-tank guns prevented him from getting into proper position.' Shulman, *Defeat in the West*, p. 105. For his part, Max Wünsche would later insist in interrogations that he was not present in the Ardenne Orchard initially as Meyer claims, but only later because of Allied air attacks.

26. 'With his reconnaissance unit he had several times penetrated Russian lines and permitted himself to be encircled, but preserving, if he could, a way out. He would then destroy an entire village with all its inhabitants; men, women and even small children. When

questioned about this, he said that the shooting of prisoners in such a situation was necessary because they could not be brought back to the German positions.' Bruce J.S. MacDonald, *The Trial of Kurt Meyer* (Toronto: Clarke, Irwin and Co., 1954), p. 75. Hauptmann Fritz Steger, one of Meyer's battalion commanders, testified that Meyer often told him that, in Russia while with the Leibstandarte, it was necessary to shoot prisoners and that Meyer had given such orders. See MacDonald, *Trial of Kurt Meyer*, p. 137. And Meyer's efficient adjutant of the 15 Kompanie, Hauptsturmführer Horst von Büttner, repeated what Meyers had told him just before the invasion: 'I don't care what others do, this company takes no prisoners.' (MacDonald, *Trial of Kurt Meyer*, p. 108).

27. Ian J. Campbell, *Murder at the Abbaye* (Ottawa: Golden Dog Press, 1996), pp. 77, 143. See also Foster, *Meeting of Generals*, pp. 315–317. The statements of both surviving soldiers and local French citizens from the trial attested to the brutal murder of Canadians in Authie on 7 June 1944.

28. MacDonald, *The Trial of Kurt Meyer*, p. 171.

29. Jesionek was a young Polish soldier who had been impressed into service with the Hitlerjugend Panzer Division. 'Case No. 22: The Abbaye Ardennes Case Trial of SS Brigadeführer Kurt Meyer, Canadian Military Court 10–28 December, 1945', *Law Reports of Trials of War Criminals*, The United Nations War Crimes Commission, Vol. IV, London, HMSO, 1948. For 'my regiment takes no prisoners', see p. 102 of the above report. Yet there was likely no written order against taking prisoners: 'I would not commit such an order to writing,' he rightfully pointed out. 'When you have enough old comrades in such a company, they know how the commander fights.' MacDonald, *The Trial of Kurt Meyer*, p. 167.

30. MacDonald, *The Trial of Kurt Meyer*, summary of charges on pp. 15–36. See also Tony Foster's impressive and balanced account of Meyer's trial: *Meeting of Generals*. Meyer claimed to have learned of the executions only on 11 June and then recommended investigation of the incident by Fritz Witt, the division commander. Not surprisingly, nothing came of that. 'I do not know today who committed the deed and I have no idea of incriminating my regiment without exact information,' said Meyer. He sought to justify the killings by claiming to have personally observed executed German prisoners in a vehicle at La Villeneuve south of Rots. That was disputed by the Canadians, however, who showed that the German

vehicle in question had been ambushed in conventional operations. MacDonald, *The Trial of Kurt Meyer*, pp. 139–144.

31. Ian Sayer and Douglas Botting, *Hitler's Last General: The Case Against Wilhelm Mohnke* (New York: Bantam Press, 1989), pp. 156–169.

32. C.P. Stacey, *The Victory Campaign* (Ottawa: Roger Duhamel, 1960). That the Canadians responded in kind was admitted by candid accounts of the fighting in Normandy by reporters from the *London Telegraph* who witnessed the slit throats of German dead and wounded on the captured battlefield: Foster, *Meeting of the Generals*, p. 334.

33. 'A subject to fill an evening's discussion': Peiper to Weingartner, 9 April 1976.

34. General Major Fritz Kraemer, *I SS Panzer Corps in the West*, NA: RG 338, MS No. C-024.

35. 'Report About the War Years 1939–45', Sepp Dietrich, prepared for Burton Ellis in Schwäbisch Hall, 1946, Ellis Papers, in author's possession.

36. Lehmann and Tiemann, *Die Leibstandarte*, vol. IV/1, p. 104–105.

37. Kurt Meyer, *Grenadiers*, p. 220.

38. 'For a commander of a panzer or motorized division to leave his headquarters without a radio set was considered tantamount to travelling without his head.' Kraemer, *I SS Panzer Corps in the West*.

39. PRO: DEFE 3, KV 6605. ULTRA decrypt signalled at 2 pm on 6 June.

40. 'Interrogation of Kurt Meyer', First Canadian Army Interrogation Report, PRO: WO 205/1021.

41. See Shulman, *Defeat in the West*, pp. 104–105.

42. 'SS Panzergrenadier Regiment 2, Befehl für den Vormarsch', 9 June 1944, NA: T-354, R 624, F000714.

43. Edmund Martin on 7 June 1944: Agte, *Michael Wittmann and the Tiger Commanders*, p. 355. 'We are working night and day to make sure our tanks are ready for battle. The exhortation of the Führer to us on the Western Front has given each of us an honourable obligation: hold our assigned sector to the last man.'

44. Tiemann, *Chronicle of the 7. Panzerkompanie*, p. 89.

45. Leo Geyr von Schweppenburg, 'Panzer Group West', NA: RG 338, MS B-466.

46. 'Kriegstagebuch Panzerarmeeoberkommando 5, I. Teil', entry by Oberleutnant Erlenwein for 10 June 1944, NA, T-313, Roll 420, 8213531.

47. PRO: DEFE 3, KV 7171 and 7225, signalled on the evening of 9 June and provided to Allied Supreme Command at 4:39 am on 10 June.

48. For insight into Montgomery's failed strategy before Caen, see Carlo D'Este, *Decision in Normandy* (New York: HarperCollins, 1991), pp. 160–211.

49. Peiper, as related to Heinz Stuttecker, Stutterecker, interview with author, 28 February 2009.

50. 'Unsere Heldensage: Eine kühne Tigerprüfung', *SS Leithefte 10*, Heft 11, October 1944, p. 6, NA: RG-242, T-611, R 44.

51. Kalinowsky had been a brewmaster before the war, coming to the Eastern Front with Das Reich in 1942. He eventually joined the Tigers of schwere SS Panzer Battalion 101 in July 1943. Patrick Agte, *Michael Wittmann and the Tiger Commanders*, p. 458.

52. For the criminal complexion within the SS Totenkopf Division, see Charles W. Syndor Jr., *Soldiers of Destruction* (Princeton, NJ: Princeton University Press, 1977), pp. 313–342.

53. BDC file for Heinz Lammerding: 'SS Personalakte Lammerding, Dienstlaufbahn', NA: RG-242, A3343 SSO 236A F1376-1494. For his operations with Totenkopf and Bach-Zelewski's promotional transfer to 2nd SS Panzer Division, see Sydnor, *Soldiers of Destruction*, p. 320. For problems with assimilating the Alsatians into the Waffen SS, see NA, captured and translated order: 'Desertion of Alsatians', SS Pz. Gr. Regiment 4, 24 July 1944, Otto Weidinger, FUSA, G-2 Records,101-2.1, Box 1392

54. 'Partisan Fighting and Atrocities: Consolidated Report on Information from SS Obscharführer Wimmer and SS Schütze Kuntzelmann', CSDIC (UK) SIR 778, RG 338, 290/56/1/1-2, Box 4.

55. SS Schütze Kuntzelmann: 'It was said that the Germans were ordered to lay down their arms and that the partisans would then allow them to pass unharmed. After the company had complied with order, they were all killed.' CSDIC (UK) SIR 778.

56. '2. SS Panzer Division Das Reich, Order of the Day: The Position with Regard to Guerrilla Bands and Tactics for Combating Them, 9 June, 1944,' Max Hastings, *Das Reich: The March of the 2nd SS Panzer Division Through France* (New York: Holt, 1981), Appendix A. (It is important to note that even though interviewing many of the SS men involved at Oradour, Hastings remained unconvinced of their innocence.)

57. 'Bekämpfung von Terroristen und Saboteuren in den besetzten Gebieten; Der Führer WFSt/Qu.2/Verw. 1 Nr. 009169', 30 July 1944, Toland Papers, FDR Library, Box 49.

58. 'The inhabitants [of Tulle] were forced to face the ropes so they were compelled to watch relatives and friends as they were hanged. After

this had been done, the 20 hangmen fetched 10 or 15 victims … One after another they were forced by kicks and blows with rifle butts up the ladders which were placed under the ropes. Nooses were placed around their necks and ladders were pulled away … The victims died as heroes, most of them without flinching; many of them cried *"Vive la France!"* with their last breath; not one of them cried or asked for mercy.' CSDIC (UK) SIR 778. Members of the SS Panzer Grenadier Regiment 4 with the 2nd SS Panzer Division captured in late August, corroborated witnessing more than a hundred civilians killed in Tulle as the division leadership believed the area teeming with partisans. 'Combined Interrogation Report', September 1944, NA RG-407, VII Corps Records, 607-2.6–3.0, Box 3299. Also, 'Interrogation of SS Sturmman Erwin Hanck', PWIS(H)/LDC/740, NA, RG 498, US 118, Box 1250. Hanck, part of the 2nd Company of the 2nd SS Panzer Reconnaissance Battalion, was captured on 27 August near Bernay. Hanck claimed to have witnessed as dozens of civilians in Tulle were hanged—even children.

59. On 11 June a further fifty French were put to death at the village of Mussidan south-west of Perigeux. For background on the Oradour massacre, see Hastings, *Das Reich*; Sarah Farmer, *Martyred Village: Commemorating the 1944 Massacre at Oradour-sur-Glane* (Berkeley: University of California Press, 1999). For the Waffen SS view, see Otto Weidinger, *Tulle and Oradour: A Franco-German Tragedy* (privately published, 1985). I reviewed archival records from the U.S. Army Judge Advocate General's war crimes investigations into the incident: 'Crimes de Guerre: Oradour sur-Glane', report of E.O. Munn, SHAEF, 13 October 1944, RG 153, Entry 151, 'French War Crimes', Box 5. Graphic description of the atrocity, including many photographs are found in this collection. Approximately 695 were killed.

60. James Lucas, *Das Reich* (London: Arms and Armour Press, 1991), p. 128.

61. A recent German account (Wolfgang Scheider, *Die Waffen-SS, Das Buch zur Serie im Ersten* [Berlin: Rowohlt Berlin Verlag G.m.b.H., 1999], p. 167) claims that 'after a sniper from the French resistance kills an officer of the SS elite division, Das Reich, the soldiers burn the village down and murder all 642 occupants, 190 children among them. The daily report of the unit reports this mass murder as a military operation.' Other possible motives for the Oradour massacre have come to light. One story suggests that resistance fighters captured a shipment of gold bars looted from south-west France that were the personal stash of the division commander, Heinz Lammerding. The

maquis ambushed a convoy transporting the gold, killing most of those in the SS party and kidnapping and killing a popular SS major. Given its proximity, Oradour-sur-Glane became the centre of reprisals and a search for the missing loot. For that controversial tale: Robert Mackness, *Massacre at Oradour* (New York: Random House, 1989). Lammerding, who had much explaining to do about the massacre, died in 1971. The conventional evidence was that the reprisal was due to a resistance shooting of a driver and the kidnapping and execution of Sturmbannführer Helmut Kaempfe, who then ordered the village destroyed: 'Report on the Interrogation of SS Oscha. Karl Lenz: Additional Notes on the Atrocity of Oradour sur-Glane', PoW Interrogation Section (MIS-Y) PWIS(H)/LDC/741, RG 498, UD 228, Box 1250. See also PWIS(H)/LDC/213.

62. PRO: DEFE 3, KV 7707, issued on 12 June 1944.
63. 'Verhalten gegenüber der franz Zivilbevölkerung, Leibstandarte SS Adolf Hitler, Rgt.Gef.Std., den 21.7.44', T-354, R622, F001105. In the Waffen SS, rape was considered an egregious offensive. In Caen in 1944 Kurt Meyer claimed to have had one of his NCOs shot by firing squad for rape. '[By allowing that], we undermine all that is best in our troops.' GRGG 226, Kurt Meyer on 1–20 November 1944, PRO: WO 208/4364.
64. For a discussion of the great deception of D-Day that left Peiper and his division idle in Belgium, see Brown, *Bodyguard of Lies*.
65. Heiber, *Hitlers Lagebesprechungen*, Adolf Hitler to Jodl, Fragment 40, 6 April 1944. During this session Hitler had argued for strongly reinforcing Normandy but was later swayed that the Pas-de-Calais should be bolstered instead.
66. Percy E. Schramm, *Die Invasion 1944: Aus d. Kriegstagebuch der Oberkommandos der Wehrmacht* (Munich: Dt. Taschebuch Verlag, 1963), p. 315. For Hitler's comments on the prospects of the V-weapons, see Max Domarus, *Hitler: Speeches and Proclamations*, vol. IV (Wauconda, IL: Bolchazy Carducci, 2004), p. 2900.
67. For Rommel on 10 June: Irving, *Trail of the Fox*, p. 380.
68. Geyr to von Rundstedt: 'Information Obtained from German C-in-C West, Field Marshal von Rundstedt', MS B-823, 6 August 1945, RG 407, Entry 427, Box 2620, 270/52/19/3-4.
69. 'Kriegstagebuch, Heeresgruppe D', 11 June 1944, T-311, R24, F702917.
70. For von Rundstedt's 11 June prediction of the need for 'fundamental decisions', see Dieter Ose, *Entscheidung im Westen* (Stuttgart: Deutsche Verlagsanstalt, 1985). Those who knew von Rundstedt

believed that 'fundamental decisions' could only mean peace negotiations.

71. 'Information Obtained from Gen.d. Panzertruppe von Geyr von Schweppenburg', SAIC/X/6, 28 May 45, '7th Army Interrogation Centre', RG 338, 290/56/2/4-5, Box 73. 'When it was reported that the British fleet was outside Caen, that they could fire as far as 30 km inland, and that it would be senseless to leave our panzer divisions within the range of their artillery, someone would simply maintain that they couldn't fire that far ... they got all their experience at sessions around conference tables.'

72. For Witt's death from an 'unlucky hit': PRO: WO 208/4516, BBC telegraph intercept of German telegraph service on 16 June 1944.

73. 'Laut Mittagsmeldung Feindangriff gegen Tilly abgewiesen', KTB Heeresgruppe D.

74. 'Special Interrogation Report: Oberstgruppenführer Sepp Dietrich', 29 August 1945, 'Miscellaneous Intelligence and Interrogation Reports', RG 338, 290/56/3/4, Box 121.

75. Irving, *Trail of the Fox*, p. 379.

76. The location is the expansive estate built in 1675, Château de Saint Joris ten Distel par Beernem east of Knesselare. Philippe van Pottelberghe de le Potterie and Jean De Lanier, interview with author, 4 July 2002. Thanks to Johan Gussé in Knesselare for helping to determine the location. The Luftwaffe had occupied the house from 1941 to 1943, frequently importing Parisian ladies for wild parties and keeping a small bear as a mascot! After the Luftwaffe left, the SS took over and then the Canadians after the Germans departed. 'They all broke many things.'

77. Within Himmler's SS mythos, the Hagall Rune symbolized unshakeable faith in the Nazi philosophy and was thus featured with the marriage ceremony.

78. This was SS Haupsturmführer Christian Jochum, who served as the legal representative for the wedding.

79. Proper marriage and siring of children had recently been a featured topic in Leibstandarte. Weltansschauung instruction—instruction on National Socialist Ideology. 'Gattenwahl im Krieg', LSSAH, May 1944. 'Marriage is not for its own, but is to breed and to spread the art and race. The task is to preserve the race and to make more of it. It is sufficient only to satisfy the desire for mating at war. By this desire for mating at war, the soul should not be allowed to fall back into Jewish ways.' BA-MA, RS 3-1, V 97.

80. For 'it struck us as peculiar': Peiper's chiding that unmarried officers marry and married SS officers have more children: Tiemann, *Chronicle of the 7. Panzerkompanie*, p. 101. An example of the similarity to Himmler's sentiments: On 22 October 1943 Himmler threatened a 44-year-old bachelor, SS Hauptsturmführer Franz Schwarz, with ex-communication from the SS if he was not married by the end of the war. Helmut Heiber, *Reichsführer: Briefe an und von Himmler* (Stuttgart: Deutsche Verlagsanstalt, 1968), p. 239. On the need for offspring: Himmler to Hitler, 15 August 1942, regarding Waffen SS officers, particularly only sons: 'It is your duty to see to it as quickly as possible that you birth and begat children of good blood.' NA: T-175, R161, F2693305. Himmler went on to complain 'in spite of all propaganda in favour of Germanic, blonde, blue-eyed women, his Waffen SS men persisted in marrying brunettes.' Kersten, *Memoirs*, p. 99.
81. Hans Siptrott, interview with author, 15 July 2012.
82. Junker Diary, 16 June 1944.
83. Hans Speidel, *Invasion 1944: Ein Beitrag zu Rommels und des Reiches* (Stuttgart: Wunderlich, 1949), pp. 113–118; also Nicolaus von Below, *At Hitler's Side* (London: Greenhill Books, 2001), p. 201.
84. Von Below, *At Hitler's Side*, p. 204.
85. Rommel's chief of staff, General Hans Speidel, quoted by Ellis, *Victory in the West*, vol. I, p. 118.
86. Warlimont, *Inside Hitler's Headquarters*, p. 432.
87. Hart, *Rommel Papers*, pp. 478–479, 496.
88. That the numerous launching platforms for the V-1 were not far inland at the Pas-de-Calais only reinforced Hitler's worry that a second more powerful invasion would be launched there.
89. Speidel, *Invasion 1944*, p. 92. If the V-1s were so effective, Rommel countered to Hitler's enthusiasm, why were they not directed at the invasion beaches?
90. Speer, *Inside the Third Reich*, p. 458. Hitler's doubts about Rommel were well founded. As early as March 1944 the field marshal had confided to Hans Speidel that 'the time has come that we must tell the Führer that we cannot continue the war'. B.H. Liddell Hart, *The German Generals Talk* (New York: Quill, 1979), p. 260.
91. 'Kriegstagebuch (KTB), Heeresgruppe D, 12 June 1944', NA: RG 242, T-354, R24, F7029217. Hitler also released the 9th SS and 10th SS Panzer Divisions, although it would be sometime before they appeared at the front.
92. 'Panzer Division LSSAH: Befehl für die Ausladung und Versammlung der Division', 19 June 1944, T-354, R622, F1117.

93. Harrison, *Cross Channel Attack*, pp. 422–426.
94. Nigel Hamilton, *Monty: The Making of a General* (New York: McGraw Hill, 1981), p. 272.
95. 'KTB Panzerarmeeoberkommando 5', T-313, R420, F 8713755, 21 June 1944. The actual mapped attack plans (Studie I und Studie II) for the Panzer attempt to wipe out the Allied beachheads can be seen on Frames 8714140-42.
96. 'Übersicht über die Unterkunftsräume der Verbände, vom 19.6.1944', NA: RG 242, T-354, Roll 624, F000707.
97. 'Fernschreiben an Panzergruppe West', 22 June 1944, T-311, R420, F8713753.
98. Mechanical problems with tanks: Pflughaupt Report.
99. For the extensive photographic coverage of the move of the Leibstandarte tanks through Paris: Cazenave, *Panzers Normandie 44*, pp. 72–83.
100. 'Notes on SS Pz Div LAH: Report on Information obtained from PW Schütze Pichler, 17 Ko. 1SS Pz GR', CSDIC (UK) SIR 599, Combined Services Detailed Interrogation Service, RG 338, 290/56/1/1-2, Box 3.
101. Redecker, 'Die Lötlampe, 1943'. Hermann Löns (1866–1914) was a German author, famous for his love of nature and the seminal poet of the German youth movement. As an army volunteer, he was killed in action in the autumn of 1914.
102. Operation Bagration was named for a Russian war hero from the battles that destroyed Napoleon's armies in 1812. David Glantz, *Soviet Military Deception in the Second World War* (London: Frank Cass, 1989), pp. 348–358. For the Soviet operation: Glantz and House, *When Titans Clashed*, pp. 195–215' also, Overy, *Russia's War*, pp. 236–245.
103. 'KTB Panzergruppe West', NA, T-313, Roll 420, 29 June 1944, F3536.
104. 'KTB Panzergruppe West', 28 June 1944.
105. 'Information Obtained from Obstgruf Paul Hausser', SAIC/X/6. 28 May 1945, NA: RG-549, 290/56/2/4-5, 7th Army Interrogation Centre, ETO-MIS-Y, Box 73.
106. 'Hausser's Personal Experiences', SAIC/FIR, 9 July 1945, 7th Army Interrogation Centre, ETO-MIS-Y, RG 549, 290/56/2/4-5, Box 74.
107. Dietrich warning to Panzergruppe West: 'Vorgänge: Kriegstagebuch Panzer-Armeeoberkommando 5', 28 June 1944, NA, T-313, Roll 420, F8713534.
108. Oberst Paul Tzschökell's 7th Nebelwerfer Brigade had deployed on both sides of Hill 112, firing hundreds of tons of rockets against the British in the fighting around Caen. '7th Werfer Brigade', General Major Kurt Paape, RG 338, MS B-131.

109. 'KTB Panzergruppe West', 29–30 June 1944, F8713535-37.
110. 'The action of SS Pz Rgt 12 on 28/29 June 1944 south-west of Caen foiled the enemy intention of forming a bridgehead ... across the Orne River ... Wünsche was already wounded on the second day during close hand-to-hand combat. Despite this, he remained with his regiment and led it with great bravery.' 'Begründung und Stellungsnahme der Zwischenvorgesetzten', signed by Kurt Meyer, 1 July 1944, BDC file for Max Wünsche, RG-242, A3343 RS-G5406. Wünsche was wounded five times in the war: once in Greece, twice in Russia and France in 1940, and also during the invasion in 1944.
111. 'Way to Paris Blocked: Gen. Dietrich in Interview', German telegraph service, 7 July 1944, PRO: WO 208/4452.
112. This unit would be developed under Oberst Heinz Heigel of the 5th Staffel of the secretive, KG 200 as the SS *Selbstopferkommando Leonides Staffel*. Main Source: 'Interrogation of Hanna Reitsch', 28 November 1945, AIU/IS/10, Hanna Reitsch Papers, NL 130, Box 101a, Deutsches Museum, Munich. Additional details: Hannah Reitsch, *The Sky My Kingdom: Memoirs of the Famous German World War II Test Pilot* (Drexel, PA: Casemate, 2009), pp. 189–198.
113. Werner Wendt was with 1 Kompanie, SS schwere Panzer Battalion 101 in Normandy with the Tigers. 'It was bad in the West. You could not take a shit without being attacked by fighter-bombers. My tank was attacked while driving down the road; my driver was hit. We marched backwards. It was quiet. Suddenly, the fighter-bombers came. We hit the ground fast. The U.S. air force ruined us that way.' Werner Wendt, interview with author, 21 May 1996.
114. Heinz von Westernhagen, Letter to family, 3 July 1944, Westernhagen, *Die Kinder der Täter*, p. 43.
115. 'That's meant for us!' Lehmann and Tiemann, *Die Leibstandarte*, vol. IV/1, p. 127.
116. In actuality there were only fifteen Allied divisions still waiting in England. This German intelligence gaff is from Irving, *Hitler's War*, p. 649.
117. For an account on the 29 June meeting, see 'The Papers and Diaries of General Karl Koller', Irving Collection, Microform, DI-17.
118. 'Interrogation of Field Marshal von Rundstedt', PRO WO 205/1022.
119. 'Special Interrogation of Field Marshal Karl Rudolf Gerd von Rundstedt', 1 February 1946, Canadian M.I. HQ Hist. Sec., London, SIR, NA: RG 407, Entry 427, 7th Army Interrogation Centre, Box 1954P.
120. Account of von Kluge's encounter with Rommel: Speidel, *Invasion 1944*, pp. 104–108.

121. Von Kluge, 'En shricken sie mir Truppen mit einem Spazierstock'. 'G-2 Periodic Report No. 54: Interrogation of Cpl. Heinz Gerkmann, 84th Army Corps', Aug 2, 1944, Records of U.S. XIX Corps, G-2 Records, RG-407, entry 427, 2.19-2.1, Box 4371.

Chapter 18: Normandy

1. Lewis Carroll, *Through the Looking-Glass, and What Alice Found There.*
2. 'Our Army lacks discipline. Ever since Cherbourg, as soon as a place is captured, the American soldier sits himself down and gets dead drunk, and the junior officers, if they stay sober, say, well, he's been through hell, he's entitled to it … Generals spend too much time running regiments, colonels spend too much time running platoons.' Lt. Col. C.A. Jones, 12 July 1944, letter to Col. G.S. Eyster from Col. W.A. Ganoe, Theatre Historian, 17 July 1944, NARA, RG-498, UD 602, Historical Division, Miscellaneous Records of the Theatre Historian, Box 4061.
3. 'KTB Panzergruppe West', 6 July 1944. F8713541.
4. 'AEAF Historical Record, 7 July 1944', PRO: AIR 37/1057. The controversial last-minute decision to bomb Caen was made on 6 July by Montgomery with Eisenhower present. Some said that Churchill had much to do with the decision, having informed Montgomery that 'you will take Caen by Monday or you are out'. Montgomery replied that he would take it the next day had he the support he needed. When Churchill asked what that might be, Montgomery supposedly said an attack on Caen by the heavy bombers. See E.J. Kingston-McCloughy, *The Direction of War* (London: Jonathan Cape, 1955). Whether Churchill was actually behind the bombing attack will only become known when Churchill's personal papers are released later this century.
5. 'Observations on Bomber Command Attack on Caen, 7 July 1944', E.J. Kingston-McCloughry and S. Zuckerman, PRO: AIR 37/1255.
6. Harry C. Bucher, *My Three Years with Eisenhower* (London: Heinemann, 1946), p. 531.
7. 'KTB, Herresgruppe D: Bericht über die Frontfahrt des Gen. Fldm. v. Kluge am 14.7.44 zur Panzergruppe West', T-311, R28 F7034537. Although only a paltry thousand replacements were available for the totality of I SS Panzerkorps, the tank workshops managed to repair and return 137 Tigers and Panthers in a space of a month. Weingartner, *Hitler's Guard*, p. 122.
8. 'KTB Panzergruppe West', 9 July 1944, F8713543.

9. Alexander McKee, *Caen: Anvil of Victory* (New York: St. Martin's Press, 1984), pp. 197–199.

10. Interrogation of Leibstandarte SS grenadier Röthling: SRM 643, 13 July 1944, PRO, WO 208/4138, Kew, London.

11. CSDIC (UK) S.R. report: Oberstleutenant von der Heydte, captured 23 December 1944. PRO: WO 208/4140, SRM 1150, 30 December 1944. 'In the South of France they set a village on fire because they thought there were partisans in it … anyhow it was the wrong one. All the people had to go into the church and then they set fire to the church. An "SS-Führer" told me with a laugh that it was the wrong village. "It was just too bad for them."'

12. Hubert Meyer, *The History of the 12.SS-Panzerdivision Hitlerjugend*, pp. 146–147.

13. General der Pztruppen Hans Eberbach, 'Panzer Group Eberbach and the Falaise Encirclement', NARA, RG-338, FMS, MS A-922, February 1946. The reason for Eberbach's negative assessment on 10 July? 'Absolute superiority of the British and American air forces … absence of our own reconnaissance. No air observation … constant large losses of men and material through enemy ground attack, aeroplanes and fighter-bombers. Big morale effect … our attacks are only possible during bad weather or at night … movement during daytime severely retarded. Enemy can move three times faster than us … [our] supply service is strained.'

14. Comte and Comtesse de Perthuis de Laillevault, owners of the chateau in Garcelles where Peiper made his headquarters, interview with author, 7 July 2002. Interestingly, the Linden trees under which Peiper hid his tanks had been planted after the chateau was built in 1721 to herald the American Revolution. Several years before our interview the gardener at the chateau had found a skull and an identity disc while tilling the soil on the south grounds. The German government came to remove the remains. For another account of the fighting in this sector: Georges Bernage, 'La Bataille de Tilly et Garcelles 18 juillet–août 1944 de la Garde de Hitler aux Highlanders', *39/45 Magazine*, Nr. 108, June 1995.

15. Pflughaupt Report.

16. Description of the fighting for Hill 112: Wilhelm Tieke, *In the Firestorm of the Last Years of the War* (Winnipeg: J.J. Fedorowicz, 1999), pp. 115–125.

17. Pflughaupt Report. Although Pflughaupt was cagey, the British provided him with a planted cellmate from the 17th SS Panzer Grenadier Division and secretly microphoned quarters.

18. Recorded conversation of Reinhardt and Pflughaupt, 25 July 1944, TNA: WO 208/4138, SRM 668. 'The German Air Force can't have been totally destroyed. That's impossible. I assume it is being saved up somewhere to be released in one fell swoop.'

19. Cazenave, *Panzers Normandie 44*, p. 89.

20. Percy E. Schramm, ed., *Kriegstagebuch des Oberkommandos der Wehrmacht*, vol. IV (Frankfurt am Main: Bernard & Graefe Verlag für Wehrwesen, 1961), pp. 1572–1573.

21. For Kurt Meyer's conversation with Rommel, see Kurt Meyer, *Grenadiers*, pp. 270–271.

22. Conversation between Rommel and Dietrich: 'Affidavit of Helmuth Lang', 27 May 1950, Sch. Gmünd, RG-549, Case 6-24, Box 51.

23. Rommel was taken to the hospital in Bernay and later sent to his hometown of Ulm to convalesce. Speidel, *Invasion 1944*, pp. 112–113.

24. Account of Werner Josupeit of 7th Company, SS Panzer Grenadier Regiment 2. Georges Bernage, 'La Bataille de Tilly et Garcelles 18 juillet–août 1944 de la Garde de Hitler aux Highlanders', *39/45 Magazine*, Nr. 108, June 1995.

25. 'Special Interrogation Report: Oberstgruppenführer Sepp Dietrich', 29 August 1945, 'Other Records, Miscellaneous Intelligence and Interrogation Reports', RG 549, 290/56/3/4, Box 121.

26. John Keegan, *Six Armies in Normandy* (New York: Viking Press, 1982), p. 213.

27. 'Special Interrogation Report of Brigadeführer Theodor Wisch, Comdr 1 SS Panzer Division "Adolf Hitler", 6 June 44–25 August 44', August 1945, U.S. First Army, PWI Interrogations, NA, RG-407, 101.1-3.2, Box 1515. 'The commander was interviewed at the Berman Hospital, Watford, England, where he is slowly recovering from wounds received on 20 August 1944 in the Falaise Pocket. For a year now, he has laid on his back … Pleasant faced with sunken eyes and a mild speaking voice, he is the opposite of the person that normally would be considered as the commander of the best known of all divisions.'

28. 'KTB Panzergruppe West', F8713551-3552. The available German tanks would have been still less if not for the rapid work of the Panzer repair shop in the Cinglais Forest. So impressive had the mechanics been at repairing and returning damaged tanks that Sepp Dietrich himself visited the workshop to pin an Iron Cross Second Class onto to the busy mechanics. 'Dietrich Interrogation', CSDIC (UK) SIR.

29. Members of the Regiment, *The Story of the 23rd Hussars* (Germany: publisher unknown, 1946), p. 76.
30. For British losses: Chester Wilmot, *The Struggle for Europe* (London: Harper & Row, 1952), pp. 358–360. German losses: Kraemer, 'I SS Panzer Corps in the West in 1944', p. 40.
31. Ellis, *Victory in the West*, vol. I, p. 346.
32. 'KTB Panzergruppe West', 19 July 1944, F8713552-53.
33. The four hundred tanks lost represented 36 per cent of the British tank strength in Normandy. In spite of the bulk of the armour being replaced within days, the failure of Goodwood was a crippling event to Allied plans. Max Hastings, *Overlord* (London: Simon & Schuster, 1984), p. 236.
34. Prisoner of War Interrogation Report, 15 August 1944, G-2 Periodic Report No. 69, U.S. 1st Infantry Division, G-2 records, RG 407, 101.2.13, Box 5055.
35. 'An Interview with SS Obergruppenführer Karl Wolff', 15 June 1945, Rome, TNA, WO 204/6384, AFHQ 525.
36. 'PW Report No. 47', 3rd Armoured Division G-2 Records, 103-2.13, Box 12255, 19 August 1944. '2 PWs reported that members of the 6 and 8 Companies of the first battalion of the 9th Panzer Division's Panzer Regiment were told in early July that from now on, they "belonged" to the Leibstandarte Adolf Hitler.'
37. 'KTB Panzergruppe West', 19 July 1944, F8713553-54.
38. Carlo D'Este, *Decision in Normandy* (New York: HarperCollins, 1983), pp. 467–473.
39. Manfred Thorn, 'Unforgettable Tilly!', manuscript prepared for author (Nuremberg: 1994).
40. Thorn, 1994 manuscript.
41. Stacey, *The Victory Campaign*, pp. 189–190. The Highlanders suffered 139 casualties and reported that its opponent, 'the Leibstandarte Adolf Hitler had fought with genuinely fanatical determination and much skill.'
42. German account of the action on 21 July in Tilly: BDC file for Werner Wolff, Box 011C, 'Vorschlag Nr. 1 für die Nennung im Ehrenblatt des Deutschen Heeres', Joachim Peiper, 2 November 1944. At the same time Wolff was fighting in Tilly the Panthers of the division and Max Hansen's grenadiers successfully ousted the Canadians defending Saint-Martin-de-Fontenay.
43. Reiser, interview with author, 15 May 1997.
44. Hitler's Rastenburg consisted of some sixty above-ground buildings. Although extensive efforts were made at camouflage,

the woods were neither dense nor continuous, and the complex was not invisible from the air. There was also copious intelligence showing that Hitler's main headquarters was located near Rastenburg during 1943–1944. The reason the Western Allies or Russians did not attack Hitler's complex from the air remains a puzzle, with pertinent archival evidence still classified. See Richard Raiber, 'The Führerhauptquartiere', no. 19 (London: After the Battle, 1977), p. 38.

45. The Fritz Darges episode is described by Irving, *Hitler's War*, pp. 660–661. The larger reason for Darges's expulsion from Hitler's inner circle came from his unwillingness to marry Eva Braun's reportedly promiscuous sister, Gretl. Flings aside, Darges let it be known that he preferred to remain single. Accordingly, on 3 June 1944 Hermann Fegelein, another of Hitler's oversexed adjutants, had married Gretl in a big ceremony at Berchtesgaden. Upon leaving Hitler, Darges soon became the Panzer regiment leader for 'Wiking', the 5th SS Panzer Division, where he eventually received the Ritterkreuz for his exploits in Hungary in February 1945.

46. SS officer Fritz Darges (8 February 1913) from Dülseberg/Salzwedel joined the SS in April 1933. From 1936 to 1939 the SS Obersturmführer served as Reichsleiter Martin Bormann's personal adjutant. Later Darges was a company commander in SS Regiment 'Deutschland', being transferred to the Panzer troops and made commander of the 3rd Company of SS Panzer Regiment 5 in Wiking in early 1942. Darges was later selected as a personal adjutant for Hitler, serving from 1 March 1943 through 18 July 1944. Even though dismissed by Hitler on the later date, Darges remained one of Hitler's favourites, such that the German leader made a birthday gift to him in 1944 of 5,000 RM—a benefaction he extended to his driver, SS Sturmbannführer Erich Kempka and SS favourite Obersturmbannführer Max Wünsche. Darges died on 25 October 2009.

47. Himmler's speech at Jägerhöhe, 21 September 1944. For context of the immense suffering in the Polish city, see Norman Davies, *Rising '44: The Battle for Warsaw* (New York: Viking, 2003).

48. Peter Hoffmann, *Stauffenberg: A Family History* (Cambridge: Cambridge University Press, 1995), p. 151.

49. Von Stauffenberg himself had cancelled two previous attempts, one at the Berghof on 11 July, when he learned that although Hitler and Göring would be present at the meeting, Himmler would not be. They decided to wait to try to get all three. On 15 July at the *Wolfsschanze* Stauffenberg made another try, only to cancel again

when Hitler suddenly left the briefing room just before he intended to arm his briefcase bomb. For an overview of the convoluted bomb plot, see Toland, *Adolf Hitler*, pp. 789–816.

50. Was Himmler aware of the move against Hitler? Although one can have many doubts about the source, according to his astrologer Wilhelm Wulff, the SS Reichsführer was already doubting the outcome of the war. In the spring of 1944 Himmler met with Wulff at Bergewald, the beautiful old castle and park at Aigen outside Salzburg that had once belonged to Prince Schwarzenberg. Himmler engaged Wulff in a long rambling conversation, discussing astrology, ancient India and even Atlantis before getting around to divination of the Reich's crumbling prospects. Himmler wanted to know what Hitler's natal chart promised. Wulff told Himmler that Hitler's path was disastrous—he would meet his end in 1945. 'There may well be an assassination attempt, but it will not cost him his life.' At that Himmler winced. 'Surely it's not too late to save the situation. We still have reserve divisions in Russia.' He began to speak of 'secret weapons'. When Wulff dismissed them, Himmler seemed perturbed. 'What do you think I should do?' 'Overthrow Hitler,' said Wulff. Himmler did not even hesitate. 'That wouldn't be difficult. I could send Berger with a panzer division and my men could take over all the other important posts.' Wulff sensed that Himmler had already thought through a coup. 'You know, Herr Wulff, what we two are discussing is high treason.' 'I know that this task is difficult and dangerous ... That is why you must act! Your police force is still intact. For the immediate future your constellations are favourable and Hitler's are bad. Do not wait until it is too late.' Wulff continued naively. 'I am convinced that foreign attitudes towards you would change, if you could make peace now and put an immediate end to the concentration camps.' With mention of the KZ, Himmler grew pensive. 'The only thing I am afraid of is the people.' From 'Lunch with Himmler' in Wulff's book, *Zodiac and Swastika* (New York: Coward, McCann & Geoghegan, 1973).

51. Kersten, *Memoirs*, p. 201.

52. Details of the configuration of the *Wolfsschanze* are from Raiber, 'The Führerhauptquartiere'. Thanks also to Dr Raiber for his review of this brief section.

53. Warlimont, *Inside Hitler's Headquarters*, p. 440. Also see Warlimont, interview with Toland, 15 March 1971, FDR Library, Box 59 (hereafter Warlimont Interview). Heinz Brandt had, in fact, been one of the co-conspirators. No one had seen fit to inform him of the assassination attempt so that he could avoid the deadly meeting.

54. Heinz Linge, *Bis zum Untergang. Als Chef des persönlichen Dienstes des Hitler* (Munich: Herbig, 1980), p. 225.
55. Irving, *Secret Diaries of Hitler's Doctor*, p. 168.
56. Alan Bullock, *Hitler and Stalin: Parallel Lives* (New York: Vintage Books, 1993), p. 837.
57. Hasselbach, interview with John Toland, June 9, 1975, FDR Library, Box 60.
58. Warlimont Interview.
59. See Allen W. Dulles, *Germany's Underground* (New York: Macmillian, 1947); also, *Abwehr* dispatch to Allen Dulles from Edward von Waetjen, OSS dispatch from Bern, Switzerland, dated 6 March 1944. NA: RG 226, Records of the Office of Strategic Services.
60. Padfield, *Himmler*, pp. 509–516.
61. Kersten, *Memoirs*, p. 201.
62. On the evening of 12 August 1944 Kersten returned from a visit to Himmler with the news that, 'The Reichsführer himself has been placed in a very difficult position as a result of this assassination attempt and wants you to check his horoscope for him ... This crazy business will get us all into trouble!' Wulff, *Zodiac and Swastika*, p. 129.
63. 'SS Panzergrenadier Regiment 2, Führerhauptquartier den 21.7.1944: Abschrift!', T-354, R623, F000644.
64. The military plan of Hitler's would-be assassins? 'The plan called for holding the Eastern Front under all circumstances to protect the German border from a Russian invasion. It was intended that the British–American invasion of the West would not be opposed; German troops were to be withdrawn to the interior of the Reich and to reinforce the Eastern front. The plan was to let in the Americans and British without fighting and as fast as possible, far into Germany.' 'The 20 July Putsch: Genmaj. Alexander von Pfuhlstein', 7th Army Interrogation Centre, 10 April 1945, SAIC/2, 290/56/2/4-5, Box 72.
65. Hans Adolf-Jacobsen, *Germans Against Hitler* (Bonn: Press and Information Office of the Federal Government of Germany, 1969), pp. 186–188. For Himmler's declaration on the Sippenhaftung, see Padfield, *Himmler*, p. 528.
66. Hedwig Maier, 'Die SS und der 20. Juli 1944', *Vierteljahrshefte für Zeitgeschichte 14*, July 1966.
67. 'SS Panzer Grenadier Regiment 2: Nachstehender Tagesbefehl des Kommandierenden Generals den Einheiten zur Kenntnis', 24 July 1944, NA: RG 242, T-354, R604, F000370.
68. 'OB West (6 June–24 July 1944', Gunther Blummentritt, NARA, RG-549, Foreign Military Studies, MS- B-284; also Microfiche M1035.

69. 'Meine Begegnungen mit Joachim Peiper', Fritz Kosmehl, manuscript provided to author.
70. 'KTB Panzergruppe West', 25 July 1944, T-313, R420, F8713559.
71. Thorn, 1994 manuscript.
72. Stacey, *The Victory Campaign*, p. 190.
73. Story of Manfred Thorn in fighting at Tilly on 25 July 1944. Tiemann, *Chronicle of the 7. Panzerkompanie*, p. 99.
74. 'Interrogation of Members of 12 SS Panzer Division "Hitlerjugend" in the Matter of the Murder of Canadian PWs in Normandy in 1944', WCIU/LDC 1617, London, 1947, Testimony of SS Sturmmann Heinrich Albers, WCIU/LDC/1617(a). PRO: WO/208/4684. Bernard Siebken would later be executed as a result of the accusations.
75. 'Testimony of SS Sanitätssturmann Eberhard Heinrich', PRO: WO/208/4684, WCIU/LDC/1599 (a).
76. 'Interrogation of PW Kp 22243 Withold Stangenberg, Regt. HQ Company, SS Pz Gren Rgt 26', 10 July 1944, PRO: WO 208/4295. Stangenberg reported that the incident was witnessed by four other men in his unit; two were disgusted by the event and the other two thought it was a good thing that 'should be done more often'.
77. 'Before attacks start, they use artillery and bombers to destroy the position. If the attack starts and is stopped, they pull back and start again with the artillery. If they capture anything, they immediately set up for defence.' '1. SS Panzer Division LSSAH Abt. Ic Nr. 458/44 geh. B/Ha', 16 July 1944, NA T-354, R622, Frame 1103.
78. Joachim Peiper: Russian Theatre, p. 234.
79. Antony Beevor, *D-Day: The Battle for Normandy* (London: Viking, 2009), p. 341.
80. Fischer, interview with author, 15 May 1997. 'Near Kharkov, one of our companies was encircled. In a counterattack two weeks later we captured the area where they had been. All had been brutally killed. That was the significant difference between the East and the West.' Fischer then looked seriously at the author and confided seriously: 'There is a difference, you know, between shooting prisoners and not taking them.'
81. Feldvoss: 'He [Wolff] made the victims lie down in [a] line, head to head and had their heads crushed by the chains.' 'Voluntary Declaration of Karl-Walter Becker', 4 October 1944, PRO: WO 208 4295, Report No. WIS (H)/LDC/395. Becker was with the 2/12 SS Panzer Reconnaissance Battalion when captured. He was interrogated at the London District PoW Cage.

Chapter 19: Operation Lüttich

1. The fierce German–Canadian battle has become the subject of a book: Ken Tout, *The Bloody Battle for Tilly* (Gloucestershire: Sutton Publishing, 2000).

2. 'The well dug in infantry was smashed by heavy bombs in their foxholes and dugouts or killed and buried by blast ... During the bombardment which lasted for three hours, some of the men got crazy or paralyzed and were unable to do anything ... the whole bombed area was transformed into a field covered with craters in which no human being was alive. Tanks and guns were destroyed and overturned and could not be recovered ... every kind of telephone communication was eliminated ... Dugouts and foxholes were smashed, the men buried and we were unable to save them.' Fritz Bayerlein, 'Panzer Lehr Division (23–25 July 1944)', NARA, RG-338, FMS, MS A-902.

3. 'The tempo of the invasion seems to be pushing all before it.' SS Hauptsturmführer Wilhelm Alvatter was with the 17th SS Panzer-grenadier Division, SS Panzer Grenadier Regiment 38, 12th Company and was captured near Roncey on 30 July and then interrogated at Fort Hunt in the United States on 25 August 1944. RG 165, Entry 179B, Box 442.

4. 'Handwritten Report of Company F of 117th Infantry Regiment', U.S. 30th Infantry G-2 Journal and File, 31 July 1944, NARA, 330-2.2, RG 407, Entry 427.

5. Martin Blumenson, *Breakout and Pursuit* (Washington, DC: Office of Chief of Military History, U.S. Government Printing Office, 1961), p. 315.

6. 'Ferngespräch Feldmarschall v. Kluge-Gen. d. Inf. Blumentritt', 31 July 1944, T-311, R28, 7034950.

7. Eberbach, 'Panzer Group Eberbach and the Falaise Encirclement'.

8. 'Bezug: gez. Jodl OKW, WFSt/ Op.(H) West geh.Kdos.Ch. Vom 2.8', T-311, R28, 7035065-66.

9. 'Information Obtained from Genobst. Heinz Guderian', U.S. 7th Army Interrogation Report, SAIC/X/6. 28 May 1945, NA: RG-549, 290/56/2/4-5, 7th Army Interrogation Centre, ETO-MIS-Y, Box 73.

10. Stacey, *The Victory Campaign*, p. 205.

11. Thorn, 1994 manuscript. 'Up to that point, I had personally only fought on the Russian Front ... I had nothing from my previous experience that could compare with that of Tilly. This tactic of hour-long unbroken artillery fire was gruesome. One could, without a

doubt, speak of battle fatigue [shell shock] when speaking of Tilly. It was mental torture.'

12. Calgary Highlanders' diarist for 2 August 1944. Stacey, *The Victory Campaign*, p. 206. 'At 1800 hours, the Typhoons [rocket firing fighter-bombers] arrived and Tilly went up and down in a mess of smoking rubble ... Shortly afterwards our artillery played terrifically heavy fire into the rubble and many air bursts were fired directly over Tilly as well. It is a seemingly impossible thing for anyone to live under such fire. Snipers continue to be very active and the seemingly impossible has happened because we are once again receiving machine gun fire from the slits at Tilly. The Hun is like a rat and comes up for more no matter how hard we pound him.'

13. 'Vorschlag Nr. für Verleihung des Deutschen Kreuzes in Gold', 20 October 1944, Hans Siptrott: BDC file, NA: RG-242, A3343 SM-R070, F001056-86.

14. 'Testimony of Josef Frank', PRO: WO 309/256. Frank, the medical officer, was 21 years old, having been with the Waffen SS since 1941.

15. BDC file for Werner Wolff, NA: RG-242, A3343 SSO, Box 011C, 'Vorschlag Nr. 1 für die Nennung im Ehrenblatt des Deutschen Heeres', Joachim Peiper, 2 November 1944. In that action Peiper claimed that 'this outstanding soldier' destroyed two of the five tanks in the assault. At Tilly Peiper credited Wolff with the destruction of thirteen tanks, two halftracks, assorted guns and vehicles, including two hundred Canadian soldiers killed and wounded and thirty prisoners taken.

16. For Wolff's love of Friedrich Hölderlin, see Agte, *Michael Wittmann and the Tiger Commanders*, p. 369. Hölderlin (1770–1843) was a lyrical German poet emphasizing a classic Greek style and a favourite of Nietzsche towards the end of his life. Wolff's favourite poem was the featured selection from the summer celebration held that June (1944), as recorded in the weekly propaganda publication of the Leibstandarte, *Politische Wochenschau*: 'Die Sonnwendfeier', NA: RG 242, Roll 622, F 1046–1049.

17. The extant war diaries reveal that the Canadian troops involved were from the Calgary Highlanders and the Royal Regiment of Canada. PRO: WO 309/256.

18. 'Statement from SS Unterscharführer Josef Frank to Sgt. A. Salomons of 21st Army Group Special Investigation Branch B.A.F.O.', 6 March 1946, and Deposition of Josef Frank to G.W. Low of Canadian War Crimes Investigation Team,' 17 February 1947, PRO: WO 309/256.

19. 'Statement from Rolf Ehrhardt, SS Unterscharführer, Lodged at No. 2 Internee Prison', 6 March 1946, PRO: WO 309/256. 'I heard Obersturmführer Wolff giving the order that in case the transport did not arrive, the prisoners had to be "bumped off". The cause of this order was an expected night attack, for in such a case prisoners would have meant a danger … the next day Unterscharführer Josef Frank told me that he carried out the order. The shooting was in a cafe near the headquarters. At about 2230 hours on 1 August 1944 I came back to the company headquarters and heard Wolff shouting that one prisoner had escaped from the shooting.'

20. 'Statement from Georg Fleps to Sgt. A. Salomons', 21 Army Group B.A.F.O., 6 March 1946. PRO: WO 309/256.

21. 'Deposition of Willi Edmund Bolze to Geoffrey W. Low', 19 February 1947, PRO: WO 309/256.

22. 'Statement from Rolf Ehrhardt, SS Unterscharführer', PRO: WO 309/256.

23. 'I later reported this incident to Obersturmführer Wolff. Wolff said, "That is not your business. I have ordered this."' 'Deposition of Willi Edmund Bolze to Geoffrey W. Low'.

24. 'Peiper developed heart trouble in the early stages of the invasion'. PRO: WO/208/4139, 'Kurt Meyer', CSDIC (UK) SRM 1022, CS/648, 15 November 1944. The intelligence came from a secret taping by British intelligence of Meyer in his cell with others. Peiper's real problem was hepatitis.

25. See account of Georg Preuss in Tiemann, *Chronicle of the 7. Panzer-kompanie*, p. 186.

26. Statement of Joachim Peiper to Police in Vesoul, 22 June 1976, Courtesy of the Thomson archive.

27. See statement of Ehrhard Gührs, in Agte, *Michael Wittmann and the Tiger Commanders*, p. 370. 'The boys were terribly afraid, not only because they had fallen into the hands of the SS, but also because they had certainly heard many fables of our cruelty from their propaganda. Our field kitchen had just arrived with coffee and we were happy to give them some. We then turned them over to the regimental staff.'

28. 'Allegmeine Befehle und Anordnungen des Generalkommando I.SS-Panzer-Korps Leibstandarte Adolf Hitler', Enthält auch SS Korps Sanitäts Abteilung 501, BA-MA, RS 9/8.

29. 'Krankenbuchlager Berlin: Joachim Peiper, Res. Laz. Tegernsee, 2.8.44', Wehrmachtsauskunftstelle (WASt) Archives, Berlin. The record shows that Peiper was admitted on 6 August to Feldlaz 501.

For Peiper's shrapnel injury: 'Bestätigung der Verwundungen und Erkarnkungen des SS-O_Stubanf. Joachim Peiper, Kdr. Pz. Rgt.1 zwecks Einlage in das Soldbuch', Kurt Sickel, Rgt-Gef.-Std., 30 January 1945, NA: Peiper BDC file. Sickel misdiagnosed the problem as a gall bladder infection, as listed in some medical reports. The shrapnel would later be removed at Landsberg on 20 October 1950.

30. Elke M., Letter to author, 15 July 2017.
31. Himmler's one concession to reality in his ramblings was recognizing the importance of air power: 'Our technical knowledge,' he said, 'can already tell us that a future war with the frontiers of today is lost from the outset for a nation whose air warning posts are not at least 2,000 km from its frontier.' And, 'The war consists fourthly in the solid extension of the German population frontier eastwards at least 500 km from the frontier of 1939. It means the settling of this space with German sons and German families to produce a nursery of German blood.' Himmler's 26 July 1944 speech, as published in Das Reich, 24 September 1944. PRO: WO 208/4474.
32. General Hans Eberbach in captivity at Trent Park wondered aloud: 'I can't make Himmler out at all, on the one hand because he decided to have all the Jews massacred consciously.' SS General Kurt Meyer, his cellmate, was emphatic: 'Do you know why? Himmler was the most faithful executor of the Führer's order. The Führer used to say: "Should the Jews succeed once again in involving Europe in a war, it will not mean the destruction of the German people, but the annihilation of the Jewish race."' GRGG 226, Hans Eberbach and Kurt Meyer on 1–20 November 1944, PRO: WO 208/4364.
33. 'Betr.: Vichy und Perier Quellen', Pohl to Rudolf Brandt, 10 July 1944, T-175, Roll 25, Folder 1032.
34. In spite of tank losses in July, the Panzer strength of the Leibstandarte had been built back up by 1 August: sixty-one Mk IVs, forty Mk Vs and twenty-three StuGs operational. Lefevre, Panzers in Normandy, p. 126.
35. Manfred Thorn, letter to author, 1 February 2018: 'Somehow we would recuperate from the hell of the previous three weeks.'
36. Hitler: 'The more troops they squeeze through the gap and the better they are, the better for us when we reach the sea and cut them off!' Victor Brooks, The Normandy Campaign: from D-Day to the Liberation of Paris (Cambridge, MA: DaCapo, 2002), p. 140.
37. Ralph Bennett, ULTRA in the West (New York: Charles Scribner's Sons, 1980).

38. 'Bezug: gez. Jodl OKW/WFSt vom 2.8.44 23.15 Uhr', T-311, R28, 7035065.

39. The other Panzer divisions in the Lüttich operation were: 2nd Panzer, 2nd SS Das Reich, 116th Panzer and part of the 17th SS Panzer Grenadier Division. Among them they had about 160 tanks available in the first wave. Should the assault be successful, the attack would be nourished by additional forces from the 9th SS and 10th SS Divisions as well as the Panther Battalion from the 9 Panzer Division. Michael Reynolds, *Steel Inferno* (New York: Sarpedon, 1995), p. 211.

40. Account of SS Oberführer Georg Preuss of the 10th Company, SS Panzer Grenadier Regiment 2: Tiemann, *Chronicle of the 7. Panzer-kompanie*, p. 186.

41. 'Hausser's Personal Experiences', SAIC/FIR, 9 July 1945, 7th Army Interrogation Centre, ETO-MIS-Y, RG 549, 290/56/2/4-5, Box 74.

42. Records of captured telephone conversation with von Kluge and other army-level leaders of Operation Lüttich on 7 August 1944, NA, RG-407, 101-2.1, U.S. First Army G-2 Records, Box 1392, June–October 1944.

43. Fischer, interview with author, 15 May 1997.

44. 'Oberbefehlshaber West: 15.25 Uhr Anruf Genobst. Jodl bei Chef des Gen.St.Ob.West', T-311, R28, F7035204-5207.

45. Hitler's pronouncement: 'KTB 5. Panzer Armee', 7 August 1944. For 'into the sea', see Dietrich von Choltitz, *Soldat unter Soldaten* (Zurich: Konstanz Europa, 1951), p. 222–223.

46. Werner Haupt, *Rückzug im Westen* (Friedberg: Motorbuch Verlag, 1970), p. 93.

47. These were 116th Panzer Division, 2nd Panzer Division and 2nd SS Panzer Division.

48. ULTRA Decrypt of Luftwaffe radio traffic encoded on Enigma, PRO: DEFE, 3/114, XL 5135, 7 August 1944.

49. 3rd Armoured Division G-2 Journal, NARA, RG-407, 103-2.13, 5 August 1944.

50. Theodor Wisch, 'Leibstandarte Adolf Hitler in Aug 1944', 1946, NA RG-549, Foreign Military Studies, MS B-358.

51. 'Our panzers stood on the asphalt road': Werner Josupeit on 7 August, Lehmann and Tiemann, *Die Leibstandarte*, vol. IV/1, p. 185.

52. Letter Jupp Steinbüchel to Timo Worst, 26 April 2012.

53. Kraemer, 'I SS Panzer Corps in the West'.

54. Fischer, interview with author, 15 May 1997: 'The Lord would have helped us, if he had left that fog in place.'

55. 'Then as I moved up, I was shot down again four or five hours later by P-38s. I remember their distinctive tail as they dived at us.' Fischer, interview with author, 15 May 1997.
56. Paul Zwigart, interview with author, 20 May 1997.
57. Statement of Paul Zwigart, 11 February 1946, NA, Case 6-24, RG-549, Box 9.
58. Peiper's comment: Heinz Stutterecker, interview with author, 28 February 2009.
59. 'Special Interrogation Report', Interrogation of medical officer with the 1st SS Panzer Division, 15 August 1944, U.S. VII Corps G-2 Report, NA, RG-407, 607-2.1, Box 3279.
60. 'The remnants of the Leibstandarte are still available for employment in the push. Where do you want them?' Intercepted telephone log of von Kluge on 7 August: NARA, RG-407, 101-2.1, U.S. First Army G-2 Records, Box 1392, June–October 1944.
61. Oberkommando der Wehrmacht (OKW), vol. IV, pp. 338–339.
62. General Lieutenant Paul Danhauser, '271st Infantry Division (March–13 August 1944)', NARA, RG-338, FMS MS B-256, 1946. See also Oberst Hasso Neitzel, '89th Infantry Division (March–6 Aug 1944)', NARA, RG-338, FMS, B-012, 1946. The 271st had entered Normandy with 12,500 men but was nearly completely destroyed in less than a month.
63. 'Interrogation of Kurt Meyer', PRO: WO 205/1021.
64. 'KTB 5. Panzer Armee', 8 August 1944, F8713601-5.
65. Peiper on Wittmann: Agte, *Michael Wittmann and the Tiger Commanders*, p. 373.
66. 'Von Kluge to Eberbach', 7 August 1944 at 2140 hours.

Chapter 20: Falaise to the Seine

1. 'It was a Führer's order. What else could we do?' Sepp Dietrich, interview with Shulman, September 1945, p. 151.
2. Dietrich's aside to General Lieutenant Friedrich August Schack: Wilmot, *The Struggle for Europe*, p. 417. For Dietrich's award, see *Das Schwarze Korps*, 'Höchste Tapferkeitsauszeichnung für Sepp Dietrich', 17 August 1944, Dietrich BDC file, NA, BDC A3343 SSO-152. Dietrich was only the sixteenth soldier in the German armed forces to receive that award.
3. 'KTB Pz AOK 5', 13 August 1944, F8713621. Leibstandarte operational armoured strength at midday: fourteen Mk IVs, seven Mk Vs and eight assault guns.

4. Eberbach, 'Panzer Group Eberbach and the Falaise Encirclement'.
5. Blumenson, *Breakout and Pursuit*, p. 505.
6. 'KTB Pz AOK 5', 14 August 1944, T-314, R420, 8713624.
7. 'Falaise to Geber', narrative by Manfred Thorn, prepared for author, 1 February 2018.
8. OKW Kriegstagebuch KTB, vol. IV, p. 339.
9. 'KTB Pz AOK 5', 15 August 1944, F 8713625.
10. For von Kluge's 'fatalistic resignation', see Speidel, *Invasion 1944*, pp. 125–129.
11. Helmut Heiber, ed., *Hitlers Lagebesprechungen im Führerhauptquartier 1942–1945* (Stuttgart: Deutsche Verlags Anstalt, 1962), p. 273.
12. 'KTB Pz AOK 5', 17 August 1944, F 8713629. See also Wilmot, *The Struggle for Europe*, p. 419.
13. 3rd Armoured G-2 Records, 'G-2 Periodic Reports: Order of Battle', NARA, 103-2.2, Box 12252. 1st Infantry Division G-2 Records for a week later on 22 August 1944 (Box 5056) estimated that the Leibstandarte then consisted of only five thousand men.
14. General der Waffen SS Georg Keppler, 'Fighting of the I SS Panzer Corps in Northern France (16 August–October 1944)', MS B-623, NARA, RG-338, FMS, 28 March 1947.
15. Eberbach, 'Panzer Group Eberbach and the Falaise Encirclement'.
16. 3rd Armoured Division, G-2 Journal and File, 17 August 1944, 103.2.13, Box 12255.
17. Ernst Jung: Lehmann and Tiemann, *Die Leibstandarte*, vol. IV/1, p. 199. 'It was dangerous to use the roads. The Americans had firm control of them. Anyone venturing onto a road fell victim to anti-tank guns or the fighter-bombers circling like a swarm of bees.'
18. 'KTB Pz AOK 5', 18 August 1944, F 8713630-33.
19. Reiser, interview with author, 15 May 1997.
20. Agte, *Michael Wittmann and the Tiger Commanders*, p. 456.
21. Lehmann and Tiemann, *Die Leibstandarte*, vol. IV/1. New translation of Stiller Account.
22. Lehmann and Tiemann, *Die Leibstandarte*, vol. IV/1, pp. 210–211.
23. In the Waffen SS since 1938 Armberger had been with the Leibstandarte with the flak battalion in all campaigns since France in 1940. He was wounded four times in Russia before recovering in Vienna to return to join the Leibstandarte as a tank company commander in May 1944. For his fatal actions at Falaise north-east of Mossey, Armberger earned the Ritterkreuz, awarded posthumously on 31 October 1944. The recommendation bore Peiper's own signature, although Peiper was not with the tank regiment during the period

when Armberger sacrificed himself. BDC file for Josef Armberger: NA, RG-242, A3343-SSO-012, Armberger, of the 8th Company of the 1st SS Panzer Regiment, shot down four Sherman tanks with *panzerfausts* and was stalking a fifth when he fell north-east of Mossey/Evreux. He was awarded the Knight's Cross posthumously.

24. Eberbach, 'Panzer Group Eberbach and the Falaise Encirclement'.

25. 'Falaise to Geber', Manfred Thorn, prepared for author, 1 February 2018.

26. SS Brigadeführer Heinz Harmel tended to Wisch at the height of the Falaise battle, pleading with General Heinrich von Lüttwitz of the 2nd Panzer Division to provide them with an ambulance to escape the encirclement. 'Why should I?' the Army commander complained. 'They have their own vehicles, they won't get any from me.' Covertly tapped conversation of SS Standartenführer Heinz Lingner, 17th SS Panzergrenadier Division, with unnamed captain of the 276th Volksgrenadier Division, 10 January 1945, PRO: C.S.D.I.C. (U.K.) 1541, SRM 1210, Kew, London.

27. Lehmann and Tiemann, *Die Leibstandarte*, vol. IV/1, pp. 223–224.

28. Gersdorff, Rudolf-Christoph von, *Soldat im Untergang* (Frankfurt am Main: Ullstein, 1979), pp. 153–159.

29. SHAEF, *Report by the Supreme Commander to the Combined Chiefs of Staff on the Operations in Europe of the Allied Expeditionary Force 6 June 1944 to 8 May 1945* (Washington, D.C.: U.S. Government Printing Office, 1946), p. 46. The exact count of prisoners from Falaise varies from a low of thirty thousand to a high of fifty thousand.

30. The actions of Kuhmann on 20 and 21 August 1944 are summarized in his application for the German Cross in Gold ('Vorschlag Nr. 357 für die Verleihung des Deutschen Kreuzes in Gold', 30 September 1944), and signed by Werner Poetschke. BDC File for Herbert Kuhlmann, NA, RG-242, SS-Officers, A3343-SSO-228A. Also Fritz Kosmehl, interview with author, 17 December 2004. The BDC file for Kuhlmann shows him wounded near Chambois on 21 August.

31. For a description of Von Kluge's demise, see Speidel, *Invasion 1944*.

32. 'Interrogation of Sepp Dietrich', U.S. 7th Army Interrogation Report, SAIC/43, 11 June 1945, NA: RG-407, Entry 143, 7th Army Interrogation Centre. A translation of von Kluge's parting letter to Hitler is contained in OCMH file R-58. 'Both Rommel and I, and probably all the leaders here in the West, who have experienced the struggle with the English and Americans with their wealth of materiel, foresaw the development that has now appeared …

Our views were not dictated by pessimism, but by sober recognition of the facts.'

33. '12th Army Group WD Observers Bd. Ltr. AGF Bd. Rpt. ETO, No. 208, Visit to Falaise Pocket', 31 August 1944. As cited in Blumenson, *Breakout and Pursuit*, p. 558. 'The grass and trees were vividly green as in all Normandy and a surprising number of houses ... untouched. That rather peaceful setting framed a picture of destruction so great that it cannot be described. It was as if an avenging angel had swept the area bent on destroying all things German ... I stood in a lane, surrounded by 20 or 30 dead horses or parts of dead horses, most of them still hitched to their wagons and carts ... As far as my eye could see ... there were vehicles, wagons, tanks, guns, prime movers, sedans, rolling kitchens, etc., in various stages of destruction. I stepped over hundreds of rifles in the mud and saw hundreds more stacked along the sheds ... I walked through a mile or more of lanes where the vehicles had been closely packed ... I saw probably 300 field pieces and tanks, mounting large-caliber guns that were undamaged. I saw no foxholes or any other kind of field fortifications. The Germans were trying to run and had no place to run. They were probably too exhausted to dig ... They were probably too tired even to surrender. I left this area rather regretting that I had ever seen it ... Under such conditions, there are no supermen—all men become rabbits looking for a hole.'

34. 'G-2 Periodic Report', G-2 Records of U.S. 90th Infantry Division, 23 August 1944, NARA, Box 5056.

35. This tragic episode described by Jean Marius Vesque (Mémorial de Caen archive) is from Beevor, *D-Day*, p. 490.

36. 'KTB Pz AOK 5', 18 August 1944, F 8713634-37. Lehmann and Tiemann (*Die Leibstandarte*, vol. IV/1, p. 228) estimate the Leibstandarte losses since the invasion at approximately five thousand officers, NCOs and enlisted men.

37. Rolf Reiser was one of those who had escaped. Reiser would later earn the Iron Cross for his mission. He drove across the Seine River in a Schwimmwagen and headed back towards Germany. As Reiser left France, he claimed to have seen Peiper once more briefly in Chantilly near Paris on 23 August. He did not see Peiper again until arriving at the training area near Witzendorf in mid-October. Reiser, interview with author, March 2006. Reiser told him of his miraculous escape at Falaise. Peiper knew Reiser was from Transylvania: 'Rumania just capitulated during the night. Is your wife going to

get out?' Reiser told him he hoped so; he had seen his family last the previous Easter. Peiper told him that he was headed for Germany. 'Pack your stuff and get ready to get out of here.' Did Reiser want to go on to Vienna? No, Reiser said he would stay with the troop.

38. Jodl relating Hitler's orders to defend before the Seine: Wehrmacht Operations Staff/Operations Section, 21 August 1944, BA-MA, RH 19/IX/7.

39. For the discussion on the Heinkel 177 on 24 August, see *Aus den Tagebüchern von Joseph Goebbels seine unterredungen mit Adolf Hitler*, 18 April 1944, p. 460, Goebbels' diary on 2 September 1944. For He 177 problems: 'He-177: Report from Captured Personnel and Material Branch,' Military Intelligence Division, U.S. War Department, 26 January 1945. The account came from a Lufwaffe electrician who had been with KG 100 before being transferred to the 5th Fallschirmjaeger Division. NARA, RG 165, Entry 179B, Box 438. In one operation flown against England by twenty-four He-177s from Chateaudun, eight planes cracked up on take-off, and five other aborted the mission to return because of various problems with the engines. And on three separate occasions in July 1944 He 177s with no other apparent problems exploded in mid-air while cruising over the field. Konigsberg: 'The pilots have so little faith in their machines that they use every expedient to avoid flying them.'

40. Typescript from telephone discussion between Hans Speidel and Sepp Dietrich, 23 August 1944, KTB Herresgruppe B, RH 19 IX/88. In response to the exchange, Model informed Hitler that the orders for the counterattack were impossible, as the identified Panzer divisions were shadows of their former strength.

41. For the warning of Gause, see Kriegstagebuch LXXXI Armeekorps, 22 August 1944, BA-MA, RH 24-81/97; also, Herresgruppe B Kriegstagebuch, 25 August 1944, BA-MA, RH 19/IX/88.

42. KTB Fifth Panzer Armee, Report dated 23–25 August 1944, BA-MA, RH 21-5/52; also, Edgar Feuchtinger, 'History of the 21 Pz Division: Normandy Campaign, Pt. II, 26 July–14 September 1944', NARA, RG-338, FMS, MS B-631. The round trip by one of the six ferries took twenty-five minutes to move troops and vehicles across.

44. 'KTB Pz AOK 5', 22 August.

45. 'KTB Pz AOK 5'. The report indicated that there were 150 German infantry from SS Das Reich and Leibstandarte Adolf Hitler, with three to five tanks in Ivry and setting up prepared positions by the bridge there across the Eure River.

46. 'An O.D. Pz. AOK SS Obergruppenführer Sepp Dietrich gez Standartenführer Mohnke', 'KTB Pz AOK 5', 24 August 1944, F 8714224-5. Mohnke to Dietrich: *Es wurden im Kampf niedergemacht 41 Terroristen'*.

47. Hans Grühle to Hubert Meyer, 28 July 1986, BA-MA, RS7/ v.507.

48. Junker Diary. Courtesy of Timm Haasler: Having been wounded in Tilly, Junker recovered in Paris on 15–17 August: 'Even now, Paris is beautiful ... I am released, but the military situation is not nice. The serious life begins again. Everything looks doubtful.' On 20 August, after sipping champagne and looking for entertainment in the City of Lights, Junker made his way back to the posted assembly point at Chantilly just north of Paris to find Werner Poetschke and Herbert Kuhlmann just arriving with what was left of the tanks and other personnel that had escaped the Falaise pocket.

49. 'The Last Days in Paris: Interrogation of Gen. der Infanterie von Choltitz', 24 August 1944, NA, RG-498, Records of the intelligence services of the ETO Historian, C.S.D.I.C. (U.K.) D11/535, Box 1373. Although von Choltitz complained on the SS and likes to paint himself as the saviour of Paris, in reality he had been a part of the Holocaust apparatus. Five days after his description of his days in Paris he was in his cell at Trent Park confiding to his cellmate, General Wilhelm Ritter von Thoma (a tank commander of Afrika Korps captured at El Alamein in 1942), unaware that their conversation was being recorded: 'The worst job I ever carried out ... was the liquidation of the Jews. I carried out that order to the last detail.' CSDIC (UK) von Choltitz in conversation with von Thoma, 29 August 1944, PRO: WO 208/6364. The mass shooting of Jews in the Crimea took place between 9 and 15 December 1941, when elements of Einsatzgruppen D killed at least ten thousand people in the City Park of Simferopol. Infantry Regiment 16 of the 22nd Infantry Division, under von Choltitz, was at Sevastopol at the time. See Sönke Neitzel, *Tapping Hitler's Generals* (Barnsley, UK: Frontline Books, 2007), p. 366.

50. 'Morale of German garrison in Paris, Consolidated PWI Interrogation Report No. 2', U.S. First Army, 30 August 1944, 101-2.1-3.0, U.S. First Army G-2 Records: Operations Reports, Box 1517.

51. 'We no longer know the meaning of the world national ... of it being a matter of honour ... I'm saying that we steal ... that man Himmler ... to cover ourselves with the shame of carrying out organized robbery under the supervision and encouragement of the state ... that's a different matter.' General Choltitz speaking with General

der Fallschirmjäger Bernhard Ramacke, GRGG 270, 9 March 1945, PRO: WO 208/4177.

52. Interrogation of Hauptmann Fritz Kraemer of the Abwehr Alarm Abteilung Riedel, stationed in Paris and captured 24 August 1944, interrogated at Fort Hunt on 24 April and 25 June 1945. NARA, RG 165, Entry 179B, Box 502.

53. Max Ketterer file, Covert surveillance with cellmate Lang on 16–22 March 1945, NARA, RG 165, Entry 179B, Box 496. Kettner was one of 280 men sent as replacements to the Leibstandarte on 27 July 1944. He had trained under the Germania leadership in April and May of 1944 in training that was so inhumane that three recruits with him committed suicide. His trainers in Unna and Arnhem, SS Untersturmführer Krueger and Unterscharführer Fuhrmann, told him of shocking atrocities witnessed in Russia—so disturbing in their cruelty that the author is loath to repeat them. During their stay at Fort Hunt in Room 10B Lang and Ketterer became suspicious that there were microphones in the room.

54. 'It was raining and we had to wait the entire afternoon and practically the whole night. Finally we got in line and the ferry took us over.' Recollection of SS flak driver Ernst Buchta, Tiemann, *Chronicle of the 7. Panzerkompanie*, p. 231.

55. 'Dietrich Interrogation', PRO: WO 208/1788; Wilmot, *The Struggle for Europe*, p. 434.

56. Larry Collins and Dominque Lapierre, *Is Paris Burning?* (London: Simon and Schuster, 1965), p. 284.

57. 'Only as a heap of rubble must Paris fall into Allied hands', Enigma decrypt from Hitler as passed on by Herresgruppe B on 20 August 1944. PRO: DEFE, XLs 7753, 7793 1712/24.

58. On 25–26 August 1944 surviving situation maps show Kampfgruppe Mohnke holding a tenuous line behind the Seine between Amfreville sur les Monts and Muids. For actions of the 15th Scottish Division, see the Division diaries (www.15thScottishdivisiondiaries.co.uk) as well as Ellis, *Victory in the West*, vol. I, p. 467.

59. Evening telephone discussion between Model and Blumentritt on 31 August 1944, BA-MA, RH 19/IX/88.

60. For Sperrgruppe Ullerich: Lehmann and Tiemann, *Die Leibstandarte*, vol. IV/1, p. 232.

61. 'G-2 Journal: Third Armored Division', NA, RG-407, 603-2.2, Box 12255, 30 August 1944; Interrogation of Major Schulte with XLVII Panzer Corps, 1944.

62. 'Interrogation of SS Pfc Ernst Ulrich, 1st Army PWI Report No. 19', G-2 Records U.S. First Army, RG-407, 101-2.2, Box 1407. Ulrich was with the 4th Panzer Company when the 12th SS Panzer Regiment had come from Paderborn to escort the tanks by rail to Reims and moved with them as far as Epernay and then moved to Soissons on orders to help unload eight new Tigers, only to be captured when surprised by U.S. armour while unloading the heavy tanks.

63. 'Tactical IPW Report No. 29', TUSA, G-2 Records U.S. First Army, RG-407, 101-2.2, 3 September 1944, with data on 1st SS Division from 29 August, Box 1407 Elements of the 4th Company, 12th SS Panzer Regiment fought with Kampfgruppe Jürgensen, which was attached to Kampfgruppe Mohnke.

64. 'Falaise to Geber', narrative by Manfred Thorn, prepared for author, 1 February 2018. Thorn and his loan tank crew would unload their tank in Metz, then drive to Monschau, Germany, where they would again beg for fuel at a local tavern! They were making their way to Geber near Siegburg, where the tank regiment was reassembling in early September.

65. Patton to his wife, Beatrice, on 21 August 1944 and Patton Diary entry for same date, Martin Blumenson, *The Patton Papers* (Boston: Houghton Mifflin, 1972).

66. SHAEF Weekly Intelligence Summary 23, Week Ending 2 September 1944, Headquarters 12th Army Group, SHAEF War Diaries, NA, RG-331, Entry 176, Box 40.

67. 'The troops are on their own': Paul Frank, 'Report on the Fighting of the *Fifth Panzer Army* from 24 August–4 September 1944, MS B-729, NARA, RG-549; also, OB West Tagesmeldungen, 31 August 1944, RH 19/IV 54.

68. 3rd Armoured Division Association, Spearhead in the West, 1945, p. 91.

69. Omar Bradley, *A Soldier's Story* (New York: Henry Holt, 1951), p. 402. Patton would let loose his frustration even more vulgarly in early September when Montgomery's Operation Market Garden was going forward at the expense of his supply. His comment to war correspondent Cornelius Ryan: 'Maybe there are five thousand, maybe ten thousand Nazi bastards in their concrete foxholes before the Third Army. Now if Ike stops holding Monty's hand and gives me the supplies, I'll go through the Siegfried Line like shit through a goose!'

70. Blumenson, *Breakout and Pursuit*, pp. 688–692. The Red Ball Express itself burned three hundred thousand gallons of gasoline a day— as much as three armoured divisions on the move.

71. 'Despite everything that has happened do not allow your firm faith in Germany's future to be shaken one whit. This moment will separate the weaklings and the real men.' 'Captured Order of the Day for Field Marshal Walther Model: G-2 Report for 3 September', 101-2.1, U.S. First Army G-2 Records, Box 1392, June–October 1944.
72. 'Special Interrogation Report: Maj. Paul Korn of Kampfgruppe Aulock', G-2 Records U.S. First Army, RG-407, 101-2.2 to 3.0, 2 September 1944, Box 1407. 'Morale at home very low … Duesseldorf almost totally destroyed and heavy industries there have largely been moved to Silesia.'

Chapter 21: Escape to the Westwall

1. Beevor, *D-Day*, pp. 490–491.
2. One order from the Army Group B: 'Danger of enemy, but stronger danger of terrorist … take all security measures. Travel of cars alone is forbidden! Hold weapons at the ready.' G-2 Journal and File, U.S. First Army; 31 August 1944, NA RG-407, 101-2.15 to 3.0, Box 1407. 'In certain parts of France the situation with French terrorists demands the greatest precautions.' Captured advisory from Kampgruppe Heintz, 4 July 1944, G-2 Records, U.S. First Army, Annex 2 to Periodic Report No. 38, NA RG-407, 101-2.1, Box 1392.
3. The damage exacted by the French and Belgian resistance on the fleeing German columns was well beyond commonly reported contemporary accounts, which tend to focus on U.S. Army military operations. See particularly the list of attacks and damage listed: 'G-3 SF 10 Det. Rpt: Resistance Groups in France, 1st Army', G-2 Records U.S. First Army, RG-407, 101-2.15 to 3.0, Box 1517, NARA.
4. 'In the morning we reached Amiens.' Lehmann and Tiemann, *Die Leibstandarte*, vol. IV/1 p. 235
5. The SS officer killed was likely SS Obersturmführer Walter Trommer, an ordnance officer with the 12th SS Panzer Division who was listed as dying on 31 August near Hirson—at the time the supply point for the I SS Panzerkorps.
6. BDC file for Gerhard Bremer (27 May 1917): NA, RG-242, BDC File: A3343-SS0-104. Bremer received the Knight's Cross on 30 October 1941.
7. For 'bullies and brawlers', see Eberbach's testimony at the trial of Kurt Meyer: Foster, *Meeting of Generals*, p. 482. After the war, after being released from French prison, Bremer retired in 1954 to Denia, Spain, where he directed a restaurant and hotel, El Tossalet,

that frequently entertained Nazi ex-patriot friends such as Otto Skorzeny, the famous SS commando; Otto Remer, commander of the Führer Begleit Brigade; Léon Degrelle, the Belgian Rexist; and SS Mauthausen concentration camp doctor, Aribert Heim. See 'Spanien: Ein Paradies für Hitlers Schergen', Holger Weber, *Mallorca Zeitung*, 17 January 2008. Bremer died in 1989.

8. 'Interrogation of SS Sgt Sepp Engshuber, 101 SS Pz Battalion', 1st Army PWI Report No. 20, G-2 Records U.S. First Army, RG-407, 101-2.2, 3 September 1944, Box 1407. Engshuber, who was captured between Epernay and Soisson in Brouillet, reported that Bremer lost a leg in Normandy, whereas he was only wounded. Considerably elaborating the story, see 'The Bremer Murders', in Howard Margolian, *Conduct Unbecoming: The Murder of Canadian Prisoners of War in Normandy* (Toronto: University of Toronto Press, 2000).

9. Excerpts from Kriegstagebuch SS-Pz Gren. Rgt. 25, 12th SS Panzer Division, military archives VHA (Vojenský Historický Archiv) in Prague; thanks to Simon Vosters. The entry from 13:10 on 30 August 1944 refers to Tavaux (Rennevall was the headquarters of SS Panzer Grenadier Regiment 25). 'In almost all the villages [around Rennevall] there are terrorist groups. A separate scout platoon of our troop is shot by terrorists. The place is burned down, the inhabitants shot.' (*'In fast allen Orten treten Terroristengruppen auff. Ein eigener Spahtrupp wird von Terroristen angeschossen. Der Ort wird niedergebrannt, die Einwohrer erschossen.'*)

10. For the death of Odette Maujean and the surrounding story, see 'Case of Tavaux-Pontsericourt', NA, RG 153, Entry 151, Records of the Office of the Judge Advocate General, USAEUR, French War Crimes Cases, File No. 000-11-127, Box 2. Also, Alain Nice, Tavaux 30-31 août 1944. Histoire d'une tragédie, compte d'auteur (Bosmont-sur-Serre), 2002, Musée de la Résistance et de la déportation de Tergnier. My appreciation for the assistance of Simon Vosters and Ann Shields in helping to research this episode. It is noteworthy that in the Leibstandarte chronology Lehmann and Tiemann (*Die Leibstandarte*, vol. IV/1, p. 234) show that battle groups were in the area of Marle on that date and only 11km from Tavaux, with one Tiger I abandoned in Marle for lack of fuel. Elements listed with this battle group: 6th, 9th and 12th Company SS Panzer Grenadier Regiment 1 and 3rd Company, SS Panzer Pionier Battalion 1. The G-2 report of the 3rd Armoured and VII Corps clearly shows that elements of the 1st SS Panzer Division were in the town, as they describe the capture and identification of 'three PW from engr

bn hq Co SS Adolf Hitler taken at 270315 near Cilly'. Intelligence showed that the 1st SS Panzer Division was concentrating its assets in the Vervins area, with Hirson serving as a supply point. The place of the prisoners' capture is the road midway between Tavaux and Montcornet [Agnicourt-et-Séchelles]. In the meantime the 4th Cavalry Group reported being held up at Montcornet by an infantry company braced by seven tanks—tanks of Kampfgruppe Berlin supporting KG Olboeter. 'G-2 Journal: Third Armored Division', NA, RG-407, 603-2.2, Box 12255. 31 August 1944.

11. 'Rapport du Captaine Couraux, Commandant le section de Vervins', 26 September 1944, NARA, RG-153, Entry 151, Records of the U.S. Judge Advocate General, French War Crimes, Box 2. The SS men had shown up in the village just east of Vervins at 5:30 pm and began gunning down Frenchmen in the village and setting houses alight. For Waldmüller having given the reprisal orders at Plomion, see 'G-2 Records of U.S. 9th Infantry Division: Miscellaneous PW Statements', 4 September 1944, NA RG-407, 109-2.1, Box 6346.

12. 'Area east of Chimay jammed with enemy vehicles … Much movement north and east of Charleroi (J-6805).' 'G-2 Journal and File, U.S. First Army; 31 August 1944', RG-407, 101-2.15 to 3.0 Box 1407, NARA. For German convoy camouflage like 'walking greenhouses', see 'Miscellaneous: Morale', 28 August 1944, U.S. VII Corps G-2 Reports, NA, RG-407, 207-2.1, Box 3279.

13. Kampfgruppe Diefenthal consisted of approximately 400 men, including 12th Company, and a platoon of 9 Company of SS Panzer Grenadier Regiment 2, as well as assorted stragglers from the divisional grenadier regiments organized into a provisional company and Einheit Woelky (SS Obersturmführer Otto Woelky). The later unit consisted of 138 men with four 7.5cm self-propelled infantry howitzers originally organized on 10 August in Saint-Germain-en-Laye, France, west of Paris, just in time for the large-scale retreat. Kampgruppe Diefenthal fought a delaying action at Avesnes aimed at delaying the advance of the 3rd Armoured Division. Only after did they reach the east bank of the Meuse River. From there they were designated as a mobile attacking force, designed to screen the gap between AOK 7 and AOK 1 to pull back with Woelky and other ragtag combat elements, including Kampgruppe Rink, to defend the Westwall bunkers near Neuerburg on 12 September. 'PW 1st Lt. Otto Woelky: First Army PWI Report No. 4', 3 October 1944, NA, 101-2.13, Box 1496. Woelky had been ordered with Kampfgruppe Diefenthal to prepare to lance the American penetration of the 4th Infantry Division

in the Schnee Eifel near Prüm when he was captured on 29 September near Rehbusch.

14. 3rd Armoured captures Leibstandarte prisoners near Buironfosse—likely stragglers from Sperrgruppe Ullerich on 2 September: 'G-2 reports', NARA, RG-407, 603-2.13, Box 12258; 6 September: At 860868 near Flavion, 9th ID captured two prisoners from LAH, 9th Infantry Division, G-2 Reports, NARA, RG-407, 309-2.1, Box 6349.

15. 'Special Interrogation Report: 5/6 September 1944', NA RG-407, 1st Infantry Division, 3.01-2.2, G-2 Journal and File, Box 5072. The PW report indicated that as they moved to the Belgian border the 1 SS Panzer and 12th SS Divisions received approximately a thousand replacements form March Gruppe Kurmark. The replacements—mostly from no longer needed Luftwaffe flak troops—were less than enthusiastic about their assignment to the Waffen SS (they only had four days training when sent to join the SS units), and a number of them took the opportunity in the confusion of early September to desert to the Americans or otherwise flee to Germany, taking their chances with evading military authorities. The German blocking force included elements of the 7th and 9th companies of SS Panzer Grenadier Regiment 2 reinforced with assault guns from the 12th SS. However, the small battle group was no match for the advancing U.S. 3rd Armoured Division. For the mission of I SS Panzer Corps, see Keppler, 'Fighting of the I SS Panzer Corps in Northern France'.

16. 'G-2 Journal: Third Armored Division', NA, RG-407, 603-2.2, Box 12255, 6 September.

17. 'Message: September 2, 1944, NA, RG-407, 607-2.2, VII Corps G-2 Journal and file, Box 3287'. For the perspective of Joseph Andlinger, who was captured near Lechateau on 1 September 1944, see covert surveillance on 6–8 March 1945 at Fort Hunt: NARA, RG 165, Entry 179B, Box 441.

18. Recorded conversation of Wilhelm Freisser with Hauswirth, 4 March 1945, NARA, RG-165, Entry 179B, Box 467. In captivity Freisser was amazed at the quantity of food—particularly *Kartoffeln*. 'We may invent the Jet Turbine Fighter,' Freisser joked, 'but the Americans will likely invent an automatic potato peeler.'

19. Waldmüller and Untersturmführer Karl Marquart rode in a motorcycle with a sidecar and driver on a stretch of road in the Ardennes between Werbomont and Stavelot. In the deep woods near Basse Bodeux the French resistance fighters pulled a cable across the road, throwing Waldmüller and the driver from the motorcycle. Marquart in the sidecar was shot through the head, and the driver was found nearby

and badly wounded. Waldmüller was only located later after having been stabbed, mutilated and dumped in a small nearby lake. Hubert Meyer, *The History of the 12.SS-Panzerdivision Hitlerjugend*, pp. 221–222.

20. Abschrift 12 SS Pz Div. Hitlerjugend, Pz Art Rgt 12, Regiments-Sonderbefehl über das Verhalten gegen Terroristen, Rgt Gef. Std. 6 September 1944, BA-MA, M-854, 12.SS-Pz.Div. Hitlerjugend. Signed by SS Obstuf. Oskar Drexler. In another order, evidently from the I SS Panzer Corps on 3 September: 'It has happened … that German soldiers were fired at and wounded by civilians. Terrorists are to be killed. All houses from which fire was delivered, or weapons are found are to be recklessly burned.' Report from 347th Inf. Division, 1st Inf Div, G-2 Report, 8 September 1944, RG 407, 101.13.

21. Kurt Meyer, *Grenadiers*, p. 300. In his unexpunged autobiography Meyer anticipated post-war criticism for his troops' actions in late August and September: 'The "glorious" fight of the so-called partisans was nothing more than mean, common murder. The originators of partisan war were the real war criminals of that war … the so called partisans only raised their heads when they did not have to fear for their own bodies and lives … Seen from a military point of view, the actions of partisans did not have any influence on the German conduct of war. The population that was not involved suffered the most harm as a result of the retaliations of German troops … The hatred between the nations was stirred according to plan.' A good number of the mixed SS troops along the Meuse were from the 3rd Battalion, SS Panzer Grenadier Regiment 4 (*Der Führer*) of the 2nd SS Panzer Division, which made their headquarters in Mesnil-Saint-Blaise east of the river. Kampgruppe Mohnke consisted of Schrott's II Battalion, SS Panzer Grenadier Regiment 25 and Siebken's II Battalion, SS Panzer Grenadier Regiment 26.

22. By 5 September the I SS Panzer Corps would report to Army Group G that the strength of their four assigned divisions (1st SS, 2nd SS, 12th SS and 2nd Panzer Division) now totalled no more than a thousand combat effectives and four tanks—an accounting that may have been pessimistic but still showed the fundamental weakness. Headquarters, Army Group G, Operations Section, 5 September 1944, BA-MA, RH 19 IV/55.

23. William I. Hitchcock, *The Bitter Road to Freedom* (New York: Free Press, 2008), p. 63. The author's source is Commission de Crimes de Guerre of the Belgian government, with reports covering civilian testimony: CEGES, AA 120, VII, 1 and 1bis; index to this series: www.cegesoma. be/docs/Invent/AA_120_CommissieOorlogsmisdaden.pdf.

24. Records of G-2, 9th Infantry Division, NARA, RG 407, 309-2.1, G-2 Journal and File, Box 6346. On 4 September civilians reported seventeen houses in Profondeville burned.
25. Records of G-2, 9th Infantry Division, 4–5 September: 'Repulse [of Meuse crossing] was orchestrated by 88mm guns, some SPWs with flame-throwers and SPWs with mortars—all SS equipment.' Along the Meuse River line both the 12th SS and 2nd SS Divisions were identified. In later investigations elements of SS Panzer Grenadier Regiment 25 were accused of committing war crimes near Godinne.
26. 'Enemy Situation at End of Period: G-2 Periodic Report No. 52', 5 September, U.S. 9th Infantry Division, NARA, RG 407, 309-2.1, G-2 Journal and File, Box 6346. See also G-2 Records (101-2.2) of FUSA, Box 1408: Conversations overhead in the PW Cage on 7 September: Army PW: 'Look at those [redacted] from the SS. As usual they always want to be the first on the trip backwards.' SS man: 'Ignore those deserting Army Swine. They know damned well that they can thank the SS if Germany today is still free from the Bolshevik and Jewish carpet baggers.' Army: 'Thank you like hell. We can thank you for the fact that because of you the French population is throwing rocks at us now as we pass by.' VII Corps G-2 Report for 8 September 1944: 'All reinforcements go to the SS and stragglers are collected and under SS control … army troops do the fighting while the SS hold a gun in their backs.' 'U.S. First Army G-2 Records', NA, RG-407, 101-2.2, 8 September 1944, Box 1408.
27. 'G-2 Journal: Third Armored Division', NA, RG-407, 603-2.2, Box 12255, 6 September. 'Germans in the woods around K857120'.
28. After the war the Sovet, Belgium, atrocity loomed large enough concern in Allied war crime investigations that Kurt Meyer was suspected as he was taken prisoner two days later in a chicken coup in Spontin, near Ciney, just south-east of Sovet and not far from Anhée, where a maelstrom of shootings took place. 'Subject: General Kurt Meyer', 24 July 1946, PRO: WO 311/691, BOAR/3796/90/A. Thanks to Carol Byrne for alerting me to this source.
29. Testimony of Maurice Crickx: Rapport historique concernant des crimes commis en septembre 1944 à Verdenne, Marenne et Marche-en-Famenne (CEGE SOMA AA 120/A/IX/2/26). Thanks to Simon Vosters.
30. Westemeier, *Himmlers Krieger*, p. 316. Westemeier's findings are based on examination of previously unexamined records of the 12th SS Panzer Division held at the military archives VHA in Prague. For the war crimes at Odet, see *Les Crimes de Guerre commis lors de la*

libération du territoire national Septembre 1944, Région de Dinant (Liège: Georges Thones, 1946), pp. 13–19. See also '1st Infantry Division G-2 Records', NARA, RG-407, 101.-2.2, 8 September 1944.

31. On 1 September Obersturmführer Rink was in Charleroi when he received orders to form a battle group around his 2nd Battalion of the SS Panzer Grenadier Regiment 1 with other elements. Initial strength was 120 men, two 75mm SP guns and six SPWs. His unit fought a series of delaying actions near Fleurus north-east of Charleroi and in Belgium at Ohey west of Dinant and Modave and Wibrin. On 8 September Kampfgruppe Rink was ordered to re-join Kampfgruppe Diefenthal, assembling in the region of Vaux Chavanne in the Ardennes and, after fighting against Belgian resistance fighters near Nadrin on 11 September, eventually pulled east towards the German border near Trois Vierges the following day, crossing the German border near Burg Reuland. NARA, RG 407, G-2 records of 9th Infantry Division, Box 6346. Rink's Kampfgruppe moved via Charleroi (1 September), Fleurus–Gembloux–Éghezée–Huy–Ohey (7 September), Modave–Ouffet (8 September), area Vaux-Chavanne (9–10 September), area Houffalize–Nadrin–Wibrin–north of Bastogne (11 September), Limerlé and Troisvierges, (12 September), Oudler–Burg Reuland–Vianden. They were in the Ohey–Modave area protecting the Meuse riverfront, with elements of the Deutschland regiment (2nd SS Panzer Division) on their left flank. When units of the 3rd Armoured Division started to advance towards Huy on 6 September, they probably started to make contact with Rink's men, who became temporarily attached to Kampfgruppe Milius in the Modave area after Milius's men had retreated from the Meuse River.

32. Keppler, 'Fighting of the I SS Panzer Corps in Northern France', 4 September. See also Roge and Helmuth Reinhardt, 'The FFI Before and After D-Day', NARA, RG-338, FMS, B-035, 14 October 1950.

33. Kriegstagebuch der Heerresgruppe B, 1–30 September 1944, 4 and 8 September 1944, BAMA.

34. 'Message from VII Corps G-2, Journal File', September 2 1944, U.S. VII Corps G-2 Journal Files', NA, RG-407, 607-2.2, Box 3287.

35. Junker Diary, 31 August–September 1944. For the 'battle at Rocourt', see Peter Taghon, *Belgique 44*, pp. 179–182. Junker would later be court-martialed for the event for which he was blamed.

36. Adolph G. Rosengarten Jr., 'With Ultra from Omaha Beach to Weimar, Germany—A Personal View', *Military Affairs* 42, no. 3 (October 1978), pp. 127–133.

37. 'Message from VII Corps G-2', September 2 1944, U.S. VII Corps G-2 Journal Files, NA, RG-407, 607-2.2, Box 3287. 'Prisoner reports SS HQ at Philippeville [HQ of 2.SS-Pz.Division] with multiple SS units assembling in Couvins prior to departure for Liège'. The declared staging point the previous day from additional prisoners had been Hirson.

38. 'G-2 Records for U.S. 3rd Armored Division', 103-2.13, Box 12258, 6–7 September 1944. On 6 September 1944 PWs reported that elements of the 2nd SS Panzer Division made their headquarters in the town of Celles just east of Dinant. The headquarters of the 12th SS (less Kampgruppe Milius) reached the village of Wanne in Belgium on 8 September and pulled back to Plettenberg, Germany, east of the Rhine three days later.

39. 'U.S. First Army G-2 Records', NA, RG-407, 101-2.2, 9 September 1944, Box 1408. Major General Konrad Heinrichs, commander of 89th Infantry Division, was killed on the night of 7–8 September trying to pass a roadblock north-east of Liège as the U.S. 3rd Armoured Division surged towards the German border.

40. On Himmler's condemnation of SS surrender, see Karl-Günther Zelle, *Hitlers zweifelnde Elite* (Paderborn: Schöningh Verlag, 2010), p. 209. For Peiper's 'last round is for yourself', see Schramm, 'Der siebenteTag'.

41. 'Report of SS-Sgt. Karl Heinz Beckert', taken prisoner on 31 August 1944 at Rosoy-sur-Serre; report from 4 September, 'U.S. First Army G-2 Records', NA, RG-407, 101-2.2, September 1944, Box 1407.

42. 'U.S. First Army G-2 Records', NA, RG-407, 101-2.2, 9 September 1944, Box 1408.

43. Michael J. Neufeld, *The Rocket and the Reich: Pennemunde and the Coming of the Ballistic Missle Era* (New York: Free Press, 1994), pp. 287–295. As most Allied fighters were faster than the V-1s, the British soon learned that they could be shot down in the ten minutes over the English Channel before the AA and barrage balloon defences were reached over south London. Of the 4,361 V-1s launched at London in the first month of the robot bomb attack, some 1,240 were shot down and barely three in ten of those launched reached the target area. Although Hitler's propaganda minister, Joseph Goebbels, claimed on 10 July 1944 that life in London was irreparably harmed, with large communities destroyed, the actual damage was comparatively slight, although the 'doodlebugs' remained a dangerous nuisance (Tagebuch Joseph Goebbels, entry for 7 October 1944). As the invasion continued on and the bombing of Germany increased,

Hitler's public began to realize that the V-1 had failed expectations. On the streets some whispered of it as the *Versager-1* (Failure No. 1). Even so, the bombs and rockets killed an estimated nine thousand civilians (most in London, Antwerp and Liège). An additional twelve thousand forced labourers at Mittelbau-Dora perished in the production of the V-2 rocket weapons.

44. OB West, Operations Section, BA-MA, RH 19/IV 55, Nr. 805/44, 7 September 1944. Von Runstedt, who had recently been recalled by Hitler to command, recommended to army high command that at least five fresh divisions should be immediately brought up to the Westwall behind the Ardennes.

45. 'U.S. First Army G-2 Records: Secret Ciropearl Report for 10 September: Elmts 4 SS PGR', NA, RG-407, 101-2.2, 10 September 1944, Box 1408. The 3rd Battalion of the SS Panzer Grenadier Regiment 4 radioed a total counted strength of 299, with a single Mk V Panther tank, coming to its headquarters at Aywaille on 9 September. The unit would move to the area between Manderfeld and Krewinkel on the Belgian–German border on 12 September 1944.

46. Recollection of SS battle group commander Herbert Rink, Tiemann, *Chronicle of the 7. Panzerkompanie*, p. 238. Rink's small battle group, built around remainders of SS Panzer Grenadier Regiment 1, was assigned to the Westwall sector in the Eifel from Dasburg to Sevenig with the 81 Army Corps.

47. Erich Brandenberger, Northern France, vol X: 7th Army, 1–20 September 1944, MS-730, NA, RG-549, FMS.

48. 'Die eisernen Särge', *Das Schwarze Korps*, 10 February 1944.

49. 'But in the flow of combat, even the most courageous one may have the misfortune to fall into the hands of the enemy alive. For him, the oath to the flag is binding when one is a prisoner and obligates him to continued full endeavour for his Fatherland. International law requires that no force can be exerted on a prisoner of war to make him give information about the troops to which he belongs or their country. If the enemy threatens, the honour of the German soldier requires him to maintain a dignified position against threats and bad treatment. Give only rank, name, place and date of birth and place of residence ... Decline to answer any other questions because in all cases it is of use to the enemy and can endanger the life of comrades, constitutes treason and after the end of the war will be seriously punished.' 'Verhalten als Kriegsgefangener: Anlage zu Gen. Kdo I. SS Pz Korps', 27 May 1944, T-354, R604, 00458.

50. For the Hitlerjugend Division, Hubert Meyer gives an incomplete list of 8,626 casualties. Hubert Meyer, *The History of the 12.SS-Panzerdivision Hitlerjugend*, p. 222. The Leibstandarte had lost at least five thousand men in Normandy and likely closer to six thousand—about 30 per cent of their strength of twenty-two thousand on 1 June 1944. See Lehmann and Tiemann, *Die Leibstandarte*, vol. IV/1, p. 228. The U.S. 3rd Armoured Division evaluated the losses to the Leibstandarte that they faced from compiled PoW interrogations. They noted on 17–18 August that 3rd Company of SS Panzer Grenadier Regiment 2 was wiped out, with the leftovers from 10, 11th and 12th companies formed into a single battle group, and the SS Panzer Grenadier Regiment 1 formed into a combat team of approximately 164 men: 3rd Armoured Division G-2 Records, NA, RG-407, 603-2.1, Box 12252.
51. For the capture of Max Wünsche: Interview with Georg Isecke, courtesy of Duward Massey. See also PRO WO 208/4139. Wünsche went to Great Britain as a POW, to be released in 1948.
52. Wünsche, interview with John Toland, 3 November 1971, LOC. 'At the [English] hospital where I was for several months, I was treated very well. There in the hospital, I met U.S. and British pilots recovering from wounds. "You are a slave and we are slaves, so we are friends."' For more background on Wünsche's capture and interrogation, I am grateful to Carol Byrne. See also Hubert Meyer, *History of the 12th SS Panzer Division*, p. 115.
53. 'Morale in the Waffen SS: KP/55201 Ostubaf. Wünsche', 9 September 1944, CSDIC (UK) SIR 933, Combined Services Detailed Interrogation Service, RG 338, Box 4. After the war Wünsche described his perspective to John Toland in less-than-apologetic tones: 'I was very idealistic, and I did the job working for Hitler with great pleasure. I was convinced of the historical greatness of that time. I recognized that he was a very important person for Germany. I was convinced that except for him, there would be Bolshevism in Germany. But a great number of mistakes were made that could not be forecast ... Perhaps we won the early battles too easily and did not suspect the hard fighting that was ahead.' LOC, Interview, 3 November 1971.
54. H.R. Trevor Roper, ed., *The Bormann Letters* (London: Weidenfeld & Nichols, 1954), p. 90. Bormann's wife, Gerda, was a true believer, as evidenced in her response on 29 August: 'I can't get it into my head that Wünsche is no longer alive. I hadn't been worrying about him although he was in the front line all of the time. It seemed to me that he was absolutely necessary for the future reconstruction, so I believed that Destiny would have to preserve him. Perhaps it isn't

true after all and he will fight his way through again or be rescued by his comrades … Every word the Führer spoke during the years of our hardest struggle goes round and round in my head again. "If I saw the future completely black I wouldn't go on fighting," he said in December 1924 when he was sitting around our tiled stove and it is the same now. Whenever you say the Führer is well, it is better than any other important news.'

55. 'Washington urged that he [Wünsche] be exchanged. Important reasons why he should not be—war criminal. Colonel Starr, 2 December 1944; Bissel letter to me, re Wash. cables, that he not be repatriated.' CSDIC (UK) 905, 'Notes on Hitler: information obtained from Ostubaf. Wünsche,' NA: RG 226, Entry 190, Box 743, courtesy of Richard Breitman review of material declassified under the Nazi War Crimes Disclosure Act, October 2000. SS General Karl Wolff continued diplomatic feelers with the British to try to arrange to have Wünsche freed in a prisoner exchange. As late as 4 April 1945 Wolff reported to Himmler that he was pursuing an exchange of British secret agent 'Tucker' for Max Wünsche as a birthday present for Hitler on 20 April. 'Operation Sunrise', 4 April 1945, NA, Records of the Central Intelligence Agency, RG 263, File: CIA- RDP78T03194A000200010001-2, p. 90, Declassified 13 April 2005.

56. Astrid Hommert and Charlotte Zimmermann, interviews with author, 17 August 2003.

57. Peiper to Ernst Klink, 1 April 1975, BA-MA, Klink Papers.

58. Years after the war Peiper still complained bitterly about the failure in Normandy. Peiper to Heinz Stuttecker, as related in Stuttecker, interview with author, 28 February 2009.

59. 'Panzergruppe Eberbach bei Alençon und beim Durchbruch aus dem Kessel von Falaise', BA-MA 20/7/149.

60. Kraemer, 'I SS Pz Corps in the West in 1944'.

61. For the training course, see Richard Schulze Kossens, *Militärischer Führernachwuchs der Waffen SS: Die Junkerschulen* (Coburg: Nation Europa Verlag, 1999), p. 312.

62. 'Interrogation of SS Major General Kurt Meyer', no date, German Generals Collection, Liddell Hart Papers, King's College, London. The interviewer's commentary on Meyer: 'As he described his actions and those of his men, it seemed as though he liked to consider himself as Siegfried leading his warriors to their death.'

63. Shulman, *Defeat in the West*, p. 314. Shulman interviewed Meyer in July 1945.

64. Francine Vico was surprised and much relieved to later learn that her husband, Roland, survived Mauthhausen concentration camp— particularly given its ghastly reputation. Jacques and Jean-Marie Vico ended their fight with de Gaulle and the Free French at the end of the war. Jacques Vico, detailed interview with author, Abbaye d'Ardennes, 8 July 2002. See also Campbell, *Murder at the Abbaye*.
65. *Nazi Conspiracy and Aggression* (Washington D.C.: U.S. Government Printing Office, 1946), vol. 2, p. 229. 2997-PS, 'Supplementary Report of Supreme Headquarters, Allied Expeditionary Force, Court of Inquiry, concerning the shooting of Allied Prisoners of War in Normandy, France', vol. V, p. 677.
66. Although there was little denying that the Canadians prisoners had been shot—a point Meyer grudgingly acknowledged—there was only circumstantial evidence to establish the culpability of the SS leader in ordering their execution. The charges that stuck were those charging him with inspiring others in the Hitlerjugend Division to deny any quarter for the enemy. See MacDonald, *The Trial of Kurt Meyer*. For the SS officer's self-serving account: Kurt Meyer, *Grenadiers*, pp. 354–368.
67. MacDonald, *The Trial of Kurt Meyer*, p. 193.
68. Harry Foster to son Tony Foster in 1958; Foster, *Meeting of the Generals*, p. xxiii.
69. 'Should losing generals be hanged?' This was the question Canadian authorities struggled with after his death sentence. In fact, Kurt Meyer was almost executed by a firing squad on 7 January 1946, but was given a last-minute reprieve after an appeal by his wife moved Canadian General Chris Vokes to commute his sentence to life imprisonment. The key point was that there was not any evidence that Meyer himself had ordered the prisoners shot at the abbey. This outraged many Canadian citizens; Meyer was brought in secrecy to Dorchester Penitentiary in New Brunswick. Serving his sentence with common Canadian criminals, Meyer made a positive impression in his work at the prison library. He learned English and made friends among lawyers in Halifax, who looked to have him freed. Eventually Meyer was returned to Germany to serve the remainder of his sentence at Werl Prison. There his sentence was further commuted, and he was released on 7 September 1954. Foster, *Meeting of the Generals*, pp. 484–511.
70. Even today the locals around Stavelot, Belgium, describe this incident with pride. Author's anonymous interviews 1996–1997.
71. '4th Cavalry Message to VII Corps G-2', 10 September 1944, U.S. VII Corps G-2 Journal Files,' NA, RG-407, 607-2.2, Box 3287. German

stragglers out of contact with their units were being pointed to assemble in Aachen.

72. Jeannine Goffin-Kalbusch, interview with author, La Gleize, 29 March 1996. Around 10 September the Germans had killed a father and son in La Gleize who were well-known members of the Belgian resistance (Monsieur Becker) who had unwisely planted American flags in the windows of their home, anticipating the liberation by the Americans.

73. Gerard Gregoire, interview with author, 28 March 1996. The Belgians remained in the cellar after the Germans left, to be liberated a day later.

74. 'SHAEF Intelligence Summary No. 22 of 19 August', Headquarters 12th Army Group, SHAEF War Diaries, NA, RG-331, Entry 176, Box 40.

75. War Diary of General Courtney Hodges, Major William C. Sylvan, Wednesday, 6 September 1944.

76. Ellis, *Victory in the West*, vol. II, p. 55.

77. Hodges largely halted the U.S. First Army on 10 September, even though the Germans were poorly organized before him. His hesitation over the following week came from a critical lack of ammunition and fuel as well as the fact that armoured battalions were in poor repair—many at only thirty per cent of established strength after crossing the length of France. The delay proved critical for the Germans on the Western Front, as fresh forces arrived with which to man the Westwall line.

78. '28th Inf. Div. G-2 Records', September 1944, NA, RG-407, 328-2.3, Box 7386.

79. An interview with General Lieutenant Fritz Bayerlein, 'Critique of the Normandy Breakthrough', NARA, RG-549, FMS, ETHINT 67, August 15, 1945. For German losses, see Robert J. Kershaw, *It Never Snows in September* (New York: Ian Allan, 1990), p. 14.

80. For the briefing of Hitler and OKW to Generalfeldmarschal Von Rundstedt between 1 and 3 September: General Lieutenant Bodo Zimmermann, 'OB West: Command Relationships', NA, RG-549, FMS, MS-B-308.

81. Zimmermann, 'OB West: Command Relationships'. On 5 September Von Rundstedt assumed command of OB West as the supreme field commander in the West.

82. 'He is in contact with me daily by telephone.' For Martin Bormann to Gerda Bormann on 3 September 1944: H. Trevor Roper, ed., *The Bormann Letters* (London: Weidenfeld and Nicholson, 1954). In many of the period letters Gerda Bormann tells her husband that

'Uncle Heinrich's' mistress in the Obersalzberg and their neighbour, Hedwig Potthast, was now very comfortable at their new home with his two children out of wedlock. See also Peter Longerich, *Heinrich Himmler: A Biography* (New York: Oxford University Press, 2012), p. 711. By mid-month the replacement army had sent more than 160,000 stragglers back to the German front lines along the Westwall— an accomplishment that figured large in the sudden resilience of German lines along the border by October 1944.

83. 'Tactical Echelon: 30 August–6 September 1944', U.S. First Army G-2 Records, 101-2.2, Box 1476.

84. Tiemann, *Chronicle of the 7. Panzerkompanie*, p. 110.

85. 'Falaise to Geber', narrative by Manfred Thorn, prepared for author, 1 February 2018.

86. Redecker, 'Die Lötlampe, 1943'.

87. 'U.S. First Army G-2 Records', NA, RG-407, 101-2.2, 6 September 1944, Box 1407.

88. 'U.S. First Army G-2 Records: PW Interrogations', NA, RG-407, 101-2.2, 8 September 1944, Box 1408; also, General Lieutenant Hugo Seemueller, 'Medical Comments on "Stomach" Units', NARA, RG-338, FMS, MS B-275.

89. Staatsanwaltschaft Flensburg 2 Js 437/56 AR 491/66, now on file at Bundesarchiv Ludwigsburg 124 AR 491/1966. Peiper's testimony about Leibstandarte replacements in 1944 from 30 July 1956.

90. Extract from Jodl's diary: Warlimont, *Inside Hitler's Headquarters*, p. 457.

91. *Aus den Tagebüchern von Joseph Goebbels seine unterredungen mit Adolf Hitler*, 23 August 1944, p. 455.

92. 'Until we get a peace that will secure the life of the German nation for the next 50 to 100 years': Max Domarus, *Hitler: Speeches and Proclamations, 1932–1945*, vol. IV (Wauconda, IL: Bolchazy-Carducci Publishers, 2004), p. 2946.

93. SS Gruppenführer Karl Gebhardt to Himmler, 5 September 1944, BA-Lichterfelde, R19/ 751. Folder 4.

94. Kurt Meyer, *Grenadiers*, p. 297. Yet Meyer soon worried of German prospects: 'If Bolshevism triumphs today, then it will be a question of the biological annihilation of our people.' This came from a surreptitious taping of Meyer speaking with Gen. Dietrich von Choltitz at Trent Park, CSDIC (UK), 18–20 February 1945, GRGG 262, PRO: WO 208/4177.

95. Elke M., Letter to author, 15 July 2017. In one of the bicycle trips in the autumn of 1944 Sigurd took four-year-old Elke along on the

bicycle to see her father. For Jochen Peiper's statement: 'During six bloody years I fought and bled in all European Theatres and became a preferred favorite of the God of Hosts! In spite of it all—it was proud and heroic time. Where we were standing was Germany and as far as my tank gun reached was my kingdom! We had no personal aspirations! Our vision always has been the "Dream of the Reich".' Peiper to Willis Everett, 14 July 1946, Everett Papers, letter in author's possession.

Chapter 22: P.O. Box 1142

1. This incident is covered extensively in the author's detailed treatment: Danny S. Parker, *Fatal Crossroads: The Untold Story of the Malmédy Massacre* (Cambridge, MA: DaCapo Books, 2011).
2. Pam Fessler, 'Former GIs Spill Secrets of WWII POW Camp', National Public Radio, 18 August 2008. See also Matthew Laird, *By the River Potomac: An Historic Resource Study of Fort Hunt Park* (Mt Vernon, VA: National Park Service, 2013).
3. Beyond Werner von Braun, Operation Paperclip included many rocket scientists who were prominent in the U.S. space programme in the 1950s through to the 1970s, including Kurt Debus, Arthur Rudolf, Ernst Geissler, Ernst Steinoff and Hubertus Strughold. However, most of these men were not without blemish relative to their roles in Hitler's Third Reich—in particular Rudolf and Strughold—and Paperclip even brought over odious scientists such as Dr Otto Ambros, who had worked at Auschwitz but was retained for the CIA as a nerve gas specialist. See Annie Jacobsen, *Operation Paperclip: The Secret Intelligence Program to Bring Nazi Scientists to America* (New York: Little, Brown and Co., 2014).
4. 'During the many interrogations, I never laid hands on anyone,' remembered George Frenkel. 'We extracted information in a battle of wits. I'm proud to say I never compromised my humanity.' Fessler, 'Former GIs Spill Secrets of WWII POW Camp'.
5. 'The Hidden History of PO Box 1142', Michael Lee Pope, *Northern Virginia Magazine*, 4 October 2016.
6. Interrogation files for LSSAH men: Peter Lantschner and Wilhelm Reichert, NARA, RG 165, Entry 179A, Boxes 506 and 530, interrogations on 13 and 3 March 1945, respectively.
7. File for Max Ketterer, NARA, RG 165, Entry 179B, Box 496. The author is not willing to repeat particulars of the sadistic episodes that Ketterer related to interrogators.

8. File for Georg Blunder, NARA, RG 165, Entry 179B, Box 450.
9. Peupelmann, Heinz, NARA, RG 165, Entry 179B, Box 525, 21–26 April 1945. *'Peiper in Russland deh Befehl gab, das keine Gefangene gemacht warden, dieser nie Gefangene abstransportieren liess, sonder sie erschoss.'*
10. 'Report of the Supreme Headquarters Allied Expeditionary Force Court of Inquiry re Shooting of Allied Prisoners of War by the German Armed Forces near Malmédy, Liege, Belgium, 17 December 1944', 13 January 1945, NARA, RG 331, Entry 46, Box 127.
11. These numerous screening interrogations in the various PoW camps around the United States conducted by a roving team from P.O. Box 1142 can be seen in RG 153, War Crimes Cases Tried, Case 6-24, Boxes 71 and 75.
12. SS Obersturmführer Sepp Salmutter, previously with the 2nd SS Panzer Division, was being utilized, although there were some questions of his trustworthiness even though he was a deserter. 'Memorandum to Capt. Holbrook, P/Ws Working as Trustees', 31 January 1946, NARA, RG 165, Entry 179B, Box 502.
13. Harsch, Anton, NARA, RG 165, Entry 179B, Box 479, 18 February 1946; also Hoffmann, Ewald, in Box 486. It is possible that Fritz Reuss may have been referring to U.S. paratroopers captured and then executed along the road to Petit-Spai near Trois Ponts on the afternoon of 21 December by elements of the 1st SS Panzer Reconnaissance Battalion. See Timo Worst, *Career, Crimes and Trial of SS Sturmbannführer Gustav Knittel* (self-published, 2016), p. 392.
14. Grimberg, Helmut, NARA, RG 165, Entry 179B, Box 475. Grimberg to Heeke: 'We have no reason to be afraid as we have done no war crimes.'
15. 'We reached Stavelot the evening of the same day' on 17 December 1944, said Braun, who then would be made prisoner in that town on 21 December. Braun, Willi, NARA, RG 165, Records of the War Department General and Special Staffs, Entry 179B, Box 453.
16. 'Sworn Testimony of Helmuth Haas', at Ft. Knox, KY, 27 February 1946, to Paul E. Custer and Lt. Youkstetter, NARA, RG 153, War Crimes Cases Tried, Case 6-24, Box 71.
17. Testimony of Herbert Haeusgen, 5 March 1946, Camp Forrest, Capt. Paul E. Custer and Frederick S. Youkstetter, NARA, RG 153, War Crimes Cases Tried, Case 6-24, Box 71. The testimony of Otto Burckhardt in which he denies seeing the massacre field is in the same location and was taken on the same date. Haeusgen directly contradicts Burckhardt, who had personally related to him of coming

across the field with the numerous dead Americans. For the guilt of Helmuth Haas, see Parker, *Fatal Crossroads*, pp. 133–136.

18. Hartig, Lothar, NARA, RG 165, Entry 179B, Box 480, 5 March 1946. Hartig, a native of Chemnitz-Altendorf, had been 18 at the time of the Ardennes Offensive. A Hitler Youth during the early years of the war, he became a member of the NSDAP on 1 May 1944 and joined the Leibstandarte that August during the retreat from France. Taken prisoner on Christmas Eve in 1944, he was eventually sent to the United States from Le Harve on 8 February 1945, arriving in New York to shuttle from Camp Forrest in Tennessee to Camp Rucker in Alabama to Camp Shelby in Mississippi before being sent to Fort Hunt.

19. Kappermann, Heinz, NARA, RG 165, Records of the War Department General and Special Staffs, Entry 179B, Box 493. Kappermann was determined to be a key witness and was kept at P.O. Box 1142 for an extended time. He was assigned to a room with Franz Hekl, also with the Leibstandarte (6th Company, SS Panzer Grenadier Regiment 2) on 18–20 February 1946. Later he roomed with Willi Braun and Lothar Hartig, who also both knew about the incident, in 21A from 27 February–5 March. Franz Hekl's file is in Box 481. 'I cannot say whether the *Strafgruppe* of my company received orders from the company commander to shoot the American soldiers.' In overheard conversation with Franz Hekl on 18 February 1946 Kappermann told Hekl of deeply regretting the shooting of the American prisoners. 'I told the interrogating officer everything I knew.' For context of Kappermann's account, see Parker, *Fatal Crossroads*, pp. 130–132.

20. Kappermann statement, 26 February 1946: both transcribed statement in German as well as translation and original pencilled drawings are included in the file in Box 493.

21. 'I recall that an engineer unit proceeded in front of us and the armoured regiment in front of that unit.' Fritz Wesch, SS Sturmann with 12th Panzer Grenadier Company, was captured in La Gleize on 23 December after having been wounded on 18 December 1944. Wesch joined the Leibstandarte in May 1944 in Belgium. NARA, RG 165, Entry 179B, Box 559, testimony of 2–3 April 1946.

22. 'Testimony of German Prisoner of War, Fritz Wesch', Fort Knox, KY, to Capt. Paul E. Custer with qst Lt. Frederick S. Youkstetter from P.O. Box 1142, NARA, RG 153, War Crime Cases Tried, Case 6-24, Box 71. Wesch ventured that there were at least seventy tanks and perhaps twenty to twenty-five halftracks associated with the Panzer engineers ahead of his company at the time they came across the massacre field—'an exceedingly bad deed'.

23. Testimony of Morris Ellowitz on 22 April 1949, Malmédy Massacre Investigation Hearings before a Subcommittee on the Armed Services, U.S. Senate, 81st Congress (Washington D.C.: U.S. Government Printing Office, 1949), pp. 132–133.
24. A simple stone monument is the only remaining landmark for P.O. Box 1142.

Epilogue

1. Special Agent Richard C. Lang, 1st CIC Detachment, U.S. 1st Infantry Division, interview with author, 3 February 1999. Lang and his interpreter, John M. Centner, were investigators at Langwasser. The place was raw—something like a Wild West for twilight National Socialists. Clouds of DDT hovered over the camp to control head lice, and beyond twilight mayhem reigned. 'Every night they were killing each other,' Centner remembered. Many of these were concentration camp guards killing off those they knew could be important witnesses against them. After sunrise Lang and Centner would find the bodies laying out in the street between the facilities or sprawled in the trench latrines, strangled with strands of barbed wire. 'It was a dangerous place.' John Marie Centner, interview with author, 25 December 2001.
2. 'Preliminary Interrogation Report: Peiper, Joachim, AIC 1807', Headquarters Third U.S. Army Intelligence Centre, 24 August 1945, NA, RG 319, CIC Files, Records on J. Peiper.
3. Peiper's direct testimony during the trial in his own defence, paper copy of trial record, R1885, NA, Case 6-24, RG 153, Box 73. Also, RG 153, Roll 2, Frame 000107-88.
4. Dwight Fanton, interview with author, 27 January 1997. On Peiper: 'He was a very personable individual, and you could not help but admire him as a person. On the other side, he was a dedicated Nazi. I interviewed him early on in August 1945 and then saw him later in the trial. He never changed at all.'
5. 'Affidavit: Joachim Peiper', 5 June 1948, Landsberg/Lech, Case 6-24, NA, RG-549, Box 60. 'As adjutant to Himmler I'm supposed to have been the only one who kept his personal integrity.' Peiper claimed the report of American Major McCown would reveal his proper behaviour during the Ardennes Offensive.
6. 'In Freising, Mr. Paul informed me as follows': Peiper testimony, Ellis Papers, no date. 'In view of the hopeless situation, I am prepared to admit all charges. It is my duty to save decent fellows by taking

the blame of the incident upon myself. Otherwise to save face and die as a soldier.' Peiper refers to the initial article about him: 'GI's No. 1 War Criminal Seized—CO of Malmédy Murders', *Stars & Stripes*, 20 August 1945. 'Peiper has been the object of an intense search by the whole U.S. Army, which has been relentlessly investigating the Malmédy slayings as the biggest atrocity of the war.'

7. Fanton, interview with author, 27 January 1997; also Fanton testimony on 5 May 1949, Malmedy Massacre Investigation Heatings, 1949, Subcommittee on Armed Services, U.S. Senate (Washington, DC: U.S. Government Printing Office, September 1949) (hereafter MMIH), p. 279.

8. 'An Interview with Joachim Peiper, 1 SS Pz Regt: ETHINT-10', 7 September 1945, Freising, Germany, NA, RG-549, Foreign Military Studies. Burton Ellis would later claim that Peiper prepared a seventy-page operations analysis of his participation in the Ardennes Offensive at Freising on 25 and 26 August 1945, although this document was never found, even during later deliberations for the Senate investigations and numerous trial reviews (see Royce L. Thompson, 'The ETO Ardennes Campaign, Operations of the Combat Group Peiper, 16–26 December 1944', OCMH, Washington D.C., 24 July 1952). The Freising interrogation was, however, extensively quoted within the trial itself: *U.S. v. Bersin et al.*, 1946, Case 6-24, War Crimes Cases Tried, NA, RG-549, pp. 2532–2547. A long effort by the author to locate this document was unsuccessful.

9. Ken Hechler, interview with author, 15 December 1994. Hechler would later become a congressman and secretary of state for West Virginia.

10. PRO: WO 208/4517: Karl Wolff: CSDIC/CMF/X 189: 9 July 1945, conversation with Dr Leyers. 'You are an optimist, sir. I think we shall be banished a la Napoleon!'

11. PRO: WO 208/4169, SRGG 1125: Meyer on 27 January 1945: 'In my opinion, the Führer hasn't been quite himself since the winter of 1941–1942, as a result of all the happenings ... Despite all that he achieved ... even if the whole Reich collapses once more, he is responsible for a tremendous awakening in the German people; he gave them back their self-confidence.' For Meyer's lecture to the demoralized German army officer: PRO: WO/4168, 19 February 1945.

12. PRO: WO/208/4139, 'Interrogation with Kurt Meyer', CSDIC (UK) SRM 1022, CS/648, 15 November 1944.

13. 'General Correspondence: 1939–1947, 333.9 Personnel: McCown Hal D., Interrogation of Col. Joachim Peiper, 30 October 1946', NA, RG

159, Entry 26E, Box 531. According to Peiper, McCown jested to him at one point during their long evening chat: 'Well, I guess the war is over on this front for me, so I'll help you fight the Russians.'

14. 'Operation Unthinkable: Russia: Threat to Western Civilization', War Cabinet Joint Planning Staff, report prepared for Winston Churchill, 22 May 1945, PRO: CAB 120/691, Kew, London.

15. 'Operation Unthinkable'. Churchill himself had instructed his staff to undertake the war planning exercise but was unhappy with its prospects, which showed the Soviet ground forces possessing a two-to-one strength advantage. While Churchill had called for a short decisive jab, the report opined that 'there is virtually no limit to the distance which it would be necessary for the Allies to penetrate into Russia in order to render further resistance impossible. It is hardly conceivable that the Allies could penetrate even as far as, or as quickly as the Germans.'

16. 'W.S. Churchill to General Ismay, C.O.S. Committee', 10 June 1945, PRO: CAB 120/691.

17. Kurt Meyer, interview with Shulman, July 1945, Shulman, *Defeat in the West*, pp. 314–315.

18. E.H. Cookridge, *Gehlen: Spy of the Century* (New York: Random House, 1972), pp. 127–128.

19. Ladislas Fargo, Letter to John Toland, 1971, FDR Library, Toland Papers, Box 109. Also see Ladislas Farago, *Patton: Ordeal and Triumph* (New York: Dell, 1963), p. 768. Patton thought Russian war hero Marhshal Georgi Zhukov looked ridiculous with an overweight chest gaudily covered with medals. 'He has a prehensile chin like an ape with good blue eyes.'

20. Patton, the warless warrior, died in a fatal car crash just two months later.

21. For the investigation and trial, see Parker, *Hitler's Warrior*, pp. 147–184.

22. Benoni Junker, *Unter dem Galgen gesungen* (Darmstadt: C.W. Leske, 1954), pp. 5–7.

23. Peiper's entrance information from Landsberg Prison is contained in his CIC file at the National Archives: RG 319, Investigative Repository Reports, 'Records on J. Peiper', no box.

24. Peiper to Lehmann, 14 December 1947, BA-MA. 'On the outside, our women starve in an incredible attitude, while the freed population salutes the coming winter with Cassandra warnings, and you are constructively engaged in maintaining world peace. I enjoy quiet and concentration offered as advantages of my monkish seclusion and observe with fatherly benevolence the camel caravan flowing

towards Damascus. As progress in technology, science, civilization, and other deviant manifestations stand in a direct relationship with the retrogression of humanity, my devolution from homo sapiens to a unicellular being is merely logical. As long as one does not lose one's inner freedom, one gets used to this condition—even though, admittedly,—I rather would sit with you in "La Florence".'

25. Others under the death sentence for Malmédy: Valentin Bersin, Friedel Bode, Paul Zwigart, Hubert Huber and Josef Diefenthal. 'Memorandum for Deputy Judge Advocate, Landsberg Prisoners under Death Sentences', 16 January 1950, Landsberg Records, Box 6.

26. 'Im Krieg ist es so, wär die Gewalt hat, hat das Recht und er kann damit tun, was er will.' 'During war, he who has might is right.' This quote, freely lifted from the 1890 book *Might is Right*, was invoked by General Major Carl Wahle after his capture in France, where he was asked if he still supported Hitler and believed the wild rumours circulating among his men. 'Yes, there was widespread belief that prisoners of the Americans would be castrated ... If you hear something often enough, you start believing it.' 'U.S. First Army G-2 Records', NA, RG-407, 101-2.2, 6 September 1944, Box 1407.

27. Perry's recollection of his conversation with Peiper in February 1947: MMIH, pp. 935–937.

28. 'General Handy Announces Decision in War Crimes Trial', HQ European Command, Public Information Division, 31 January 1951, Landsberg Files, RG 549, 'Records of Post Trial Activities,' Box 4.

29. General Handy to Major General George P. Hays, 25 March 1952, NA, RG 549, USAREUR Files, General Administration, Box 461.

30. Peiper to Everett, 6 February 1951, Everett Papers. On this same day Sepp Dietrich, the nominal head of the Red Jackets at Landsberg, composed an ornate certificate on parchment that was sent to Willis Everett in Atlanta: 'There is no one among us who would not have a deep and true feeling of gratitude towards you for all the work, the pains and sacrifices that you have borne in the course of 5 long years in order to save us ... May we assure you that we, all through our life will not forget this act of individual person against a world eager to satisfy the spirit of revenge. We do not feel we say too much when stating that the name Everett has become a conception in Germany. A conception representing justice, decency and fairness ... Landsberg, 30th January, 1951 when the last 6 of 43 death sentences of the Malmédy Case were commuted.' Signed Sepp Dietrich, Everett Papers.

31. Elke Peiper, Letter to Charles Whiting, as described in a letter to the author on 29 December 1998.

32. Peiper to Rudolf Lehmann, 4 April 1951.

33. Peiper to Kosmehl, 11 August 1951. 'We were all recently brought up before the so-called Modifications board a month ago ... But you can imagine the result when it takes only ten minutes for careful review of each man. Humanity is deluded.'

34. 'Ex Nazi General Paroled by British After 10 Years', 8 September 1954, NA, RG-319, IRR File for Kurt Meyer, Box 473, XE-013591. See also Kurt Meyer, *Grenadiers*, pp. 390–391. Thanks also to the detailed recollections and photographs of Kurt Meyer Jr in our interview on 28 September 2013.

35. For confirmation that Kurt Meyer did, in fact, return to Normandy, see Gunter d'Alquen, Letter to Hubert Meyer, 12 December 1975, BA-MA, RS/7, vol. 480.

36. Jacques Vico, interview with author, 8 July 2002. See also Ian J. Campbell, interview with Jean-Marie Vico, as given in Campbell, *Murder at the Abbaye*, pp. 171–172. Thanks to Mr Campbell for permission to use his material.

37. Details from Jacques Vico, interview with author, 8 July 2002.

38. Kurt Meyer, *Grenadiers*, p. 392. However, when asked during his captivity about his knowledge of the concentration camps, Meyer said he knew nothing about them—he had been too busy fighting at the front. 'He was then given a detailed description of the frightful treatment given two persons. Meyer listened quietly and did not reply for a few seconds; then, slowly turning, he said, somewhat defiantly, that our soldiers had descended to the mean trick of taking away watches, rings and private papers of his men. When asked if he honestly considered this a reasonable comparison, he offered no reply.' MacDonald, *Trial of Kurt Meyer*, p. 79.

39. See author's detailed treatment of the incident that figured so prominently in Peiper's post-war life: Parker, *Fatal Crossroads*.

40. Enlisted men and NCOs released in 1954: Willi von Chamier, Max Hammerer, Joachim Hoffmann, Friedel Kies, Gustav Neve, Max Rieder, Theo Rauh, Hans Siptrott, Gustav Sprenger, Heinz Stickel, August Tonk, Johann Wassenberg and Paul Zwigart. Officers: Werner Kühn, Hermann Priess, Heinz Rehagel, Erich Rumpf, Dr Kurt Sickel. NA, RG549 Records of Headquarters, U.S. Army Europe, Records Related to Parolee Case Files, 1945–1958.

41. While at Landsberg before his release Hans Siptrott developed a reputation as a lacklustre worker who maintained communication with all the old cronies, including Rolf Reiser, Arndt Fischer and Otto Dinse. Hans Siptrott's transfer into civilian life on 30 April 1954

from a combat veteran in the Waffen SS back to Esslingen did not go smoothly. His parole officer, Theodor Knapp, was frustrated by his client, who had many problems at his work (R. Hirschmann in Stuttgart)—absence, indifference and an argumentative manner with workers. Indeed, one employer after another was happy to see him move on. 'Siptrott is suffering acute neurosis,' Knapp wrote in September 1954. His employer questioned his mental viability: a physician pronounced him 'in poor health' and 'a human ruin'. His records also show that Siptrott complained to higher-ups and, moved without permission—and in direct contradiction to parole policies—maintained communication with his old SS pal, Manfred Thorn. NA, RG-549, Records of U.S. Army Europe (USAREUR), Records Related to Parolee Case Files, 1945–58, (290/59/30/2), Box 119.

42. Peiper: Malmédy was not 'Amok laufender Nazihorden' but rather a 'bedauerliches Kampfgeschahen inmitten der Hitze und des Laerms der Schlacht'. NA, RG-549, Records Related to Post Trial Activities (290/59/8/1), 'Record Officer's Summary of the Cases', Case 6-24, Box 16.

43. 'Application for Clemency of Joachim Peiper, Case 6-24', 20 December 1954, RG-549, Landsberg Stayback files, Box 5.

44. Tonk, who wrote HIAG often from prison, soon showed his unreconstructed nature after his release by blatantly violating his parole conditions. This happened when his parole officer became aware that he had visited other paroled Malmédy men, Guenther Weiss, on his birthday along with parolees Axel Rodenburg and Joachim Hoffmann, who had all been released in the preceding six months. All four came into trouble by this action, which was strictly forbidden within their parole conditions. 'At the institution, before you were released, I warned you to avoid such visits, evidently you forget easily.' Gernert to Tonk, 25 May 1954, NA, RG549 Records of Headquarters, U.S. Army Europe, Records Related to Parolee Case Files, 1945–58, August Tonk.

45. In charge of the Landsberg Library was Dr Franz Six, who had been with Heydrich's SD. Peiper recalled his tenure during their time there. Strafsache gegen Dr Werner Best u.a. wegen Mordes, Joachim Peiper, 19 January 1967, 1 JS 12/65 Aussage Joachim Peiper vom 2 September 1970, Zwentralenstelle, Ludwigsburg. Dr Six was to have run the Einsatzgruppen killing teams for both England and Moscow that, luckily for him, were never utilized, but his work with Heydrich had got him into trouble enough to wind up at Landsberg. After his release in 1953, like Peiper, Dr Six was employed by Porsche automotive.

46. Peiper to Kosmehl, 20 September 1955. 'Ortega's polished language is going to be good company on the coming long winter evenings.' José Ortega y Gasset was best known for his work on the nature of truth: The Revolt of the Masses (1930), which showed the influence of Friedrich Nietzsche in this thinking. 'Under fascism' from this work.

47. Kurt Briesemeister was released on the same date. Others released in 1955 included Valentin Bersin, Friedel Bode, Friedrich Christ, Sepp Dietrich and Franz Sievers.

48. Diefenthal to Everett, 3 August 1955, Everett Papers. 'I am very happy to be able to tell you that I was released on parole ... Now after a ten-year confinement, I could go home in order to live together with my brave wife and my 12-year-old daughter. We, my family and me, are happy and able to catch our luck. We know that you are the man who made that possible ... We will never forget you.'

49. 'Institutional Records', *Parole files*, Major Elliot F. Ashford, 12 June 1956. '[Peiper] has made a favourable impression by his efforts to improve his general outlook. This inmate was an instructor in the Prison School for two years. He has completed courses in English, French, commercial law, book keeping, civics and engineering. He is also head of the prison school system ... this inmate has the character and ability to make a good citizen if released.' Certainly Peiper had used his prison school time to advantage. He had taken English since 1951 and became so proficient that he passed an interpreter's examination in August 1952. After that he taught courses and gave lectures at the prison school, and studied French from 1952 to 1954. For 'time has stopped', Peiper on 7 September 1955: 'Although those years of idealism and belief are over—that is a certainty—sometimes the dreams and illusions must replace the silence with which we cannot otherwise come to terms with the present.'

50. *Anständige* was the term that Heinrich Himmler vociferously advo-cated for himself and other SS men: 'tough, but decent'. See *Der Anständige*, a documentary film by Vanessa Lapa (Real Works, February 2014) based on original Himmler diaries discovered in Israel. Philip Oltermann, 'Himmler Hoard of Letters and Diaries Discovered in Israel', *Guardian*, 26 January 2014. Himmler often used the term to describe 'decent hardness in battle', which included executions. 'Most of you know what it means when 100 corpses are laid out along with each other, or when 500 or a 1000 are laid out. To have gone through that and—aside from exceptions of human weakness—remain decent [*anständige*], that is what makes us tough.' Himmler's

Posen speech, 4 October 1943. IMT, PS-1919. Peiper's use of the term here reflects his unreconstructed choice of words fourteen years after being Himmler's adjutant.

51. Jochen Peiper, Letter to Franz Reisner, 5 July 1955, copy courtesy of Heinz Stutterecker. Members of Peiper's little Nachkommando at Landberg in midsummer 1955: Sepp Dietrich, Georg Preuss and Hubert Huber, who were the last members of the Malmédy 'Red Jackets' still held at War Criminal Prison Nr. 1.

52. 'Interview Report: Josef (Sepp Dietrich)', 5 February 1954, NA, Case 6-24, RG-549, Box 51. In an interview with Dietrich's parole officer. Ursula protested her husband's parole plan that would send him back to Karlsruhe to live with her and three sons. Frau Ursula Dietrich was now no longer using Dietrich's name, having returned to her maiden name of Moninger. Further, she told U.S. Parole Officer Paul J. Gernert that she was planning to divorce her husband, a fact she had told Sepp in a visit to Landsberg on 22 January 1954. She also said that her husband (20 years older) and some of the other prisoners with him were 'fresh, arrogant and still believe they are important people'. In any case, Frau Dietrich was convinced to stay married to Sepp at least long enough for him to be paroled. They were divorced soon thereafter.

53. Ken McAuliffe, detailed email to author regarding his father's decision to retire, 26 August 2010. Information supplied by Michael Stern, a Second World War correspondent who was a close friend of McAuliffe during and after the war. For the controversy from Dietrich's release: 'Debate on Parole Stirs DC', and Stern and McAuliffe's explanation, 'USAREUR Explains Release of Dietrich', 28 October 1955, *Stars & Stripes*. Thanks to Pat Spayd for putting the author into contact with Mr McAuliffe.

54. 'Commander of Hitler's Elite Guard Is Released', *New York Times*, 25 October 1955. The Army reaction to the public outcry: 'U.S. Says Dietrich Free Under Tight Restrictions', *Stars & Stripes*, 3 November 1955. McAuliffe complained that he 'had no choice but to parole Dietrich', saying that this condition arose with the change in the Bonn Conventions, which granted West Germany sovereignty in May 1955.

55. 'Institutional Record: Clemency Application of Joachim Peiper, WCP No. 99', 10 January 1955, NA RG 549, Records of Parolee Files, 1945-1958, Box 94.

56. 'Peiper to Raimund Hergt', State Department, Bonn, no date, but autumn 1955. NA, Peiper Parole Files.

57. 'Supplement to Parole Plan for Joachim Peiper', Paul J. Gernert, 14 November 1955, RG-549 Parole Files.
58. 'Joachim Peiper: Parole Applicant', 21 February 1956, Parole Files.
59. Robert Walz, Letter to Association for Probation Assistance, Frau Ursula Wolff, 11 November 1955. Karl Heinz Brohl had been the commander of the 4th Machine Gun Company of the Leibstandarte before the war but was killed in France while leading a section of the artillery regiment of the Totenkopf Division at Arras. The action that day had countered the most significant British armoured attack in France, where Eicke's Totenkopf was only able to turn back the heavy English Matilda tanks by countering them with artillery guns firing over open sights. Casualties in this action were exceedingly heavy, with Brohl among them. BA-MA, III SS, 41/1, 'KTB Nr. 2', and BA-MA, III SS, 46/1, 'Divisions Arzt: KTB Nr. 4'.
60. Peiper to Kosmehl, 12 January 1956.
61. Peiper to Kosmehl, 12 February 1955.
62. "His future life will, in any case, be difficult." Theodor Knapp to Deforest Barton, 1 November 1956, NA, RG-549, Peiper Parole Files, Records Related to Parolee Files, 1945-1958. Leaving Landsberg, Peiper checked into his new one room apartment at the home of Dr. August Hartmann at Klagenfurterstr. 4 in Stuttgart. As required for a parolee, he attempted to register with the police in Feuerbach, but could not as the authorities were on holiday. He consulted his parole officer, Dr. Theodor Knapp, and also phoned Alfred de Maight, his sponsor at Porsche, to coordinate appearance for work at Zuffenhausen. With permission, Peiper proceeded to Sinzheim for reunion with his family at Bergstr. 2. There, he would remain for the holiday from 24 – 31 December 1956. Yet, the ghost of Himmler's old *Zauberkreis* remained. Not by coincidence, Sigurd Peiper and Hedwig Potthast were living as next door neighbors in Sinzheim since 1953. Before the war, both had worked for Himmler as secretaries and were now doing the same for a wood treatment company, Dr. Wolman GmbH, headed by Hans Joachim von Kruedener. Von Kruedener had coordinated one of Oswald Pohl's wartime SS industrial firms aimed at extracting fuel from oil shale.

As Peiper always told it, his first assigned task when he began his job at Porsche in January 1957 was to wash cars. Hinrich Peiper, interview 19 May 1999. Peiper repeated this apocryphal story to everyone and the tale took on a life of its own. See Benno Müller, Letter to Willis Everett (Müller to Everett, 10 September 1959, Everett Papers).

Equivalent Ranks of Waffen SS, German Army and U.S. Army in 1944

SS	Abbrev.	German Army	Abbrev.	US-Army
Reichsführer-SS	RFSS	Generalfeldmarschall	Genflm.	General of the Army
SS-Oberst-Gruppenführer	Obstgruf.	Generaloberst	Gen.O.	General
SS-Obergruppenführer	Ogruf.	General	Gen.	Lieutenant General
SS-Gruppenführer	Gruf.	Generalleutnant	Gen.Lt.	Major General
SS-Brigadeführer	Brigf.	Generalmajor	Gen.Maj.	Brigadier General
SS-Oberführer	Of.	–	–	
SS-Standartenführer	Staf.	Oberst	O	Colonel
SS-Obersturmbannführer	Ostubaf.	Oberstleutnant	OTL	Lieutenant-Colonel
SS-Sturmbannführer	Stubaf.	Major	M	Major
SS-Hauptsturmführer	Hstf.	Hauptmann	Hptm.	Captain
SS-Obersturmführer	Ostf.	Oberleutnant	Olt.	1st Lieutenant
SS-Untersturmführer	Ustf.	Leutnant	Lt.	2nd Lieutenant
SS-Standartenjunker	Stjk.	Fähnrich	Fhr.	Cadet
SS-Sturmscharführer	Stuscha.	Hauptfeldwebel	HFw.	Sergeant-Major
SS-Hauptscharführer	Hscha.	Oberfeldwebel	Ofw.	Master Sergeant
SS-Oberscharführer	Oscha.	Feldwebel	Fw.	Staff Sergeant (T/5)
SS-Unterscharführer	Uscha.	Unteroffizier	Uffz.	Sergeant (T/4)
SS-Rottenführer	Rttf.	Obergefreiter	OG	Corporal
SS-Sturmmann	Strm.	Gefreiter	G	Private 1st Class
SS-Mann	Man.	Schütze	Schtz.	Private

Index